W9-BNR-352

RACE
IDENTITY
AND REPRESENTATION
IN EDUCATION

RACE
IDENTITY
AND REPRESENTATION
IN EDUCATION

Edited by Cameron McCarthy and Warren Crichlow

Routledge • New York & London

Published in 1993 by

Routledge
29 West 35th Street
New York, NY 10001

Published in Great Britain by

Routledge
11 New Fetter Lane
London EC4P 4EE

Copyright © 1993 by Routledge

Printed in the United States of America on acid-free paper.

All rights reserved. No part of this book may be reprinted or reproduced or utilized in any form or by any electronic, mechanical or other means, now known or hereafter invented, including photocopying and recording, or in any information storage or retrieval system, without permission in writing from the publisher.

Library of Congress Cataloging-in-Publication Data

Race, identity, and representation in education / edited and with an introduction by
    Cameron McCarthy & Warren Crichlow.
        p.   cm. — (Critical social thought)
    Includes bibliographical references and index.
    ISBN 0-415-90557-5 — ISBN 0-415-90558-3 (paper)
    1. Education—Social aspects United States. 2. Multicultural
education—United States. 3. Minorities—Education—United States.
4. Race awareness—United States. 5. Discrimination in education—
United States. 6. Educational equalization—United States.
7. Curriculum change—United States. I. McCarthy, Cameron.
II. Crichlow, Warren. III. Series.
    LC191.4.R33 1993
370.19'342'0973—dc20   93-25989
                                                                                    CIP

British Library Cataloging-in-Publication Data also available.

Contents

III CULTURAL INTERVENTIONS IN RACE RELATIONS IN SCHOOL AND SOCIETY

Series Editor's Introduction to Race, Identity, and Representation in Education

RACE IS NOT a stable category. It has changed over time. What it means, how it is used, by whom, how it is mobilized as a social discourse, its role in educational and more general social policy, all of this is contingent and historical. Of course, it is also misleading to talk of race as an "it." "It" is not a thing, a reified object that can be tracked and measured as if it were a simple biological entity. Race is a set of fully social relations (Omi and Winant, 1986). Much the same needs to be said about identity. It is not necessarily a stable, permanent, united center that gives consistent meaning to our lives. It too is socially and historically constructed, and subject to political tensions and contradictions (Hall, 1992).

The complex issues surrounding race, identity, and representation cannot be understood through the lenses of only one discursive tradition. Rather, our approach must be multidisciplinary. It needs to draw from studies of popular culture, literature, the role of the state in struggles over race, class, and gender relations, national and international economic structures, and the cultural politics of imperialism and postcolonialism. And, at the same time, all of this needs to be connected to a set of liberatory projects. This is not simply about understanding for its own sake. Real people's histories and collective memories, languages, and futures—their very minds and bodies—are at stake here, as the so often alienating daily experiences of so many persons of color inside and outside of "our" educational institutions so clearly document.

If race is not a thing, but what critical cultural commentators have called a performance, neither is it an innocent word. It has played a considerable role in the attempted building of a new hegemonic alliance based upon rightist social, economic, and cultural principles (Apple, 1993). The conservative restoration in many Western capitalist nations has played the "race card" with distressing regularity. Economically and culturally dominant groups have been able to "export the blame" from the disastrous effects of their own policies and practices to others with much less power in the public arena (Apple, 1985). The word OTHERS here is pregnant with meaning since it is through this very process of creating "the other" that racial logics have some of their most telling effects.

Behind much of the conservative discourse about education—the supposed decline of standards, the call for the return to the western tradition, a reassertion of toughness and discipline in schools—lies this vision (if that is not too positive of a word) of the Other. It symbolizes an immense set of fears, including cultural ones. In particular, there is a fear that unless "we" return to an utterly romanticized) common culture, we will have a void, chaos, no serious culture at all. The racial subtext may be tacit here, but it is quite remarkably present nevertheless (Education Group II, 1991).

But how do we deal with concepts such as culture? Like race, words such as this do not (or at least should not) signify an already existing and unitary thing. Rather, they are place markers for a complex political arena in which the fundamental educational question of "What knowledge is of most worth?" is transformed—as it should be—into the even more challenging question of "Whose knowledge is of most worth?. Knowledge and power become inextricably linked here. Thinking about this relationship in terms of the politics of race is crucial.

At all levels of the educational system, aside from the growing conservative pressures to return to a Eurocentric curriculum, the dominant approach in dealing with the issue of race and culture is either to engage in "mentioning" (the adding to the curriculum of a few "representative" women and men of color by, usually briefly, discussing their contributions, but never seeing the world through their eyes) or by becoming a total relativist (see Apple and Christian-Smith, 1991 and McCarthy, 1990). This has usually resulted in programs based on a position that "we are all equally ethnics." Therefore, we should celebrate the contributions of all to the melting pot (or salad bowl) of our society. This has had the effect of marginalizing the structures and experience of racial oppression of specific groups and uses a logic of equivalence that denies the importance of cultural struggles in the politics of identity.

In opposition to these multicultural approaches, a movement toward Afrocentrism has developed specifically based on the politics of identity. Only by centering the African experience(s) as the core of the curriculum can, say, African American students sustain themselves and their culture and history.

Without denying the emancipatory possibilities in Afrocentrism and without suggesting that no progress was made under multiculturalism, *Race, Identity, and Representation in Education* seeks to go beyond what the editors believe are still limited perspectives. Cameron McCarthy and Warren Crichlow are themselves very clear on what this volume seeks to do. They intend it as a specific "strategic intervention" into the debates that are currently so very powerful about racial difference, identity politics, and the relations of exploitation and domination in societies such as our own. As they put it, on the one hand, "We reject current models of radical pluralism and cultural relativism that have been promoted in certain strains of multiculturalism quite popular within mainstream circles in education" (Introduction in this volume), yet, on the other hand, in their rejection of the usual forms of multiculturalism they are equally clear that they are uncomfortable with many of the essentializing alternatives that have been proposed. Again, in their words, "A central and unifying theme in this volume is a critique of tendencies toward dogmatism and exclusionary theories and ideologies that have now overtaken debates within and across hegemonic and subaltern camps" within education.

In taking this position, they recognize that we need ways of understanding race theoretically as a social and cultural production. This is important in and of itself. But, since this is a book on race, identity, and education, we need to see what race means and does in those institutions that play so large a part in defining what counts as official knowledge and in helping to form identities around these definitions. Finally, there is the crucially important issue of intervention. What can be done actively to interrupt dominant racial discourses? What are the positive and negative moments and the contradictions of such oppositional practices? These are among the most significant interests and questions taken up by the contributors to this volume.

By treating issues of race and identity with the seriousness and complexity that they deserve, and by refusing to totally separate race from class, gender, sexuality, and other relations, McCarthy and Crichlow have produced a volume that will surely prove to be a critical interruption itself.

Michael W. Apple
The University of Wisconsin, Madison

REFERENCES

Apple, M. W. (1985). *Education and Power.* New York: Routledge.

_____. (1993). *Official Knowledge: Democratic education in a conservative Age.* New York: Routledge.

Apple, M. W., & Christian-Smith, L. (1991). *The Politics of the Textbook.* New York: Routledge.

Education Group II. (1991). *Education Limited.* London: Unwin–Hyman.

Hall, S. (1992). The question of cultural identity. In S. Hall, D. Held, & T. McGrew (eds.). *Modernity and Its Futures* (pp. 273–316). Cambridge, England: Polity.

McCarthy, C. (1990). *Race And Curriculum.* London: Falmer.

Omi, M. & Winant, H. (1986). *Racial Formation in the United States.* New York: Routledge.

Acknowledgements

FROM START TO FINISH, *Race, Identity, and Representation* required more effort, goodwill, solidarity, and support than could be supplied by Warren Crichlow and myself. Special funding and technical support for this volume were provided by Colgate University's working research grants and by a Department of Speech Communication Visiting Fellowship offered to Cameron McCarthy by the University of Illinois at Urbana-Champaign. Similar support was offered to Warren Crichlow at the University of Pennsylvania in the form of a Ford Foundation Summer Fellowship in the area of African American Studies and Popular Culture at the Center for the Study of Black Literature and Culture. We are grateful for the acts of collaboration, collective spirit, and good, solid advice that came to us from many quarters during our preparation of this volume. We would especially like to thank Michael W. Apple and Jayne Fargnoli and Anne Sanow at Routledge for their invaluable support and guidance. They helped to shepherd *Race, Identity, and Representation* from conception to final production. We would like to acknowledge the wonderful editorial work done by Laura U. Marks, whose many suggestions for revision helped to focus, tighten, and strengthen the manuscript considerably. Lawrence Grossberg and Jesse Delia were particularly generous in offering advice and support at critical moments in the production of the volume. Special thanks is due to Lisa Reilly, who read and offered critical insights on individual essays at a very early stage. We are particularly grateful for the word processing, typing, and general assistance that Mary Rudder, Margaret Abbott, Thelma Mayer, and Mary Elizabeth Baird provided us throughout the preparation of the manuscript. Finally, we would like to say that we feel particularly privileged to have collaborated on this volume with such a wide diversity of fellow contributors, whose rich and varied treatments of the topics of race, identity, and representation foreground new theoretical and methodological directions in the areas of race relations, cultural studies, and education.

Versions of some of the essays in this book were published elsewhere. We are grateful to the publishers for their permission to make use of the following essays: Manthia Diawara's "Black Studies, Cultural Studies: Performative Acts," previously appeared in *Afterimage 20* (3) (October 1992); Elizabeth Ellsworth's "I Pledge Allegiance: The Politics of Reading and Using Educational Films" was published in *Curriculum Inquiry 21* (1) (1991); a version of Lawrence Grossberg's "Cultural Studies and/in New Worlds" will be published in *Critical Studies in Mass Communication*; Edward Said's "The Politics of Knowledge" first appeared in *Raritan 11* (1) (Summer 1991); Michele Wallace's "Multiculturalism and Oppositionality" was previously published in *Afterimage*, 19 (3) (October 1991); and Cornel West's essay "The New Cultural Politics of Difference" appeared in *October, 53* (Summer 1990).

Introduction:
Theories of Identity, Theories of Representation, Theories of Race

CAMERON MCCARTHY AND WARREN CRICHLOW

Don't you think that the white neo-Nazis and some of these black nationalists should unite, so as to save on overhead?
Ishmael Reed, "Hiphoprisy"

It is clear to the most reductionist intellect that…the time for undiscriminating racial unity has passed. [We are] in a new arena, and the contestants defy the mold.
Toni Morrison, "Introduction: Friday on the Potomac"

A single overmastering identity at the core of the academic enterprise, whether that identity be Western, African, or Asian, is a confinement, a deprivation. The world is made up of numerous identities interacting, sometimes harmoniously, sometimes antithetically.
Edward Said, "Identity, Authority, and Freedom: The Potentate and the Traveler"

IN A RECENT *New York Times Book Review* article, Henry Louis Gates Jr. (1991) relates a story that has made its rounds in the jazz world. The story takes the form of an answer to what Gates calls "the perennial question: Can you really tell?" The question is about racial authenticity, racial identity, and racial origins and their predictive capacity with respect to cultural behavior and the meaning of style. Can you really tell who is the black one, who is the white one? Can you really tell? According to Gates:

> The great black jazz trumpeter Roy Elridge once made a wager with the critic Leonard Feather that he could distinguish white musicians from black ones—blindfolded. Mr. Feather duly dropped the needle onto a variety of record albums whose titles and soloists were concealed from the trumpeter. More than half the time, Elridge guessed wrong.
> (Gates, 1991, p. 1)

What Gates fails to mention is the fact that the blindfold test has been an institution of *Down Beat* jazz magazine for well over a quarter century now and that white jazz musicians presented with the blindfold test regularly confuse black musicians with white ones and vice versa. The problem of racial origins and racial authenticity is a problem all around. The elusiveness of racial identity not only affects blacks, it affects whites. No matter how hard some people may try, racial identities can never be gathered up in one place as a final cultural property. And, as we approach the end of the twentieth century, what seemed like stable white ethnicities and heritages in an earlier era are now entering a zone of recoding and redefinition. Michael Omi and Howard Winant (1992) put the problematic of waning white ethnicity in the following terms:

> Most whites do not experience their ethnicity as a definitive aspect of their social identity. They perceive it dimly and irregularly, picking and choosing among its varied strands to exercise, as Mary Waters (1990) suggests, an "ethnic option." The specifically ethnic components of white identity are fast receding with each generation's additional remove from the old country. Unable to speak the language of their immigrant forbears, uncommitted to ethnic endogamy and unaware of their ancestors' traditions (if in fact they can still identify their ancestors as, say, Polish or Scots, rather than a combination of four or five European—and non-European!—groups) whites undergo a racializing pan-ethnicity as "Euro-Americans." (p. 17)

Of course, this story of ethnic instability is no less true of more recent Asian, Latino, and Middle Eastern immigrants to the United States. For instance, Andrew Hacker (1992) informs us in his provocative book, *Two Nations*, that

> in 1990, the census located 7,687,938 residents of California who selected the Latin or Hispanic designation. Within this group, just under half—49.5 percent—chose to say that they also had a race: black or white, or, in a few cases, Asians or Native Americans. However, the other 50.5 percent told the census that in their own view, they had no "race" at all....The same eschewal of "race" may be observed among Islamic immigrants from the Middle East. (Hacker, 1992 p. 6)

Young Asian American students express a similar ambivalence about racial/ethnic identity, as Keith Osajima (1992) found out in a recent study of Asian American students' perspectives on ethnicity. One Chinese American female student poignantly articulated this ambivalence:

> I grew up in a white suburb and my parents are also very Americanized, and spoke mostly English at home, so I don't speak Chinese....I also grew up trying to identify as much as possible with white people and feeling very inadequate because I would never be like them....I mean it's a constant conflict with me now. I assume it's going to be for the rest of my life...you know either being with white Americans and not feeling I'm like them, or going to the Chinese environment, like Chinatown or something and not feeling like I fit in there. (quoted in Osajima, 1992, p. 1)

These individual and collective stories of racial/ethnic instability come at a critical juncture in debates over racial inequality, racial identity, and curriculum reform in the educational field in the United States. They also point to the crisis in the theorization of race and racial logics in education. But it is also, paradoxically, a time when there is a peculiar language of racial and ethnic certainty driving ideological and cultural approaches to racial antagonism in education and society—a time of pan-ethnic camps drawn tightly around specular origins. The world is a vast Lacanian mirror in which theorists of racial purity and racial essence see themselves standing in front of their ancestors. It is the perfect image, the snapshot of history collected in the nuclear family photo album. It is the story of the singular origin, the singular essence, the one, true primary cause. The old Marxist and neo-Marxist orthodoxies of class and economic primacy in education debates are rapidly being replaced by the new pan-ethnic cultural orthodoxies of racial origins and racial identity. The proponents of Western Civilization and Eurocentrism and their critics, and the proponents of Afrocentrism, now struggle over the heart and soul of the educational enterprise. (This is not, of course, to suggest that there is an equivalence in the deployment of material and political resources in this struggle; for in some ways, the playing out of this conflict involves a certain project of encirclement of black intellectual thinking.) Conservative educators like Dianne Ravitch join conservative ideologues such as George Will who insist, for instance, that "Our country [the United States] is a branch of European civilization...'Eurocentricity' is right, in American curricula and consciousness, because it accords with the facts of our history, and we—and Europe—are fortunate for that" (Will, 1989, p. 3). Europe, through this legerdemain, is collapsed into the United States without any difficulty. History and tradition in this country are seen as interchangeable with the history and tradition of Europe.

On the other hand, Afrocentric theorists such as Molefi Asante (1987) argue for the pan-ethnic unity of all black people of the diaspora, pointing to the origins of African people in the "spatial reality of Africa." We are in the historical moment of what Stanley Aronowitz and Henry Giroux (1991) call the "politics of clarity." Of course, it is important to emphasize here that Afrocentrism is a liberatory discourse. When one reads the work of Asante, Jawanza Kunjufu, and others one recognizes immediately a sustained effort to connect to an intellectual and political history of struggle waged by racially subordinated groups in the U.S. But Afrocentrism also contains within its discourse a language that masks issues of contradiction and discontinuity within the diaspora, between the diaspora and Africa, between different economically and socially situated African Americans and other minority groups, and between differently situated men and women.

Beyond these concerns is the issue of the intellectual and cultural worker and his or her problematic relationship to anything that begins to sound like a singular cultural heritage or cultural stream. It is a necessary condition of dynamic intellectual and cultural work that the intellectual worker have the flexibility to draw on the well-ground of history, to draw on the variety of cultural resources that fan out across the myriad groups that make up this society and the world (Said in this volume). "Culture," as writers such as Coco Fusco, Cornel West, and Stuart Hall suggest, is a hybrid. For that matter, racial identity is a hybrid too! It is the product of encounters between and among differently located human groups. This fact is deeply etched and written into the history and present of the formation of racial identities in this country. In saying this, we do not seek to deny that there are certain stabilities associated with race. We are not here denying that there is the persistence of what Stuart Hall calls "continuities" between, say, the peoples of Africa and the peoples of the Afro–New World diaspora (Hall, 1989). We are not seeking to contest that there are brutal realities associated with the patterns of racial exclusion that affect minorities in the United States. What we are saying is that racial difference is the product of human interests, needs, desires, strategies, capacities, forms of organization, and forms of mobilization. And that these dynamic variables which articulate themselves in the form of grounded social constructs such as identity, inequality, and so forth, are subject to change, contradiction, variability, and revision within historically specific and determinate contexts. We maintain that "race" is a social, historical, and variable category.

Against the grain of this historical variability, Afrocentrics and Eurocentrics now argue for school reform based on the narrow limits of ethnic affiliation. For the Afrocentric, the intolerable level of minority failure in schooling has to do with the fact that minority, particularly African American, cultural heritage is suppressed in the curriculum. Black students fail because schools assault their identities and destabilize their sense of self and agency (a good example of this thesis is to be found in "The conspiracy to destroy black boys" by Kunjufu, 1985). For the proponents of Western Civilization, the Western cultural emphasis in the curriculum is color-blind. Black students fail because of the cultural deprivation that exists in their homes and in their communities. As E. D. Hirsch Jr. (1987) claims, broad cultural literacy would help disadvantaged black youth enter the mainstream. Literacy in the canon of Western civilization would be the best antidote for failure among the black poor. Of course, parallels to the great struggles over race, identity, and representation that are taking place in the American education system now also exist in other metropolitan countries such as England, Australia, and Canada, as well as in the postcolonial societies in the third world (McGee in this volume; Said, 1992). Edward Said in a recent article (a reprint of a lecture that the author gave at the University of Cape Town, South Africa) calls attention to these parallels:

> I spoke earlier about the debate between upholders and opponents of the Western canon in the American university; I also spoke of how in the post-independence, postcolonial Arab universities a great deal of emphasis was placed on the *Arabness* of what was being offered. In both cases therefore, ordinarily so different and so far removed from each other, one idea—that of national identity—shines through. (1992, p. 10)

As one of us has noted elsewhere, "over the past decade, there has been an unmistakable rise in the demands for recognition of difference and diversity" (Crichlow, 1990, p. 1). However, in many quarters these demands are being articulated in essentialist and exclusionary terms that ignore the historical and contemporary variability of race and the crucial roles of gender, class, sexuality, and nation in the process of racial identity formation and structuration. The immediate consequence of this in education and elsewhere is a considerably fragmented political space in which meaningful dialogue over difference has virtually collapsed and concerted collective action across racial, class, and gendered divides is significantly stymied (in contrast, for some promising examples of multiracial alliance see Brecher and Costello, 1990). All this has led to an increasing contraction of democratic focus and momentum on the issue of racial inequality and racial difference in the United States and other metropolitan countries.

As a collective and interdisciplinary effort, *Race, Identity, and Representation in Education* is intended as a strategic intervention in debates over racial difference and inequality in an educational arena that has become increasingly balkanized and marked by a paralysis of the will. We reject current models of radical pluralism and cultural relativism that have been promoted in certain strains of multiculturalism quite popular within mainstream circles in education. Nevertheless, a central and unifying theme in this volume is a critique of tendencies toward dogmatism and exclusionary theories and ideologies that have now overtaken debates within and across hegemonic and subaltern camps in the curriculum and educational fields. This effort to resuscitate an expanded democratic discourse over issues of racial difference leads us inevitably beyond "the coalface of the classroom" (Williamson, 1980) and outside the corridors of schooling to a rendezvous with literature, popular culture, the state, and the deep imbrication of racial logics in current developments in national and global capitalism and in the economic and cultural processes associated with imperial domination of postcolonial societies.

Specifically, *Race, Identity, and Representation in Education* fulfills three objectives. First, the contributors to this volume present a much-needed multidisciplinary appraisal of the status of the conceptualization of the race category in contemporary educational and social science research. Particular attention is paid to theorizing the intersection of race with other dynamic variables operating in the school setting and in popular culture, namely, the variables of class, gender, sexuality, and nation. Second, the volume foregrounds a wide range of original theoretical and methodological perspectives that centrally address the marginalized issues of racial identity and representation in education. By "identity and representation in education," we are not simply referring to mimesis or the presence or absence of "positive" images of minorities and third world people in textbooks and other curriculum materials. By identity and representation, we are referring to the question of the social power that resides in the specific arrangement and deployment of subjectivity in cultural and ideological practices in schooling and society. We call attention to the complex relationships that exist between culture, knowledge, and power. Issues of identity and representation directly raise questions about who has the power to define whom, and when, and how. We particularly want to emphasize the fact that often minorities do not have central control over the production of images about themselves in this society. So that when events like the Los Angeles riots and the Howard Beach and the Bensonhurst attacks on black people occur, minorities, particularly Hispanics and African Americans, do not have "equal access" to the media to "tell their side of the story." Third, *Race, Identity, and Representation in Education* offers a forum for dialogue among national and international and first world and third world scholars and cultural activists on the topic of cultural intervention in race relations in schooling and society. This dialogue is long overdue.

CONTRADICTIONS OF EXISTENCE

> What is at issue here is the recognition of the extraordinary diversity of subjective positions, social experiences and cultural identities which compose the category "black," that is the recognition that "black" is essentially a politically and culturally constructed category, which cannot be grounded in a set of fixed transcultural or transcendental racial categories and which therefore has no guarantees in Nature. (Hall, 1988, p. 28)

The subject of racial domination has, to say the least, been treated problematically in modern educational and social theories. Racial logics and mechanisms have been difficult to specify, their persistence difficult to explain, and their dynamics and trajectories difficult to predict. Indeed, the very slippery nature of what has come to be known in the educational literature as "the race question" challenges in fundamental ways the entire tapestry of curriculum and educational thought, particularly with respect to nonclass social antagonisms and domination relations in general. That is to say, the race question brings into the foreground omissions and blind spots. It exposes callouses and bottlenecks in even the most radical and ameliorative of approaches to social themes of "exploitation," "domination," "resistance," and "human emancipation." The intractability of racial logics within contemporary research frameworks, for instance, raises questions about unequal relations in the production of educational theory itself. Who produces it? About whom? And for whom? What social and ideological functions does educational theory serve? And how is it socially deployed with respect to policies and programs that address and "target" minority youth? Furthermore, the race question brings into the open in the most provocative manner, as Cornel West (1982, 1988) suggests, methodological and ethical questions with respect to the privileging of establishment and instrumental agendas in curriculum research and practice.

Specifically, there is something of a divide within the curriculum and educational literature in terms of its discussion of racial antagonism. For neo-Marxist school critics such as Ronald Edari (1984) and Allan Jackobowitz (1985), and also in the early work of Samuel Bowles and Herbert Gintis (1976), racial antagonism is theorized as an effect of the capital-labor contradiction. Schools merely help to flesh out this story by delivering minorities, via a differentiated curriculum, to the secondary labor market. Such approaches lead ultimately to paralysis and pessimism: race relations reform in education must await the abolition of capitalism. Though recent neo-Marxist writing (Spring, 1989) offers more culturally sophisticated accounts of race, the latter seems still to be regarded as an adjunct of class divisions, a secondary matter in an otherwise dynamic social system. On the other hand, mainstream and liberal theorists such as Eleanor Orr (1987) and Signithia Fordham (1990) are decidedly idealist in their formulations. These sociologists of schooling have sought to show the connections between minority failure and differential patterns of socialization, individual teacher values, preferences, expectations, and so on. Mainstream explanations of racial inequality also tend to be situated in pathological constructions of minority cognitive capacities (Jensen, 1984; deParle, 1990), child-rearing practices (Bell, 1975), family structures (Moynihan, 1965), and linguistic styles (Orr, 1987). Mainstream theorists have in this sense tended to "blame the victim." Curriculum practices and interventions predicated on these approaches attempt to influence positive changes in minority school performance through the manipulation of specific school variables, such as teacher behavior, methods of testing, placement, and counseling (Cortes, 1986).

Common to these approaches to race and education, as well as the more emergent discourses of Afrocentrism and multiculturalism, is a tendency to undertheorize race. Within these paradigms of educational theory, racial antagonism is conceptualized as a kind of deposit or disease that is triggered into existence by some deeper flaw of character or society. In this sense, both mainstream and radical conceptualizations of racial inequality can be described as essentialist and reductionist in that they effectively eliminate the "noise" of multidimensionality, historical variability, and subjectivity from their explanations of racial differences in education. Let us clarify what we mean by essentialism and reductionism. By essentialism, we refer to the tendency in current mainstream and radical writing on race to treat social groups as stable or homogeneous entities. Racial groups such as "Asians," "Latinos," or "blacks" are therefore discussed as though members of these groups possessed some innate and invariant set of characteristics that set them apart from each other and from "whites." Feminist theorists such as Coco Fusco (1988), Teresa de Lauretis (1984), and Michele Wallace (1990) have critiqued dominant tendencies in mainstream research to define differences in terms of transcendental essences. Wallace (1990), for example, maintains that differences in the political and the cultural behavior of minority women and men are determined by social and historical contingencies and not some essential checklist of innate, biological, or cultural characteristics. It is our contention in this volume that current tendencies toward essentialism in the analysis of race relations significantly inhibit a dynamic understanding of the operation of race and race-based politics in education and in society. Reductionist strategies, on the other hand, tend to locate the "source" of racial differences in schooling in a single variable or cause. Current approaches to racial inequality therefore tend to rely too heavily on linear, monocausal models or explanations that retreat from the exploration of the political, cultural, and economic contexts in which racial groups encounter each other in schools and society. Carlos Cortes (1986) points to these limitations in his examination of current approaches to racial inequality in education:

> Some analyses [of racial differences in education] have relied too heavily on single-cause explanations. Group educational differentials have been attributed, at various times, to language difference, to cultural conflict, to discriminatory instruments (such as I.Q. tests), or to the cultural insensitivity of educators. Yet as surely as one of these has been posited as "the," or at least "the principal," cause of group achievement differentials, then other situations are discovered in which these factors exist, and yet group achievement differentials do not occur....There has been a tendency to decontextualize explanations. That is, explanations about the relationship between sociocultural factors and educational achievement often posit causation without consideration of the context in which these factors operate. (p. 16)

As Cortes points out, without an examination of institutional and social context it is difficult to understand how racial inequality operates in education. Current mainstream and radical conceptual frameworks do not effectively capture the heterogeneous and variable nature of race relations in either the school setting or society. Theoretical and practical insights that could be gained from a more relational and dialectical method of analyzing racial domination in education—one that attempts to show in detail the links between social structures (whether they be economic, political, or ideological) and what real people such as teachers and students do—have been forfeited (Pérez in this volume).

In *Race, Identity, and Representation in Education,* we seek to inflect the discussion of race away from the language of cultural deprivation and ideological and economic essentialism that now dominates the popular and research literatures on racial inequality in education. We point to the fact that racial differences are produced. These differences, as Said (1985) points out, are "the product of human work." We call attention to the organization and arrangement of racial relations of domination and subordination in cultural forms and ideological practices of identity formation and representation in schooling—what Louis Althusser (1971) calls the "mise-en-scène of interpellation." We are therefore interested in the ways in which moral leadership and social power are exercised in "the concrete" (Hall, 1981, 1986) and the ways in which regimes of racial domination and subordination are constructed and resisted in education.

The theoretical and methodological issues concerning race are complex, and therefore analysis and intervention in unequal relations in schools require a relational and multidisciplinary approach. Such analysis and intervention must pay special attention to contradiction, discontinuity, and nuance within and between embattled social groups (what one of us has called "nonsynchrony" [McCarthy, 1990]). Rather than treat minority groups as homogeneous entities, we point to the contradictory interests, needs, and desires that inform minority educational, cultural, and political behavior and define minority encounters with majority whites in educational settings and in society. These discontinuities in the needs and interests of minority and majority groups are expressed, for example, in the long history of tension and hostility that has existed between the black and the white working class in this country (Baran, 1971; Hill, 1987). Also of crucial importance within this framework are the issues of the "contradictory location" (Wright, 1978) of the "new" black middle class within the racial problematic and the role of neoconservative black and white intellectuals in redefining the terrain of contemporary discourse on racial inequality toward the ideal of a "colorblind" society (McCarthy, 1990). Just as important for a relational and nonessentialist approach to race and curriculum is the fact that minority women and girls have radically different experiences of racial inequality than do their male counterparts, because of the issue of gender. A relational and nonessentialist approach to the discussion of racial identities allows for a more complex understanding of the educational and political behavior of minority groups. We do not wish to imply that the politics of race, identity, and representation only addresses the experiences of minority groups. Rather we firmly believe that the same contradictions, discontinuities, and nuances also apply to whites. Much work needs to be done to understand and intervene in the ways in which whites are positioned and produced as "white," in the language, symbolic, and material structures that dominate culture in the West and the U.S. in particular. There is a need to move beyond static definitions of whites and blacks as they currently pervade existing research in education (Fusco, 1988; Roman, Sleeter, Wallace in this volume).

As Michael Burawoy (1981) and Mokubong Nkomo (1984) make clear with respect to South Africa, economic divides that exist between the black underclass from the Bantustan and their more middle-class counterparts working for the South African state (the police, nurses, Bantustan bureaucrats, etc.) often serve to undermine black unity in the struggle against apartheid. Similar examples exist in the United States, where some middle-class minority intellectuals such as Shelby Steele and Thomas Sowell have spoken out against multicultural education, affirmative action, and minority scholarship programs in higher education, suggesting that such ameliorative policies discriminate against white males. A case in point is the 1990 ruling by the U.S. Department of

Education's former Assistant Secretary for Civil Rights, Michael Williams, that maintained that it was illegal for a college or university to offer a scholarship only to minority students (Jaschik, 1990). The irony of this situation is underlined by the fact that the former Assistant Secretary for Civil Rights is a black man. The tragic fact is that without these scholarships a number of very talented minorities would not be able to pursue higher education. Here again, the "point man" on a policy that effectively served to undermine the material interests of African Americans and other minority groups is a neoconservative member of the emergent minority middle class.

Linda Grant (1984) calls attention to these discontinuities in terms of the operation of gender at the classroom level. Based on findings from a study of "face-to-face interactions" in six desegregated elementary school classrooms in a midwestern industrial city, Grant concludes that "Black females' experiences in desegregated schools…differ from those of other race-gender groups and cannot be fully be understood by extrapolating from the research on females or research on blacks" (p. 99). Among other things, Grant contends that the teachers (all women, three blacks and three whites) she observed did not relate to their black students and white students in any consistent or monolithic way. Grant places particular emphasis on the way in which black girls were positioned in the language of the classroom and in the informal exchanges between teachers and students. She notes that while white girls "spent more [instructional] time with teachers, prolonging questions into chats about personal issues," black girls' formal and informal contacts with teachers "were briefer, more task related, and often on behalf of a peer rather than self" (p. 107). Although these teachers tended to avoid contact with black male students, they were still inclined to identify at least one black male student in their individual classrooms as a "superstar." In none of the six desegregated classrooms was any of the black girls identified as a high academic achiever. Instead, Grant maintains, black girls were typified as "average achievers" and assigned to average or below average track placements and ability groups. Gender differences powerfully influenced and modified the racially inflected ways that teachers evaluated, diagnosed, labeled, and tracked their students. Grant therefore points to a hidden cost of desegregation for black girls:

> Although they are usually the top students in all-black classes, they lose this stature to white children in desegregated rooms. Their development seems to become less balanced, with emphasis on social skills.…Black girls' everyday schooling experiences seem more likely to nudge them toward stereotypical roles of black women than toward [academic] alternatives. These include serving others and maintaining peaceable ties among diverse persons rather than developing one's own skills. (1984, p. 109)

The point that we want to make here, then, is that you can not read off the educational, cultural, or political behavior of minority and majority groups from assumptions about race pure and simple. Different gender and class interests within minority and majority groups often cut at right angles to racial politics. In a related sense, to predicate race relations reform in education on the basis of static definitions of what white people are like and what minorities are like can lead to costly miscalculations that can undermine the goal of race relations reform in education itself.

Our principal theoretical and practical concern—one that contributors to this volume all share—is therefore to stress the importance of social context, nuance, and language in understanding the dynamics of race relations. We also want to emphasize the need to pay attention to the differential patterns of historical and contemporary incorporation of minority and majority groups into the social and cultural relations that exist in the school setting. Of course, in affirming the positive moment in history and culture, we should not fall back on the idea of race as some essential or primordial expression of language and cultural solidarity. Neither should we rush headlong into the politics of cultural exceptionalism or the celebration of cultural diversity for its own sake. For as Abdul JanMohamed and David Lloyd argue, "Such pluralism tolerates the existence of salsa, it even enjoys Mexican restaurants, but it bans Spanish as a medium of instruction in American schools" (1987, p. 10). Rather than taking the easy path to exceptionalism, we maintain that subaltern educational activists must begin to see racial difference as one (not the only) of the starting points for drawing out the various solidarities among subordinated minorities and working-class women and men over our separate but related forms of oppression. Indeed, it is the failure of some elements within the progressive movement to see the limitations of a calcified position around racial identity that contributed to the paralysis around the recent nomination of the ultra-conservative black judge, Clarence Thomas, to the Supreme Court. Again, one cannot diagnose racial interests or politics by looking at racial experience alone—even if this experience places you in Pin Point, Georgia, the ominous location of Thomas's origins. Such intensely complex problematics help to underline the fact, as Toni Morrison has forcefully put it, "that the time for undiscriminating racial unity has past....[We are] in a new arena, and the contestants defy the mold" (1992, p. xxx).

The challenge before us is to move beyond tendencies to treat race as a stable, measurable deposit or category. Racial difference is to be understood as a subject position that can only be defined in what Homi Bhabha (1992) calls "performative terms"—that is, in terms of the effects of political struggles over social and economic exploitation, political disenfranchisement, and cultural and ideological repression (see also Diawara in this volume). In this respect, discourses over racial inequality in education cannot be meaningfully separated from issues such as police brutality in African American and Latino neighborhoods or the sexual and mental harassment of minority women on the shop floor. Nor can oppression and inequality be meaningfully confronted by simply adding more "sensitive" curriculum materials to or including new voices in the school syllabus (Carby, 1990, 1992). We come to recognize that examining race relations is critical not simply for an understanding of social life as it is expressed in the margins of industrial society, but ultimately for an understanding of life as it is expressed in its very dynamic center. For as Stuart Hall (1981) maintains:

> If you try to stop the story about racial politics, racial divisions, racist ideologies short of confronting some of these difficult issues; if you present an idealized picture of a "multicultural" or "ethnically varied" society which doesn't look at the way racism has acted back inside the working class itself, the way in which racism has combined with, for example, sexism working back within the black population itself; if you try to tell the story as if somewhere around the corner some whole constituted class is waiting for a green light to advance and displace the racist enemy...you will have done absolutely nothing whatsoever for the political understanding of your students. (p. 68)

The contradictory dimensions of the operation of race in daily life that Hall identifies serve as a caution against dogmatism and totalizing solutions to the problems of racial inequality and antagonism in education and society. But it is these same contradictions that behoove us to guard against quietism and cynicism. A vigorous attempt to read schools as dynamic and complex cultural institutions that are deeply infiltrated by society, and stratified by difference, unstable alliances, needs, desires, and interests is a vital first requirement in thinking through the parameters of race relations reform in education.

MODELS OF MULTIDISCIPLINARITY: CONVERSATIONS ACROSS THE DIVIDE

A common theoretical and practical ground shared by the essays included in this volume is an opposition to racial inequality and logics of oppression and exclusion. As the reader will discover, however, there is no unified point of view or narrative among the contributors. There are many points of agreement and equally as many, if not more, disagreements, tensions, and contradictions among the positions voiced in these pages. We hope this multidisciplinary dialogue across geographic location, theory, methodology, and lexicon will extend current lines of discourse and foster new questions on the themes of *Race, Identity, and Representation in Education.*

The essays are grouped into three parts that foreground specific themes. In Part One, "The Problem of Race" is explored in eight essays that draw on critical, postcolonial, and feminist theories, philosophical and psychoanalytical curriculum studies, and cultural studies. Michael Omi and Howard Winant establish the general tone for the political and cultural analysis of race in their essay, "On the Theoretical Status of the Concept of Race." Omi and Winant trace the movement of the conceptualization of race from that of a fixed essence to race as subordinate to "objective" material conditions such as social class to the present-day discourse on race as an illusory or ideological construct. All three perspectives resonate to varying degrees in contemporary theories of race, identity, and representation. Omi and Winant argue that all three positions are ultimately inadequate in accounting for the salience of race in changing international and national contexts. They conclude by proposing an alternative "racial formation approach." Omi and Winant draw out the implications for this process-oriented approach whose minimum theoretical conditions require critical interrogation of political relationships, the global context, and historical time.

In "The New Cultural Politics of Difference," Cornel West argues that the present historical moment has given rise to new forms of cultural critique that depart—though not completely—from previous cultural perspectives and attitudes. He sketches a genealogy of crucial historical coordinates that account for transformations in intellectual life and critical practice in the postwar U.S. From this perspective, West elaborates a new cultural politics of difference whose basic challenges are intellectual, existential, and political. The distinctive features of this new cultural politics are not specifically race-bound, but intellectual and activist commitments that forge new conceptions of the vocation of the critic, artist, and teacher. West insists that the new cultural politics are constituted by a rejection of status quo forms of self-representation, a keen sense of the flow of history, and an alignment with counterhegemonic struggles for empowerment on a global scale.

In "Constructing the 'Other': Rightist Reconstructions of Common Sense," Michael W. Apple analyzes how the tactics and principles of the new right work in ideological ways to command a highly persuasive position in popular conceptions of race, economics, and educational equality in the U.S. He reviews theoretical work on the nature of ideology to uncover the limits and possibilities of counterhegemonic cultural and political action in the context of an expanding conservative cultural agenda. Apple concludes by showing how tensions within the new right and resistance from countervailing though fragmented forces in local communities are important obstacles to the consolidation of the conservative restoration. He argues for the crucial role of intensive educational work, aligned with social movements and multiracial coalitions, in sustaining the collective struggle for equality and person rights in societal institutions.

In "Traveling to Teach: Postcolonial Critics in the American Academy," Ali Behdad examines the predicament of postcolonial practices and the new conditions of postcolonial subjects in the American academy. He employs a complex and nuanced theoretical framework to explore the contradictions of differences within "other" communities. These differences and discontinuities simultaneously displace and privilege some postcolonial travelers through "ironic accidents of place," differential processes of spatial mobility, and configurations of institutional and cultural power relations. Behdad argues that these historical, epistemological, and political problematics of alterity are often unaddressed in postcolonial theory and are absent in generalized appropriations in contemporary academic theory in the West. In posing questions about institutional space, travel, hybridity, displacement, contingent communities, and tokenized inclusion, Behdad mounts a critique of static notions of knowledge, but also addresses—through the metaphoric practices of "wild anthropology"—the situatedness of postcolonial critique in the context of postcolonial mobility.

In "Racism, Sexism, and Nation Building in Canada," Roxana Ng continues the focus on the postcolonial critic in the Western academy by discussing her experience of being "in limbo," as a woman of Chinese decent, a "woman of color," in the first world academy. Employing a neo-Gramscian analysis, Ng reveals not only the politically and socially constructed character of race but also the interrelatedness of race, class, and gender in specific historical moments in the formation of the Canadian nation-state.

Like other contributors, William F. Pinar asserts that race is a complex, dynamic, and changing construct. Yet sustained critical discussions of race have been conspicuously absent in contemporary curriculum theorizing. Pinar's "Notes on Understanding Curriculum as a Racial Text" employs psychoanalytic theory to understand the meaning of curriculum in the American South as a racialized place. He argues that curricular debates over the canon are also debates over the constitution of the American self as a racial self.

Also located in the racial politics of the American South, Leslie Roman's "White Is a Color! White Defensiveness, Postmodernism and Anti-Racist Pedagogy" confronts whiteness as the absent color of race in feminist scholarship and theorizing. She examines the interrelatedness among dynamics of race, class, and gender and argues for the development of alternatives to the dominant conceptions of race as a reified set of meanings. Roman proposes a "socially transformative critical realism" as a provisional alternative to the relativism of postmodernist discourses and practices. She then outlines a framework for a dialogical politics of "speaking with" racial others. Roman's new theoretical framework challenges white teachers to confront the issue of "white defensiveness." It is a challenge, in her view, that some postmodernist theorists desperately try to defer.

Part One concludes with Lawrence Grossberg's "Cultural Studies and/in New Worlds." Echoing the themes of global space and time raised by Omi and Winant and Behdad, Grossberg considers the impact on cultural studies of its increasing internationalization. He argues for a conception of cultural studies that will enable it to escape from the consequences of its links with "modern" forms of power. In opposition to the temporalizing logic of modernity, Grossberg proposes a spatial and machinic model of power. Critiquing three figures of difference—fragmentation, hybridity, and differance—Grossberg attempts to rethink the meaning and place of race, identity, and representation within the contemporary politics of culture.

Part Two of the volume addresses the question of how racial inequality is produced in schools. Written within contexts in the U.S. and abroad, the essays report on studies of racial awareness and processes of identity formation among children and adolescents, mechanisms of teachers' resistance to multicultural in-service training, student teachers' engagement with multicultural ideas, and racial identity and representational practices in educational film, popular music, and literature.

British analysts Richard Hatcher and Barry Troyner and Australian sociologist Fazal Rizvi examine racial formation among young schoolchildren. In "Racialization and Children," Hatcher and Troyner critique research on the racialization of young children's interpretation of their worlds. They report findings from a recent ethnographic study of nine-, ten-, and eleven-year-old children in mainly white schools in England. Hatcher and Troyner provide an account of how racism is reproduced as a popular ideology that provides a meaningful way of understanding and acting in daily life. The account demonstrates the extent to which the culture of childhood, framed by the family, the school, and the neighborhood, has become racialized. The authors conclude by outlining curricular and pedagogical strategies for tackling popular racism in school contexts.

Rizvi's "Children and the Grammar of Popular Racism" discusses findings from research on how children construct the idea of racial difference and how the curriculum practices of schools help to organize and reproduce racial differentiation. From his investigations, Rizvi derives implications for the development of effective anti-racist educational interventions. He argues for pedagogical approaches that equip children with the critical thinking skills that would enable them to imagine alternatives to the popular racism that pervades the social organization of everyday practices.

Adolescent racial identity formation processes are addressed in different ways and different national contexts by Catherine Raissiguier and Glenn M. Hudak. In "Negotiating Work, Identity and Desire: The Adolescent Dilemmas of Working-Class Girls of French and Algerian Descent in a Vocational High School," Raissiguier employs a comparative perspective to analyze the relationship between school experience and identity formation processes for working-class female Algerian and French students. Her account describes how school is viewed and responded to by young women. She shows how their processes of identity formation differ as a function of the specific conjuncture of schooling, family, sexual desire, and an opportunity structure shaped by ethnic and racial forces. Raissiguier's ethnographic case accounts illustrate the multifaceted and fluid qualities of these young women's identities. Her analysis reveals the complex ways in which these identities are mediated by the social, cultural, and discursive contexts to which the young women have access.

Hudak's "Technologies of Marginality: Strategies of Stardom and Displacement in Adolescent Life" employs comparative case studies to explore racial formation in the parallel yet different experiences of two adolescent males, one Latino and one white, in a suburban high school in the U.S. The analytic "micro-stories" Hudak constructs suggests that each adolescent's self-definitional pathway, one toward and the other against marginality, is grounded in concrete, material conditions of racial discrimination on the one hand and privilege on the other. His analysis reveals the operation of different dimensions and "technologies" of marginality and the ethical strategies employed by a Latino and a white adolescent to negotiate power relations within their respective worlds.

Christine Sleeter and Deborah Britzman and colleagues shift the focus to teachers and classrooms. In "How White Teachers Construct Race," Sleeter critiques perspectives on teacher education and teacher in-service training that affirm multiculturalism without specifically interrogating the racial identities of a predominantly white teaching force. She analyzes findings from a two-year study of a staff development project that serve to illustrate how white teachers process education about race. Problematizing apolitical notions of multicultural sensitivity training, Sleeter argues that teachers bring to the profession perspectives about what race means, ones they construct mainly from their own life experiences and vested interests. She suggests necessary forms of intervention to politicize multicultural teacher education practices.

Deborah Britzman, Kelvin Santiago-Válles, Gladys Jiménez-Muñoz, and Laura M. Lamash collaborate in the essay "Slips That Show and Tell: Fashioning Multiculture as a Problem of Representation." They explore the racialized, gendered, sexualized, and class-based tensions operating between the real and the imaginary in the representational practices of multiculturalism. Britzman and colleagues examine a pedagogical experiment implemented by two high-school English student teachers and analyze the identities that are both unintentionally invoked and displaced in the classroom. The authors argue that the commitment to rationality—and to rational persuasion—is antithetical to teaching multiculturalism insofar as such a stance actively erases the complex, contested, and highly charged emotional investments students and teachers confront when their subject positions are called into question.

Part Two concludes with essays by Elizabeth Ellsworth, Susan Huddleston Edgerton, and Hazel Carby that explore themes of race and inequality through analyses of educational media and intertextual readings of literature. In "I Pledge Allegiance: The Politics of Reading and Using Educational Films," Ellsworth examines how visual representation and language in educational films organize knowledge through discourses of truth, desire, fear, and control and thereby inflect knowledge with meanings that support particular gender, race, and class interests. Ellsworth argues that educational documentaries in the 1950s, and in the 1980s as well, offer students a viewing experience that attempts to make pleasurable a particular position: that of the subject-of-paternalism, rationalism, and scientism. Ellsworth's analysis shows how such positioning blocks students' consideration of other factors that help to account for social inequality.

Edgerton begins her essay, "Toni Morrison Teaching the Interminable" with a question: "How is it that some things come to be sources of knowledge and some things do not?" The question serves as a point of departure to explore unauthorized sources of knowledge and knowing, how these sources become unauthorized, and why they are influential for those who encounter them. Drawing on reflective readings of psychoanalytic theory, her students' autobiographical writing, and Toni Morrison's novel *Beloved,* Edgerton examines two sources of nonauthoritative knowing/knowledge: popular literature and autobiographical fiction. She argues that the politics of identity are reflected in and produced by such nonauthoritative sources.

In "Encoding White Resentment: *Grand Canyon*—A Narrative for Our Times," Hazel Carby draws attention to the "inscription of national issues on black bodies." Carby contends that popular narratives in film and literature work as pedagogic texts for the production and stabilization of racial meanings. In her intriguing textual analysis of Lawrence Kasdan's film *Grand Canyon,* Carby identifies traces of white paternalism, anxiety, and resentment that echo a much earlier popular work, Harriet Beecher Stowe's *Uncle Tom's Cabin.* But *Grand Canyon* is a narrative for our times. Black bodies in Kasdan's film are framed in the glow of the Los Angeles riots and the real and imaginary dangers American middle classes attribute to the inner cities.

Part Three completes the volume with critical cultural reflections on a variety of themes introduced in the two previous parts. In this final section of the book, authors scrutinize tensions and dilemmas that continue to challenge contemporary "multi-cultural criticism" and intervention in the crucial issues of race relations in school and society. Michele Wallace's "Multiculturalism and Oppositionality" sets the tone with a critical examination of multiculturalism against the backdrop of deteriorating material conditions and social effects of late multinational capitalism. She argues that even as multiculturalism is being debated in the mainstream press and celebrated by cultural events in the art world, the symbolic and political menace faced by the nonwhite populations of American cities has invested these events with "a certain quality of hyperreality." Wallace takes as her point of departure media representations that reveal the dominant culture's contradictory attitudes toward events that take place "at the interstices of racial and social difference." She then examines how parallel conflicts are "played out in the programming and attitudes of the art world and the cultural left."

Wallace argues that within the multicultural debate, an understanding of difference cannot be derived from the privileging of one difference over others in an a priori manner. For Wallace it is important to see how various contradictions articulate and interrupt each other. Hence she places a special emphasis on theorizing differences—"sexuality, the body, and gender"—from a variety of cultural perspectives.

In "Black Studies, Cultural Studies: Performative Acts," Manthia Diawara examines tensions and interrelationships of theory, place, and practice in cultural studies. He traces the genealogy and elaboration of cultural studies from the Birmingham Centre for Contemporary Cultural Studies and the London-based black British Cultural Studies to emergent strains of U.S. cultural studies. Diawara points out that a distinct and relevant cultural studies in the U.S. can develop only through dialogue with, not importation of, British variants. A critical area of conflict in this encounter is reflected in current debates over essentialist and anti-essentialist theorizations of race and culture. Diawara argues that cultural studies of race, identity, and representation must provide new meanings that engage the material conditions of culture in the U.S. Drawing on attempts to integrate cultural studies with racial, ethnic, and gender oppression studies in the U.S., Diawara describes a shift in black studies to "performance studies" as a potentially promising alternative to the current fragmentation.

Evoking an autobiographical memory of an "emblematic encounter," Laura Elisa Pérez's "Opposition and the Education of Chicana/os" describes the "discriminatory logic, practices, and institutional structures" that marked her academic sojourn as a Chicana woman. This memory is a point of departure for contextualizing the current conditions of the Chicana/o population as a whole. Pérez finds that the educational experiences of Chicana/os differentially produce these subaltern subjects as disempowered and oppressed minorities. She critiques simplistic notions of identity politics, while disputing the claim that minority identity politics is obsolete or counterproductive. Drawing on the recent work of Chicana/o intellectuals Chela Sandoval and Tomás Ybarra-Frausto, Pérez argues for "an oppositional, tactical politics of identity aimed at eventually reconstructing a new discourse of multiple, mobile, and unhierarchized identities."

In "Decolonization and the Curriculum of English," Patrick McGee also draws on personal anecdotes to situate his critique of curriculum reform in university departments of English in response to multicultural challenges to canonicity and tradition. McGee argues that instead of reform, incremental revisions are enacted; ironically, because threatening political questions are displaced onto already politicized academic programs like cultural studies, or satisfied by appending new programs with new canons. Hence, radical questioning is contained and the depoliticized organization of English studies is itself sustained. Drawing on critiques of English and literary studies from postcolonial writers such as Ngũgĩ wa Thiong'o, Edward Said, and Gauri Viswanathan, McGee argues that much more than revision is needed in English studies. He suggests a strategy of curriculum expansion to include literature, theory, and criticism by women, African Americans, and postcolonial writers, but warns that such curricular gains can only be meaningful if linked to a broader critique of the discipline's role in the reproduction of hegemony in educational institutions.

Cameron McCarthy's "After the Canon: Knowledge and Ideological Representation in the Multicultural Discourse on Curriculum Reform" critiques current variants of multicultural discourse on race and racial identity in the U.S. McCarthy argues for rethinking multiculturalism in critical and emancipatory terms that emphasize the relationality and social production of knowledge and representation, as well as "issues of unequal distribution of material resources and power outside the school door." He concludes by outlining an alternative approach to multicultural education that draws directly on some of the more critical insights in the curriculum and cultural studies literatures.

Finally, in "The Politics of Knowledge," Edward Said considers some of the historical ways in which the politics of identity have been constructed during the high period of European imperialism and the anticolonial and nationalistic resistance movements it precipitated. As a point of departure, Said recalls a personal episode that illustrates the contemporary play of identity politics that underlies these debates within the humanities and the wider society and culture. From this perspective, he critiques an impoverished politics of knowledge "based upon the assertion and reassertion of identity, an ultimately uninteresting alteration of presence and absence." Said concludes by arguing for a relational application of ideas that seriously and non-coercively links texts and the world in which victims of race, class, and gender still exist. For Said, unlike Lyotard, the end of meta-narratives is not yet at hand.

CONCLUSION

We believe that the theoretical, methodological, and practical issues concerning race are complex, and that paradoxically, one cannot understand racial inequality by studying race alone (Hall, 1981). As the essays collected in this volume attest, the study of race in education must engage with the variables of class, gender, sexuality, and nation and their material expression in the discursive practices of social life. Moreover, the study of "race" must not exclude the study of "whiteness" as though it were a category that stands, unmarked, outside of history. We must also work toward the dissolution of whiteness as a "transparent racial identity" (Omi & Winant in this volume).

Along with the contributors, the editors wish to put these developments affecting subaltern groups in the United States in a broader international and world context of center and periphery relations. Above all, we fully intend, through the acts of writing and interpretation in this book, to intervene in the rather cloudy debate over racial inequality and educational and social reform. Such an activist, interventionist stand with respect to race relations requires a much broader conception of the theater of education than the one that currently exists in mainstream educational thinking—a notion that confines education within the walls of the classroom. What we need is a much more "popular," democratic, and strategic thinking about schooling that would allow us to begin to break down the walls that now exist between education and other disciplines and between education and the wider national and global political cultures. We are interested in thinking through strategies and practices that can make a difference in the educational experiences of minority and third world children in U.S. schools and elsewhere in metropolitan countries.

Throughout this volume, emphasis is placed on multidisciplinary approaches and analyses that seek to integrate the contemporary issues concerning race and education in the United States within a broader global context of imperial and center-periphery relations. This kind of broad-based, flexible response is almost mandatory in light of recent developments: the Los Angeles riots, the new racisms and xenophobias of Europe, the Persian Gulf, the unilateral declaration of a "New World Order" by the imperialist powers of the West, and the virtual institutionalization of neoconservative attacks on the material interests of minorities and women and other embattled subaltern groups in this country. A final development for which we must equip ourselves is the rise of the "Great Debate" over the issue of diversity versus the dominant Eurocentric cultural orientation of curriculum and education in light of the radical demographic and ethnic changes taking place in the major industrial centers, workplaces, and school sites in the United States and elsewhere. We hope this volume makes a contribution to readers' efforts to critically confront the enormous challenges these developments present to their practices in education and society.

REFERENCES

Althusser, L. (1971). Ideology and ideological state apparatuses. (Notes towards an investigation). In L. Althusser, *Lenin and philosophy and other essays* (pp. 121–173). New York: Monthly Review.

Aronowitz, S. & Giroux, H. (1991, Oct.). The politics of clarity. *Afterimage,* 19 (3), 5, 17.

Asante, M. (1987). *The Afrocentric Idea.* Philadelphia: Temple UP.

Baran, H. M. (1971, March-April). The demand for black labor: Historical notes on the political economy of racism. *Radical America,* 1–46.

Bhabha, H. (1992). Post-colonial authority and post-modern guilt. In L. Grossberg, C. Nelson, and P. Treichler (eds.), *Cultural Studies* (pp. 56–68). New York: Routledge.

Bell, R. (1975). Lower class Negro mothers' aspiration for their children. In Stub, H. (ed.), *The Sociology of Education: A sourcebook* (pp. 125–136). Homewood, IL: Dorsey.

Bowles, S., & Gintis, H. (1976). *Schooling in Capitalist America.* New York: Basic.

Burawoy, M. (1981). The capitalist state in South Africa: Marxist and sociological perspectives on race and class. In M. Zeitlin (ed.), *Political Power and Social Theory* (Vol. 2, 279–335). Greenwich, CT: JAI.

Brecher, J. and Costello, C. (eds.). (1990). *Building Bridges: The emerging grassroots coalition of labor and community.* New York: Monthly Review.

Carby, H. (Sept./Oct. 1990). The politics of difference. *Ms.,* 84–85.

_____. (Fall 1992). The multicultural wars. *Radical History Review,* 54, 7–20.

Cortes, (1986). The education of language minority students: A contextual interaction model. In California State Department of Education (ed.), *Beyond Language: Social and cultural factors in schooling language minority students* (pp. 3–33). Los Angeles: Evaluation, Dissemination, and Assessment Center, California State University.

Crichlow, W. (1990). Theories of representation: Implications for understanding race in the multicultural curriculum. Unpublished paper. Graduate School of Education, University of Rochester.

de Lauretis, T. (1984). *Alice Doesn't: Feminism, semiotics, cinema.* Bloomington: Indiana UP.

deParle, J. (1990, Nov. 28). An architect of the Reagan vision plunges into inquiry on race and I.Q. *The New York Times,* Section A, 22.

Edari, R. (1984). Racial minorities and forms of ideological mystification. In M. Berlowitz & R. Edari (eds.), *Racism and the Denial of Human Rights: Beyond ethnicity* (pp. 7–18). Minneapolis: Marxist Educational.

Fordham, S. (1990). Racelessness as a factor in black students' school success: Pragmatic strategy or pyrrhic victory? *Harvard Educational Review. Reprint Series 21,* 232–262.

Fusco, C. (1988). Fantasies of oppositionality. *Screen,* 29 (4), 80–95.

Gates, H. L., Jr. (1991, Nov. 24). "Authenticity," or the lesson of Little Tree. *The New York Times Book Review,* 1991, 1, 26–30.

Grant, C., & Sleeter, C. (1988). *Turning on Learning: Five approaches for multicultural teaching plans for race, class, gender, and disability.* Columbus: Merrill.

Grant, L. (1984). Black females' "place" in desegregated classrooms. *Sociology of Education,* 57, pp. 98–111.

Hacker, A. (1992). *Two Nations.* New York: Scribners.

Hall, S. (1981). Teaching race. In A. James & R. Jeffcoate (eds.), *The School in the Multicultural Society* (pp. 58–69). London: Harper.

_____. (1986). Gramsci's relevance to the analysis of race. *Communication Inquiry,* 10, 5–27.

_____. (1988). New ethnicities. In K. Mercer (ed.), *Black Film, British Cinema*. ICA documents, 7 (27–31). London: ICA.

_____. (1989). Cultural identity and cinematic representation. *Framework, 36*, 68–81.

Hill, H. (Winter 1987). Race, ethnicity and organized labor: The opposition to affirmative action. *New Politics*, 1 (2) 23–62.

Hirsch, E. D., Jr. (1987). *Cultural Literacy*. Boston: Houghton.

Jackobowitz, A. (1985). State and ethnicity: multiculturalism as ideology. In F. Rizvi (ed.), *Multiculturalism as Educational Policy* (pp. 43–63). Geelong, Victoria: Deakin UP.

JanMohamed, A. & Lloyd, D. (1987). Introduction: Minority discourse—What is to be done? *Cultural Critique*, 7, pp. 5–17.

Jaschik, S. (1990). Scholarships set up for minority students are called illegal. *The Chronicle of Higher Education*, 37 (15), A 1.

Jensen, A. (1984). Political ideologies and educational research. *Phi Delta Kappan*, 65 (7), p. 460.

Kunjufu, J. (1985). *The Conspiracy to Destroy Black Boys*. Chicago: African American Images.

McCarthy, C. (1990). *Race and curriculum*. London: Falmer.

Morrison, T. (1992). Introduction: Friday on the Potomac. In T. Morrison (ed.), *Race-ing Justice, En-gendering Power: Essays on Anita Hill, Clarence Thomas and the construction of social reality* (pp. vii–xxx). New York: Pantheon.

Moynihan, P. (1965). *The Negro Family: The case for national action*. Washington, D.C.: United States Department of Labor, Office of Policy, Planning, and Research.

Nkomo, M. (1984). *Student Culture and Activism in Black South African Universities: The roots of resistance*. Westport, CT: Greenwood.

Omi, M. & Winant, H. (1992). Contesting the meaning of race in the post–civil rights period. Paper presented at the Annual Meeting of the American Sociological Association, August 23–27.

Orr, E. (1987). *Twice as Less*. New York: Norton.

Osajima, K. (1992). Rethinking Asian American identity. Unpublished paper, Department of Education, Colgate University.

Reed, I. (1992). Hiphoprisy (Interview with M. Franti). *Transition*, 56, 152–165.

Said, E. (1985). Orientalism reconsidered. *Race and Class*, 26 (1), 1–15.

_____. (1992). Identity, authority, and freedom: The potentate and the traveler. *Transition*, 54, 4–18.

Spring, J. (1989). *American Education* (4th ed). New York: Longman.

Wallace, M. (1990). *Invisibility Blues*. New York: Verso.

Waters, M. (1990). *Ethnic Options: Choosing identities in America*. Berkeley: U of California P.

West, C. (1982). *Prophesy Deliverance: Afro-American revolutionary Christianity*. Philadelphia: Westminister.

_____. (1988). Marxist theory and the specificity of Afro-American oppression. In C. Nelson & L. Grossberg (eds.), *Marxism and the Interpretation of Culture* (pp. 17–33). Urbana, Illinois: U of Illinois P.

Will, G. (1989, Dec. 18). Eurocentricity and the school curriculum. *Baton Rouge Morning Advocate*, 3.

Williamson, B. (1980). *Education, Social Structure and Development*. London: Macmillan.

Wright, E. O. (1978). *Class, Crisis and the State*. London: New Left Review.

1 THE PROBLEM OF RACE

On the Theoretical Status of the Concept of Race

MICHAEL OMI AND HOWARD WINANT

INTRODUCTION

RACE USED TO BE a relatively unproblematic concept; only recently have we seriously challenged its theoretical coherence. Today there are deep questions about what we actually mean by the term "race." But before (roughly) World War II, before the rise of Nazism, before the end of the great European empires and before the decolonization of Africa, before the urbanization of the U.S. black population and the rise of the modern civil rights movement, race was still largely seen in Europe and North America (and elsewhere as well) as an essence, a natural phenomenon, whose meaning was fixed—constant as a southern star.

In the earlier years of this century only a handful of pioneers, people like W.E.B. DuBois and Franz Boas, conceived of race in a more social and historical way. Other doubters included avant-garde racial theorists emerging from the intellectual ferment of the Harlem Renaissance; black nationalists and pan-Africanists who sought to apply the rhetoric of national self-determination expressed at Versailles to the mother continent, and who returned from the battlefields of France to the wave of antiblack race riots that swept the country in 1919; a few Marxists (whose perspectives had their own limitations); and to some extent the Chicago school of sociology led by Robert Ezra Park. But even these intellectuals and activists made incomplete breaks with essentialist notions of race, whether biological or otherwise deterministic.

That was then; this is now. Today the theory of race has been utterly transformed. The socially constructed status of the concept of race, which we have labeled the *racial formation* process, is widely recognized (Omi and Winant, 1986), so much so that it is now often *conservatives* who argue that race is an illusion. The main task facing racial theory today, in fact, is no longer to problematize a seemingly "natural" or "common sense" concept of race—although that effort has not been entirely completed by any means. Rather our central work is to focus attention on the *continuing significance and changing meaning of race*. It is to argue against the recent discovery of the illusory nature of race; against the supposed contemporary transcendence of race; against the widely reported death of the concept of race; and against the replacement of the category of race by other, supposedly more objective categories like ethnicity, nationality, or class. All these initiatives are mistaken at best, and intellectually dishonest at worst.

In order to substantiate these assertions, we must first ask, what is race? Is it merely an illusion, an ideological construct utilized to manipulate, divide, and deceive? This position has been taken by a number of theorists, and activists as well, including many who have heroically served the cause of racial and social justice in the U.S. Or is race something real, material, objective? This view too has its adherents, including both racial reactionaries and racial radicals. From our perspective both these approaches miss the boat. The concept of race is neither an ideological construct nor does it reflect an objective condition. In this essay we first reflect critically on these two opposed viewpoints on the contemporary theory of race. Then we offer an alternative perspective based on the approach of racial formation.

RACE AS AN IDEOLOGICAL CONSTRUCT

The assertion that race is an ideological construct—understood in the sense of a "false consciousness" that explains other "material" relationships in distorted fashion—seems to us highly problematic. This is the position taken by the prominent historian Barbara Fields in a recent, well-known article, "Slavery, Race and Ideology in the United States of America" (1990). Although Fields inveighs against various uses of the concept of race, she directs her critical barbs most forcefully against historians who "invoke race as a historical explanation" (p. 101).

According to Fields, the concept of race arose to meet an ideological need: its original effectiveness lay in its ability to reconcile freedom and slavery. The idea of race provided "the means of explaining slavery to people whose terrain was a republic founded on radical doctrines of liberty and natural rights" (p. 114). But, Fields says, to argue that race—once framed as a category in thought, an ideological explanation for certain distinct types of social inequality—"takes on a life of its own" in social relationships, is to transform (or "reify") an illusion into a reality. Such a position could be sustained "only if race is defined as innate and natural prejudice of color."

> Since race is not genetically programmed, racial prejudice cannot be genetically programmed either, but must arise historically....The preferred solution is to suppose that, having arisen historically, race then ceases to be a historical phenomenon and becomes instead an external motor of history; according to the fatuous but widely repeated formula, it "takes on a life of its own." In other words, once historically acquired, race becomes hereditary. The shopworn metaphor thus offers camouflage for a latter-day version of Lamarckism. (p. 101)

Thus race is either an illusion that does ideological work, or an objective biological fact. Since it is certainly not the latter, it must be the former. No intermediate possibility—for instance the Durkheimian notion of a "social fact"—is considered.

Some of this account—for example, the extended discussion of the origins of North American race-thinking—can be accepted without major objection.[1] Furthermore, Fields effectively demonstrates the absurdity of many commonly held ideas about race. But her position is so extreme that at best it can only account for the origins of race-thinking, and then only in one social context. To examine how race-thinking evolved from these origins, how it responded to changing sociocultural circumstances, is ruled out. Why and how did race-thinking survive after emancipation? Fields cannot answer, because her theoretical approach rules out the very perpetuation of the concept of race. As a relatively orthodox Marxist, Fields could argue that changing "material conditions" continued to give rise to changes in racial "ideology," except that even the limited autonomy this would attach to the concept of race would exceed her standards. Race cannot take on "a life of its own"; it is a pure ideology, an illusion.

Fields simply skips from emancipation to the present, where she disparages opponents of "racism" for unwittingly perpetuating it. In denunciatory terms she concludes by arguing for the concept's abolition:

Nothing handed down from the past could keep race alive if we did not constantly reinvent and re-ritualize it to fit our own terrain. If race lives on today, it can do so only because we continue to create and re-create it in our social life, continue to verify it, and thus continue to need a social vocabulary that will allow us to make sense, not of what our ancestors did then, but of what we choose to do now. (p. 118)

Fields is unclear about how "we" should jettison the ideological construct of race, and one can well understand why. By her own logic, racial ideologies cannot be abolished by acts of will. One can only marvel at the ease with which she distinguishes the bad old slavery days of the past from the present, when we anachronistically cling, as if for no reason, to the illusion that race retains any meaning. We foolishly "throw up our hands" and acquiesce in race-thinking, rather than…doing what? Denying the racially demarcated divisions in society? Training ourselves to be "color-blind"?[2]

We venture to say that only a historian (however eminent) could have written such an article. Why? Because at the least a sociologist would know W. I. Thomas's famous dictum that if people "define situations as real, they are real in their consequences" (Thomas and Thomas, 1928, p. 572). Nor is Fields alone in claiming that racial ideology persists because people insist on thinking racially. Her position is espoused by many, on both the left and the right of racial debates.[3]

In any case the view that race is a kind of false consciousness is not held only by intellectuals, based on both well-intentioned and ulterior motivations; it also has a common sense character. One hears in casual discussion, or in introductory social science classes, variations on the following statement: "I don't care if a person is black, white, or purple, I treat them exactly the same; a person's just a person to me." Furthermore, some of the integrationist aspirations of racial minority movements, especially the civil rights movement, invoke this sort of idea. Consider the famous phrases from the "I Have a Dream" speech, the line that made Shelby Steele's career: "…that someday my four little children will be judged, not by the color of their skin, but by the content of their character."

The core criticisms of this "race as ideology" approach, in our view, are two. First, it fails to recognize that the salience of a social construct can develop over half a millennium or more of diffusion, or should we say enforcement, as a fundamental principle of social organization and identity formation. The longevity of the race concept, and the enormous number of effects race-thinking (and race-acting) have produced, guarantee that race will remain a feature of social reality across the globe, and *a fortiori* in our own country, despite its lack of intrinsic or scientific merit (in the biological sense). Our second, and related, criticism of this approach is that it fails to recognize that at the level of experience, of everyday life, race is an almost indissoluble part of our identities. Our society is so thoroughly racialized that to be without racial identity is to be in danger of having no identity. To be raceless is akin to being genderless. Indeed, when one cannot identify another's race, a microsociological "crisis of interpretation" results, something perhaps best interpreted in ethnomethodological or perhaps Goffmanian terms. To complain about such a situation may be understandable, but it does not advance understanding.

RACE AS AN OBJECTIVE CONDITION

On the other side of the coin, it is clearly problematic to assign objectivity to the race concept. Such theoretical practice puts us in quite heterogeneous, and sometimes unsavory, company. Of course the biologistic racial theories of the past do this: here we are thinking of the prototypes of fascism such as Gobineau and Chamberlain (see Mosse,

1978), of the eugenicists such as Lothrop Stoddard and Madison Grant, and of the "founding fathers" of scientific racism such as Agassiz, Broca, Terman, and Yerkes (See Kevles, 1985; Chase, 1977). Indeed up to our own time we can find an extensive legacy of this sort of thinking. Stephen Jay Gould makes devastating critiques of such views (1981).

But much liberal and even radical social science, though firmly committed to a social, as opposed to biological, interpretation of race, nevertheless also slips into a kind of objectivism about racial identity and racial meaning. This is because race is treated as an *independent variable* all too frequently. Thus, to select only prominent examples, Daniel Moynihan, William Julius Wilson, Milton Gordon, and many other mainstream thinkers theorize race in terms that downplay its variability and historically contingent character. Even these major thinkers, who explicitly reject biologistic forms of racial theory, fall prey to a kind of creeping objectivism of race. For in their analyses a modal explanatory approach emerges: As sociopolitical circumstances change over historical time, racially defined groups adapt or fail to adapt to these changes, achieving mobility or remaining mired in poverty, etc. In this logic there is no problematization of group identities, of the constantly shifting parameters through which race is understood, group interests are assigned, statuses are ascribed, agency is attained, and roles performed.

Contemporary racial theory, then, is often "objectivistic" about its fundamental category. Although abstractly acknowledged to be a sociohistorical construct, race in practice is often treated as an objective fact: one simply *is* one's race; in the contemporary U.S., if we discard euphemisms, we have five color-based racial categories: black, white, brown, yellow, and red.

This is problematic, indeed ridiculous, in numerous ways. Nobody really belongs in these boxes; they are patently absurd reductions of human variation. But even accepting the nebulous—"rules" of racial classification—such as "hypodescent" (see Harris, 1964; Davis, 1991) many people don't fit anywhere. Into what categories should we place Arab Americans, for example? Brazilians? South Asians? Such a list could be extended almost indefinitely. Objectivist treatments, lacking a critique of the *constructed* character of racial meanings, also clash with experiential dimensions of the issue. If one doesn't act black, white, etc., that's just deviance from the norm. There is in these approaches an insufficient appreciation of the *performative* aspect of race, as postmodernists might call it.[4]

To summarize the critique of this race-as-objective-condition approach, then, it fails on three counts. First, it cannot grasp the process-oriented and relational character of racial identity and racial meaning. Second, it denies the historicity and social comprehensiveness of the race concept. And third, it cannot account for the way actors, both individual and collective, have to manage incoherent and conflictual racial meanings and identities in everyday life. It has no concept, in short, of what we have labeled racial formation.

TOWARD A CRITICAL THEORY OF THE CONCEPT OF RACE

The foregoing clearly sets forth the agenda that any adequate theorization of the race concept must fulfill. Such an approach must be constructed so as to steer between the Scylla of "race as illusionary" and the Charybdis of "racial objectivism." Such a critical theory can be consistently developed, we suggest, drawing upon the racial formation approach. Such a theoretical formulation, too, must be explicitly historicist. It must recognize the importance of historical context and contingency in the framing of racial categories and the social construction of racially defined experiences.

What would be the minimum conditions for the development of such a critical, process-oriented theory of race? We suggest that it must meet three requirements:

- It must apply to contemporary political relationships
- It must apply in an increasingly global context
- It must apply across historical time.

Let us address each of these points briefly.

CONTEMPORARY POLITICAL RELATIONSHIPS

The meaning and salience of race are forever being reconstituted in the present. Today such new relationships emerge chiefly at the point where some counterhegemonic or postcolonial power is attained. At that point the meanings and the political articulations of race proliferate.

A central example is the appearance of competing racial projects, by which we mean efforts to institutionalize racial meanings and identities in particular social structures, notably those of individual, family, community, and state (see Winant, 1990, 1991). As egalitarian movements contend with racial "backlash" over sustained periods of time, as binary logics of racial antagonism (white/black, ladino/indio, settler/native, etc.) become more complex and decentered, political deployments of the concept of race come to signal qualitatively new types of political domination, as well as new types of opposition.

Consider the U.S. case. It is now possible to perpetuate racial domination without making any explicit reference to race at all. Subtextual or "coded" racial signifiers, or the mere denial of the continuing significance of race, may suffice. Similarly, in terms of opposition, it is now possible to resist racial domination in entirely new ways, particularly by limiting the reach and penetration of the political system into everyday life, by generating new identities, new collectivities, new (imagined) communities that are relatively less permeable to the hegemonic system.[5] Much of the rationale for Islamic currents among blacks in the U.S., for the upsurge in black anti-Semitism, and to some extent for the phenomenon of Afrocentrism, can be found here. Thus the old choices, integration vs. separatism and assimilation vs. nationalism, are no longer the only options.

In the "underdeveloped" world, proliferation of so-called postcolonial phenomena also has significant racial dimensions, as the entire Fanonian tradition (merely to select one important theoretical current) makes clear. Crucial debates have now been occurring for a decade or more on issues such as postcolonial subjectivity and identity, the insufficiency of the simple dualism of "Europe and its others," and the subversive and parodic dimensions of political culture at and beyond the edges of the old imperial boundaries.[6]

THE GLOBAL CONTEXT OF RACE

The geography of race is becoming more complex. Once more easily seen in terms of imperial reach, in terms of colonization, conquest, and migration, racial space is becoming *globalized* and thus accessible to a new kind of comparative analysis. This only becomes possible now, at a historical moment when the distinction "developed/underdeveloped" has been definitively overcome. Obviously by this we don't mean that now there are no disparities between North and South or rich and poor. We mean that the movement of capital and labor has internationalized all nations, all regions. Today we have reached the point where "the empire strikes back" (see Centre for Contemporary Cultural Studies, 1982), as former (neo)colonial subjects, now redefined as "immigrants," challenge the majoritarian status of the formerly metropolitan group (the whites, the Europeans, the "Americans" or "French," etc.). Meanwhile such phenomena as the rise of "diasporic" models of blackness, the creation of "pan-ethnic"[7] communities of Latinos and Asians (in such countries as the U.K. or the U.S.), and the breakdown of borders in both Europe and North America all seem to be internationalizing and racializing previously national polities, cultures, and identities. To take just one example, popular culture now internationalizes racial awareness almost instantaneously, as reggae, rap, samba, and various African pop styles leap from continent to continent.

Because of these transformations a global comparison of hegemonic social/political orders based on race becomes possible. We think that in a highly specified form, i.e., not as mere reactions to or simple negations of "Western" cultural/theoretical dominance, such notions as diasporic consciousness or racially informed standpoint epistemologies deserve more serious attention as efforts to express the contemporary globalization of racial space (see Mudimbe, 1988; Rabinow, 1986; Harding, 1986). Indeed, recent developments such as the construction of new racial identities or the phenomenon of pan-ethnicity simply cannot be understood without recognizing that the territorial reach of racial hegemony is now global.

The dissolution of the transparent racial identity of the formerly dominant group, that is to say, the increasing racialization of whites in Europe and the U.S., must also be recognized as proceeding from the increasingly globalized dimensions of race. As previous assumptions erode, white identity loses its transparency and the easy elision with "racelessness" that accompanies racial domination. "Whiteness" becomes a matter of anxiety and concern.

THE EMERGENCE OF RACIAL TIME

Some final notes are in order in respect to the problem of the epochal nature of racial time. Classical social theory had an enlightenment-based view of time, a perspective that understood the emergence of modernity in terms of the rise of capitalism and the bourgeoisie. This view was by no means limited to Marxism. Weberian disenchantment and the rise of the Durkheimian division of labor also partake of this temporal substrate. Only rarely does the racial dimension of historical temporality appear in this body of thought, as for example in Marx's excoriation of the brutalities of "primitive accumulation":

> The discovery of gold and silver in America, the extirpation, enslavement, and entombment in mines of the aboriginal population, the beginning of the conquest and looting of the East Indies, the turning of Africa into a warren for the commercial hunting of blackskins, signalized the rosy dawn of the era of capitalist production. These idyllic proceedings are the chief momenta of primitive accumulation. On their heels treads the commercial war of the European nations with the globe for a theater. It begins with the revolt of the Netherlands from Spain, assumes giant dimensions in England's AntiJacobin War, and is still going on in the opium wars with China, etc. (Marx, 1967, p. 751)

Yet even Marx frequently legitimated such processes as the inevitable and ultimately beneficial birth-pangs of classlessness—enacted by the ceaselessly revolutionary bourgeoisie.

Today such teleological accounts seem hopelessly outmoded. Historical time could well be interpreted in terms of something like a racial *longue durée*. For has there not been an immense historical rupture represented by the rise of Europe, the onset of African enslavement, the *conquista,* and the subjugation of much of Asia? We take the point of much poststructural scholarship on these matters to be quite precisely an effort to explain "Western" or colonial time as a huge project demarcating human "difference," or more globally, as Todorov, say, would argue, of framing partial collective identities in terms of externalized "others" (Todorov, 1985). Just as, for example, the writers of the *Annales* school sought to locate the deep logic of historical time in the means by which material life was produced—diet, shoes, etc. (Braudel, 1981)—so we might usefully think of a racial *longue durée* in which the slow inscription of phenotypical signification took place upon the human body, in and through conquest and enslavement to be sure, but also as an enormous act of expression, of narration.

In short, just as the noise of the "big bang" still resonates through the universe, so the overdetermined construction of world "civilization" as a product of the rise of Europe and the subjugation of the rest of us still defines the race concept. Such speculative notes, to be sure, can be no more than provocations. Nor can we conclude this effort to reframe the agenda of racial theory with a neat summation. There was a long period—centuries—in which race was seen as a natural condition, an essence. This was only recently succeeded, although not entirely superseded, by a way of thinking about race as subordinate to supposedly more concrete, "material" relationships; thus we have become used to thinking about race as an illusion, an excrescence. Perhaps now we are approaching the end of this racial epoch too.

We may, to our dismay, have to give up our familiar way of thinking about race once more. If so, there may also be some occasion for delight. For it may be possible to glimpse yet another view of race, in which the concept operates neither as a signifier of comprehensive identity, nor of fundamental difference, both of which are patently absurd, but rather as a marker of the infinity of variations we humans hold as a common heritage and hope for the future.

Notes

1 Minor objections would have to do with Fields's functionalist view of ideology, and her claim that the race concept only "came into existence" when needed by whites in North American colonies beginning in the late 17th century. The concept of race, of course, has a longer history than that. (Fields, 1990, p. 101)

2 Fields's admirer David Roediger also criticizes her on this point. "At times she nicely balances the ideological creation of racial attitudes with their manifest and ongoing importance and their (albeit ideological) reality....But elsewhere, race disappears into the 'reality' of class." (see Roediger, 1991, pp. 7–8)

3 Another important thinker who has at least flirted with the idea of race as illusion is Kwame Anthony Appiah. See "The Uncompleted Argument: DuBois and the Illusion of Race" (Gates, ed., 1985); idem, "Racisms" (Goldberg, ed., 1990).

4 "The question of identification is never the affirmation of a pregiven identity, never a self-fulfilling prophecy—it is always the production of an image of identity and the transformation of the subject in assuming that image" (Bhabha, 1990, p. 188).

5 The work of Paul Gilroy, which focuses on the British racial situation, is particularly revealing in regard to these matters. Gilroy's analysis of the significance of popular music in the African diaspora is indispensable (see Gilroy, 1991).

6 There is a vast literature by now on these matters, whose founding statement is undoubtedly Edward Said's *Orientalism* (Said, 1978); also useful is Bhabha, ed., 1990.

7 David Lopez and Yen Espiritu define pan-ethnicity as "...the development of bridging organizations and solidarities among subgroups of ethnic collectivities that are often seen as homogeneous by outsiders." Such a development, they claim, is a crucial feature of ethnic change—"supplanting both assimilation and ethnic particularism as the direction of change for racial/ethnic minorities." While pan-ethnic formation is facilitated by an ensemble of cultural factors (e.g., common language and religion) and structural factors (e.g., class, generation, and geographical concentration), Lopez and Espiritu conclude that a specific concept of race is fundamental to the construction of pan-ethnicity. (Lopez and Espiritu, 1990, p. 198)

References

Appiah, K. A. (1985). The uncompleted argument: DuBois and the illusion of race. In H. L. Gates (ed.), *"Race," Writing, and Difference*. Chicago: Chicago UP.

_____. (1990). Racisms. In D. T. Goldberg (ed.), *Anatomy of Racism*. Minneapolis: Minneapolis UP.

Bhabha, H. K. (ed.) (1990). *Nation and Narration.* New York: Routledge.

_____. (1990). Interrogating identity: The postcolonial prerogative. In D. T. Goldberg (ed.), *Anatomy of Racism.* Minneapolis: Minneapolis UP.

Braudel, F. (1981). *The Structures of Everyday Life: The limits of the possible,* vol. 1 of *Civilization and capitalism, 15th-18th century.* (S. Reynolds, trans.). New York: Harper.

Centre for Contemporary Cultural Studies. (1982). *The Empire Strikes Back: Race and racism in 70s Britain.* London: Hutchinson.

Chase, A. (1977). *The Legacy of Malthus: The social costs of the new scientific racism.* New York: Knopf.

Davis, F. J. (1991). *Who Is Black: One nation's definition.* University Park: Pennsylvania State

Fields, B. (1990). Slavery, race, and ideology in the United States of America. *New Left Review,* 181, 95–118.

Gilroy, P. (1991). *"There Ain't No Black in the Union Jack": The cultural politics of race and nation.* Chicago: Chicago UP.

Harding, S. (1986). *The Science Question in Feminism.* Ithaca: Cornell UP.

Harris, Wilson. (1964). *Patterns of Race in the Americas.* New York: Norton.

Kevles, D. J. (1985). *In the Name of Eugenics: Genetics and the uses of human heredity.* New York: Knopf.

Lopez, D., & Espiritu, Y. (1990). Panethnicity in the United States: A theoretical framework. *Ethnic and Racial Studies,* 13, 198–224.

Marx, K. (1967). *Capital,* vol. 1. New York: International Publishers.

Mosse, G. L. (1978). *Toward the Final Solution: A history of European racism.* New York: Fertig.

Mudimbe, V. Y. (1988). *The Invention of Africa: Gnosis, philosophy, and the order of knowledge.* Bloomington: Indiana UP.

Omi, M., & Winant, H. (1986). *Racial Formation in the United States: From the 1960s to the 1980s.* New York: Routledge.

Rabinow, P. (1986). Representations are social facts: Modernity and post-modernity in anthropology. In J. Clifford & G. E. Marcus (eds.), *Writing Culture: The poetics and politics of anthropology.* Berkeley: U of California P.

Roedinger, D. (1991). *The Wages of Whiteness: Race and the making of the American working class.* London: Verso.

Said, E. (1978). *Orientalism.* New York: Pantheon.

Thomas, W. I., & Thomas, D. S. (1928). *The Child in America: Behavior problems and programs.* New York: Knopf.

Todorov, T. (1985). *The Conquest of America: The question of the other.* (R. Howard, trans.). New York: Harper.

Winant, H. (1990). Postmodern racial politics in the United States: Difference and inequality. *Socialist Review,* 90 (1), 121–47.

_____. (1991). Rethinking race in Brazil. *Journal of Latin American Studies,* 24 (1), 173–92.

2 The New Cultural Politics of Difference

CORNEL WEST

IN THE LAST FEW YEARS of the twentieth century, there is emerging a significant shift in the sensibilities and outlooks of critics and artists. In fact, I would go so far as to claim that a new kind of cultural worker is in the making, associated with a new politics of difference. These new forms of intellectual consciousness advance new conceptions of the vocation of critic and artist, attempting to undermine the prevailing disciplinary divisions of labor in the academy, museum, mass media, and gallery networks while preserving modes of critique within the ubiquitous commodification of culture in the global village. Distinctive features of the new cultural politics of difference are to trash the monolithic and homogeneous in the name of diversity, multiplicity, and heterogeneity; to reject the abstract, general, and universal in light of the concrete, specific, and particular; and to historicize, contextualize, and pluralize by highlighting the contingent, provisional, variable, tentative, shifting, and changing. Needless to say, these gestures are not new in the history of criticism or art, yet what makes them novel—along with the cultural politics they produce—is what constitutes difference and how it is constituted, the weight and gravity it is given in representation, and the way in which highlighting issues like exterminism, empire, class, race, gender, sexual orientation, age, nation, nature, and region at this historical moment acknowledges some discontinuity and disruption from previous forms of cultural critique. To put it bluntly, the new cultural politics of difference consists of creative responses to the precise circumstances of our present moment—especially those of marginalized first world agents who shun degraded self-representations, articulating instead their sense of the flow of history in light of the contemporary terrors, anxieties, and fears of highly commercialized North Atlantic capitalist cultures (with their escalating xenophobias against people of color, Jews, women, gays, lesbians, and the elderly). The nationalist revolts against the legacy of hegemonic party henchmen in second world excommunist cultures, and the diverse cultures of the majority of inhabitants on the globe smothered by international communication cartels and repressive postcolonial elites (sometimes in the name of communism, as in Ethiopia) or starved by austere World Bank and IMF policies that subordinate them to the North (as in free-market capitalism in Chile), also locate vital areas of analysis in this new cultural terrain.

The new cultural politics of difference are neither simply oppositional in contesting the mainstream (or *male*stream) for inclusion nor transgressive in the avant-gardist sense of shocking conventional bourgeois audiences. Rather they are distinct articulations of talented (and usually privileged) contributors to culture who desire to align themselves with demoralized, demobilized, depoliticized, and disorganized people in order to empower and enable social action and, if possible, to enlist collective insurgency for the expansion of freedom, democracy, and individuality. This perspective impels these cultural critics and artists to reveal, as an integral component of their production, the very operations of power within their immediate work contexts (i.e., academy, museum, gallery, mass media). This strategy, however, also puts them in an inescapable double bind—while linking their activities to the fundamental, structural overhaul of these institutions, they often remain financially dependent on them. (So much for "independent" creation.) For these critics of culture, theirs is a gesture that is simultaneously progressive and co-opted. Yet without social movement or political pressure from outside these institutions (extraparliamentary and extracurricular actions like the social movements of the recent past), transformation degenerates into mere accommodation or sheer stagnation, and the role of the "co-opted progressive"—no matter how fervent one's subversive rhetoric—is rendered more difficult. In this sense there can be no artistic breakthrough or social progress without some form of crisis in civilization—a crisis usually generated by organizations or collectivities that convince ordinary people to put their bodies and lives on the line. There is, of course, no guarantee that such pressure will yield the result one wants, but there is a guarantee that the status quo will remain or regress if no pressure is applied at all.

The new cultural politics of difference faces three basic challenges—intellectual, existential, and political. The intellectual challenge—usually cast as a methodological debate in these days in which academicist forms of expression have a monopoly on intellectual life—is how to think about representational practices in terms of history, culture, and society. How does one understand, analyze, and enact such practices today? An adequate answer to this question can be attempted only after one comes to terms with the insights and blindnesses of earlier attempts to grapple with the question in light of the evolving crisis in different histories, cultures, and societies. I shall sketch a brief genealogy—a history that highlights the contingent origins and often ignoble outcomes—of exemplary critical responses to the question.

THE INTELLECTUAL CHALLENGE

An appropriate starting point is the ambiguous legacy of the Age of Europe. Between 1492 and 1945, European breakthroughs in oceanic transportation, agricultural production, state consolidation, bureaucratization, industrialization, urbanization, and imperial dominion shaped the makings of the modern world. Precious ideals like the dignity of persons (individuality) or the popular accountability of institutions (democracy) were unleashed around the world. Powerful critiques of illegitimate authorities—the Protestant Reformation against the Roman Catholic Church, the Enlightenment against state churches, liberal movements against absolutist states and feudal guild constraints, workers against managerial subordination, people of color and Jews against white and gentile supremacist decrees, gays and lesbians against homophobic sanctions—were fanned and fueled by these precious ideals refined within the crucible of the Age of Europe. Yet the discrepancy between sterling rhetoric and lived reality, glowing principles and actual practices, loomed large.

By the last European century—the last epoch in which European domination of most of the globe was not substantively contested or challenged—a new world seemed to be stirring. At the height of England's reign as the major imperial European power, its exemplary cultural critic, Matthew Arnold ([1855]1969), painfully observed in his "Stanzas from the Grand Chartreuse" that he felt some sense of "wandering between two worlds, one dead/the other powerless to be born" (p. 302). Following his Burkean sensibilities of cautious reform and fear of anarchy, Arnold acknowledged that the old glue—religion—that had tenuously and often unsuccessfully held together the ailing European regimes could not do so in the mid-nineteenth century. Like Alexis de Tocqueville in France, Arnold saw that the democratic temper was the wave of the future. So he proposed a new conception of culture—a secular, humanistic one—that could play an integrative role in cementing and stabilizing an emerging bourgeois civil society and imperial state. His famous castigation of the immobilizing materialism of the declining aristocracy, the vulgar philistinism of the emerging middle classes, and the latent explosiveness of the working-class majority was motivated by a desire to create new forms of cultural legitimacy, authority, and order in a rapidly changing moment in nineteenth-century Europe.

For Arnold ([1869]1925), this new conception of culture

> seeks to do away with classes; to make the best that has been thought and known in the world current everywhere; to make all men live in an atmosphere of sweetness and light....

> This is the *social idea* and the men of culture are the true apostles of equality. The great men of culture are those who have had a passion for diffusing, for making prevail, for carrying from one end of society to the other, the best knowledge, the best ideas of their time, who have laboured to divest knowledge of all that was harsh, uncouth, difficult, abstract, professional, yet still remaining the best knowledge and thought of the time, and a true source, therefore, of sweetness and light. (p. 67)

As an organic intellectual of an emergent middle class—as the inspector of schools in an expanding educational bureaucracy, professor of poetry at Oxford (the first noncleric and the first to lecture in English rather than Latin), and an active participant in a thriving magazine network—Arnold defined and defended a new secular culture of critical discourse. For him, this discursive strategy would be lodged in the educational and periodical apparatuses of modern societies as they contained and incorporated the frightening threats of an arrogant aristocracy and especially of an "anarchic" working-class majority. His ideals of disinterested, dispassionate, and objective inquiry would regulate this secular cultural production, and his justifications for the use of state power to quell any threats to the survival and security of this culture were widely accepted. He aptly noted, "Through culture seems to lie our way, not only to perfection, but even to safety" (Arnold, [1869]1925, p. 200).

For Arnold, the best of the Age of Europe—modeled on a mythological mélange of Periclean Athens, late republican/early imperial Rome, and Elizabethan England—could be promoted only if there were an interlocking affiliation among the emerging middle classes, a homogenizing of cultural discourse in the educational and university networks, and a state advanced enough in its policing techniques to safeguard it. The candidates for participation and legitimation in this grand endeavor of cultural renewal and revision would be detached intellectuals willing to shed their parochialism, provincialism and class-bound identities for Arnold's middle-class-skewed project: "Aliens, if we may so call them—persons who are mainly led, not by their class spirit, but by a general humane spirit, by the love of human perfection" ([1869]1925, p. 107). Needless to say, this Arnoldian perspective still informs much of academic practice and secular cultural attitudes today: dominant views about the canon, admission procedures, and collective self-definitions of intellectuals. Yet Arnold's project was disrupted by the collapse of nineteenth-century Europe—World War I. This unprecedented war—in George Steiner's words, the first of the bloody civil wars within Europe—brought to the surface the crucial role and violent potential not of the masses Arnold feared but of the state he heralded. Upon the ashes of this wasteland of human carnage—including some of the civilian European population—T.S. Eliot emerged as the grand cultural spokesman.

Eliot's project of reconstituting and reconceiving European highbrow culture—and thereby regulating critical and artistic practices—after the internal collapse of imperial Europe can be viewed as a response to the probing question posed by Paul Valéry in "The Crisis of the Mind" ([1919]1962) after World War I:

> Will Europe become *what it is in reality*—that is, a little promontory on the continent of Asia? Or will it remain *what it seems*—that is, the elect portion of the terrestrial globe, the pearl of the sphere, the brain of a vast body? (p. 31)

Eliot's image of Europe as a wasteland, a culture of fragments with no cementing center, predominated in postwar Europe. And though his early poetic practices were more radical, open, and international than his Eurocentric criticism, Eliot posed a return to and revision of tradition as the only way to regain European cultural order and political stability. For Eliot, contemporary history had become, as James Joyce's Stephen declared in *Ulysses* ([1922]1934), "a nightmare from which he was trying to awake" (p. 35); "an immense panorama of futility and anarchy," as Eliot put it in his renowned review of Joyce's modernist masterpiece (Eliot, [1923]1948, p. 201). In his influential essay, "Tradition and the Individual Talent" ([1919]1950), Eliot stated that:

> Yet if the only form of tradition, of handing down, consisted in following the ways of the immediate generation before us in a blind or timid adherence to its successes, "tradition" should positively be discouraged. We have seen many such simple currents soon lost in the sand; and novelty is better than repetition. Tradition is a matter of much wider significance. It cannot be inherited, and if you want it you must attain it by great labour. (p. 4)

Eliot found this tradition in the Church of England, to which he converted in 1927. Here was a tradition that left room for his Catholic cast of mind, Calvinist heritage, puritanical temperament, and ebullient patriotism for the old American South (the place of his upbringing). Like Arnold, Eliot was obsessed with the idea of civilization and the horror of barbarism (echoes of Joseph Conrad's Kurtz in *Heart of Darkness*), or, more pointedly, the notion of the decline and decay of European civilization. With the advent of World War II, Eliot's obsession became a reality. Again, unprecedented human carnage (fifty million died)—including an indescribable genocidal attack on Jewish people— throughout Europe as well as around the globe put the last nail in the coffin of the Age of Europe. After 1945, Europe consisted of a devastated and divided continent, crippled by a humiliating dependency on and deference to the United States and Russia.

The second historical coordinate of my genealogy is the emergence of the United States as *the* world power (in the words of André Malraux, the first nation to do so without trying to do so). The United States was unprepared for world power status. However, with the recovery of Stalin's Russia (after losing twenty million lives), the United States felt compelled to make its presence felt around the globe. Then, with the Marshall Plan to strengthen Europe, it seemed clear that there was no escape from world power obligations.

The post-World-War-II era in the United States, or the first decades of what Henry Luce envisioned as "The American Century," was a period not only of incredible economic expansion but of active cultural ferment. The creation of a mass middle class— a prosperous working class with bourgeois identity—was countered by the first major emergence of subcultures among American non-WASP intellectuals; the so-called New York intellectuals in criticism, the abstract expressionists in painting, and the bebop artists in jazz music. This emergence signaled a vital challenge to an American male WASP elite loyal to an older and eroding European culture.

The first significant blow was dealt when assimilated Jewish Americans entered the higher echelons of the cultural apparatuses (academy, museums, galleries, mass media).

Lionel Trilling is an emblematic figure. This Jewish entree into the anti-Semitic and patriarchal critical discourse of the exclusivistic institutions of American culture initiated the slow but sure undoing of male WASP cultural hegemony and homogeneity. Trilling's aim was to appropriate Arnold's project for his own political and cultural purposes—thereby unraveling the old male WASP consensus while erecting a new post-World-War-II liberal academic consensus around cold war, anticommunist renditions of the values of complexity, difficulty, variousness, and modulation. In addition, the postwar boom laid the basis for intense professionalization and specialization in expanding institutions of higher education—especially in the natural sciences, which were compelled to respond somehow to Russia's successful ventures in space. Humanistic scholars found themselves searching for new methodologies that could buttress self-images of rigor and scientific seriousness. The close reading techniques of New Criticism (severed from their conservative, organicist, anti-industrialist ideological roots), the logical precision of reasoning in analytic philosophy, and the jargon of Parsonian structural-functionalism in sociology, for example, helped create such self-images. Yet towering cultural critics like C. Wright Mills, W.E.B. DuBois, Richard Hofstadter, Margaret Mead, and Dwight MacDonald bucked the tide. This suspicion of the academicization of knowledge is expressed in Trilling's well-known essay "On the Teaching of Modern Literature" ([1961]1965):

> Can we not say that, when modern literature is brought into the classroom, the subject being taught is betrayed by the pedagogy of the subject? We have to ask ourselves whether in our day too much does not come within the purview of the academy. More and more, as the universities liberalize themselves, turn their beneficent imperialistic gaze upon what is called Life Itself, the feeling grows among our educated classes that little can be experienced unless it is validated by some established intellectual discipline. (p. 10)

Trilling laments the fact that university instruction often quiets and domesticates radical and subversive works of art, turning them into objects "of merely habitual regard." This process of "the socialization of the anti-social, or the acculturation of the anti-cultural, or the legitimization of the subversive" leads Trilling to "question whether in our culture the study of literature is any longer a suitable means for developing and refining the intelligence" ([1961]1965, p. 26). He asks this question in a spirit not of denigrating and devaluing the academy but rather of highlighting the possible failure of an Arnoldian conception of culture to contain what he perceives as the philistine and anarchic alternatives becoming more and more available to students of the '60s—namely, mass culture and radical politics.

This threat is partly associated with the third historical coordinate of my genealogy—the decolonization of the third world. It is crucial to recognize the importance of this world-historical process if one wants to grasp the significance of the end of the Age of Europe and the emergence of the United States as a world power. With the first defeat of a Western nation by a non-Western nation—in Japan's victory over Russia (1905); revolutions in Persia (1905), Turkey (1908), Mexico (1911–12), and China (1912); and much later the independence of India (1947) and China (1948) and the triumph of Ghana (1957)—the actuality of a decolonized globe loomed large. Born of violent struggle, consciousness raising, and the reconstruction of identities, decolonization simultaneously brings with it new perspectives on that long-festering underside of the Age of Europe (of which colonial domination represents the *costs* of "progress," "order," and "culture"), and requires new readings of the economic boom in the United States (wherein the black, brown, yellow, red, white, female, gay, lesbian, and elderly working class live the same *costs* by supplying cheap labor at home as well as in U.S.-dominated Latin American and Pacific Rim markets).

The impetuous ferocity and moral outrage that motor the decolonization process are best captured by Frantz Fanon in *The Wretched of the Earth* (1963):

> Decolonization, which sets out to change the order of the world, is, obviously, a program of complete disorder....Decolonization is the meeting of two forces, opposed to each other by their very nature, which in fact owe their originality to that sort of substantification which results from and is nourished by the situation in the colonies. Their first encounter was marked by violence and their existence together—that is to say the exploitation of the native by the settler—was carried on by dint of a great array of bayonets and cannons....

> In decolonization, there is therefore the need of a complete calling in question of the colonial situation. If we wish to describe it precisely, we might find it in the well-known words: "The last shall be first and the first last." Decolonization is the putting into practice of this sentence....

> The naked truth of decolonization evokes for us the searing bullets and bloodstained knives which emanate from it. For if the last shall be first, this will only come to pass after a murderous and decisive struggle between the two protagonists. (pp. 36–37)

Fanon's strong words describe the feelings and thoughts between the occupying British Army and the colonized Irish in Northern Ireland, the occupying Israeli Army and the subjugated Palestinians on the West Bank and Gaza Strip, the South African Army and the oppressed black South Africans in the townships, the Japanese police and the Koreans living in Japan, established armies and subordinated ethnic groups in the former Soviet Union. His words also partly invoke the sense many black Americans have toward police departments in urban centers. In other words, Fanon is articulating century-long, heartfelt, human responses to being degraded and despised, hated and hunted, oppressed and exploited, and marginalized and dehumanized at the hands of powerful, xenophobic European, American, Russian, and Japanese imperial nations.

During the late 1950s, the '60s, and the early '70s in the United States, these decolonized sensibilities fanned and fueled the civil rights and black power movements, as well as the student, antiwar, feminist, gray, brown, gay, and lesbian movements. In this period we witnessed the shattering of male WASP cultural homogeneity and the collapse of the short-lived liberal consensus. The inclusion of African Americans, Latino/a Americans, Asian Americans, Native Americans, and American women in the culture of critical discourse yielded intense intellectual polemics and inescapable ideological polarization that focused principally on the exclusions, silences, and blindnesses of male WASP cultural homogeneity and its concomitant Arnoldian notions of the canon.

In addition these critiques promoted three crucial processes that affected intellectual life in the country. First is the appropriation of the theories of postwar Europe—especially the work of the Frankfurt School (Marcuse, Adorno, Horkheimer), French/Italian Marxisms (Sartre, Althusser, Lefebvre, Gramsci), structuralisms (Levi-Strauss, Todorov), and poststructuralisms (Deleuze, Derrida, Foucault). These diverse and disparate theories—all preoccupied with keeping alive radical projects after the end of the Age of Europe—tend to fuse versions of transgressive European modernisms with Marxist or post-Marxist left politics and unanimously to shun the term "post-modernism." Second, there is the recovery and revisioning of American history in light of the struggles of white male workers, African Americans, Native Americans, Latino/a Americans, gays and lesbians. Third is the impact of forms of popular culture such as television, film, music videos, and even sports on highbrow, literate culture. The black-based hip-hop culture of youth around the world is one grand example.

After 1973, with the crisis in the international economy, America's slump in productivity, the challenge of OPEC nations to the North Atlantic monopoly of oil production, the increasing competition in high-tech sectors of the economy from Japan and West Germany, and the growing fragility of the international debt structure, the United States entered a period of waning self-confidence (compounded by Watergate) and a nearly contracted economy. As the standards of living for the middle classes declined—owing to runaway inflation and escalating unemployment, underemployment, and crime—the quality of living fell for most everyone, and religious and secular neoconservatism emerged with power and potency. This fusion of fervent neo-conservatism, traditional cultural values, and "free market" policies served as the groundwork for the Reagan-Bush era.

The ambiguous legacies of the European Age, U.S. preeminence, and decol-onization continue to haunt our postmodern moment as we come to terms with both the European, American, Japanese, Soviet, and third world *crimes against* and *contributions to* humanity. The plight of Africans in the New World can be instructive in this regard.

By 1914 European maritime empires had dominion over more than half of the land and a third of the peoples in the world—almost seventy-two million square kilometers of territory and more than 560 million people around colonial rule. Needless to say, this European control included brutal enslavement, institutional terrorism, and cultural degradation of black diaspora people. The death of roughly seventy-five million Africans during the centuries-long, transatlantic slave trade is but one reminder, among others, of the assault on black humanity. The black diaspora condition of New World servitude—in which people of African descent were viewed as mere commodities with production value, who had no proper legal status, social standing, or public worth—can be characterized, following Orlando Patterson, as natal alienation. This state of perpetual and inheritable domination that diaspora Africans had at birth produced the *modern black diaspora problematic of invisibility and namelessness*. White supremacist practices—enacted under the auspices of the prestigious cultural authorities of the churches, print media, and scientific academics—promoted black inferiority and constituted the European background against which African diaspora struggles for identity, dignity (self-confidence, self-respect, self-esteem), and material resources took place.

An inescapable aspect of this struggle was that the black diaspora peoples' quest for validation and recognition occurred on the ideological, social, and cultural terrains of non-black peoples. White supremacist assaults on black intelligence, ability, beauty, and character required persistent black efforts to hold self-doubt, self-contempt, and even self-hatred at bay. Selective appropriation, incorporation, and rearticulation of European ideologies, cultures, and institutions alongside an African heritage—a heritage more or less confined to linguistic innovation in rhetorical practices, stylizations of the body as forms of occupying an alien social space (e.g., hairstyles, ways of walking, standing, and talking, and hand expressions), means of constituting and sustaining camaraderie and community (e.g., antiphonal, call-and-response styles, rhythmic repetition, risk-ridden syncopation in spectacular modes in musical and rhetorical expressions)—were some of the strategies employed.

The modern black diaspora problematic of invisibility and namelessness can be understood as the condition of *relative lack of power for blacks to present themselves to themselves and others as complex human beings, and thereby to contest the bombardment of negative, degrading stereotypes put forward by white supremacist ideologies*. The initial black response to being caught in this whirlwind of Europeanization was to resist the misrepresentation and caricature of the terms set by uncontested non-black norms and models and to fight for self-recognition. Every modern black person, especially the cultural disseminator, encounters this problematic of invisibility and namelessness. The initial African diaspora response was a mode of resistance that was *moralistic in content and communal in character.* That is, the fight for representation and recognition highlighted moral judgements regarding black "positive" images over and against white supremacist stereotypes. These images "re-presented" monolithic and homogeneous black communities in a way that could displace past misrepresentations of these communities. Stuart Hall has discussed these responses as attempts to change the "relations of representation."

These courageous yet limited black efforts to combat racist cultural practices uncritically accepted non-black conventions and standards in two ways. First, they proceeded in an *assimilationist manner* that set out to show that black people were really like white people—thereby eliding differences (in history and culture) between whites and blacks. Black specificity and particularity were thus banished in order to gain white acceptance and approval. Second, these black responses rested upon a *homogenizing impulse* that assumed that all black people were really alike—hence obliterating differences (class, gender, region, sexual orientation) between black peoples. I submit that there are elements of truth in both claims, yet the conclusions are unwarranted owing to the basic fact that non-black paradigms set the terms of the replies.

The insight in the first claim is that blacks and whites are in some important sense alike—i.e., positively, in their capacities for human sympathy, moral sacrifice, service to others, intelligence, and beauty; or negatively, in their capacity for cruelty. Yet the common humanity they share is jettisoned when the claim is cast in an assimilationist manner that subordinates black particularity to a false universalism, i.e., non-black rubrics and prototypes. Similarly, the insight in the second claim is that all blacks are in some significant sense "in the same boat"—that is, subject to white supremacist abuse. Yet this common condition is stretched too far when viewed in a *homogenizing* way that overlooks how racist treatment vastly differs owing to class, gender, sexual orientation, nation, region, hue, and age.

The moralistic and communal aspects of the initial black diaspora responses to social and psychic erasure were not simply cast into binary oppositions of positive/negative, good/bad images that privileged the first term in light of a white norm, so that black efforts remained inscribed within the very logic that dehumanized them. They were further complicated by the fact that these responses were advanced principally by anxiety-ridden, middle-class black intellectuals (predominantly male and heterosexual) grappling with their sense of double-consciousness—namely their own crisis of identity, agency, audience—caught between a quest for white approval and acceptance and an endeavor to overcome the internalized association of blackness with inferiority. And I suggest that these complex anxieties of modern black diaspora intellectuals partly motivate the two major arguments that ground the assimilationist moralism and homogeneous communalism just outlined.

Kobena Mercer has talked about these two arguments as the *reflectionist* and the *social engineering* arguments. The reflectionist argument holds that the fight for black representation and recognition—against white racist stereotypes—must reflect or mirror the real black community, not simply the negative and depressing representations of it. The social engineering argument claims that since any form of representation is constructed—i.e., selective in light of broader aims—black representation (especially given the difficulty for blacks to gain access to positions of power to produce any black imagery) should offer positive images, thereby countering racist stereotypes. The hidden assumption of both arguments is that we have unmediated access to what the "real black community" is and what "positive images" are. In short, these arguments presuppose the very phenomenon to be interrogated and thereby foreclose the very issues that should serve as the subject matter to be investigated.

Any notions of "the real black community" and "positive images" are value laden, socially loaded, and ideologically charged. To pursue this discussion is to call into question the possibility of such an uncontested consensus regarding them. Hall has rightly called this encounter "the end of innocence or the end of the innocent notions of the essential Black subject...the recognition that 'black' is essentially a politically and culturally constructed category"(Hall, 1988, p. 28). This recognition—more and more pervasive among the postmodern African diaspora intelligentsia—is facilitated in part by the slow but sure dissolution of the European Age's maritime empires and the unleashing of new political possibilities and cultural articulations among ex-colonized peoples across the globe.

One crucial lesson of this decolonization process remains the manner in which most third world authoritarian bureaucratic elites deploy essentialist rhetorics about "homogeneous national communities" and "positive images" in order to repress and regiment their diverse and heterogeneous populations. Yet in the diaspora, especially among first world countries, this critique has emerged not so much from the black male component of the left as from the black women's movement. The decisive push of postmodern black intellectuals toward a new cultural politics of difference has been made by the powerful critiques and constructive explorations of black diaspora women (e.g., Toni Morrison). The coffin used to bury the innocent notion of the essential black subject was nailed shut with the termination of the black male monopoly on the construction of the black subject. In this regard, the black diaspora womanist critique has had a greater impact than have the critiques that highlight exclusively class, empire, age, sexual orientation, or nature.

This decisive push toward the end of black innocence—though prefigured in various degrees in the best moments of W.E.B. DuBois, James Baldwin, Amiri Baraka, Anna Cooper, Frantz Fanon, C.L.R. James, Claudia Jones, the later Malcolm X, and others—forces black diaspora cultural workers to encounter what Hall has called "the politics of representation." The main aim now is not simply access to representation in order to produce positive images of homogeneous communities—though broader access remains a practical and political problem. Nor is the primary goal here that of contesting stereotypes—though contestation remains a significant albeit limited venture. Following the model of the African diaspora traditions of music, athletics, and rhetoric, black cultural workers must constitute and sustain discursive and institutional networks that deconstruct earlier modern black strategies for identity formation, demystify power relations that incorporate class, patriarchal, and homophobic biases, and construct more multivalent and multidimensional responses that articulate the complexity and diversity of black practices in the modern and postmodern world.

Furthermore, black cultural workers must investigate and interrogate the other of blackness/whiteness. One cannot deconstruct the binary oppositional logic of images of blackness without extending it to the contrary condition of blackness/whiteness itself. However, a mere dismantling will not do—for the very notion of a deconstructive social theory is oxymoronic. Yet social theory is what is needed to examine and *explain* the historically specific ways in which "whiteness" is a politically constructed category parasitic on "blackness," and thereby to conceive of the profoundly hybrid character of what we mean by "race," "ethnicity," and "nationality." Needless to say, these inquiries must traverse those of "male/female," "colonizer/colonized," "heterosexual/homosexual," et al., as well.

Demystification is the most illuminating mode of theoretical inquiry for those who promote the new cultural politics of difference. Social structural analyses of empire, exterminism, class, race, gender, nature, age, sexual orientation, nation, and region are the springboards—though not the landing grounds—for the most desirable forms of critical practice that take history (and herstory) seriously. Demystification tries to keep track of the complex dynamics of institutional and other related power structures in order to disclose options and alternatives for transformational praxis; it also attempts to grasp the way in which representational strategies are creative responses to novel circumstances and conditions. In this way the central role of human agency (always enacted under circumstances not of one's choosing)—be it in the critic, artist, or constituency, and audience—is accented.

I call demystificatory criticism "prophetic criticism"—the approach appropriate for the new cultural politics of difference—because while it begins with social structural analyses it also makes explicit its moral and political aims. It is partisan, partial, engaged, and crisis centered, yet it always keeps open a skeptical eye to avoid dogmatic traps, premature closures, formulaic formulations, or rigid conclusions. In addition to social-structural analyses, moral and political judgements, and sheer critical consciousness, there indeed is evaluation. Yet the aim of this evaluation is neither to pit art objects against one another like racehorses nor to create eternal canons that dull, discourage, or even dwarf contemporary achievements. We listen to Laurie Anderson, Kathleen Battle, Ludwig van Beethoven, Charlie Parker, Luciano Pavarotti, Sarah Vaughan, or Stevie Wonder; read Anton Chekhov, Ralph Ellison, Gabriel García Márquez, Doris Lessing, Toni Morrison, Thomas Pynchon, William Shakespeare; or see the works of Ingmar Bergman, Le Corbusier, Frank Gehry, Barbara Kruger, Spike Lee, Martin Puryear, Pablo Picasso, or Howardena Pindell—not in order to undergird bureaucratic assents or enliven cocktail party conversations, but rather to be summoned by the styles they deploy for their profound insights, pleasures, and challenges. Yet all evaluation—including a delight in Eliot's poetry despite his reactionary politics, or a love of Zora Neale Hurston's novels despite her Republican Party affiliations—is inseparable from, though not identical or reducible to, social structural analyses, moral and political judgements, and the workings of a curious critical consciousness.

The deadly traps of demystification—and any form of prophetic criticism—are those of reductionism, be it of the sociological, psychological, or historical sort. By reductionism I mean either one-factor analyses (crude Marxisms, feminisms, racialisms, etc.) that yield a one-dimensional functionalism or hypersubtle analytical perspectives that lose touch with the specificity of an artwork's form and the context of its reception. Few cultural workers of whatever stripe can walk the tightrope between the Scylla of reductionism and the Charybdis of aestheticism—yet demystificatory (or prophetic) critics must. Of course, since so many art practices these days also purport to be criticism, this also holds true for artists.

THE EXISTENTIAL CHALLENGE

The existential challenge to the new cultural politics of difference can be stated simply: How does one acquire the resources to survive and the cultural capital to thrive as a critic or artist? By cultural capital (Pierre Bourdieu's term), I mean not only the high-quality skills required to engage in cultural practices but more importantly, the self-confidence, discipline, and perseverance necessary for success without an undue reliance on the mainstream for approval and acceptance. This challenge holds for all prophetic critics, yet it is especially difficult for those of color. The widespread modern European denial of the intelligence, ability, beauty, and character of people of color puts a tremendous burden on critics and artists of color to "prove" themselves in light of norms and models set by white elites whose own heritage devalued and dehumanized them. In short, in the court of criticism and art—or any matters regarding the life of the mind—people of color are guilty (i.e., not expected to meet standards of intellectual achievement) until "proven" innocent (i.e., acceptable to "us").

This is more a structural dilemma than a matter of personal attitudes. The profoundly racist and sexist heritage of the European Age has bequeathed to us a set of deeply ingrained perceptions about people of color, including, of course, the self-perceptions that people of color bring. It is not surprising that most intellectuals of color in the past exerted much of their energies and efforts to gain acceptance and approval by "white normative gazes." The new cultural politics of difference advises critics and artists of color to put aside this mode of mental bondage, thereby freeing themselves both to interrogate the ways in which they are bound by certain conventions and to learn from and build on these very norms and models. One hallmark of wisdom in the context of any struggle is to avoid knee-jerk rejection and uncritical acceptance.

Self-confidence, discipline, and perseverance are not ends in themselves. Rather they are the necessary stuff of which enabling criticism and self-criticism are made. Notwithstanding inescapable jealousies, insecurities, and anxieties, one telling characteristic of critics and artists of color linked to the new prophetic criticism should be their capacity for and promotion of relentless criticism and self-criticism—be it the normative paradigms of their white colleagues that tend to leave out considerations of empire, race, gender, and sexual orientation, or the damaging dogmas about the homogeneous character of communities of color.

There are four basic options for people of color interested in representation—if they are to survive and thrive as serious practitioners of their craft. First, there is the Booker T. Temptation, namely the individual preoccupation with the mainstream and its legitimizing power. Most critics and artists of color try to bite this bait. It is nearly unavoidable, yet few succeed in a substantive manner. It is no accident that the most creative and profound among them—especially those who have staying power beyond being mere flashes in the pan to satisfy faddish tokenism—are usually marginal to the mainstream. Even the pervasive professionalization of cultural practitioners of color in the past few decades has not produced towering figures who reside within the established white patronage system, which bestows the rewards and prestige for chosen contributions to American society.

It certainly helps to have some trustworthy allies within this system, yet most of those who enter and remain tend to lose much of their creativity, diffuse their prophetic energy, and dilute their critiques. Still, it is unrealistic for creative people of color to think they can sidestep the white patronage system. And though there are indeed some white allies conscious of the tremendous need to rethink identity politics, it is naive to think that being comfortably nested within this very same system—even if one can be a patron to others—does not affect one's work, one's outlook, and most important, one's soul.

The second option is the Talented Tenth Seduction, namely, a move toward arrogant group insularity. This alternative has a limited function—to preserve one's sanity and sense of self as one copes with the mainstream. Yet it is, at best, a transitional and transient activity. If it becomes a permanent option it is self-defeating in that it usually reinforces the very inferiority complexes promoted by the subtly racist mainstream. Hence it tends to revel in parochialism and encourage a narrow racialist and chauvinistic outlook.

The third strategy is the Go-It-Alone Option. This is an extreme rejectionist perspective that shuns the mainstream and group insularity. Almost every critic and artist of color contemplates or enacts this option at some time in his or her pilgrimage. It is healthy in that it reflects the presence of independent, critical, and skeptical sensibilities toward perceived constraints on one's creativity. Yet it is, in the end, difficult if not impossible to sustain if one is to grow, develop, and mature intellectually, as some semblance of dialogue with a community is necessary for almost any creative practice.

The most desirable option for people of color who promote the new cultural politics of difference is to be a Critical Organic Catalyst. By this I mean a person who stays attuned to the best of what the mainstream has to offer—its paradigms, viewpoints, and methods— yet maintains a grounding in affirming and enabling subcultures of criticism. Prophetic critics and artists of color should be exemplars of what it means to be intellectual freedom fighters, that is, cultural workers who simultaneously position themselves within (or alongside) the mainstream while clearly being aligned with groups who vow to keep alive potent traditions of critique and resistance. In this regard one can take clues from the great musicians or preachers of color who are open to the best of what other traditions offer, yet are rooted in nourishing subcultures that build on the grand achievements of a vital heritage. Openness to others—including the mainstream—does not entail wholesale co-optation, and group autonomy is not group insularity. Louis Armstrong, Ella Baker, W.E.B. DuBois, Martin Luther King, Jr., Jose Carlos Mariatequi, Wynton Marsalis, M.M. Thomas, and Ronald Takaki have understood this well.

The new cultural politics of difference can thrive only if there are communities, groups, organizations, institutions, subcultures, and networks of people of color who cultivate critical sensibilities and personal accountability—without inhibiting individual expressions, curiosities, and idiosyncrasies. This is especially needed given the escalating racial hostility, violence, and polarization in the United States. Yet this critical coming together must not be a narrow closing of ranks. Rather it is a strengthening and nurturing endeavor that can forge more solid alliances and coalitions. In this way prophetic criticism—with its stress on historical specificity and artistic complexity—directly addresses the intellectual challenge. The cultural capital of people of color—with its emphasis on self-confidence, discipline, perseverance, and subcultures of criticism—also tries to meet the existential requirement. Both are mutually reinforcing. Both are motivated by a deep commitment to individuality and democracy—the moral and political ideals that guide the creative responses to the political challenge.

THE POLITICAL CHALLENGE

Adequate rejoinders to intellectual and existential challenges equip the practitioners of the new cultural politics of difference to meet the political ones. This challenge principally consists of forging solid and reliable alliances to people of color and white progressives guided by a moral and political vision of greater democracy and individual freedom in communities, states, and transnational enterprises—i.e., corporations and information and communications conglomerates. Jesse Jackson's Rainbow Coalition is a gallant yet flawed effort in this regard: gallant due to the tremendous energy, vision, and courage of its leader and followers; flawed because of its failure to take seriously critical and democratic sensibilities within its own operations.

The time has come for critics and artists of the new cultural politics of difference to cast their nets widely, flex their muscles broadly, and thereby refuse to limit their visions, analyses, and praxis to their particular terrains. The aim is to dare to recast, redefine, and revise the very notions of "modernity," "mainstream," "margins," "difference," "otherness." We have now reached a new stage in the perennial struggle for freedom and dignity. And while much of the first world intelligentsia adopts retrospective and conservative outlooks that defend the crisis-ridden present, we promote a prospective and prophetic vision with a sense of possibility and potential, especially for those who bear the social costs of the present. We look to the past for strength, not solace; we look at the present and see people perishing, not profits mounting; we look toward the future and vow to make it different and better.

To put it boldly, the new kind of critic and artist associated with the new cultural politics of difference consists of an energetic breed of new world *bricoleurs* with improvisational and flexible sensibilities that sidestep mere opportunism and mindless eclecticism; persons of all countries, cultures, genders, sexual orientations, ages, and regions, with protean identities, who avoid ethnic chauvinism and faceless universalism; intellectual and political freedom fighters with partisan passion, international perspectives, and, thank God, a sense of humor to combat the ever-present absurdity that forever threatens our democratic and libertarian projects and dampens the fire that fuels our will to struggle. We will struggle and stay, as those brothers and sisters on the block say, "out there"—with intellectual rigor, existential dignity, moral vision, political courage, and soulful style.

Published with the permission of the author. This essay first appeared in *October* 53 (Summer 1990), pp. 93–109.

REFERENCES

Arnold, M. ([1869]1925). *Culture and Anarchy: An essay in political criticism.* New York: MacMillan.

————. ([1855]1969). Stanzas from the Grand Chartreuse. In C. B. Tinker & H. F. Lowry (eds.), *Poetical Works* (299–306). London: Oxford.

Eliot, T. S. ([1919]1950). Tradition and the individual talent. In *Selected Essays* (pp. 3–11). New York: Harcourt.

————. ([1923]1948). Ulysses, order, and myth. In S. Givens (ed.), *James Joyce: Two decades of criticism* (198–202). New York: Vanguard.

Fanon, F. (1963). *The Wretched of the Earth.* New York: Grove.

Hall, S. (1988). *New Ethnicities.* In K. Mercer (ed.), *Black Film, British Cinema.* ICA documents, 7 (27–31). London: ICA.

Joyce, J. ([1922]1934). *Ulysses.* New York: Random.

Trilling, L. ([1961]1965). On the teaching of modern literature. In *Beyond Culture: Essays on literature and learning* (3–30). New York: Viking.

Valéry, P. ([1919]1962). The crisis of the mind. In D. Folliot & J. Mathews (eds.), *The Collected Works of Paul Valéry* (Vol. 10, 23–36). New York: Bollingen.

3 Constructing the "Other": Rightist Reconstructions of Common Sense

Michael W. Apple

Introduction

In 1988, Kenneth Baker, the former British Secretary of Education and Science in the Thatcher Government, evaluated nearly a decade of rightist governmental efforts by saying that "the age of egalitarianism is over" (quoted in Arnot, 1990, p. 2). He was speaking positively, not negatively. At the same time in the United States, high-level right-wing government officials also spoke eloquently of their accomplishments in returning education to what was important if we were to reverse "our economic and cultural decline" (Bennett, 1988).

Seen from above, the "success" of the conservative attacks on egalitarian norms and values has largely been that, a success. Seen from below—from the perspective of, say, inner-city schools or from the perspectives of the majority of people of color—this signifies another in a long history of race and class attacks on the least advantaged members of this society, attacks that ignore the oppressive realities of these people's lives in and out of schools. It ignores the fact that for many chronically ill poor school districts, after years of "benign neglect" the fiscal crisis has gotten so severe that textbooks are used until they literally fall apart. Basements, closets, gymnasiums, and any "available" spaces are used for instruction. Teachers are being laid off, as are support staff, counselors, and others.[1]

In some towns and cities in the United States, it will be nearly impossible for schools to remain open for the full academic year. And even when they are open, the financial plight is now so distressing that in cities such as Detroit it is not unusual to have three entire elementary school classes share one set of textbooks (Kozol, 1991, p. 198).

Yet, while all this is occurring, there has been a movement toward a more widespread public acceptance of both the diagnoses and the solutions offered by neoconservatives (with their emphasis on "traditional" culture and values) and neoliberals (with their emphasis on a totally market-driven society). Even though one could argue that such cultural absolutism is often a new form of racism and could show the destructiveness of unregulated markets (Johnson, 1991, p. 97), one is still left with the fact that analyzing how the discourses of race and economics work ideologically has become very complicated.

On Ideology

The conventional approach to understanding how ideology operates assumes by and large that ideology is "inscribed in" people simply because they are in a particular class position.

Either the power of dominant ideas is treated as a given in which dominance is guaranteed, or the differences in "inscribed" class cultures and ideologies are seen as generating significant class conflict. In either case, ideology is seen as something that somehow makes its effects felt on people in the economy, in politics, in culture and education, and in the home without too much effort. It is simply *there*. The common sense of people becomes common sense "naturally" as they go about their daily lives, lives that are prestructured by their class position. If you know someone's location in the class structure, you know her or his sets of political, economic, and cultural beliefs, and you don't really have to inquire into *how* dominant beliefs actually do become dominant. It is usually not assumed that these ideas "should positively have to *win* ascendancy (rather than being ascribed it) through a specific and contingent (in the sense of open-ended, not totally determined) process of ideological struggle" (Hall, 1988, p. 42).

Yet the current political situation in many Western capitalist nations presents us with evidence that such a conventional story is more than a little inadequate in understanding the shifts that are occurring in people's common sense. We are seeing a pattern of conflicts within dominant groups that has led to significant changes in their own positions, and, even more importantly, we are witnessing how elements of ideologies of groups in dominance become truly *popular*. There is a rupture in the accepted beliefs of many segments of the public who have historically been less powerful (Hall, 1988), a rupture that has been worked upon and expanded by economically and politically strong forces in the society. And these ideological shifts in common sense are having a profound impact on how a large portion of the public thinks about the role of education in that society.

In this chapter, I shall describe and analyze a number of the most important changes in popular conceptions. A particular concern will be how ideologies actually become a part of the popular consciousness of classes and class fractions who are not among the elite. The construction, use, and history of racial discourse will be a crucial part of the story I wish to tell. In order to understand this, I shall employ theoretical work on the nature of how ideology functions that has developed over the past decade. I don't want to do this because of some disembodied commitment to the importance of "grand theory." Indeed, as I have argued at greater length in *Teachers and Texts* (Apple, 1988b), we have been much too abstract in our attempts to analyze the role of education in the maintenance and subversion of social and cultural power. Rather, I intend to provide an instance of the use of theories to uncover the limits and possibilities of cultural and political action by actually applying them to a concrete situation that is of major importance today, the new right's reconstruction of our ideas about equality.

Stuart Hall stresses exactly this point in his criticism of the abstractness of much critical literature on culture and power in the last two decades. After a period of "intense theorization," a movement has grown that has criticized "the hyperabstraction and overtheoretism that has characterized theoretical speculation, since...the early 1970s" (Hall, 1988, p. 35). As he puts it, in what seemed to be the pursuit of theory for its own sake, "we have abandoned the problems of concrete historical analysis" (p. 35). How do we counteract this tendency? Theoretical analysis should be there to allow us to "grasp, understand, and explain—to produce a more adequate knowledge of—the historical world and its processes; and thereby to inform our practice so that we may transform it" (p. 36). This is what I shall do here.

RECONSTRUCTING EDUCATION

Concepts do not remain still very long. They have wings, so to speak, and can be induced to fly from place to place. It is this context that defines their meaning. As Wittgenstein so nicely reminded us, one should look for the meaning of language in its specific contextual use. This is especially important in understanding political and educational concepts, since they are part of a larger social context, a context that is constantly shifting and is subject to severe ideological conflicts. Education itself is an arena in which these ideological conflicts work themselves out. It is one of the major sites in which different groups with distinct political, economic, and cultural visions attempt to define what the socially legitimate means and ends of a society are to be.

In this chapter, I want to situate the concern with "equality" in education within these larger conflicts. I shall place its shifting meanings both within the breakdown of the largely liberal consensus that guided much educational and social policy since World War II and within the recent growth of the new right and conservative movements. Over the past two decades, conservatives have had a good deal of success in redefining what education is *for* and in shifting the ideological texture of the society profoundly to the right (Apple, 1993; 1988b; Giroux, 1984). In the process, I want to document how new social movements gain the ability to redefine—often, though not always, in retrogressive ways—the terms of debate in education, social welfare, and other areas of the common good. At root, my claim will be that it is impossible fully to comprehend the shifting fortunes of the assemblage of concepts surrounding equality (equality of opportunity, equity, etc.) unless we have a much clearer picture of the society's already unequal cultural, economic, and political dynamics that provide the context in which education functions.

As I have argued at considerably greater length elsewhere, what we are witnessing today is nothing less than the recurrent conflict between *property rights* and *person rights* that has been a central tension in our economy (Apple, 1985; 1988b). Herbert Gintis defines the differences between property rights and person rights in the following way:

> A *property right* vests in individuals the power to enter into social relationships on the basis and extent of their property. This may include economic rights of unrestricted use, free contract, and voluntary exchange; political rights of participation and influence; and cultural rights of access to the social means for the transmission of knowledge and the reproduction and transformation of consciousness. A *person right* vests in individuals the power to enter into these social relationships on the basis of simple membership in the social collectivity. Thus, person rights involve equal treatment of citizens, freedom of expression and movement, equal access to participation in decision-making in social institutions, and reciprocity in relations of power and authority (Gintis, 1980, p. 193).

It is not surprising that in our society dominant groups "have fairly consistently defended the prerogatives of property," while subordinate groups on the whole have sought to advance "the prerogatives of persons" (Gintis, 1980, p. 194).[2] In times of severe upheaval, these conflicts become even more intense. So, given the current balance of power in society, advocates of property rights have once again been able to advance their claims for the restoration and expansion of their prerogatives not only in education, but in all of our social institutions.

The United States economy is in the midst of one of the most powerful structural crises it has experienced since the Depression. In order to solve it on terms acceptable to dominant interests, as many aspects of the society as possible need to be pressured into conforming with the requirements of international competition, reindustrialization, and (in the words of the National Commission on Excellence in Education) "rearmament." The gains made by women and men in employment, health and safety, welfare programs, affirmative action, legal rights, and education must be rescinded since they are "too expensive" both economically and ideologically.

Both of these latter words are important. Not only are fiscal resources scarce (in part because current policies continue to transfer much of them to the military despite the discussion of a "peace dividend"), but people must be convinced that their belief that person rights come first is simply wrong or outmoded given current "realities." Thus, intense pressure must be brought to bear through legislation, persuasion, administrative rules, and ideological maneuvering to create the conditions right-wing groups believe are necessary to meet these requirements (Apple, 1988b).

In the process, not just in the United States, but in Britain and Australia as well, the emphasis of public policy has materially changed from issues of employing the state to overcoming disadvantage. Equality, no matter how limited or broadly conceived, has been redefined. No longer is it seen as linked to past *group* oppression and disadvantage. It is now simply a case of guaranteeing *individual choice* under the conditions of a "free market" (Anderson, 1985, pp. 6–8). Thus, the current emphasis on "excellence" (a word with multiple meanings and social uses) has shifted educational discourse so that underachievement is once again increasingly seen as largely the fault of the student. Student failure, which was formerly at least partly interpreted as the fault of severely deficient educational policies and practices, is now being seen as the result of what might be called the biological and economic marketplace. This is evidenced in the growth of forms of Social Darwinist thinking in education and in public policy in general (Bastian, Fruchter, Gittell, and Haskins, 1986, p. 14).

In a similar way, behind a good deal of the rhetorical artifice of concern about the achievement levels in, say, inner city schools, notions of choice have begun to evolve that assert deep-seated school problems will be solved by establishing free competition over students. These assume that by expanding the capitalist marketplace to schools, we will somehow compensate for the decades of racism and economic and educational neglect experienced by the communities in which these schools are found.[3] Finally, there are concerted attacks on teachers (and curricula) based on a profound mistrust of their quality and commitments.

All of this has led to an array of educational conflicts that have been instrumental in shifting the debates over education profoundly to the right. The effects of this shift can be seen in a number of educational policies and proposals now gaining momentum throughout the country: 1) proposals for voucher plans and tax credits to make schools more like the idealized free-market economy; 2) the movement in state legislatures and state departments of education to "raise standards" and mandate both teacher and student "competencies" and basic curricular goals and knowledge, thereby centralizing even more at a state level the control of teaching and curricula; 3) the increasingly effective assaults on the school curriculum for its supposedly anti-family and anti-free enterprise bias, its "secular humanism," its lack of patriotism, and its neglect of the norms and values of the "Western tradition"; and 4) the growing pressure to make the needs of business and industry into the primary goals of the educational system (Apple, 1988b; Apple and Christian-Smith, 1991). These are major alterations, ones that have taken years to show their effects. Though I shall paint in rather broad strokes here, an outline of the social and ideological dynamics of how this has occurred should be visible.

THE RESTORATION POLITICS OF AUTHORITARIAN POPULISM

The first thing to ask about an ideology is not what is false about it, but what is true. What are its connections to lived experience? Ideologies, properly conceived, do not dupe people. To be effective they must connect to real problems, real experiences (Apple, 1990; Larrain, 1983). As I shall document, the movement away from social democratic principles and the acceptance of more right-wing positions in social and educational policy occur precisely because conservative groups have been able to work on popular sentiments, to reorganize genuine feelings, and in the process to win adherents.

Important ideological shifts take place not only through powerful groups "substituting one, whole, new conception of the world for another" (Hall, 1985, p. 122). Often, these shifts occur through the presentation of novel combinations of old and new elements. Let us take the positions of the Reagan administration—positions that helped define and were largely continued by Bush—as a case in point, for as Clark and Astuto (1986) have demonstrated in education and Piven and Cloward (1982) and Raskin (1986) have shown in the larger areas of social policy, during the Reagan-Bush years, significant and enduring alterations occurred in the ways policies are carried out and in the content of those policies.[4] Some of these policies have been continued by Clinton for political reasons.

The success of the policies of the Reagan administration, like that of Thatcher's (and, later, Major's) tenure in Britain, should not simply be evaluated in electoral terms. They need to be judged by their success as well in disorganizing other more progressive groups, in shifting the terms of political, economic, and cultural debate onto the terrain favored by capital and the right (Hall and Jacques, 1983, p. 13; Education Group II, 1991). In these terms, there can be no doubt that the current right-wing resurgence has accomplished no small amount in its attempt to construct the conditions that will put it in a hegemonic position.

The right in the United States and Britain has thoroughly renovated and reformed itself. It has developed strategies based upon what might best be called an *authoritarian populism* (Hall, 1980, pp. 160–161). As Hall has defined this, such a policy is based on an increasingly close relationship between government and the capitalist economy, a radical decline in the institutions and power of political democracy, and attempts at curtailing "liberties" that have been gained in the past. This is coupled with attempts to build a consensus, one that is widespread, in support of these actions (p. 161). The new right's "authoritarian populism"[5] has exceptionally deep roots in the history of the United States. The political culture here has always been influenced by the values of the dissenting Protestantism of the seventeenth century. Such roots become even more evident in periods of intense social change and crisis (Omi and Winant, 1986, p. 214). As Burnham has put it:

> Whenever and wherever the pressures of "modernization"—secularity, urbanization, the growing importance of science—have become unusually intense, episodes of revivalism and culture-issue politics have swept over the social landscape. In all such cases since at least the end of the Civil War, such movements have been more or less explicitly reactionary, and have frequently been linked with other kinds of reaction in explicitly political ways. (Burnham, 1983, p. 125)

The new right works on these roots in creative ways, modernizing them and creating a new synthesis of their varied elements by linking them to current fears. In so doing, the right has been able to rearticulate traditional political and cultural themes and because of this has effectively mobilized a large amount of mass support.

As I noted, part of the strategy has been the attempted dismantling of the welfare state and of the benefits that working people, people of color, and women (these categories are obviously not mutually exclusive) have won over decades of hard work. This has been done under the guise of anti-statism, of keeping government "off the backs of the people," and of "free enterprise." Yet, at the same time, in many valuative, political, and economic areas the current government is extremely state-centrist both in its outlook and very importantly in its day-to-day operations (Hall, 1985, p. 117).

One of the major aims of a rightist restoration politics is to struggle in not one but many different arenas at the same time, not only in the economic sphere but in education and elsewhere as well. This aim is grounded in the realization that economic dominance must be coupled with "political, moral, and intellectual leadership" if a group is to be truly dominant and if it wants genuinely to restructure a social formation. Thus, as both Reaganism and Thatcherism recognized so clearly, to win in the state you must also win in civil society (Hall, 1985, p. 119). As the noted Italian political theorist Antonio Gramsci would put it, what we are seeing is a war of position. In Hall's reconstruction of this argument, "it takes place where the whole relation of the state to civil society, to 'the people' and to popular struggles, to the individual and to the economic life of society has been thoroughly reorganized, where 'all the elements change'" (Hall, 1980, p. 166).

The right then has set itself an immense task, to create a truly "organic ideology," one that seeks to spread throughout society and to create a new form of "national popular will." It seeks to intervene "on the terrain of ordinary, contradictory common sense," to "interrupt, renovate, and transform in a more systematic direction" people's practical consciousness. It is this restructuring of common sense, which is itself the already complex and contradictory result of previous struggles and accords, which becomes the object of the cultural battles now being waged (Hall, 1988, p. 53).

In this restructuring, Reaganism and Thatcherism did not create some sort of false consciousness, creating ways of seeing that had little connection with reality. Rather, they "operated directly on the real and manifestly contradictory experiences" of a large portion of the population. They did connect with the perceived needs, fears, and hopes of groups of people who felt threatened by the range of problems associated with the crises in authority relations, in the economy, and in politics (Hall, 1983, pp. 19–39).

What has been accomplished is a successful translation of an economic doctrine into the language of experience, moral imperative, and common sense. The free-market ethic has been combined with a populist politics. This has meant the blending together of a "rich mix" of themes that have had a long history—nation, family, duty, authority, standards, and traditionalism—with other thematic elements that have also struck a resonant chord during a time of crisis. These latter themes include self-interest, competitive individualism (what I have elsewhere called the possessive individual) (Apple, 1985; 1990),[6] and anti-statism. In this way, a reactionary common sense is partly created (Hall, 1983, pp. 29–30).

The sphere of education has been one of the most successful areas in which the right has been ascendant. The social democratic goal of expanding equality of opportunity (itself a rather limited reform which, when it came to issues of race, was never given total ideological and material support by the state) has lost much of its political potency and its ability to mobilize people. The "panic" over falling standards and illiteracy,[7] the fears of violence in schools, the concern with the destruction of family values and religiosity, all have had an effect. These fears are exacerbated, and used, by dominant groups within politics and the economy who have been able to move the debate on education (and all things social) onto their own terrain, the terrain of standardization, productivity, and industrial needs (Hall, 1983, pp. 36–37).[8] Since so many parents are justifiably concerned about the economic futures of their children—in an economy that is increasingly conditioned by lowered wages, unemployment, capital flight, and insecurity (Apple, 1988b)—rightist discourse connects with the experiences of many working-class and lower-middle-class people.

However, while this conservative conceptual and ideological apparatus does appear to be rapidly gaining ground, one of the most critical issues remains to be answered. How *is* such an ideological vision legitimated and accepted? How was this done (Jessop, Bonnett, Bromley, and Ling, 1984, p. 49)?

The right-wing resurgence is not simply a reflection of the current crisis. Rather, it is itself a response to that crisis. Beginning in the immediate post-World War II years, the political culture of the United States was increasingly characterized by American imperial might, economic affluence, and cultural optimism. This period lasted for more than two decades. Socially and politically, it was a time of what has been called the *social democratic accord,* in which government increasingly became an arena for a focus on the conditions required for equality of opportunity. Commodity-driven prosperity, the extension of rights and liberties to new groups, and the expansion of welfare provisions provided the conditions for this compromise both between capital and labor and between capital and historically more dispossessed groups such as African Americans and women. This accord has become mired in crisis since the late 1960s and early 1970s (Hunter, 1987, pp. 1–3).

Allen Hunter gives an excellent sense of this in his own description of this accord.

> From the end of World War II until the early 1970s world capitalism experienced the longest period of sustained economic growth in its history. In the United States a new "social structure of accumulation"—"the specific institutional environment within which the capitalist accumulation process is organized"—was articulated around several prominent features: the broadly shared goal of sustained economic growth, Keynesianism, elite pluralist democracy, an imperial America prosecuting a cold war, anti-communism at home and abroad, stability or incremental change in race relations and a stable home life in a buoyant, commodity-driven consumer culture. Together these crystallized a basic consensus and a set of social and political institutions which was hegemonic for two decades. (Hunter, 1987, p. 9)

At the very center of this hegemonic accord was a compromise reached between capital and labor in which labor accepted what might be called "the logic of profitability and markets as the guiding principles of resource allocation." In return they received "an assurance that minimal living standards, trade union rights and liberal democratic rights would be protected" (Bowles, 1982, p. 51). These democratic rights were further extended to the poor, women, and people of color as these groups expanded their own struggles to overcome racially and sexually discriminatory practices (Hunter, 1987, p. 12). Yet, this extension of (limited) rights could not last, given the economic and ideological crises that soon beset American society, a set of crises that challenged the very core of the social democratic accord.

The dislocations of the 1960s and 1970s—the struggle for racial and sexual equality, military adventures such as Vietnam, Watergate, the resilience of the economic crisis—produced both shock and fear. "Mainstream culture" was shaken to its very roots in many ways. Widely shared notions of family, community, and nation were dramatically altered. Just as importantly, no new principle of cohesion emerged that was sufficiently compelling to recreate a cultural center. As economic, political, and valuative stability (and military supremacy) seemed to disappear, the polity was itself "balkanized." Social movements based on difference—regional, racial, sexual, religious—became more visible (Omi and Winant, 1986, pp. 214–215). The sense of what Marcus Raskin (1986) has called "the common good" was fractured.

Traditional social democratic "statist" solutions, which in education, welfare, health, and other similar areas took the form of large-scale attempts at federal intervention to increase opportunities or to provide a minimal level of support, were seen as being part of the problem, not as part of the solution. Traditional conservative positions were more easily dismissed as well. After all, the society on which they were based was clearly being altered. The cultural center could be *built* (and it had to be built by well-funded and well-organized political and cultural action) around the principles of the new right. The new right confronted the "moral, existential [and economic] chaos of the preceding decades" with a network of exceedingly well-organized and financially secure organizations incorporating "an aggressive political style, an outspoken religious and cultural traditionalism and a clear populist commitment" (Omi and Winant, 1986, pp. 215–216).[9]

In different words, the project was aimed at constructing a "new majority" that would "dismantle the welfare state, legislate a return to traditional morality, and stem the tide of political and cultural dislocation which the 1960s and 1970s represented." Using a populist political strategy (now in combination with an aggressive executive branch of the government), it marshaled an assault on "liberalism and secular humanism" and linked that assault to what some observers have argued was "an obsession with individual guilt and responsibility where social questions are concerned (crime, sex, education, poverty)" with strong beliefs against government intervention (Omi and Winant, 1986, p. 220).[10]

The class, racial, and sexual specificities here are significant. The movement to create a conservative cultural consensus in part builds on the hostilities of the working and lower middle classes toward those above and below them and is fueled as well by a very real sense of antagonism against the new middle class. State bureaucrats and administrators, educators, journalists, planners, and so on, all share part of the blame for the social dislocations these groups have experienced (Omi and Winant, 1986, p. 221).[11] Race, gender, and class themes abound here, a point to which I shall return in the next section of my analysis.

This movement is of course enhanced within academic and government circles by a group of policy-oriented neoconservatives who have become the organic intellectuals for much of the rightist resurgence. A belief in a society based on individualism, market-based opportunities and the drastic reduction of both state intervention and state support runs deep in their work (Omi and Winant, 1986, p. 221). The neoconservatives provide a counterpart to the new right and are themselves part of the inherently unstable alliance that has been formed.

BUILDING THE NEW ACCORD

Almost all of the reform-minded social movements—including the feminist, gay and lesbian, student, and other movements of the 1960s—drew upon the struggle by blacks "as a central organizational fact or as a defining political metaphor and inspiration" (Omi and Winant, 1986, p. 164). These social movements infused new social meanings into politics, economics, and culture. These are not separate spheres. All three of these levels exist simultaneously. New social meanings about the importance of person rights infused individual, family, and community identities, and penetrated state institutions and market relationships. These emerging social movements expanded the concerns of politics to all aspects of the "terrain of everyday life." Person rights took on ever more importance in nearly all of our institutions, as evidenced in aggressive affirmative action programs, widespread welfare and educational activist programs, and so on (Omi and Winant, 1986, p. 164).[12] In education this was very clear in the growth of bilingual programs and in the development of women's, black, Hispanic, and Native American studies in high schools and colleges.

There are a number of reasons the state was the chief target of these earlier social movements for gaining person rights. First, the state was the "factor of cohesion in society" and had historically maintained and organized practices and policies that embodied the tension between property rights and person rights (Apple, 1985; 1988b).

As such a factor of cohesion, it was natural to focus on it. Second, "the state was traversed by the same antagonisms which penetrated the larger society, antagonisms that were themselves the results of past cycles of [social] struggle." Openings in the state could be gained because of this. Footholds in state institutions dealing with education and social services could be deepened (Omi and Winant, 1986, pp. 177–178).

Yet even with these gains, the earlier coalitions began to disintegrate. In the minority communities, class polarization deepened. The majority of barrio and ghetto residents "remained locked in poverty," while a relatively small portion of the black and brown population was able to take advantage of educational opportunities and new jobs (the latter being largely within the state itself) (Omi and Winant, 1986, pp. 177–178). With the emerging crisis in the economy, something of a zero-sum game developed in which progressive social movements had to fight over a limited share of resources and power. Antagonistic rather than complementary relationships developed among groups. Minority groups, for example, and the largely white and middle-class women's movement had difficulty integrating their programs, goals, and strategies.

This was exacerbated by the fact that, unfortunately, given the construction of a zero-sum game by dominant groups, the gains made by women sometimes came at the expense of blacks and browns. Furthermore, leaders of many of these movements had been absorbed into state-sponsored programs which—while the adoption of such programs was in part a victory—had the latent effect of cutting off leaders from their grass-roots constituency and lessened the militancy at this level. This often resulted in what has been called the "ghettoization" of movements within state institutions as movement demands were partly adopted in their most moderate forms into programs sponsored by the state. Militancy was transformed into constituency (Omi and Winant, 1986, p. 180).

The splits in these movements occurred as well because of strategic divisions, divisions that were paradoxically the results of the movements' own successes. Thus, for example, those women who aimed their work within existing political/economic channels *could* point to gains in employment within the state and in the economic sphere. Other, more radical, members saw such "progress" as "too little, too late."

Nowhere is this more apparent than in the black movement in the United States. It is worth quoting one of the best analyses of the history of these divisions at length.

> The movement's limits also arose from the strategic divisions that befell it as a result of its own successes. Here the black movement's fate is illustrative. Only in the South, while fighting against a backward political structure and overt cultural oppression, had the black movement been able to maintain a *de*-centered unity, even when internal debates were fierce. Once it moved north, the black movement began to split, because competing political projects, linked to different segments of the community, sought either integration in the (reformed) mainstream, or more radical trans-formation of the dominant racial order.
>
> After initial victories against segregation were won, one sector of the movement was thus reconstituted as an interest group, seeking an end to racism understood as discrimination and prejudice, and turning its back on the oppositional "politics of identity." Once the organized black movement became a mere constituency, though, it found itself locked in a bear hug with the state institutions whose programs it had itself demanded, while simultaneously isolated from the core institutions of the modern state (Omi and Winant, 1986, p. 190).

In the process, those sectors of the movement that were the most radical were marginalized or, and this must not be forgotten, were simply repressed by the state (Omi and Winant, 1986, p. 190).

Even though there were major gains, the movements' integration into the state latently created conditions that were disastrous in the fight for equality. A mass-based, militant grass-roots movement was defused into a constituency, dependent on the state itself. *And very importantly, when the neoconservative and right-wing movements evolved with their decidedly anti-statist themes, the gains that were made in the state came increasingly under attack and the ability to recreate a large-scale grass-roots movement to defend these gains was weakened considerably* (Omi and Winant, 1986, p. 190). Thus, when there are right-wing attacks on the more progressive national and local educational policies and practices that have benefitted people of color, it becomes increasingly difficult to develop broad-based coalitions to counter these offensives.

In their failure to consolidate a new "radical" democratic politics, one with majoritarian aspirations, the new social movements of the 1960s and 1970s "provided the political space in which right-wing reaction could incubate and develop its political agenda" (Omi and Winant, 1986, p. 252). Thus, state reforms won by, say, minority movements in the 1960s in the United States, and the new definitions of person rights embodied in these reforms, "provided a formidable range of targets for the 'counter-reformers' of the 1970s." Neoconservatives and the new right carried on their own political "project." They were able to rearticulate particular ideological themes and to restructure them around a political movement once again (Omi and Winant, 1986, p. 155). And these themes *were* linked to the dreams, hopes, and fears of many individuals.

Let us examine this in somewhat more detail. Behind the conservative restoration is a clear sense of loss: of control, of economic and personal security, of the knowledge and values that should be passed on to children, of visions of what counts as sacred texts and authority. The binary opposition of we/they becomes very important here. "We" are law-abiding, "hard working, decent, virtuous, and homogeneous." The "theys" are very different. They are "lazy, immoral, permissive, heterogenous" (Hunter, 1987, p. 23). These binary oppositions distance most people of color, women, gays, and others from the community of "worthy" individuals. The subjects of discrimination are now no longer those groups who have been historically oppressed, but are instead the "real Americans" who embody the idealized virtues of a romanticized past. The "theys" are undeserving. They are getting something for nothing. Policies supporting them are "sapping our way of life," draining most of our economic resources, and creating government control of our lives (Hunter, 1987, p. 30).

These processes of ideological distancing make it possible for anti-black and anti-feminist sentiments to seem no longer racist and sexist because they link so closely with other issues. Once again, Allen Hunter is helpful.

> Racial rhetoric links with anti-welfare state sentiments, fits with the push for economic individualism; thus many voters who say they are not prejudiced (and may not be by some accounts) oppose welfare spending as unjust. Anti-feminist rhetoric... is articulated around defense of the family, traditional morality, and religious fundamentalism (Hunter, 1987, p. 33).

All of these elements can be integrated through the formation of ideological coalitions that enable many Americans who themselves feel under threat to turn against groups of people who are even less powerful than themselves. At the very same time, it enables them to "attack domination by liberal, statist elites" (Hunter, 1987, p. 34).

This ability to identify a range of "others" as enemies, as the source of the problems, is very significant. One of the major elements in this ideological formation has indeed been a belief that liberal elites within the state "were intruding themselves into home life, trying to impose their values." This, neoconservatives argued, was having serious negative effects on moral values and on traditional families. Much of the conservative criticism of textbooks and curricula rests on these feelings, for example. While this position certainly exaggerated the impact of the "liberal elite," and while it certainly misrecognized the power of capital and of other dominant classes (Hunter, 1987, p. 21), there was enough of an element of truth in it for the right to use it in its attempts to dismantle the previous accord and build its own.

A new hegemonic accord, then, is partly reached. It combines dominant economic and political elites intent on "modernizing" the economy, white working-class and middle-class groups concerned with security, the family, and traditional knowledge and values, and economic conservatives (Hunter, 1987, p. 37). It also includes a fraction of the new middle class whose own advancement depends on the expanded use of the accountability, efficiency, and management procedures that are their own cultural capital (Apple, 1988b; 1992). This coalition has partly succeeded in altering the very meaning of what it means to have a social goal of equality. The citizen as "free" consumer has replaced the previously emerging citizen as situated in structurally generated relations of domination. Thus, the common good is now to be regulated exclusively by the laws of the market, free competition, private ownership, and profitability. In essence, the definitions of freedom and equality are no longer democratic, but *commercial* (Hall, 1986). This is particularly evident in the proposals for voucher plans as "solutions" to massive and historically rooted relations of economic and cultural inequality.

In sum, then, the right in both the United States and Britain has succeeded in reversing a number of the historic post-World War II trends.

> It has begun to dismantle and erode the terms of the unwritten social contract on which the social forces settled after the war. It has changed the currency of political thought and argument. Where previously social need had begun to establish its own imperatives against the laws of market forces, now questions of "value for money," the private right to dispose of one's own wealth, the equation between freedom and the free market, have become the terms of trade, not just of political debate…but in the thought and language of everyday calculation. There has been a striking reversal of values: the aura that used to attach to the value of the public welfare [that is, the value of the common good] now adheres to anything that is private—or can be privatized. A major ideological reversal is in progress in society at large; and the fact that it has not swept everything before it, and that there are many significant points…of resistance, does not contradict the fact that, conceived not in terms of outright victory but more in terms of the mastery of an unequal equilibrium, [the right] has…begun to reconstruct the social order. (Hall, 1988, p. 40)

This reconstruction is not imposed on unthinking subjects. It is not done through the use of some right-wing attempt at what Freire has called "banking" where knowledge and ideologies become common sense simply by pouring them into the heads of people. The ruling or dominant conceptions of the world and of everyday life "do not directly prescribe the mental content of the illusions that supposedly fill the heads of the dominated classes" (Hall, 1988, p. 44). However, the meanings, interests, and languages we construct are bound up in the unequal relations of power that do exist. To speak theoretically, the sphere of symbolic production is a contested terrain just as other spheres of social life are. "The circle of dominant ideas does accumulate the symbolic power to map or classify the world for others," to set limits on what appears rational and reasonable, indeed on what appears sayable and thinkable (Hall, 1988, p. 45). This occurs *not* through imposition, but through creatively working on existing themes, desires, and fears and reworking them. Since the beliefs of people are contradictory and have tensions because they are what some have called polyvocal (Mouffe, 1988, p. 96), it is then possible to move people in directions where one would least expect given their position in society.

Thus, popular consciousness can be articulated to the right precisely because the feelings of hope and despair and the logic and language used to express these are "polysemic" and can be attached to a variety of discourses. Hence, a male worker who has lost his job can be antagonistic to the corporations who engaged in capital flight or can blame unions, people of color, or women "who are taking men's jobs." The response is *constructed*, not preordained, by the play of ideological forces in the larger society (Mouffe, 1988, p. 96). And, though this construction occurs on a contradictory and contested terrain, it is the right that seems to have been more than a little successful in providing the discourse that organizes that terrain.

WILL THE RIGHT SUCCEED?

So far I have broadly traced out many of the political, economic, and ideological reasons that the social democratic consensus that led to the limited extension of person rights in education, politics, and the economy slowly disintegrated. At the same time, I have documented how a new "hegemonic bloc" is being formed, coalescing around new right tactics and principles. The question remains: Will this accord be long lasting? Will it be able to inscribe its principles into the very heart of the American polity?

There are very real obstacles to the total consolidation within the state of the new right political agenda. First, there has been something of a "great transformation" in, say, racial identities. Omi and Winant describe it thusly:

> The forging of new collective racial identities during the 1950s and 1960s has been the enduring legacy of the racial minority movements. Today, as gains won in the past are rolled back and most organizations prove unable to rally a mass constituency in racial minority communities, the persistence of the new racial identities developed during this period stands out as the single truly formidable obstacle to the consolidation of a newly repressive racial order. (Omi and Winant, 1986, p. 165)

Thus, even when social movements and political coalitions are fractured, when their leaders are co-opted, repressed, and sometimes killed, the racial subjectivity and self-awareness that were developed by these movements has taken permanent hold. "No amount of repression or co-optation [can] change that." In Omi and Winant's words, the genie is out of the bottle (Omi and Winant, 1986, p. 166). This is the case because, in essence, a new kind of person has been created within minority communities.[13] A new, and much more self-conscious, *collective* identity has been forged. Thus, for instance, in the struggles over the past three decades by people of color to have more control of education and to have it respond more directly to their own culture and collective histories, these people themselves were transformed in major ways.[14] Thus:

> Social movements create collective identity by offering their adherents a different view of themselves and their world; different, that is, from the world view and self-concepts offered by the established social order. They do this by the process of *rearticulation*, which produces new subjectivity by making use of information and knowledge already present in the subject's mind. They take elements and themes of her/his culture and traditions and infuse them with new meaning. (Omi and Winant, 1986, p. 166)

Even with the highly publicized sponsorship of black conservatives by right-wing organizations and administrations, these meanings will make it exceedingly difficult for the right to incorporate the perspectives of people of color under its ideological umbrella and will continually create oppositional tendencies within the black and brown communities. The slow, but steady, growth in the power of people of color at a local level in these communities will serve as a countervailing force to the solidification of the new conservative accord.

Added to this is the fact that even within the new hegemonic bloc, even within the conservative restoration coalition, there are ideological strains that may have serious repercussions on its ability to be dominant for an extended period. These tensions are partly generated because of the class dynamics within the coalition. Fragile compromises may come apart because of the sometimes directly contradictory beliefs held by many of the partners in the new accord.

This can be seen in the example of two of the groups now involved in supporting the accord. There are both what can be called "residual" and "emergent" ideological systems or codes at work here. The residual culture and ideologies of the old middle class and of an upwardly mobile portion of the working class and lower middle class—stressing control, individual achievement, "morality," etc.—have been merged with the emergent code of a portion of the new middle class—getting ahead, technique, efficiency, bureaucratic advancement, and so on (Apple, 1988b).

These codes are in an inherently unstable relationship. The stress on new right morality does not necessarily sit well with an amoral emphasis on careerism and economic norms. The merging of these codes can only last as long as paths to mobility are not blocked. The economy must pay off in jobs and mobility for the new middle class or the coalition is threatened. There is no guarantee, given the unstable nature of the economy and the kinds of jobs being created, that this payoff will occur (Apple, 1988b; Carnoy, Shearer and Rumberger, 1983).

This tension can be seen in another way that shows again that, in the long run, the prospects for such a lasting ideological coalition are not necessarily good. Under the new, more conservative accord, the conditions for capital accumulation and profit must be enhanced by state activity as much as possible. Thus, the "free market" must be set loose. As many areas of public and private life as possible need to be brought into line with such privatized market principles, including the schools, health care, welfare, housing, and so on. Yet, in order to create profit, capitalism by and large also requires that traditional values be subverted. Commodity purchasing and market relations become the norm and older values of community, "sacred knowledge," and morality will need to be cast aside. This dynamic sets in motion the seeds of possible future conflicts between the economic modernizers and the new right cultural traditionalists who make up a significant part of the coalition that has been built (Apple, 1988b).[15] Furthermore, the competitive individualism now being so heavily promoted in educational reform movements in the United States may not respond well to the somewhat more collective senses of traditional working-class and poor groups.

Finally, there are counter-hegemonic movements now being built within education itself. The older social democratic accord included many educators, union leaders, minority-group members, and others. There are signs that the fracturing of this coalition may only be temporary. Take teachers, for instance. Even though salaries have been on the rise throughout the country, this has been countered by a rapid increase in the external control of teachers' work, the rationalization and deskilling of their jobs, and the growing blame of teachers and education in general for most of the major social ills that beset the economy (Apple, 1993; 1988b; 1985). Many teachers have organized around these issues, in a manner reminiscent of the earlier work of the Boston Women's Teachers' Group (Freedman, Jackson, and Boles, 1982). Furthermore, there are signs throughout the country of multiracial coalitions being built among elementary and secondary school teachers, university-based educators, and community members to act collectively on the conditions under which teachers work and to support the democratization of curriculum and teaching and a rededication to the equalization of access and outcomes in schooling. The Rethinking Schools group based in Milwaukee provides an example here, as does the

Southern Coalition for Educational Equity (Apple, 1993; 1991; 1988b; Bastian, Fruchter, Gittell, Greer, and Haskins, 1986; Livingstone, 1987).

Even given these emerging tensions within the conservative restoration and the increase once again of alliances to counter its attempted reconstruction of the politics and ethics of the common good, this does not mean we should be at all sanguine. It is possible that, because of these tensions and counter movements, the right's economic program will fail. Yet its ultimate success may be in shifting the balance of class forces considerably to the right and in changing the very ways we consider the common good (Hall, 1983, p. 120). Privatization, profit, and greed may still substitute for any serious collective commitment.

We are, in fact, in danger both of forgetting the decades of hard work it took to put even a limited vision of equality on the social and educational agenda and of forgetting the reality of the oppressive conditions under which so many of our fellow Americans live. The task of keeping alive in the minds of the people the collective memory of the struggle for equality, for person rights in *all* of the institutions of our society, is one of the most significant tasks educators can perform. In a time of conservative restoration, we cannot afford to ignore this task. This requires renewed attention to important curricular questions. Whose knowledge is taught? Why is it taught in this particular way to this particular group? How do we enable the histories and cultures of the majority of working people, of women, of people of color (these groups, again, are obviously not mutually exclusive) to be taught in responsible and responsive ways in schools?

Given the fact that the collective memory that *now* is preserved in our educational institutions is more heavily influenced by dominant groups in society (Apple, 1990; Apple and Christian-Smith, 1991), the continuing efforts to promote more democratic curricula and teaching are more important now then ever. For it should be clear that the movement toward an authoritarian populism will become even more legitimate if our public institutions make available only the values embodied in the conservative restoration. The widespread recognition that there were, are, and can be more equal modes of economic, political, and cultural life can only be accomplished by organized efforts to teach and expand this sense of difference. Clearly, there is educational work to be done.

NOTES

I would like to thank the Friday Seminar at the University of Wisconsin, Madison for their comments on the various drafts of this chapter. A briefer treatment of these arguments can be found in Giroux and McLaren (1989). A more extensive discussion can be found in Apple (1993).

1 For further discussion of these and other conditions see Apple (1993) and Kozol (1991).

2 See also Bowles and Gintis (1986).

3 I wish to thank my colleague Walter Secada for his comments on this point. The effects of such policies are described in Kozol (1991).

4 Clark and Astuto (1986) point out that during Reagan's terms, the following initiatives characterized the administration's educational policies: reducing the federal role in education, stimulating competition among schools with the aim of "breaking the monopoly of the public school," fostering individual competition in the name of "excellence," increasing the reliance on performance standards for students and teachers, an emphasis on the "basics" in content, increasing parental choice "over what, where, and how their children learn," strengthening the teaching of traditional values in schools, and expanding the policy of transferring educational authority to the state and local levels (p. 8).

5 I realize that there is a debate about the adequacy of this term. See Hall (1985) and Jessop, Bonnett, Bromley, and Ling (1984).

6 For an interesting discussion of the gendered nature of possessive individualism, one that needs to be extended to an analysis of race, see Nancy Fraser's *Unruly Practices* (1989), pp. 144–160. The racial structuring of our legal concepts of individual rights is poetically analyzed in Patricia J. Williams's *The Alchemy of Race and Rights* (1990).

7 See the discussion of whether there actually is a new crisis in literacy in Carl Kaestle et al., *Literacy in the United States* (1991).

8 For an illuminating picture of how powerful groups manipulate these issues, see Hunter (1984).

9 See also Hunter (1984).

10 For a more complete discussion of how this has affected educational policy in particular, see Clark and Astuto (1986) and Apple (1988b).

11 I have elsewhere claimed, however, that some members of the new middle class—namely efficiency experts, evaluators, testers, and many of those with technical and management expertise—will form part of the alliance with the new right. This is simply because their own jobs and mobility depend on it. See Apple (1988b). For further discussion of the rightist attack on "professional intellectuals," see Johnson (1991).

12 The discussion in Bowles and Gintis (1986) of the "transportability" of the struggle over person rights from, say, politics to the economy is very useful here. I have extended and criticized some of their claims in Apple (1988a).

13 I say "new" here, but the continuity of, say, black struggles for freedom and equality also needs to be stressed. See the powerful treatment of the history of such struggles in Vincent Harding's *There Is a River* (1981). A personal account of the meanings of these transformations is seen in the published dialogue between bell hooks and Cornel West (1991).

14 See Hogan (1983) for a discussion of this in relationship to class dynamics.

15 For a comprehensive analysis of the logic of capitalism, one that compares it with other political and economic traditions, see Levine (1984).

REFERENCES

Anderson, M. (1985). *Teachers Unions and Industrial Politics.* Unpublished doctoral dissertation, Macquarie University, Sydney.

Apple, M. W. (1985). *Education and Power.* New York: Routledge.

————. (1988a). Facing the complexity of power: For a parallelist position in critical educational studies. In M. Cole (ed.), *Rethinking Bowles and Gintis.* (pp. 112–130). Philadelphia: Falmer.

————. (1988b). *Teachers and Texts: A political economy of class and gender relations in education.* New York: Routledge.

————. (1990). *Ideology and Curriculum* (2nd ed.). New York: Routledge.

————. (1991). Conservative agendas and progressive possibilities. *Education and Urban Society, 23,* 279–291.

————. (1992). Education, culture and class power. *Educational Theory, 42,* 127–145.

————. (1993). *Official Knowledge: Democratic education in a conservative age.* New York: Routledge.

————. (forthcoming). Creating the captive audience. *International Studies in the Sociology of Education.*

Apple, M. W., and Christian-Smith, L. K. (eds.). (1991). *The Politics of the Textbook.* New York: Routledge.

Arnot, M. (1990). *Schooling for Social Justice.* Paper presented at the 12th national conference of the New Zealand Association for Research in Education, Auckland, New Zealand.

Bastian, A., Fruchter, N., Gittell, M., Greer, C., & Haskins, K. (1986). *Choosing Equality: The case for democratic schooling.* Philadelphia: Temple UP.

Bennett, W. (1988). *Our Children and Our Country.* New York: Simon and Schuster.

Bowles, S. (1982, Sept.-Oct.). The post-Keynesian capital-labor stalemate. *Socialist Review,* pp. 45–72.

Bowles, S. and Gintis, H. (1986). *Democracy and Capitalism.* New York: Basic.

Burnham, W. D. (1983, Nov.-Dec.). Post-conservative America. *Socialist Review,* pp. 123–132.

Clark, D. & Astuto, T. (1986). The significance and permanence of changes in federal education policy. *Educational Researcher*, 15, 4–13.

Carnoy, M., Shearer, D., & Rumberger, R. (1983). *A New Social Contract: The economy and government after Reagan*. New York: Harper.

Education Group II (eds.). (1991). *Education Unlimited: Schooling, training, and the new right in England since 1979*. London: Unwin.

Fraser, N. (1989). *Unruly Practices: Power, discourse, and gender in contemporary social theory*. Minneapolis: U of Minnesota P.

Freedman, S., Jackson, J., & Boles, K. (1982). *The Effects of the Institutional Structure of Schools on Teachers*. Somerville, MA: Boston Women's Teachers' Group.

Gintis, H. (1980, March-June). Communication and politics. *Socialist Review*, pp. 189–232.

Giroux, H. A. (1984). Public philosophy and the crisis in education. *Harvard Educational Review*, 54, 186–194.

Giroux, H. A. & McLaren, P. L. (1989). *Critical Pedagogy, the State, and Cultural Struggle*. Albany: State U of New York P.

Hall, S. (1980). Popular democratic vs. authoritarian populism: Two ways of taking democracy seriously. In A. Hunt (ed.), *Marxism and Democracy*. London: Lawrence and Wishart.

————. (1983). The great moving right show. In Hall & Jacques (pp. 19–39).

————. (1985). Authoritarian populism: A reply. *New Left Review* 151, 115–124.

————. (1986). Popular culture and the state. In T. Bennett, C. Mercer, & J. Wollacoot (eds.), *Popular Culture and Social Relations* (pp. 22–49). Milton Keynes, England: Open UP.

————. (1988). The Toad in the Garden: Thatcherism among the theorists. In Nelson & Grossberg (pp. 34–57).

Hall, S. & Jacques, M. (1983). Introduction. In Hall & Jacques (pp. 9–16).

Hall, S. & Jacques, M. (eds.). (1983). *The Politics of Thatcherism*. London: Lawrence and Wishart.

Harding, V. (1981). *There Is a River: The black struggle for freedom in America*. New York: Vintage.

Hooks, B. & West, C. (1991). *Breaking Bread: Insurgent black intellectual life*. Boston: South End.

Hogan, D. (1983). Education and class formation. In M. Apple (ed.), *Cultural and Economic Reproduction in Education* (pp. 32–78). Boston: Routledge.

Hunter, A. (1984). Virtue with a vengeance: The pro-family politics of the new right. Unpublished doctoral dissertation, Brandeis University.

————. (1987). *The politics of resentment and the construction of middle America*. Paper presented at the American Institutions Program, University of Wisconsin, Madison.

Jessop, B., Bonnett, K., Bromley, S., & Ling, T. (1984). Authoritarian populism, two nations, and Thatcherism. *New Left Review*, 147, 33–60.

Johnson, R. (1991). My new right education. In Education Group II (pp. 87–113).

Kaestle, C., et al. (1991). *Literacy in the United States: Readers and reading since 1880*. New Haven: Yale UP.

Kozol, J. (1991). *Savage Inequalities: Children in America's schools*. New York: Crown.

Larrain, J. (1983). *Marxism and Ideology*. Atlantic Highlands, NJ: Humanities.

Livingstone, D. W. (ed.). (1987). *Critical Pedagogy and Cultural Power*. South Hadley, MA: Bergin and Garvey.

Levine, A. (1984). *Arguing for Socialism: Theoretical considerations*. Boston: Routledge.

Mouffe, C. (1988). Hegemony and new political subjects: Toward a new concept of democracy. In Nelson & Grossberg (pp. 89–101).

Nelson, C., & Grossberg, L. (eds.). (1988). *Marxism and the Interpretation of Culture*. Urbana: U of Illinois P.

Omi, M. & Winant, H. (1986). *Racial Formation in the United States: From the 1960s to the 1980s*. New York: Routledge.

Piven, F. F. & Cloward, R. A. (1982). *The New Class War: Reagan's attack on the welfare state and its consequences*. New York: Pantheon.

Raskin, M. (1986). *The Common Good: Its politics, policies, and philosophy*. New York: Routledge.

Williams, P. J. (1990). *The Alchemy of Race and Rights*. Cambridge: Harvard UP.

4

Traveling to Teach:
Postcolonial Critics in the
American Academy

ALI BEHDAD

> Time would pass, old empires would fall and new ones take their place, the relations
> of countries and the relations of classes had to change, before I discovered that it is
> not quality of goods and utility that matter, but movement: not where you are or what
> you have, but where you have come from, where you are going and the rate at which
> you are getting there.
> C.L.R. James, *Beyond a Boundary*

IN A 1990 INTERVIEW, Gayatri Spivak recalls a conversation with Edward Said after a
lecture he gave on anthropology. Surprised by Said's dismissal of some students'
questions about "the people," Spivak reproached him, "'You really need to say this. After
all, look at the two of us. We are postcolonials. We are in fact wild anthropologists.' We,
because of our class alliance, went out to do our field work...we went out to do field
work in the West, not in the disciplinary sense, but pushed by class alliance and power
lines, and we became successful" (1990, p. 165). Spivak's self-reflexive remarks provide an
interesting point of departure toward understanding the predicaments of postcolonial
practices in the American academy and their politics of affiliation.[1] Her emphasis on the
"anthropological" nature of postcolonial traveling, embedded in a whole series of
institutional and cultural power relations, draws attention to the complexities of what she
calls the "scandal of our production" as displaced subjects of oppositional consciousness
in Western universities. As in C.L.R. James's remarks in my epigraph, which underline
the significance of movement, Spivak's comments to Said define the new conditions of
postcoloniality in terms of spatial mobility. Her reflections particularly interest me here
because they problematize the facile politics of alterity that generalize the notion of
displacement and thus fail to address differences within "other" communities and the
specificity of various subject positions. While critical of "cultural determinism" that
reduces postcolonial subjectivities to some biographical details, she stresses the particular
configuration of power relations that has enabled some postcolonial subjects to write
back to the center, to use Salman Rushdie's words. Spivak underscores the ironic
accidents of place and privilege that have produced the new kind of cosmopolitan
intellectual—the "wild anthropologist" whose field work has simultaneously displaced
him/her in the global village and privileged her/him as intellectually elite.

In what follows, I want to explore the predicaments of postcolonial practices of
wild anthropology in the U.S. academy. What does it mean for postcolonial critics to
inhabit the institutional space of Western academies? How do these intellectuals negotiate
the relations of power involved in the inclusion of the cultural "periphery" in

metropolitan institutions? What are the political and epistemological implications of the traveling theories of these "anthropologists" in the context of what Paul Rabinow has called "micropractices of the academy"? In what ways does the trope of travel depend on *actual* geographical mobility? How does the temporal space of the academy figure into postcolonial practices? And finally, what is the relation between the privileged itineraries of the postcolonial elite and those of their contingent communities in Western metropolises? Obviously the answers to these questions are complex and well beyond the scope of a short essay like this, but I pose them nonetheless as guiding principles to direct my discussion of the predicaments of postcoloniality in the U.S. academy. As points of departure for this essay, these questions raise two sets of problematics: a historical and political set of issues concerning the actual displacement and travel of these critics in the postcolonial era, and an epistemological set of problems involving the very situational, relational, and mobile nature of knowledge. Needless to say, these problematics are interconnected, and my essay attempts to, on the one hand, make a general critique of static notions of knowledge, and on the other, argue for the situatedness of such a critique in the context of postcolonial mobility—in the world of global contacts, knowledge loses its objectivity, neutrality, and naturalness.

TRAVELING CRITICS AND THEORIES OF TRAVEL

A slogan on what one may call a "postcolonial" T-shirt in London reads, "We are here because you were there." This oppositional message interestingly situates the postcolonial relations of travel as an effect of Europeans' colonial journeys. The T-shirt's message responds oppositionally to the racist images of "swarthy aliens" flooding Western metropolises, by pointing out that the displacing practices of colonialism are precisely what have produced the new set of geographical and cultural movements between the ex-colonies and the West. Colonial expansion was dependent on a whole series of localizing strategies that enabled Europeans to exercise power over the indigenous populations of those regions where they traveled and conquered. The geopolitics of colonialism, as Johannes Fabian has shown (1983), had its ideological foundations in "chronopolitics," the politics of time that was constructed in spatial terms: the farther from European centers the indigenous people were located, the more primitive they were claimed to be: geographical distance here meant distance in time. The postcolonial condition, in contrast to that unilateral journey and the colonialist denial of coevalness, enables or *forces* Europe's "others" to immigrate or travel to the metropolitan centers of the West. The postcolonial world, in contrast to the polarized colonial situation, has become a "confusing world, a world of crisscrossed economies, intersecting systems of meanings, and fragmented identities" (Rouse, 1991, p. 8). I will return later to the problematic and unequal geography of such boundary crossings, but for the moment suffice it to say that notions such as coherent communities and unified identities have become inadequate, for no longer can the boundaries of center and periphery, home and abroad, self and other be drawn so distinctly. As Roger Rouse has suggested, "we have all moved irrevocably into a new kind of social space," a crucial shift necessitating a new cartography that would include the complexities of postcolonial spaces (Rouse, 1991, p. 8).

Given the itinerant condition of postcoloniality, it is no surprise that many intellectuals of the diaspora have used various figures of spatial movement—such as travel, exile, displacement, etc.—not only to reflect on their own hybrid position but to describe and theorize new conditions of possibility in the new social space. These spatial tropes, I will argue, have been both enabling and problematic—enabling in that they constitute a discursive space to reflect on postcolonial displacements and to politicize the empirical discussions of immigration and exile in social sciences, and yet problematic in that, in their generality, they fall short of articulating the particular socioeconomic conditions that privilege some forms of mobility and render others oppressive. I will return to the problematic aspects of the tropes of mobility in the context of academic practices later, but for the moment I want to address some useful features of the trope of travel.

James Clifford has recently suggested a rethinking of culture in terms of travel in order to question the naturalizing tendencies that are associated with culture (1992). Critiquing the localizing strategies of traditional anthropology that, as a science of imperialism, confined non-Western people within cultural "types," he posits the "chronotope" of travel to account for the complex systems of mobility and intercultural exchanges that mediate the relation of the researcher to the researched. (Postcolonial) culture is here viewed more accurately as a site of contestation traversed by people and their spatial practices of moving, mapping, migration, immigration, and so on. The point of the chronotope of travel is not to privilege displacement over localization, but to provide a comparative perspective to "work on the complexities of cultural localizations in post- or neocolonial situations" (Clifford, 1992, p. 105). This comparative project recognizes correctly that the movements of postcolonial travelers are overdetermined by a whole range of cultural, economic, and political conditions—conditions that, as I have already stated, privilege some and yet oppress others. The mutable and wavering nature of postcolonial spaces allows for unequal modes of travel and uneven destinies depending on the traveler's access to power and its discourses. But travel's generality and contingency make it nonetheless a useful term of comparison to broach the predicaments of postcolonial diasporas and describe intercultural relations. In short, what makes the chronotope of travel so attractive to intellectuals like Clifford and others is "precisely…its historical taintedness, its associations with gendered, racial bodies, class privilege, specific means of conveyance, beaten paths, agents, frontiers, documents, and the like" (Clifford, 1992, p. 110).

Using the chronotope of travel, postcolonial intellectuals have taken the diasporic condition of the new social space as an invitation to reconceptualize the very nature of intellectual practice itself. Clifford, following Said's essay "Traveling Theories" (1983), has therefore suggested the return of theory to its etymological root, *theorein*; that is, a "practice of travel and observation, a man sent by the polis to another city to witness a religious ceremony" (1989, p. 177). (Dis)placed in a world of global contacts where communities, economies, and subjectivities constantly crisscross, theory, Clifford argues, "is no longer naturally 'at home' in the West" (1989, p. 179); it has been destabilized by other locations, contested by other trajectories of subjectivity, and displaced by other forms of knowledge. Theory therefore becomes a kind of itinerary conceived through a complex network of diasporic conjunctures, conditions of displacement, and transplantation.

The implications of such destabilizing theories are crucial to postcolonial critics' academic practices not only for their connections and references to these critics' self-fashionings but also for their consequences in the everyday life of the institutional space. In a recent article, "Identity, Authority, and Freedom: The Potentate and the Traveler," Said (1991a) uses the figure of the traveler to critique the notion of national identity for its infringement on academic freedom. Relegating social heterogeneity and cultural differences to the margin, overmastering and monologic notions of identity such as "Arabness," "Americanness," or "Western identity" impair intellectual freedom and suppress creative interaction. "Our model for academic freedom," Said goes on to suggest, "should therefore be the migrant or the traveler" (Said, 1991a, p. 17). The figure of the traveler is used here to imply mobility and motion in both metaphoric and literal senses, that is, "a willingness to go into different worlds, use different idioms, and understand a variety of disguises, masks, and rhetorics" (p. 18). The university, according to this model, should provide students with a cultural space where they can "discover and travel among other selves, other identities, other varieties of the human adventure" (p. 17). Abandoning fixed positions and ideologies of mastery and detachment, the academic model of the traveler makes it possible to traverse different intellectual domains and explore a plurality of subject positions.

Crucial to such a project of pedagogic reorientation is the crossing of disciplinary boundaries in the academy. Because the dominant mode of knowledge, as a disciplinary discourse, renders invisible the plurality of subject and ideological positions it produces as its effects, any critical reflections on it can only be accomplished effectively through interdisciplinary praxis. Postcolonial and other "minority" critics have played a major part in challenging the dominant politics of knowledge through their "wild" practices that have been in general counter-systemic, contestatory, and antidisciplinary. Said, for example, has persistently renounced the disciplinary space of a compartmentalized academy, arguing against the dominant principle in American universities that "knowledge ought to exist, be sought after and disseminated in a very divided form" (1983b, pp. 140–141). The problematics and politics of postcolonial conditions demand a counter-disciplinary mode of knowledge that undermines the social, political, and economic reasons behind the principle of compartmentalization. Following Gramsci and Foucault, Said argues cogently that the dominant culture in the West achieves its hegemony by making invisible the "actual *affiliations* that exist between the world of ideas and scholarship, on the one hand, and the world of brute politics, corporate and state power, and military force, on the other" (Said, 1983b, p. 136).[2] While universities play a central role in the production of "experts" and of the professional knowledge often used by corporate and state power, any political discussion of knowledge encounters disciplinary resistance on campus. Social and political processes and economic interests are always immanent in the pursuit of knowledge and the production of power, though the effects of differentiation, separation, and denial render them opaque. With counterdisciplinary practices, postcolonial critics attempt, through their "decentered consciousness," to expose the internal conditions of these strategies of differentiation. In the place of the dominant will to specialize, Said suggests that "there must be *interference*, crossing of borders and obstacles, a determined attempt to generalize exactly at those points where generalizations seem impossible to make" (1979, p. 157).

Said's own work provides a fascinating example of antidisciplinary practice. In *Orientalism* (1979), to cite an example, he demonstrates how Europe's geopolitical awareness of its "exotic" others was distributed into aesthetic representations as well as within economic, sociological, anthropological, historical, and philosophical texts, all of which provided a heterogeneous discourse of power through which the Orient was colonized. Said describes in great detail how culture becomes a productive site where a plurality of interests are articulated and brought into contact with the kinds of military, economic, and political strategies that produce a complex system of domination. Given the multifarious and composite network of power relations, a critique of Orientalism can only be produced in an interdisciplinary project addressed to a large spectrum of audiences. Said, therefore, situates his work within a plurality of interests and readers. He addresses his book not only to various university scholars who would benefit from his example of the interrelations between culture, history, and texts but to policymakers and Orientalists, to present them with their "intellectual genealogy" and question their false assumptions about the Middle East, as well as to the general public in the U.S. and the "third world," to expose the "*strength* of Western cultural discourse" (1979, p. 24). In short, the aim of postcolonial antidisciplinarity is to expose how seemingly specialized discourses are in fact linked in ways that allow for the complexities of Western cultural hegemony.

Beyond such general critiques of dominant culture's epistemology and politics, the interventionary practices of postcolonialist, feminist, gay/lesbian, and "minority" critics[3] have exerted a strong "local" influence in bringing about pedagogic changes in the U.S. academy—such as the inclusion of multicultural perspectives in curricula, the democratization of the institutional space through "minority" hiring and student recruitment, and so on. The oppositional discourses of diasporic and U.S. minority intellectuals in the academy have functioned as catalysts for the emergence of a general recognition of the multiethnic, multicultural imperatives demanded by students whose textbooks have excluded their histories. No longer does the Eurocentric paradigm of knowledge seem "natural" or impartial in the educational system, a recognition that has made social, cultural, and historical diversity a necessity and educational democracy imperative.

SITUATED TRAVELERS, UTOPIAN JOURNEYS

And yet, oppositional as the interventions of diasporic critics have been in the U.S. academy, a whole series of unresolved predicaments surrounds the politics of affiliation and difference in postcolonial praxes. Above all, with the trope of travel has emerged a discourse of utopian mobility that fails to address the "situatedness" of postcolonial practices. Although most critics are percipient about the "historical taintedness" of the metaphor of travel, acknowledging its connection with gendered, racial, and class identities, one often encounters a sense of utopian optimism among many, even sophisticated, readers who sometimes seem to conflate the clearing of a "space for the 'other' question"[4] in the academy with the needs, aspirations, and deteriorating conditions of many neo-colonized communities in the "third world" as well as in the West. Even more problematic in the discourse of mobility is the unreflected privileging of hybridity as a utopian product of postcolonial movements, not taking into consideration the horrendous effects and conditions of the hybrid state for disempowered "split" communities. While many postcolonial artists and theoreticians, such as Coco Fusco (1991) and Trinh T. Minh-ha (1989, 1991), celebrate the massive immigrations of the twentieth century as a hybridizing phenomenon, for many immigrants to the metropolitan centers of the West hybridity has been anything but salutary. Even a cursory glance at some diasporic communities—such as Chicanos in the U.S., North Africans in France, and Pakistanis and Indians in England—would confirm that the everyday conditions of living have actually deteriorated for most recent immigrants as a result of a whole series of sociopolitical changes, ranging from the Immigration Reform and Control Act of 1986 in the U.S. to the busting of the manufacturing industry and its replacement with high-technology fields or the transference of certain industries to "third world" countries. My aim here is not to play a set of empirical data against the theoretical notions of hybridity and alterity; it is rather to draw attention to the discrepancy between the salutary explorations of postcolonial demographic shifts by academics and artists *and* the dead-end itineraries of many immigrants caught in a tailspin away from their desires for upward mobility and into a state of economic and cultural disenfranchisement. This discrepancy, I want to argue, points to two disparate narratives of postcolonial immigrations that have often separated diaspora intellectuals from underprivileged immigrant communities. Sarat Maharaj describes these split narratives perceptively:

The one recounts entry into the Western world, becoming part of its modernity, its thrills, speeds, sensations, drifting with its fashions of life and living....The second tale speaks of those who arrived in the modern West only to find themselves left behind by it, marooned, cut off within it. (1991, p. 78)

Although neither of these narratives tells the whole story, they are useful in situating the uneven itineraries of postcolonial travelers. A journey is always undertaken within particular relations of power, and the traveler's access to these relations and the discourses that surround them transforms his or her status both on the road and at a given destination. This is an obvious but crucial point to consider because it calls into question the free-floating metaphors of travel and hybridity so prevalent among postcolonial artists and theoreticians. Consider, for example, Papo Colo's opening remark at an exhibition titled "The Hybrid State": "Hybrid is a word in a world for utopia. Multiples measure time" (1991, n. p.).

The alternative to general, not to say homogenizing, theories of hybrid identities is "partial, locatable, critical knowledges sustaining the possibility of webs of connections called solidarity in politics and shared conversations in epistemology," to use Donna Haraway's argument in a different context (1991, p. 191). Postcolonial theories of travel, I will argue, ought to address the contingent and partial locations in which they are produced, while remaining attentive to the significance of political alliances in the general struggle against the neocolonial regime of truth. Traveling is a worldly phenomenon, always inscribed within material and symbolic fields of power that are open-ended, contradictory, and vulnerable to recuperation as well as open to resistance.

TRAVELING IN/TO THE U.S. ACADEMY

To return to the specific context of the academy, I want to argue that inattention to the situatedness of travel has led to two fundamental predicaments of postcolonial displacement: the uneven distribution of the production of knowledge and the misappropriation of the discourse of victimhood in new claims to alterity. First, postcolonial discussions of alterity, hybridity, and travel have subtly evaded the problem of unequal distribution of knowledge, and therefore power. Mostly contained within the institutional boundaries of the "first world," critics have rarely addressed the ways in which their discursive productions have been in many ways complicitous with the geopolitical divisions of the "first" and "third worlds," reflecting the unequal distribution of power that existed between the imperial powers and their colonies.[5] This is especially evident in the disparity of educational systems and access to knowledge, research materials and facilities in the "first" and "third worlds." As a Sri Lankan graduate student of mine pointed out to me, only in the University of Sussex library could he find the ethnographic data he sought about a particular region in his country. Not only has the metropolitan West maintained its cultural and political hegemony but its material and symbolic power has enforced the conditions of displacement and exile for many "wild anthropologists." Although it is true that in the late twentieth century the nation is losing its centrality as a "home" base, as many critics have argued, one must remain attentive to the fact that such a decentering process has nonetheless maintained crucial material and symbolic differences between Gastarbeiter and Western tourists in Southeast Asia, between American businessmen in Saudi Arabia and Pakistani immigrants in England, or between Indian intellectuals in American universities and Mexican farm workers in Texas. Many diasporic critics may acknowledge the point as obvious, but it is ironically undermined, if not completely forgotten, in the neo-romantic tropes of writer/artist as exile and culture as travel. Many postcolonial critics tend to valorize the experiences of a few intellectuals who happen to have gained access to the privileged institutions of the West by virtue of their class and/or academic background, or even sometimes to conflate in their oppositional discourses such privileged experiences with those of disenfranchised underclass immigrants in the metropolitan West in their claims of being "the oppressed." Spivak's remarks at the start of my essay begin to address the "scandal" of postcolonial critics' production in Western universities, situating the particular relations of power that have allowed these critics to operate as wild anthropologists from the "other world." In view of the uneven relations of power not only between the West and its others, but also between diasporic intellectuals and disenfranchised immigrant communities, it becomes crucial to raise the forbidden question of to what extent postcolonial practices have actually contributed to that depressing mode of intellectual neocolonialism in which the ex-colonies provide yet again the "raw materials" for Western academic consumption. Add to this the familiar issue of brain drain from the "third" to "first world," and one gets a disturbing picture of traveling to teach.

In the context of such inequality in power/knowledge, the predicament of postcolonial claims to alterity, or worse to represent the "other," surfaces as a political site of contradiction. The claim to alterity is not merely a positional choice for postcolonial critics but it functions also as an effective strategy of containment of them. Ghettoization through tokenization is not a new strategy to control and discipline oppositional forces, but in the context of the American academy it has become a subtle and powerful means for the hegemonic discourse of neocolonialism to force diasporic critics to occupy the tokenized positions of spokespersons for "other" communities. The strategy is complex and powerful because it works out of both "third world" intellectuals' misappropriation of a generic alterity and the discourse of authenticity that the academy as an institution perpetuates. The discourse of power in the academy has shifted in the past decade from an exclusionary practice to one of selective inclusion, which inscribes certain positions of desire and success for those "oppositional" elements who consent, perhaps uncon-sciously, to the position of alterity—a position that is sanctioned only as the exception. The example of one person teaching all postcolonial literatures in a traditional English department that has two Renaissance scholars and three nineteenth-century critics is symptomatic of the practice of tokenized inclusion. In sum, in spite of the inclusion of "postcolonial" or "minority" critics, the academic system has maintained its traditional approaches to knowledge and its disciplinary divisions—for example, the ongoing pursuit of national literatures or the emphasis on Western philosophy.

In her essay "Who Claims Alterity?" Spivak cautions postcolonial critics against making the sorts of uncritical and false claims to alternative histories that underlie the discourse of authenticity in the academy. Recognized and singled out as "native informants," members of the postcolonial elite, she argues, are often the "site of a chiasmus, the crossing of a double contradiction: the system of production of the national bourgeoisie at home, and, abroad, the tendency to represent neocolonialism by the semiotic of 'internal colonization'" (1989, pp. 274–275). The practice of tokenized inclusion can force the intellectual elite abroad to become the victim of two kinds of ahistoricity: a misrepresentation of alternative histories of colonialism, and a misconception of the neocolonized story/history. Drawing attention to the "disenfranchised *female* in decolonized space," Spivak is to the point in criticizing the "indigenous elite woman abroad" who obliterates her difference with the doubly displaced figure of the disempowered woman in the "third world." The critic's problematic self-identification as "other" fails to address both his or her privilege as a member of a national bourgeoisie and the plurality of alterity, thus conflating the "indigenous" bourgeois, whose "class alliance and power lines" enable him or her to occupy an elite position abroad, with the disempowered subjects in the "third world." Furthermore, "the stories (or histories) of the postcolonial world," Spivak points out, "are not necessarily the same as the stories coming from 'internal colonization,' the way the metropolitan countries discriminate against disenfranchised groups in their midst" (1989, p. 274). The point here is not to play one kind of alterity against another but to make the crucial distinction between, say, a working-class Chicana and the "indigenous elite woman" who comes to the West with heavy cultural and economic baggage.

These conflations have dangerous consequences, most recognizably, the misrepresentation of neocolonial struggles in diaspora and "third world" communities and the ironic complicity with what Spivak calls the "benevolent third worldism" of the Euroamerican academy. The academy's discourse of authenticity plays a fundamental part in perpetuating this form of benevolence. Even a cursory glance at the MLA job recruiting system would confirm the academy's profound belief in authenticity; the positions in so-called "postcolonialism" and "minority literatures" have been consistently filled by "natives," while minority scholars are being excluded in other fields. While it is true that the elision of their histories in the educational system has made diasporic intellectuals most interested in pursuing these fields, the uncritical identification of a "postcolonial" identity with postcolonial fields of research may actually work to further racist misconceptions that pigeonhole these intellectuals into compartmentalized ghettos. Identified as native informants, postcolonials are often encouraged, if not sometimes forced, to "speaking as," to be representatives of the contingent communities whose culture, literature, and history they are to "cover." Authenticity here entails positioning the investigating subject in a compartmentalized category that assumes final determinacy; that is to say, the authenticity of a racial or national category finally determines the content of what the "minority" critic has to say. Although one cannot deny the oppositional, liberatory nature of speaking for oneself and the danger of representing others, the discourse of authenticity categorically divides the field of interests according to a crude "chromocentric" ideology. In spite of over two decades of poststructuralist "deconstruction" of essentialist and transcendental notions of subjectivity, the recuperative strategies of the U.S. academy have, in a gesture of benevolent pluralism, reinscribed the problematic categories of "race" and "gender." Always couched as an attempt to liberalize the educational space, tokenized inclusion has in fact rendered the conservative grip more efficient and powerful, in that voices of resistance are now somewhat contained in the compartmentalized ghettos of the academy.

Only recently have some postcolonial critics begun to respond to these local predicaments. Said, for example, has argued against the politics of blame and nationalist identity politics. In "The Politics of Knowledge" he remarks:

> Our [postcolonial] point...cannot be simply and obdurately to reaffirm the paramount importance of formerly suppressed or silenced forms of knowledge and leave it at that, nor can it be to surround ourselves with the sanctimonious piety of historical or cultural victimhood as a way of making our intellectual presence felt...The whole effort to deconsecrate Eurocentrism cannot be interpreted, least of all by those who participate in the enterprise, as an effort to supplant Eurocentrism with, for instance, Afrocentric or Islamocentric approaches. (1991b, p. 24; in this volume)

Neither the discourses of victimhood nor reactionary theories of national exclusiveness are capable of disturbing, let alone dismantling, the new practices of discrimination in the academy, for they reinforce the discourse of authenticity. An oppositional practice must begin by denouncing such de-negating strategies of containment in the educational system—strategies that produce the relatively comfortable and depoliticized sites of alterity, strategies that work in accordance with the benevolent third worldism of the academy that excludes in its very gestures of inclusion.

If the problems I have outlined above seem too academic, it is because I agree with Pierre Bourdieu (1984), Michel Foucault (1980), and Paul Rabinow (1986) that the kinds of political issues that we, as postcolonial teachers and critics, ought to address and explore are precisely academic politics. In "Representations Are Social Facts: Modernity and Post-Modernity in Anthropology," Rabinow criticizes euphoric proclamations of anticolonialism—by critics of anthropology like Clifford—arguing that "these proclamations must be seen as political moves within the academic community" (p. 252). Following Bourdieu's sociology of cultural production that draws attention to the particular position of the writer/intellectual in a specific field of power, Rabinow calls for an exploration of the micropractices of the academy that surround us and in which our cultural productions are inscribed. The lack of attention to the particular positions postcolonial critics occupy in the academic field of power has led some intellectuals to displace the "crisis of representation within the context of the rupture of decolonization," ignoring, as Rabinow cogently points out, the obvious facts that neither are they writing in the late 1950s nor are their audiences the colonized masses and colonial officials. Although I would not go so far as to argue that "situating the crisis of representation within the context of the rupture of decolonization is...basically beside the point," for one cannot deny or forget the historical baggage with which this crisis has traveled to our particular cultural context, I do agree with Rabinow's general suggestion that postcolonial teachers ought to look more seriously at "the conditions under which people are hired, given tenure, published, awarded grants, and feted" (1986, p. 253).

Foucault is to the point in arguing that with the disappearance of the "universal intellectual" or the writer as figurehead, "the university and the academic emerge, if not as principal elements, at least as 'exchangers,' privileged points of intersection" (p. 127). As "specific intellectuals" postcolonial teachers and writers play a crucial part in the general functioning of the apparatus of truth in the neocolonial era, but that general function does and must work out of the specific positions these intellectuals occupy in the cultural space of the academy—a specificity that includes race and class positions, conditions of work and life, and the particular access to discourses of truth in our society—but without breaking or splintering political alliances. The new direction of postcolonial journeys, in sum, ought to be toward a return to local and specific struggles, struggles whose effects and implications go beyond the academic profession, struggles that are linked to the general project of dismantling the neocolonial regime of truth.[6]

Notes

1 The predicaments I will discuss here have many important connections to themes of exile, return, hybridity, and displacement in the literary works of such postcolonial writers as James Baldwin, Driss Chraïbi, Assia Djebar, C.L.R. James, and George Lamming, to name only a few, but given the focus of my discussion and the limited space of this essay, I will not address them specifically.

2 Recently this superficial disciplinary division has been insidiously appropriated by new conservatives who, despite their own affiliations with state power—e.g., Dinesh D'Sousa, who served as a White House domestic policy analyst—have charged academic intellectuals with deploying a "politics of race and sex on campus" (1991).

3 I group these different types of critic together because their conditions and experiences of marginality have allied them in their oppositional practices against mainstream and dominant systems of power/knowledge, although I recognize the plurality of interests, terrains, and constituencies from which they work.

4 Though I use it to generalize here, the phrase is Homi Bhabha's in "The Other Question: Difference, Discrimination and the Discourse of Colonialism" (1986).

5 As examples of this problem, see the otherwise illuminating essays by Homi Bhabha (1992), Vivek Dhareshwar (1989), and Mary John (1989).

6 I would like to express my gratitude to my traveling companions, Ross Chambers, Cameron McCarthy, Laura Pérez, and Janet Wolff, for many helpful comments and stimulating conversations.

REFERENCES

Bhabha, H. K. (1986). The other question: Difference, discrimination and the discourse of colonialism. In F. Barker et al. (eds.), *Literature, Politics, and Theory* (pp. 148–172). London: Methuen.

_____. (1992). Postcolonial authority and postmodern guilt. In Grossberg, Nelson, & Treichler (pp. 55–66).

Bourdieu, P. (1984). *Homo Academicus*. Paris: Editions de Minuit.

Clifford, J. (1989). Notes on theory and travel. *Inscriptions, 5,* 177–188.

_____. (1992). Traveling cultures. In Grossberg, Nelson, & Treichler, (pp. 96–112).

Colo, P. (1991). Hybrid: World word on the vision of film. In Fusco (n. p.).

Dhareshwar, V. (1989). Toward a narrative epistemology of the postcolonial predicament. *Inscriptions, 5,* 135–158.

D'Souza, D. (1991). *Illiberal Education: The politics of race and sex on campus*. New York: Free Press.

Fabian, J. (1983). *Time and the Other: How anthropology makes its object*. New York: Columbia UP.

Foucault, M. (1980). *Power/Knowledge*. New York: Pantheon.

Fusco, C. (1991). *The Hybrid State*. New York: Exit Art.

_____. (1991). Stateless hybrids: An introduction. In Fusco (n. p.).

Grossberg, L., Nelson, C., & Treichler, P. (eds.). (1992). *Cultural Studies*. New York, London: Routledge.

Haraway, D. (1991). *Simians, Cyborgs, and Women: The reinvention of nature*. New York, London: Routledge.

James, C. L. R. (1984). *Beyond a Boundary*. New York: Pantheon.

John, M. E. (1989). Postcolonial feminists in the Western intellectual field: Anthropologists *and* native informants?" *Inscriptions, 5,* 49–78.

Maharaj, S. (1991). The Congo is flooding the Acropolis: Art in Britain of the immigration. *Third Text, 15,* 77–90.

Rabinow, P. (1986). Representations are social facts: Modernity and post-modernity in anthropology. In J. Clifford & G. E. Marcus (eds.), *Writing Culture: The poetics and politics of ethnography* (pp. 234–261). Berkeley: U. of California P.

Rouse, R. (1991). Mexican migration and the social space of postmodernism. *Diaspora, 1,* 8–21.

Said, E. W. (1979). *Orientalism*. New York: Vintage Books.

_____. (1983a). *The World, the Text, and the Critic*. Cambridge: Harvard UP.

_____. (1983b). Opponents, audiences, constituencies and community. In H. Foster (ed.), *The Anti-aesthetic: Essays on postmodern culture* (pp. 135–159). Port Townsend, Washington: Bay Press.

_____. (1991a). Identity, authority, and freedom: The potentate and the traveler. *Transition, 54,* 4–18.

_____. (1991b). The politics of knowledge. *Raritan,* II(1), 17–31 [Reprinted in this volume].

Spivak, G. C. (1990). *The postcolonial critic: Interviews, strategies, dialogues* (ed. S. Harasym). New York, London: Routledge.

_____. (1989). Who claims alterity? In B. Kruger & P. Mariani (eds.), *Remaking History* (pp. 269–292). Seattle: Bay Press.

Trinh, T. M. (1989). *Woman, Native, Other*. Bloomington: Indiana UP.

_____. (1991). *When the Moon Waxes Red: Representation, gender, and cultural politics*. New York, London: Routledge.

5   Racism, Sexism, and Nation Building in Canada

Roxana Ng

I.

STUDIES OF RACE and ethnic relations have by and large ignored class and gender as essential constituents of the structuring of these relations. Similarly, gender analysis in the North American context bypasses race and ethnicity, and to a lesser extent class, as crucial elements in the gendered experiences of members of society. As a woman of Chinese descent, a "woman of color," a feminist working in the field of race relations and anti-racist education in the "first world" context, my experience in the academy is much like that of being in limbo: I don't fully belong to either "camp," because I insist on bringing a feminist perspective to bear on the issue of race and ethnicity and a minority perspective to the analysis of gender relations. Meanwhile, being in this position of marginality has challenged me to search for a way of understanding race, gender, and class not as stable or homogeneous categories for analysis but as dynamic relations integral to the construction of contemporary social life. It is from this marginal and contradictory location that I speak, write, and put forward the analysis to be presented in this essay.

Nowadays, "gender race and class"[1] has become a popular phrase in scholarly circles. (I remember a time when the mention of this phrase only produced frowns of puzzlement on the faces of my colleagues.) This phrase appears in many papers I read. Practically every student thesis I am supervising is about "gender race and class." Reading these writings, however, it is unclear how these concepts operate. The phrase is frequently used to gain scholarly and ideological legitimacy within certain circles rather than taken up as a matter for serious empirical investigation and analysis.

In the past these terms have been used as competing categories for determining social status. I want to move away from treating race, gender, and class as *categories* designating different and separate domains of social life to *discovering* how they are *relations* that organize our productive and reproductive activities, located in time and space. That is, these are *not* merely abstract theoretical categories; they are concrete social relations that are discoverable in the everyday world of experience.[2]

My insistence on treating race, gender, and class as relations, instead of theoretical categories, is consistent with the way in which Marx and Engels speak of "class" in the *German Ideology* (1970) and the *Communist Manifesto* (1967). Class, according to them, refers to people's *relations* to the means of production. Class is not a static category or a thing; it is a *process* that indicates how people construct and alter their relations in terms of the productive and reproductive forces of society, using whatever means they have at their disposal (Braverman, 1974).

This understanding of class goes beyond the standard treatment of the concept in stratification and classical Marxist theories, which confine it to the narrowly defined realm of economic activities, giving rise to the incorrect notion of economic determinism in Marxist analysis. My understanding of class (and of race and gender as well) is more in line with the broader understanding of the concept put forward by cultural Marxists (e.g., Williams, 1961; Thompson, 1963; Cockburn, 1983) and poststructural theorists (e.g., Weedon, 1987) who assert its relational and dynamic character. This latter understanding also implies that classes do not just emerge at an appointed time; they are made in the course of history as people group together and set themselves apart in their ongoing struggles and engagements in productive and reproductive activities.

Reviewing the historical development of Canadian society, we find that family and kinship, perceived or real, are means people deploy to exert their domination or overcome their subordination. Ethnic theorists have identified the deployment of kin ties and common descent as the salient features of ethnic groups. However, as Max Weber has pointed out, descent itself is not a sufficient condition for the formation of ethnic groups. He correctly observes:

> It is primarily the political community, no matter how artificially organized, that inspired the belief in common ethnicity. This belief tends to persist even after the disintegration of the political community, unless drastic differences in the custom, physical types, or above all, language exist among its members. (1978, p. 389)

Thus race and ethnicity are ideological constructions that arise from the struggles for dominance and control in which Canada emerged as a colony of Britain and France. While I am aware of the technical differences between concepts of "ethnicity" and "race," I am using them as though they were interchangeable to draw attention to their politically and socially constructed character. The struggle between the English and the French was perceived by themselves as the struggle between two "races," as members of these nations competed for hegemonic control over the new colony. Meanwhile, while the differences between people of Irish and Scottish descent in Atlantic Canada are seen today as subcultural or ethnic, at one time they treated each other as people belonging to different races with distinct and distinguishable characteristics. Certainly the Acadians were, and to an extent still are, treated as people from an inferior race, distinguishable from the Anglo-Saxons and the Celts by social and physical differences. These differences have been deployed by the dominant groups (the Scots and the English) to organize the subordinate class positions of the Acadians historically and presently.[3]

Similarly, gender is a social construction whereby "men and women are represented as naturally different categories of persons" (Miles, 1989, p. 88). That is, biological and sexual characteristics are identified as absolute differences, which then serve as justification for and conclusion about their differential social, economic, and political participation in society (Miles, 1989; Cockburn, 1983).

To summarize and reiterate, race, gender, and class are *relations* that have to do with how people define themselves and how they participate in social life. They are not *mere* theoretical categories. The conception I put forward allows us to see how relations of race, gender, and class converge, diverge, and change over time as people's relations to productive and reproductive activities change within a given society. These are real and concrete relations, not just abstract and imaginary categories.

Following this line of thinking, I use the terms "racism" and "sexism" to point to systems of domination and subordination that have developed over time as taken-for-granted societal features. These terms usually refer to people's prejudicial attitudes toward individuals of a certain ethnic/racial background (e.g., Afro-Caribbean) and/or a certain gender (e.g., women). They are also used to indicate certain discriminatory practices (e.g., in employment) directed at these groups. While these attitudes and practices are important elements of racism and sexism, I draw attention to them as *systems* of oppression and inequality based on the ideology of the superiority of one race and/or gender over others. Thus in Canada, white European men, especially those of British and French descent, are seen to be superior to women and to people from other racial and ethnic origins. Systems of ideas and practices have been developed over time to justify and support this notion of superiority. These ideas become the premise on which societal norms and values are based, and the practices become the "normal" ways of doing things.

While some theorists refer to these beliefs as "ideology," I prefer Gramsci's notion of "common sense" to indicate the taken-for-granted character of ideological thinking. The term "common sense," used in the everyday vernacular, denotes ordinary good sense. My usage here refers to the incoherent and at times contradictory assumptions and beliefs held by the mass of the population (Sassoon, 1982, p. 13). Treating racism and sexism as "common sense" draws attention to the norms and forms of action that have become ordinary ways of doings things, of which we have little consciousness, so that certain things, to borrow Himani Bannerji's description, "disappear from the social surface" (1987, p. 11). In developing an antiracist feminism, Bannerji states:

> Racism becomes an everyday life and "normal" way of seeing. Its banality and invisibility is such that it is quite likely that there may be entirely "politically correct" white individuals who have a deeply racist perception of the world. It is entirely possible to be critical of racism at the level of ideology, politics and institutions...yet possess a great quantity of common sense racism. This may coexist, for example, with a passively racist aesthetic. Outside the area which is considered to be "political" or workplace...this same white activist (feminist or solidarity worker) probably associates mainly or solely with white middle class people. That fine line which divides pleasure and comfort from politics is constituted with the desire of being with "people like us." (1987, p. 11)

This understanding also suggests that racism and sexism do not denote the same phenomena at all times but are historically specific. For example, they took a particular form under slavery. Blacks were subordinated in particular ways during this era: as slaves rather than free laborers. Black women's sexuality (in addition to their labor power) was exploited by white men to perpetuate slavery. This is how Marx puts it:

> What is a Negro slave? A man of the black race. The one explanation is as good as the other. A Negro is a Negro. He becomes a slave in certain *relations* [my emphasis]. A cotton spinning Jenny is a machine for spinning cotton. It becomes *capital* only in certain relations. Torn from these relationships it is no more capital than gold itself is money or sugar is the price of sugar. (1971, p. 28)

II.

To treat race, gender, and class as *relations* enables us to see how racism and sexism were deployed to subordinate particular groups of people in the colonization of Canada and its subsequent development as a modern nation-state. The most obvious example is the struggle between England and France for control and domination of the colony. I will not examine the historical development of this tension here; suffice to say that this contestation has given rise to Canada's unique political configuration as a bilingual country with two nations: English Canada and Quebec. It also explains how the "two nations" conceptualization (e.g., Elliott, 1983) completely eclipsed the nationhood of the Native people. Historically the antagonism between the two nations was also fundamentally a class question (see Rioux, 1971; Milner and Milner, 1973; Vallières, 1971).

In this section I will discuss in general terms how race, gender, and class relations converged in the colonization of the Native people in Canada. I will show that racism and sexism, as ideologies and systems of subordination concretized as common sense practices, were integral to the formation of class relations and the implantation and development of capitalism.[4]

The first group of people to be racialized and subordinated in the colonization of Canada was the Native people.[5] To underscore my earlier point that "race" is an ideological category, I would remind the reader that prior to colonization it would have been impossible to consider the Native people as a "race" (the "Indians"). (For a discussion, see Frideres, 1983, especially chapter 1.) Before the "discovery" of North America and during the fur trade period, the continent was inhabited by a myriad of tribal groups who were nomadic. The mode of existence was that of subsistence.

Initially during the fur trade, both the English and the French recruited Native men to act as intermediaries between them and the Native tribes. In the wars between the French and English, as well as that between the English and the U.S., alliances were made between the colonizers and different Native tribes. Indeed, the procurement of Upper Canada by the English was largely due to the military efforts of the Iroquois confederacy (Hall, quoted in Clubine, 1991, p. 3).

In this period Native women's sexuality was also deployed politically and economically. In addition to being slaves to English and French officials, they were taken as wives and concubines. This was one way that white men, both traders and officials, gained access to the Native kinship system and lured Native groups into trading relations with Europeans. These relations, initially established to facilitate the fur trade, ultimately destroyed the communal way of life characteristic of hunting and gathering societies and transformed this mode of production into one that facilitated the implantation of mercantile capitalism in Canada (see Bourgeault, 1991, pp. 93–102).

The offspring of these alliances gave rise to a new "race," the Métis, who first acted as intermediaries between Native people and Europeans. But as trading relations stablilized, they were denigrated by Europeans and Native people alike (see Frideres, 1983; St-Onge, 1991). As Maria Campbell's touching autobiographical novel, *Halfbreed* (1973), reveals, the Métis became the most oppressed people in the new colony.

Once the wars ended and the colony was secured, Native people's position changed from ally to subject of the Crown. It was in this period of imperialist expansion by the Europeans that an ideology of superiority and inferiority of different "races" came to be developed (see Miles, 1989). According to Christopher Clubine (1991, pp. 7–10), the works of Francis Bacon, John Locke, and William Robertson began to establish a notion of European supremacy that was intimately tied to private property, farming, and Christianity. Farming and land ownership were seen to be a superior economic system, pertaining to a superior civilization, vis-à-vis other forms of subsistence. Reviewing the works of social historians of the eighteenth and nineteenth centuries on the progress of societies, Clubine observes:

> The criteria for ranking cultures into a hierarchy of superior-inferior stocks was [sic] based on the group's means of production. For example, William Robertson's popular work, the *History of America* (1777), ranked cultures from savage to civilized by this criterion....Robertson's evaluation of [the Native people's] mode of subsistence appeared in his *History of America* when he wrote that "[i]n America, man appears under the rudest form in which we can conceive him to subsist."...The Europeans were "civilized" and by implication the Indians were "rude" and "uncivilized" since they lacked the traits and hallmarks of English culture. (1991, pp. 8–9)

This ideology was later used, in the Canadian context, to justify the colonization of the

Native people (Clubine, 1991, pp. 7–10). A statement by Anna Jameson, an English woman visiting Upper Canada in 1837, indicates the common sentiment of the time:

> The attempts of a noble and a fated race to oppose, or even to delay for a time, the rolling westward of the great tide of civilization, are like efforts to dam up the rapids of Niagara. The *moral* world has its laws, fixed as those of physical nature. The hunter *must make way for the agriculturalist,* and the Indian must learn to take the bit between his teeth, and set his hand to the plow share or perish. (Maclean, 1978, p. 68, quoted in Clubine, 1991, p. 9; emphasis in Clubine)

It is important to point out that the ideology of European supremacy rooted in the notion of private property and Christian morality, and the deployment of this ideology for the subordination of the native people, had a material base. As the colonial economy evolved from mercantilism to industrial capitalism, agricultural development to provide food for England and Upper Canada became a priority. Later, as we shall see, Canada's westward expansion by railways and roads also necessitated securing parcels of "free" land. If the Native people's nomadic way of life had been incompatible with the fur trade, it was more so with an agrarian-based economy and the exigencies of the modern nation-state.

In this context education played a central role in the entrenchment of racist and sexist ideologies. In Canada formal education has always served as an assimilationist tool. It was designed by the dominant groups to impose cultural conformity upon subordinated groups by eliminating the latter's cultural heritage (see Clubine, 1991, p. 2). Nowhere is this function more visible than in the education of the Native people.

Initially education of the Native people was carried out by the missionaries. It had a two-fold purpose: to make the "Indians" into dutiful and loyal subjects of the Crown and to prepare them to adopt a new mode of production. This process was racist in the sense that it was through religion and education that the ideology of European superiority and supremacy was inculcated among the Native people. It was sexist in that while men were taught farming skills, such as how to clear land and hold a plow, women, under the tutelage of the missionaries' wives and daughters, were taught "civilized domestic skills" (Clubine, 1991, p. 15). As Clubine observes, the perceived differences between men and women

> were used by nineteenth-century missionaries to organize Indians into white-approved male and female roles. For example, a man's place was to be in the economic food production world, while a woman's was in the domestic food preparation world. This moved the prime economic unit from the tribe to the European version of the family, the nuclear family. (p. 16)

This kind of education in effect prepared Native men later to become farm laborers and women for wage labor using domestic skills. It involved de-constructing traditional male/female relations among the Native people, and re-constructing and socializing them into male/female roles appropriate to and approved by English colonial society, in which the Native people were to participate in new ways (Clubine, 1991, St-Onge, 1991). Native people's sexuality, labor, and social acumen were deployed both in their own subordination and as a means to subordinate other Native people. This is an example of the dynamic interplay of gender and race in the organization of productive and reproductive (class) relations. In this process racism and sexism, as ideology, were entrenched as normal and rational ways of doing things. The displacement of the Native people, the exploitation of their labor power and sexuality, and their assimilation through Christian education were seen as "common sense" practices.

III.

Race, gender, and class relations took different forms in different periods. Historians frequently refer to the years between 1880 and 1920 as the nation-building period (see

Roberts, 1990, p. 110). This period witnessed Canada's transition from a primarily rural agrarian society to an urban industrialized one. It saw the emergence of Canada from a British colony to a modern nation-state. With this development came the progressive centralization of ruling activities in an expanded state apparatus, as the ruling elite consolidated its power.

Re-examining this period from a feminist perspective, Barbara Roberts observes that two types of nation building took place. The first was economic. It involved developing the infrastructure for economic growth (such as building a nationwide transportation system) and developing the national system of manufacturing and national markets, as well as intensifying agricultural production and resource exploitation (Roberts, 1990, p. 110). This aspect of nation building was dominated by men.

The second was the creation of the human nation: the building of a population base and communities. Women's work was fundamental to this aspect of nation building. In particular, women reformers of the ruling class in England and the new colony, whom Roberts calls "ladies" (1990, p. 108), worked relentlessly to organize the immigration of single working-class women from Europe, especially the British Isles, to become domestic servants and wives. Beginning in the mid-nineteenth century, their work was crucial in supplying the labor markets of the Empire (see also Lay, 1980).

While the efforts of the lady reformers might have been motivated initially by their own need for domestics, their vision in organizing female immigration went beyond self-interest. According to Roberts, these immigrationists often spoke of themselves as empire builders. Their aim was to build strong communities in the Dominion of which everyone could be proud. "Canada was to be a British country, founded upon the moral, patriotic and racial influence (and unpaid labor) of British wives and mothers in Canadian homes" (Roberts, 1990, p. 111). Clearly, women cannot be treated as an undifferentiated and homogeneous group; their experiences were, and continue to be, divided by class position and interests. Lady reformers played a critical role in organizing the labor force participation, and hence the livelihood, of working-class women on the basis of their class and racial backgrounds.

Roberts' study further reveals a shift of control over immigration matters from the ladies to state officials during this period of forty years. Upper-class ladies were the first to set up immigration societies across the country to facilitate the settlement of these working-class women. While they received some funding from the government, they worked primarily on a voluntary basis. They were ready and willing to cooperate with government officials and businessmen, as they saw their goals to be compatible with those of the ruling classes in the empire, although from time to time their methods conflicted with those of the men. But as men consolidated their power in the state apparatus, control over immigration matters increasingly shifted from the lady reformers to professionals employed by the government (Roberts, 1990, p. 111). Their activities were incorporated as part of the coordinated functions of the state, which was controlled and dominated by men.[6] Here we see how class interests fragmented along gender lines. As ruling-class men consolidated their power in the state apparatus to facilitate the expansion of capitalism, they also took over areas of activities that had previously resided with women. Women's work was relegated to the "private" domestic sphere (see also Smith, 1985).

In the continuing efforts of nation building and the consolidation of political and economic power by the Anglo-Saxons and the Scots in English Canada, migrant labor was used in specific ways. For example, Chinese men were brought into Canada through an indentured labor system to build the railway that would facilitate the expansion of commercial interest and state control to western Canada. But in order to preserve Canada as an essentially white and Christian nation, these men were not allowed to bring their wives and children with them, or to have sexual relations with white women, for fear of spreading the "yellow menace" (see Chan, 1983; H. Con, R. Con, Johnson, Wickberg, and Willmott, 1982). Immigration, deployed to meet demographic and economic needs, was and continues to be a mechanism for organizing people's differential access to resources on the basis of their race and gender. This in turn shapes how different groups of people participate in labor-market (class) relations.

The relations of race, gender, and class discussed above do not pertain only to the Canadian past. They continue to operate in the organization of contemporary social life. Elsewhere I have examined in depth the racist and sexist subtext in apparently neutral and objective immigration policy. (Ng, 1988; forthcoming). Here I will summarize some of its aspects.

People applying for landed immigrant status (comparable to resident alien status in the U.S.) are classified into categories of "independent class" and "family class." This tends to disadvantage married women, whose livelihood is assumed to be dependent upon the household head (assumed to be the husband). This classification system ignores the fact that the wife may have comparable education and work experience to the husband and have made essential contributions to the family income before immigration. While immigration procedures do not distinguish between people's ethnic and racial origins as such, immigration officers have a great deal of discretionary power, which they exercise according to their assumptions about gender and racial stereotypes. These stereotypes, together with the accreditation process that gives more weight to education and training obtained in the Western, English-speaking world, mean that non-white women from the so-called "third world" face more discrimination in the immigration selection and assessment process.[7] Furthermore, once categorized as "family class" immigrants, these women are ineligible for social assistance and many subsidized language and job-training programs available to their "independent class" counterparts and other Canadians (see Ng, forthcoming). This is another way in which racism and sexism structure people's daily reality.

The recruitment of (female) domestic workers in the contemporary period is yet another example of how race, gender, and class operate in interlocking ways. Unlike other workers who can apply for landed immigrant status to enter Canada, domestic workers, most of them from the Caribbean and the Philippines, enter the country under the Foreign Domestic Worker (FDW) program. These women are in Canada as temporary workers and are issued temporary employment authorizations for a specific period of time. Prior to 1981, women who entered Canada as domestic workers had to return home when their work permits expired. Since then, as a result of agitation by civil rights, immigrant women's, and domestic workers' organizations, they can apply for landed immigrant (permanent resident) status from within Canada after they have been in the country for two years. The main criterion governing the admissibility of domestic workers as landed immigrants is self-sufficiency (Ng, forthcoming).

Again, a closer look at this admissibility criterion reveals many sexist and racist assumptions. Workers are assessed on the basis of their education, experience, skills, financial security, and social adaptation. Whereas many domestic workers from Europe (such as Scotland and the Scandinavian countries) have formal training, including "nanny" training, this kind of formal education is unavailable to women from the Caribbean and the Philippines. This, coupled with the general lack of recognition of training from "third world" countries, means that non-white, non-European women are disadvantaged in the assessment process (Ng, forthcoming). A recent federal legislative proposal states that nannies entering the country should have a minimum of Grade 12 education. This legislation, if passed, would further prohibit many women from developing countries from coming to Canada as domestic workers, thereby rendering the FDW program racist in yet another way (Ng, 1992, p. 23).

Racism and sexism take different, interwoven, and complex forms under different historical conjunctures. As well, these examples show that the development of capitalism and the emergence of Canada as a nation-state cannot be separated from racism and sexism as systems of domination and subordination. These systems are integral to this mode of production, but take different *forms* in different times and places, depending on the means and relations of production already existing in a particular locality and historical moment.

IV.

As capitalist society has developed to its present form, there has been a tendency to treat class as an analytical category that refers only to economic activities (for a critique, see Smith, 1985; 1987). In tracing the transformation of family relations in Canada, this is how Dorothy Smith puts it:

> In pre-capitalist societies, gender is basic to the "economic" division of labour and how labour resources are controlled. In other than capitalist forms, we take for granted that gender relations are included. In peasant societies for example, the full cycle of production and subsistence is organized by the household and family and presupposes gender relations. Indeed, we must look to capitalism as a mode of production to find how the notion of the separation of gender relations from economic relations could arise. It is only in capitalism that we find an economic process constituted independently from the daily and generational production of the lives of particular individuals and *in which therefore we can think economy apart from gender.* (1985, p. 2; emphasis in original)

My analysis, which insists on examining class as a process having to do with people's struggle over productive and reproductive activities, recommends an expanded understanding of class that goes beyond the economic realm. Class, in this formulation, is the embodiment of ideological and economic processes that structure how people relate to each other socially *as well* as how they are able to think about social relationships (see also Sayer, 1979).

Gramsci's notion of "common sense" is useful here to point out how ideological processes are not merely superstructural, that is, not only located in particular sites like the school—as theorized by Althusser (1977), for example. They are embodied in people's daily practices as the normal ways of doing things; in other words, ideology, including racist and sexist ideology, is taken for granted and normalized. In the above discussion I have attempted to show how racism and sexism were and continue to be an integral part of the way things are done in Canadian society, which in turn illuminates the connectedness of race, gender, and class relations in organizing social life.

By examining class as an actual activity (rather than as a purely theoretical category) in the building of Canada as a modern nation state, my analysis shows that class cannot be understood without reference to race and gender relations. Similarly, gender and race cannot be understood without reference to class relations. To think in relational terms, then, is to insist on discovering how race, gender, and class are expressed concretely in everyday practice lodged in time and space. It is to insist that race, gender, and class cannot be treated as universal and fixed. They must be understood as fluid, constantly changing, interactive, and dialectical.

The sketches of the dynamic interplay of race, gender, and class I have given throughout this essay do not provide an encompassing picture of how these relations permeate Canadian history. They are presented as illustrations of how we may (re)examine historical and contemporary realities not as independent and separate—as with the assumption of the separation between the private and public realms—but as interrelated and interactive. Each piece of the puzzle is connected to the others, and changes in one set of relations will lead to changes in other relations. The challenges for critical pedagogy are to show how the relations named above work to create, sustain, and reinforce existing forms of inequality, and to rupture our common sense ways of thinking and being in the world.

NOTES

1 I am using the unpunctuated phrase "gender race and class" to indicate the rhetorical usage of concepts of race, gender, and class. As I mention in the essay, the phrase is used frequently to gain legitimacy, rather than as a basis for analysis. There are, of course, writings that show how these concepts organize social life. For an example, see Angela Davis's book on *Women, Race and Class* (Davis, 1981). Various writings by bell hooks also explore the interrelatedness of these concepts (e.g., hooks, 1990).

2 The term "experience" is used here to refer to how people manage their daily life, for instance, how they go about the business of doing their jobs and taking care of their families. It does not refer to people's feelings and inner psychological states.

3 Acadian writers have poignantly captured the inferior position of the Acadians by virtue of their race/ethnicity and class. See, for example, the works of Antonine Maillet (e.g., Maillet, 1979).

4 For this discussion I have drawn extensively on research by Christopher Clubine (1991) and Ron Bourgeault (1991). I am indebted especially to Christopher Clubine for making available to me his unpublished work.

5 Many terms have been developed to refer to the aboriginal peoples of Canada. The changing terminology—from "Indians" to "First Nations people"—reflects the changing political and economical reality of Canada from the "discovery" of the Americas to Canada's emergence as a modern nation-state, as well as the progressive and militant demands of the aboriginal peoples for self-government. I am using the term "Native people" throughout this discussion to include all the people who are identified as such under the Indian Act and who self-identify as Native, including the Métis. To avoid confusion, I will not use other terms.

6 This is not the place to theorize the formation of the Canadian state. For a more elaborate discussion, see Ng (1989) and Ng, Walker, and Muller (1990, especially the introduction and conclusion).

7 I must hasten to add that other factors, such as demographic trends and economic needs, prevent utter discrimination against selected groups. The increasing number of immigrants from non-European countries, in the face of immigration trends that have historically favored certain European groups, is an example. Yet even as more Chinese "business class" immigrants are admitted as a way for the Canadian government to attract foreign investment, they are subject to racism in their daily lives, especially when they are perceived by Canadians to be competitors in the labor market.

REFERENCES

Althusser, L. (1977). *For Marx.* London: NLB.

Bannerji, H. (1987). Introducing racism: Notes towards an anti-racist feminism. *Resources for Feminist Research*, 16 (1), 10–12.

Bourgeault, R. (1991). Race, class and gender: Colonial domination of Indian women. In J. Vorst et al.

Braverman, H. (1974). *Labor and Monopoly Capital: The degradation of work in the twentieth century.* New York: Monthly Review.

Campbell, M. (1973). *Halfbreed.* Toronto: McClelland.

Chan, A. B. (1983). *The Gold Mountain: The Chinese in the new world.* Vancouver: New Star.

Clubine, C. (1991). *Racism, Assimilation and Indian Education in Upper Canada.* Unpublished manuscript, Ontario Institute for Studies in Education, Department of Sociology, University of Toronto.

Cockburn, C. (1983). *Brothers: Male dominance and technological change.* London: Pluto.

Con, H., Con, R. J., Johnson, G., Wickberg, E., & Willmott, W. E. (1982). *From China to Canada: A history of the Chinese communities in Canada.* Toronto: McClelland.

Davis, A. Y. (1981). *Women, Race and Class.* New York: Vintage.

Elliott, J. L. (ed.). (1983). *Two Nations, Many Cultures: Ethnic groups in Canada* (2nd ed.). Scarborough: Prentice-Hall Canada.

Frideres, J. S. (1983). *Native People in Canada: Contemporary conflicts* (2nd ed.). Scarborough: Prentice-Hall Canada.

hooks, b. (1990). *Yearning: race, gender and cultural politics.* Toronto: between the lines.

Lay, J. (1980). To Columbia on the Tynemouth: The emigration of single women and girls in 1892. In B. Latham & C. Kess (eds.), *In Her Own Right: Selected essays on women's history in B. C.* Victoria: Camosum College.

Maillet, A. (1979). *La Sagouine* (L. de Cespedes, trans.) Toronto: Simon & Pierre.

Marx, K. (1971). *Wage, Labor and Capital.* Moscow: Progress.

Marx, K. & Engels, F. (1967[1888]). *The Communist Manifesto.* Middlesex: Penguin.

_____. (1970). *The German Ideology.* New York: International Publishers.

Miles, Robert. (1989). *Racism.* London and New York: Routledge.

Milner, S. H. & Milner, H. (1973). *The Decolonization of Quebec: An analysis of left-wing nationalism.* Toronto: McClelland.

Ng, R. (1988). Immigrant women and institutionalized racism. In S. Burt, L. Code, & L. Dorney (eds.), *Changing Patterns: Women in Canada.* Toronto: McClelland.

_____. (1989). Sexism, racism and Canadian nationalism. In J. Vorst et al. (pp. 10–25).

_____. (1992). Managing female immigration: A case of institutional sexism and racism. *Canadian Woman Studies,* 12 (3), 20–23.

_____. (forthcoming). Racism, sexism, and immigrant women. In S. Burt, L. Code & L. Dorney (eds.), *Changing Patterns: Women in Canada* (2nd ed.). Toronto: McClelland.

Ng, R., Walker, G., & Muller, J. (eds). (1990). *Community Organization and the Canadian State.* Toronto: Garamond.

Rioux, M. (1971). *Quebec in Question* (J. Boake, trans.). Toronto: Lewis.

Roberts, B. (1990). Ladies, women and the state: Managing female immigration, 1880–1920. In Ng, Walker & Muller (pp. 108–130).

Sassoon, A. S. (ed.). (1982). *Approaches to Gramsci.* London: Writers and Readers.

Sayer, D. (1979). *Marx's Method: Ideology, science and critique in "Capital."* Sussex: Harvester.

Smith, D. E. (1985). Women, class and family. In V. Burstyn & D. E. Smith, *Women, Class, Family and the State.* Toronto: Garamond.

_____. (1987). *Feminist Reflections on Political Economy.* Paper presented at the annual meeting of the Association of Political Science and Political Economy, Learned Societies Meetings, Hamilton, Ontario.

St-Onge, N. (1991). Race, class and marginality in a Manitoba interlake settlement: 1850–1950. In J. Vorst et al.

Thompson, E. P. (1963). *The Making of the English Working Class.* New York: Vintage.

Vallières, P. (1971). *White Niggers of America.* Toronto: McClelland.

Vorst, J., et al. (eds.). (1991). *Race, Class, Gender: Bonds and barriers* (2nd rev. ed.). Toronto: Garamond.

Weber, M. (1978). *Economy and Society.* Berkeley: U of California P.

Weedon, C. (1987). *Feminist Practice and Poststructuralist Theory.* Oxford: Blackwell.

Williams, R. (1961). *Culture and Society.* Middlesex: Penguin.

6 Notes on Understanding Curriculum as a Racial Text

WILLIAM F. PINAR

The issues of culture and identity must be seriously incorporated into a nonsynchronous approach to racial domination in schooling.
Cameron McCarthy, "Rethinking Liberal and Radical Perspectives on Racial Inequality in Schooling"

The trauma of racism is, for the racist and the victim, the severe fragmentation of the self.
Toni Morrison, "Unspeakable Things Unspoken: The Afro-American Presence in American Literature"

PREFACE: RACE, TEXT, AND IDENTITY

I WISH TO SUGGEST that curriculum debates about what we teach the young are, in addition to being debates about what knowledge is of most worth, debates about who we perceive ourselves to be and how we will represent that identity, including what remains as "left over," as "difference." To think about curriculum in this way I rely on three interrelated concepts: race, text, and identity. Relying on these concepts I will suggest that understanding curriculum as a racial text implies understanding the American national identity. I want to point to the complex interrelation of race and identity, specifically how racial representation—including the splitting off and projection of difference—portrays, suppresses, and reformulates racial identity. Curriculum is one highly significant form of representation, and arguments over the curriculum are also arguments over who we are as Americans, including how we wish to represent ourselves to our children. While I speak of an American "self," of an American identity, clearly "self" and "identity" are multivocal concepts. I ask readers not to mistake the implicit unity of a concept of "American self" or "American identity" for its constituent diversity.

Why employ the concept of "text"? The concept of text implies both a specific piece of writing and, much more broadly, social reality itself. A term borrowed from poststructuralism, and particularly from the work of Jacques Derrida, "text" implies that human reality is fundamentally discursive. In contrast to the phenomenological view (Pinar and Reynolds, 1992) that language is derived from a fundamental substratum of preconceptual experience, the poststructuralist view is that all experience has been deferred (hence the famous construct *differance*) from original experience, and in this "gap" occurs language and history. Reading, in Derrida's words,

> cannot legitimately transgress the text toward something other than it, toward a reference (a reality that is metaphysical, historical, psychobiographical, etc.) or toward a signified outside the text whose content could take place, could have taken place outside language. (1986, p. 158)

In one sense, race originates in the "gap" between self and other. I aspire to read this text in such a way as to contribute to understanding curriculum as a discursive formation of identity and difference. What discursive formations are written in our unconscious, which selectively we represent in the curriculum, splitting off the excess as "difference?" Of course, what is "different" from majority culture is not reducible to the unconscious of the majority culture. As Toni Morrison asserts, "we are not, in fact, the 'other'" (1989, p. 9).

What is the meaning of race? It is hardly an unchanging, biological concept. Race is a complex, dynamic, and changing construct. Historically, those groups identified as "people of color" have changed according to political circumstance. For instance, before the Civil War, southern Europeans, Jews, even the Irish were considered "non-white" (Omi and Winant, 1983). The racial category of "black" grew out of slavery. "Whites" collapsed the diversity of African—and native—peoples into monolithic, racialized categories.

> By the end of the seventeenth century, Africans, whose specific identity was Ibo, Yoruba, Dahomeyan, etc., were rendered "black" by an ideology of exploitation based on racial logic. Similarly, Native Americans were forged into "Indians" or the "red man" from Cherokee, Seminole, Sioux, etc. people. (Omi and Winant, 1983, p. 51)

In nineteenth-century California the arrival of large numbers of Chinese provoked a "crisis" of racial classification. In *People v. Hall* (1854) the Supreme Court of California ruled that the Chinese should be regarded as "Indian" and thereby ineligible for those political rights afforded whites (Omi and Winant, 1983).

Identity becomes a central concept in the effort to understand curriculum as a racial text. Identity is not a static term either, reflective of a timeless, unchanging inner self. Rather identity is a gendered, racialized and historical construct. For involuntary immigrants such as African Americans, the notion of "caste" is not inappropriate. Castelike minorities tend to construct a collective identity, arising from the experience of oppression, in opposition to the dominant group (Ogbu and Matute-Bianchi, 1986). Additionally, "the formation of a collective oppositional identity system is usually accompanied by an evolution of an oppositional cultural system or cultural frame of reference that contains mechanisms for maintaining and protecting the group's social identity" (p. 94). Identity formation is constructed and expressed through representation, i.e., the construction of "difference," and negotiated in the public sphere. Curriculum is one significant site of negotiation. What is at stake is not only the identity of majority and minority groups but of the American nation as a whole.

I: Curriculum and Identity

A Fragmented Self

"We are what we know." We are, however, also what we do not know. If what we know about ourselves—our history, our culture, our national identity—is deformed by absences, denials, and incompleteness, then our identity—both as individuals and as Americans—is fragmented. This fragmented self is a repressed self, that is, it "contains" repressed elements. Such a self lacks access both to itself and to the world. Repressed, the self's capacity for intelligence, for informed action, even for simple functional competence is impaired. Its sense of history, gender, and politics is incomplete and distorted.

I seek to link current debates regarding the "canon" with questions of self and identity. Such an understanding might shift the curricular debate from preoccupations with equity or with multiculturalism to debates regarding the relationship between knowledge and ourselves. It is clear that the Eurocentric character of the school curriculum functions not only to deny "role models" to non-European American students but to deny self-understanding to "white" students as well. The American self is not exclusively or even primarily a European American self. Fundamentally, it is an African American self. I refer here not only to well-publicized demographic trends; I refer to the American past and the present. To a still unacknowledged extent, the American nation was built by African Americans. African Americans' presence informs every element of American life. For European American students to understand who they are, they must understand that their existence is predicated upon, interrelated to, and constituted in fundamental ways by African Americans (Goldberg, 1990).

The absence of African American knowledge in many school curricula in the United States is not a simple oversight. Its absence represents an academic instance of racism, or in Houston Baker's apt phrase, "willful ignorance and aggression toward Blacks" (quoted in E. O'Brien, 1989). Just as African Americans have been denied their civil rights in society generally, they have been denied access to their history and culture in school. Not only African Americans have been denied self-understanding, however. Institutional racism deforms "white" students as well. By refusing to comprehend curriculum as a racial text, students misunderstand who they are as racialized, gendered, historical, political creatures. Such deformity occurs—for most "whites"—almost "unconsciously." Many European American students and their parents—and perhaps many curriculum specialists—would deny that curriculum is a racial text. Such denial is done "innocently"; it represents an instance of repression in its psychoanalytic sense. Socially, psychological repression expresses itself as political repression (Schwartz and Disch, 1970; Kovel, 1971; Thomas and Sillen, 1972).

Freudian imagery of the self provides a provocative analogy here. During the decades of the 1980s the businessman represented the American prototype. Lee Iaccoca, Donald Trump, Michael Milken: white, male, savvy, shrewd, calculating, devoted to the bottom line. If this prototype represented the American ego—realistic, adaptive, adjusting in self-profiting ways to "reality"—then representations of African Americans alluded to the id—pleasure-seeking, unpredictable, accomplished in athletics and the arts. American culture projected African Americans as the id and, in classical Freudian style, maintained relative repression of the "pleasure principle" so that, presumably, ego stability and hegemony could be maintained. Continuing the analogy, fundamentalist religious groups, those elements of life in the U.S. that could be said to represent the superego, were permitted by the "business" ego to grow in size and influence. Those groups marginal to this version of the ego—African Americans, other marginalized ethnic groups, women, children, gays—were undermined, via public policy and in political practice.

Christopher Lasch (1984) has argued that the conservative political prescriptions for schools and society during the 1980s can be characterized as superegolike in nature. Illustrative of this "superego" voice are slogans such as "more homework," "just say no," "work not welfare." Conservatives insisted that the problem with American society was simple laziness (not their own, of course), and in this simpleminded analysis African Americans were assigned a major blameworthy role. True enough, liberals continue to call for rational deliberation, incorporating aspects of the unconscious (African Americans, in the analogy) into the conscious ego (mainstream society), but in controlled and planned ways (as with the liberal conceptualization of an orderly, incremental civil rights movement). My point is that the question of school curriculum extends to a question about the self, the American self. Understanding curriculum as a racial text means understanding this country as fundamentally a racialized place, as fundamentally an African American place, and the American identity as inescapably

African American as well as European, Hispanic/Latino, American Indian and Asian American. African Americans are ego and superego as well as id. Debates over the canon are also debates over the constitution of the American self.

European Americans and African Americans are two sides of the same cultural coin, two interrelated narratives in the American story. The former cannot hope to understand themselves unless they are knowledgeable and knowing of the latter, and vice versa. The sequestered suburban white student is uninformed unless he or she comes to understand how, culturally, he or she is also African American. As Baldwin (1971, 1985) has pointed out, "white" does not exist apart from "black." The two coexist and intermingle, and the repression of this knowledge deforms us all, especially those who are white and male. All Americans are racialized beings; knowledge of who we have been, who we are, and who we will become is a text; curriculum—our construction and reconstruction of this knowledge—is indeed a racial text.

During the past decade much has been made of the failure of public school students to learn even the most elementary and necessary facts regarding their history, geography, and culture. Cultural literacy is a noncontroversial requirement for any citizenry. What becomes controversial is the composition of such literacy. Voices in the popular press express views of cultural literacy that are informed primarily by Eurocentric and patriarchal knowledge systems. Without question American students must know and understand the European antecedents of contemporary American culture. However, this knowledge ought not be used as a defense against "otherness," a denial of our cultural unconscious.

I believe that to understand curriculum as a racial text is especially urgent given the present ascendancy of neoconservatism, during which time racial attacks and racial antagonism have increased (Omi and Winant, 1986; *Chronicle of Higher Education*, 1990). As you no doubt know, David Duke's white supremacy candidacy for the Louisiana governorship in 1991 brought him fifty-five percent of the white vote. I have been struck by the silence of curriculum specialists during the public debates of the past decade. I suspect this silence results from both ignorance and avoidance. While making enormous strides during the recent reconceptualization of the field (1969–80) toward understanding curriculum multidimensionally, mainstream curricularists have yet to incorporate racial considerations in any significant way (Pinar et al., forthcoming). Even multiculturalism remains marginalized and largely unincorporated in the scholarly effort to understand curriculum. Even those scholars who accept and study the profound ways in which curriculum is a political text seem reluctant to assert and teach curriculum as a racial text. Instead, race tends to be subsumed under politics (McCarthy, 1988a, b). It is past time for the curriculum field to change.

To understand curriculum as a racial text suggests understanding ourselves as racial texts. By exploring the denied past, we might push back the blacked-out, repressed areas and in so doing understand our nonsynchronous identity as Americans. One place to begin in this labor of self-understanding is remembering where our national identity became repressed. As I have argued elsewhere (Pinar, 1991), that place is the American South, for it is there that slavery, the Civil War, and the consequent struggle over civil rights scarred the psyche of the nation. Despite claims that the South is "new"—indeed well-worn claims (M. O'Brien, 1979)—only the veneer has changed. As the Duke election results indicate, white racism runs broad and deep. Additionally, Duke's success with Louisiana white voters in two statewide elections (he collected an even higher percentage of votes in the U.S. Senate election in 1990) indicates continued white reaction to a civil rights movement largely dismantled by twenty-five years of Republican (or conservative, a broader designation that includes the Carter administration) control of the White

House. Bluntly stated, the South is not only a terrible problem unto itself; it is a terrible problem for the United States. It is well-known that Republicans have appealed to the South—through playing the "race card"—in order to shift the ideological center of national political debate rightward and provide a safe and significant electoral basis for their conservative "restoration." Permit me now to review in abbreviated fashion selected racial, and related, aspects of Southern history to underscore the historical role of the South in U.S. race relations and in the deformation of the American national identity. Understanding the role of the South in the American identity and imagination, and considering a curricular provocation to study this role, might help point us toward understanding curriculum as a racial text.

II: SOUTHERN STUDIES AS SOCIAL PSYCHOANALYSIS

THE ANTEBELLUM SOUTH

Slave historians have debated how barbaric the American system of slavery was, on its own terms and compared to other systems. For instance, Stanley Elkins's controversial study suggests that the stereotype of "Sambo"—ignorant, innocent, and loyal—was rooted in reality (1968). Elkins attempts to reconstruct the psychosocial process of slavery, a process he characterizes as "mass infantalization." That is, adults were sufficiently psychosocially crushed that they regressed to an infantile state. In contrast to the sentimentalized view of slavery expressed in, say, Margaret Mitchell's *Gone with the Wind*, Elkins likens the American system to the Nazi death camps.

Eugene Genovese regards Elkins's theory as one-sided (1971). While agreeing that the American system was bestial, Genovese argued that the mass-infantalization model obscures the slaves' struggles to contest slaveholders' control. Further, the model ignores the slaves' development of self-affirmative rituals. Genovese views slaves and slaveholders as culturally as well as politically intertwined. For him the "South" is a black as well as a white concept. Dissenting from the mainstream view of Christianity as politically conservative, G.S. Wilmore found that the Christian church played an important role in slaves' rebellions (1983). He traces recent expressions of African American radicalism to these antebellum revolts.

The Civil War was no moral crusade to free the slaves. While emancipation was the paramount issue for abolitionists, it is clear that Lincoln and others regarded emancipation as a political threat. For Lincoln as for the Southerners, the war was a political struggle, not a moral one. Indeed, the North profited from the slave trade. Further undermining the view that the North was morally superior in this conflict is the experience of those escaped slaves who joined the Northern army. These soldiers faced racial prejudice, despite which they performed loyally and bravely. The Civil War's residue today in mass culture is a sense of moral self-righteousness in the North. Indeed, the North constructs the South as other, as a racist, primitive place, a splitting off of its own racism and cultural underdevelopment. Yet as African American experience in the North makes clear, this moral self-righteousness is unwarranted.

In the South remains a defensiveness regarding race, including the denial of guilt and responsibility for enslavement and consequent segregation, prejudice, and violence. As the Genovese thesis of inseparability implies, Southern whites and African Americans probably need to reexperience their past intimacy, however politically vertical its structure was, and renegotiate its terms horizontally. Until that complicated psychosocial and political process is lived through, distortions in both personalities will linger, a persistent sense of defeat among Southern blacks and a false sense of superiority among Southern whites. While racially born, these issues become, in the present era, also class issues.

The myth of a Southern aristocracy is as powerful as it is false. As Wilbur J. Cash and other students of the "mind of the South" have observed, a true aristocracy does not travel a dangerous ocean and settle a primitive frontier (1941). Those who immigrated to the American South sought economic opportunity and sometimes political escape. The creation of slavery and plantation life hardly represented an extension of an aristocratic life lived in Europe; indeed the early plantation owners, relatively few in number, were as primitive as the land they settled. Many more whites were "yeomen," small landowners with fewer than five slaves or no slaves at all. The class differences between these two groups were obscured by the presence of slaves, who provided a permanent class "floor" to Southern white society. The personalism of an agrarian culture in which many residents of a particular region were members of the same extended family numbed working-class and poor whites to class difference and economic inequities. Within slavery, house slaves tended to assume superior class positions to those who worked in the fields. The former group may have formed the beginnings of the African American middle class (Genovese, 1965).

While African Americans remain the underclass in the South today, there are hints of change. (At this writing, both Atlanta and New Orleans have black mayors, for instance.) Despite change, still absent in the South are the aggressiveness and willingness to contest racism visible among a number of African Americans living in the North. Southern African Americans know that Southern whites fought and died to keep them enslaved and then devised systems of segregation that they fought to maintain. Northern African Americans know that the self-righteousness of Northern whites is just pretense, and they respond at times with indignation. In the South the issue is decidedly class, intertwined as it with race. African Americans were condemned by many whites to a permanent underclass status due to their race; now their economic and cultural emergence undermines the white-defined class structure of the South. Poor whites have permitted their racial prejudice to keep them complacent. No matter how defeated, no matter how poor, no matter how ruined poor whites' lives may be, they are able to believe that there is always a group worse off. Faulkner has described in vivid ways how the self-destructiveness of the Southern system of racism and classism destroys poor and working-class whites as well as blacks (1946). The Duke campaigns provided false hope to poor and racist whites who misunderstand their class status and interests.

Clearly, supporting educational accomplishment for Southerners cannot be merely technical; it must take to heart these profound distortions in Southern history and in the Southern character. What curricular form would such an educational initiative for Southerners take?

THE CASE FOR SOUTHERN STUDIES

Curriculum as social psychoanalysis aspires to recover memory. As Lewis Simpson has noted, the South lost both history and memory in defending its agrarian way of life, in its denial of its status as a "garden of chattel" (1983). The Southern literary renaissance of the early twentieth century, most prominently associated with the names of William Faulkner, Robert Penn Warren, Eudora Welty, Thomas Wolfe, and others, involved the recovery of both history and memory. This achievement in Southern letters has yet to be accomplished, however, in Southern mass culture. Recent economic gains are accompanied, ironically, by the erasure of Southern culture (Southern voices continue to disappear from television and radio, for instance), which supports Southerners in their repression of history, a history that differs painfully from that of the North. This pain comprises, in part, the South's history of relative poverty and the absence of that self-righteousness associated with the legacy of New England Puritanism, with its pervasive senses of invincibility, optimism, and guilt. White Southerners can still be enraged when they remember they lost the only war they waged, a condition illustrated by the controversy surrounding Ken Burns's documentary of the Civil War, recently aired on public television. This pain when repressed produces pessimism, which in turn produces nostalgia (witness the agrarian movement, M. O'Brien [1979]), which in turn leads to provincialism, conservatism, and the racial class system. Recall that the democratic legacy of the New England town meeting is absent in the plantation South with its acute, if denied, system of racial caste (Woodward, 1968). Despite Southern as well as federal efforts to integrate the South with the American cultural mainstream, the South has remained—stubbornly—true to its racist and militaristic history (Odum, 1930, 1936).

The repression of memory and history is accompanied by vigorous distortions of various kinds—political, social, racial, and psychological. These distortions undermine intelligence in its various modes, including technical, psychosocial, and aesthetic intelligences (Gardner, 1983). Aside from questions of social ethics, then, the racism and classism of the South must be confronted for the sake of functional competence. Put simply, racism makes one stupid. The denials and distortions of memory and history it requires guarantee malignant intellectual development. The most refined science and mathematics curriculum—as important as it is—cannot respond to this cultural crisis. Perhaps a social psychoanalytic curriculum of Southern studies might. Such a curriculum seeks not to erase the Southern "place" and thereby support "homelessness" (Urban, forthcoming); on the contrary, such a program supports Southerners in understanding and living through exactly who they are. Through such intellectual, psychosocial, and political work, Southerners might finally return home: to an authentic home, not a mystification of a South that never existed, except through denial and fantasy.

It almost goes without saying that such a curriculum of Southern studies would not function as an occasion for nostalgia. It would comprise political, critical and informed analyses of race and class in the South. Genovese's studies of slavery and of African American history in general represent one such analysis (1965, 1969, 1971). This analysis should be supplemented by the work of others, including, but hardly limited to, the work of African American historians and writers such as Maya Angelou, James Baldwin, W.E.B. DuBois, Alice Walker, and Richard Wright. A central theme of these Southern studies would be the multiracial character of the South and the nation and the profound ways in which African Americans and European Americans are two ethnic sides of the same cultural coin. Indeed, they are the same, split apart only by projection and fantasy. Only when Southern whites understand that their experience is inseparable from that of Southern African Americans (and vice versa) can the history of each group, merged and denied as it is now, be reexperienced and psychologically integrated and its genocidal aspects perhaps forgiven and surpassed.

Of course, this is an enormous curricular and cultural task. Yet the size and complexity of what faces Southerners—especially white Southerners—cannot be a pretext for failure to make the effort. The educational development of the South as well as the political fate of the nation, in a postindustrial era when cultural and economic development are intertwined, depends upon it. Within both European American and African American sectors, the history of class as well as race must be made explicit. The presence of slaves, as I have observed, blurred class distinctions between the small aristocracy and the much larger working-class and poor white groups, with the effect of blinding these white lower classes to their true status and undermining their efforts to further themselves economically and culturally. Indeed, poor and lower-middle-class whites continue to misunderstand their status vis-à-vis the white upper class and to displace their frustrations onto each other and onto African Americans. Racism is the central issue, of course, and it must be the central thematization in this social-psychoanalytic curriculum of Southern studies. Due to its inseparability from race, class would be a second theme of curricular organization. Third, a history of gender would be required to explicate the ways that women, both white and African American, were socially constituted and located (Fox-Genovese, 1988). The often heroic history of African American women, as they supported slave families from which African American men were marginalized by white slaveowners, needs to be taught and its psychological implications incorporated. The passive aggression of slaveholders toward their wives and daughters, as they mystified them into objects of hyperfemininity and social uselessness, needs to be theorized and taught. Also to be taught would be the complex responses of these women, including their strategies of self-affirmation, empowerment, and retaliation, as well as their displacement of frustration onto each other and upon their racial captives. Without question the struggle and triumph of African American men, as they appeared to comply with their masters while retaining and sometimes strengthening an autonomous and undefeated psychological cultural core—which led a hundred years later to African American nationalism and separatism—needs to be detailed. Each of these thematizations needs to be studied, reexperienced, and integrated in the present (Genovese, 1969). What is necessary here is not simply memorization but a social-psychoanalytic recovery of history and memory and a fuller entry into a present characterized by horizontal social and economic relations.

While history and literature would comprise the two major disciplines in this curriculum of Southern studies, the other disciplines comprising the humanities, the arts, and the social sciences also have curricular roles to play. Departments of black and women's studies need to be involved, probably in leadership capacities. While courses in Southern history and literature have been taught for decades, systematic programs of Southern studies are rare (Pinar, 1991). Offerings in the lower levels of schooling are even more scarce. The potential here is for a social-psychoanalytic curriculum of Southern studies, which communicates clearly and profoundly an understanding of curriculum as a racial text, to be the means for the South to enter fully (not only in literary ways) and on its own terms into the twentieth century. Not only the fate of the South depends upon this accomplishment but the fate of the nation as well.

III: CONCLUSION

"UNDER EVERY DARK SKIN A JUNGLE"

When we acknowledge that we are racial creatures, that we are both what we know and what we do not know, we acknowledge that curriculum is a racial text. In its representations of race, difference, and identity, the school curriculum communicates images of who we are as individuals and civic creatures. As Americans we live a complex, nonsynchronous identity. We are multicultural, multiclassed, and multigendered. Despite this fundamental truth, various elements in the American national character continue to be devalued, indeed repressed. Morrison observes in this regard: "Certain absences are so stressed, so ornate, so planned, they call attention to themselves; arrest us with intentionality and purpose, like neighborhoods that are defined by the population held away from them" (1989, p. 11).

What do "stressed absences" imply for understanding race and representation? Susan Edgerton understands that marginality is created by centrality (and vice versa), that marginality "lives within the very language/world that makes it necessary and that it must oppose" (forthcoming). Marginality can suggest invisibility, as portrayed in Ralph

Ellison's *Invisible Man* (1952). As that novel indicates, it is possible to be invisible to others yet not to oneself; by the end of it Invisible Man realizes that he is "invisible, not blind" (p. 563). Others so marginalized may internalize their social invisibility and may suppress their interior life, indeed their humanity. Edgerton quotes from the Ellison novel: "Already he's learned to repress not only his emotions but his humanity. He's invisible, a walking personification of the Negative....The mechanical man!" (Ellison, 1952, p. 92). Hidden perhaps not only to himself, the African American is hidden to "white" America. Again, Edgerton quotes from Ellison's novel: "You're hidden right out in the open....They wouldn't see you because they don't expect you to know anything, since they believe they've taken care of that" (Ellison, 1952, p. 152).

The second novel Edgerton consults, Morrison's *Beloved* (1987), enables her to depict how the fantasies of European Americans become realized through the marginalized "other." Edgerton quotes Morrison's novel:

> White people believed that whatever the manners, under every dark skin was a jungle. Swift unnavigable waters, swinging screaming baboons, sleeping snakes, red gums ready for their sweet white blood. In a way, he thought, they were right. The more colored people spent their strength trying to convince them how gentle they were, how clever and loving, how human, the more they used themselves up to persuade whites of something Negroes believed could not be questioned, the deeper and more tangled the jungle grew inside. But it wasn't the jungle Blacks brought with them to this place from the other (livable) place. It was the jungle whitefolks planted in them. And it grew. It spread. In, through and after life, it spread, until it invaded the whites who had made it. Touched them every one. Changed and altered them. Made them bloody, silly, worse than ever they wanted to be, so scared were they of the jungle they had made. The screaming baboon lived under their own white skin; the red gums were their own. (Morrison, 1984, pp. 198–199)

This passage vividly portrays the inextricability—psychological and cultural—of whites and blacks. This inextricability is not only an empirical, historical fact but a psychological reality. European Americans are also what they displace onto others, and their self-repression requires repression of the "other." The dynamics of racism are complex, much deeper than a catalogue of attitudes that workshops might aspire to change. The very complexion of one's skin, the nature of one's blood, one's view of the world are all experienced racially (Edgerton, forthcoming).

"DECONSTRUCT STRATEGIES FOR IDENTITY FORMATION"

Not only the repressed suffer—although surely their suffering is the greatest, the most intolerable. Americans of European ancestry suffer as well. In their ignorance that they are racial creatures, that their knowledge is racial knowledge, indeed that their material and cultural wealth is in significant measure the product of others, especially of African Americans, they forget history and politics—and themselves. They have lost touch with reality, their own and others'. They cannot grasp that they "have been shaped and transformed by the presence of the marginalized" (Carby, 1989, p. 39).

What does understanding curriculum as a racial text imply for African American scholars? One answer is provided by the distinguished philosopher Cornel West, who suggests:

> Black cultural workers must constitute and sustain discursive and institutional networks that deconstruct earlier modern black strategies for identity formation, demystify power relations that incorporate class, patriarchal, and homophobic biases, and construct more multivalent and multidimensional responses that articulate the complexity and diversity of black practices in the modern and postmodern world. (West, in this volume, p. 19)

Euro-Americans might take West's advice as well. A fragmented American national identity has been predicated upon exclusions, and, in the imagery of an intrapsychic politics of the self, it is replicated by the politics of repression evident in the public sphere. These politics of identity are represented in the school curriculum and in the curriculum field.

Curriculum is "cultural capital," and under current politically conservative conditions, African American culture is "black-market currency." Because knowledge of American culture is characterized by distortions, repressions, and silences—what holds true for the South holds true in regionally different ways across the nation—American identity is deformed. Estranged from African Americans, European Americans are estranged from themselves. Being repressed, unfortunately, also means being stupid, and in order to realize our national intelligence we need to remember—in social-psychoanalytic fashion—those denied and repressed elements of who we are. This means, in part, that we must incorporate African American experience throughout the school curriculum, rather than marginalize it as "black studies" (although it also necessary to institutionalize it in that form as a space for separatist, intellectually autonomous research and action).

Obviously these are complicated issues. I have proposed that debates over the canon are also debates over identity and that history and culture make it clear that we European Americans are—in a fundamental sense—also African American. It is not only African Americans who are deprived when their history is underemphasized; European and other Americans are deprived as well. It is in our own self-interest—read European American self-interest—to incorporate an expanded and more accurate concept of who we are as individuals and as civic creatures. Educationally, this requires understanding curriculum as a racial text.

REFERENCES

Baldwin, J. (1971). Author's notes, in Blues for Mister Charlie. In J. Glassner & C. Barnes (eds.), *Best American Plays*. New York: Crown.

_____. (1985). White man's guilt. In *The Price of the Ticket* (pp. 409–414). New York: St. Martin's/Marek.

Carby, H. (1989). The canon: Civil War and Reconstruction. *Michigan Quarterly*, 28 (1), 35–43.

Cash, W. J. (1941). *The Mind of the South*. New York: Knopf.

Cleaver, E. (1968). *Soul on Ice*. New York: McGraw Hill.

Cooper, W. J., Jr. (1978). *The South and the Politics of Slavery 1828–1856*. Baton Rouge: Louisiana State UP.

Current, R. (1983). *Northernizing the South*. Athens: U of Georgia P.

Dabbs, J. M. (1964). *Who Speaks for the South?* New York: Funk.

Davenport, F. G. (1970). *The Myth of Southern History: Historical consciousness in twentieth-century Southern literature*. Nashville: Vanderbilt UP.

Derrida, J. (1986). The last word in racism. In H. L. Gates, Jr. (ed.), *"Race," Writing and Difference*. Chicago: U of Chicago P.

Edgerton, S. H. (forthcoming). Love in the margins: Notes toward a curriculum of marginality in Ralph Ellison's *Invisible Man* and Toni Morrison's *Beloved*. In L. Castenell, Jr., & W. F. Pinar (eds.), *Understanding Curriculum as a Racial Text*. Albany: State U of New York P.

Elkins, S. (1968). *Slavery: A problem in American institutional and intellectual life* (2nd ed.). Chicago: U of Chicago P.

Ellison, R. (1952). *Invisible Man*. New York: Vintage.

Faulkner, W. (1946). *The Sound and the Fury*. New York: Vintage.

_____. (1948). *Intruder in the Dust*. New York: Random.

Fox-Genovese, E. (1988). *Within the Plantation Household: Black and white women of the old South.* Chapel Hill, NC: U of North Carolina P.

Freyre, G. (1963). *New World in the Tropics: The culture of modern Brazil.* New York: Vintage.

Gardiner, H. (1983). *Frames of the Mind.* New York: Basic.

Genovese, E. D. (1965). *The Political Economy of Slavery: Studies in the economy and society of the slave South.* New York: Pantheon.

_____. (1969). *The World the Slaveholders Made: Two essays in interpretation.* New York: Pantheon.

_____. (1971). *In Red and Black: Marxian explorations in Southern and Afro-American history.* New York: Pantheon.

Goldberg, D. T. (ed.). (1990). *Anatomy of Racism.* Minneapolis: U of Minnesota P.

Grumet, M. (1988). Women and teaching. In Pinar (pp. 531–540).

Kovel, J. (1971). *White Racism: A psychohistory.* New York: Pantheon.

Lasch, C. (1984). *The Minimal Self: Psychic survival in troubled times.* New York: Norton.

McCarthy, C. (1988a). Rethinking liberal and radical perspectives on racial inequality in schooling: Making the case for nonsynchrony. *Harvard Educational Review,* 58 (2), 265–279.

_____. (1988b). Slowly, slowly, slowly, the dumb speaks: Third world popular culture and the sociology for the third world. *JCT,* 8 (3), 7–22.

Miller, J. L. (1988). The resistance of women academics: An autobiographical account. In Pinar (pp. 486–494).

Morrison, T. (1989). Unspeakable things unspoken: The Afro-American presence in American literature. *Michigan Quarterly,* 28 (1), 1–34.

O'Brien, E. (1989). Debates over curriculum expansion continues. *Black Issues in Higher Education,* 6 (8), 1–26.

O'Brien, M. (1979). *The Idea of the American South, 1920–1941.* Baltimore and London: Johns Hopkins UP.

Odum, H. W. (1930). *An American Epoch: Southern portraiture in the national picture.* New York: Holt.

_____. (1936). *Southern Regions of the United States.* Chapel Hill: U of North Carolina P.

Ogbu, J. & Matute–Bianchi, M. (1936). Understanding social factors in education: Knowledge, identity and school adjustment. in California State Department of Education (ed.), *Beyond Language: Social and cultural factors in schooling and language minority students* pp. (73–142). Los Angeles: Evaluation, Dissemination and Assessment Center, California State University.

Omi, M. & Winant, H. (1983). By the rivers of Babylon: Race in the United States. *Socialist Review,* 13 (5), 31–65.

Phillips, U. B. (1957). *Life and Labor in the Old South.* Boston: Little.

Pinar, W. F. (1988). (ed.). *Contemporary Curriculum Discourses.* Scottsdale, AZ: Gorsuch.

_____. (1991). Curriculum as social psychoanalysis: On the significance of place. In J. Kincheloe & W. F. Pinar (eds.), *Curriculum as Social Psychoanalysis: The significance of place* (165–186). Albany: State U of New York P.

Pinar, W. F & W.M. (1992). *Understanding Curriculum as Phenomenological and Deconstructed Text.* New York: Teachers College.

Pinar, W. F., Reynolds, W.M., Edgerton, S.H., & Slattery, P. (eds.) (forthcoming). *Understanding Curriculum.* New York: Longman.

Potter, D. (1968). *The South and the Sectional Conflict.* Baton Rouge: Louisiana UP.

Schwartz, B. & Disch, R. (1970). *White Racism.* New York: Dell.

Simpson, L. P. (1983). *The Dispossessed Garden: Pastoral and history in southern literature.* Baton Rouge: Louisiana State UP.

Thomas, A. & Sillen, S. (1972). *Racism and Psychiatry.* New York: Brunner.

Urban, W. J. (forthcoming). A curriculum for the south. *Curriculum Inquiry.*

Wilmore, G. S. (1983). *Black Religion and Black Radicalism* (2nd ed.). Mary Knoll, NY: Orbis.

Woodward, C. V. (1968). *The Burden of Southern History.* Baton Rouge: Louisiana State UP.

West, C. (In this volume) The new cultural politics of difference.

7 White is a Color!
White Defensiveness, Postmodernism, and Anti-racist Pedagogy

Leslie G. Roman

WHITE IS A COLOR! This simple, declarative statement addresses a central paradox within contemporary cultural studies, feminist scholarship, and the sociology of education. Within these debates, as well as in popular culture, "race," like the concept of gender, all too often has been used as a synonym for groups and persons who have been positioned as racially subordinate. One need look neither far nor wide for evidence of this usage. For example, it underlies the ambivalent and oxymoronic phrase "people of color," a phrase that developed as one of the positive achievements of multiculturalism's celebration of diverse "racial" and "ethnic" communities. The phrase "people of color" has been an important alternative to pejorative "racial" distinctions made by whites who were not part of the groups we attempted in ignorance to define.

However, given the tendency of the multicultural discourse to celebrate diversity without adequately analyzing power differentials among groups positioned by racial categorizations and inequalities, the phrase "people of color" still implies that white culture is the *hidden norm* against which all other racially subordinate groups' so-called "differences" are measured. Within certain contexts, the phrase can convey the mistaken idea that racially subordinate groups are essential subjects of a single experience or system of racism. At the same time, it can be used to imply that whites are *colorless,* and hence without racial subjectivities, interests, and privileges. Still worse, it can convey the idea that whites are free of the responsibility to challenge racism.

What becomes apparent is that the phrase "people of color," like other acts of naming and identification, cannot be separated from the more pervasive discourses of structural racism, or resistance to them, which locate the struggles of the various groups to be included in its name. This is not to suggest that the phrase is inherently regressive— even though I am critical of the larger problematic discourse of pejorative racial distinctions in which it is located. Clearly, it has been put to empowering and oppositional uses by racially oppressed groups and need not be taken up in a relativistic fashion. Yet in the current context of intensified racism and its attendant ultra-conservative attacks on the formerly progressive elements of multiculturalism, feminists and others on the left cannot afford to presume that the phrase has inherently or exclusively progressive meanings, or that socially just consequences will prevail from its use. The current celebration of ubiquitous or essential "racial differences" (permitted by the discourse of multiculturalism) is itself already in danger of becoming an expression of rearticulated white defensiveness. By white defensiveness, I mean the relativistic assertion that whites, like "people of color," are history's oppressed subjects of racism.

The multiculturalist ideology of *difference as pluralism* raises many questions for feminist scholarship concerning what postcolonial critic Chandra Talpade Mohanty calls "a hastily derived notion of 'universal sisterhood'" (1990, p. 181). Mohanty argues . compellingly that while the "blossoming" feminist scholarship around questions of "racial difference" and "pluralism" has been an

> important corrective to earlier middle-class (white) characterizations of sexual difference, the goal of the analysis of difference and the challenge of race was not the proliferation of discourse on ethnicities as discrete and separate cultures. The challenge of race resides in a fundamental reconceptualization of our categories of analysis so that differences can be historically specified and understood as part of larger political processes and systems. The central issue, then, is not one of merely *acknowledging* difference; rather, *the more fundamental question concerns the kind of difference that is acknowledged and engaged.* Difference seen as benign variation (diversity), for instance, bypasses power as well as history to suggest a harmonious empty pluralism (1990, p. 181; my emphasis).

Returning to the title of this paper, to say that white is a color does not rescue the concept of "race" from similar forms of empty pluralism and dangerous relativism invoked by the larger essentialist discourse of "race." Try as I might to recognize whiteness as a structural power relation that confers cultural and economic privileges, the phrase, spoken declaratively by the racially privileged, can also become a form of white defensiveness.[1] I write of these issues with an urgency to understand the consequences of adhering to either racial relativism or essentialism, having witnessed the reactions of my former students to the October 1990 statewide campaign and election results in Louisiana. There, David Duke, a former Ku Klux Klan and Nazi Party member, led a nearly successful bid for U.S. Senator. Duke appropriated the category of racial oppression with the support of his organization, the so-called National Association for the Advancement of White People, in order to appeal to the anxieties of racial displacement and racist scapegoating among white voters.

However, the implications of the ways in which the claim *to know* or to be able *to represent the diverse experiences of the racially oppressed*, within the context of the backlash against the gains of various oppressed groups, are not confined to the supporters of David Duke, the regional politics of Louisiana, or those outside "enlightened" liberalism or progressivism. For example, after sharing the title of this paper with one of my new white academic colleagues in Canada, I was surprised to learn that her reaction, although in no way sympathetic to the protestations of Duke's ultra-conservativism, nonetheless echoed white defensiveness. She stated: "Oh good, I'm glad you've challenged that idea of 'people of color.' I've always felt excluded by it." To appreciate the complexity and the contradictory range of attitudes that constitute white defensiveness means questioning, if not abandoning, simplistic explanations of racial inequalities as the consequence of unambivalent prejudices held by individuals. It means focusing attention on the variability of racist discourses and the contextual nuances in which they are articulated.

Those who have benefited from structural racism nonetheless claim or proclaim to know or represent the reality of racial oppression as an all-embracing, relativistic, and ubiquitous category of experiences to which anyone can belong. In this essay, I contend that this tendency is but a symptom of treating the concept of "race" as a reified synonym for racially subordinate groups. I argue that such an equation contributes to white misrecognition of the effects of our own racially privileged locations, that is, the ways in which institutionalized whiteness confers upon whites (both individually and collectively) cultural, political, and economic power.

Following the important insights of James Donald and Ali Rattansi in their introduction to *"Race," Culture, and Difference* (1992), I begin by acknowledging that "race" must be challenged as a stable category of cultural and ideological meaning on any grounds—whether biodeterminist or socially constructivist—in order to provide an alternative to its reified conceptualization. To ask how "race" operates in daily practice as a set of complex and changeable meanings is to take one modest step away from the essentialist discourse of race and toward a focus on the *unequal effects of racism* for different groups of people.[2] It means drawing attention to the dynamic interconnections between the representational practices of discourses of "race" and the power (or lack thereof) of various groups to voice *oppositional difference from* or *solidarity with* the racialized hegemonic centers of white power.

My argument finds resonance with Chandra Talpade Mohanty's conclusion that

> difference defined as asymmetrical and incommensurate cultural spheres situated within hierarchies of domination and resistance cannot be accommodated within a discourse of "harmony in diversity." A strategic critique of the contemporary language of difference, diversity, and power thus would be crucial to a feminist project concerned with making revolutionary change. (1990, pp. 181–182)

My interest in developing alternatives to the dominant conception of race as a reified set of meanings which are equitable with racially subordinate groups emerges from my attempt to apply a relational conception of racial interests to the concrete political and ethical problems I confronted as a middle-class, white, feminist teacher of secular Jewish background living and working amid the embattled reactionary politics of Louisiana. It also emerges from my desire to make interconnections between recent feminist scholarship on the *politics of identity, voice, and difference* and the agendas of postcolonial and anti-racist feminist scholars in the arena of critiques of imperialism and racism.

First, I consider the presuppositions of recent feminist debates influenced by postmodernism and variously referred to by terms such as *identity politics* or the *politics of difference and voice*. I foreshadow the kinds of stances they would authorize or discourage feminists to adopt in the struggle to advocate anti-racist pedagogical positions. I shall argue that one consequence of a feminism that would practice the avowed *a priori* relativism of particular versions of postmodernism—often expressed as a rejection of all realist epistemologies—would be political paralysis. By political paralysis, I mean the inability to make difficult critical choices that require distinguishing among adequate and inadequate claims to be a member of a systemically oppressed group. When, as feminists, we adjudicate between, or find it necessary to distinguish between, the epistemic standpoints of fundamentally oppressed groups and of those in more privileged positions who, nonetheless, claim to be oppressed, we are implicitly practicing a form of *critical realism* and, hence, refusing both essentialism and relativism. By taking critical, socially transformative stances, which I call *feminist materialist standpoint positions*,[3] in our classroom pedagogy, we are ruling out the unacceptable knowledge claims of some to be included in one or more categories of fundamentally oppressed groups. In the current national backlash against the gains made by various social justice movements—one that is primarily characterized by members of more privileged groups erroneously claiming to be history's oppressed or disadvantaged victims by appropriating the rhetoric of the oppressed and discriminated against—I argue that an anti-racist feminist pedagogy increasingly requires us to evaluate these claims without resorting to essentialism or relativism. Instead, we must make such evaluative distinctions by weighing the person's or group's subjective claims against and in relation to adequate structural analyses of their objective social locations without also falling into objectivism or universalism. Put more sharply, even the practice of postmodernist feminists may not be as indifferent to *differences* or to different claims *to know* and *represent the real* as is required by relativistic versions of postmodernism.[4]

Second, I briefly compare the political agendas (whether implicit or explicit) that emerge from feminist postmodernist scholarship on the *"politics of identity, voice, and difference"* with those of postcolonialism and anti-racism. I ask whether convergence of their agendas is possible and desirable. I argue for a shift within Western Anglo feminism from "identity politics" to the *politics of coalition* across different groups of women (and men) for the purpose of challenging racism, imperialism, sexism, and homophobia in their interrelated and contradictory forms. In both these ways, I aim to contribute retrospectively and theoretically to what Mohanty (1990) calls "a strategic critique" of my own attempts to forge an anti-racist and postcolonial feminist pedagogy in the Southern United States (Roman, 1993).

Third, based upon my recent analysis of *emergent* forms of *white defensive racism* as they manifested themselves in one racially mixed graduate class I taught at Louisiana State University, I develop what I call a *critical socially contested realism* (Roman, 1993). I use this concept to discuss the ways in which individuals' and groups' representations of reality are linked to their material and ideological interests in a struggle for hegemony. The extent to which those struggles become articulated with counter-hegemonic practices within larger emancipatory movements becomes a matter for critical pedagogy. Lastly, I formulate a provisional alternative politics of classroom discourse that challenges both racial essentialism and relativism, which are part of the discourse of the current resurgence of racism.

POSTMODERN RELATIVISM: WHOSE DIFFERENCES SPEAK FOR WHOM?

Feminists as well as others on the left face a material and self-definitional crisis that socialist feminist Jenny Bourne Taylor recognizes as being "at once theoretical and strategic" (1990, p. 298). According to Bourne Taylor, the crisis confronting British feminism hinges most centrally and paradoxically on the insights produced by recent postmodernist debates over "identity and difference"(p. 298). She contends that, once the category of gender has been pluralized by recognizing its intersections with the conflicting interests of "class, ethnicity, sexuality, region, age, and so on," it is no longer clear whether feminism as political practice and as a movement can transcend local contingent struggles and identities to propose radical social reform in a wider context (p. 299).[5] Thus, as she assesses the dominant view of the strategical consequences of postmodern theory, the impasse for feminism is that "it paradoxically undermines and is undermined by actual local contingent struggles for progressive change" (p. 299).

Poststructural feminist Linda Alcoff similarly argues against a ubiquitous "retreat response," which she finds particularly problematic among segments of the U.S. feminist movement (1991/92). For Alcoff, this response involves the curious assertion that in all cases we can only speak for ourselves, which articulates a pervasive skepticism about the possibility of ever adequately or justifiably taking advocacy positions. In her view, the "retreat response" paradoxically arises from the important recognition by feminists that the practice of privileged persons engaging in advocacy—or what she calls "the problem of speaking for" less privileged others—often further silences those whose voices it seeks to empower (pp. 17–24). Alcoff observes, however, that this important recognition has been taken to its paralyzing limits, denying feminists any epistemically salient conditions for advocacy as feminist practice. Although Alcoff does not directly attribute "the retreat response" to postmodernism's assertions of a fragmented, individualistic, and particularistic self, her concerns are well founded. Curiously, most of the scholars she finds to be retreating from advocacy identify themselves as postmodern feminists and use postmodernism to warrant or justify such retreats—a tendency that has become all too commonplace in work within this tradition. Thus, I believe Alcoff would concur with me that closer scrutiny needs to be made of the warrants postmodernist feminism provides to privileged academics (many of whom are among its own proponents) to hide in the light of reflexive exposure and to talk of representing multiple voices and subjectivities, while obscuring their own structural locations, ethical responsibilities, and epistemic standpoints in relationship to those they/we represent.

While Alcoff locates the evidence of such a crisis in the debates concerning the "politics of voice," or what she calls the problem of "speaking for" others, Bourne Taylor finds the crisis hinging on the terms of "identity and difference" (1990, p. 298). One thing is strikingly clear: Whether implicitly or explicitly, their understandings of the symptoms and consequences of this crisis (whether explicitly or implicitly) implicate the relativistic variants of postmodernism in providing some of the conditions for widespread political and moral paralysis among feminists and others on the left. There is, however, another angle or view on the source of this paralysis. It emerges from postcolonial and anti-racist feminist scholars and struggles.

WHITE NOISE AND WHITE SPACE: THE CRISIS OF "RACE" AND REPRESENTATION IN POSTMODERNISM

To locate the "crisis of retreat" (or what postmodernists so often call the "crisis" of representation in the disciplines of Western humanism) *solely* within terms internal to postmodernism is ahistorically to circumscribe its discourse to its own neocolonial referents. It means ignoring the production of knowledge about third and first world people of color emergent from the contexts and agendas of postcolonial and anti-racist scholarship and struggles. To say there is a general state of "crisis" within left and feminist scholarship does not tell us which groups are experiencing the crisis, who gets to claim territorial membership in it, and why such a crisis of representation, voice, difference, and identity emerges now. Nor does it tell us whose voices it has silenced, or how this crisis may be related to other discursive and political struggles. Getting answers to these questions may tell radical scholars more about the cartography of intellectual discourses within Western imperialism than we asked to know.

An examination of the historical relationship between postmodernist and postcolonial feminist scholarship at once produces the regrettable and angering insight that the former has largely marginalized, if not colonized and appropriated, the latter in the circulation of scholarly work.[6] Postcolonialism and, more specifically, postcolonial feminism have critiqued trenchantly Western national narratives of imperialism. Yet while Anglo Western feminists acknowledge the insights from these critiques, less often do we use them to revise our own terms of debate and bases for political struggle and coalition around women's differential forms of oppression.

A few years prior to her call for a "strategic critique of the contemporary language of difference, diversity and power," Mohanty wrote prophetically of Western feminism's difficulties in formulating a self-critical discursive space within which to study and represent the oppression of different groups of third world women (1988, pp. 181–182). She analyzed a wide-ranging body of literature, particularly critiquing the international development studies of the late 1970s and early 1980s. Mohanty demonstrated how Western feminist representations of third world women mobilized the largely undifferentiated categories of "women" and "gender" in studies of women's participation in familial systems, religious ideologies, and economic development processes. She showed how

Western feminism's language of sexual difference and women's oppression was often mistakenly universalistic or reductionistic. These tendencies, Mohanty argued, resulted in the representations denying not only the necessary cultural and material specificity of third world women's diverse experiences of oppression, but also their active agency as subjects of history. Mohanty argued powerfully that the "over-determined discourse" and ideologically vested representations of Western "first-world women" as "secular, liberated," and autonomously in control of their lives were enabled by an equally loaded discourse of "third world women" as "passive victims" or romanticized, exotic "others" (e.g., "the veiled woman," "the powerful mother," "the chaste virgin," "the obedient wife," etc.). The resulting binary oppositions, argued Mohanty, reinforced Western cultural imperialism within feminist scholarship.

Of additional significance is the fact that at the strategic core of her postcolonial critique of Western feminist scholarship about third world women were some of the foremothers and fathers of poststructuralist/postmodernist feminism's "identity politics" (e.g., Foucault, Derrida, Kristeva, Deleuze, Irigaray, and Cixous), whose important, but nonetheless equally ethnocentric, works were susceptible to similar criticisms. Moreover, Western Anglo feminism, in her view, missed an opportunity to revise its own imperialist understandings of the sexual division of labor and of conditions for women's independence by confusing or blurring the distinctions and relations between discursive representations and material realities.

To shift one's location from the questions and issues postmodernist literature entertains to those engaged by postcolonial scholars is often like voyaging between two strategically different communities whose politics and discourses share little apparent common ground. Shantu Watt and Juliet Cook (1991), for example, speak out in a collection of essays assessing the impact and direction of women's studies and feminism in the 1990s.[7] Their concerns are not the infinite play of fragmented subjectivities in language or texts (as so often is the case with relativistic versions of postmodernism); rather, they emphasize basic material issues. Drawing upon the work of Hazel Carby (1982), Michelle Barrett and Mary McIntosh (1985), Pratibha Parmar (1982; 1989), and Caroline Ramazanoglu (1989), they speak of the vital efforts within their own British context of black and white women's groups to undertake coalitions. The shift from identity to coalition politics emphasizes the enactment of occasions for independence, as well as unity, between these groups on a range of issues and priorities that have challenged fundamentals of Anglo Western feminist theory. These have included

> notions that *the* family is the site of women's oppression; reproductive rights when they mean only or primarily the right to abortion; notions of paid work as necessarily liberatory for women; and the significance of domestic labor in women's lives.
> (Watt and Cook, 1991, pp. 133–134)

Warning of the dangers of feminist "identity politics" as they are currently formulated, Watt and Cook quote Parmar, who observes that such politics have become a force for destructiveness, divisiveness, and immobilization among women's groups—reducing public issues of the women's movement to individual identities competing among hierarchies of oppression. In such a context, the temptation is to retreat into "ghettoized lifestyle politics," a retreat that renders women "unable to move beyond personal and individual experience" (Parmar, quoted in Watt and Cook, p. 133). The time has come, they insist, to move beyond identity politics to the hard work of coalition politics, that is, building coalitions among differentially oppressed groups for the purpose of agitation and activism for the civil rights of the racially oppressed. The task of collectively theorizing women's "shared and different experiences of oppression, including the oppression of women on [the] grounds of 'race,'" creates a "positive practice for the future by developing a basis for action against the structures of racial inequality" and thus becomes "an urgent priority for the 1990s" (Watt and Cook, 1991, p. 133).

In light of these criticisms, what can we make of the political implications of the last several years of Western Anglo scholarship on the politics of identity, voice, and difference? Certainly, many of the efforts to de-essentialize "identity" could become responsive to the kinds of criticisms and agendas generated within postcolonial feminist and anti-racist scholarship and political struggles. However, as Carby compellingly asks:

> Have we, as a society, successfully eliminated the desire for achieving integration through political agitation for civil rights and opted instead for knowing each other through cultural texts? (Carby, 1992, p. 17)

While we would not want to make the false idealist distinction between representation and materiality, it may serve as powerful reminder to suggest that homeless people cannot eat discourse. On the issue of refusing orthodox Marxism's idealism, Western feminism's identity politics has been an admirable theoretical leader, even if lagging behind in the specification of concrete political agendas that might come from such insights. For example, admirably, within the last fifteen years, Western feminist scholarship has strived to engage in self-reflexive analyses of gender in which it advocates that researchers locate our own interests and subjectivities on the same critical plane with those we research. This has created the space within Western humanism to critique the manner in which masculinist gender interests are mystified as "objective" and value-free—what feminists now call pseudo-objectivity or objectivism (Harding, 1987). It has also made possible the recognition that divisions between men and women are salient to the adequacy and validity of knowledge claims researchers make about the social world.

If, however, we are to extend the reach of our own insights concerning the limits of Western humanism, then our quests for critical reflexivity will need to be examined for their implications in relations of racial domination and colonial and neocolonialism. Closer scrutiny will need to be made of certain contemporary radical and postmodern critiques of the Subject and subjectivity that pretend to create, in the name of fragmented subjectivity and authorial enunciation, the possibility of the non-Western disenfranchised being able to speak on his or her own behalf while using the language(s) of the West as Subject. As Gayatri Spivak disturbingly asks in her critique of contemporary theorists such as Foucault, Gilles Deleuze, and Félix Guattari, do they actually provide anything more than "an interested desire to conserve the subject of the West or the West as Subject[?]" (1990, p. 271).

Similarly, we might ask of recent feminist scholarship concerned to articulate the *politics of identity, voice, and difference* in an effort to be critically reflexive whether it could also amount to an interested desire to conserve the subjects of Western feminism or Western feminism as Subject. Why, after all, does so much of the current literature written from a postmodernist and feminist postmodernist perspective on the *politics of difference, identity, and voice* nonetheless fail to locate whiteness and Westernness within the studies of women's experiences of differential power and lived culture? Could some of the noise about "difference" be white noise in response to postcolonial critics' charges of ethnocentrism within the leftist and feminist ranks? (Barrett and McIntosh, 1985, Brah, 1991, 1992; Parmar, 1989)

Taking such criticism seriously means altering some fundamental research assumptions and priorities. For example, along with attending the divisions that exist between men and women, we will need to examine equally profound racial interests and inequalities among women within global social relations (Brah, 1991, 1992). We will need to locate ourselves within these relations, going beyond the usual confessions (e.g.,

"I am a white, middle-class, heterosexual feminist") that function as little more than disclaimers of privilege.

In order to problematize the apparent intractability of "race" as a conceptual category and as a system of representation in which political agendas are formed, Anglo first world feminist scholars will need to take ownership in the overdetermination of "race" and racism in the sites where we may exercise some control: the curriculum of the so-called non-traditional programs of women's, ethnic, and African American studies, the traditional disciplines, and the research we produce. We can no longer afford to equate "race" with the anthropological and sociological approach of what Sandra Harding (1987, pp. 1–14) calls "studying down" in the power structure. The anti-dialectical study of racism qua the reified category of "race" unwittingly enables the discourse and practice of multiculturalism to have easy targets within current educational structures: the inclusion (or exclusion) of token representations of minorities in texts or as members of school faculties, staff, and student bodies. For example, Mohanty (1990) and Carby (1992) compellingly argue that efforts in the 1980s to integrate the curricula and the student bodies of universities under the aegis of "diversity" and "multiculturalism" (code words for racially subordinate groups) now serve as apologies for not living up to the promise of necessary affirmative action and widescale reform in higher education. In fact, such efforts, argue Mohanty (1990) and Carby (1992), commodify and manage the structural problems that are symptomatic of persistent racial inequalities through an extraordinary proliferation of prejudice-reduction and multicultural-awareness workshops on issues of cultural diversity and difference.

Aligning feminist inquiry with a multiculturalist ideology of difference and studying down in the power structure leads to the crippling criticism of ethnocentrism within feminist theory within women's studies, as well as traditional departments such as literature. Carby laments warily that within the curricula of such programs

> black women writers have been used…and abused as cultural and political icons…to produce an essential black female subject for its own consumption, one that represents a single dimension: either the long-suffering or the triumphantly noble aspect of black community throughout history. Because the black female subject has to carry the burden of representing what is otherwise significantly absent in the curriculum, issues of complexity disappear under the pressure to give meaning to blackness. (1992, p. 11)

Instead of focusing our attentions almost exclusively upon racially oppressed groups of women and men as either heroic icons or victims of racist practices and structures, we need to study the enactment of power and ideologies in a relational way.

What would a relational alternative to the study of racism look like? Provisionally speaking, it would entail studying up in the power structure (the board and locker rooms where institutional decisions are made), as well as studying down—that is, the cultural practices of marginalized and less powerful groups. It would entail democratizing the process of research such that the rights of the oppressed are protected by asking tough political, epistemological, and methodological questions concerning whose interests are served in any research endeavor (Roman, 1992).

If we begin to destabilize the concept of "race," supplanting it with analyses of our own locations within the cultural processes and structural effects of racism, we start (however modestly) to cross the historical and political borders of segregated sisterly schisms, which are the consequences of racism within and outside of the women's movement. Perhaps, then, there would be less reality to Carby's contention that cultural texts of multiculturalism and the "others" of feminist theory have become "fictional substitutes" for sustained social relationships on the parts of white, middle-class faculty and students with racially oppressed people in a society that "retains many of its historical practices of apartheid in housing and schooling" (1992, p. 12).

In other words, the rhetorical question Gayatri Chakravorty Spivak asks (1990), "Can the subaltern speak?", needs to be reframed.[8] We need to shift the burden of proof to the institutional deafness and defensiveness of scholarship produced within first world European and North American contexts, especially when it has been confronted with postcolonial and anti-racist critiques of the colonizing functions of Western humanism. The question for scholars working within such contexts (including Anglo feminists), who now confront the crisis of representation, is *not* whether the subaltern can speak. Instead, it is whether privileged (European and North American) white groups are willing to listen when the subaltern speaks and how whites can know the difference between occasions for responsive listening and listening as an excuse for silent collusion with the status quo of racial and neocolonial inequalities.

Questions for Feminisms: Dialogues of Border Crossing[9]

Postmodernist skepticism as to whether anyone has or ought to have the authority to speak in the name of social change is not altogether misguided. As Alcoff states,

> The impetus to speak must be carefully analyzed, and in many cases (certainly for academics!), fought against....If one's immediate impulse is to teach rather than to listen to a less-privileged speaker, one should resist that impulse long enough to interrogate it carefully. Some of us have been taught that by right of gender, class, or race, letters after our name, or some other criterion we are more likely to have the truth. (1991/92, 24–25)

The risk of imposing one's authority and authorial voice is at stake in representational politics and in the politics of defining whose needs and rights constitute urgent priorities for social transformation. But the refusal of the privileged to make difficult choices about who can and should speak in the interests of oppressed groups does not solve in a responsible or responsive manner the problem of being privileged in the first place. Nor does it solve the contradictory implications of advocacy for and with others who are less privileged than oneself. In fact, "the very decision to move over or retreat" altogether, argues Alcoff, "can occur only from a position of privilege" (Alcoff, 1992, p. 24). If silence is one of the effects of one's subordination, then "retreat from an action" is a recourse one may not employ as the oppressed (p. 24).

Moreover, postmodernism's attendant tendency to reduce such complex political problems to aesthetic textual ones raises the question of whether a relativist version of postmodernism is compatible with feminism as a political movement and whether women's experiences of oppression are so divergent that no single feminist movement is possible (Barrett, 1989). Within (Western Anglo) feminist theorizing and the women's movement, many feminists have used postmodernism (at least as a *slogan system*) to show that it is no longer possible to accept an essential or singularly interested category of *woman* or *gender*. Feminists have also employed the discourses of postmodernism to conceive of the social world and "reality" as plurally interested according to the determinants of race, class, sexual orientation, and age, as well as gender. On this basis, the pluralism of postmodern feminism means to avoid resorting to modernism's alleged reduction of these interests to a coherent ensemble of social relations or what they see as the grand narrative of "social totality" to which feminist discourses and politics have addressed themselves (Barrett, 1989, pp. 41–42).

Postmodernist feminists have sought to pluralize the categories of difference and oppression while rejecting realist epistemologies, and indeed often rejecting epistemology altogether. Leading proponents of postmodern feminism tell us that unlike modernism's discourses of Marxism and feminism, postmodern feminism avoids the master narratives of universality and totality, with their dominating hierarchies of oppression (Flax, 1987; Jamison, 1984; Lyotard, 1984). By now, arguments attesting to the benefits of abandoning modernist projects of emancipation in favor of inflecting feminist discourses with those of postmodernism are well rehearsed. Their typical formulations often entail the assertion that feminism and postmodernism can serve as important correctives to one another. Nancy Fraser and Linda Nicholson, for example, emphasize the necessity for a critical encounter between feminism and postmodernism:

> Postmodernists offer sophisticated and persuasive criticisms of foundationalism and essentialism but their conceptions of social criticism tend to be anemic. Feminists offer robust conceptions of social criticism, but they tend, at times, to lapse into foundationalism and essentialism. (1988, p. 84)

Fraser and Nicholson's assertion implies that the "anemic" stances of postmodern discourses toward engaged social critique of prevailing theories and social structures are politically and ethically neutral. Thus they argue that postmodernism could be combined as unproblematically with the feminist commitment to social criticism and emancipation as with reactionary epistemologies and politics. While we might find it important to produce explanations that are the subjects neither of totalism nor of essentialism, to suggest that postmodernism's lack of robust social criticism is just as minor a deficiency as is feminism's essentialism is to treat all partialities as having relatively equal political consequences.[10]

Despite their conflicting epistemologies and conceptions of women's oppression, most traditions of feminism admirably recognize that all theories and epistemologies are *interested* and thus demand ongoing revaluations of the social world, including their own terms for representing feminism. I argue along with Alison Jaggar (1983) and Sandra Harding (1987) that with the exception of liberal feminism, which accepts liberalism's empiricist claims to value neutrality, the major traditions of feminism (radical, materialist, and poststructuralist) offer us some moral, political, and epistemological principles to correct the terms of their own essentialist tendencies as well as the gender, class, and racially specific blind spots of prevailing epistemologies. And they stand their different self-correcting grounds without recourse to relativistic versions of postmodernism that fail to locate their own celebration of the indeterminacy of knowledge or reality claims in an interested perspectival way (Radhakrishan, 1989).[11]

It is therefore difficult to fathom the ultimate value for feminist political practice of uniting feminism with a relativistic postmodernism. This becomes especially problematic when we consider the implications of relativism for the strategic decisions involved in building effective coalitions across diverse interests. Coalition building necessarily entails the ability of feminist activists to set priorities for interests that require immediate or long-term political attention—in short, to avoid treating all interests relativistically. Nonetheless, the sloganeering around a relativist version of postmodernism as a complementary epistemology that corrects the deficiencies of feminism has reached a fevered pitch, extending into educational debates over what counts as critical and socially transformative pedagogy.

EDUCATION AND THE CONUNDRUM OF POSTMODERNISM

Within education, Carol Nicholson takes the call for unification between the feminist and postmodernist discourses one step further than do Fraser and Linda Nicholson. After recognizing that the variants of postmodernism à la Lyotard and Rorty are not only *not* neutral but in fact reinforce certain reactionary tendencies, she alleges that their appropriation within feminism will form the "basis of a new radical pedagogy" (Nicholson, 1989, p. 203). As she puts it,

> A postmodern feminism that is sensitive to differences can serve as an important corrective to postmodernism's tendencies toward nihilism on the one hand and apologies for the status quo on the other. (p. 203)

But can we afford to presume that the relativism of particular postmodernist discourses is intrinsically neutral, and thus able to be appropriated as a matter of willful voluntarism to effect progressive rather than reactionary pedagogical consequences?[12] Is it sufficient, for example, to follow the recommendation by feminist postmodernist Patti Lather that as educators we should "just say no to nihilism," and thus we can rest assured that nihilistic or reactionary choices and appropriations will not follow or be effected (1991, p. 314)? Such a response seems particularly inadequate, "especially insofar as the emblematic principle of postmodernism as such may be the 'principle' of never saying 'no' to anything" (Whitson, 1991, p. 77).

Lather responds to the critics of relativistic postmodernism by suggesting that the relativity of truth and reality claims is not problematic in itself. Rather, it is only a problem for those who are possessed by a "Cartesian obsession" with foundationalist epistemologies, causing them to engage in a "search for a privileged standpoint as the guarantee of certainty" (p. 115). As a feminist materialist, I share Lather's cogent critique of privileged or universalizing standpoints authorized by objectivist accounts. But her argument does not address the more dangerous implications of cultural and political contexts in which all reality claims are treated as representing equally valid accounts of the social world. In my experience, for example, how was I, a white, middle-class, feminist teacher to evaluate the claim of a white, middle-class student that she had been the subject of racial discrimination simply because she and the three other white women in a course were outnumbered by the five African American women taking the course? On what basis can such a teacher challenge the idea that whites are in this delimited context "racial minorities" and hence free to appropriate this category of oppression so as to then speak for or in the place of the African American students in the class? How broadly can the categories of difference and oppression be drawn? Who gets to draw them? How might we recover the critically evaluative and historicizing uses of realism to discover whose standpoints have epistemic salience on both objective and subjective grounds? Conversely, whose standpoints are more blinded by their own sexist, racist, and classist ideologies by virtue of their interests and privileged social locations? What are the moral and political consequences of a teacher resorting to postmodern relativism in the classroom; in this situation, for example, of failing to challenge the epistemic standpoints of white students claiming to be oppressed on racial grounds? Can teachers avoid the worst fears of postmodernists, that is, the imposition of our own critiques as master-narratives of authority upon what counts as *the real* in the service of radical social change?

THE RELATIVISM OF ADVOCATING NON-ADVOCACY

One indication of the hegemonic success of the right in the United States during the Reagan and Bush era has been its forceful and yet wrongful representation of its own moral agenda, policies, and visions of a just society as neutral and interest-free in opposition to those of the liberal and radical left, which it casts as disqualifiable on the grounds of its so-called extremist discourses of advocacy, bias, and ideology.[13] The implied directive to advocate non-advocacy may seem like an oxymoronic project. However, as educators we cannot afford to ignore the implications of its relativism—

whether advanced in the name of attacks on the progressive elements of multicultural efforts or in the service of commodifying racial inequalities as "cultural diversity." It is a project that attempts to deny our pedagogical responsibility to engage students in critical evaluation of their own and others' claims to *belong* to particular oppressed or privileged groups and, therefore, to *know* and *represent* their realities.

Because relativism erroneously treats all knowledge claims as equally reliable guides to describing and representing the social world, it denies their interestedness and unequal effects. When educators *assert* or *protect* relativistic claims in the classroom, what emerges is an implicit endorsement, if not advocacy, of the existing social inequalities, or, worse yet, of emergent practices that appropriate the experiences and discourses of the oppressed in order to deny their struggles for emancipation and equality.

Elsewhere (Roman, 1993), I have elaborated in some detail *emergent* forms of *defensive racism* in one of my own graduate classrooms in Louisiana. I illustrated how and why a socially transformative critical realism is preferable, in its political, ethical, and educational consequences for students and teachers, to the relativism of postmodernist discourses and to the reactionary discourses espousing non-advocacy and neutrality. While space does not permit me to describe the occasions for emergent white defensiveness in that context, my own experience suggests that are many potential and actual dangers of teachers either taking *a priori* relativistic stances themselves, or colluding with such stances—unwittingly or not—taken by students in the classroom. I shall also suggest from my previous findings (Roman, 1993) that the pedagogical politics of speaking with oppressed groups invites students and teachers to enjoy the rewards of engaging in the socially transformative practice of critical realism in order to evaluate in a relational way the objective and subjective bases for *conflicting claims to belong to, know, and represent the reality* of differentially oppressed and privileged groups.

SPEAKING WITH RATHER THAN FOR/INSTEAD OF OTHERS

The provisional alternative I propose as a non-totalizing means to achieve a socially transformative practice of critical realism may be best expressed as *speaking with rather than for*, the interests of oppressed groups who are engaged in critically evaluating and transforming existing social relations—whether or not members of such groups are physically present in the classroom. In contrast to the dominant meaning of *speaking for*, which implies that one group's voice can replace and stand for another's, I introduce the concept of *speaking with* to convey the possibility for tendential and shifting alliances between speakers from different, unequally located groups. *Speaking with* refers to the contradictions of voices engaged in dialogue with one another without suggesting that they are reducible to the same voice or epistemic standpoint. While the politics of *speaking with* cannot be defined in any *a priori* or absolutist way, we can specify the *relational politics of dialogue—or the lack thereof*—between unequally located groups. It also means that we can specify the conditions under which effective coalitions for social transformation may or may not be possible.

To use the term "relationally" means avoiding the conclusion that we can only address each conjuncture of dialogue—or the lack thereof—between unequal groups as dislocatable from a history of power relations in which they are embedded and thus necessarily subject to treatment only on a case-by-case basis. The concept of *speaking with* suggests that effective coalition politics relies upon groups rigorously evaluating the strategic value of their integrating with or separating from other groups in any decision to speak in behalf of the oppression of one's group or of others.

In the context of education, this alternative conceives of the aims of constructing, deconstructing, and transforming curriculum and pedagogy as dialogic in their form and democratically collective in their process—aims which do not result in teachers or students *imposing* their definitions of critical reality upon others in the classroom. As I argued at the outset, I use the notion of *a socially contested realism* to discuss the ways in which individuals' and groups' representations of reality are linked to their material and ideological interests in a struggle for hegemony. Classrooms are one significant context in which struggles for hegemony amidst unequal power relations take place. I am arguing for an ontology of *socially contested realism*, one which aspires to democratize the production of theory in the classroom as pedagogy, research, and political process. Such a process aims to treat as its legitimate texts for collective deconstruction all claims *to know* and *represent reality* made in the classroom, including those of the teacher, those manifest in the formal and hidden curriculum, and those implicit in classroom social relations. The politics of *speaking with* the interests of the oppressed confronts educators with the fact that social subjects occupy a range of contradictory and asymmetric interests that make it impossible to bracket or contain the pedagogical politics of who can speak for whom to an individualistic and essentialist conception.

Speaking with the interests of the oppressed presents the possibility of educators and students scrutinizing the common ground, as well as the conflicting moral and political stakes, of the discourses of multiculturalism and anti-racism within and outside of educational institutions. It means approaching anti-racist and multicultural ideologies and discourses on the same critical plane as we would common sense claims to know and represent reality, such as classroom speech and dialogue. Though ultimately we would expect theoretical "models" of anti-racism, for example, to offer more adequate accounts of racism than unexamined common sense propositions, both discourses contain contradictions that should become grist for critical analysis in the effort to socially contest racist ideologies of "the real."

Since both the discourses of anti-racism and multiculturalism are enabled or constrained by the institutional structures in which they are articulated, students and teachers can analyze them in light of what Phil Cohen calls their "hidden narratives" within theories of "race" and racism (1992, p. 97). "Hidden narratives" mobilize and articulate a "minefield of vested interests" and "powerful structures of feeling—anger, hatred, pain, and envy" (1992, p. 97). On the ground, for example, anti-racist and multicultural discourses and strategies may be constrained to similar institutional limits and interests, despite their often explicitly different ideological accounts of racism and agendas for social transformation. While the ideology of multiculturalism lacks an adequate account of the structural features of racism, many activists may use such a discourse to build anti-racist coalitions. This would suggest that what goes on beneath the labels of each of these discourses may be relatively autonomous from their dominant hidden narratives. In other words, analyzing the historical and political context for the articulation of these discourses places educators and students in an open rather than a doctrinaire atmosphere of critique and analysis. Such an atmosphere encourages the collective scrutiny of the kinds of practices authorized or limited by both the ideological claims of the discourses of anti-racism and multiculturalism and the institutional structures in which they operate.

Unfinished Postscript: Coalition Politics and White Defensiveness Revisited

While advocating more openness and careful pluralism within what constitutes anti-racist work, I have offered a provisional alternative to both relativism and essentialism in classroom pedagogy. The politics of speaking with the interests of the racially oppressed does not offer demagogic theories of anti-racist pedagogy. Nor can it in-and-of-itself adequately resolve the structural dimensions of racism that shape classroom conversation. It can, however, underwrite dialogical ethics in which classroom conversation can be opened, tested, and redefined between and among unequally located speakers. It can also prefigure, if not set the example for, the kinds of dialogue that make anti-racist coalitions possible.

The provisional alternative I have described here in theoretical terms and substantiated in practical pedagogical terms elsewhere (Roman, 1993) raises important questions about what educators ought to do with that moment when white students not only recognize that racism exists at levels deeper than the expression of individual prejudices (as a multiculturalist ideology would suggest), but also feel ashamed to be implicated in its structural practice—ashamed to face those who have suffered from racism. Ashamed, contradictory white subjects are not absolved of their responsibility to build effective social alternatives to structural racism. If white students and educators are to become empowered critical analysts of their/our own claims to know the privileged world in which their racial interests function, then such privileges and the injustices they reap for others would necessarily become the *objects* of analyses of structural racism. This allows white students and educators, for example, to move from *white defensiveness* and *appropriative speech* to stances in which we/they take effective responsibility and action for "disinvesting" in racial privilege.

I have offered a provisional alternative for handling conflicting knowledge and reality claims to be racially oppressed, showing how such a conversational ethic avoids treating "race" as a reified essentialist or relativistic category. The politics of speaking with others permits white educators or other members of dominant groups to struggle with what it means to make choices about one's political allegiances rather than to use one's privileged location as an excuse for paralysis, guilt, and shame. Keeping this alternative narrative in view and making it explicit means recognizing that I, like other white teachers, am *in* the stories of structural racism. We (who occupy racially privileged positions) have much to learn about how to work with white students to transform their (our) desire to be included in the narratives of racial oppression as its disadvantaged victims into a willingness to be included in narratives which fully account for the daily ways we (whites) benefit from *conferred* racial privilege as well as from our complicity in the often invisible institutional and structural workings of racism.

As a white teacher, I remain my responsible to work with racially privileged students to help them to understand that their (our) attempts to assume the positions of the racially oppressed are also the result of our contradictory desires to misrecognize and recognize the collective shame of *facing* those who have been *effaced* in the dominant texts of culture, history, and curricular knowledge. Such (mis)representations, or the allowance for them to speak in the name of the *real*, are only successful if we as educators permit them to go unchallenged. Left unchallenged, they may silence, or, worse yet, eclipse any memory of the historical, economic, and cultural conditions under which they were produced.

Our task as educators is not to reproduce demagogic theories of exclusiveness in which only racially subordinate students can be allowed to comprehend the experiences of racism. As I learned in my own experience in Louisiana (1993), this only intensifies existing white defensiveness, rather than promoting knowledge of one's role in the structural narratives of racism. I am in these narratives, but only to the extent that I can begin to hear that neither myself nor other racially privileged students are their central subjects. Learning when to move over in order to permit the speech of those who have been silenced and when to speak against racism in an alliance with others would mark a profoundly postcolonial rupture in the texts of curriculum theorizing and pedagogy. And if, for some, feminism is the happy "victim of the postmodern breakdown of authority," then "ironically it can benefit from the modernist virtue of risk-taking" (Frueh and Raven, 1991, p. 9) in the act of deciding with whom we shall speak, how we shall listen, and what we shall now do.

NOTES

My discussion of postmodern relativism appears as part of Roman (1993). I wish to acknowledge the constructive criticism of John Willinsky and Mutindi Ndunda.

1 Peggy McIntosh's work (1988) within feminist theory to understand how taken-for-granted privileges of whiteness confer cultural, political, and economic power upon whites has been instructive here. Vron Ware (1991) historicizes white women's political power as racial subjects in the women's movement in relation to anti-racist movements for equality. Beryl Tsang (1992) and Becky Thompson and Estelle Disch (1992) struggle with some of the practical implications of white privilege and anti-racist feminist pedagogy.

2 To distinguish the asymmetrical effects of structural racism and its expression by whites from the reactive prejudices of individual members of racially subordinate groups is to acknowledge that racism clearly advantages whites as a group, while it has injurious consequences for everyone. On this point, see the important work of Beverly Daniel Tatum (1992).

3 I use the concept as it is informed by feminist materialism to mean the political, theoretical, and methodological project of women and other groups subordinated by class, race, national culture, sexual orientation, and/or age collectively and democratically theorizing what is common and different in their experiences of oppression and privilege. Certainly, the aim would be to avoid *universalizing* such a standpoint from a prior specified position implicitly written as norm. Increasingly, however, I find the language of women's or feminist standpoints to be understood (whether justifiably or not) as underwriting a kind of universalism. As a counterpoint to such an understanding, I will further refine the concept's political commitments and its possibilities to recognize the inequalities of power that operate in classroom dialogue between and among groups of women and men. The works of Alison Jaggar (1983), Sandra Harding (1986 and 1987), and Dorothy Smith (1988), to name a few, have been important to me in the formulation of a provisional alternative to the idea of women being merely the objects of feminist or any other kind of analyses.

4 Here I join other scholars who also observe that postmodernism and poststructuralism's laudable project to deconstruct the categories of the self, subject, identity, and voice, etc., "fails to ground historically its own capacity for this far-sighted intervention," particularly when its analyses celebrate and reify what postcolonial poststructuralist R. Radhakrishan calls "indeterminacy-as-such" and thus lose sight of their actual constituencies "as though nothing were at stake." (See Radhakrishan, 1989, p. 190.)

5 For a recent example of this position see Knowles and Mercer (1992), who argue that because "there is no general relationship between race and gender," anti-racist and feminist political coalitions can only be formed on a case-by-case basis (p. 104). They clearly reject the idea of specifying how longer-term or broader coalitions between differentially oppressed groups can be built, arguing that broader constituencies for the purposes of mounting campaigns are unnecessary. This position, however, seems to rely on voluntarist notions of the ways in which people identify their oppression and form alliances. It appears to underestimate how oppression is constituted systematically and institutionally rather than in any voluntary or short-term way. The involuntary nature of oppression thus may dictate with far less individual choice how people identify with particular struggles against specific forms of oppression than their analysis suggests. Without recourse to middle-range theories concerned with the relationship of racism to sexism as well as the ways effective coalitions form, it is difficult to imagine how systematic forms of oppression could be combatted.

6 A number of postcolonial critics have made this point. See, for example, Mohanty (1988); Hicks (1988); Said (1986, 1989); and Spivak (1990).

7 Ironically, their essay appears in the section of the book entitled "Working with Diversity," whose contributors were representatives of many of the "others" of academic Western Anglo feminism, including other women of color, lesbian feminists, and third world feminists. Their marginalization and simultaneous commodification in this manner did not go unnoticed by them.

8 Spivak's closing anecdote describes a young woman who hangs herself in mute testimony to her own disenfranchisement, confirming the non-European non-Subject's understanding of her own double bind. The anecdote hauntingly suggests suicide as the final appropriation of an imposed mutism (1990, p. 313). On this point, see Mira Kamdar's (1990) discussion of the constitution of the European (non) Subject through the assimilation of different colonized voices who are made to speak as "others" in its name.

9 My analysis of what it means to do border work has been influenced by the work of Celia Haig-Brown (1990), Emily Hicks (1988), and John Willinsky (forthcoming).

10 Diana Fuss (1989) makes this point well when she argues to other poststructuralists that their critiques of essentialism may have forgotten that "'essentially speaking,' we need both to theorize essentialist spaces from which to speak and, simultaneously, to deconstruct those spaces to keep them from solidifying" as universals (p. 118).

11 On several grounds, feminist poststructuralism can and ought to be distinguished from relativistic versions of postmodernism. Chief among these reasons is the importance and primacy poststructuralism has given to social structuration and processes of determinacy. Careful appropriation, if not reinvention of poststructuralism, deconstruction, and psychoanalysis by feminists has created new epistemological and methodological insights into the relations among the subjectivity, language, and processes of psychic and social structuration (Fuss, 1989 and 1991; Hollway, 1984; Walkerdine, 1992), which offer alternatives to the determinism of their structuralist predecessors without concluding that structures are a fiction.

12 I am indebted to philosopher of education James A. (Tony) Whitson (1991) for an insightful critique of willful voluntarism, which he applies to the work of Stanley Aronowitz, but which I believe is apropos for some postmodernist feminists as well.

13 This illogic of pseudo-neutrality and disinterest renews a McCarthyist atmosphere of intellectual and cultural politics. The fervor to reshape issues of academic and intellectual freedom in the interests of the right is part of the recent attack on the left through the discourse of "politically correct" criticism. See, for one notable example, George Jonas (1991).

REFERENCES

Alcoff, L. (Winter 1991/92). The problem of speaking for others. *Cultural Critique*, 23, 5–32.

Amos, V. & Parmar, P. (1984). Challenging imperial feminism. *Feminist Review*, 17, 3–19.

Barrett, M. (1989). Some different meanings of the concept of "difference": Feminist theory and the concept of ideology. In E. Meese & A. Parker (eds.), *The Difference Within: Feminism and critical theory* (pp. 37–48). Amsterdam: Benjamins.

Barrett, M. & McIntosh, M. (1985). Ethnocentrism in socialist feminist theory. *Feminist Review*, 20, pp. 23–47.

Bourne Taylor, J. (1990). Raymond Williams: Gender and generation. In T. Lovell (ed.), *British Feminist Thought: A reader* (pp. 296–308). London: Blackwell.

Brah, A. (1991). Questions of difference and international feminism. In J. Aaron & S. Walby (eds.), *Out of the Margins: Women's studies in the nineties* (pp. 168–176). London: Falmer.

_____. (1992). Difference, diversity and differentiation. In Rattansi and Donald, (eds.), (pp. 126–148).

Carby, H. (1982). White Woman Listen. Black feminism and the boundaries of sisterhood. In Centre for Contemporary Cultural Studies, *The Empire Strikes Back: Race and racism in '70s Britain*. London: Hutchinson.

_____. (Fall 1992). The multicultural wars. *Radical History Review*, 54, pp. 7–20.

Cohen, P. (1992). 'It's racism what dunnit': Hidden narratives in theories of race. In Rattansi and Donald, (eds.), (pp. 62–104).

Dworkin, D. & Roman, L. G. (1993). Introduction: The politics of location. In Dworkin & Roman (pp. 1–17).

Dworkin, D. & Roman, L. G. (eds.). *Views Beyond the Border Country: Raymond Williams and cultural politics.* New York: Routledge.

Flax, J. (1987). Postmodernism and gender relations in feminist theory. *Signs,* 12 (4), 621–643.

Fraser, N. & Nicholson, L. (1988). Social criticism without philosophy: An encounter between feminism and postmodernism. In A. Ross (ed.), *Universal Abandon? The politics of postmodernism* (pp. 83–104). Minneapolis: U of Minnesota P.

Frueh, J. & Raven, A. (1991). Feminist art criticism: Its demise and resurrection. *Art Journal,* 50 (2), 6–10.

Fuss, D. (1989). *Essentially Speaking.* New York: Routledge.

_____. (ed.). (1991). *Inside/Out: Lesbian theories, gay theories.* New York: Routledge.

Haig-Brown, C. (1990). Border work. In W. H. New (ed.), *Native writers and Canadian writing.* Vancouver: U of British Columbia P.

Harding, S. (1986). *The Science Question in Feminism.* Ithaca: Cornell University Press.

_____. (ed.) (1987). *Feminism and Methodology: Social science issues.* Bloomington: Indiana UP.

Harding, S. & Hintikka, B. (eds.). (1983). *Discovering Reality: Feminist perspectives on epistemology, metaphysics, methodology, and philosophy of science.* Dordrecht, Holland: Reidel.

Hicks, E. (1988). Deterritorialization and border writing. In R. Merrill (ed.), *Ethics/Aesthetics: Postmodern positions* (pp. 47–58). Washington: Maisonneuve.

Hollway, W. (1984). Gender difference and the production of subjectivity. In J. Henriques, W. Hollway, C. Urwin, C. Venn, & V. Walkerdine (eds.), *Changing the Subject: Psychology, social regulation, and subjectivity.* London: Methuen.

Jaggar, A. (1983). *Feminist Politics and Human Nature.* New Jersey: Rowman.

Jamison, F. (1984). The politics of theory: Ideological positions in the postmodern debate. *New German Critique,* 33, 53–65.

Jonas, G. (1991). *Politically Incorrect: Notes on liberty, censorship, social engineering, feminism, apologists, and other topics of our times.* Toronto: Lester.

Kamdar, M. (1990). Subjectification and mimesis: Colonizing history. *The American Journal of Semiotics,* 7(3), 91–100.

Knowles, C. & Mercer, S. (1992). Feminism and antiracism: An exploration of the political possibilities. In Rattansi and Donald (pp. 104–125).

Lather, P. (1991). *Getting Smart: Feminist research and pedagogy with/in the postmodern.* New York: Routledge.

Lyotard, J. F. (1984). *The Postmodern Condition: A report on knowledge.* Minneapolis: U of Minnesota P.

McIntosh, P. (1988). White privilege and male privilege: A personal account of coming to see correspondences through work in women's studies. Unpublished working paper 89, Wellesley College, Wellesley, MA.

Mohanty, C. T. (1988, Autumn). Under Western eyes: Feminist scholarship and colonial discourses. *Feminist Review,* 30, 61–88.

_____. (Winter 1989/1990). On race and voice: Challenges for liberal education in the '90s. *Cultural Critique,* 18 (14), 179–208.

Nicholson, C. (1989). Postmodernism, feminism and education: The need for solidarity. *Educational Theory* 39 (3), 197–205.

Parmar, P. (1982). Gender, race, and class: Asian women in resistance. In Centre for Contemporary Cultural Studies, *The Empire Strikes Back: Race and racism in '70s Britain.* London: Hutchinson.

Parmar, P. (1989, Spring). Other kinds of dreams. *Feminist Review,* 31, 55–65.

Radhakrishan, R. (1989). Feminist historiography. In E. Meese and A. Parker (eds.), *The Difference Within: Feminism and critical theory* (pp. 189–203). Amsterdam: Benjamins.

_____. (1993). Cultural theory and the politics of location. In Dworkin & Roman (pp. 275–294).

Ramazanoglu, C. (1989). *Feminism and the Contradictions of Oppression.* London: Routledge.

Rattansi, A. & Donald, J. (eds.) *"Race," Culture and Difference.* London: Open UP.

Roman, L. G. (1992). The political significance of other ways of narrating ethnography. In M.

LeCompte, W. Millroy, & J. Preissle Goetz (eds.), *The Handbook of Qualitative Research in Education* (pp. 555–594). San Diego: Academic.

_____. (1993). "On the ground" with anti-racist pedagogy and Raymond Williams's unfinished project to articulate a socially transformative critical realism. In Dworkin & Roman (pp. 158–214).

Said, E. (1986). Intellectuals in the postcolonial world. *Salmagundi,* 70/71, 44–64.

_____. (1989). Representing the colonized: Anthropology's interlocutors. *Critical Inquiry,* 15 (2), 205–225.

Smith, D. (1988). *The Everyday World as Problematic: A feminist sociology.* Milton Keynes: Open UP.

Spivak, G. C. (1990). Can the subaltern speak? In S. Harasym (ed.), *The Post-Colonial Critic: Issues, strategies, dialogues* (pp. 271–313). New York: Routledge.

Tatum, B. D. (1992, Spring). Talking about race, learning about racism: The application of racial identity development theory in the classroom. *Harvard Educational Review* 62(1), 1–24.

Tsang, B. Anti-racist Education: A career in social and political change. *Women's Education,* 9(3), 25–28.

Thompson, B. and Disch, E. (1992, Spring). Feminist, anti-racist, anti-oppression teaching: Two white women's experience. *Radical Teacher,* 41, 4–10.

Walkerdine, V. (1992). Progressive pedagogy and political struggle. In C. Luke & J. Gore (eds.), *Feminisms and critical pedagogy* (pp. 25–53). New York: Routledge.

Ware, V. (1991). *Beyond the Pale: White women, racism, and history.* London: Verso.

Watt, S. & Cook, J. (1991). Racism: Whose liberation? Implications for women's studies. In J. Aaron & S. Walby (eds.), *Out of the Margins: Women's studies in the nineties* (pp. 131–142). London: Falmer.

Whitson, J. A. (1991). Post-structuralist pedagogy as counter-hegemonic praxis (Can we find the baby in the bathwater?). *Education and Society,* 9 (1), 73–86.

Willinsky, J. (in press, 1993). After 1492-1992: A post-colonial supplement for the Canadian curriculum. *Journal of Curriculum Studies.*

8 Cultural Studies and/in New Worlds

Lawrence Grossberg

I BEGIN WITH a rather obvious observation: cultural studies is going through changes. But I also want to emphasize that this is not a "crisis," for cultural studies has always been changing. That is part of what makes it so attractive: Cultural studies is always remaking itself as it responds to a world that is always being remade. This is possible, even necessary, precisely because it matters to cultural studies itself that this field, one with competing questions, projects, and positions, always remain open. Cultural studies is always more than one thing, but its openness should not be construed as pluralism. Its openness should rather be considered the necessary condition for its own commitment to "go on theorizing" in the face of changing historical demands.

But certainly the present moment in cultural studies is not exactly like previous ones; there is no reason to think that it should be. One reason it is not the same is that cultural studies has to deal with its own "success," a transformation not so much of its status as of its place. Prior to this "success" cultural studies could be conceived of as a minoritarian critical practice that existed in a number of different places and traditions, both intellectually and nationally. The connections between these places, the degrees of familiarity and influence, were highly varied and often relatively invisible.

So what has success transformed? Perhaps it can be described as the degree of cultural studies' dispersion: that is, the proliferation of its speaking positions (defining where and by whom it is spoken) across ethnicities and nationalities and across traditions and disciplines. But more, I would suggest that the grid of lines connecting these positions is changing—the density, intensity, and visibility of the lines themselves.

And this raises a significant question: How should cultural studies travel? How should it locate itself in the relations between its local speaking positions and the increasingly dense and intense lines connecting these positions? Certainly cultural studies has become something of a global intellectual commodity. We may not like this, at least in principle, but it need not necessarily negate cultural studies' "use value," to use a rather simple image.

Perhaps more dangerously, cultural studies has become something of a global fantasy, so that the more we talk about it, the less clear it is what we are talking about. There is a danger that cultural studies then becomes an idealized but empty vision of a politically and/or theoretically informed intellectual practice. It remains empty because its status as a fantasy relieves us of the obligation of recognizing that it also matters to the field itself that not everything is cultural studies, that the field is not entirely open. In other words, it does matter what cultural studies is in any specific context. The fact is that cultural studies takes work—work that must partly be directed to remaking cultural studies in response to its context, even as it is responding to that context (see Hall, 1992a).

It may be useful at this point to offer at least some preliminary description of the terrain, if only in terms of the struggle over how the signifier of cultural studies is being deployed. British cultural studies is not the only space of cultural studies, but it has recently provided a common vocabulary and iconography for diverse traditions to come together. Of course, even if we acknowledge the diversity of positions that come together in "British cultural studies," we are, in the words of John Clarke (personal conversation), still only acknowledging "the diversity that won." I am aware that policing the frontiers of cultural studies is a dangerous endeavor. Still, as "cultural studies" as a description of a certain body of work becomes increasingly content-free, we will increasingly need to ask, what is being lost? What specific bodies of work have no name?

If it matters how cultural studies is defined contextually, I would argue that it is less a question of theoretical positions than of critical practices. Cultural studies is obviously a set of approaches that attempt to understand and intervene in the relations of culture and power, but the particular relationship between theory and context in cultural studies is equally central to its definition. Cultural studies neither applies theory as if answers could be known in advance nor is empiricism without theory. Cultural studies is committed to the detour through theory even though it is not theory driven; it is driven by its own sense of history and politics. Furthermore, cultural studies is committed to contestation, both as a fact of reality (although not necessarily in every instant) and as a strategic practice in itself.

Finally, and perhaps most importantly, cultural studies is radically contextual. Culture itself cannot be defined autonomously of the context any more than theory can. This contextuality can be described at three levels. First, the concept of "culture" in cultural studies is caught between community (social formations), totality (a whole way of life) and aesthetics (representational practice)—to use the more common notions. I have argued elsewhere (Grossberg, 1992) that, as a result, cultural studies always operates within the ambiguous space of "culture," refusing to give it a singular definition and refusing, at the same time, to reduce reality to its cultural representations. Second, the very significance not only of culture but of the relationship between culture and power depends upon the particular space into which cultural studies imagines itself to intervene. Third, the cultural "text" is neither a microcosmic representation of nor the embodiment of a meaning related to some social other (whether a totality or a specific set of relations). It is a place at which a multiplicity of forces (determinations and effects) are articulated. As Meaghan Morris (1988) argues, such practices have to be seen as places where different things can and do happen, where different possibilities of use and effects intersect. In other words, a cultural practice is itself a complex and conflictual place that cannot be separated from the context of its articulation. It can have no existence or identity outside of that context. For this reason cultural studies is never merely a practice of textual interpretation and/or audience ethnography.[1]

At the same time I want to separate myself from another strategy that closes off the terrain of cultural studies by identifying it with a particular speaking position. Tony Bennett (1992) calls this a "charismatic closure." Such a move assumes that the speaking position of cultural studies is identical to the speaker's biographical one (thus demanding "proof" of the speaker's actual political commitment). At the same time, a charismatic closure demands a *particular* political commitment by equating the speaking position of cultural studies with the abstract position of the subordinate. Consequently the biographical identity of the speaker becomes a measure of the acceptability of his or her version of cultural studies. (This obviously echoes the "political correctness" debates.)

Too much of the contemporary discussion about cultural studies is trapped in the fruitless opposition between the global and the local. The former tends to see cultural studies as "traveling theory" and consequently often to fetishize and reify theory. The latter tends to emphasize local exigencies and political demands, often with the result of substituting "political necessity" for theoretical work. It underestimates the values of the lines linking the various sites of cultural studies. Both positions fail to take seriously Stuart Hall's admonition that "theory is always a [necessary] detour on the way to something more important" (1991b, p. 42). If the relation between the global and the local is itself an articulated one, with each existing in and constituting the other, cultural studies needs to map the lines connecting them. Only then can it begin to challenge some of these relations and offer new possibilities. This work has already begun, but I want to suggest that it has not gone far enough.

For those, like myself, who are positioned somewhere within the space opened up by British cultural studies or for whom it is a touchstone of sorts, this rearticulation of cultural studies has involved a questioning of the complicity of its own intellectual frameworks (culture/society, relative autonomy, ideology) and practices (a hermeneutics of understanding) with "the modern," with modern institutions and technologies of power. This is the moment of the "post" in cultural studies—I would rather not refer to it as "postmodern"[2]—a moment when its place within broader discursive spaces is problematized, a moment when it is recognized that cultural studies' own conditions of possibilities also articulate both its limits and its complicitous silences. It is too easy to reduce these complicities to some singular criticism such as Eurocentrism, as if concepts were intrinsically spatially placed or all worked in the same way (for example, universalization) to claim power. But it is also too easy to explain the moment of the "post" as if it were simply "the return" of the voices repressed by Eurocentric discourses.

For the most part, the attempt to disarticulate cultural studies from "the modern" has focused on the concept of culture and the practice of cultural interpretation (for example, Hunter, 1988; Bennett, 1990; Miller, forthcoming; and Viswanathan, 1991). These authors have identified a paradox in the way "culture" is used in cultural studies: culture is both autonomous of and deeply implicated in social and historical processes. This division has to be both maintained and reconciled. Culture's autonomy must be maintained as the domain of aesthetic value or social cultivation if it is to serve a normative function as a technology of power. Only in this way can culture remain apparently untainted by its constitutive role in, for example, imperialism. These authors propose that we change our conception of culture from the field in which power is symbolized to a set of practices that apply power. In their terms, culture "civilizes" the population by altering its behavior.

Simultaneously, but from a different trajectory—one involving the effort to reconsider questions of race and ethnicity—cultural studies has moved from a practice of critical interpretation to one of articulation, from the attempt to uncover a relation that necessarily exists (for example, between a text, a meaning, and a political position) to the project of looking at the continuous production of relations that are never guaranteed in advance. This leads cultural studies to reinterpret its interventionism and contextualism so that it sees both history and its own practice as the struggle to produce one context out of another, one set of relations out of another. Articulation transforms cultural studies from a model of communication (production-text-consumption; encoding-decoding) to a theory of contexts.[3]

Both of these moves within cultural studies are predicated on the recognition of one of the constitutive features of "the modern": that it fragments the social formation into a number of isolated realms—whether Rousseau's "society sui generis" or the invention of civil society and culture, always separated from economics and politics— each with its own history and its own temporality. But I want to turn to another constitutive feature of "the modern," one that points to a different possible trajectory for cultural studies' rearticulation.

THE MODERN, TIME, AND SPACE

"The modern" is always defined, positioned, in relation to an other. It is finally conceivable only in terms of the apparently undefinable rupture separating it from others. In its own terms "the modern" implies an alienation from some imaginary past or future (for example, the traditional), which is in fact the projection of a position and a measure from which "the modern" can both describe and judge itself. This temporal displacement, as Raymond Williams suggested, is precisely what constitutes the notion of culture as an autonomous realm.

A number of authors, including Eric R. Wolf (1982) and Samir Amin (1989), have offered a different interpretation of this displacement. (In the following discussion I deal only with the latter's arguments.) Amin refuses to identify Eurocentrism with provincialism or ethnocentrism or even the claim of Europe to have the right to represent others. Instead he locates the specificity of Eurocentrism as a certain prejudice or mythology necessary for Europe to reconcile its supposed superiority with its universalist ambitions. Europe constructed its exceptionality not on the basis that "the modern" (or capitalism—although the two are not quite identical) was born there but rather that it could not have been born elsewhere. This mythology is based on two conflicting assumptions, according to Amin. The first is that internal factors peculiar to each society are decisive for its evolution. Thus Europe located its claim to uniqueness in its Christian faith and its supposed Greek ancestry.

It is important to notice that this assumption identifies history with the notion of an isolatable, autonomous culture, closed off from its outside, from its others.

The second assumption underlying Eurocentrism is that the Western model of "the modern" (or capitalism) can be generalized. To the European imagination the only thinkable future was the progressive Europeanization of the world. This universalization, embodied in a rhetoric of homogenization—they would become like us—legitimated a project of world conquest and colonial violence. Of course, this universality was never actually descriptive; it was distributive and normative or, in Amin's term, polarizing. As Hall (1992b) describes it, it organized the world into "the West and the rest." The conjunction of these two conflicting assumptions—one that defined the local conditions of possibility of the modern, the other that proposed to universalize the modern and ignore local conditions—instituted and legitimated the unequal distribution of both power and value across space. And this inequality was produced both inside and outside of every nation-space colonized by capitalism.

On this reading we might argue that Eurocentrism—and the technologies of power of the modern—temporalizes space and rearticulates the other into the different. This opens a problematic which could only be solved by the search for or construction of a self-enclosed, isolated identity. And for just this reason, Amin rejects any politics in which modernization is treated as Westernization and opposed by the search for an alternative cultural identity. But I am getting ahead of myself. I need first to say something about time and space in "the modern"; namely that, by temporalizing reality and human existence, "the modern" effectively erased space.[4]

In fact, modernism has often been described as embodying a temporalizing logic and a specific temporality. Modern time is linear, irreversible, and unrepeatable: change, the transitory, the immanent, replaced the Kantian transcendental ideal (giving rise to the paradox of a relativism that must be resisted). Even the modernist avant-garde, which offered itself as the adversary of "the modern," was caught in this specific sense of time. These artists assumed that the present was by definition unprepared for their art; that its worth could only be recognized in the future; and the only contemporary proof of its validity was its shock effect (giving rise to the paradox of an aesthetic that demands experiment and compels repetition).

In more philosophical terms, according to Robert Young (1990), Hegel is the key figure behind the temporalizing logic of the modern. Hegel simultaneously viewed space as a product and residue of historical time; fetishized a particular space—the nation-State; and idealized historical time as History. In response to this idealization, the great philosophers who followed Hegel—Marx, Bergson, Husserl—all sought to restore the immanence of time. But, consequently, they all failed to challenge the identification of space with reification, false consciousness, and the distortion of time. (As Morris [1992] has pointed out, this privileging of time continues in such celebrated works as David Harvey's *The Condition of Postmodernity*.) It was Sartre who asked, if Hegel defined History as the continuity and coherence of time, as a historical totality, how there can be such a totalization without a totalizer? In other words, what is the relation of individual practice to this totality?

But it was not until Levi-Strauss and Foucault, Young argues, that the real question was raised: Is History, historicity, historical consciousness, essential to human existence? Or is it a construct imposed upon differential histories across space? If the latter is correct, this implies what Foucault calls "a transformation of history into a totally different form" (cited in Young, 1990, p. 61). And this transformation has radical implications for how we think of power. For example, metaphors like the "survival" or "reproduction" of capitalism over time as defining images of power would have to be rethought; and of course, this is exactly what Foucault attempted to do.

This would also obviously require a rearticulation of the concept of space in "the modern," a reconsideration not only of where it was excluded, but where and how it was included as well. This for me is not a question of the changing structures of history, as it is for John Berger: "Prophesy now involves a geographical rather than a historical projection. It is space not time that hides consequences from us" (cited in Soja, 1989, p. 22). Even Foucault has at times treated space as a historical issue, as in his description of the present age as

> an epoch of space. We are in the epoch of simultaneity; we are in the epoch of juxtaposition, the epoch of the near and the far, of the side by side, of the dispersed....Time probably appears to us only as one of the various distributive operations that are possible for the elements that are spread out in space. (1986, pp. 22–23)

Such strategies merely privilege time once again and reproduce the structure of "the modern" in arguments about "the postmodern." Nor is the relation of time and space in modernity a question that can be entirely addressed at the level of critical social theory or philosophical anthropology. Such theories assert the mutability of history, its social production, against the claim of a necessary and universal History. One can imagine theories that assert the mutability or social production of geographies of space against the assumption of a necessary and universal—what shall we call it—Geography (whether on the model of world-system or center-periphery or any other). That is, such theories would argue that human beings make space but in conditions not of their own making, to echo Marx. They would see space, following Henri Lefebvre (1991), as both the presupposition or medium and the outcome or embodiment of human life.

I do not want to deny the need for such work, as in the efforts of the new critical geographers, but they do not go far enough. They often continue to understand temporality as the precondition of spatiality, so that, for example, Edward W. Soja (1989) can still identify sequence with time and simultaneity with space. They often reduce the relation of space and power to an instrumental one, as if power merely manipulates space. And they often take spatial figures or images to be metaphorical rather than real (for example, Rosi Braidotti's otherwise brilliant analysis of feminism and philosophy [1991]). A more promising path might be found in the distributive maps of Pierre Bourdieu (1984).

CULTURAL STUDIES AND THE SPACE OF POWER

As cultural studies moves into different sites—"new" worlds, to speak ironically, worlds that have been irretrievably reconstructed by the violence of the various forms of modern power, including those of colonialism, imperialism, racism, sexism, disciplinization, and normalization—it too will have to be irretrievably reconstructed in some fundamental ways. It will have to rethink its articulations of culture and power. I want to propose two related trajectories of such a rearticulation. First, cultural studies must move from a temporal to a spatial logic of power; second, it must move from a structural to a machinic theory of power.

To begin to try to conceive of power spatially does not mean that we erase history but that we see it as singular events or "becomings" (in the terms of Gilles Deleuze and Félix Guattari [1987]) rather than as continuity or reproduction. It also requires that we recognize that on certain maps, where a map is a geography of becomings, the places marked as history, time, and reproduction can be invested with a great deal of intensity or even power. History, then, becomes inseparable from memory, not as a dis-placed "popular memory" but precisely as "placed time," as a geography of temporalities (Hay, forthcoming).

But the project of mapping the spaces of power will inevitably raise different and other questions: questions about mobilities rather than change, about intensities rather than identities. Spatial power is a matter of orientations and directions, of entries and exits, rather than of beginnings and ends. Let me emphasize here that by describing this as a spatial logic, I do not mean only that we need to look at the organization of space in literal or material terms as the site of power, or that we need to look at the nontextual existences of culture. As Foucault says, "A whole history remains to be written of spaces—which would at the same time be the history of powers (both of these terms in the plural)—from the great strategies of geopolitics to the little tactics of the habitat" (cited in Soja, 1989, p. 21). Culture itself must be understood spatially before it is seen hermeneutically. To say that space is material does not mean that it is reducible to material space. To look at different spatial organizations and the different technologies that produce them is to consider the vectors, intensities, and maps of space as regimes of power rather than simply structures of relationality. But such regimes are often defined as well by structures of what we might call "the spatial imaginary" (Wark, forthcoming).

Similarly, thinking of power machinically requires a significant shift in the questions we ask. For example, as Deleuze and Guattari put it, "the question...is not whether the status of women, or those on the bottom, is better or worse, but the type of organization from which that status results" (1987, p. 210). This suggests that we give up a view of the critical project that merely constantly rediscovers what we already know: that structures of domination and subordination are reproduced, that representations of difference and inequality are reinscribed. But we must also give up our willingness to be satisfied with finding the cracks in the processes of reproduction and reinscription, with discovering that people are indeed active and capable of struggle and even resistance. I would propose that cultural studies needs to move beyond models of oppression, both the "colonial model" of the oppressor and the oppressed and the "transgression model" of oppression and resistance, and toward a model of articulation or "transformative practice" (Cameron McCarthy, personal conversation). Both models of oppression seem not only inappropriate to the contemporary relations of power but also incapable of creating alliances, because they cannot tell us how to interpellate fractions of the "empowered" into the struggle for change in something other than a masochistic (guilt-ridden) way.

I am suggesting that cultural studies explore the concrete ways in which different machines—or, in Foucault's terms, apparatuses—produce the specific spaces, configurations, and circulations of power. These spaces, configurations, and circulations constitute not only specific conjunctures or social formations but also the relations between the local and the global. In this regard, I would argue that we need (and the project is being carried out by others more capable) to rethink not only the history of capitalism but the very nature of capitalism—in spatial terms. If I can offer a very small and simple piece of this puzzle as an example, we might begin to understand Taylorism— a crucial aspect of the Fordist articulation of capitalism—as an apparatus that quite precisely and intentionally temporalized the space of the production of surplus value. And on the other hand, many of the strategies that have been discussed as "post-Fordist" (for example, subcontracting, the construction of what Manuel Castells [1989] calls "informational" or "dual cities," the spatial redistribution of labor and wealth) are all part of a set of apparatuses that is reorganizing the spatial distribution of capital and respatializing the time of production. In fact, any analysis of contemporary capitalism should recognize that there is a struggle over the spatial distribution of different articulations of capitalism itself. The goal seems to be an increasingly rapid but controlled flow of capital, people, and commodities in order to remonetarize capitalism through the creation of a globally circulating debt.

IDENTITY AND DIFFERENCE

I want to turn my attention to some themes that may have a more immediate and obvious relevance (although they are not by that fact more important) to the questions facing an international cultural studies. I want to try to consider, perhaps even demonstrate, the significance of the move to a spatial and machinic model of power by turning to a central and particularly difficult set of questions that have arisen from the philosophical inheritance of "the modern." Many people date the beginning of modern philosophy to the Cartesian problematic of the relations between the individual and reality, understood as the epistemological problematic of truth. Descartes of course solved it by postulating a self-reflective consciousness. Kant identified this consciousness with the mediating position of experience (giving rise on the one hand to phenomenology and on the other to structuralism).

This privileging of consciousness (or in romanticism, of imagination) as the space in which opposition is mediated depended upon an identification of subjectivity with temporality. Only in this way was consciousness capable of totalizing and transcending chaos: the unity of the subject depended upon the unity of time, an assumption that continues at least through Heidegger (if not Derrida). In political terms, this traditional set of assumptions gives rise to what Rosalind O'Hanlon (1988) calls "the virile figure of the subject-agent." In other words, the modern "humanistic" individual is predicated on the articulation or assumed identification of three distinct events: the subject as a unified source of knowledge and experience; the agent as a position of activity; and the self as the bearer of a social identity.

If "maps of identification and belonging" define how and where individuals and groups are located in the world, the articulation of these three different aspects of our maps of identification and belonging into a singular and presumably coherent figure inevitably gave rise to a paradox. This paradox only became painfully visible when anti-essentialist arguments were successfully mounted against any claim to the unity of both the subject and the self, and critical arguments were successfully mounted to demonstrate the social construction of both the subject and the self. The paradox is simple: How can the individual be both cause and effect, both subject and subjected? Or, in other words, how does one locate agency? This problem has animated the large body of contemporary political and theoretical work on the production of subordinate identities and the possibilities of resistance, whether in the name of the subaltern, feminism, anti-racism, postcolonialism, or the new ethnicities. I do not intend to rehearse the positions and debates that have made such work so exciting and so important in both theoretical and political terms.

Instead, I merely want to identify three dominant strategies operating in this field, all of which oppose a search for essential origins as the basis for subaltern identity. But I emphasize that I am isolating these from their discursive contexts to construct something like "ideal types" or rhetorical figures. Often a single author will use more than one, and this need not necessarily result in a contradictory or paradoxical position. All three of these figures can be seen as models of articulation, or in more spatial terms, as figures of borders. And all of them are predicated on a principle of difference or negativity. As Hall says, "identity is a structured representation which only achieves its positive through the narrow eye of the negative. It has to go through the eye of the needle of the other before it can construct itself" (1991a, p. 21). Moreover, because all of them ground identity, in one way or another, in language and signification, they can all be read as grounding identity in the temporality of consciousness or what Homi K. Bhabha calls the "temporal nonsynchronicity of signification" (1991, p. 58).

Before turning to these three figures of identity, however, I need to say something more about the sense of negativity and difference operating here in order to distinguish this notion of difference as a negative relation from a more positive notion of the other. In common sense terms, difference makes the identity of one term depend totally on its relation to, its difference from, another term, while otherness recognizes that the other exists in its own place, independently of any specific relation of difference.

In more philosophical terms, we can see that the distance between these two positions (difference and otherness) corresponds to the argument between Derrida and Foucault, an argument I will briefly summarize and, no doubt, oversimplify (see Foucault, 1979). Derrida, for example, argues that Descartes's exclusion of madness from the realm of reason constituted the possibility and identity of reason itself. The relation (difference) between reason and madness is an originary structure of differance, a difference which always exists at the center of identity. And in this sense, for Derrida, Descartes is still alive, still relevant for our world. For Foucault, on the other hand, Descartes's exclusion of madness was a historical event. And while it was necessary to establish the status of reason and to enable an identification of reason and subjectivity, the exclusion itself is not constitutive, either of reason or of madness. Each has its own positivity or exteriority that effects the other. And consequently, the exclusion of madness was not entirely discursive; it was as much a material and spatial exclusion of real practices and peoples. And so, for Foucault, Descartes is irrelevant today.

Having briefly explained my use of difference, as opposed to otherness, let me now briefly describe the three dominant figures of difference or borders operating in contemporary theories of subaltern identity: fragmentation, hybridity, and differance. (I realize the terms can be confusing, especially since they do not necessarily correspond to how different authors use the terms within their own theories.)

The figure of fragmentation is one in which the border is a space of articulations across differences. Here identity or subjectivity is "a kind of disassembled and reassembled unity." A fragmented identity is a contradictory and always partial identity or, as in Donna J. Haraway's image of a cyborg identity, "a potent subjectivity synthesized from the fusion of outsider identities" (1991, p. 174). Similarly, Hall (1991b) describes "diaspora identities" as those that are constantly producing and reproducing themselves anew, through transformation and difference. Here identity is a temporary and arbitrary closure constructed across differences, as in Dick Hebidge's image of "cut 'n' mix" and Paul Gilroy's image of "syncretism."

The figure of hybridity is one in which the border is itself a place inhabited by the subaltern; it is literally an "in-between" place or, in Bhabha's terms (1991), "a third space." Here the subaltern are different from the identities on either side of the border, but they are not simply the fragments of both. The subaltern exists as different from either alternative, in the place between the colonizer and the (imagined) precolonial subject or, in Gloria Anzaldua's borderland, between the Mexican and the American: "A borderland is a vague and undetermined place created by the emotional residue of an unnatural boundary....People who inhabit both realities...are forced to live in the interface between the two" (1987, pp. 3, 37). Anzaldua describes this third space as "a shock culture, a border culture, a third culture, a closed country" (p. 11).

Finally, the figure of differance is one in which the border is a necessary and internal force of destabilization. Here the subaltern is seen as the necessary and constitutive other of the dominant position, who at the same time threatens the very possibility of the unity of the dominant position. This is usually seen as the result of the very nature of language and signification; it is often strongly influenced by a Derridean view that sees an inherent ambiguity or instability at language's center, which constantly undermines language's power to define a unified, stable identity. There are many examples of the figure of differance, including both Derrida's and Luce Irigaray's very different interpretations of Woman, as well as Jean François Lyotard's (1990) vision of "the jew" as that which European culture cannot identify because its exclusion, its unnameability, is itself constitutive of European identity. We might also include here a strong line of Bhabha's (1984) work embodied in the notion of mimicry as a ("mis")appropriation of the dominant discourse. Mimicry is a kind of textual insurrection in which the subaltern is defined only by its difference, only negatively. Similarly, Michel de Certeau's (1984) attempt to define the subordinate only by their difference, by their lack of a place that would entitle them to their own practices or strategies, presents a figure of differance. And finally, the figure of differance dominates a very common (mis)reading of Edward Said's (1978) theory of Orientalism in which the dominant power constructs its other as a repressed and desired difference.

There are a number of important and provocative critiques of these three positions, in excellent articles by Benita Parry (1987), O'Hanlon (1988), and Morris (1990), for example. All three positions ignore the fragmentary and conflictual nature of colonial discourse (or the dominant discourse), both at home and abroad. They ignore the heterogeneity of (colonial) power, often apparently reducing it to discourses of representation and ignoring its material realities. And they ignore the "positivity" of the subaltern, as the possessors of other knowledges and traditions and as located within their own history, in which there is domination and subordination within the ranks of the subordinate.

I want to raise one additional question against these three figures of the subaltern: What is the status of the "subordinate," or the marginal, or the subaltern in these arguments? On what grounds do we assume that subaltern identity is, if not a privileged, then at least an inherently different structure of subjectivity? If, as Hall (1991a) suggests, the marginal has become central in the contemporary world, then are not such figures at the very least descriptive of the contemporary subject? But if that is true, then where is the difference to be located? That is, too often such descriptions of the subject are reserved for certain, usually marginalized or subordinated, subject groups, as if they belonged only to those who had no other power. The other side of this question is equally important: can one form of subordination (for example, colonialism) become the model of all structural domination? Gayatri Spivak (1987), for example, has argued that the critique of imperialism cannot be identified with the critique of racism. Is the same not true of colonialism and patriarchy? In the end, all three figures seem too universalistic, providing answers to any local struggle before we have even begun the theoretical and empirical work. In all three figures, we always find the production of the other as different. Dare one ask how far that gets us?

IDENTITY AND SPACE

I do not wish to underestimate the importance of the theoretical and political work represented by these three figures of difference. And yet, I want to place them in the context of my own frustrations. I do not mean to reject the concept of identity or its importance in certain political struggles; but I do reject the subsumption of identity within a logic of difference and the assumption that such structures of identity necessarily belong to particular subject groups. And I believe it is important to ask whether every struggle over power can or should be organized around issues of identity. At the very least, it may be necessary to rearticulate the category of identity and its place in cultural studies and politics. Debates about multiculturalism, for example, too quickly assume a necessary relation between identity (ethnicity) and culture. I would argue instead that the question of the desirability of a multicultural society is a normative one (to what extent can a society continue to exist without a common—albeit constantly rearticulated and negotiated—culture), while the fact that the United States is (and has been) a multiethnic society with a wide range of cultural practices cannot be ignored.

After all, if, as I believe, cultural studies is to be judged by whether and how it opens up new possibilities and enables new political strategies, then something is wrong. It may be that such work has constrained our possibilities as much as it has advanced them. This seems especially true in the context of contemporary events and trends in the United States. Let me point to two examples. At the broader level, any critical perspective has to begin by acknowledging our apparent inability to comprehend, to say nothing about challenging, the power of the new conservatism and the increasingly conservative tone of American life. At a more specific, and in some ways even more disturbing, level, I would point to the 1992 violence in Los Angeles—I refuse to call it either a riot or an uprising. It seems that in Los Angeles the lessons of anti-essentialism disappeared—assuming we believe that they ever took hold. The fact of the matter is that when people actually took to the streets, all of their anger, their disappointment, and their antagonism came out in the most essential of terms. And for all the struggle and suffering to which this event gave witness, we know that little or nothing is likely to change for the urban populations of the United States.

It seems to me that, in part, we have become so fascinated with theory that we have forgotten a fundamental lesson: that people cannot be successfully changed or moved politically if one begins by telling them that their deepest beliefs and investments are mistaken. Or, to put it another way, we must begin where people already are if we want to move them to somewhere else. This does not mean that we accept the common sense grounds of the often ineffective forms of contemporary struggle. It does mean that we have to find a theoretical project that would enable us to do two things: first, to draw the lines that make the local and the global always inseparable; and second, to rearticulate the forms and sites of people's antagonisms and hopes.

It is this project that has led me to seek a different way of looking at identity, alterity, and agency—spatially and machinically. Let me begin then by looking at three different machinic productions involved. First, there is the production of subjectivity or, in other words, of a phenomenological field. I would argue that insofar as everyone experiences the world, subjectivity is a universal, if unequally distributed, value. But everyone has subjectivity in the sense that everyone exists at the center of their own phenomenological field; consequently, they have access to some experience, to some knowledge about themselves and the world. And to a certain extent, as Althusser argued, subjectivity "authorizes" experience. Such a notion of experience, however, is not ontological. Subjectivity is a machinally produced value rather than a prediscursive or preterritorial reality.

But of course, subjectivity in this sense is abstract, and it must be articulated to and within a second "differentiating machine," a machine that discursively (or ideologically) produces differentially valued subject positions (through a discursive interpellation), which, when articulated to maps of meaning, produce what we more commonly call identities. Thus, although everyone exists within what we might call these "strata" of subjectivity, they are also located at particular positions within the strata, each of which enables and constrains the possibilities of experience, but even more, of representing and legitimating those representations. In this sense, we can agree with the various positions described above that the subject exists only after the inscription of historical difference. As Lefebvre says, the subject "can never be caught red-handed, because it is made up after the event" (1984, p. 92).

However, because people take up their different identities in different ways and do not always internalize or live the discursive interpellation, we need yet another machine, a machine in which individuality is constructed as a vector through an affective interpellation. This third machinic production is more difficult to describe. It involves a more explicit spatial territorialization—an organization of places and spaces—and it requires a notion of affective investment. To explain, let me begin with some quotations, first two from Hall:

> By ethnicity, we mean the astonishing return to the political agenda of all those points of attachment which give the individual some sense of place and position in the world, whether these be in relations to particular communities, localities, territorialities, languages, religions, or cultures. (1989, p. 33)

> …the recreation, the reconstruction of imaginary knowable places in the face of the global postmodern which has, as it were, destroyed the identities of specific places.… So one understands the moment when people reach for these groundings…and the reach for those groundings is what I call ethnicity. (1991a, pp. 35–36)

Rudolfo Anaya and Francisco Lomelí describe Aztlán as the simultaneously historical and imaginary place within which Chicanos and Chicanas increasingly come to place their ethnicity:

> The element of identity is but a fragment of the totality that permits the experiencing of origins as a comfort zone which enhances our development. Aztlán localizes this process in a particular milieu in relation to a complex network of historical events and

happenings. In other words, through Aztlán we come to better understand psychological time (identity), regional makeup (place), and evolution (historical time). Without any one of these ingredients, we would be contemporary displaced nomads, suffering the diaspora in our own land, and at the mercy of other social forces. Aztlán allows us to come full circle with our communal background as well as to maintain ourselves as fully integrated individuals. (1989)

Here we turn our attention to the relations of spaces, places, things, and people. But this is not meant as a return to a Cartesian dualism in which we separate psychology from the material world. Rather we must raise the question of psychology in new and, perhaps, sometimes disconcerting ways. I want to describe a territorializing machine that distributes subjectivity and subject positions in space. A territorializing machine diagrams lines of mobility and placement; it defines or maps the possibilities of where and how people can stop and *place* themselves. Such places are temporary points of belonging and identification, of orientation and installation, of investment and empowerment. Such places create temporary addresses or homes. But as Morris points out, such places or homes do not pre-exist the lines of mobility, the space. They are not origins. They are the product of an effort to organize a limited space, as Deleuze and Guattari describe it (1987, p. 311). They define forms of empowerment or agency, ways of going on and going out. Around such places, maps of meaning, of desire, and of pleasure can be articulated.

A territorializing machine attempts to map the sorts of places people can occupy and how they can occupy them. It maps how much room people have to move, and where and how they can move. A territorializing machine produces lines of specific vectors, intensities, and densities that differentially enable and enact specific forms of mobility and stability, specific lines of investment (or anchoring) and flight. It maps the ways in which people live the always limited freedom to stop in and move through a field of force.

Within the structured mobility of such machinic operations, as O'Hanlon has observed, "the subaltern is not a social category but a statement of power"(1988, p. 207). And power and resistance are defined by the spatial relations of places and spaces and the distribution of people and practices within them. In this sense marginalization is neither an identity nor a spatial position but a vector or distribution defining access, mobility, and the possibilities of investment and agency.

> The subaltern is rendered marginal in quite a different way—in part through his inability, in his poverty, his lack of leisure and his inarticulacy, to participate to any significant degree in the public institutions of civil society, with all the particular kinds of power which they confer, but most of all, and least visibly, through his consequently weaker ability to articulate civil society's self-sustaining myth. (O'Hanlon, 1988, p. 221)

It is within the machinic operation of territorialization that agency is constructed and its possibilities distributed. Particular places define specific forms of agency and empower specific populations. In this sense we can inquire into the conditions of possibility of agency, for agency—the ability to make history, as it were—is not intrinsic either to subjectivity or to subjects. It is not an ontological principle that distinguishes humans from other sorts of beings. Agency is defined by the articulations of subject positions into specific places (sites of investment) and spaces (fields of activity) on socially constructed territorialities. Agency is the empowerment enabled at particular sites and along particular vectors. Thus, when we speak of the agent of articulation, we need to distinguish between the fact that people do things that have effects, often while they are struggling to change their circumstances or even history, and the existence of agents—

places and vectors—that make history. Agency points to the existence of particular formations of practices as places on social maps, where such places are at least potentially involved in the making of history. Agency as a site is, of course, only realized if specific investments are enabled and articulated.

A number of consequences follow from this. First, resistance cannot be explained by an abstract metaphysical (or philosophical-anthropological) principle, or by an appeal to the return of the repressed, or by the fact of contradictory interpellations and subject positions. It can only be explained as the concrete, overdetermined articulation of fractions of the population to particular sites of agency. Second, we need to radically rethink our assumptions about the nature, possibility, and effectivity of alliances. Too often we get captured by the assumed equivalence of subject and agent, resulting in such bizarre debates as the place of "men in feminism." A more fruitful approach, especially in the context of the resurgence of racism, sexism, and homophobia in the United States, might be to reconsider the civil rights movement as a model in which affect and agency were successfully articulated to morality and politics.

The question of agency, then, is how access and investment are distributed within a particular structured mobility. And this suggests that political identity is not the same as subject position or cultural identity. We need a different conception of political identity and of politics: a politics of commitment, of affect, of identification and belonging. Here we might, once more, return to Hall:

> Political identity often requires the need to make conscious commitments. Thus it may be necessary to momentarily abandon the multiplicity of cultural identities for more simple ones around which political lines have been drawn. You need all the folks together, under one hat, carrying one banner, saying we are this, for the purpose of this fight, we are all the same, just black and just here. (cited in Grossberg, 1992, 380).

Hall's proposal, albeit too voluntaristic and individualistic for my tastes, nevertheless seems to me to take the diaspora literally, to see the subaltern in spatial, affective, and machinic terms. And it sees agency and ethnicity as a struggle over the articulation of places and investments. It is a matter of what I (following Rebecca Goldstein) have called mattering maps, which define where and how one can and does invest, and where and how one is empowered, made into an agent. Here, as Deleuze and Guattari say (1987, p. 316), the proper name is not the mark of a subject but the constituting mark of an abode.

TOWARD A CONCRETE POLITICS OF SPACE

In concluding, I have two possible vectors before me. One leads me to the abstract theoretical question of how we map the space of power, remembering that we are interested in how that space is produced. I have offered something like a model of triangulation, which suggests that any such space is produced by the simultaneous operation of three types of machines, three active organizations of power: an abstract or stratifying machine of value; a coding/decoding machine of differentiation; and a territorializing/deterritorializing machine of distribution. Not only are these three machines or structurations of power complexly articulated, but each is itself multiple and internally articulated. The three machines operate on each other but not in any temporal sequence. Moreover, the whole operation, as well as the operation of each machine, is a site of contestation. Hence, the relations between them are not guaranteed, nor is any one equivalent to, for example, capitalism, patriarchy, racism or colonialism. Each is articulated by specific relations, although one assemblage (for example, capitalism) may deploy others (for example, racism, patriarchy). This means that any analysis of the machinic production of power must always be conjunctural. A map of the conjunctural operation of such a machinic complex describes what Foucault calls a "diagram" (Deleuze, 1988).

It may be helpful to say a little more about each of these machines in the abstract. The first—abstract—machine produces value (axioms) by what Deleuze and Guattari (1987) describe as a double articulation or "acts of capture" (connective synthesis). It produces strata by bringing together two planes, the plane of content and the plane of expression. It is, therefore, a machine of production or positivity. The second—coding—machine establishes relations within the strata (on each plane). It is a differentiating machine of subjectivation and normalization, which, through negativity and exchange, produces a striated space marked by dimensionality (lines of extension). The third—territorializing—machine establishes relations between strata, between expression and content. It is a distributive machine of alterity, which produces a smooth space marked by intension (vectors or lines of intensity) and the possibility of nonextensional relations (voyage in place). Alterity then becomes a distribution of places and spaces where each place is not only the site of expressivity but also of multiple vectors (hybridity) and agency.[5]

The second vector leads me back to the new conservatism of the United States (see Grossberg [1992]) and to Los Angeles, about which I want to say a few words in conclusion. Thinking about Los Angeles, I am reminded of Mike Davis's (1985) critique of Fredric Jameson's "reading" of the Bonaventura Hotel as a postmodern text—a classic interpretation and a classic part of Jameson's analysis of the postmodern. Davis, rather than reading the hotel as a text with its own aesthetic, points instead to the "savagery of its insertion into the surrounding city" (p. 112) and identifies it as part of a larger project to "polarize [the city] into radically antagonistic spaces" (p. 113). It is an outpost, part of the fortifications, of the newly emerging "fortress America" that is arising in the midst of the dual or multiple cities of global capitalism.

The question is how we can rearticulate the antagonisms that erupted between African Americans, Latinos, and Koreans, antagonisms that seem to be based on assumptions of essential identities. The traditional answer—that we must use education to overcome cultural relativism—not only assumes that the problem is one of understanding and communication (probably a mistaken assumption), but also seems to preclude the possibility of effective alliances as much as does the antagonism itself.

I offer the following suggestion only as a possibility and only in the briefest terms since, as I must acknowledge, I have not yet done the research necessary to make my analysis concrete at the local level, nor have I got very far in my efforts to make the connections between Los Angeles and regional, national, and global political and economic developments. I want to suggest that the antagonisms can be displaced from questions of identity to the more sympathetic question of the relations among the different maps of territorialized marginality that have come to define postwar U.S. urban space. This space cannot even be described as a dual city in which two different maps (two different populations, two different economies, two different structured mobilities) coexist; it is a complex and overlapping system of spatial empowerment and disempowerment, of mobility and placement, of openness and closure. It is a polyspatial city.

In particular, I think we can identify four different modes of spatial existence, four different territorializing maps or structured mobilities existing within the common space of the city: a population that is increasingly demobilized, with no access to any places of agency (and which is, of course, largely black); a highly mobile diasporic population that also has almost no access to places of agency (largely Latino); and a population with a highly constrained but nevertheless extensive line of mobility. The Korean population, like the Jews before them, find that they must work in South Central Los Angeles, but that they are free to live elsewhere (although certainly not anywhere; their mobility is also constrained by racism). Moreover, like the Jews, the Koreans come with their own economic and cultural capital, which allows them to establish alternative places and institutions of agency and empowerment (such as communal and interfamilial "banks").

If we can understand the antagonisms that exist among these three groups as a matter not of identities but of the conflicts constructed among these different spatial configurations, can we begin to rearticulate them into a common opposition to the fourth spatial map? This fourth map describes the increasingly "fortresslike" organization of significant fractions of the white (but not entirely) and wealthy (how far down into the middle class does this map extend?) dominant populations. Yet it is a fortress that, through a variety of technologies and capital flows, allows for an extraordinary degree of mobility. And more than anything, I think, it is this apparent paradox that defines the existence of domination in urban centers like Los Angeles.

Obviously, a fuller discussion would need to recognize historical and economic determinations. It would need to explore how class distinctions operated; after all, not the entire black population was involved. It would need to explore the operation of the changing economic context, in which the contradiction between the forces and relations of production is itself being rearticulated: Is it that the forces are becoming socialized while the relations are becoming privatized? It would also need to consider the specific circumstances that defined the condition of emergence of this particular event.[6]

But the question remains: was the violence aimed at a specific people understood in terms of a subject-identity? If that is true, then education should help to overcome the implicit cultural relativism that underlies such misunderstandings. But if the violence is defined by and aimed at the role that people play in the lives of black people, we need to ask how that role is to be defined. My answer is, obviously, spatially. And if this is the case, then education would quickly be made irrelevant, for new surface features would quickly be found to justify the antagonism. In this sense, local racisms are increasingly a matter of place rather than of race, or even ethnicity as it is commonly used. Regarding political strategies, I believe we should not eliminate any possibility to begin with. After all, political strategies must themselves be conjuncturally determined. In spatial terms a social movement can be understood as a territorializing map that attempts to reorganize space and to create new places. A social movement must be seen as an affective alliance that does not merely bring together multiple interests but finds affective investments that unite them "under one banner." But this can only be accomplished if we strategically consider the proper level of abstraction at which a political struggle must operate.

I do not know the answer to this question. I do not know if such a model can help to open up new possibilities. But it seems to me that this is the only justification for the privileged position of political intellectuals and for the labor of cultural studies. What I do know is that finally the answer will only be available as we open up the lines that are making cultural studies into a global as well as a local endeavor. For that reason, perhaps the answers to the questions I am raising about the United States can only come from those who are caught up in its lines of power, but who also define its exterior whether from within or from outside its spaces.

NOTES

1 For the best description of the specificity of cultural studies, see the introduction to Morris and Frow (forthcoming). See also the introduction to Grossberg (1992) for a discussion of the disciplinary and historical articulation of the specificity of cultural studies.

2 I am reluctant to use "postmodern" here, not only because it constructs a homogeneous "before" but also because it too often assumes a necessary relation between cultural forms and their

effects. Moreover, it tends to reduce the multiple levels of cultural effectivity to questions of aesthetics and economics/history. Similarly, I do not mean to suggest that "the modern" is a singular or homogeneous structure.

3 For a discussion of articulation, see Grossberg (1992) and Centre for Contemporary Cultural Studies (1982).

4 I want to privilege space not merely because it has been left off the agenda but because it has been "intentionally" left off the agenda. But I do not mean to close off the possibility of, and even the necessity for, reintroducing a temporal or historical dimension (albeit one radically rearticulated). There is an important difference between criticizing an argument for not having addressed a specific issue (every argument ignores some important issues) and claiming that it does not have the theoretical and political space to address it.

5 The problem with Deleuze and Guattari's theory of the politics of the diagram is that they equate the politics of becoming in the three moments of the diagram: becoming body-without-organs; becoming different (for example, woman; and by the way, it is only at this level that real women are not erased); and becoming minor (other).

6 I want to thank Mark Reid for reminding me of this.

REFERENCES

Amin, S. (1989). *Eurocentrism.* New York: Monthly Review.

Anaya, R. A., & Lomelí, F. (eds.). (1989). *Aztlán: Essays on the Chicano homeland.* Albuquerque: Academia/El Norte.

Anzaldua, G. (1987). *Borderlands/La Frontera: The new mestiza.* San Francisco: Spinsters/Aunt Lute.

Bennett, T. (1990). *Outside Literature.* London: Routledge.

_____. (1992). Coming out of English. Paper presented at Trajectories: Toward an Internationalist Cultural Studies, Tapei, Taiwan, July 1992.

Bhabha, H. K. (1984). Of mimicry and man: The ambivalence of colonial discourse. *October,* 28, 125–33.

_____. (1991). Postcolonial authority and postmodern guilt. In Grossberg, Nelson, & Treichler (pp. 56–66).

Bourdieu, P. (1984). *Distinction: a social critique of the judgement of Taste.* (R. Nice, Trans.). Cambridge: Harvard UP.

Braidotti, R. (1991). *Patterns of Dissonance.* (E. Guild, Trans.). New York: Routledge.

Castells, M. (1989). *The Informational City.* Oxford: Blackwell.

Centre for Contemporary Cultural Studies. (1982). *The Empire Strikes Back: Race and racism in '70s Britain.* London: Hutchinson.

Davis, M. (1985). Urban renaissance and the spirit of postmodernism. *New Left Review.* 143, 106–13.

de Certeau, M. (1984). *The Practice of Everyday Life.* (S. F. Rendall, trans.). Berkeley: University of California.

Deleuze, G. (1988). *Foucault.* (S. Hand, Trans.). Minneapolis: U of Minnesota P.

Deleuze, G. & Guattari, F. (1987). *A Thousand Plateaus: Capitalism and schizophrenia.* (B. Massumi, Trans.). Minneapolis: U of Minnesota P.

Foucault, M. (1979). My body, this paper, this fire. *Oxford Literary Review,* 4, 9–28.

_____. (1986). Of other spaces. *Diacritics,* 16, 22–28.

Grossberg, L. (1992). *We Gotta Get Out of This Place: Popular conservatism and postmodern culture.* New York: Routledge.

Grossberg, L., C. Nelson, & P. Treichler. (eds.) *Cultural Studies.* New York: Routledge.

Hall, S. (1989). The meaning of new times. In S. Hall & M. Jacques (eds.), *New Times: The changing face of politics in the 1990s* (pp. 116–134). London: Lawrence & Wishart.

_____. (1991a). The local and the global: Globalization and ethnicity. In King (pp. 19–40) .

_____. (1991b). Old and new identities, old and new ethnicities. In King (pp. 41–68).

_____. (1992a). Cultural studies and its theoretical legacies. In Grossberg, Nelson, & Treichler (pp. 277–294).

_____. (1992b). The West and the rest. In S. Hall & B. Gieben (eds.), *Formations of Modernity* (pp. 275–331). Cambridge: Polity.

Haraway, D. J. (1991). *Simians, Cyborgs, and Women: The reinvention of nature.* New York: Routledge.

Hays, J. (forthcoming). Invisible cities/visible geographies. *Quarterly Review of Film and Video.*

Hunter, I. (1988). *Culture and Government: The emergence of literary education.* London: Macmillan.

King, A. D. (ed.). (1991). *Culture Globalization and the World-System.* London: Macmillan.

Lefebvre, H. (1984). *Everyday Life in the Modern World* (S. Rabinovitch, Trans.). New Brunswick: Transaction.

_____. (1991). *The Production of Space.* (D. Nicholson-Smith, Trans.). Oxford: Blackwell.

Lyotard, J.F. (1990). *Heidegger and "the jews".* (A. Michel & R. Roberts, Trans.). Minneapolis: U of Minnesota P.

Miller, T. (forthcoming). *The Well-tempered Self: Formations of the cultural subject.*

Morris, M. (1988). At Henry Parkes Motel. *Cultural Studies,* 2, pp. 1–47.

_____. (1990). Banality in cultural studies. In P. Mellencamp (ed.), *Logics of Television* (pp. 14–43). Bloomington: Indiana UP.

_____. (1992). The man in the mirror: David Harvey's *Condition of Postmodernity.* In M. Featherstone (ed.), *Cultural Theory and Cultural Change* (pp. 253–279).

Morris, M. & J. Frow. (forthcoming). *Australian cultural studies: A reader.*

O'Hanlon, R. (1988). Recovering the subject: Subaltern studies and histories of resistance in colonial South Asia. *Modern Asian Studies,* 22, 189–224.

Parry, B. (1987). Problems in current theories of colonial discourse. *Oxford Literary Review,* 9, 27–58.

Said, E. W. (1978). *Orientalism.* New York: Vintage.

Soja, E. W. (1989). *Postmodern Geographies: The reassertion of space in critical social theory.* London: Verso.

Spivak, G. C. (1987). *In Other Worlds: Essays in cultural politics.* New York: Routledge.

Viswanathan, G. (1991). Raymond Williams and British colonialism. *Yale Journal of Criticism,* 4, 47–66.

Wark, K. (forthcoming). *Logic Bombs: Living with global media events.* Bloomington: Indiana UP.

Wolf, E. R. (1982). *Europe and the People without History.* Berkeley: U of California P.

Young, R. (1990). *White Mythologies: Writing history and the West.* London: Routledge.

CONTRADICTIONS OF EXISTENCE: THE PRODUCTION OF RACIAL INEQUALITY IN SCHOOLING

9 Racialization and Children

RICHARD HATCHER AND BARRY TROYNA

THE TERM *racialization* entered the lexicon of "race relations" in the early 1970s. Its analytical purpose, according to Robert Miles, has been to specify "any process or situation wherein the idea of 'race' is introduced to define and give meaning to some particular population, its characteristics and actions" (1988, p. 246). The extent, nature, and significance of young children's racialized conceptions of themselves and their social worlds are, of course, a highly contentious and contested domain. On the one hand, the proposition that young children perceive and interpret the world through this ideological lens sits uncomfortably with common sense understandings about childhood innocence. These assumptions, in themselves, constitute one of the central tenets of the ideology of primary education (Carrington and Troyna, 1988). Consider, for instance, the following recommendations offered by the Assistant Masters and Mistresses Association (AMMA), one of Britain's largest teacher unions. In its statement on multicultural and anti-racist education it advises members to ensure that "pupils learn about the nature and mechanisms of group prejudice...in the formal curriculum, *probably at secondary level when children are more likely to benefit from the approach of 'knowing the enemy'*" (1987, p. 103; emphasis added).

On the other hand, social psychological research, often conducted under experimental conditions using quantitative methods, has developed a strong tradition of teasing out the salience of "race" in the way young children perceive and evaluate themselves and members of other ethnic groups (see Aboud, 1988). But it has lacked persuasive powers for two compelling reasons. First, it has failed to account adequately for the disjunction between children's expressed racialized attitudes and their routine judgements and actions. Rather glibly, perhaps, Gordon Allport asserted that (white) children's rejection of other ethnic and religious groups was "chiefly verbal." In his view, while children "may damn the Jews, the wops, the Catholics they may still *behave* in a relatively democratic manner" (1954, p. 310; original emphasis). Second, this body of research has not resolved satisfactorily the ideological dilemma that many people, young and old, experience in relation to "race" and other controversial matters. In everyday discourse this apparent contradiction is often expressed in phrases such as "Some of my best friends are..." or "I'm not prejudiced, but...." Social psychological research in Britain (Billig, et al., 1988), Australia (Walker, 1988), and the Netherlands (van Dijk, 1991) consistently has highlighted this dilemma.

We want to elaborate our critique of research into the racialization of young children's interpretation of their worlds as a critical backdrop to our own investigation of this thorny issue. Drawing on a recently completed ethnographic study of nine-, ten-, and eleven-year-old children in mainly white schools in England (Troyna and Hatcher, 1992), we want to explain how, in their specific social milieu, racism is reproduced as a popular ideology by providing children with meaningful ways of understanding and acting in daily life. In short, we want to demonstrate the extent and ways in which the cultures of childhood, framed by the family, the school, and the neighborhood, may become racialized.

LIVING DOLLS

Research into whether or not young children recognize and evaluate themselves and others along perceived racial lines has a long history (Aboud, 1988). Until recently studies in this area have tended to be embedded in the research orthodoxy pioneered by Kenneth and Mamie Clark in the late 1930s in the United States (Clark and Clark, 1939). By using photographs and, later, differently colored dolls, the Clarks invited black children to select the appropriate representation in response to various questions associated with their ethnicity: how they identified themselves, their preferred identity, and their sensitivity to and awareness of ethnic differences. Complementary to these identity studies, and using broadly similar research tools, have been inquiries into white children's perceptions and conceptions of their own and others' ethnicity. As long ago as 1929 Bruno Lasker, using a mail questionnaire to establish adults' views of children's racialized attitudes, concluded that young children "are made to notice outer differences and to accept them as signs of inner differences of value" (1929, p. 370).

In Britain identity studies couched within the same theoretical, methodological, and interpretive paradigm established in the United States flourished in the late 1970s and early 1980s. Despite an almost forty-year gap, the research of David Milner (1975; 1983) and Alfred Davey (1983) in Britain generated conclusions that bore more than a passing resemblance to those of the Clarks' studies: namely, a strong trend toward "misidentification" and "out-group preferment" by black[1] children and, as a corollary, white children's strong attachment to their own ethnic identity. The recommendations that flowed from these identity studies met with a warm response from educational policy makers. It's not difficult to see why. To begin with, black children's allegedly negative self-image was seen to be linked causally to their persistent educational "underachievement." In an attempt to mitigate these effects, schools were exhorted to shed their monocultural skin in favor of curricular, organizational pedagogic and appraisal arrangements based on a cultural-pluralist ideology. The rationale? If the expressive and historical features of minority ethnic cultures were promoted, it was expected that black children's motivation to succeed would be enhanced, their self-worth affirmed, and ultimately, their academic performance improved. The identity studies, then, played a catalytic role in presaging the intercultural movement in the U.S. and comparable multicultural education initiatives in Britain (Olneck, 1990; Troyna, 1992). Meanwhile, white children's apparent hostility to (and devaluation of) black children would be further countered by putting into operation the contact hypothesis: the "widely-held belief that interaction between individuals belonging to different groups will reduce ethnic prejudice and intergroup tension" (Hewstone and Brown, 1986, p. 1). In substantive terms, the desegregation of schools in the U.S., busing, and school exchanges were justified and championed more or less in terms of this rationalist policy.

"Flawed theory," wrote Thomas Boston in 1987, "creates flawed policy" (p. 196). Now, while we do not accept the sharp distinction between theory and policy that Boston presumes, the failure to bear fruit of the policy initiatives derived from the identity studies leads us to question the theoretical framework in which these studies resided and the understandings of racialization that they conveyed.

According to Liz Gordon, "quantitative methods can only report what is happening; qualitative look at the why and how" (1984, p. 106). In both the studies of black children's identity and the more general investigations of children's "racial" attitudes, researchers have given priority to the "what." Their principal concern has been to explicate and document children's perceptions and conceptions of "race" rather than explore the processes that underpin those attitudes. In this scenario, then, children have been presented with a range of stimuli (dolls, photographs, word completion tests, and so on) that establish physical characteristics as the main tool for characterizing humankind. Put simply, researchers collude, wittingly or otherwise, in legitimating "race" as a valid criterion for differentiating the population. And the children are constrained to respond in similar terms, partly because of the relationship between the (adult) researcher and the (young) researched; partly also because under these experimental conditions children are compelled to highlight spurious "racial" characteristics. After all, they are the only resource available to them. Ultimately, then, it is difficult to dissent from Olivia Foster-Carter's argument that the research constructed along these lines is manipulated in ways that ensure that children's perceptions and responses are "color-struck" (1986).

These caveats do not lead us to believe that theories about the early onset of children's racialized attitudes are simply an artifact of this methodology. But we are convinced that researchers working within this positivistic paradigm have tended to sacrifice understandings of the racialization process on the altar of description. Their theorizations, then, bifurcate into structural and individualized interpretive frameworks. In our view these are at best reductionist, at worst obfuscatory. The overtly deterministic social reflection theory, for instance, privileges structural determinants but conceives of young children as passive and indiscriminate recipients of a racist ideology that circulates within sociocultural norms and mores. Microinterpretations, in contrast, eschew any concern with structural factors. These localized analyses focus purely and simply on cognitive and affective developments in children, especially those that are in one way or another aberrant (Aboud, 1988, pp. 18–43).

Against this background the limitations of policy designed to tackle young people's racism become clearer, if not more justified. Multicultural education, for instance, privileges knowledge of minority ethnic cultures as a means of preempting or undermining racist conceptions. Elsewhere we have mounted serious criticisms of this orthodoxy, and there is insufficient space to rehearse those arguments in full here (Troyna and Hatcher, 1992; Troyna, 1993). But it is pertinent to note our reservation about the illogical use of "racial" and "ethnic" categories to combat racism. As our own and other work has demonstrated, children and adults use (spurious) "racial" categories as a means to understand and deal with particular situations (Cashmore, 1987; Phizackiea and Miles, 1980; Troyna, 1989). "Racial" categories, then, have certain functional properties. If racism is to be tackled effectively, the conditional status of these categories must be challenged by alternative frameworks that provide people with superior and more plausible explanations for the way things are. As Stuart Hall reminds us, social scientists need to deconstruct the obvious; to "show people that the things they immediately feel to be 'just like that' aren't quite 'just like that'" (Hall, 1980, p. 6). Educators who structure children's experiences around "racial" conceptions of reality are in danger of legitimating "race" as an organizing and differentiating category.

Similarly, the contact hypothesis presumes that racial prejudice and the discriminatory practices to which it sometimes gives rise can be dispelled by the positive experiences of interethnic contact in schools (and elsewhere). But as Mike Hewstone and Rupert Brown remind us, "contact is not enough" (1986, pp. 1–44). Although the contact hypothesis is an appealing and seductive proposition, it is predicated on individualized grounds, and blind to the wider social influences that affect intergroup contact. Indeed, as John Turner (1987) has argued, the contact hypothesis often fails to differentiate between interpersonal attraction, by which he means favorable attitudes toward people as unique individuals, and group cohesion, the mutual attraction between in-group members qua group members. The conflation of interpersonal relationships, say, between children of different ethnic backgrounds with an individual's perception and valuation of other ethnic groups is elliptical; it is one of the dubious grounds on which the contact hypothesis often rests.

We now want to turn to our study *Racism in Children's Lives* (1992) in which we attempt to clear up some of the enduring misconceptions about the racialized complexion of children's perceptions of and relationships with their peers.

Our research was conducted in three predominantly white primary schools in working-class districts of medium-sized towns in England. Most of our data came from discussions with some 160 children, of whom twenty-nine were black (twenty-four of Indian or Pakistani descent, and five Afro-Caribbean).

"It's Everybody's World"?

In each of the school classes that we studied there was a spectrum of views about "race" among the white children. A significant number had explicitly anti-racist views. Many appealed to a common humanity. Some had more socially informed understandings. They invoked the principle of equality of treatment to defend the right of black people to migrate and settle in Britain, by contrasting the racist treatment of black immigrants with the treatment that white British people found when they went to other countries. They also placed black immigration in the historical context of white colonialism. However, many children, black and white, acknowledged that some white children, perhaps a minority, perhaps a majority, had racist beliefs. Their fundamental underlying theme was the concept of British identity, as Kevin, an Afro-Caribbean boy, explained:

> They think this is their country and that we should go back to our own country. Like they say to Pakistanis....I was born here but they still think that I wasn't, but the only thing that changes it is because of my color.

This theme is illustrated by a discussion we had with two white boys, Paul and David. They had said that white children sometimes told black children to "go back to your own country," and we asked them why.

Paul:	Because they think that being as most white people here, they don't want them there because they've got their own.
David:	Well this is our own country, isn't it?...We don't really want that many more here, do we, because they take over, don't they? They have all the shops and everything.
Paul:	Yes, all the corner shops.
David:	I wouldn't mind if they didn't do that, but they do.
Paul:	They get away with more things than white people, I think.
Interviewer:	Like what?
Paul:	Pickpocketing, probably. They probably blame it on somebody else. That other person will believe them.
David:	Yes, I mean, black people can call white people names in their own language, but we don't understand what they are saying, do we?
Paul:	I read in the papers quite a few weeks ago now that there was this black man and he was walking around with an eighteen-inch knife, and then a few weeks ago I read it, and there was the bloke walking around with this little knife about that big, and this white bloke he got put in jail and the black person got away with a warning, I think, or a fine.

Interviewer: And are you saying that that was unfair and the black person wasn't treated the same as the white person?

David: I think a colored is more dangerous.

David and Paul introduce three of the most common themes of white children's racist beliefs: black people are taking over the country, they are given unfair advantages, and they are associated with violence and crime. What makes racist interpretations of social processes at the level of the wider society so credible for children like David and Paul is that those same interpretations also seem to make sense of congruent social processes at the level of their own personal experiences. In their neighborhood Asians are taking over local shops from white people. Asian children do on occasion put white children at a disadvantage by calling them names in Asian languages. This dual movement between the societal and the personal, each reinforcing the other, is characteristic of children's racist discourses. In a later discussion David expanded on why he thought that white British identity was under threat: "Probably because they will be more than us, like prime ministers, soon there might be a black one and so on, and then they will be ruling us, and then instead of our Christmases and that, making a song and dance about it, there will be theirs."

David explained why black people want to "take over" in this way in terms of "natural" ethnic solidarity. He thought that black people were more likely to favor black people than white people, and white people were more likely to favor other whites, and that this was "normal." He went on to describe a personal experience:

We used to live next to black people and when somebody died—because our entry came off theirs as well—and when somebody died millions of them came down the entry and we just couldn't do with it, so we moved.

David's experience of mourners from a different cultural tradition blocking the side passage of his house serves as a symbol of the process of "taking over the country," just as Christmas serves as the embodiment of the cultural tradition that is seen to be at risk. Racism gains a powerful purchase precisely because it seems able to make sense of circumstances and problems at the level of personal everyday life—the local shop, name calling in the playground, a crowd in a shared passageway—by bringing them into conformity with larger ideological constructions of national identity.

We want to explore further this process of constructing racist interpretations by turning to a discussion with another white boy, Adam. He didn't share David's vision of black people "taking over."

I mean I think it would be quite a good world if people were mixed up. I reckon it's everybody's world. It's not just our world, it's their world as well. I don't mean that people have to go to Pakistan—black people have to go to Pakistan—and white people just stay in England. I reckon it ought to be a mix up, because it's their world as well as our world.

But there are other elements in Adam's understanding of "race," relating particularly to the connections he made between black people and violence. They emerged as Adam led our conversation through a chain of five instances in his experience. To appreciate their significance it is necessary to bear in mind that Adam was the smallest child in the class, was often teased about it by other children, and often got into trouble for responding violently.

He began by telling us about how, the previous year, a group of Asian boys in the top class used to harass people, including him. "Nasar, he used to be really bossy, and he used to go around causing trouble in a great big bunch, all of them in a great big bunch, just going around stirring up trouble, beating everybody in for nothing." They "just wanted a bit of fun I suppose. Liked seeing people cry....But I didn't take it. Every time he hit me I just punched him back because I just wasn't taking it."

"Nasar was the strongest Asian in the school," Adam continued, "but now there's nothing to compare to what Nasar was. They've all gone down, and we've gone a bit up." We asked what he meant by "we." "Well, what I mean is like us, our color, because they used to go up and start beating everybody in, but now it's gone like down and we've grown a bit."

From this account we want to focus on two points. First is Adam's vulnerability to tougher boys, including Asian boys whose own display of toughness might be at least partly the product of experiences of racism, as well as a phenomenon of male assertiveness. Second is the high salience of toughness and of "race" for Adam as categories of social cognition. The playground hierarchy is understood in terms of a combination of a racialized "us" and "them" and a hierarchy of toughness.

Immediately after his account of Nasar and his friends, Adam told us a story about a man called David who lived in the block of flats that he used to live in. One day Adam went round to see him and found that he had just been attacked by two Pakistani men. Adam interpreted this episode as evidence that "if they don't control themselves while they are this age, when they grow up they are going to be even worse....I suppose really it can just prove how they can get really vicious when they grow up if they don't stop beating other people up."

Adam then went to explain that Asians saw "things on the telly. They take it for granted and think, 'Oh, I'll do that at school.'...Films like people going round in their language they are saying—not in English, their Pakistan language—and just like films, like kings. There is a king sitting there and he orders his men to go and kill somebody and starts bossing them around and using them as slaves, so I suppose that is what they think."

We asked why he thought Asian people were more likely to behave like that than white people.

> I suppose it's their mums' fault really. Mr. H. [the head] sends loads of letters to their mums and he says "I want this letter back and if it's not back intact, I'm going to go round and see mum." It comes back and it says "Dear such and such, your son is behaving very badly at school being a great big bully. If he does not pack it in in the next few days we will expel him from school." And then the lady will sign and most of them just think it is not very good and it gets put in the bin, so they never get back.

He added that this had happened to Zabeel, a boy in his class, and the mention of his name reminded him of another incident, one that had happened some two years earlier. A group of children, Asian and white, including Zabeel, had met him in the street and started pushing him around. He had felt frightened and opened up his penknife to defend himself.

This must be one of those "critical incidents" in Adam's life, representative of many experiences of harassment, in which his small size is an important factor. He interprets personal experiences of harassment involving Asian children in terms that reinforce racist schemas linking black people and violence, for which he finds further evidence in the incident with David and the scene depicting a king and slaves from an Asian film on television. He explains the connection between child and adult violence in terms of lack of parental control (here drawing on his own experiences of complaints made by the head teacher to Adam's mother about his own violent outbursts). The notion of black people having a propensity to violence is a key one in racist discourse. What is important here is that Adam is reconstructing it for himself in terms of his own personal experience, to make sense of some of the critical incidents in his life.

However, as we have noted, this was not the only element in Adam's understanding of "race." It coexisted with explicit racially egalitarian views. Adam was typical in this respect of many children whom we talked to. Their understandings of "race" were a fluid mixture of elements, often contradictory, often not fully formed but tentative and partial.

Hurting Their Feelings

All the black children we spoke to had some personal experience of racist behavior. For some it was a frequent event, for others rare. For all it was particularly hurtful. By far the most common form was racist name calling and verbal abuse. There was also some evidence of white children excluding black children from activities, and of racist remarks, including jokes, among white children. The black children told us that incidents of racist physical harassment were very rare. We will focus here on racist name calling and taunts, and their meanings for white children.

The white children exhibited a range of behavior. Some of them never used racist name calling or similar behavior, for a number of very different reasons. For some it was because they held strong anti-racist beliefs. For others it was fear of retaliation by black children. However, many of the white children did use racist names on occasion. The use of the same language forms does not, however, necessarily signify the same meanings, as Jane and many of the children recognized.

> Some people think, "Oh I'm going to be cruel and just call someone a name," and they go ahead and they hurt people, but some people really believe that they shouldn't be in the country and think, "Well, get lost," and some people just don't think, they are getting so angry, they just say it and they don't know what they are saying.

Racist name calling most commonly took took place when children got angry, used racist names or remarks in the heat of the moment, and then felt sorry for having done so. Often this took place between friends, and so was especially hurtful to the black children involved. Many white children described experiences to us in terms similar to those used by Stuart and Nicola.

Stuart:	I've done it before.
Interviewer:	What happened?
Nicola:	You don't mean to say it. You say something like "Go and have a wash" or something. It's horrible, you wouldn't like it, but it just like gets on your nerves, like Sandeep gets on my nerves, but I never call her names. Sometimes she's alright but sometimes she walks round me and gets on my nerves a bit, and I don't like upsetting her really.
Stuart:	I wouldn't call her names.
Nicola:	I probably would if I was that mad.
Interviewer:	When you say "Why don't you go and have a wash," something like that, is that something that you have said?
Nicola:	I've seen loads of people saying that. From like different schools to someone, and sometimes you like feel sorry for them, don't you?
Stuart:	When you get angry it just slips out. You hurt their feelings and you have to go and apologize. It's happened to me.
Interviewer:	What happened, can you remember?
Stuart:	No, I can't remember, but I know it has happened.
Interviewer:	Did you apologize?
Stuart:	Yes, I did.
Interviewer:	Why did you?
Stuart:	Because it's not very nice—it's not their fault that they are a different color to us. It's just the way they were born. Older people call them

horrible names. We've heard them on the telly and things like that, and we've got them in our minds, and then when you get angry with them, we say it, but we don't mean to.

We define this category of racist name calling as "hot" and "nonstrategic," by which we mean that it was not part of what the white children who used it saw as their legitimate repertoire of interaction strategies; this is why they felt guilty afterwards. It was so common because it was the product of conflict situations, which for many children occurred most frequently among friends. We contrast it with "strategic" racist name calling. This illustration by Katy, a white girl, is typical of many:

Interviewer: Why do you think you called him that particular name rather than just calling him another name not to do with his color?

Katy: Because I'd heard people calling him that name and I know he gets upset about it, so if I know he gets upset about it, I call him that name.

She continued by mentioning a time when she had called Claire, an Afro-Caribbean girl in her class, "Blacky."

Interviewer: Is it different calling Claire say "Blacky" from calling her "cow" or something like that?

Katy: It's not different, it's just a name. If there's a name about someone then you call it them. If you think they are then you call it them.

For Katy, racist name calling was a legitimate part of her interactional repertoire, functionally no different from the non-racist forms of name calling that were a crucial interactional resource in the conflictual world of children.

We can in fact distinguish two forms of strategic racist name calling, "hot" and "cold." Some children regarded name calling as legitimate in any social situation, including the "cold" use of racist abuse for aggressive purposes; others reserved it as a legitimate tactic for defensive purposes in "hot" situations only. James, for example, said that he would use racist names against Imran to defend himself against Imran's aggressive behavior, but would never do so against Bindi because the latter didn't harass other children.

THEIR "WEAK SPOTS"

The question we now want to address is the relationship between racist behavior, in particular name calling, in its various forms, and children's beliefs about "race." Does the use of racist name calling necessarily express a commitment to racist beliefs?

Many of the children we talked to made a distinction between what can be called the instrumental and the expressive functions of racist name calling. Tricia regarded most racist name calling, like other forms of name calling, as purely instrumental, without any necessary underlying racist beliefs. Racist names were no different from other abusive terms. She had been explaining how boys might call girls "fat cow" if they got in the way of their football game in the playground.

Interviewer: Supposing it was Ghazala who got in the way of their game, what might they say to her?

Tricia: They would call her a "Paki" or a "burnt sausage" or they'd tell her to "get back to her own country."

Interviewer: And do you think that is just the same as calling you a "fat cow"?

Tricia: Yes.
                    …

Interviewer: If they say that to you, is it because they think that all girls are "cows" or they don't like people who they think are fat? Is that what they really think?

Tricia: No, I just think that they say that name just so you will go off the football pitch and let them carry on with their game, because you'll just go and leave them. Sometimes they just say the first thing that comes into their head.

Simon voiced similar views. We asked him if children who used racist name calling really didn't like black people being in this country.

Simon: But when I say this, they haven't got such serious feelings about it, they just say it and mocking them and everything. They're not really serious or anything, but they really say it when they get mad or something, or whenever they see them that's what they use against them. The same with Tony, they use against him "four eyes" and they use against Zabeel "Paki" and if they use against David they use "titch" or something. Things like that.

Interviewer: So are you saying that calling somebody "Paki" or "go back to your own country" is just the same as saying "four eyes" and "titch"?

Simon: Virtually, yes.

We asked Simon if he would use racist name calling against, for example, Kevin, a black boy, if he had an argument with him. "Probably if I had an argument. It's something to use against him, isn't it?"

This distinction between the instrumental function of racist name calling and its expressive function—the beliefs about "race" that the child holds—was made by almost all the white children we spoke to. It was also recognized by the black children. Nina, for example, felt that remarks such as "Go back to your own country" were only said to hurt, with no necessary commitment to their content.

Interviewer: Why do you think that people say things like that? Do you think that they really do want you to go from this country?

Nina: I don't think so. They just get angry inside and it just comes out and they say it.

Interviewer: So where do they get this idea from if they don't believe it?

Nina: They just think of it like people say it. They hear it and they just say it. Because they get angry.

Yvette and Natasha thought the same.

Nina: They say "Go back to your own country." America or somewhere like that—a hot country.

Yvette: No, they say Africa or Jamaica or something like that.

Interviewer: Do you think, I mean it's difficult to say, do you think they really want you to go away, or do you think they are just saying that for something to hurt you?

Nina: They just want to hurt us.

Yvette: To get at us.

How can we explain the distinction that children make between the instrumental and expressive functions of racist name calling? Is it simply a ritual disclaimer of racist beliefs on the part of white children, a rhetorical strategy used in reporting racist behavior? Or does it represent a real ideological disjuncture and contradiction?

Teun van Dijk (1987) has analyzed the strategies of conversational discourse about "race" used by white people. He explains the contradiction in the characteristic form of "I'm not racist but…" as one between the speakers' real racist attitudes and their desire to create an impression of not being prejudiced. These strategies of self-presentation and impression management serve to persuade the listener by presenting the speaker favorably as rational and unprejudiced.

In a discussion of van Dijk's ideas, Michael Billig notes his distinction between "the effective expression of semantic macrostructures (themes)" and the "interactional and social goal" of creating the desired impression in the hearer (1988, p. 96). He goes on to assert that "these two different sets of goals may be sometimes in conflict: a direct or 'honest' expression of the beliefs or the opinions from the speaker's situation model may lead to negative social evaluation of the speaker by the hearer" (p. 384).

Billig argues rightly that for van Dijk this is a contradiction between ideology and interactional strategy, not a contradiction within ideologies themselves. But for Billig, interactional strategies are themselves ideological, and therefore the conflict embodied in "I'm not racist but…" is one "within individuals, who have two contrasting ideological themes on which to draw. To use Althusser's…terminology it is this ideological contradiction which 'interpellates' the subject" (1988, p. 97).

At this point we want to clarify our concept of ideology. Gramsci made an important distinction between elaborated and common sense ideologies. Elaborated ideologies were the coherent bodies of thought produced and disseminated by intellectuals. In popular consciousness, elements of elaborated ideologies intervene in common sense understandings. For Gramsci, "common sense is not something rigid and immobile, but is continually transforming itself, enriching itself with scientific ideas and with philosophical opinions which have entered ordinary life" (Gramsci, 1971, p. 326n). Racist ideologies find a purchase in children's cultures because they provide answers to the problems of everyday life, problems of making sense of the world, and problems of negotiating social interaction with other children. Robert Miles emphasizes how ideologies are actively reworked in everyday life: "Ideologies are never only received but are also constructed and reconstructed by people responding to their material and cultural circumstances in order to comprehend, represent and act in relation to those circumstances" (1989, p. 132). But common sense is not uniform: for Gramsci it is "an ambiguous, contradictory and multiform concept" (Forgacs, 1988, p. 346) containing elements of both cultural reproduction and contestation.

On this basis we want to develop the distinction between what Billig calls thematic ideologies and interactional ideologies in order to clarify what we have referred to as processes of racialization of children's subcultures. In this context children operate with two ideological structures. The first is a thematic ideology of "race." It consists of elements of elaborated ideologies made available by the wider society, together with elements of common sense understandings circulating within the cultures of the child's family and community, all subject to reinterpretation in terms of the child's own social knowledge, values, and experiences. This ideological ensemble may be structured into a relatively unified system, predominantly racist or anti-racist in orientation, or it may be less coherent and stable, more fluid and contradictory. The second ideological structure is that which governs everyday interpersonal interaction. Again, it combines elements of elaborated societal ideologies, for example of social morality and social identity, with subcultural and personal elements to construct for each child a matrix of understandings of how social interaction works and a repertoire of social goals and interactional strategies, which receive continuous feedback and reshaping from experiences of social interaction.

These two ideological domains, the thematic and that of interactional strategy, can be articulated in more than one way. Billig and van Dijk only explore one possible variant: racist beliefs combined with reporting strategies designed to present non-racialized accounts. But if we translate this model from "secondary" episodes of accounts of "race" given to researchers to "primary" episodes of racialized interaction, in our case to racist name calling by children, it opens up another possible combination. Here the interactional goals, and the ideologies in which they are embedded, are very different from the van Dijk/Billig scenario.

The interactional goal is not to persuade the listener that one is not racist but to achieve offense and hurt by using racist terms. This interactional ideology may be associated with thematic ideologies of "race" that are racist or that are non-racist or anti-racist.

Furthermore, the concept of ideology allows for the possibility of inconsistency and contradiction. Billig notes this in warning against the frequent practice of social psychologists, uncomfortable with notions of cognitive or attitudinal ambivalence, who impose a unitary model of consciousness by claiming that one attitude is more deeply held and therefore is the "real" attitude. Billig uses this idea to discuss the contradiction between speakers' attitudes and opinions, governed by racist ideologies, and speakers' accounts of racialized episodes, governed by non-racist liberal-rationalist ideologies. But he doesn't address the possibility of anti-racist elements within discourse and therefore of contradictions within ideologies of "race" themselves. Nor does he pose the question of contradictions within ideologies of interaction.

The model we are proposing to account for racist name calling (and by extension other forms of racist behavior) is presented in Figure 1. It locates racist name calling incidents in relation to two axes. One axis represents the user's beliefs and attitudes to "race," ranging from racist to anti-racist. The other represents the user's interactional repertoire, and ranges from racist to non-racist. Individual children's "thematic" attitudes and their interactional repertoires may be more or less internally consistent.

Our point is therefore that the existence of racist beliefs cannot be simply read off from incidents of racist name calling, any more than racist beliefs automatically generate

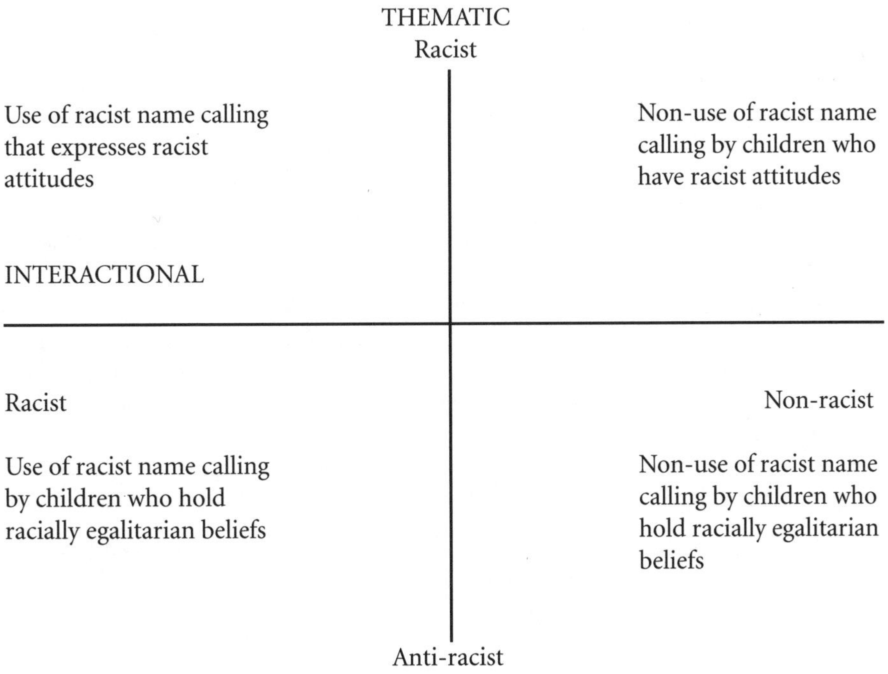

Figure 1. A model for locating racist name calling.

racist name calling. Society makes available to children a powerfully charged vocabulary of racist terms, but their use, while trading on the negative meanings that they bear, does not necessarily imply a commitment to the racist ideologies from which they derive. Each incident of choosing to use racist name calling (whether "hot" or "cold," strategic or nonstrategic), or of choosing not to use it, needs to be concretely analyzed to determine the specific combination of the two dimensions of behavior, thematic and interactional, that it represents.

We are not saying that nonexpressive racist name calling (i.e., the use of racist names by children that is not expressive of racist beliefs) is not racist. We would argue that it is racist in two other senses. First, it is a form of hurtful discrimination against black children. Second, it trades on a racist frame of reference and thus tends to reinforce its legitimacy within children's culture.

We can illustrate our model by referring to Adam and David, two of the children whose beliefs about "race" we have examined. Following on our earlier discussion, Adam explained that he would use racist taunts in certain situations.

Adam: Well, I mean if somebody says like, "Go back to your own country," the Asians have got to do something to make them really angry before they can say that. I mean, I wouldn't say that unless they did something to me and made me angry. But I've just thought that is one of their weak spots. That is another one of their weak spots if you say, "Go back to your own country, you don't belong here." That's their baddest weak spot.

Interviewer: I don't quite understand. You said that you thought it would be best if anybody belonged here and everybody was sort of mixed up, but you said also that sometimes you might say "Go back to your own country."

Adam: Well, if they got me angry, I would.

Interviewer: Does that mean that you would want them really to go back to their own country?

Adam: No, I don't really, it's just that that's their weak spot. It just gets me so angry and I say that, and I don't really mean it. I say that—I said it to Zabeel. He's got me so angry in the end I've said "Sorry."

Adam explained this incident to us. He had been writing and Zabeel had kept mocking his writing and nudging him. "Every time I tried to do better he kept on nudging me, so in the end I got so angry that I said that to him. After school I said sorry. I felt really guilty because I said that, and I didn't really mean it."

From this we know something of the competing ideas about "race" that coexist within Adam's understanding. We do not interpret Adam's racist remark as primarily expressive of, or motivated by, racist beliefs on his part. Its explanation lies in the interactional domain rather than the thematic. We see it as an example of "nonexpressive," "hot," "nonstrategic" name calling.

We know that racist ideas helped David to "make sense" of the wider society. David was a member of a friendship group of half a dozen or so boys, all white except for Zabeel.

Interviewer: If you ever got in a big argument with some of your friends, like Zabeel, do you think you would ever call him names like "Paki" or names about his color?

David: No.

Interviewer: And yet some children do. And if you got in a big argument with somebody then you might call them names. Why wouldn't you call Zabeel or other black friends names about their color?

David: Because it isn't fair. We're probably a different color to them.

Interviewer: Why is it not fair? Do you mean that calling people other sorts of
               names like "fatty" or "skinny" or whatever is fair?
David: No. I don't know really, but it isn't fair being called names.

What unifies David's interpretation of the wider society and the way he approaches
relationships with other children is the principle of equality. In the societal context his
conception of equality is colonized by racist perceptions. Black people are unfairly
privileged: they take over, they get away with things. In the peer context the principle of
equality governs interaction, with ambivalent implications for "race." It became clear
from discussions with David and the other boys in his friendship group that they
consciously managed relationships between themselves on the egalitarian basis of
reciprocity of treatment in order to minimize conflict. One aspect of this was that name
calling within the group was regarded as "out of order," and since one member of the
group, Zabeel, was black, this included racist name calling. The subculture of their
friendship group is, in Les Back's terms, "a domain within which 'race' is temporarily
deconstructed" (1991, p. 11).

Recent ethnographic studies by Back, Roger Hewitt, and Simon Jones of the
emergence of multiracial youth cultures have identified anti-racist dynamics within the
cultures of young white people. Hewitt notes that friendship between black and white
youth was extremely common and was grounded in an experience of being born and
growing up through primary school in mixed working-class neighborhoods together,
occupying the same recreational spaces, experiencing closely meshed life worlds, and
growing into adolescence with far more friendship and other network ties than had been
true of their parents' generation (1989, p. 2).

This new culture has given rise to what Hewitt calls "strongly expressed, com-
munity-based anti-racist stances (1986, p. 2). But shared experience, common cultural
orientations, and cross-racial friendships did not automatically lead to anti-racism, and
here we draw again on the Gramscian notion of common sense consciousness. Jones
speaks of the deeply contradictory nature of white responses about race. In struggling to
resolve the contradictions that resulted from their friendships and cultural-musical
influences, young whites constantly had to battle not only against the weight of peer
group pressure but also against other, more general, ideological influences (1988, p. 219).

Within youth cultures, Hewitt, Jones, and Back identify three related sources of
anti-racism: the adoption of black cultural forms, prosocial interaction with black
people, and the shared experience of working-class life in the inner city generating an
ideology of "community" based on "a set of basic values of everyday life, values of
cooperation, mutuality and reciprocity" (Jones, 1988, p. 212).

What relevance does this explanation of white anti-racism have for the situation of
children of nine, ten, and eleven years old living in predominantly white neighborhoods
and going to predominantly white primary schools? "Elaborated" anti-racist ideologies
circulating in society enter the cultures of children and young people "from outside." One
obvious source in the school context is school policies against racist name calling. But we
know that some children develop anti-racist stances even in the absence of school
policies, or largely independently of them, and so we have to look at how anti-racist
stances may be generated by the internal dynamics of children's subcultures, providing a
purchase for elaborated ideologies of racial equality.

The extent to which black culture had an impact on these children was very
limited, for two reasons. First, these children were only beginning to enter into teenage
youth culture, and any impact it might have still lay largely in the future. Second, the
schools were in areas where the black population was largely Asian, with few Afro-
Caribbeans. The direct transmission of Afro-Caribbean culture, which is by far the most

important source of cultural forms adopted by young white people, into the locality was therefore attenuated. The influence of black culture could not be more than a subsidiary source of anti-racist elements among the culture of these white children.

It is therefore to processes of interpersonal interaction that we must look for the roots of anti-racism among children in predominantly white schools. One important element is prosocial relationships between white and black children. But they are embedded in a more fundamental and extensive social structure of children's culture, based on and prefiguring the "set of basic values of everyday life, values of cooperation, mutuality and reciprocity" that Jones identifies in youth cultures (1988, p. 212). At this point it is necessary therefore to step back from the specific issue of racism and look more generally at children's culture and interaction.

THE EGALITARIAN DYNAMIC IN CHILDREN'S PEER RELATIONSHIPS

We will take as our starting point some ideas in an early work of Piaget: not the more familiar work on stages of nonsocial cognitive development, but his ideas about children's social development in *The Moral Judgement of the Child* (1932). The book's key idea is that children's social morality arises from the structure of their social relationships. Piaget argues that a new type of morality for the child, the "morality of cooperation," arises from egalitarian peer relationships as a result of the experience of cooperative play with peers. This is how Kutnick summarizes Piaget's argument:

> Collective understanding and mutuality are the bases of Piaget's further stage of moral development, the "morality of cooperation." Unlike the morality of constraint, the morality of cooperation can develop only among peers, or children of an equal status. It is in the environment of equals that children are free to explore the differences between their perceptions and understandings of rules and justice. Children come from a home/adult-dominated set of rules and modes of interaction. They quickly find that these are not an adequate background for the relationships they wish to develop among themselves. With their different backgrounds and understanding of rules, children who wish to play with one another must learn to adapt and negotiate. The understanding of intentionality becomes more fully developed. In the interests of those children concerned, rules become changeable or mutable to maintain play....Through the strength of mutuality, the peer group becomes a viable alternative to the imposition of hierarchical constraints. (Kutnick, 1988, pp. 79–80)

Piaget never returned to the themes of this early work, but his initial insights have provided a starting point for a large number of subsequent studies (see Modgil, Modgil, and Brown, 1983, for an overview). We want to outline the contribution made by James Youniss (1980), an American social psychologist, to developing Piaget's approach.

Youniss's concern is with the changes that take place as children move into and through the period of middle childhood. He argues that "the most important lesson which children learn with peers is that social business can be transacted smoothly only through a joint agreement to practice reciprocity for mutual ends" (1980, p. 271). During the years from ages eight to ten children enter a new type of relationship based on two interrelated principles. The first is that the notions of equality and reciprocity are reconstituted not as pragmatic rules of joint activity but as explicit ideal principles of relationships, based on cooperation and equal treatment. "The practice of free and open discussions where everyone's opinions have an equal chance to be heard leads naturally to a belief that fairness demands equality in treatment and in outcomes" (p. 255). The second is the individual's growth of understanding. The new peer relationship depends upon the ability to move away from an egocentric viewpoint and take the perspective of the other.

It is this egalitarian dynamic within children's culture that generates and sustains anti-racist stances. In the context of "race" the development of the two interrelated processes to which Youniss refers was testified to by many children we interviewed. Katherine at Greenshire School explained that she had stopped using racist name calling because she realized how much it hurt black children, even though their reverse name calling didn't upset her.

Katherine: I just don't say it anymore, I've just stopped saying it.
Interviewer: When do you feel like saying it?
Katherine: Like I can remember I was having an argument with someone who was black and they were saying things like "You white duck" and all things like that, and at that time I felt like saying it but I didn't, because I think that it would really upset them if we said it, but if they say it to us because it wouldn't really upset me.

The combination of the growth of psychological insight into the other and the development of an egalitarian social morality is the principal cause of the decline of racist behavior during the junior school years upon which many children remarked. This is Paul at Hillside School:

Paul: I don't do it as often, no. I used to do it when I was smaller because I thought it was funny, but I don't think it is as good now.
Interviewer: Why not?
Paul: Because I've grown up a bit more now and I understand how much they get hurt, more their feelings.

Piaget's insight into the material basis of social morality in children's relationships needs to be situated within a theory of how social relationships are socially constructed. This is where we want to render Piaget "more social."

Children do not necessarily confront each other as equals. On the contrary, they live in a social field structured by ideologies of gender, class, "race," age, ability, and so on, which tend to position children unequally in relation to each other. Other ideologies speak to them of equality, and as we have argued, drawing on Piaget's insight, the most powerful among them is that deriving from, and continuously reinforced by, everyday peer interaction.

CONCLUSION

We want to draw out five points from our study in terms of the implications for schools. First, it is clear that racism is a significant element in the experience of black children, including those in schools where they are a relatively small minority. Second, "race" is a significant element in the lives of white children, both in their social relationships and in their understanding of society. Third, "race" does not work in isolation: it is interfused with other ideologies and social processes of children's lives. Fourth, among white children there is a spectrum both of beliefs about "race" and of ways in which "race" operates in social interaction. The relationship between the two is not one of simple correspondence: interactional processes have their own dynamics. Finally, processes of racialization of children's attitudes and social behavior are often fluid, fragmented, and inconsistent.

Schools need to respond in two related ways. They need effective procedures to implement a clear and firm policy to deter and deal with racist incidents, as part of a wider policy addressing issues of conflict between children. But on its own this is not enough. It may reduce the occurrence of racist incidents on the school premises without affecting the roots of racism in children's culture. Schools therefore need to find ways in the curriculum to help children to engage with how race works in their lives. To reflect cultural diversity positively and to teach about racism in society are both vital, but it is equally important to connect these interventions with children's own lives by bringing children's relationships and the conflicts within them, including racialized forms, into the curriculum itself.

NOTES

1 It is important to note that in Britain "black" is a political category that refers to people of Indian and Pakistani, as well as of Afro-Caribbean descent.

REFERENCES

Aboud, F. (1988). *Children and Prejudice*. Oxford: Blackwell.

Allport, G.W. (1954). *The Nature of Prejudice*. Cambridge, MA: Addison.

AMMA. (1987). *Multi-Cultural and Anti-Racist Education Today: An AMMA statement*. London: Author.

Back, L. (1991). Social context and racist name-calling: An ethnographic perspective on racist talk within a south London adolescent community. *European Journal of Intercultural Studies*, 1 (3), 19–38.

Billig, M. (1988). Prejudice and tolerance. In M. Billig, S. Condor, D. Edwards, M. Gane, D. Middleton, & A. Radley (eds.), *Ideological Dilemmas: A social psychology of everyday thinking* (pp. 100–123). London: Sage.

Boston, T. (1987). *Race, Class and Conservatism*. London: Unwin.

Carrington, B. & Troyna, B. (eds.) (1988). *Children and Controversial Issues: Strategies for the early and middle years of schooling*. Lewes: Falmer.

Cashmore, E. (1987). *The Logic of Racism*. London: Allen.

Clark, K. & Clark, M. (1939). The development of consciousness of self and the emergence of racial identification in Negro preschool children. *Journal of Social Psychology*, SPSSI Bulletin, 10, 591–599.

Davey, A. (1983). *Learning to be Prejudiced: Growing up in multi-ethnic Britain*. London: Arnold.

Forgacs, D. (ed.). (1988). *A Gramsci Reader: Selected writings, 1916-1935*. London: Lawrence.

Foster-Carter, O. (1986). Insiders, outsiders and anomalies: A review of studies of identity. *New Community*, 13 (2), 224–34.

Gordon, L. (1984). Paul Willis—Education, cultural production and social reproduction. *British Journal of Sociology of Education*, 5 (2), 105–116.

Gramsci, A. (1971). *Selections from the Prison Notebooks* (Ed. Q. Hoare & G. Nowell-Smith). London: Lawrence.

Hall, S. (1980). Teaching race. *Multiracial Education*, 9 (1), 3–13.

Hewitt, R. (1986). *White Talk, Black Talk: Inter-racial friendship and communication amongst adolescents*. Cambridge: Cambridge UP.

Hewstone, M. & Brown, R. (eds.) (1986). *Contact and Conflict in Intergroup Encounters* (pp. 1–44). Oxford: Blackwell.

Jones, S. (1988). *White Youth, Black Culture*. Basingstoke: Macmillan.

Kohlberg, L. (1976). Moral stages and moralization: The cognitive-developmental approach. In T. Lickona (ed.), *Moral Development and Behavior*. New York: Holt.

Kutnick, P. (1988). *Relationships in the Primary School Classroom*. London: Chapman.

Lasker, B. (1929). *Race Attitudes in Children*. New York: Greenwood.

Miles, R. (1988). Racialization. In E. Cashmore (ed.), *Dictionary of Race and Ethnic Relations*, 2nd ed. (pp. 246–247). London: Routledge.

_____. (1989). *Racism*. London: Routledge.

Milner, D. (1975). *Children and Race*. Harmondsworth: Penguin.

_____. (1983). *Children and Race: Ten years on.* London: Ward Lock Educational.

Modgil, S., Modgil, C., & Brown, G. (eds.) (1983). *Jean Piaget: An interdisciplinary critique.* London: Routledge.

Olneck, M. R. (1990, February). The recurring dream: Symbolism and ideology in intercultural and multicultural education. *American Journal of Education,* 147–74.

Phizackiea, A. & Miles, R. (1980). *Labour and Racism.* London: Routledge.

Piaget, J. (1932). *The Moral Judgement of the Child.* New York: Free Press.

Therborn, G. (1980). *The Ideology of Power and the Power of Ideology.* London: Verso.

Troyna, B. (1989). "A new planet"? Tackling racial inequality in all-white schools and colleges. In G. K. Verma (ed.), *Education for All: A landmark in pluralism* (pp. 175–191). Lewes: Falmer.

_____. (1992). Can you see the join? An historical analysis of multicultural and anti-racist education policies. In D. Gill, B. Mayor, & M. Blair (eds.), *Racism and Education: Structures and strategies* (pp. 63–91). London: Sage.

_____. (1993). *Racism and Education: Research perspectives.* Buckingham: Open UP.

Troyna, B. & Hatcher, R. (1992). *Racism in Children's Lives: A study of mainly-white primary schools.* London: Routledge.

Turner, J.C., with M. A. Hogg, et al. (eds.) (1987). *Rediscovering the Social Group: A self-categorization theory.* Oxford: Blackwell.

van Dijk, T. (1983). Cognitive and conversational strategies in the expression of ethnic prejudice. *Text ,* 3 (4), 375–404.

_____. (1991). *Racism and the Press.* London: Routledge.

Walker, J. (1988). *Louts and Legends: Male youth culture in an inner-city school.* Sydney: Allen.

Youniss, J. (1980). *Parents and Peers in Social Development: A Sullivan-Piaget perspective.* Chicago: U of Chicago P.

10 Children and the Grammar of Popular Racism

Fazal Rizvi

Introduction

Children growing up in Australia are exposed to contradictory images of "race" relations. On the one hand, they are taught to celebrate the fact that Australia is a multicultural society that values the principles of cultural tolerance and intercultural harmony. On the other hand, they are exposed to images of Aboriginal Australians and of other minority groups that portray those groups as objects of paternalistic concern, or as aliens whose presence threatens the cultural identity and economic well-being of the majority community. Australians are often told that their future is now linked with Asia, yet most media reports represent Asians in a homogenous manner, positing them as the radical other as constructed within the discourses of colonialism. The impact of these conflicting images on the way children view "racial" difference is neither well documented nor well understood.

In this essay I want to discuss the findings of a research project that sought to explore how children construct their ideas of "racial" difference and how these ideas are socially organized through the practices of pedagogy and curriculum.[1] More specifically, I investigate the issue of how, in schools, popular forms of racism are produced, maintained, and reproduced, on the one hand, and resisted, challenged, and rearticulated, on the other. Such issues are of enormous significance, because without an adequate understanding of how children make sense of the contradictory images of the "racial" other, constructed through and within the practices of popular racism, we cannot hope to develop effective anti-racist educational policies and practices.

I want to argue that children develop their ideas of "race" within their everyday experiences and that these experiences are socially organized, determined by social processes that extend beyond the scope of everyday experience. That is, children's social construction of "race" articulates with the social relations inherent in the broader discourses and practices that express racism in Australian society. I use the notion of articulation rather than reproduction in order to stress that popular racism does not *determine* the way children construct their ideas of social difference, rather, it *articulates* with them,[2] giving them both form and content. As they grow older, children increasingly seek to locate themselves within the contradictory discourses of popular racism. The construction and development of their racial and ethnic identity are thus linked both to the way they are viewed and to their processes of self-representation.

THE PROJECT

The project upon which this discussion of children and racism is based emerged from a dissatisfaction with contemporary theories of multiculturalism that assume a relatively unproblematic account of the nature of racial formation and the reproduction of racism. Such literature often reduces "race" to ethnicity, which is in turn reified into a static category by which to differentiate groups of people, either in terms of some primordial sociobiological criteria (Van den Berghe, 1981) or because groups of people share certain cultural values that are realized in overt unity in various cultural forms (Wallman, 1979). What is missing from these accounts is any exploration of how the concept of ethnicity is related to structural and political issues and linked to various relations of ruling. Issues of power are obscured. The idea of ethnicity is naturalized, treated in an apolitical and ahistorical manner. (For a critique of this literature, see Rizvi, 1991.) The reproduction of ethnic relations is considered to be unproblematic within a framework of functionalist socialization theories. This culturalist orientation has a number of implications for understanding racism. It renders racism a matter of discrimination directed against particular "racial" or ethnic groups, which can be ameliorated by allowing ethnic groups to maintain their cultural traditions, on the one hand, and by encouraging intercultural understanding and tolerance in the majority population, on the other.

Against the background of this general critique, two colleagues and I sought to investigate the manner in which children make sense of the prevailing ideas of "racial" difference, and how the children worked with these categories to construct their social relations across people designated as having different ethnicities. The project, conducted in 1990-1991 in Victoria, Australia, involved intensive ethnographic work in four schools, two primary and two secondary. The findings discussed here are based on the research conducted in the primary schools only. The two schools were selected largely because of the many differences that existed between them.

St. Peter's Primary School[3] is an inner-city parish school with 140 students. A block of flats towers over the school, which has no grassy playing area. Sixty-five percent of the children attending the school live in these flats, which are occupied mostly by recent immigrants from Southeast Asia. Only ten percent of the children come from families where English is spoken at home. According to the principal, more than sixty percent of the parents at the school are either unemployed or are on some form of welfare. The school has fourteen teachers, and apart from the elderly Vietnamese-speaking teacher's aide, none of them speaks any language other than English. The principal of the school is an Anglo-Australian nun. She works very closely with the parish priest, a Celtic-Australian man who lives next door to the school. Additional staff include one part-time secretary and a number of support teachers, all of whom are of the dominant Anglo and Celtic backgrounds. Teachers at the school are very conscious of its "disadvantaged" label and also of the fact that they are relatively unfamiliar with most of their students' cultural backgrounds.

Birmingham Primary School is, in contrast, a wealthy public school by any standard, with a remarkable match between the cultural backgrounds of its teachers and its students. The school is located in a beachside suburb with rambling houses. It has beautiful grounds and excellent playing facilities, maintained mostly by volunteer parent labor. Most of the parents are professionals and belong to Australia's dominant Anglo-Celtic group. All of the teachers at the school also belong to this group, and most live in the local area.

Significantly, both schools are committed to the idea of multicultural education and have incorporated in their curriculum many activities that celebrate cultural diversity in Australian society. At Birmingham Primary School, for example, a major international day is held every year, which both the children and the parents are expected to attend wearing costumes that represent the various cultural groups in the country. St. Peter's, on the other hand, has been making intensive efforts to make its students of non-English-speaking background feel "comfortable" at school. According to the principal, the school is seeking to provide "a secure environment in which the children can feel safe from the harsh realities of the wider society, and in some cases their own homes."

We spent six weeks in each school, collecting data from a variety of sources. Methodologically, we adopted a team approach to the research and used many techniques developed within the ethnographic tradition. These included participant observation and individual and group interviews, as well as active involvement in most of the schools' activities. We attempted critically to observe all facets of school life, paying particular attention to the way children constructed their ideas of social difference. Extensive journal notes were kept, with significant utterances transcribed verbatim.

The team approach raised a number of issues in relation to what and how we "saw" everyday activities at the schools, how it might be possible to bring our competing interpretations together into a coherent collective account, and, given some major disagreements, whether this could be done at all. While at the beginning of the project we believed we shared a common theoretical position on the nature and scope of racism, it soon became evident that our ideas not only about the origins of racism but about its very salience were in conflict.[4]

THEORIZING POPULAR RACISM

Fundamental to the development of this research project, however, was our collective rejection of the theories of racism associated with the rhetoric of multiculturalism. Perhaps the most popular of these theories views racism as an expression of an individual's negative prejudicial attitudes that is directed against another individual or a group of individuals on the basis of some presumed physical or cultural differentiation (Lippmann, 1977). It is believed that racism manifests itself in various stereotypes about the capacities and characteristics of particular people. It is a consequence of an individual's inability to reason correctly. Racism is thus constituted as an individualized, exceptional phenomenon located in ignorance and irrationality, or even in a pathological personality. As Julian Henriques put it (1984, p. 62), this view implies a "rotten apple" theory of racism predicated upon a set of normative assumptions about the nature of the sane, rational, and unprejudiced individual. It suggests educational interventions that might seek to promote a more sympathetic understanding of cultural differences. It is assumed, as Paul Cohen observes, that racism can be "punctured by the application of a superior logic" (1987, p. 1).

Objections to this view of racism have led many theorists (for example, McConnochie, Hollingsworth, and Pettman, 1988) to emphasize the structural constitution of racism. It has been suggested, for example, that racism manifests itself not only in particular attitudes of individuals but, more insidiously, in those social structures that systematically disadvantage particular groups of people on the basis of their "race." Racism is thus viewed as a structural relationship that defines patterns of distribution of social goods and power through the operations of key social institutions. The notion of "institutional racism" has often been used to describe the way various practices of subordination have been institutionalized. To challenge institutional racism, it is argued, major structural changes are required in the way society is currently organized.

The theoretical differences between the views of racism as a phenomenon constituted by individuals, on the one hand, and as institutionally constituted, on the other, have been widely discussed, and in a way they characterize the debates that have become common between multicultural and anti-racist educators (see Brandt, 1986). However, what these debates mask are the many similarities between the two perspectives.

It is clear, for example, that both views are located within the framework of the same individual-institution dualism. For while the former view is defined in terms of the explicit intentional actions of individuals, the latter stresses the pervasive operations of institutions. The dominant social-psychological paradigm that views racism as a problem whose origins lie in the cognitive errors of individuals is replaced by a sociological thesis that seeks to explain the structural subordination of one racial group by another.

But, significantly, both perspectives *naturalize* the phenomenon they seek to describe. The former perspective assumes a Cartesian view of subjectivity, while the latter assumes institutions to have a *sui generis* character, independent of the actual practices of actual individuals. The former sees attitudes as fundamental, learned through individuals' information-processing mechanisms. Discrimination, according to one of the most influential advocates of this view, Gordon Allport (1954), is the most overt manifestation of this cognitive process. The study of attitudes is thus seen as a key to an understanding of behavior. In explaining how children develop racist ideas, Allport suggests that they are influenced by a pantechnicon of cultural messages throughout their lives. These include parents, family, peer subcultures, and schools, as well as many other systems that sustain society's normative order. Allport's explanations are largely functionalist, relying on a socialization theory that views children as passive recipients of the cultural messages that form the basis of their attitudes.

Theories of institutional racism are similarly predicated on functionalist assumptions. They treat individuals as relatively powerless in the face of the structural distribution of power. Racist institutions, they suggest, are reproduced through mechanisms internal to the operations of the institutions. Apart from the problem of treating institutions as if they were homogeneous, these theories are unable to be explained how changes can be brought about to the way institutions work. What has become increasingly clear, then, is that the individual and institutional views of racism operate from the opposite ends of the same dualism.

However, if we reject such a dualism, both accounts can be shown to be equally problematic, as indeed is the view that sees individual and institutional racism as describing two different levels at which racism operates. The talk of levels is basically misguided, because it is impossible to describe institutions that are not historically constructed through the actual practices of individuals. Nor is it possible to imagine discourses and practices in which individuals engage as having any significance outside their institutional locations.

What the rejection of this dualism suggests is that racism does not have some essential form. It is continually changing, being challenged, interrupted, and reconstructed, in the actual practices in which people engage. As Stuart Hall has pointed out, while there are no doubt certain general features to racism, what is "more significant are the ways in which these general features are modified, and transformed by the historical specificity of the contexts in which they become active" (1986, p. 23). Hall implores us to look for "not racism in general but racisms," to study racism's particular formations in actual practices.

Central to Hall's social theory is the conviction that racist meaning is constructed in and through ideology. The view of ideology to which Hall is committed is derived largely from Gramsci. Ideology, he argues, organizes the everyday practical activities in which human beings engage, think about their options, explain their predicaments, and formulate a sense of their struggle. Ideologies are organic because they are linked to common sense in ways that are disjointed, episodic, fragmentary, and contradictory; they are continually changing as people encounter and learn new ways of acting upon the world around them. Hall refuses to accept any idea of a pregiven, unified ideological subject, with a coherent set of ideas constituting his or her consciousness. Rather, he suggests that consciousness is not an individual but a relational, collective phenomenon, located in practices. He cites approvingly Gramsci's observation in *Prison Notebooks* that "the personality is strangely composite"; it contains "Stone Age elements and principles of a modern science, prejudices from all past phases of history...and institutions of a future philosophy" (Gramsci, 1971, p. 324).

Hall's insights lead us to see that at any historical juncture racism has a popular ideological form. As an ideology, popular racism describes a kind of collective practice in thinking about social relations. To think ideologically about racism is to think in a distinctive and describable way that is historically constituted. It is to engage in practices that are predicated on certain ideas, concepts, and generalizations that define a distinctive method of reasoning and of interpreting society. And like all ideological practices, popular racism is subject to change and rearticulation (Gilroy, 1987).

For example, while racism is often believed to contain a reference to visible color differences, this residual element of nineteenth-century biological racism is notably no longer essential to contemporary expressions of racism. Indeed, as Philip Cohen points out,

> racist discourses have never confined themselves just to body images. Names and modes of address, states of mind, clothes and customs, every kind of social behavior and cultural practice have been pressed into the service to signify this or that racial essence. (1988, p. 14)

Contemporary popular racism has a much more complex form, with a range of intersecting modalities and historical trajectories. For example, in Australia, racisms against Aboriginal people and Asians have very different modalities and structures of meaning. However, despite their different historical trajectories, in a structural sense both involve practices of marginalization and exclusion. And while historically such practices have involved physical violence, political repression, psychological abuse, and harassment, their more contemporary forms are no longer as overt. Covertly, they include paternalism, inequalities of access and treatment, and various other forms of ideological practices.

While many of the overt forms of marginalization and exclusion are gradually disappearing in Australia, they are being replaced by new ideological expressions that often escape recognition as racism because they are masked by the discourses of social cohesion, nationalism, and patriotism. "New" racism, as it has been called (by Castles, Kalantzis, Cope, and Morrisey, 1988, for example), takes a necessary distance from crude ideas of biological and cultural inferiority and superiority and seeks to present a normative image of a nation characterized by a requirement that all those who reside in Australia commit themselves to a uniform set of social and cultural values. It binds ideas of national culture and social cohesion into an homogenous form, an ethnic essence, in which minority cultures are often regarded as alien. Marginalization and exclusion are thus not so much legal as ideological, informed by a theory of human nature that presumes that human beings have a deep-seated desire to prefer the company of "their own kind" and that it's "only common sense" for people to be hostile to other groups and thus protect their territory from "aliens."

A number of writers (for example, Pettman, 1992) have recently argued that contemporary popular expressions of racism in Australia are tied to this alleged common sense. But, as Gramsci observed (1971), common sense does not appear in a coherent and logical form. In its hegemonic form, it is contradictory, made secure ideologically and practically in a generalized set of ideas and practices. It enables people to make sense of their everyday experiences by making them seem natural. Practices of popular racism are thus predicated on an essentialist view of human nature and social relations, which, as Errol Lawrence points out, naturalizes "the social order, by obscuring the historical struggles that produced the present configurations of social forces" (1982, p. 50).

What the foregoing discussion indicates is that popular racism represents a practical ideology, rooted in everyday cultural practices. It is an ideology that works through certain cultural practices of representation, which make it possible to sustain particular racist constructions of social difference. But how do children relate to this ideology and learn to make an imaginative sense of their social identity and difference through it? To explore this issue, we now turn to discuss the findings of the project.

PRACTICES OF POPULAR RACISM IN SCHOOLS

Children entering a primary school at the age of five or so have already been exposed to racially constructed images of social relations. They already engage in certain ideological practices of popular racism, which inform their engagement in the learning tasks they perform in schools. Thus we found that in a Grade One art class at Birmingham Primary School almost half of the children depicted robbers as blacks, while those who were robbed were invariably white. The lesson in which these representations were produced was about crime. The teacher began the lesson by asking the children what crime was and what could be done to prevent it. The children put forward various ideas which were derived mostly from the familiar cops-and-robbers stories and cartoons, as well as personal anecdotes. They were then asked to draw, using colored pencils, an imaginary scene where a crime was being committed.

The representational images the children produced relied heavily on the stereotypes of the cops-and-robbers stories. The images demonstrated clearly how their imaginations were socially organized. The ideology of popular racism helped most of them construct representations of robbers as blacks, while none of the police, nor the people robbed, were so depicted. One child, for example, drew a robber whose face was shaded, who was dragging a chain as two white policeman looked over him. It should be noted further that none of the robbers, nor the police, were women, suggesting an imagery that was not only racially formed but also gendered.

Toward the end of the lesson the teacher asked a number of children to describe what they had drawn. None of their accounts referred to color, nor indeed to gender, despite the fact that the representations of robbers were inherently racialized and gendered. What was also significant was that the teacher had not noticed this social formation, as she did not raise it as an issue, allowing its reproduction to go unchallenged. Children's racialized images rested on a set of taken-for-granted assumptions; the children drew spontaneously without engaging in any reflexive practice.

It is important to note, however, that such taken-for-granted assumptions are located in a wider, complex web of social relations. It is not possible to understand the representations of robbers produced by the children without also recognizing how class factors mediated these representations. For such is the classed nature of "race" relations in Australia that very few of the children in middle-class Birmingham had ever had a direct social relation with a black person, let alone made friends with one. Instead, the children's racial imagery had been developed mostly through television and other media of popular communication. But racial images are not simply reproduced in a mechanical fashion; they are constructed and reconstructed by children attempting to make sense of their everyday experiences.

This discussion indicates that it is not possible to understand racism without investigating the broader social relations that define children's experience of the world, for racism articulates with a variety of other factors, such as class and gender, in such a way as to render its distinctive delineation impossible. As Cameron McCarthy (1990) has argued, racism often articulates with other ideological discourses and with other forms of exclusion and oppression, often in ways that are contradictory. It is interesting to speculate, therefore, how children at the working-class St. Peter's Primary School, who encounter black people daily, might have produced very different representations of the robbers.

The complex and contradictory dynamics of the relation between race and gender expressed themselves differently at St. Peter's, where we witnessed an incident that involved a much more deliberate application of the ideology of popular racism. One of the researchers and a teacher were walking around the playground during lunch when the teacher pointed to two girls holding hands as they walked. Nothing special about that, except that the teacher felt it necessary to remark that one of the girls was white while the other was clearly of an Asian background. However, just as the teacher was stressing that this was a common occurrence at the school, an older child, David, in Grade 6, came running in to disrupt this example of intercultural harmony: he forced the girls apart. Somewhat embarrassed, the teacher scolded David and to the researcher dismissed his actions as those of a bully who had "often been in trouble picking on younger *Chinese girls.*" She also said that the Chinese boys had "often ganged up on him."

A more in-depth interview with David later that day revealed a very different picture. Initially, David showed considerable reluctance to talk about the incident, but he later explained his action in terms of his belief that "Asians and Australian people shouldn't be friendly…they are different, and should keep to their own." David also maintained that the Aboriginal people had a right to be in this country, but that "Asians are trying to take over the country…sometimes I get angry when I see so many Asians at the shops." When asked whether he had any Asian friends, David replied somewhat self-consciously, "yeah, I am not racist or somethin'. I talk to them at school, but my mum wouldn't let them come to the flat." He was then asked why his mum didn't like Asians. He said, "I don't know, really.…They are dirty, aren't they?…and they take our jobs." This response indicated David's own confusions, as well as what he viewed as the perfectly reasonable beliefs his mother had about Asians, linked as they were to her class-mediated anxieties about jobs.

The interview with David showed him to be actively struggling to make sense of his world. He was caught between the contradictory discourses of the school's commitment to multiculturalism and his mother's racist representations of both the experienced and the imagined other (see Miles, 1989, p. 15). He also had the contradictory desires to like and be liked by everyone at school and at the same time to give a practical expression to the generalizations he had gained from his mother about a putative causal link between the physical appearance of a group of people, their moral character, and Australia's dire economic circumstances. For David, his disjointed imageries, beliefs, and evaluations about the other constituted a reason sufficient to intervene in a social interaction that did not affect him directly.

St Peter's, it should be recalled, is a school of 140 students, more than 75% of whom are from minority backgrounds. At the school David was recognized by teachers and also by many students as a member of the dominant group in Australian society, though at St. Peter's he was clearly in a minority. The same was true of Erica, a Grade 4 student, who was widely disliked in her class. She was regarded by her teacher as a "loner, who enjoyed her own company." Erica was often absent from school, mostly, according to the teachers, to help her single mother look after her two-year-old brother; and when she did attend school she seemed always to find a corner in which to hide. Her academic results were uniformly poor, and she often spent hours on a task that most children could complete within minutes. She was often left alone by the teacher, who freely admitted that she disliked Erica and that she understood why the children in her class found Erica's behavior toward them irritating. The principal of the school knew of the problems the teacher had with Erica, but attempts by her and the school counselor to mediate had proved unsuccessful.

We wondered, therefore, how Erica defined her social relations and interpreted the social organization of the school. Unlike David, Erica was very keen to talk to us. She was deeply conscious of her contradictory status in school and also of what other children at St. Peter's thought of her. But in contrast to David she maintained that she "didn't need any friends...especially Asians...they like sticking together and we couldn't be friends anyway." Erica told us that she had had many Asian friends in Grade Two, but now that she was older, and presumably in grasp of greater wisdom, she did not wish to associate with such people because they "talk funny, and hang around with each other....There are too many Asians in this school....I don't like Asians any more." In contrast, Erica insisted that she liked Aborigines: "They own this country, and we should treat them better."

Erica indicated a strong moral commitment to fairness and equality, but had no problem reconciling her differing attitudes toward Asians and Aborigines. Here she used a particular form of the notion of "territorial belongingness" (Walker, 1988) to represent Asian immigrants as aliens and therefore deserving of a moral treatment very different from that applicable to Aborigines. Erica sympathized with the Aboriginal demand for racial justice and broadly supported attempts by governments to ameliorate the consequences of past racism. This commitment, she believed, rendered the charge of racism inapplicable to her, even though she held that recent immigrants were not entitled to the same positive treatment.

Samuel L. Gaertner and John F. Dovidio (1986) have identified such views as an aspect of what they call the ideology of "aversive" racism. This ideology refers to a form of liberal discourse that claims to be nonprejudiced and nondiscriminatory but at the same time contains negative evaluations of certain groups of people. This contradictory discourse is somehow able to reconcile a commitment to multiculturalism, on the one hand, with practices of marginalization and exclusion, on the other. Further, such an ideology is not only applicable to the dominant group; it also organizes the way minority children think about their social relations.

At Birmingham Primary School the case of Vincent Khoo, a recent immigrant from Hong Kong, illustrates the complex and contradictory fashion in which this ideology works. We first noticed Vincent in the playground not only because he was one of the very few children who did not belong to the dominant Anglo group, but also because he seemed always to walk around with a small cricket bat in his hand, which he often threatened to use against anyone who made fun of him. Vincent was a brilliant student who was frequently asked by teachers from across the school to troubleshoot their computing problems. At the same time, however, he was an object of much ridicule and racist name calling.

Vincent's response to his harassment was to threaten violence, something that sat very uneasily with popular racist constructions of many students and teachers who saw the Chinese, as one teacher put it, as "gentle and hardworking people." On one occasion Vincent's teacher went as far as to suggest that Vincent was not like other Chinese people. Making use of her representation of the imagined other, the teacher saw no difficulties in homogenizing the Chinese, even if they had come from Hong Kong rather than the mainland and had lived in Australia for a number of years.

Attempts by the teacher to deal with "Vincent's problem" had made him an object of considerable racialized attention. His playground response was to threaten children with a cricket bat. But in the classroom Vincent was struggling to develop a very different response, one derived from popular multiculturalist sentiments. Nowhere was this response better illustrated than in the following poem, titled "Be Happy," which Vincent wrote as part of a creative writing lesson.

> When people are teasing you
> and you are feeling down
> just pick yourself up
> and smile, don't frown
>
> If you are from Russia
> or China or some place bad
> If people tease you
> don't cut or get mad
>
> Just be happy—don't be sad
> Don't get angry—just be glad
>
> If people tease you about where you come from
> Forget about them, just leave them alone
> You don't have to tease them back
> just because they are Russian, Indian, or Black

Multiculturalist sentiments also played a major part in the way Sue and Anne, Grade Six students at Birmingham Primary School, described their experiences of other cultures. Both of them had visited Asia but, as a result, were concerned that "Australia might become a place like Bali....They have a different culture, which is okay for over there...but I don't want too many Asians here, because Australia is sort of cleaner." When asked whether they would like to have Asian friends, both said yes, but Anne insisted that "they couldn't be really good friends...[because] they prefer to stay together." And Sue added, "So do we!"

Of course, Anne and Sue did not have to mix with children from different backgrounds at Birmingham. At St. Peter's Primary School, however, there was not only an ample opportunity to mix but also a great deal of evidence that children in lower grades mixed freely. However, in higher grades there was considerable separation along ethnic lines. A friendship group of four girls, all born in Australia of parents born in Egypt, was typical. According to the girls, they had only been friends since they were in Grade Three. Earlier they had played regularly with children from other backgrounds, but now they felt more secure in each other's company. Why was this, they were asked. Nadia replied, "You're sort of expected to....Teachers are always putting us together, and our parents know each other." Another girl, Sebajh, was more assertive: "I wouldn't want to be friends with the Vietnamese anyway, they are so creepy...and the Australians I fight." At that point the other girls turned on Sebajh: "Don't be so rude....We don't think that really," one of them said reassuringly. The girls had recognized that a distinction had to be drawn between those beliefs that could be made public and those that were confidential to their racially organized friendship group.

The Social Organization of Popular Racism

The above discussion demonstrates that popular racism serves as a framework within which children develop their ideas of racial difference. However, it also shows that while popular racism is an ideology that organizes children's thinking, it does not determine it. As active organizers of their own learning, children are engaged in continually changing, challenging, interrupting, and reconstructing expressions of racism in ways that are often contradictory. We found, for example, Vincent Khoo challenging forms of racism he confronted at Birmingham Primary School both with an instrument of violence and with the resources of an ideology of romantic pluralism.

The research thus challenges both the functionalist socialization and structural-Marxist reproduction views of the ways children acquire racist ideas. It shows the articulation between the ideology of popular racism and racist practices to be much more complex, multifaceted, and contextually specific, supporting Miles's suggestion that we should avoid any assumption of simple duplication, because

> ideologies are never only received but are also constructed and reconstructed by people responding to their material and cultural circumstances in order to comprehend, represent and act in relation to those circumstances. (1989, p. 132)

If this is so, then specific forms of racism can be expected to change, and forms of popular racism are likely to be reconstituted in the actual practices in which children engage.

Thus, for example, the simplistic representation of racist images we witnessed in the drawings of Grade One children at Birmingham Primary School was largely missing in the ideas and practices of the older children at both schools. Racism was expressed in a more complex form. As the influential work of Milner has demonstrated (1983, p. 108), while young children have only rudimentary feelings about racial difference, as they grow older they begin to absorb and think and act through a more complex set of stereotypes and conceptual principles. They deal with the contradictions of popular racism in a variety of ways in order to make imaginative sense of the social world around them.

Thus our research shows that even those students who hold an affinity to the principles of multiculturalism and racial justice are comfortable with the perceptions of security derived from racial separation. As children grow older, they develop ways of expressing forms of racism that, while they are not overtly offensive, nevertheless represent a discourse that has been identified as "new" racism. The talk of "us" and "them" is a central part of this discourse, the practical manifestation of which lies in the patterns of friendship formed around ethnic differentiation. This finding is consistent with J. C. Walker's observation based on his ethnography of a boys' high school in Sydney. He maintains:

> Our overwhelming impression was that the traditional ASC working class in the locality regarded certain areas, and in the global sense the whole of Stockham, as really "ours," even if as a result of decisions made by others of another class in other places, they were invaded by unwanted outsiders and aliens—wogs, chows and coons. (1988, p. 47)

In our research David exhibited the sentiments described by Walker. In a school where he felt he was in a very small minority, he was nevertheless convinced that he belonged to the dominant group outside the school and that the school itself was structured around cultural values that were his.

Our research also supports Michael Billig's contention that recent forms of racism trade on their supposed "reasonableness" (1988). Billig has pointed out that popular racism operates in such a way as to accommodate simultaneously a commitment to the values of justice and representations of minorities that sustain racist images. He has suggested that it is necessary to understand modern racism in its rhetorical context, in which opposition to racism is often stated in a preliminary clause followed by an assertion of an overtly racist belief. This rhetorical device is most clearly evident in such phrases as "I am not prejudiced, but…" and "Some of my best friends are Asians, but…." Contradictions of popular racism are simply put aside as its form is reconstituted.

However, our research also shows that *expressions* of popular racism in textbooks, in educational policies, and in the discourse of teachers are not necessarily the same as their *reception*. Children do not always accept what teachers tell them; nor do they unquestioningly accept the popular racism inherent in much of the talk in the media and textbooks about a unitary Australian identity structured around a uniform set of cultural values. They are capable of making their everyday world problematic. The idea of making the everyday world problematic is one that can be found in the writings of Dorothy Smith (1987; 1990). Smith has described a method of thinking for a sociology for women that, in my view, is also useful in understanding how popular racism articulates with children's actual conceptual practices.

If we follow Smith's method, then everyday practices can be investigated in terms of the way they are organized as social relations, or indeed as a complex of social relations beyond the scope of any one individual's experience. The local organization of everyday experience, Smith suggests, "is determined by the social relations of an immensely complex division of labor knitting lives and local settings to national, international, social, economic and political processes" (1987, p. 154). A local practice is thus articulated with certain conceptual practices of power. Smith argues that "the relation between the local and particular to generalized social relations is not a conceptual or methodological issue, it is a property of social organization" (p. 157). The everyday world, Smith insists, "is not fully understandable within its own scope. It is organized by social relations not fully apparent in it nor contained in it." What Smith calls "relations of ruling" (1990), that is, public discourses and practices that are historically formed and institutionalized, define the everyday world.

In my view it is possible to conceptualize popular racism as expressing certain relations of ruling. The ideology of popular racism provides children with a framework of thoughts, images, generalizations, and modes of expression within which to think about, act upon, and imagine the world. But how do children acquire this ideology?

Children learn by instruction and by engaging in practices that enable them to differentiate between classes of objects, discriminate between categories of actions, and develop a sense of what are considered appropriate practices in particular circumstances. To use an idea that is central to Wittgenstein's later philosophy (1973), this is how children learn the "grammar" of a linguistic practice, initially by imitating and using the expression in an unproblematic and unreflexive way as part of a conventional practice. According to Wittgenstein, the grammar of a concept determines the relation between an expression and what in the world that expression is used *for*. It establishes the concept's place in a system of concepts and the discursive practices that that system articulates. The goal of any training is to draw individuals into an established grammar, a shared practice; to initiate them into a community of persons bound together by their allegiance to the rules of a particular discourse. To have learned the grammar of a concept is to demonstrate in practice that one can "go on in the same way, to show an agreement in judgement which is necessarily also a judgement in form of life" (Wittgenstein, 1973, para 241).

Such learning is not passive, however. We must be careful, Wittgenstein maintains, not to think of the grammar of a conceptual practice as a closed, rule-bound system. Although grammar regulates the possibilities, that is, both permits and guides our practice, Wittgenstein insists it is not circumscribed everywhere. He argues, "Our grammar, that is, our conceptual formation, which directs our experience in certain channels, is often such that only through it do we see a definite kind of fact" (1969, para 357). Grammar is open in this way; it regulates the possibilities of how a particular practice might be recognized or interpreted.

Thus children often have to make judgements between competing claims and interpretations within a discourse, for no discourse is entirely complete and coherent. And as we have already noted, as a discourse that claims to express common sense, popular racism is contradictory and contains interpretations of social relations that can be and often are challenged by children. Popular racism thus does not so much determine the way children view the world as *steer* them toward certain interpretations. It is hegemonic in this way.

Popular racism is hegemonic because it expresses itself as an authoritative discourse inviting the kind of rhetorical appeal that is by its very nature uncritical. Its claim to common sense and naturalness is predicated on the assumption that it constitutes a shared practice that is embodied in institutions—and that it could not be otherwise. It claims to represent an objective discourse in terms of which social life must inevitably be arranged in the way it currently is; that is, the very participation in that form of life demands that we accept the epistemic authority it represents.

Through many of the message systems of schools, children learn that the beliefs that constitute popular racism are authoritative because in many different ways they are presented as a model for sound social thinking. Thus such beliefs as that it is natural to stick to one's own kind, that it is appropriate to protect one's own territory, and that interethnic competition is inevitable appear to children as not only reasonable but also authoritative. Children's ability to imagine their social relations is linked to these presumptions, as are their abilities to understand everyday practices in terms of their social organization and to project alternative courses of action.

All explanation takes place relative to a background space of alternatives (see Garfinkel, 1981), a set of assumptions about what needs to be explained, what questions are appropriate, and what counts as an adequate explanation. Children attempting to understand everyday practices take a great many assumptions for granted. These assumptions constitute the relations of ruling that organize children's practices of popular racism. As we have already noted, these relations of ruling steer the imagination. But given that such relations are not fixed and that popular racism is inherently contradictory, children are not entirely complicit in the social practices they define.

The grammar of popular racism is compelling, but it does not determine in any absolute sense the way children must think and act. Our public discourses contain canons of criticism that can be used to imagine a different way of organizing social relations. Children can and do object to particular racist assertions and practices, but often only because "it doesn't seem right" or "it's not fair" and not necessarily because they have a reflexive understanding of popular racism and the way it defines those practices and their social organization.

It should not be inferred from this discussion that intellectual understanding of these processes is enough to tackle racism. The epistemic authority of popular racism is not sustained by reason but through a wide variety of practices of marginalization and exclusion beyond the scope of the school. It is linked to social and political factors that define the formation of the state (see Omi and Winant, 1986), including the way schooling is structured.

It has become commonplace to observe that contemporary schools are structured in such a way as to curb imagination and discourage critical and speculative thinking. In my view, however, unless this feature of schooling is challenged, popular racism will continue to have an effective steering capacity in the social organization of everyday practices. To challenge its hegemonic influence, children therefore need to be equipped with critical skills that enable them to imagine alternative moral configurations. For while the grammar of popular racism directs their experience in certain channels, it does not circumscribe their critical imaginative capacity. Nothing rules out the possibility of children using their faculty of moral imagination to represent to themselves how things might be different and better.

CONCLUSION

What are the curricular and pedagogic implications of this analysis of the grammar of popular racism and the way it steers children's thinking and activities? We need to remind ourselves that schools are not the only site where children learn the grammar of popular racism. Such institutions as families, peer groups, the church, and the media in its various forms all have the capacity morally and politically to steer children in ways that are often contradictory. At the same time children do not all receive popular racist constructions in the same way. Popular racism, as has already been noted, is contradictory. Its epistemic authority is ambiguous and tentative, allowing a space for imagining an alternative understanding of social relations, and of possible futures.

To tackle popular racism it is essential to challenge not only the attitudes and beliefs that signify its grammar but, more importantly, its practical ideological form, the epistemic authority that sustains its practices, enabling children to make sense of the everyday world in racist terms. As Cohen has argued:

> Popular racism cannot be tackled by simply giving students access to alternative sources of experience, or new means of intellectual authority; rather it is a question of articulating their lived cultures to *new practices of representation*, which make it possible to sustain an imaginative sense of social identity and discourse without recourse to racist constructions. (1987, p. 2)

Such an anti-racist education must, however, be predicated on a realization that the faculty of critical imagination cannot be exercised in isolation but only as part of a collective struggle and as part of a project to undermine popular racism's epistemic authority in an effort to replace it by more socially just practices of representation.

Schools cannot, of course, be the only site where this might happen. Given that many teachers themselves occupy contradictory positions in relation to racism and are often complicit in such discriminatory practices as grading according to norms that rest on assimilationist assumptions, it is necessary for school-based initiatives to link up with anti-racist struggles taking place at other sites. It is important, therefore, for teachers and communities not only to equip students with the general critical skills that might help them to deconstruct representations of popular racism, but also to unmask those institutional practices that sustain racist ideologies, with a view to dismantling them.

NOTES

1 This research project, titled "Forms of Racism," was funded by the Australian Research Council, whose support is gratefully acknowledged, as is the contribution of my coresearchers, Dr. Alan Rice and Dr. Margaret Woodward of Monash University, Australia. Thanks also to Vicki Crowley, John Knight, and Bob Lingard for their comments on an earlier draft of this paper.

2 The idea of articulation is explored by Stuart Hall, most notably in his essay "The Problem of Ideology: Marxism Without Guarantees" (1986b).

3 The names used of the schools and children throughout this essay are pseudonyms.

4 The contested nature of the interpretations of racism raises a number of very difficult issues, both personal and methodological. These are discussed in "Myths, Metaphor and Methodology: some issues in team ethnography" (1990).

REFERENCES

Allport, G. W. (1954). *The Nature of Prejudice*. Cambridge: Addison.

Billig, M. (1988). Prejudice and tolerance. In M. Billig et al. (eds.), *Ideological Dilemmas: A social psychology of everyday thinking* (pp. 95–111). London: Sage.

Brandt, G. L. (1986). *The Realization of Anti-Racist Teaching*. London: Falmer.

Castles, S., Kalantzis, M., Cope, B., & Morrisey, M. (1988). *Mistaken Identity: Multiculturalism and the demise of nationalism in Australia*. Sydney: Pluto.

Cohen, P. (1987). *Racism and Popular Culture: A cultural studies approach*. London: Centre for Multicultural Education, University of London.

_____. (1988). The perversions of inheritance: Studies in the making of multi-racist Britain. In P. Cohen & H. S. Bains (eds.), *Multi-Racist Britain*. London: MacMillan.

Gaertner, S., & Dovidio, J. F. (1986). The aversive form of racism. In J. F. Dovidio & S. Gaertner (eds.), *Prejudice, Discrimination, and Racism* (pp. 61–90). New York: Academic.

Garfinkel, A. (1981). *Forms of Explanation: Structures of inquiry in social science*. New Haven: Yale UP.

Gilroy, P. (1987). *"There Ain't no Black in the Union Jack": The cultural politics of race and nation*. London: Hutchinson.

Gramsci, A. (1971). *Prison Notebooks*. London: Lawrence.

Hall, S. (1986a). Gramsci's relevance to the analysis of racism and ethnicity. *Journal of Communication Studies*, 10 (2), 5–27.

_____. (1986b). The problem of ideology: Marxism without guarantees. *Journal of Communication Studies*, 10 (2), 28–44.

Henriques, J. (1984). Social psychology and the politics of racism. In Henriques, J., et al. (eds.), *Changing the Subject: Psychology, social regulation and subjectivity*. London: Methuen.

Lawrence, E. (1982). Just plain common sense: the "roots" of racism. In Centre for Contemporary Cultural Studies (ed.), *The Empire Strikes Back* (pp. 47–94). London: Hutchinson.

Lippman, L. (1977). *The Aim Is Understanding: Educational techniques for a multicultural society*. Sydney: Australia and New Zealand.

Miles, R. (1989). *Racism*. London: Routledge.

Milner, D. (1983). *Children and Race: Ten years on*. London: Ward Lock Educational.

McConnochie, K., Hollingsworth, D., & Pittman, J. (1988). *Race and Racism in Australia*. Wentworth Falls, N.S.W.: Sydney Social Science.

McCarthy, C. (1990). *Race and Curriculum*. London: Falmer.

Omi, M., & Winant, H. (1986). *Racial Formation in the United States*. Boston: Routledge.

Pettman, J. (1992). *Living in the Margins*. Sydney: Allen.

Rizvi, F. (1990). *Myths, Metaphor, and Methodology: Some issues in team ethnography*. Paper presented at the annual conference of the Australian Association for Research in Education, Sydney.

_____. (1991). The idea of ethnicity and the politics of multicultural education. In D. Dawkins (ed.), *Power and Politics in Education* (pp. 161–196). London: Falmer

Smith, D. E. (1987). *The Everyday World as Problematic: A feminist sociology*. Boston: Northeastern UP.

_____ (1990). *The Conceptual Practices of Power: A feminist sociology of knowledge*. Boston: Northeastern UP.

Van de Berghe, P. L. (1981). *The Ethnic Phenomenon*. New York: Elsevier.

Wallman, S. (1986). Ethnicity and the boundary process in context. In J. Rex & D. Mason (eds.), *Theories of Race and Ethnicity Relations* (pp. 226–245). Cambridge: Cambridge UP.

Walker, J. C. (1988). *Louts and Legends: Male youth culture in an inner city school*. Sydney: Allen.

Wittgenstein, L. (1969). *Zettel*. Oxford: Blackwell.

_____. (1973). *Philosophical Investigations*. Oxford: Blackwell.

11 Negotiating Work, Identity and Desire:
The Adolescent Dilemmas of Working-Class Girls of French and Algerian Descent in a Vocational High School

Catherine Raissiguier

Snapshots of Working-Class Girls

Farida: See, I consider myself Algerian, but I don't have the mentality, I don't have...For them—I call them "Arabs" [laughter]—for the Arabs in general, as soon as the girl is eighteen she's got to think about marriage, immediately! But not for me! For me it's freedom first. For me studies come first, employment comes first. And I'm definitely not getting married now.

Alexandra: I don't see myself as a homemaker, not at all. I am not someone who'll stay at home and raise my kids. I see myself dynamic—with a profession I like.

FARIDA IS EIGHTEEN. She was born in France of Algerian parents. She has maintained a dual nationality. Her father came to work in France thirty-three years ago. A few years later his wife and his two kids came to join him. Farida's parents had four more children born on French soil. Farida's mother has never worked outside the home; her father is a welder in the auto industry. The whole family lives in a large housing project heavily populated by North Africans. Alexandra is also eighteen. She is French of French ancestry. Her father is a house painter and her mother a clerical worker. Her parents are now divorced, and she lives with her mother and younger brother in a small housing project.

In the fall of 1989 both young women were enrolled in their second and last year of a short vocational training program. They had been geared toward this clerical track at the outset of junior high school. At the end of the academic year—depending on their performance and the results of a final examination—they would either enter the labor force or transfer to a longer track that might lead them to a vocational *baccalauréat* and perhaps, for a lucky few, beyond.[1]

The present essay is about these young women who, at the junior high school level, have been allocated to short vocational tracks and for whom upward mobility in the future is seriously limited.[2] How do they, given their social class, their educational records, and their racial/ethnic and gender locations, understand their present and future position in society? What are their hopes and visions of themselves in that future? How do they negotiate and construct possibilities for themselves, and what importance do they give to education and schooling?

This essay starts with the working assumption that Farida, Alexandra, and their classmates are active agents crafting their selves through an ongoing process of analysis, interpretation, and negotiation of their actual social positions as they exist within specific structural and discursive boundaries. The larger study from which this essay develops (Raissiguier, forthcoming) asks questions such as the following: What kinds of individual and collective identities do working-class female students develop in a French vocational high school? Is the process of identity formation different for girls of Algerian descent than for girls of French descent and, if so, in what ways? Here I explore these questions around the specific issues of employment, work, family, marriage, and romance.

METHODS AND SOURCES OF DATA

This study is based on data collected over the academic year 1989-1990. During that time I spent several days a week in the vocational school Lycée Lurçat. The school, located in a working-class suburb of Paris, offers primarily short tertiary training programs to working-class students, of whom the great majority are female. At the time of the study, approximately seventy percent of the students were female, half were of migrant descent or were migrants themselves, and over twenty-five percent were of North African parentage.

For the purpose of the study, I "followed" two classes of girls in a short secretarial track, who were studying for a Brevet d'Etudes Professionnelles (BEP, or vocational studies certificate). Among the two classes (forty eight students), eleven students were of Algerian descent, twenty of French descent, and the rest of other migrant parentage. Out of the two classes only one student was male. I spent the first trimester observing classroom processes and the last two trimesters doing semi-directive student interviews (individual and collective) as well as intermittent classroom observations. I also interviewed school officials and informally talked to teachers.

ON WAGE LABOR

Before embarking on a close analysis of the data, let us briefly set up the backdrop against which Farida's and Alexandra's stories unfold. Since World War II, the French economy has undergone deep structural changes. While these changes are similar to those observable within other Western industrialized economies, it is important to note here that in the French context they have been deeply shaped by gendered and ethnic/racial dynamics (Jenson, 1988; Noiriel, 1988; Lipietz, 1990). Because of human labor shortages after the war, the French economy rebuilt itself by relying heavily on female and migrant labor. Women and migrants were incorporated into the economy, but only to occupy the most de-skilled forms of manual and service labor. Both groups were constructed as marginal workers within the discursive logics of a patriarchal and postcolonial society. Indeed migrants, because transient (they don't really belong here), and women, because "secondary" (they really belong in the home), formed the ideal pool of cheap, tractable, and flexible labor necessary for modernizing the French economy.

The first oil crisis in 1973 marked the beginning of a long period of economic recession and restructuration. French deindustrialization has been clearly visible in the dramatic decline of industrial jobs and the soaring of national unemployment rates. Parallel to this process, France also experienced a tremendous growth of its tertiary sector, which pulled even more women into wage labor. This tertiarization and feminization of the labor force since the '70s has been accompanied, however, by worsening working conditions (precarious work, unemployment, part-time work, night work, etc.) for women in particular, but also for youth and migrants.

With deindustrialization and the shrinking of its traditional sources for work, migrant labor has also been deeply affected by the economic downturn.[3] As a result, France has moved toward greater state regulation of migratory flows. The present policy has favored immigration on a permanent basis for migrants of European origin, but encouraged returning home for African and North African workers (Abadan-Unat, 1984; Taguieff and Weil, 1990). In 1974 the French government halted all work migration and allowed migrants into the country for family reunification purposes only. Ironically, the policy changed what had started as a transient male worker immigration into an immigration of family settlement.

We can now turn to the core of this essay and explore the ways in which the two groups of working-class female students respectively position themselves in relation to wage labor as well as how they come to this particular positioning. Previous studies of working-class girls in school have generated a set of interesting and sometimes contradictory findings. My own data about working-class girls of French descent echo the analysis of Lois Weis in *Working-Class Without Work* (1990) and contrast with earlier studies, such as those of Angela McRobbie (1978), Jane Gaskell (1983), and Linda Valli (1986), that suggested that white working-class female students developed marginalized wage labor identities because they were secondary to their home or "domestic" identities. Indeed, most of the female students in this study have as a central goal to work and be engaged in some form of wage labor. This is true of girls of Algerian and French descent alike. My data about girls of Algerian descent also corroborate findings about "minority" female students in other societies that have pointed out that under certain circumstances these students, in contrast to their male counterparts, do not develop anti-school, anti-education subcultures (Fuller, 1980; Miles, 1984; Weis, 1985).

While wage labor is definitely a priority for most of these young women, most also conceive of their future in terms of emotional attachments, even if these are not restricted to traditional marriage arrangements. At this level there are some discrepancies between the two groups: young women of French descent are more likely to talk in terms of romantic attachments outside the traditional bond of marriage. In both groups, however, few young women spontaneously addressed the issues of emotional links, marriage, and children. While employment is certainly something that they all "see themselves" engaged in five or seven years down the road, love, romance, marriage, and motherhood take on a different importance for different young women.

Nathalie:	Well, first I'd like to have a good profession.
Monique:	[I want] the life I have now—that is my life outside school [laughter]—and a job I like!
Mireille:	I want to work to make money; that's the most important!
Danielle:	Logically, I think I'll be working.
Catherine:	In five to seven years; I'll be twenty-five! Wow! [laughter] I have no idea. But I hope that I'll have my own place. I'll be working, that is, if I find a job.
Alexandra:	I don't see myself as a homemaker, not at all. I am not someone who'll stay at home to raise my kids. I see myself dynamic, with a profession I like.
Claude:	[I'll be an] executive secretary! [laughter] No, really I don't know. A job I like, an apartment, and a car.

All these students seem to sense that in their mid-twenties they will be finished with their schooling and will be working—"that is, if [they] find a job." It is almost as if a young working-class woman in France in 1990 could not but think of her future in terms of wage labor. Danielle clearly captures the quasi-inevitability of a wage labor future for herself and her peers: "*logically*, I think I'll be working." And indeed, this is quite logical given the way in which the French labor force has become feminized within the larger restructuration of the economy since the '70s.

My data suggest, however, that a primary identification with wage labor is not necessarily antithetical to love, romance, and domesticity. Indeed, even for the students who spontaneously include domestic and emotional arrangements in their visions for the future, employment remains a key element.

Lili: I see myself working, I see myself working and living alone or with someone.

Noëlle: In five years...I'd like my life to be good, a good job that pays well. A man whom I love and who loves me...and a family.

Mirabelle: In five years I'll be working, and [I will have] found the ideal man that I'm already looking for.

Corinne: I'll have a part-time job so I can take care of my children. I want to get married but not immediately.

Among the girls of French descent Corinne is the only one to suggest that she will take up part-time employment in order to take care of her children, and Stéphanie is actually the only one who does not put her employment first when answering my question:

Stéphanie: In five years! Be with someone, I hope! [laughter] Well, and have a job, you know.

This pattern of thinking of oneself primarily as a wage earner is also present among girls of Algerian descent. Here the phenomenon is even more interesting since, for the most part, Algerian mothers were not engaged in paid employment.

Farida: Well, I'll be working. Maybe I'll have my own place, who knows? I don't want to dream too much.

Fatma: In five years, I have a job, I live alone, I have a car, and I live real close to my parents—that's it!

Aïcha: I'm not optimistic; I'll be working as a secretary. Depending on my income, I'll be living alone, with a girlfriend, or still at my parents'.

Nasma: I have no idea. But I'll be working; that I know.

Interestingly enough, young women of Algerian descent seem to be aware of the economic difficulty of living on one's own. Even though they express the desire to do so, they also mention the possibility of having to stay with their parents. This awareness might be compounded by the fact that the Algerian family, as in many other Mediterranean ethnic groups, is a close network, which manages to maintain extended links in spite of the dominance of nuclear units in the French context. Fatma's comment about wanting to stay "real close" to her parents is a sign of such adaptative strategies.

More often than among the French group, young women of Algerian descent spontaneously bring to the fore marriage along with their engagement in wage labor:

Acia: I see myself working, with my apartment, married and one child [laughter]. I hope it will work out.

Fella: I'll be working, and if I'm lucky I'll be going steady with someone.[4]

Anifa: I'd like to find myself a nice little job in a small [travel] agency or working with youth; something where I'm in contact with people...and

	then I don't know…then, perhaps the man of my life [laughter].
Abla:	In seven years I'll be a computer specialist, I'll be married, and I'll have children—in this order.
Soraya:	In five or six years…I don't know but I see myself, perhaps I'll be married, I don't know. If I'm not married yet I'll be living at home, working…but at twenty-four I'll be married, yeah, five years from now I'll be married, no problem!

Soraya is the only one among the students of Algerian descent to concentrate primarily and so heavily on marriage. In fact, she is also the only one to express her desire to quit her job in order better to take care of her children. While Soraya knows she might jeopardize her ability to work in the future, she is willing to take the chance, because she feels the double burden of wage labor and domestic work is something that might prevent her from enjoying life and might be detrimental to her children.

> Soraya: I see myself married and working, but I tell myself as soon as I have my first child I quit, but I…the problem is that if you quit your job for some time, then when you want to work again you've got to get more training because things will have changed. So I wonder whether I'll quit or keep my job, but I think I'll quit. Because you've got to choose between working or raising your kids. Because I see people, the little kids when they come back from school, they are waiting outside—the poor kids—waiting for their parents to come and get them.…I don't like that, it breaks my heart. Or else they've got to stay in childcare until 6:30; [mothers have] no time to cook meals. I don't like this kind of life. I want the time to enjoy life. We see them [these working mothers]: 6:30 childcare, 7:00 home, no time to buy bread, to go shopping. It's not the life I want for myself!

For all the others it is clear that marriage and family will have to coexist with paid labor. What is interesting here is that girls of Algerian descent are both challenging and abiding by "traditional" expectations. While they are committed to moving away from a future of domesticity and dependence (on a husband or on parents), they are also attached to traditional marital arrangements and show in this respect a certain degree of solidarity with their group of origin and in particular with their parents. This point corroborates studies conducted in France among various migrant groups (Camillieri, 1980; Charlot, 1981; Saoud, 1985, cited in Dubet, 1989).

Employment, therefore, is a primary goal for these young women regardless of their ethnic origin. But what kind of work do they envision for themselves? What is their understanding of this "secretarial work" that might await them at the end of the academic year?

ON BEING A SECRETARY

Most of these students did not choose to take secretarial training, and at the end of the two-year cycle the majority have yet to learn to like the profession for which they are being trained. Very few of them "see" themselves as secretaries. Girls of Algerian descent are more intense in their dislike for the profession and are very articulate about their reasons for it. On this topic girls of French descent do not seem to have much to say and often simply suggest that in spite of their training they aspire to do something different when they get out of school.

Catherine:	I'd like to be a stewardess, or work in the tourism industry and travel lot.
Martine:	Yeah, I like it [secretarial training], but it's not because I'm in secretarial training that I'll be a [administrative] secretary later. I'd like

	to work as a paralegal secretary in fact. I like law, I'd rather work for a law firm than for a company....I don't know, it sounds more exciting!
Monique:	No [I wouldn't like to be a secretary], not at all! At first I wanted to be a child caretaker. I hate to sit around all day doing nothing [laughter].

Martine thinks that secretarial training can lead to something "more exciting." Catherine, too, envisions something only remotely connected to secretarial work. Among the French girls, however, Monique is the only one who clearly indicates her dislike for the profession; she assumes that secretaries "sit around all day doing nothing." Female students of Algerian descent discuss secretarial work much more extensively, and many are very critical of the type of work that they would have to perform.

Soraya:	I don't see myself working as a secretary. No thank you! Perhaps as a secretary but definitely not as an administrative one...yeah, a paralegal job, why not a lawyer's secretary? But an administrative secretary, no way, that's hell!...I feel that it's the type of work that becomes really boring after a while. It's repetitive: always typing letters, correcting them, making xerox copies, sending them out...it's boring after a while.
Fatma:	Me as a secretary, no way! I don't see myself as a secretary all day long behind a desk. I want to be able to move, I want to travel!

It is in an informal collective interview that the girls of Algerian descent were most articulate about their reticence vis-à-vis the profession:

Nasma:	First, they put us in a track where we didn't want to be. They told us: "You're destined to be secretaries." But, I don't see myself as a secretary, and I'm not the only one either. Everything but a secretary, really!...I don't see myself being bossed around all the time, my boss telling me "type this, type that."...I'd much rather study accounting.
Daïla:	Or sales/business.
Fella:	Yes, business.
Interviewer:	Why accounting, why business?
Nasma:	Well, first you can move up. But a secretary will always stay a secretary. And during my internship, I remember, accountants were more independent, the boss wouldn't give them orders like he did for the secretaries....An accountant knows what he's [sic] doing, he knows his job!...
Interviewer:	What about business?
Nasma:	There are lots of opportunities right now...
Fella:	Yeah, like in sales...
Nasma:	No, not sales, not saleswoman, no way!
Fella:	I'm talking about opening your own business...

The collective and informal context of the interview in some ways allowed for more oppositional responses from individuals in the group.[5] The other interesting element of the collective interview is that girls of Algerian descent were able to formulate, through the dynamics of dialogue, the reasons for their dislike of clerical work. Through their evaluation of secretarial work we can see how clear-minded they seem to be with regard to the actual working conditions of secretaries. Their understanding seems to emerge both from common sense representations of clerical work and from their own experiences in internships. What Nasma and Fella are saying is that they don't want to become secretaries because of their lack of control over work processes: "I don't see myself being bossed around all the time, my boss telling me 'type this, type that.'" They are also very clear about their awareness of the lack of upward mobility for secretarial workers: "You can't move up." Similarly, they seem to have picked up and internalized the way in which clerical workers are perceived as "unskilled" workers: "An accountant knows what he's doing, he knows his job." It is telling, here, that Nasma refers to accountants as a counter-example. Men are much better represented in the accounting profession, and the very sex-segregation of office work has contributed to the devaluation of clerical work, in particular data entry, and helped men in offices to preserve the status of their work (Crozier, 1973; Maruani and Nicole, 1989).

While girls of Algerian descent do not offer elaborate accounts of the gender dynamics at work here, they nevertheless grasp the dead-end quality of the jobs that they are being trained for. Girls of French descent, on the other hand, seem to have developed a less acute aversion to clerical work. They seem to be able to envision "ways out" of their unglamorous future roles as overworked, underpaid, undervalued clerical workers. Instead of resenting—like girls of Algerian descent—these future roles, they seem to think that they will be able to negotiate more interesting, more exciting positions for themselves.

Michelle: I'll take the exam to become a secretary in the police department and then take the internal exam to become a police officer.
Stéphanie: I'll try to get in [the police] as a secretary and then try to take the internal exam.
Catherine: I'd like to be a stewardess, or work in the tourism industry.
Martine: I'd like to work as a paralegal secretary.

Whether it be in the police force, in paralegal work, or in the tourism industry, girls of French descent seem to want to use their degree as a stepping stone to something more valorizing than regular administrative clerical work. Girls of Algerian descent too, at times, suggest that they are thinking of different and better possibilities for themselves.

Anifa: I'd like to work in a travel agency where you are in contact with people, and I wouldn't like to stay in an office all the time. I'd like to do different tasks, move around...I don't see myself as a secretary!
Soraya: Yeah, [I'd like to have] a paralegal job, why not a lawyer's secretary?

In the case of girls of Algerian descent, the desire to occupy seemingly more rewarding positions in the labor force may clash with a more or less well articulated understanding of the structural limitations that this group of the French population faces at this point in time. I am suggesting that girls of Algerian descent develop a more oppositional relation to clerical work because somehow they know that, if they manage to find work, they can indeed get "stuck" and locked in the lower ranks of the French labor force. Djamila most clearly addressed this issue when, refusing to tell me what it was that she really wanted to do for work, she proceeded to explain what made it difficult for her to think that this much desired career was indeed a real possibility for her.

Djamila: I can't tell you [what I'd like to do in the future]. If my father or my mother were famous or rich I would have done it already...but every year that goes by there is a piece of my hope that goes down the drain and I tell myself: "No, you won't be able to do it." Because I'm not French [on paper she is], because I haven't got blue eyes, because I'm not blond, because my parents aren't rich, because I'm studying for a pitiful BEP, and because I will have lost so many years anyway. This job, see, it's for certain people and it's mostly done by men. It's for the privileged and the winners. You see very few women doing it.

In a more prosaic way, Laïla echoed Djamila's awareness of structural limitations linked to asymmetric racial relations in France when she said to me:

Laïla: As far as work is concerned, a boss will hire a French woman more easily than a migrant. I have [female] cousins who have been telling

me about all this; they have a hard time finding work. One of them did
not get a job because they hired a French woman instead.

Given the more limiting structural boundaries for girls of Algerian descent, it is not
surprising that the group of students I interviewed seemed to have developed, to a greater
degree than girls of French descent, a contradictory relationship to secretarial work.
While girls of French descent might be able to entertain some hope of landing "better"
jobs for themselves, the sharp awareness of girls of Algerian descent of the structure of
opportunities in France makes it very difficult for them to think that they might be able
to do something else in the future. As a result, they seem to dislike the idea even more
than their schoolmates of French descent.

French sociologists Anni Borzeix and Margaret Maruani insist on the necessity to
distinguish between employment and work:

> or, more specifically the relation a person has to each of these. The relation to work
> refers to the ways that individuals experience their jobs, especially how they react to
> the conditions under which they have been hired and actually work. This relation
> involves wages, authority relations, promotions, qualifications and working
> conditions, among other things. The relation to employment, on the other hand,
> involves access to the labor market and to jobs. It refers not only to oppositions such
> as working/non-working, employed/non-employed or precarious/steady
> employment, but also to the opinions, attitudes, and behaviors that a person adopts
> when losing a job or looking for one. (1988, p. 253)

In light of these remarks, it is clear that while girls of Algerian descent (and in a different
form girls of French descent) express their dislike for their future of clerical work, they by
no means suggest that they refuse to be employed or that wage labor is only a secondary
goal. On the contrary, in spite of their awareness of the alienation of wage labor, they are
quite clear about the importance of having access to some form of employment for
themselves and other women. For many of these young women this understanding is
deeply connected to their self-positioning vis-à-vis men, love, and domestic arrangements.

ON MARRIAGE, ROMANCE, DOMESTICITY, AND WAGE LABOR

This is the point of juncture between the public and the private for these young women.
Indeed, for the most part they see employment as a way to maintain some independence
and some control over their domestic life. Girls of French descent often indicate a vivid
awareness that employment will provide them some financial autonomy which in turn
will allow them to "stand on their own," something that, in their eyes, their mothers have
often failed to accomplish. Quotes that follow are answers to my probing on the issue of
marriage or to the question "Do you think your life will be different from that of your
mother, and how?"

Catherine: Yeah [I want to get married], and I want children too. But I want to
              keep working because I want to be independent. Because I'll do what I
              want with my money....If I need some I won't have to ask.

Martine: I'll be married, yes. But of course, I'll work, and I'll have one child. But
              I'll keep working. Marriage is important for my mother, otherwise
              marriage for me is just a formality, that's all. But I won't stay at home,
              cleaning the house and raising the kids. That's what my mom did and I
              don't want to do like her. I'll work, I'll raise my kid. I can do both. I
              won't stay in the house, no way!

Stéphanie: Oh yes, it's going to be different from [my mother's life]. Well, first I'm
              going to have the job I want and I'll be able to stand on my own.

Alexandra: No [I don't see myself married], not necessarily.
Interviewer: What about children?
Alexandra: No, not yet. Before I have children I prefer to have a stable position so I
                can give them a decent life.
Michelle: [In the future I see myself] with a job, an apartment and a child.
Interviewer: Do you see yourself married?
Michelle: No, a man is not indispensable. In life they come and go. I don't mind
                having different relationships. As long as I make a good living.

It should be noted here that French law allows "domestic partners" some of the privileges of married couples. In the recent past many young couples who do not want a "lifetime" commitment have opted for this alternative.

When we turn to girls of Algerian descent, the situation seems to be slightly different. On the one hand they don't seem to reject the notion of marriage as widely. When some of them do, they seem to think of employment as a way to gain greater freedom within their lives as well as a means better to control the very process of getting married.

Farida: [I'll be] working. Perhaps living in a place of my own.
Interviewer: What about marriage?
Farida: See, I consider myself Algerian, but I don't have the mentality, I don't
                have…For them—I call them "Arabs" [laughter]—for the Arabs in
                general, as soon as the girl is eighteen she's got to think about
                marriage, immediately! But not for me! For me it's freedom first. For
                me studies come first, employment comes first. And I'm definitely not
                getting married now.
Nasma: I'll be working…maybe I'll still be at my mother's. But when I start
                giving her money she'll leave me alone; I'll be freer.
Aïcha: I'll work. It depends on how much I'll be making; maybe I'll live alone
                or with a girlfriend. If I don't make enough money I'll live with my
                folks. But I'll have more freedom.
Interviewer: Do you see yourself married?
Aïcha: No, not even if my mother imposes this idea on me. No, I don't want
                to depend on my husband. I depend on my parents already—that's
                enough. My sister did not get married. My sister managed to be lucky.
                She got a *baccalauréat* and a Certificate of Specialized Technician in
                administration. I don't know really what my parents think, but I feel
                that when I am twenty-five I won't be ready to live with a man. I want
                to enjoy life when it's possible. So far I haven't enjoyed life. I have yet
                to know many things. With a job I'll be able to live my life.
Fatma: I don't see myself married. Having children, yes, but not married. I
                know it's against my religion, but I would like that.

While these four young women clearly indicate that they'd rather avoid getting married, for most of the others marriage does not seem to be such a big issue, even if they have to postpone it for a little while in order to enjoy life.

Soraya: I see myself married and working.
Acia: I see myself working, with an apartment, married with a child. I hope
                it comes through.
Abla: In seven years I'll be a computer specialist, I'll be married, and I'll have
                kids. In this order. I'll keep working though, even with children,
                because I love to work.
Fella: I think that if I weren't married I'd still be with my parents. But I'd like
                to have two kids, be married and keep working.
Anifa: [Working] and, I don't know, maybe the man of my life [laughter],

both things at the same time, I hope. But I don't see myself married yet. Not at all, because I see myself going out every weekend with friends, as a group, see, travel, see.

Daïla: I don't know, I'll enjoy life to the max…maybe [I'll be] with someone.

Interviewer: Married?

Daïla: No, not at twenty-three, I'd rather wait a little.

Interviewer: Do you mean living with someone?

Daïla: No, just a boyfriend…because we, the Muslims, have got principles. No, I'd like to do it right [and get married later].

Among working-class girls of Algerian descent, community, religious, and parental pressures are fairly strong with regard to what is possible in terms of domestic arrangements. In this respect, seeing oneself married might be perceived as the "right" thing to do. It is interesting to note here that these young women are thinking of having few children in comparison to their mothers. Controlling that aspect of their life seems to be important to these young women and indicates, on their part, a selective appropriation of French mores and values.

Let us digress a little and explore how the two different groups of women relate to romance and how this might interfere with their visions for the future. Girls of French descent seem to be pulled into an ideology of romance to a degree that is not visible among girls of Algerian descent. Most of them have boyfriends, around whom they often construct their leisure time. One girl of French descent dropped out in the middle of the second trimester because she "fell in love" with a young man; another came to me and explained that she thought she might be pregnant and how that might alter her educational plans for the future; yet another told me she would quit school at the end of the year to move in with her boyfriend. However, because of personal experiences—mostly the lives of their mothers—their idea of romantic attachments, and of marriage in particular, has lost some of its luster.

Catherine: Yeah, I'd like to get married, but when I'm still young, and I want kids too. But ideally I'd like one kid and no husband…maybe it's because I am myself a child of divorced parents and I've seen my mom. I don't see myself with a husband, I don't see myself being bothered by a husband.

Alexandra: Maybe I'll be luckier than [my mother]. I saw how she lived her life and that taught me a lesson. My parents were divorced, so that's something. Before you get married you think because you've seen how your parents didn't get along, got divorced and all that, so.…It's not always easy, so you think twice, see, I don't know.

Aurore: Yes, [my life] will be different [from that of my mother]. Especially as far as my love life is concerned. My parents got married because they were kind of forced to. It was a marriage of reason not of love.… They've been together for seventeen years, and at night it's, "Good evening. What's for supper?" [My father] never thinks that they can do something fun together…they never talk, they never go out.

Noëlle: My mom never enjoyed life; she was eighteen when she got pregnant.…She's very submissive, she never enjoyed life, she never went out, she never did anything, she always stayed at home; she says that she was never free, she has regrets now.…I don't want to be a submissive wife. That's it; I've seen scenes [between my parents], things that happened.

Mirabelle: I'm afraid of my father. He never hit me, but I've witnessed scenes between my parents…Okay, in couples there are often arguments…but not to the point of sticking a knife under my mother's throat. Although that only happens when he's smashed for Christmas

> or weddings....I'm afraid to meet somebody who hits me because he feels like it. My mom, she tells me everything. Yeah, it's difficult to find the man of your life.

While Mirabelle's experience seems to be extreme, the existence of problems—and in some cases of domestic violence—in the homes of the students of French descent I interviewed might explain their doubts about love and romance. However, at another point in the interview Mirabelle suggested that romance was nevertheless something she was hoping to find.

> Mirabelle: [I'd like] to find the ideal man that I am looking for now. A warm man who'd be here when I need him and who'd understand me.

Like Mirabelle, other young women who suggested that marriage could result in unpleasant situations nevertheless voiced their desire to be involved with men outside the bonds of matrimony.

> Lili: I see myself working, living alone or with someone, but what I would really like is to travel...visit a lot of countries and be free to do what I want.
> Interviewer: Married?
> Lili: Yes, I would like it. But not really because I can end up with someone who is nasty, who beats me up, who can become mean. Sometimes it's better not to get married.
> Mireille: I want to work and make money, that's the most important, and live with my boyfriend, and have fun. I want to succeed where my mother has failed.
> Interviewer: Married?
> Mireille: No, I'm against marriage. When you are young...you never know what might happen.

Mireille, who explained at great length how her mother had failed in her professional and emotional life, seems to equate marriage with formal ties that sometimes lock women in unhappy relationships.

> Mireille: As far as love is concerned, until now my mom has failed on everything. She never loved her first husband; that marriage was mostly a way to escape her own mother and her older brother. Then she met my father, but thank god they didn't get married...they had lots of problems. I always told myself, "It won't happen to me."

While remaining unmarried obviously does not solve all problems, it is clear that these young women prefer to maintain a high level of independence both by securing employment for themselves and by loosening their emotional bonds.

Girls of Algerian descent seem not to share such mixed feelings. In fact they seem to have less access to notions of idealized heterosexual pairings, because in their communities and families marriage is still separate at some level from "romance" and because romance outside of wedlock is highly problematical. Moreover, marriage is often used and perceived as a form of punishment. In this context, and in spite of the romanticization of heterosexual pairing in France, marriage, love, and romance cannot be simply seen as desirable. Because the girls of Algerian descent I interviewed were not, for the most part, in total conflict with their families and their expectations, they often opted to postpone marriage—perhaps as a way to choose their partner—through education and employment, but did not reject marriage as a whole.

> Soraya: I've got girlfriends who went back to Algeria. We still write and they tell me their miseries. One of them got married there....Her parents

had something to do with it, but she said she wanted it too. If she hadn't married she wouldn't have been able to do what she wanted. Among Muslims it's like...if you want to go out, to do what you haven't done when you were younger, you've got to marry. If your husband doesn't let you go out then that's too bad!

Interviewer:	What about here?
Soraya:	Here you've got to tell stories to your parents, you've got to lie. But here it's less dangerous. There everybody knows you, everybody talks, everything is dangerous.
Interviewer:	What happens when you get caught?
Soraya:	Marriage! Immediately, you've got to get her married, that's the only solution, to get her in a safe place.
Fatma:	My sister Fouad got into trouble, so my parents had to react.
Interviewer:	What do you mean by "got into trouble"?
Fatma:	Well, boys and drugs. She wasn't going to school any longer...and she kept running away....They had to react.
Interviewer:	How did they react?
Fatma:	They sent her back to Algeria to my father's father.
Interviewer:	Did she agree to go?
Fatma:	No, of course not! She didn't want to go, she ran away and all that. But finally she left for Algeria and she got married there.
Interviewer:	Did she want to?
Fatma:	No, she didn't, it [the marriage] was an escape.

Marriage for Fatma's sister is an escape because the alternative would be to stay at her grandfather's. Marriage, in a limited sense, holds the hope of a future of adulthood for these young women. Both testimonies show the ways in which marriage is constructed within the Algerian community in France. Even though such pressures are loosening because some young women have managed to gain greater control over this whole process, for some of the students I interviewed this lack of "freedom" was a great source of anxiety and anger. Djamila, the most rebellious of all the young women I interviewed, is a case in point.

Djamila:	I don't know if my mother really knows what love is all about. She married my father without loving him, she had twelve children with a man she didn't love. She tells us, "You know love isn't all in life; you learn to love someone." This is absolutely wrong....I don't think you can learn to love somebody who gives you orders, I really don't think so. Because the Muslim man can do what he likes at home. He can shut you up, he can tell you "do this, do that," and you can't say anything....My mom, she has one thing on her mind; she is obsessed by marriage! She is running our lives, she really is. First marriage for her daughters and then for her sons.

Djamila articulates very clearly what seems at stake here for several of the students of Algerian descent: staying in school is a way to push certain boundaries in a way that is acceptable and legitimate within the Algerian community.

Djamila:	As women we know that we are studying and that after we're going to get married; so why not spend our life studying if we feel like we need it, if we desire it.

What emerges from these interviews is that for girls of Algerian descent marriage is difficult to avoid and that, within this particular set of constraints due to the organization of patriarchal relations within the Algerian community in France, young women are trying to create conditions enabling them better to control this part of their life. In this context, schooling and employment become central.

Some of these young women's willingness to work within a set of precise expectations cannot be seen as mere acceptance of "traditional" roles but must also be read as a subtle understanding that romance and sexual freedom are not the be-all-and-end-all of women's lives and that seemingly freer (Western) patriarchal structures do not necessarily always work to the advantage of women. Young women of Algerian descent have different takes on this issue.

> Fella: I see how some of my friends are with their boyfriends…it does not appeal to me. See, I think it's kind of stupid to go out with someone for a week, two weeks. See, I don't like it. I think it's kind of stupid.
>
> Abla: I will marry a Muslim mostly for the family, but for me too. I wouldn't want to bring shame to my family. But even me in my head I prefer [to marry] a Kabyle [Berber people of Algeria], because at least I won't have any problems and they respect women. With French men after a year or so the woman gets dropped and she can get lost.
>
> Djamila: Some French girls, when they talk about their boyfriend, they say, "my man is everything to me. If he were to drop me I'd kill myself." We don't say that.…We know it's not everything…we don't trust men.

Abla seems to find "traditional" arrangements safer for women; she perceives French men as not loyal and likely to divorce their wife early after marriage. Fella and Djamila simply seem to be very cautious about emotional ties with men. In different ways these young women are showing that they have not simply internalized the Western ideology of romance. In a slightly different way, girls of French descent seem to have been disillusioned by romance while hoping to be in a better position than their mothers in terms of their own romantic life.

Girls of Algerian descent have not embraced the ideology of romance to the same extent as their schoolmates of French descent because it is simply not directly available to them. Marriage, as we have seen, is still often constructed as punishment and reprisal against a woman who has trespassed gender-defined boundaries. Romance is often perceived as dangerous and out of reach. This particular situation might have enabled young women of Algerian descent to think of their futures more in terms of their own achievements rather than in terms of romantic pursuit. Both groups, however, seem to think that education will bring some independence in their domestic life.

ON EDUCATION AND SCHOOLING: CONCLUDING REMARKS

> Danielle: Yes, school is useful because we're going to use it in our job.
>
> Lili: Computer, accounting, secretarial training—I'll use all this in the future.
>
> Martine: Anyway you've got to go to school, if you don't go to classes you don't get a diploma and then what do you do in the future?
>
> Corinne: I study because I know I'll need it [for a job], but in fact it doesn't interest me.

While girls of French descent value their schooling primarily because it will allow them to work, girls of Algerian descent also put some value on the noneconomic outcomes of their education.

> Djamila: You can criticize school all you want, but at the end of the day that's where you learn a lot. Okay, there's TV, but with your parents…even among the French they don't talk about certain things like menstru-

	ation, drugs, etc. Okay, I'm not saying that teachers talk easily about all this, but at school you can know more and the contact with your schoolmates teaches you a lot.
Aïcha:	We learn our rights, not to let others step on us…to live in society like a civilized person.
Fella:	I tell myself if I've had the opportunity to go to school I deserve a good life.
Nasma:	I always wanted to keep the pen. I don't want to lose those skills…in order to keep up because if you don't keep the pen you're apart…yeah, apart from the rest of the world. It's important, if you don't express yourself well they don't consider you…you're underpaid, forgotten. Nobody will listen to you, see!
Anifa:	I want to succeed in school, I hope it will bring me independence.…I also want to be able to help my children [with school work], because my parents were workers and they couldn't help us.
Soraya:	They put something in your head. It's important to have some culture, not to come out stupid. When I was five or six the social security person yelled at my father—it struck me, see. This woman was talking to my father in a mean way because, then, he didn't speak French very well. When the phone rings at home I don't let my father answer, I answer myself. I don't want the same thing to happen to me.

The difference in the way each group values education and school knowledge must be understood here against specific sets of social relations that have shaped and are shaping the lived reality of different subsets of the French working-class.

Working-class girls of French descent value school knowledge primarily because they think it will provide them greater economic autonomy in their adult life and because they have understood that they cannot dispense with a future of wage labor. With the feminization and the tertiarization of the French labor force, young working-class women with vocational degrees can hope to occupy positions in the growing service sector of the economy. Moreover, the changing nature of household arrangements and the growing awareness within the working class that women cannot rely on men to bring home a "family wage," combined with young women's desire to "stand on their own," has made wage labor and education a priority for working-class female students of French descent.[6]

Girls of Algerian descent value education for the same reasons, but they also have inherited from their parents a great respect for education. While the notion of "voluntary" migration posed by Ogbu (1988) cannot totally apply to the experience of Algerians in France, it is clear here that Algerian parents broke away from their original milieu in order to open up possibilities for themselves and their children.[7] The colonial and postcolonial destruction of the Algerian economy did not leave many "choices" to impoverished North African rural dwellers, and their migration cannot be viewed simply in terms of voluntary action. However, many Algerians who initially had come to France on a temporary basis eventually brought their families and settled in France. It has been suggested that their strong investment in education is a clear continuation of their migrant trajectory (Charlot, 1990). In the context of the economic crisis in France and the shrinking number of low-skilled jobs, usually allocated to the migrant population, children of migrant parents are increasingly seeking qualification and schooling at a time when French society itself is making efforts to raise the educational level of the population at large. The increase of low-skilled jobs in the service sector of the economy at the expense of traditional industrial jobs might also work to the advantage of young women of migrant parentage.

The changing nature of the non-European migrant population in France from a single-male-transient-worker to a settled-family type of immigration has also generated increased feelings of racism and xenophobia. The experience and the mounting threat of racism that lie at the core of the lived reality of Algerian youth in France make it quite crucial to become—to feel—integrated in French society. In this context education again emerges as a key tool. Where girls are concerned, this is compounded by the sense that French society might allow greater opportunities for women and looser boundaries within which they can hope better to control their personal lives. School, then, is not simply the place to get credentials, but also becomes the avenue through which to gain access to full-fledged citizenship and a means to increase one's independence as a woman.

The comparative nature of this essay has enabled me to analyze the ways in which the construction of class and gender identities at Lurçat are deeply shaped by ethnic/racial forces. Farida and Alexandra share many similar experiences, and yet their lived realities and the ways in which they negotiate them are clearly mediated by different structural and discursive boundaries. While both of them are interpreting, challenging, and displacing common sense ideas (as well as practices) about women, women's work, and women's roles in society, they do so from different social locations and from differing understandings of these locations. Women's identities are multifaceted and fluid; this essay begins to explore the complex ways in which these identities are mediated by the social, cultural, and discursive contexts to which these young women have access.[8]

NOTES

1 According to the school statistics, about fifty percent of the students enrolled in these short vocational tracks transfer to *baccalauréat* streams.

2 In spite of a remarkable broadening of the social base of the French educational system since World War II, educational outcomes are still widely unequal. It has been documented that, at the beginning of the '80s, out of 100 children starting in the sixth grade; fourteen would leave junior high school with no diplomas; forty-six would go into secondary short vocational tracks, with only half obtaining a diploma at the end of the cycle; and forty would go into long academic tracks, of whom less than twenty-six would pass the competitive *baccalauréat* enabling them to go on to higher education (Boulot and Boyzon-Fradet, 1988, p. 138). Needless to say, working-class youth and students of migrant parentage are systematically overrepresented in short vocational tracks. Girls, regardless of class and ethnic/racial background, are slightly underrepresented in them. However, it is interesting to point out for this study that in 1983 the proportion of female students was slightly above nine percent in industrial vocational tracks, while they represented more than eighty percent of the short tertiary tracks.

3 Since the '70s unemployment rates have been systematically higher for migrants than for nationals. In 1979 when 5.6 percent of the French workers were unemployed, 9.8 percent of migrant workers were out of work; in 1983 the figures were respectively 8.1 percent and 11.7 percent (Noiriel, 1990, p. 225). Needless to say, these unemployment rates have been harsher for women. In 1982, among the Algerian population, 18.3 percent of the male workers were unemployed, while 45.1 percent of the female workers were jobless (Lebon, 1985).

4 It is clear that the girls of Algerian descent who I interviewed do not envision themselves living with a man outside of wedlock. When they say "being with someone" or "going steady" they don't mean living with their lover, or even being sexual with their boyfriend.

5 Unfortunately, mostly because girls of French descent tended to hang out in pairs rather than larger groups, I do not have similar data (from collective interviews) for both groups of students.

6 While beyond the scope of this particular essay, it is clear here that these changes are also due to the counter-hegemonic influence of feminist discourses in France.

7 John Ogbu differentiates between castelike minorities that have been integrated into "host" societies on an involuntary basis and immigrant (voluntary) minorities who have opted of their own choice to enter and settle within the "host" societies. Algerians and their children in France, I

would argue, combine "caste-like" and "voluntary" characteristics because of the postcolonial context of the Algerian immigration.

8 For the theoretical underpinnings of these observations I am particularly indebted to the work of Teresa de Lauretis (1984) and Linda Alcoff (1988).

REFERENCES

Abadan-Unat, N. (1984). International labour migration and its effects upon women's occupation and family roles: A Turkish view. In UNESCO, *Women on the Move.* Paris: UNESCO.

Alcoff, L. (1988). Cultural feminism versus post-structuralism: The identity crisis in feminist theory. *Signs*, 13 (3), 405–437.

Borzeix, A. & Maruani, M. (1988). When a strike comes marching home. In J. Jenson, E. Hagen, & C. Reddy (eds.), *Feminization of the Labor Force: Paradoxes and promises.* New York: Oxford UP.

Boulot, S. & Boyzon-Fradet, D. (1988). *Les immigrés et l'ecole: Une course d'obstacles.* Paris: L'Harmattan et CIEMI.

Camillieri, C. (1980). Les immigrés Maghrébins de la seconde génération: Contribution à une étude de leurs évolutions et de leurs choix culturels. In *Bulletin de Psychologie*, 347, 985–995.

Charlot, M. (1981). The education of immigrant children in France. In J. Bhatnagar (ed.), *Educating Immigrants.* London: St. Martin's.

Charlot, B. (1988). Les Familles immigrées entre certitudes et doutes. *Migrants-Formation*, 75, 38–43.

_____. (1990, June). Penser l'échec comme événement, penser l'immigration comme histoire. *Migrants-Formation*, 81, 8–24.

Charlot, B. & Figeat, M. (1985). *Histoire de la Formation des Ouvriers: 1789–1985.* Paris: Minerve.

Crozier, M. ([1965]1973). *The World of the Office Worker.* (D. Landau, Trans.). New York: Schocken.

de Lauretis, Teresa. (1984). *Alice Doesn't: Feminism, semiotics, cinema.* Bloomington: Indiana UP.

Dubet, F. (1989). *Immigrations: Qu'en savons nous?* Paris: La Documentation Française.

Fuller, M. (1980). Black girls in a London comprehensive school. In R. Deem (ed.), *Schooling for Women's Work.* London: Routledge.

Gaskell, J. (1983). The reproduction of family life: Perspectives of male and female adolescents. In *British Journal of Sociology of Education*, 4(1), 19–38.

Jenson, J., Hagen, E., & Reddy, C. (eds.). (1988). *Feminization of the Labor Force: Paradoxes and promises.* New York: Oxford UP.

Lebon, A. (1985). Second generation foreigners in France. In R. Rogers (ed.), *Guests Come to Stay.* London: Westview.

Lipietz, A. (1990). Après Fordisme et démocratie. *Les Temps Modernes*, 524, 97–121.

Maruani, M., & Nicole, C. (1989). *Au labeur des dames: Métiers masculins, emplois féminins.* Paris: Syros Alternatives.

McRobbie, A. (1978). Working-class girls and the culture of femininity. In Women's Studies Group, Centre for Contemporary Cultural Studies (ed.), *Women Take Issue: Aspects of women's subordination.* London: Hutchinson.

Miles, S. (1984). Asian girls and the transition from school to...? In S. Ball (ed.), *Comprehensive Schooling: A reader.* Bristol: Falmer.

Noiriel, G. (1990). *Le Creuset Français: Histoire de l'immigration XIX–XX siècle.* Paris: Seuil. *Workers of French Society in the Nineteenth and Twentieth Centuries.* (H. McPhail, Trans.). New York: St. Martin.

Ogbu, J. (1988). Class stratification, racial stratification, and schooling. In L. Weis (ed.), *Class, Race and Gender in American Education.* Albany: State U of New York P.

Raissiguier, C. (forthcoming). *Becoming Women/Becoming Workers: Identity Formation in a French Vocational School.* New York: SUNY.

Taguieff, P.-A., & Weil, P. (1990). "Immigration," fait national et "citoyenneté," *Esprit*, 161, 87–102.

Valli, L. (1986). *Becoming Clerical Workers.* Boston: Routledge.

Weis, L. (1985). *Between Two Worlds: Black students in an urban community college.* London: Routledge.

_____. (1988). High school girls in a de-industrializing economy. In L. Weis (ed.), *Class, Race and Gender in American Education.* Albany: State U. of New York P.

_____. (1990). *Working-class Without Work: High school students in a de-industrializing economy.* New York: Routledge.

12   How White Teachers Construct Race

Christine E. Sleeter

In the education literature one finds frequent reference to the fact that the teaching population in the U.S. is becoming increasingly white while the student population becomes increasingly racially diverse. The significance of teacher race is usually framed in terms of the degree to which a white teaching force is appropriate for students of color. For example, educators discuss teachers' expectations for and interactions with children of color (Aaron and Powell, 1982; Irvine, 1991; Simpson and Erickson, 1983), teachers as role models (Baez and Clarke, 1990), and the gap between the cultures of the community and the classroom (Metz, 1990; Tewell and Trubowitz, 1987). One can read most discussions of teacher race as tacitly assuming that the system of education is basically as it should be but that it functions most effectively when there is cultural congruence between teachers and students. To help address issues related to congruence between students and teachers, some educators strongly advocate recruiting more teachers of color (Contreras and Engelhardt, 1991; Haberman, 1989; Justiz and Kameen, 1988).

Many educators concentrate on the need to make teacher-education course work critical and multicultural, without specifically interrogating the racial identities of a predominantly white teaching force (Lee, 1989; Liston and Zeichner, 1990; Shor, 1986). In such discussions congruence between teachers and students of color is less an issue than is the orientation toward social justice issues that teachers bring, an orientation that presumably can be cultivated in anyone regardless of race.

In this chapter I will argue that it is terribly inadequate to address racism in education primarily by trying to educate white teachers. Teacher race *does* matter, and for reasons that include and extend beyond issues of cultural congruence in the classroom. I locate this chapter within a body of literature that examines how schools reproduce structures of inequality and oppression and that advocates schools undergo fundamental restructuring for all students (see, for example, Banks and Banks, 1989; Cummins, 1986; Grant and Sleeter, 1986; Nieto, 1992; Oakes, 1985; Sleeter and Grant, 1988). I will argue that teachers bring to the profession perspectives about what race means, which they construct mainly on the basis of their life experiences and vested interests. I will examine specifically perspectives of teachers of European descent in order to argue that a predominantly white teaching force in a racist and multicultural society is not good for anyone, if we wish to have schools reverse rather than reproduce racism.

Theoretical Perspectives about Racism

To "solve" racism by educating whites is to locate racism mainly in biased individual actions, which in turn are assumed to stem from ideas and assumptions in people's heads: prejudiced attitudes, stereotypes, and lack of information about people of color. A psychological view of racism assumes that if we can change and develop what is in the heads of white people, they in turn will create significant changes in institutions. Viewing racism as prejudice and misperception assumes "that racist attitudes are very rarely rational. Even in those cases where the attitudes are regarded as rational, they are not considered to be in the interests of the person expressing them" (Wellman, 1977, p. 14). Prejudice and misperception can be corrected by providing information. With more information, white people will abandon racist ideas and behaviors and (presumably) work to eliminate racism.

Educational approaches to addressing racism usually adopt this theoretical perspective. However, educators who try to teach white people about racism often experience tenacious resistance. For example, based on a study of twenty-three white preservice students who experienced intensive course work that involved both instruction about concepts and issues related to multicultural education and over 100 hours of experience with low-income minority children in schools, Haberman and Post observed "the remarkable phenomenon of students generally using these direct experiences to selectively perceive and reinforce their initial preconceptions" (1992, p. 30). Teacher education reinforced, rather than reconstructed, how the white students viewed children of color. Results of other studies of preservice and in-service education about multicultural teaching are only slightly more encouraging. While some studies find white students' attitudes to improve somewhat immediately after receiving instruction, studies do not report lasting changes in whites' perspectives and/or behavior patterns (e.g., Baker, 1977; Bennett, 1979; Grant, 1981; Redman, 1977; Washington, 1981).

By contrast, a structural analysis views racism not as misperception but as a structural arrangement among racial groups. Racist institutions, according to Frederickson, are controlled by whites, who restrict the access of nonwhites to "power and privileges" (1981, p. 240), in order to retain and regulate "a reservoir of cheap and coercible labor for the rest of the country" (p. 245). While a psychological analysis of racism focuses on what is in people's heads and asks how to change it, a structural analysis focuses on distribution of power and wealth across groups and on how those of European ancestry attempt to retain supremacy while groups of color try to challenge it. A structural analysis assumes that how white people view race rests on their vested interest in justifying their power and privileges. White people's common sense understandings of race "are ideological defenses of the interests and privileges that stem from white people's position in a structure based in part on racial inequality" (Wellman, 1977, p. 37).

A structural analysis of racism suggests that education will not produce less racist institutions as long as white people control them. As Beverly Gordon has argued, expecting white educators to reconstruct racist institutions ignores the fact that they face

> the sticky dilemma of attempting to educate the masses in a way that allows them accessibility to high status knowledge and places them on an equal footing to compete. Most assuredly in time, they will compete with our children and ostensibly with us for a share of the power and the reallocation of resources. And while most people do have good intentions, when our social status is threatened, we tend to become even more conservative in order to protect our material gains. (1985, p. 37)

In what follows, I will discuss data from a study of a staff development program to illustrate how white teachers process education about race. I will argue that it is important to educate white people as well as people of color about racism, but not with the assumption that white people on their own will then reconstruct racist institutions. As a white teacher educator, I do not believe most of us will do that. After discussing how white teachers construct race, I will then attempt to refocus discussion about the implications of the "whitening" of the teaching force and the role of teacher education.

A STUDY OF TEACHERS

In 1987 a colleague and I secured funding to offer what became a voluntary two-year staff development project for thirty teachers in schools in which at least one-third of the students were from low-income or racial minority (mostly African American or Latino) families. Twenty-six of the teachers were Euroamerican, three were African American, and one was Mexican American. They taught in grade levels ranging from preschool through high school (most taught grades one–six); seven taught special education, two taught English as a second language, and the rest taught in the general education program.

The teachers attended nine all-day staff development sessions during the first year of the study and five sessions during the second year. The sessions were conducted by a series of outside consultants and addressed a variety of topics such as demographic changes, culture and learning style, curriculum, working with parents, and cooperative learning. My main role was to conduct classroom observations and interviews with the teachers over the two-year period to find out what they were learning, what sense they were making of the sessions, and how they were relating the material to their teaching and their understanding of their students. The staff development sessions, research methods, and findings are described in detail elsewhere (Sleeter, 1992).

The teachers taught in two contiguous school districts located in two small cities in the Rust Belt that had developed as industrial manufacturing centers. Both cities—New Denmark and Gelegenheit (pseudonyms)—were established in the mid-1880s, when "Old Immigrants" from northern and western Europe and the British Isles, as well as Yankees from New England, came to the area to better their lives, in the process pushing Native people off the land. In the early 1900s a second wave of "New Immigrants" from southern and eastern Europe were encouraged to come to the area to work as industrial laborers. Throughout most of the 1900s descendants of the second wave of immigrants engaged in various forms of conflict with descendants of "Old Immigrants"; for example, they unionized; they combated prejudice and disdain in the community; and they created community organizations to resist attempts to "Americanize" them (Buenker, 1976; 1977). Many teachers in the community were descendants of both waves of immigrants and could draw on their own family histories to understand how mobility is achieved in the U.S.

Although small numbers of African Americans and Mexican Americans had lived in the communities since the 1800s, these groups did not begin to grow significantly until the 1960s. By the late 1980s New Denmark's population was about eighteen percent African American and eight percent Latino, and Gelegenheit's was about six percent African American and six percent Latino, both minority groups growing much more rapidly than the white population. To most residents, African Americans and Mexican Americans were simply the latest (and not too welcome) newcomers in a series of immigrant groups and would have to engage in the same process of self-help, assimilation, and perseverance that previous groups had experienced.

New Denmark School District had instituted a school desegregation plan in the mid-1970s, accompanied by a series of multicultural education workshops; Gelegenheit School District had not begun to do this. On various indicators, African American and Latino students were experiencing large problems in the schools. For example, in New Denmark a series of newspaper articles (published after the conclusion of this study) reported that white students in one of the cities received a progressively disproportionate share of the "A" grades, from eighty-seven percent in the sixth grade to ninety-one percent in the twelfth (students in the district were sixty-nine percent white). By then "the percentage of Hispanic and Black students who received four or more D's and F's remained above sixty percent. For majority [white] students, that rate was thirty percent" (Taylor, 1990, p. 5A). However, neither district engaged in much open discussion about this kind of racial problem, even after the series of articles was published.

The dominant discourse around issues of race during the late 1980s was quite conservative. Nationally the media stressed the United States' loss of undisputed world hegemony. Schools were blamed for being too lax and spreading a "rising tide of mediocrity" (National Commission on Excellence in Education, 1983). News magazines and news programs discussed the most recent immigrants, suggesting that racial and cultural diversity posed new problems for the U.S.; most of the discussion centered around trying to identify what we have in common in order to promote national unity (see, for example, Henry, 1990). The media frequently connected African Americans and Latinos with social problems that many Americans regarded as the result of moral depravity: drug use, teen pregnancy, and unemployment. Asian Americans were hailed as the "model minority," portrayed as achieving success in the U.S. through hard work and family cohesiveness (Suzuki, 1989), following the same route to success that many whites believed their ancestors had followed. Most school reforms that were discussed emphasized raising standards and requiring students to work harder, and the "at risk" discourse emerged to describe those who were falling behind (who were mainly children of color and children from low-income backgrounds). In New Denmark and Gelegenheit School Districts, problems students of color faced in schools were generally conceptualized through a cultural-deficiency perspective in which the main causes of their difficulties were located in their homes and communities (such as parental attitudes, gang influence, and "deficient" language skills), and supplementary programs were provided to remedy presumed deficiencies.

As David Wellman (1977) has discussed, a paradox of white consciousness is the ability not to see what is very salient: the visible markers of social categories that privilege people of European ancestry. Racial boundaries and racial privileges, highly visible and ubiquitous in the U.S., were becoming increasingly so in New Denmark and Gelegenheit. One had only to turn on the TV or drive through the community to see people of European ancestry dominating mainstream institutions and the most desirable resources, while people of non-European ancestries were clustered and compartmentalized into the least desirable spaces and rendered through media as either invisible or satisfied with or deserving of their lot. White people usually seek to explain persistent racial inequality in a way that does not implicate white society. In this chapter, I will focus on how the twenty-six white teachers viewed race.

RACE = EUROPEAN ETHNICITY

Most of the white teachers in the program interpreted race and multicultural education through the European ethnic experience. As Michael Omi and Howard Winant explain,

> ethnicity theory assigned to blacks and other racial minority groups the roles which earlier generations of European immigrants had played in the great waves of the "Atlantic migration" of the nineteenth and early twentieth centuries. (1986, p. 20)

Ethnicity theory holds that the social system is open and that individual mobility can be attained through hard work. Over time, ethnic ancestry will disappear as a determinant of life chances.

Equating race with European ethnicity provided white teachers with a way to explain mobility in U.S. institutions. A few made direct reference to their own ethnic backgrounds; for example, a daughter of Italian immigrants commented,

> One of my pet peeves, that I know if you want to work, you can work....I know what my father did when he was in need,...and we didn't have the free lunches and we didn't have the clothes that other kids wore. (Teacher interview, Dec. 15, 1987)

I asked twenty-two of the white teachers about their fathers' occupations: four fathers had held jobs that normally require college education, two had owned small businesses, and the other sixteen had worked as laborers of various sorts. The teachers had attained upward mobility by earning college degrees and becoming teachers; their own families' life experiences had taught them that mobility is attainable, but not necessarily easy.

Ethnicity theory denies the significance of visible, physiological marks of ancestry and of the history of colonization and harsh subjugation that Europeans and Euroamericans extended over other peoples (Omi and Winant, 1986; Ringer and Lawless, 1989). In so doing it denies white social institutions any complicity in the subordinate status of people of color. White teachers of students of color need some way of understanding why people of color have not done as well in society as whites have. Teachers generally like their students—including their students of color—and wish to help them. How do white teachers explain racial inequality without either demeaning their students or questioning their own privileges? I observed two strategies: denial of race altogether, and defining students of color as "immigrants."

Denying the Salience of Race

> What's the big hangup, I really don't see this color until we start talking about it, you know. I see children as having differences, maybe they can't write their numbers or they can't do this or they can't do that, I don't see the color until we start talking multicultural. Then, oh yes, that's right, he's this and she's that. (Teacher interview, May 16, 1988)

> I really believe that elementary teachers feel that kids are kids....People would say, "Well, what's your minority breakdown?" And teachers would really have a rough time saying, you know, it was like asking how many of your kids are wearing glasses. (Teacher interview, December 15, 1987)

White teachers commonly insist that they are "color-blind": that they see children as children and do not see race (Rist, 1978). Many of the twenty-six white teachers began the program with a "color-blind" perspective, and throughout the two years, seven steadfastly maintained it; by the second year, these teachers' attendance at sessions dwindled because of the program's focus on race. What does it mean to construct an interpretation of race that denies it?

Francisco Rios (1992) asked sixteen teachers in an inner-city high school to think aloud about twelve classroom scenes and then analyzed their responses in terms of the salience of three scene characteristics: student gender, student race, and type of action (instructional, disciplinary, and personal). He found that student race was the only statistically significant characteristic; student gender and type of action were not. In other words teachers' responses varied with student race, but not with student gender. While teachers may deny that race is important, race is still quite salient to them.

People do not deny seeing what they actually do not see. Rather, they profess to be color-blind when trying to suppress negative images they attach to people of color, given the significance of color in the U.S., the dominant ideology of equal opportunity, and the relationship between race and observable measures of success. Many of the white teachers in our study associated people of color—and particularly African Americans and Latinos—with dysfunctional families and communities, and lack of ability and motivation. Several expressed these associations rather freely in discussions of their students and their parents; for example:

> I have a very close family,...[my husband and I] have been very strong disciplinarians and we encourage the work ethic....I realize how foolish and presumptuous [it is] to think all these kids are coming from the same thing....Just to have a totally helter-skelter house where there is nothing regular and the people who are your parent figures come and go....(Teacher interview, May 16, 1988)

> All these blacks, they're coming to school late every day. Well, nobody takes care of these children, you know, they have to get up and everything like that. (Teacher interview, December 7, 1988)

For the most part, teachers took for granted that the U.S. social structure is fairly open (after all, they "made it"). Some reacted angrily to suggestions that it is not.

> I am wrestling with the last two sessions...where the women's issue was brought up, and also the issue of the blacks. From my standpoint, I left those two meetings so depressed, because I started teaching in the '60s when we were told to instill pride in these people, treat them as adults, I'm speaking now of blacks, women, you know.... I've walked away from those meetings thinking I've wasted twenty-five years now, and I got shot down again, and once again, as a teacher, it's my fault.... I thought we were doing well. (Teacher interview, February 22, 1988)

> The three ladies up there telling us about their experiences as multicultural people in an all-white class and so on, how they interpreted things, and how it stuck with them today,...I couldn't understand why they...couldn't understand now that most of those kinds of days are gone....These are things they are hanging on to years ago. I don't think it is that way any more. (Teacher interview, February 23, 1988)

These examples to the contrary, most of the white teachers did not focus directly on the distribution of resources across groups or the ideology of equal opportunity. Instead they conceptualized racism as the unfair application of (probably) accurate generalizations about groups to individuals, in a way that biases one's treatment of them. Individuals should be able to succeed or fail on their own merit and should not be held back by "deficiencies" of their race as a whole. As long as a teacher does not know for certain which students will be held back by "cultural deficiencies," it is best to treat them as if one did not see their skin color. Therefore, in an effort not to be racist themselves and to treat all children equally, many white teachers try to suppress what they understand about people of color, which leads them to try not to "see" color.

Trying not to see what is obvious (color) and to suppress the negative and stereotypical imagery with which one is bombarded requires considerable psychological energy. Education about race conflicts with many white teachers' strategies of denial, compounding the psychological energy they must expend to continue being "blind" to color. Many simply avoid such discussions or staff development programs. Some of the teachers who participated in this two-year program did so with ambivalence and resented the attention given in sessions to African Americans and Latinos:

> I've had a lot on multicultural, you know, I taught in an inner-city school, and we had a lot about habits of the Hispanic, habits of the blacks, so probably that's kind of redoing it. (Teacher interview, March 24, 1988)

> To me, all of the speakers were slanted for blacks or Hispanics only, and I think that's an injustice....Get Indian children, get their views as to what they feel about American playgrounds and classrooms. (Teacher interview, May 18, 1988)

The teachers perceived staff development on multicultural education as useful if it gave them new information about groups they did not already "know all about," or if it reaffirmed what they were doing in the classroom. However, since they did not perceive that there would be anything worthwhile to learn about African Americans and Latinos, or about racism, and since constant and direct attention to these groups brought their own negative associations, as well as white guilt, to the surface, some of the white teachers stopped coming. Of the pool of teachers in both districts who had been invited to participate, I assume many did not apply precisely because they did not see value in acknowledging their own negative associations with people of color, or any suggestion that racism still exists.

USING CULTURE TO EASE THE PROCESS OF ASSIMILATION

Most of the white teachers who participated in the staff development sessions, and who did not vigorously assert a "color-blind" stance, believed that some degree of mutual cultural adaptation between the school and immigrant and minority communities would ease the transition of minority students into the dominant culture. While they did not view the dominant culture or its institutions as a problem, they recognized that cultural differences can interfere with the successful transition from one cultural context to another and sought adaptations in their own routines that might facilitate the process for some of their students. As one teacher put it,

> At least we can make a dent in the problem by the methods that we're using in teaching and like changing the style a little bit and trying to adapt to the students, rather than expecting them to make the swing and adapt to the way that we're teaching. (Teacher interview, May 18, 1989)

Several of the staff development sessions provided material from which teachers drew for adaptations, such as two sessions on culture and cognitive style, two sessions on parent involvement, and a session on cooperative learning. Teachers came away from these sessions with a variety of insights about cultural compatibility. Some began to reinterpret students' behavior as cultural rather than as simply "wrong."

> It kind of answers some questions as to why do I have certain students who can't seem to stay in their seats and pay attention....And why I have some that are a little bit more, you know, quiet and withdrawn....It doesn't always help me to know exactly what to do with them, but at least I have a little better understanding. (Teacher interview, May 17, 1988)

Several teachers added to their repertoire additional strategies for communicating with parents, such as sending or telephoning home positive messages or translating messages into Spanish. A few stopped insisting that students look them in the eye. Many teachers were intrigued by the possibility that students might enjoy and learn more from cooperative learning than from whole-class or individual teaching strategies.

> I remember the first time that I heard that different kinds of different cultures learned in different ways, it made me remember and think about how some of my kids would be reacting in class sometimes, you know, where they would be helping each other and a couple of instances where kids may have just been helping each other instead of copying. I concluded that they were copying, or cheating. (Teacher interview, February 28, 1988)

Increased use of cooperative learning was the greatest observable impact the staff development program had on the teachers' classroom behavior. By the end of the two-year period about half had begun to use this method. And as we found out in the classroom observations, the proportion of teaching time in which children engaged in cooperative learning and other group work had jumped from eleven to thirteen percent in the first observations to thirty percent in the last. Teachers attributed their own interest in cooperative learning to its connection with learning style; the fact that colleagues in their buildings had been trained in it and could provide help; students' positive reactions to it; and their perception that cooperative learning can be broken down into steps to master. Several teachers also liked the fact that cooperative learning could be incorporated into the form and structure of their teaching without changing other things too much.

These kinds of adaptations do have considerable value, reducing the stress students of color must deal with when the culture of the classroom conflicts with their home culture and building on strengths and preferences students have for learning. The teachers appear to have accepted the validity of such adaptations because they fit within ethnicity theory, according to which "newcomers" face difficulties due to cultural differences and these difficulties can be eased during the process of transition. I should emphasize that several of the staff development facilitators were African Americans who did not adhere to ethnicity theory and did not regard changes in school process as temporary bridges to ease cultural assimilation. Nevertheless, the facilitators focused on presenting useful strategies, and this had some success in that it led to greatly increased use of cooperative learning.

However, there seemed to be a difference between the goals the facilitators had in mind and those most white teachers accepted. An African American facilitator explicitly voiced her commitment to promoting high achievement among students of color. However, in none of the sessions was there rigorous discussion of what should constitute high achievement. When, in one interview, I asked a teacher to compare the achievement of her school with that of a predominantly white suburban school, she interpreted my question as changing the subject from multicultural education to something else (and said of course, the achievement in her school was lower, what else would one expect?). Since the time of this study my attempts to get groups of white teachers in local schools to define exactly what should constitute a standard for high achievement in inner-city schools have become an interesting study in avoidance behavior. Teachers say, for example, that success is different for different children, that existing measures of achievement are biased and therefore do not count, or that it is irrelevant how they define achievement because their efforts will be undone by the homes or the next teacher students have. Relatively few white teachers argue that inner-city students can and should be attaining the same levels of achievement as white suburban students, a pattern that is consistently found in studies of schools (e.g., Anyon, 1981; Fine, 1991; Grant and Sleeter, 1986).

Schools are one of the main gatekeepers in the allocation of social resources. I suspect that most white teachers are at once unsure how much intelligence students of color (and poor white students) can actually display, fearful that well-educated African American, Latino, and Native American students might launch a bold critique of white institutions and white people, and aware that parity in achievement across groups would threaten a major advantage white people and their children currently enjoy. But few teachers will admit to these fears, and they may not even be conscious of them. Instead, many try to implement strategies that might reduce failure and make the system of schooling work more smoothly, and they regard their support for these actions as evidence that they are not racist. From the perspective of ethnicity theory, such actions help those on the bottom to gain mobility in an open system. From the perspective of a theory of racial oppression, however, such actions may serve mainly to mask the oppressiveness of the education system.

Culture as Symbolic of Family and Individual Differences

Using interviews, Richard Alba (1990) investigated the symbolic meaning white Americans attached to ethnicity in the 1980s. He was interested in why Euroamericans continue to express interest in ethnicity in spite of the belief that European ethnicity in the U.S. no longer structures life chances to any significant degree. What he found describes very well the meanings with which many white teachers infuse multicultural education when they try to work with it in the classroom.

Alba argues that Euroamericans view participation in ethnic identity as an individual choice. Euroamericans stress the commonality of ethnic immigrant histories and value expressions of ethnicity that can be shared across ethnic lines: food was the most widespread expression mentioned; holidays, festivals, and related activities were also mentioned. Many whites in his sample equated ethnicity with one's private family history, rather than viewing it as a group's collective experience. Whites rarely connected ethnicity with social structures, such as neighborhood, friendship group, occupation, or political organizations. The symbolic meaning Euroamericans attach to ethnicity today upholds the ideology of individuality and mobility within an open system and the myth that everyone came to the U.S. in search of a better life and had to work equally hard to better themselves. It attempts to place all groups on an equal status in which ethnicity is a private matter and otherwise not very important. In so doing, this meaning averts a structural analysis of racism and inequality in contemporary U.S. society, implicitly reaffirming the superior position of Euroamericans.

If white teachers wish to regard race and ethnicity in a positive manner, and if they wish to try to reduce tensions among students in multiracial schools, the Euroamerican ethnic experience provides a repertoire of concepts to use, focusing on customs a group brought from the "old" country. About half of the white teachers in my study encoded Alba's symbolic expressions of ethnicity into lessons they occasionally added to the "regular" curriculum. Essentially these lessons tried to teach students that one should be proud of family and individual differences and not stereotype others negatively.

Some teachers taught lessons oriented around family heritage. Typically such lessons began with a discussion of where (what country) their families came from, and what customs the family has retained.

> We are talking a lot about their heritage and they have gone back and found all these neat things that are going on in their families, and now they've started bringing in recipes because we're going to make a recipe book from some recipes that have been handed down in their families. (Teacher interview, May 16, 1988)

Several white teachers incorporated food, music, and holidays from different countries into their teaching, although these lessons tended to retain a Eurocentric bias. For example, a music teacher developed a "Children Around the World" concert that was very creative but included more countries from Europe than from any other continent and represented Africa in terms of animals and Tarzan whoops. Some teachers developed lessons comparing the customs of different groups. For example, an English teacher concluded the discussion of a story about a Puerto Rican family with a comparison of customs in New York with those in Puerto Rico, and an ESL teacher had immigrant students compare customs for celebrating holidays in their countries with customs for celebrating Christmas in the U.S.

Even Native American experience was interpreted within the ethnicity paradigm. For example, a fifth-grade teacher taught a social studies lesson about how Indians immigrated over the land bridge from Asia, and later in the year her students read a story about the dancer Maria Tallchief's success in ballet and retention of her Indian name because of pride in her ancestry.

Prejudice and stereotyping were the focus of a few lessons I observed. In these lessons, teachers viewed prejudice and stereotyping as resulting from generalizations individuals incorrectly apply to other individuals and groups. For example, one teacher had students consider how labels can hurt and limit options. Another taught an extensive unit about prejudice, focusing on the Holocaust and *The Diary of Anne Frank.* Prejudice was interpreted as an irrational feeling with damaging consequences; from the unit, students should gather that they should not harbor prejudice toward others.

Several teachers taught lessons about individual differences and self-concepts, connecting these loosely with race and ethnicity. For example, an elementary teacher had students create personal coats of arms that expressed various positive images about themselves and their families. Another teacher created a classroom flower in which each petal included the name of a student and positive words other students had written about her/him. Role models were another theme of several lessons and classroom decorations. Several teachers occasionally put up posters of famous African Americans or other Americans of color, and their textbooks occasionally featured stories about famous Americans of color. Generally white teachers use role models to instill pride in children and show them that members of their group can succeed if they work hard.

At times African American students resisted participating in lessons about ethnic origins, and this puzzled the teachers. For example, a teacher who taught a lesson about family heritage remarked that,

> I only have three black students in my room and they have not gone back further than Mississippi, and it's been, no way are they going to go back further....The one little boy said, "we didn't come from Africa," that was the first thing he said when we started from where our ancestors came. (Teacher interview, May 16, 1988)

When another teacher began a lesson with a discussion of where students' ancestors came from, she was similarly surprised that no African American students located their ancestry in Africa. During the two-year staff development project, none of the teachers connected such responses with the celebration of Europe and silence about Africa that the school curriculum maintains, or with the media's depiction of Europe as industrialized and "developed" and Africa as "underdeveloped" and "primitive."

I regarded many of the lessons described above as positive experiences for students, and some of them (such as the unit on the Holocaust) taught worthy material. I would critique this body of lessons mainly on the basis of their huge silences and collective implications. By omission they implied that race no longer structures access to resources in the U.S., and that America's racial groups stand in equal status to one another, differentiated only by customs in which anyone can participate. Lessons added token representations of Americans of color (mainly by adding personal knowledge about the students in the classroom) to a curriculum that heavily favored Europe and Euro-americans, without reconstructing students' interpretations of the histories of Americans of color, or their knowledge of Africa, contemporary Latin America, or the pre-Columbian Americas. Even depictions of role models, by focusing on an individual's achievements and ignoring her or his difficulties in attaining them, can suggest that the system is open equally to anyone who will try.

Americans of color were lumped with immigrants who were collectively defined as "other," bringing customs that are, at best, interesting to learn about and share when there is time. "Whiteness" was taken as the norm, as natural. When teachers told me about "multicultural lessons" or "multicultural bulletin boards," what they usually drew my attention to was the flat representations of people of color that had been added; multidimensional representations of whiteness throughout the school were treated as a neutral background not requiring comment. In a discussion of Rosaldo's (1989) concept of "cultural stripping," McLaren critiques whites' naturalization of their identities: "Being white is an entitlement, not to preferred racial attributes, but to a raceless subjectivity. That is, being white becomes the invisible norm for how the dominant culture measures its own civility" (1991, p. 244). Whites so internalize their own power and taken-for-granted superiority that they resist self-questioning. Whites appropriate the idea of culture to mean "sub-categories of whiteness (Irishness, Jewishness, Britishness)" (Dyer, 1988, p. 46), which can be fleshed out in personal subjective meanings or residual expressions of life in other countries and other times. This provides a "positive" as well as nonthreatening template for whites to apply to discussions of race.

BEGINNINGS OF ANALYSES OF WHITE SUPREMACIST INSTITUTIONS

None of the white teachers constructed a strong critique of white-supremacist institutions during the two-year period, but three of the twenty-six (as well as all four teachers of color) expressed insights that would lead in that direction. One white special education teacher, who had described racism as an attitudinal problem early in the study, began to draw connections between racism and the structure of special education.

> [I'm] seeing basically how our system is set up, the value system our whole society is set up on. And it makes me feel like we are here because of a lot of suffering. (Teacher interview, May 19, 1988)

Later in a paper she wrote, "Many cultures and governmental systems have been established on the idea that some people were meant to rule and live in luxury and some were meant to serve and live in poverty and suffering." I did not see her translate these insights into her teaching practice, however, and she dropped the program after the first year.

A second white teacher developed similar insights, locating the beginning of her awareness of racism in her teaching in a predominantly black school in a university town, when she realized that the town tried very hard to ignore the existence of the school and its needs. Part of her job as a preschool teacher involved working with parents, and she gradually began to identify with them. After the conclusion of this study she became angry about the district's apparent disinterest in programs for low-income and minority parents, and she began talking about organizing the parents to speak out.

A third white teacher taught several social studies lessons for high school special education students about civil rights and labor issues. I observed her teach a lesson about civil disobedience, focusing on the 1960s; the lesson included ideas such as freedom riders, Black Muslims, lunch counter sit-ins, and racial riots in Detroit and Watts.

Why did these three teachers begin to focus their attention on various aspects of racism and institutional discrimination rather than cultural customs and individual differences? Two taught special education and one taught in a state-funded preschool program; all three occupied positions in the school structure that served populations that schools marginalize, where they found themselves waging battles on behalf of their students against conservative bureaucracies and, often, resistant colleagues. In the last interview, when I asked teachers how much power they believed those who participated in the staff development program had to change the school system, two of these three were the only teachers to discuss organizing and exerting pressure; the others all advocated individual solutions. I would suggest that their experience working in marginalized programs, coupled with participation in the staff development program, helped to politicize frustrations they were experiencing.

CONCLUSION

The staff development program spanned two years. I have not organized this chapter sequentially because I did not see most white teachers construct a qualitatively new understanding of race over the two-year period. Instead, I saw them select information and teaching strategies to add to a framework for understanding race that they took for granted, which they had constructed over their lifetimes from their position as white people in a racist society.

White people are aware of the efforts they and their families and friends have made to better themselves, and they are aware of the problems they encounter in everyday life. It is in their interest to assume that the problems they face are not unique and that the efforts all people make pay off according to the same rules. "Given the racial and class organization of American society, there is only so much people can 'see.' Positions they occupy in these structures limit the range of their thinking. The situation places barriers on their imaginations and restricts the possibilities of their vision" (Wellman, 1977, p. 235). Spending most of their time with other white people, whites do not see much of the realities of the lives of Americans of color nor encounter their viewpoints in any depth. Nor do they really want to, since those viewpoints would challenge practices and beliefs that benefit white people.

Faced with the paradox of liking and helping students of color while explaining away the subordination of people of color and adhering to social structures that benefit themselves and their own children, the white teachers I studied responded in patterned ways. Many simply refused to "see" color. Others searched for "positive" associations with race by drawing on the European ethnic experience, which points toward petrified vestiges of immigrant culture that add texture to the fabric of everyday life. Discussing race or multiculturalism meant discussing "them," not the social structure. The staff development program provided material they could draw from; like the program studied by Haberman and Post (1992), it did not reconstruct their basic interpretation of race.

I write this paper as a Euroamerican person who has struggled with my own understanding of race and who for years has been in the process of learning how to teach white educators about race. It is possible for a white person's understanding of race to undergo marked transformation; I experienced a reconstruction of my own under-standing over a period of years, and I know other whites who have done so also. As a teacher educator, I continually seek points of access into how Euroamerican students view the world. But at the same time, while I believe whites are educable, I have gained appreciation for the strength of our resistance to change. My own color gives me a degree of comfort, privilege, and insulation that serves me in ways I continue to take for granted. It is from this position that I offer some thoughts about what to do.

I would advocate strongly working to reverse policies that propel mainly white people into the profession, such as the use of the National Teachers Exam, the lengthening of teacher education programs, and other means of defining standards in ways that penalize rather than reward strengths and resources that teachers of color could bring. Schools as they are structured currently operate in ways that largely reproduce the racial and social class structure. Various fields of discourse, such as multicultural education, emancipatory pedagogy, and Afrocentrism, express ideas and commitments for reworking schools to serve the interests of diverse populations. What I am suggesting goes beyond interaction patterns in classrooms, role models, or linking home and school cultures. I am suggesting the need to populate the teaching force with people who bring diverse worldviews and discursive fields of reference, including those that expose, challenge, and deconstruct racism rather than tacitly accepting it.

Educators of color are much more likely to bring life experiences and viewpoints that critique white supremacy than are white teachers and to engage in activities that challenge various forms of racism (Foster, 1990; Ladson-Billings and Henry, 1990). They are also less likely to "marginalize minority intellectual discourse" (Gordon, 1990, p. 103). Although Americans of color express a wide range of analyses of racism, the strongest critiques of racism tend to come from communities of color. The life experiences of people of color can be politicized to challenge racism in education more readily than can those of white people. In my own experience I have found much richer discussions of anti-racist ideas and actions to emerge from multiracial groups, in which whites are present but in the minority, than from all-white groups.

Is there a role for multicultural teacher education? I believe that there is but that it cannot substitute for making the education profession diverse. Ultimately the best solutions to racism will come from multiracial coalitions in which white people participate but do not dominate. Multicultural teacher education has somewhat different purposes for teachers of color and for white teachers.

For teachers of color it should help to politicize and develop what they know from life experience and to translate their commitments into emancipatory action in schools. For example, some teachers of color who have successfully entered the middle class accept much about the social class structure that ought to be questioned. Further, there are bodies of content knowledge and pedagogical practice that teachers of color often find very useful but do not simply know without being taught.

White people need to learn about racism, as well as about the historic experiences and creative works of American minority groups and about the wide range of implications for schooling. This means beginning their reeducation by forcing them to examine white privilege and planning long-term learning experiences that anticipate the various strategies white people use to avoid and reinterpret education about race. For example, structured immersion experiences in which a white person spends at least a month in a minority community, coupled with instruction about racism and the history and culture of that group, as well as development of some emotional bonding with members of the group, can propel serious reexamination of his or her perspective. The aim of education for white teachers would be to encourage them to work collectively with local communities of color and to construct an ongoing process of learning from and connecting with people of color.

Conceptualized as a form of political organizing, education may be a powerful vehicle to confront racism. An educator qua organizer must directly confront the vested interest white people have in maintaining the status quo, force them to grapple with the ethics of privilege, and refuse to allow them to rest comfortably in apolitical interpretations of race and multicultural teaching.[1]

NOTES

1 I am grateful to Martin Haberman, Renee Martin, Cameron McCarthy, Carmen Montecinos, and Francisco Rios for their helpful comments and suggestions on earlier drafts of this paper.

REFERENCES

Aaron, R. & Powell, G. (1982). Feedback practices as a function of teacher and pupil race during reading group instruction. *Journal of Negro Education*, 51 (1), 50–59.

Alba, R. D. (1990). *Ethnic Identity: The transformation of white America*. New Haven: Yale UP.

Anyon, J. (1981). Social class and school knowledge. *Curriculum Inquiry*, 11, 3–41.

Baez, T. & Clarke, E. (1990). Reading, writing, and role models. *Community, Technical, and Junior College Journal,* 60 (3), 31–34.

Baker, G. (1977). Two preservice training approaches. *Journal of Teacher Education,* 28, 31–33.

Banks, J. A. & Banks, C. M. (eds.). (1989). *Multicultural Education: Issues and perspectives.* Boston: Allyn.

Bennett, C. T. (1979). The preparation of pre-service secondary social studies teachers in multiethnic education. *High School Journal,* 62, 232–237.

Buenker, J. D. (1976). Immigration and ethnic groups. In J. A. Newenschwander (ed.), *Kenosha County in the 20th Century* (pp. 1–50). Kenosha, WI: Kenosha County Bicentennial.

_____. (1977). The immigrant heritage. In N. C. Burkel (ed.), *Racine: Growth and Change in a Wisconsin County* (pp. 69–136). Racine, WI: Racine County Board of Supervisors.

Contreras, G. & Engelhardt, J. M. (1990–91). Attracting and recruiting an ethnically diverse teaching force. *Teacher Education and Practice,* 6 (2), 39–42.

Cummins, J. (1986). Empowering minority students: A framework for intervention. *Harvard Educational Review,* 56, 18–36.

Dyer, R. (1988). White. *Screen,* 29, 44–64.

Fine, M. (1991). *Framing Dropouts: Notes on the politics of an urban public high school.* Albany: State U of New York P.

Foster, M. (1990). The politics of race: Through the eyes of African American teachers. *Journal of Education,* 172 (3), 123–141.

Frederickson, G. M. (1981). *White Supremacy: A comparative study in American and South African history.* New York: Oxford UP.

Gordon, B. M. (1985). Teaching teachers: "Nation at risk" and the issue of knowledge in teacher education. *The Urban Review,* 17, 33–46.

_____. (1990). The necessity of African-American epistemology for educational theory and practice. *Journal of Education,* 172 (3), 88–106.

Grant, C. A. (1981). Education that is multicultural and teacher education: An examination from the perspectives of preservice students. *Journal of Educational Research,* 75, 95–101.

Grant, C. A., & Sleeter, C. E. (1986). *After the School Bell Rings.* London: Falmer.

Haberman, M. (1989). More minority teachers. *Phi Delta Kappan,* 70, 771–776.

Haberman, M. & Post, L. (1992). Does direct experience change education students' perceptions of low-income minority children? *The Midwestern Educational Researcher,* 5 (2), 29–31.

Henry, W. A., III. (1990, April 9). Beyond the melting pot. *Time,* pp. 28–31.

Irvine, J. J. (1991). *Black Students and School Failure: Policies, practices, and prescriptions.* New York: Praeger.

Justiz, M. J. & Kameen, M. C. (1988). Increasing the representation of minorities in the teaching profession. *Peabody Journal of Education,* 66 (1), 91–100.

Ladson-Billings, G. & Henry, A. (1990). Blurring the borders: Voices of African liberatory pedagogy in the United States and Canada. *Journal of Education,* 172 (2), 72–88.

Lee, M. (1989, June). Making child development relevant for all children: Implications for teacher education. *Early Child Development and Care,* 47, 63–73.

Liston, D. P. & Zeichner, K. M. (1990). Teacher education and the social context of schooling. *American Educational Research Journal,* 27 (4), 10–36.

McLaren, P. (1991). Decentering culture: Postmodernism, resistance, and critical pedagogy. In N. B. Wyner (ed.), *Current perspectives on the culture of schools* (pp. 232–257). Boston: Brookline.

Metz, M. H. (1990). How social class differences shape teachers' work. In M. W. McLaughlin, J. E. Talbert, & N. Bascia (eds.), *The Contexts of Teaching in Secondary Schools: Teachers' realities* (pp. 40–107). New York: Teachers College.

National Commission on Excellence in Education. (1983). *A Nation at Risk.* Washington, DC: U. S. Government Printing Office.

Nieto, S. (1992). *Affirming Diversity: The sociopolitical context of multicultural education.* New York: Longman.

Oakes, J. (1985). *Keeping Track: How schools structure inequality.* Princeton, NJ: Yale UP.

Omi, M. & Winant, H. (1986). *Racial Formation in the United States: From the 1960s to the 1980s.* New York: Routledge.

Redman, G. L. (1977). Study of the relationship of teacher empathy for minority persons and inservice human relations training. *Journal of Educational Research,* 70, 205–210.

Ringer, B. B. & Lawless, E. R. (1989). *Race—ethnicity and society.* London: Routledge.

Rios, F. A. (1992). Teachers' implicit theories of multicultural classrooms. Doctoral dissertation, University of Wisconsin.

Rist, R. C. (1978). *The Invisible Children: School integration in American society.* Cambridge, MA: Harvard UP.

Rosaldo, R. (1989). *Culture and Truth: The remaking of social analysis.* Boston: Beacon.

Shor, I. (1986). Equality is excellence: Transforming teacher education and the learning process. *Harvard Educational Review,* 56 (4), 406–426.

Simpson, A. W. & Erickson, M. T. (1983). Teachers' verbal and nonverbal communication patterns as a function of teacher race, student gender, and student race. *American Educational Research Journal,* 20 (2), 183–98.

Sleeter, C. E. (1992). *Keepers of the American Dream: A study of staff development and multicultural education.* London: Falmer.

Sleeter, C. E. & Grant, C. A. (1988). *Making Choices for Multicultural Education: Five approaches to race, class, and gender.* Columbus: Merrill.

Suzuki, B. H. & Lou, R. (1989). Asian Americans as the "model minority": Outdoing whites? or media hype? *Change,* 21 (6), 13–19.

Taylor, B. (1990, April 22). Grade gap grows as students advance through Unified. *Racine Journal Times,* pp. 4A–5A.

Tewell, K. J. & Trubowitz, S. (1987). The minority group teacher. *Urban Education,* 22 (3), 355–365.

Washington, V. (1981). Impact of anti-racism/multicultural education training on elementary teachers' attitudes and classroom behavior. *The Elementary School Journal,* 81, 186–192.

Wellman, D. T. (1977). *Portraits of white racism.* Cambridge: Cambridge UP.

13 Technologies of Marginality: Strategies of Stardom and Displacement in Adolescent Life

Glenn M. Hudak

IN THIS ESSAY I want to map out the terrain of marginality within an affluent suburban high school. The investigation focuses on the case studies of two college-bound high school boys, one Hispanic, "Jorge," one white, "Sam." Both boys are performers: one is an actor, the other a musician. Both define themselves as being on the margins of school life; however, each one presents a different map of marginality. Jorge's story is one of an attempt to move out of the margins through the use of theater and acting strategies—strategies of "stardom." Here stardom is not viewed as an identity per se, but as a strategy to define oneself within a context of power relations. Sam's story is one of attempts to question his privileged status through music and literature. He struggles to move to the margins by "displacing" conservative community values.

The strategies of stardom and displacement indicate the different ways these boys negotiate power relations within and through the margins. Neither monolithic nor static, the margins become both site and "technology" in the formation of one's racial identity.

DATA COLLECTION

The setting for this study is a suburban community with a population of approximately 40,000. The community is located in a metropolitan area with an estimated population of 1.5 million. While the larger metropolitan area contains diverse cultural groups, the community of Suburbia, as I shall call it, is primarily white and upper middle class. Politically Suburbia is a Republican stronghold. Yet with regard to schooling, citizens of Suburbia continue to vote for tax increases to support school programs, even in troubled economic times. Local schools have been recognized for their excellence and have won national awards.

The demographics for the school district Jorge and Sam attend reveal that, of a total student population of approximately 4000, ninety-seven percent are white, 1.8 percent are Asian American, one percent are African American, and 0.2 percent, or approximately nine students, are Hispanic.

I collected data for this study over a six-month period, from January through June. Data were obtained from two sources: classroom observations and interviews with individual students. Classroom observations were taken from a single, upper-level English course. I made these observations on a daily basis for one month and included descriptions of social and communicative interaction within the class. From this class I recruited student volunteers for in-depth interviews. Jorge and Sam were two such volunteers, each of whom I interviewed thirteen times.

These weekly interviews, approximately forty minutes in length, were conducted on campus during the students' free time. The interviews were taped, with transcripts for each student totaling between 150 and 200 typed pages. My questions focused on the "inner monologue" these students have with themselves as they go through the school day; that is, what strategies they used to "care for" themselves in school. How, for example, did Jorge deal with racism? Likewise, how did Sam confront conservative school values? I attempt, then, to explore the strategies they used to construct themselves as individuals with special regard to race and marginality.

The project's overall aim has been to generate a "grounded theory" to explain microdynamics of race formation and marginality within the suburban school context (Glasser and Strauss, 1967). The organization of material reflects this emphasis. First, I want to make clear the theoretical framework informing my interpretations of the data. Second, I will present Jorge and Sam's narratives on school life. Third, I will compare and contrast their narratives to generate a hypothesis grounded within a specific context. In the end it is my hope that this study will instigate further research into those cultural territories situated within the margins of school life.

I. Theoretical Frames for the Study

Jorge's and Sam's case studies are presented as a way to give specificity to the investigation and capture what Michael Omi and Howard Winant (1986, p. 66) refer to as the "micro-level" of race formation. Micro-level studies reveal the construction of racial identity at the level of individuals, focusing on the ways in which one forms an understanding of self and society in practical, everyday activity. Here it is assumed that race is neither an essentialist category, i.e., fixed or objective, nor a mere illusion that will disappear with the correct social order. Rather, race (like gender and class) is a historically contested category constantly being shaped and reshaped in everyday life. While one's racial identity is related to class and gender, it is not reducible to either category. Rather the dynamics of these categories, both at the micro and macro levels, are only determinate within a specific historic context.

My concern with how Jorge and Sam went about "constructing" themselves involves a conception of self adopted from Michel Foucault's "ethical" investigations. One aspect of Foucault's ethics emphasizes the active construction of self by oneself, within a negotiating field of power relations (Foucault, 1983). Foucault observed that in the constitution of one's identity, "these practices are...not something that the individual invents by himself. They are patterns that he finds in his culture and which are proposed, suggested and imposed on him by his culture, his society and his social group" (Foucault, 1988, p. 11). Jorge and Sam did not invent the strategies, the inner monologues, that they employ; rather these strategies show us how these boys "use" the patterns that are "proposed, suggested, and imposed" on them by our culture.

To claim that one can construct oneself within a set of historically defined discourses is not to assert that we can be anything we want to be. Rather, one's sense of self, expressed as racial or gendered identity, will always be situated within parameters, a space of meanings that is already socially established (Butler, 1990). To deviate or to lie outside "accepted norms" has real social consequences for individuals or groups. That is, those individuals who are labeled "outsiders" often find themselves ostracized, excluded, indeed marginalized.

The margin, however, cannot be viewed solely as a site of exclusion and repression, as a place to which one is "marginalized" due to one's race, class, gender, or sexual preference. To be sure, marginalization is a practice of oppression. Yet as bell hooks writes, this is not the only dimension to marginality. She argues that one can choose the margins! For hooks, marginality itself becomes a strategy, a "technology," in the construction of oneself and a source of radical social action.

hooks's article, "Choosing the Margins as a Space of Radical Openness" (1990), points to another aspect of marginality as site of resistance and possibility. hooks's way of conceptualizing the margins is firmly grounded in the often painful experience of being marginalized. "It comes from lived experience. Yet I want to talk about what it means to maintain that marginality even as one works, produces, lives, if you will, at the center" (p. 150). Lived experience refers not only to actual events that have occurred in life but also to a sense of memory: "Our experience is also a struggle of memory against forgetting" (p. 148).

By locating oneself within the margins, one refuses to forget the past, and instead keeps it alive in memory. When memory is politicized, the margins come to represent a social location that is on the one hand a place of "deprivation" and on the other hand a "particular way of seeing reality" whose intent is survival and resistance. Key to choosing the margins are the links made between past experiences and present realities. The margins become a space to renew oneself. hooks concludes, "I am located in the margins. I make the distinction between that marginality which is imposed by the oppressive structures and that marginality one chooses as a site of resistance—as occasion of radical openness and possibility" (1990, p. 153).

With this understanding of "margins" in mind, the task ahead is to investigate the dimensions of marginality that Jorge and Sam inhabit. The "technologies" of marginality, in turn, suggest those "ethical" strategies employed by Jorge and Sam to construct themselves within the margins.

II. Strategies of "Stardom": Jorge

Jorge has a high profile within the school. He is very articulate and radiates positive energy in the classroom. He is also an actor involved in school plays and the drama club. Through his story we get a glimpse of the formation of one's racial (and gendered) identity and the use of theater and acting strategies in a struggle to fight racism. Jorge's story tells us of being "caught" in the margins. Unable to move out of the margins, Jorge exploits marginality in ways that fight against racial oppression while recreating and valorizing certain gender-related stereotypes such as "the Latino Man." At the time of the interviews, Jorge was in eleventh grade.

First Encounter

Jorge: If you look around Suburbia you'll notice one thing…I'm the only Puerto Rican in the school, I think. It's very hard to deal with sometimes. Like I was talking to some kids, "Would you ever have an interracial relationship?" I have trouble. When I first got to the school district, I couldn't speak English, and little kids are vicious about things like that. I was physically, openly ridiculed, and this and that, and I had to learn to deal with it.…I had real problems dealing with people up until about eighth grade.

Interviewer: What happened in eighth grade?

Jorge: I started taking acting classes.…Acting would show me how to deal with people. Acting has shown me how to deal with people. And to look at myself, and to see what I feel, and maybe figure out what other people feel by their actions. All my life I've been watching TV and movies and things like that. You see the person. I saw the person I wanted to be. I always wanted to be the hero type. I wanted to be Zorro, and Captain Blood, and Cyrano de Bergerac, all rolled into one, and in acting I could do that. I could be anything I wanted.

Interviewer: Why acting? Why not music or sports?

Jorge: It gave me the opportunity. The acting class was a little environment away from school. Like everybody in my school knew me, and it was set. I couldn't change myself there. But I went to the acting class, it's a very small group, maybe fifteen kids, they didn't know me and I could start fresh. I was in the same level as they were, hardly any of us knew what to do, and we sort of learned things. Not all of them liked me, like half of them hated me after all anyway. But right now I'm best friends with them. I was helping a girl last night that used to hate me. I didn't like her much either, but now we're like best friends. It's incredible!

MEMORIES NOT FORGOTTEN

Jorge was born in Puerto Rico and moved to the United States when he was in first grade. His family moved to Suburbia's school district when Jorge was in third grade. In interviews Jorge tells of a very rich fantasy life derived from watching old movies on TV.

Jorge: When I was growing up, my parents for some reason kept moving us to places where there weren't many kids in the neighborhood. So I didn't have people to play with. And my sisters, I have two older sisters, they're like extra parents. So I never had any kids to play with. And I got bored pretty fast. I had a very big imagination. So I'd have all these fantastic daydreams, and battles, and I'd be a knight or Zorro or things like that. I use to watch daytime TV and all the old movies that came on.

At home Jorge's life revolved around the fantasy of being the hero, but in school the story is very different. The racism encountered by Jorge as a young child is forever present in his interviews.

Jorge: In seventh grade, there's these couple of kids. Kids are vicious, I think kids are vicious. They pick out one little thing, and it's blown out of proportion. Well, I was the only Puerto Rican kid, and this kid is like, "He's Puerto Rican, he's Puerto Rican," repeats it over and over and over again. It was the stupidest thing, but it bothered me a lot. It hurt me, and I didn't know how to deal with it. I'm like lost here. Now if that were to happen to me now…

Interviewer: What would happen?

Jorge: I didn't have an outlet for it. That was before acting.…I was miserable, I was really hurt. Things like that really hurt me, and I had no one to talk to, and nothing, nothing to like vent my frustrations and feelings and things like that. Now if that were to happen to me again, I could get back.

Interviewer: How so?

Jorge: I know I'm never gonna let someone treat me like that again. *I would use every single acting thing I know* [my emphasis]. Like it wouldn't matter. I'll act like it didn't matter.

Interviewer: How would you act like it didn't matter?

Jorge: I'll laugh with them, you know, make funny sort of comments about that. The thing is, they want to get a rise out of me, you know. If they don't see a rise out of me, maybe they'll stop, maybe I don't have to worry about it.

All points on Jorge's compass, so to speak, point to acting and the theater community of which he is a member. His life both in and out of school involves, in one form or another, this community. Jorge's acting is multidimensional in that it cannot be confined solely to the stage. Indeed, for Jorge, the theater community serves as a focal point for defining himself at Suburbia High.

THEATER AS COMMUNITY

While Jorge tends to downplay the significance and consequences of his being a cultural outsider, he nonetheless is concerned about what he calls the "arrogance of nonconformity" exhibited by those students at the center of Suburbia's school life.

> Jorge: The center [at school] is not one person, one thing, one group. I don't want to be the rapper kid, or the preppie kid, or the greek kid, or the jock kid. Everybody, all these cliques, I see as having arrogance. Everybody is being arrogant to be like themselves, but in the process they are conforming. They're striving so much to be different. But look at each other. You're the same thing over and over again.

For Jorge, the only group of people in the school who are not arrogant or striving to be different are the actors: theater people. He describes them as "the dregs of society." "The dregs" metaphorically describes the life stories of the actors in his group: Jorge says that in each person's story, "You can see that little bit of hurt." The other groups, from his vantage point, struggle to be "different"; yet in the end this is a conformist goal. The theater people, on the other hand, do not *strive* to be different; they *are* different, in that they have been hurt in social relationships and acknowledge their hurt. For Jorge, the dregs are the only group that is "real," and not faking difference. This has important consequences for Jorge's social relationships.

THE IDEAL AND THE REAL

Jorge has developed a complex system to describe the terrain of acting in his everyday life. One end of the acting spectrum Jorge calls "the actor's high." On the other end lies what Jorge calls the "when-it-counts." Situated between the actor's high and when-it-counts lie a set of strategies Jorge labels as "survival skills."

When Jorge describes his ideal acting state he talks of the "actor's high." The actor's high is that state of being during a stage performance where there is no distinction between the actor and the character he plays.

> Jorge: In the ideal sense, you would be moved. You would be in this alternate state. You would be getting that *actor's high,* where you forget that you're you. You're just the character and nothing else could possibly come to your mind but the next word that the character is gonna say. It just clicks in. Nothing else would work except that exact word and that exact thing. And that's happened to me twice in my life maybe. Twice in my life, that actor's high, it's incredible.

The actor's high represents the ideal stage experience, where subject and object merge in the performance. On the other end of the spectrum lies Jorge's conception of "the real" (the authentic) in social encounters signified by the phrase, "when it counts." This phrase comes from one of Jorge's favorite quotes, from a science fiction novel, "You are what you do when it counts."

When-it-counts has special significance for Jorge in that it represents that moment when he feels that he is not acting at all. It is a moment of action in the world where one is selfless. The difference between "when-it-counts" and "the actor's high" is that the latter is a performance that occurs in a public space, on stage. When-it-counts, on the other hand, occurs in that private space with close friends or in everyday situations where one forgets oneself.

Jorge: How do I express this? At the best moment of your life, if you're doing something incredibly good, incredibly helpful to other people, incredibly just selfless and honest, you are a selfless, honest, the best kind of person you can be. Maybe you might fall, maybe you might do something incredibly awful and cruel and despicable, but…just at that moment, you're what you are. But you're never stuck at it. You can't think of yourself as good all the time or bad all the time…When-it-counts, that's when you're being selfless.

When-it-counts is that state when one is good not by trying to be good, but rather by losing one's self-consciousness and becoming selfless. When-it-counts is acting within the moment regardless of the consequences of the actions. Between the "actor's high" and "when-it-counts" are a range of acting strategies that Jorge describes as "survival skills."

SURVIVAL SKILLS

For Jorge the center of school culture has two defining dimensions. One is racial and represents larger structures, what he calls "the large, white, Anglo-Saxon thing." The other dimension refers to those "arrogant" individuals who try to be nonconformist. Jorge's relation to the center is ambiguous in a number of ways. While he is critical of the center he also wants to be part of it, to be in the limelight. He claims that for *him* to take center stage is not an act of arrogance. Rather, for Jorge, acting is an act of survival. The primary survival skill is "masquerading."

Jorge: Masquerading is one of the tools of survival. When you're masquerading, I think there's an involvement of suspension of disbelief. An acting term…even if it's a black stage, you can use your imagination, you can suspend your disbelief and go, oh my God, this is an incredible kingdom and these guys are fighting over this and that….

Diffusing the situation, that's a tool. You can masquerade as a really funny person and people won't make fun of you. Let's put on a face. The racial thing—someone is making fun of you racially. You pretend you don't care, that's masquerading, that's the survival tool. You could masquerade and pretend it doesn't matter.

Survival skills, such as masquerading, are all grounded in Jorge's past experiences in combating racism. He uses these skills both on and off stage.

Jorge: When I'm on stage, my survival mechanism generates all these feelings. I can think, I can remember and I can get that emotional connection, and I can use all that, all those feelings I *stored up before* [my emphasis], and I can vent them on stage. It's a release, maybe. The art is finding the right place to release it.

As well as using survival skills on stage, Jorge draws upon past experiences for "offstage" performances as well. Offstage performances are very gender oriented. Gender masquerading most often occurs when Jorge is at parties. Jorge attempts to be the life of the party, have fun, and draw attention to himself, particularly the attention of girls. The masquerade represents Jorge's "party character." One of his concerns in the party context is to avoid the commitment of going steady with one girl.

Jorge: My basic theory about dating and going out is I don't like to go out boyfriend-girlfriend because commitment scares me. So I end up dating a couple of girls at a time. And I don't like to make a commitment or anything.

At parties Jorge entertains. His "balancing act," to draw attention to himself without getting committed to just one girl, is achieved by being the center of attention and entertaining all at the party, without focusing his energies on anyone in particular. Acting skills enable him to reconcile potential conflicts and remain noncommittal.

"LATINO MAN"

"Latino Man" is a term Jorge uses to describe himself. The term crosses three domains: gender, race, and the labor market for actors. Jorge sees himself on the road to being a professional actor. To this end, as well as acting in the school drama club, he has been hired to do acting jobs through a casting agency.

> Jorge: I'm constantly getting calls for the ethnic young man....Those are the parts that I constantly get. I'm not about to argue. I know a lot of kids in my acting classes that are just as talented or even more, and they don't get work. There's no jobs for them.

As this particular interview progressed, Jorge talked about the isolation of being one of the very few Hispanic students in the school. At the same time he valorized the stereotyped description of "Latino Man." He struggled to distinguish between being isolated and being special, as "Latino Man."

> Jorge: I sometimes get annoyed when someone will say, well you probably want the tacos at lunch. Or we're talking in an English course, and a Spanish word comes up, and everybody turns to me and goes, ah, what's that word mean, Jorge? That bothers me on occasion.
>
> Interviewer: If you were in a high school with more Hispanic students, say fifty or sixty percent, how would it be different?
>
> Jorge: I'd sort of lose. I think I'd start losing a little bit of my specialness, if you will. I feel very special, you know. Like hey, I'm me. If there were so many around me, I wouldn't be so special.
>
> Interviewer: But doesn't this kind of work as a double edge? On the one hand, you're special. But on the other hand, you mentioned you were feeling isolated, alienated. And the struggle against racism?
>
> Jorge: Well, the difference is being seen and not being seen. I'd blend right in if there were a lot of kids. Like Latino kids in the school. And I'm not into blending. I'm really not into blending in. I'm an actor. I'm a performer.
>
> Interviewer: Couldn't you be a performer in a school where there's a lot of Latino kids?
>
> Jorge: Part of the hope is the Latino. I'm a Latino Lover Man....It's my hope for acting. For getting paying parts, paying roles. I'm not about to go and say, okay, I want to be just like everybody else. I'm in it too long not being everybody else.

STRATEGIES OF STARDOM

The demands of the job market and the construction of a personal identity merge in Jorge's image of Latino Man. Latino Man is made possible through strategies of stardom. It is an image that is constructed through the reconciliation of contradictory dimensions of Jorge's life. This is not to say other adolescents do not perform a role. In Jorge's case, however, he consciously wants to be a star, "the life of the party," and explicitly refers to acting strategies as enabling him to negotiate everyday life in school. For example, the strategy of bringing the past to bear in a present situation or acting role is known as *affective memory* (Strasberg, 1991).

Furthermore, one of the ideological functions of stars is precisely their ability to reconcile contradictory aspects of everyday life. The star is able is suppress "one half of the contradiction and foreground the other half" (Dyer, 1979, p. 39). Clearly, in Jorge's performances involving struggles with racism, his strategy is to foreground certain elements from his past in a present situation.

The contradictions that Jorge works to reconcile are past memories of discrimination and present realities. The past is the everpresent background to all of Jorge's stories. This theme of the outsider is reflected by Puerto Rican writers who discuss the contradictory nature of Puerto Rican "otherness." Arturo Madrid, for example, explains that the contradictory situation facing Puerto Ricans in the United States is that "being the other frequently means being invisible," but, on the other hand, "sometimes involves sticking out like a sore thumb" (1992, p. 8).

Jorge's reconciliation of past memories with present realities suggests another dimension to the formation of his racial identity. Namely, he employs a "chameleon strategy," altering his behavior to accommodate pressures within certain situations. The notion of a chameleon strategy is suggested by Clara Rodriguez, who argues that it is a way to deal with the perceptual dissonance many Puerto Ricans in America experience. Perceptual dissonance "is the experience of being seen in a way different from the way you see yourself, particularly as it pertains to race" (Rodriguez, 1991, p. 76). Jorge's Latino Man is a prime example of this.

Jorge reconciles imposed racial stereotypes by transforming them into characters. He takes the "outsider" image, his status as a person in the margins, and brings it back into public as a character, a role to be played. Ultimately Jorge's concern is to gain control over his life, to be respected, not to be seen as the outsider or even the stereotyped "Latin lover." Rather, most important for Jorge is that he be seen as a good person, one of the "good guys" at the center. In one of our last interviews, Jorge speaks to his wanting to move out of the margins.

Interviewer:	If you could not act or be an actor what would you do?
Jorge:	Be a police officer.
Interviewer:	A police officer!
Jorge:	Yeah. When I was growing up, my sister went out with a state trooper, and he's a giant. Incredibly funny and nice and smart, and they're good guys and they go around, righting wrong. It was the most impressive thing in my childhood, one of the most impressive things, and I always wanted to be just like them.

III. Strategies of Displacement: Sam

Sam is a musician; he plays both violin and guitar. After he graduates from high school, Sam will attend a private music conservatory to study jazz guitar. Sam is white and from an affluent family. From interviews one gets the clear sense that his family supports his efforts. Two themes stand out from the extended interviews conducted with him: his "quest" for an "authentic" self and the importance of music in his life. Through extracurricular literature and music Sam is able to question middle-class life at Suburbia High and it is from this base that he moves toward the margins. Sam's story romanticizes the struggle against forces of oppression, yet he is not trying to be someone else, to invade the space of the "other," or to be a colonizer.

First Encounter

Sam:	There are people walking around with their green or purple ribbon, whatever, to protest what happened to Rodney King. I've seen a little of that. But Suburbia is out of touch with reality.
Interviewer:	In what way?
Sam:	Well, in that people in Suburbia, most of them think that everybody

with the exception of some poorer people, mostly black, everybody goes off to college and everybody can afford it....

Interviewer: Are you trying to say that somehow living in the suburbs here is less real than some other place?

Sam: I mean like reality, getting out in the real world. You know, having to make a living, having to feed yourself, having to deal, interact with other people, with other cultures and stuff. What you get here is a lot of people, having everything handed to them easily, they can afford very expensive nice clothes, very nice stuff, they don't have to look bad....I don't resent people. Because I fall into that class too. But something that really bugs me about this area is that there is so much ignorance.

Throughout the interviews I got a clear sense that there is a significant difference between Sam's out-of-school performances and his school presence. Within the school context Sam does not attempt to be the center of attention; he is not interested in being a "star." Sam's school life revolves around strategies that "displace" the conservative "unreality" of Suburbia High. In interviews he is very articulate in his critique of white, middle-class Suburbia.

BEGINNINGS

Sam is "laid back" in school; his presence is quiet. He chooses to remain in the background of classroom activities. However, he is also a performer. He has played in various rock bands for the past five years, the largest performance being the school's senior prom, at which Sam and his band played for more than 400 dancing students.

Sam: I don't know what initially made me want to play. I remember asking, or getting a plastic violin when I was three years old because I wanted to play. I remember between kindergarten and first grade seeing a movie on violins and wanting to play. Eventually my parents found somebody who taught lessons to young kids.

Sam explains that, while he studied the violin until the eleventh grade, he had a very difficult time practicing. The violin was not his instrument. He started listening to the radio at an early age, enjoyed rock music, and began to focus on the guitar as his instrument of choice.

Sam: That's the thing, the violin really didn't have any connection with the music I liked. When I was little, I didn't listen to classical music....If you asked me in third grade what I wanted to do in life, I would have said I wanted to be a rock-and-roll musician....So I would go to the music store with my dad and dream about the guitars.

Sam's older sister studied the guitar for a while, which gave him the opportunity to start playing around with the instrument. Sam told his parents that he also wanted to take guitar lessons. At first his mom resisted the idea, but when his sister stopped playing the guitar, he was able to convince his parents to let him study instead.

Sam: By the end of seventh grade I was playing with a couple of kids in my class...."Get Back" by the Beatles was the first guitar solo I learned to play.

THAT'S WHERE PEOPLE WERE LIKE ME

From sixth grade on Sam began to hang out with other musicians and become part of the school's small musical community. Sam relates that middle school, sixth grade, marks the beginning of his becoming critical of school.

Sam: I guess sixth grade was my downfall academically....You get to middle school and it's not elementary school. It's like, elementary school, everybody knew each other in classes. The only cliques that were in elementary school were the boys and the girls. When you get into middle school and you have to do this and that and you have to act in a certain way to be in with these people, and if you weren't into that, then you were a kind of outcast. So I didn't feel at home. I just hated it because people were vicious.

Sam's friends in middle school were students older than himself. When he was in seventh grade he started to hang out with a group of eighth graders, who accepted him because of his guitar playing. For his age Sam was a very talented musician. However, it was not until he attended a summer music camp that he came to feel a part of a group of people who were just like him.

> Sam: It's an overnight camp. That was always my place to look forward to. That's where people were like me. I had a lot of friends there who were like me. I had a lot of friends back home, but they were not real, because I could not relate to them.

Sam's peer group consists of many of the students he met at camp. In this interview about summer camp, he begins to refer vaguely to people who are "real" and those who are not—the former being the other, older musicians from summer camp.

> Sam: I always found the camp to be a haven because [there were] plenty of people, most of them older. I've always tended to hang out with people that are older, not because I thought I was more mature, because I have more in common with them. I can remember discussing things with these eighteen-year-olds and I'm like twelve, you know.

No Exit

Sam kept in touch with this group throughout his freshman year at high school. His involvement with them led him not only to continue to explore music and start a band, but to merge his musical talent with a budding interest in philosophy.

> Sam: By the time I got back to Suburbia people were asking me to play, you know, other older people. I was really getting into it. In late August I got back with people I had played with earlier and we formed a band.
> Interviewer: What was the band's name?
> Sam: No Exit.

The band's name, after the play by Jean-Paul Sartre, was suggested by the band's drummer, who was in eleventh grade. At that time Sam had just begun ninth grade. During that year, Sam read Sartre's play, and "even though it was tedious, there was something to be gained from it."

After the formation of No Exit came a parting of the ways between Sam's real interest and school. Sam began to read Joseph Campbell's work on mythology, particularly the hero myth, and Hermann Hesse's *Siddhartha*. For Sam "real" learning occurred more and more outside the school context. He associated the outside world with "reality," while he saw the world of school and the community of Suburbia as "unreal," a place of containment.

The Quest: Following Your Bliss

Sam was in twelfth grade at the time of our interviews. By this time he had developed a fairly complex philosophy of life. Sam quoted a phrase from Campbell as representative of his thought: "Follow your bliss, and doors will appear where there were no doors before."

Sam believes that one can only find happiness in life by following one's dream or "bliss." His dream is to become a musician. He refers to the realization of this dream as his "quest" in life, a term that also comes from Campbell's discussion of the hero myth.

> Sam: I mean in every hero quest that he talks about, there's sort of trials that they have to go through. And there's temptations that are there that can draw them off their path. They have to overcome that, and basically follow their bliss to the destination they want to get to. So I guess that's me. I don't want to own a house and live in the suburbs.... Music is what I'm following. There's other philosophies and cultures involved in music. And I'm not just taking about American music. I want to learn the other cultures.

For Sam the quest and the attendant bliss one finds come about by being a "student," although not necessarily one in the school context. The student is an individual who can learn from a teacher or by him/herself and has been able to retain the sense that there is always more to learn on the heroic quest to finding the truth. That is, the quest for wisdom never ends for a real student.

THE FANS-OF-SCHOOL

Within the school context, Sam sees fewer of what he considers "students" than adolescents who are "fans of school." This phrase came about when Sam was explaining what a fan does at a rock concert. The connection he made was that the rock fan loses her/himself to the performance, and that there is a merging between performer and audience. Fans lose their individuality at a concert and "just go wild." While the fans-of-school do not go wild about school, they do lose their individual identity to the teacher and to the official culture of school. This fan-of-school represents Sam's conception of the people at "the center."

> Sam: There are people that are fans of school. They're the people that really get into school, the whole lifestyle....[They] are very serious, and get into sitting down and learning what the teacher told them to learn, following the rules, getting into class, raising their hands, answering the questions, and getting A's on the test. So I guess they would be the fans of the whole school policy, of getting grades, and doing the homework, being good students in the eyes of the teacher.

The fans-of-school, Sam believes, lose their ability to struggle against adversity in the quest for truth. The student, however, does her/his own thinking and in the process discovers her/his true self. Along these lines, when I asked Sam if there were any other authors besides Campbell who have influenced him, he mentioned Hesse.

> Sam: It [*Siddhartha*] has major philosophical overtones to it....it is about trying to achieve some sort of mystic participation or self-actualization or oneness with the universe.

The student, like the character Siddhartha, strives to find the truth of existence on his/her own terms. While one can learn from a teacher certain philosophic principles and ideas, the actual experience of self-realization can only be accomplished by oneself; no one can do it for you.

BEYOND WORDS

For Sam music provides the integrating link between philosophic ideas and the real world of living. Through music he finds a mode of expression that offers an alternative to the written word. As a "student" Sam strives to go beyond conventional means to express himself and reach altered states of consciousness.

> Sam: I think there are some things that you can't just put into words, and with music something I found is that there is an entirely different form of communication. There's speaking and there's music. You're trying to

convey an emotion through music. But you can't put it into words, 'cause words are symbols. I mean the word "music" is a symbol. If you see it on paper, that's not music.

For Sam the realm of music goes beyond the symbolic, into an "alternate" reality. At times he refers to music as a "higher state of consciousness," which he describes with authority.

Sam: Nothing really moves me as far as music does. It's my only form of real expression. Also, it's my only spiritual out. Some people have religion. Every now and then, when I play, there's an altered state in playing.... So I guess [I] tied music and spirituality, music is a healing thing.

Music for Sam is multidimensional, serving many different yet related functions in his life. It enables him to "speak" without the hindrance of words. It connects his philosophical ideas with the experience of "alternate" states. And music serves a social function in Sam's life: it provides him a way to critique conservative, middle-class America, while expressing his desire for world unity.

WORLD UNITY

Sam defines music as a metaphorical solution for world unity and peace between peoples of different cultures. He suggested the metaphor of world unity as he described a concert organized by Grateful Dead drummer Mickey Hart. The concert, held in Sam's community, featured drummers from a variety of countries and cultures: a drummer from Nigeria, two drummers from Brazil, two from India, two more from Africa (Sam did not know which countries) and of course Hart.

Sam: [Hart] had to get all these people from very different backgrounds, very conflicting religious backgrounds too, get them all on the stage. They were all masters, so no one missed a beat of course, but it was all these guys, and they got their shit together. They really, you know, they connected...all these very different styles combined into this one thing, *and it's kinda cheesy in a sense to be saying this, but it was like a metaphor for world unity, I would think* [my emphasis]....In my opinion, that's the only way people are able to unite, is when you put your ideologies aside....The whole time I was thinking, I was seeing that there is hope for this world in a sense that people can put differences aside, and even if it is just for one night on stage.

World unity is accomplished by people working ("playing") together and putting aside their ideological differences. For Sam music allows such a displacement to occur by enabling one to forget oneself, lose oneself in the present moment. In the act of playing, the cultural self dissolves and the "true" self merges with the other players. In a very literal sense, for Sam the act of playing an instrument with others creates harmony.

IT DIDN'T WORK

Sam's political critique of white middle America is very much linked to a change in his music preference. Sam views himself as having moved from rock guitarist to jazz guitarist. This shift, for Sam, signifies a change of focus in his life; a shift from reliving the past (nostalgia rock) to studying new cultural sounds (jazz). He now critiques the past in terms of outdated '60s musical styles and outdated '60s political ideologies. He is very concerned that his generation does not have its own sound, its own identity.

Sam: I think the problem with our generation is that a lot of people want to go back to the '60s, and deal with it [politics] in a '60s sense.

Interviewer: What's wrong with that?

> Sam: It didn't work...the '60s and '70s, it's been beat to death....I don't want
>   to hear about the '60's anymore. Some good musicians came out of
>   there and some good political things came out of there, [but] now it's
>   the 1990s, and we're still doing the same exact stuff basically. We still
>   have corrupt leaders and we're still screwing over people all over the
>   world. In the '60s a few things came out of, like, the civil rights
>   concept, like Martin Luther King. But it didn't get very, not many
>   people, very far. It opened a door for a few people, but the majority of
>   blacks still live in poverty.

Sam aims toward the future and is very concerned about "the glory days," about living in
a nostalgic past. In Sam's philosophy the past is to be remembered, yet one ought not
dwell on it. He feels his generation needs to look ahead, toward the future, for political
solutions and the creation of new musical forms.

> Sam: I don't know, I mean you gotta move on. I mean obviously everybody
>   has their glory days and it's good to look back to them. When it comes
>   to politics and stuff, you gotta start looking ahead.

STRATEGIES OF DISPLACEMENT

Sam sees his world as divided into the real and the unreal. His quest involves a journey to
a reality that entails transcending the "unreality" of Suburbia. Through strategies that
displace Suburbia's conservative social values, Sam attempts to relocate himself in the
margins. The key to these strategies of displacement is the way Sam renders his
immediate school context an illusion, as unreal.

Sam did not invent these strategies of displacement; rather they were proposed by
non-school literature, popular music, and white, middle-class culture. Sam claims to be
on a "quest" to discover his true self and to express his unique vision/sound. He seeks a
timeless and transcendental unity that exists between all beings. As Robert Bellah points
out, these notions of self and reality can be located in one of the cornerstones of middle-
class ideology—the expressive individual. Bellah writes that Walt Whitman exemplifies
the expressive individual:

> Whitman identified the self with other people, with places, with nature, ultimately
> with nature....Freedom to Whitman was above all the freedom to express oneself,
> against all constraints and conventions....[For] Whitman, the ultimate use of the
> American's independence was to cultivate and express the self and explore its vast
> social and cosmic identities. (Bellah et al., 1985, pp. 34-35)

There is a great deal of similarity between Bellah's description of Whitman's thought and
Sam's struggle to express himself. Another similarity between Sam and Whitman is that
the latter was perceived as an eccentric by the establishment, and Sam considers himself
an eccentric.

> Interviewer: Do you perceive yourself as a radical, a rebel?
> Sam: Maybe eccentric, not radical....I don't fit in the scene....[I] work not
>   to be in the center. I mean I'm eccentric.

Sam perceives the world in terms of a sort of *Bildungsroman,* the German learning novel
in which each new adventure on the quest leads the hero closer to the truth. In Sam's
favorite novel, Hesse's *Siddhartha,* we find the source of Sam's insistence that words
cannot express wisdom, and teachers cannot communicate it. Hesse writes:

> Wisdom is not communicable. The wisdom which a wise man tries to communicate
> always sounds foolish....Everything that is expressed in words is one-sided, only half
> the truth; it lacks totality completeness, unity....Therefore, teachings are of no use to

me; they have no hardness, softness, no colors, no corners, no smell, no taste—they have nothing but words. (1951, pp. 115, 118)

Sam displaces school and teachers because of their reliance on words. He replaces words with music as the primary mode of expression in his life. Music holds Sam's social and spiritual worlds together. Clearly the interviews confirm Simon Frith's observations on the social functions of music, namely that "the social functions of popular music are in the creation of identity, in the management of feelings, in the organization of time" (1987, p. 144). As an eccentric, Sam is able to transcend what he sees as the mundane and conservative reality of Suburbia High by situating himself in the margins.

IV. TECHNOLOGIES OF MARGINALITY

Micro-level studies can reveal the construction of racial identity at the individual level within a specific context. In Jorge's story, we can see how he uses strategies of stardom in his attempts to survive in school and move out of the margins. Being "caught" in the margins, Jorge has learned to work with and through his marginality. The margins, in turn, are a place (a location) filled with painful memories, such that past experiences of racism frame present reality. The racism has not ceased, but Jorge has learned to develop a "survival mechanism." His story presents acting-as-art and acting-as-survival-skills.

Sam's story is framed within a culture of privilege. He acknowledges and critiques his privileged status (white, upper-middle America) by metaphorically distancing, "displacing," himself from the immediate realities of Suburbia High. Sam looks beyond the "unreality" and "ignorance" of Suburbia to other non-Western cultures. He searches for world unity and higher states of consciousness through music. Sam's narrative presents strategies and technologies to displace conservative community values. In doing so he relocates himself to the margins. In his own words, he is an "eccentric" in school.

Taken together, "stardom" and "displacement" are not viewed as an identities per se. They are historically defined strategies, technologies, that Jorge and Sam employ. Through stardom and displacement, the two young men construct themselves within a negotiating context of power relations—the school. We notice the contrasting directionality of these two strategies. Stardom, within Jorge's context, aims toward center stage. It is a strategy enabling Jorge to gain greater visibility. In the other direction, Sam's strategy of displacement aims toward the margins. There he strives to distance himself from school and community values.

Despite the contrast in their strategies, there does exist a point of commonality. As Trinh T. Minh-ha writes, "displacing is a way of surviving. It is an impossible, truthful story of living in-between regimes of truth. The responsibility involved in this motley in-between living is a highly creative one: the displacer proceeds by unceasingly introducing difference into repetition" (1990, p. 332). Sam's story is not one of escape but, as Trinh suggests, a story of survival. Sam's strategy is to introduce difference—i.e., his emphasis/interest in non-Western cultures and music as mode of expression—into the repetitive structure of school.

With this in mind, we begin to see that both Jorge's and Sam's stories are about survival within the suburban school context. Highlighting their racial formation at the micro-level, we find that "survival" within the margins is closely related to the formation of their respective sense of time. Recent research on children's learned sense of time shows that "a young child's learned awareness of time and the future is not so much a cognitive or mental conception as it is a sense that grows out of vital intersubjective experiences" (Briod, 1992, p. 7). Clearly Jorge's and Sam's interviews suggest that their intersubjective experiences are different with respect to racial formation. In each narrative we find a different set of mitigating circumstances defining their intersubjective experiences of self and society.

Within the context of this study we find that the formation of their racial identity is paralleled by the development of different ways of situating themselves, temporally, toward the world. For Jorge, past memories frame his present strategies. This is not to say that Jorge doesn't think of the future; clearly he does. But Jorge situates himself within a *past-present* time matrix in his dealings with everyday events. All Jorge's acting strategies are firmly rooted in the past. By incorporating acting methods such as affective memory (Strasberg, 1991), he is able to bring the past to bear on present situations both on and off stage.

Sam's story suggests a *present-future* time matrix. This is not to suggest that Sam doesn't remember the past; clearly he does. In Sam's case, he prefers to interpret present situations by looking to the future. Here the term "future" must also include "the higher states of consciousness" that transcend time, i.e., the timeless state of bliss. For Sam, the '60s and the past are dead and we must move forward.

What does it mean to suggest that Jorge and Sam negotiate power relations within two different time matrices? Christoph Wulf writes, "world-view and self-image are indissolubly intertwined with each other. The way man sees the world is the way he sees himself; the way he conceives himself is the way he conceives the world.... *Time is the medium that binds a man's view of the world with his view of himself*" (1989, p. 49; my emphasis). This suggests that while Jorge and Sam occupy the same space, the margins, their worlds are bound together by a different sense of time. That is, the "glue" (time) that binds their self-images and worldviews together is different; a difference that is grounded, in part, in the concrete, material conditions of racial discrimination on the one hand and privilege on the other.

REFERENCES

Bellah, R., Madsen, R., Sullivan, W., Swidler, A., & Tipton, S. (1985). *Habits of the Heart*. New York: Harper.

Briod, M. (1992). Promising futures: Mediating the early childhood experience of time. *Analytic Teaching*, 12 (2), 3–8.

Butler, J. (1990). *Gender trouble: Feminism and the subversion of identity*. New York: Routledge.

Dyer, R. (1979). *Stars*. London: British Film Institute.

Foucault, M. (1983). On the genealogy of ethics: An overview in progress. In H. Dreyfus & P. Rabinow (eds.), *Michel Foucault: Beyond structuralism and hermeneutics*. Chicago: U of Chicago P.

_____. (1988). The ethic of care for the self as a practice of freedom. In J. Bernauer & D. Rasamussen (eds.), *The Final Foucault*. Cambridge, MA: MIT.

Frith, S. (1987). Towards an aesthetic of popular music. In R. Leppert & S. McCleary (eds.), *Music and Society: The politics of composition, performance and reception*. Cambridge: Cambridge UP.

Hesse, H. (1951). *Siddhartha*. New York: New Directions.

hooks, b. (1990). *Yearning: Race, gender, and cultural politics*. Boston: South End.

Glasser, B. G., & Strauss, A. L. (1967). *The discovery of grounded theory: Strategies for qualitative research*. New York: Aldine.

Madrid, A. (1992). Missing people and others: Joining together to expand the circle. In M. Anderson & P. Hill-Collins (eds.), *Race class and gender: An anthology*. Belmont: Wadsworth.

Omi, M., & Winant, H. (1986). *Racial Formation in the United States: From the 1960s to the 1980s*. New York: Routledge.

Rodriguez, C. E. (1991). *Puerto Ricans: Born in the USA*. San Francisco: Westview.

Strasberg, L. (1991). A dream of passion: The development of the method. In J. Butler (ed.), *Star Texts: Image and performance in film and television.* Detroit: Wayne State UP.

Trinh, T. M. (1990). Cotton and Iron. In R. Ferguson, M. Gever, T. M. Trinh & C. West (eds.), *Out There: Marginalization and contemporary cultures.* Cambridge: MIT.

Wulf, C. (1989). The temporality of world-views and self-images. In D. Kamper & C. Wulf (eds.), *Looking back at the end of the world.* New York: Semiotext(e).

14 Slips That Show and Tell: Fashioning Multiculture as a Problem of Representation

Deborah P. Britzman, Kelvin Santiago-Válles, Gladys Jiménez-Múñoz and Laura M. Lamash

> Today we are adept at the all too familiar concatenation of identity politics, as if by merely rehearsing the mantra of "race, class, gender" (and all other intervening variables) we have somehow acknowledged the diversified and pluralized differences at work in contemporary culture, politics, and society. Yet the complexity of what actually happens "between" the contingent spaces where each variable intersects with the others is something only now coming into view theoretically, and this is partly the result of the new antagonistic cultural practices by hitherto marginalized artists. Instead of analogies, which tend to flatten out these intermediate spaces, I think we need to explore theories that enable new forms of dialogue.
> Kobena Mercer, "Skin Head Sex Thing: Racial Difference and the Homoerotic Imaginary"

> An understanding of language as a site of struggle or as a conductor of ideology will empower us as both readers and writers. The right to claim linguistic space is a basic human right. Rather than set the agendas for various kinds of writings, we can do no more than ask of our education system that it encourage the writer to think about how she positions herself in that political space. Reactionary positions may well be reduced or not. But readers will have to be prepared for both possibilities.
> Zoe Wicomb, *An Author's Agenda*

WHEN IT COMES to the problem of teaching about difference differently, contradictions abound. The very language we borrow to pin down identities, to situate an experience, to recognize an event, and to render intelligible the meanings of others is, as Zoe Wicomb suggests, both a linguistic right and a site of ideological struggle. Antagonizing these discursive boundaries, writes Kobena Mercer, are the contradictory and conflicting ways people embody, conceptualize, and perform the politics of identity. The familiar litany of race, class, gender, sex, and so on, is not the originary explanation. Rather these social markers are emblematic of the treacheries of representation: the unruly and contentious relations among the imagined conditions of knowledge, identity, lived experience, and social conduct. Despite the persistent claim that differences can be anchored in and assuaged by stable meaning, we argue that while knowledge of social differences is essential to teaching multiculture, there is nothing essential about the knowledge of social difference.

Generally, as practiced in compulsory education, mainstream orientations to the field of multicultural education have been preoccupied with supplying students with "accurate" and "authentic" representations of particular cultures in the hope that such corrective gestures will automatize tolerant attitudes. These newly represented cultures appear on the stage of curriculum either as a seamless parade of stable and unitary customs and traditions or in the individuated form of particular heroes modeling roles. The knowledge that scaffolds this view shuts out the controversies of how any knowledge—including multicultural—is constructed, mediated, governed, and implicated in forms of social regulation and normalization. The problem is that knowledge of a culture is presented as if unencumbered by the politics and poetics of representation. As well, mainstream orientations have not addressed how knowledge of social difference might rearrange and bother the identities of the knower. The question of how knowledge of identities and cultures is produced, encountered, and dismissed in classrooms homogeneous and heterogeneous is completely ignored. The critical point of departure is not how to make knowledge hospitable. Rather knowledge, when recast from the perspectives of those historically unaccounted for, becomes an ideological haunted house: illusory, evasive, and preying upon the rational-minded "victims." It is this tension we wish to explore.

At the same time, our critiques of multicultural education do not deny the need or the right of oppressed subjects—collective and individual—to speak and act within and outside the classroom in the affirmative and emancipatory interests of their own identity: be it as women in general, the poor and working class, people of color, lesbians and gays, and so on. The agency of the subaltern is impossible without the capacity to perceive the experiences that structure and give meaning to one's identity—however socially constructed—as essentially identical to those of other members of one's group (Spivak, 1988). Such actions, however, while they emphasize the right to representation, are without neither ideological struggle nor contradictory effects. Judith Butler suggests as much: "I'm permanently troubled by identity categories, consider them to be invariable stumbling-blocks, and understand them, even promote them, as sites of necessary trouble" (1991, p. 14). And, in the context of the classroom, Diana Fuss poses the question this way:

> How are we to negotiate the gap between the conservative fiction of experience as the ground of all truth-knowledge and the immense power of this fiction to enable and encourage student participation? (1989, p. 118)

The critique of essentialism in the field of multiculture serves as our place of departure because mainstream practices have not moved beyond the mistaken impulse to offer students "good realism" as a remedy to the "bad fictions" of stereotypes. Such an approach to "knowledge" structures the mistaken faith in the stability of representations and language, and in the obviousness of experience as the ground of truth. Sustained are the normative boundaries between the real and the imaginary, as if these boundaries themselves were beyond the reach of representations. However, as other cultural theorists have noted (see, for example, Cohen, 1988; Dyer, 1988; Ellsworth, 1989; Fuss et al., 1991; Gilman, 1991; Hall, 1988; McCarthy, 1990; Patton, 1990; Trinh, 1989), to approximate the specificities of identities and the uneasy relations between equity and difference means attending to uneven relations of power and the structuring contradictions within and between representations. What if such approaches to education simultaneously recognize, as Elaine Marks points out, that "there must be a sense of identity, even though it is fictitious" (1984, p. 110)? Can the language of multiculture begin with a recognition of the ambivalence of meaning and the detours of representing identities that are always already overburdened with meanings one may not choose but, nonetheless, must confront and transform? What if education that is multicultural is also education that is anti-essentialist?

Is There a Subject in This Text?

Michele Wallace (1991) identifies three simultaneous horizons of political practice: she tentatively names these as equity, difference, and the deconstruction and demystification of the dichotomy between the two terms. Whereas equity concerns access to the contexts and structures of inclusiveness, visibility, and attainment of civil rights—and thus references the conditions for development and progress—difference confounds the terms of equal treatment with subjectivity, relations of power, and the respective identities produced in the social realm. Difference concerns the refusal to collapse the specificities of identity with the imperatives of equal access. As Wallace states: "It is essential that we keep acknowledging differences as a process rather than as a fait accompli" (p. 141). The third horizon suggests the need to move beyond the binary opposition that poses equity as sameness and difference as disruption. Wallace warns of the difficulties of this direction: "the deconstruction of the binary opposition of equality versus difference...is the level on which language wreaks the havoc of indeterminacy versus premature closure" (p. 142). An attention to the structuring impulses of these terms means taking an anti-essentialist stance and attending to the uncomfortable fact that social power is unevenly distributed and lived.

Keeping in mind each of these "horizons," we now want to take as a problematic the work behind them, because addressing the controversies of our time means coincidently a return to the contentions and deep investments of identity. "Selves" are neither made nor changed in isolation; the cost of identity entails reformulating the self with imperatives that, even while resisting the various forms of oppression, may still contradictorily veil and coincidentally assert how culture is lived as a relation of domination and subordination. The point is that sociality is governed by relations of power, and relations of power regulate the self. A central dilemma, then, of the slippery and shifting meanings of equity and difference concerns how individual and collective perspectives on these terms become implicated in larger discourses of social regulation.

Below we offer but three examples in university contexts in which the binary opposition between equity and difference collapses the distinctions between subordination and domination and thus obscures the question of what it means to position oneself in the political space. These examples point to the unsettling facts that classrooms are not hermetically sealed worlds; that teachers and students bring to the construction of school knowledge contradictory and conflictive criteria by which knowledge and identity are deemed relevant or irrelevant; that the larger social conditions of racism, sexism, heterosexism, and class domination fashion the borders of interpretation and meaning; and that the interruption of practices that are "normal" places the speaker—as well as her knowledge—"at risk." Our fourth and final example examines these dynamics in the context of a high school classroom, where the slips that show and tell are even more explosive.

Cindy Patton, a white lesbian cultural critic and one of the foremost experts on education and the cultural meanings of Acquired Immune Deficiency Syndrome (AIDS), describes how the politics of representation—and the meanings of equity and difference—intrude on even the most "innocent" of classroom assignments in a composition class.

> The absurdity of trying to contain the discussion of one of the most controversial and fear-inspiring issues of our time produces baffling and unpredictable situations in every classroom. In the course of a freewriting exercise in my Freshman composition course, students were asked to reflect on their choice of the University of Massachusetts. One woman said she had taken her second choice over her preference to attend a Florida university because she was afraid that if she went to Miami she would get AIDS. I couldn't simply send this student off to health services or to a course in the biology department. I could not even change her views of a few basic AIDS facts

because as a writing teacher my presentation of "facts" does not bear the authority of a scientist's.…The people in the best position to explore with students the many personal and social effects of the AIDS epidemic are the most vulnerable to accusations of "being inappropriate" or non-objective. Nevertheless, it is critical to prepare…students for life in a world where old repressive ideologies are gaining new power from their association with particular representations of AIDS. (1990, pp. 105–106)

It is difficult to decide how this student was "coding" the city of Miami: whether, in her cultural map, Miami must be synonymous with Haitians, Latinos/Latinas, gay men and lesbians, or the circumstances of drug addiction, and how she conflated these signifiers of otherness with danger and disease. This student was clearly expressing what she saw as her right to remain within the realm of the normal and the universally acceptable, be it in terms of sexuality, national-cultural identity, or relationship to the law. Her desire for "escape" fashions her dismissal of identities and social practices as deviant. Just as crucially, it entailed a reprieve from considering the social effects of her views, while it protected her own sense of academic territory, what she would deem appropriate knowledge. Thus the knowledge that might challenge her particular construct of "Miami" came to signify everything that deviated from—and therefore, threatened—this life-identified norm.

Patricia Williams, an African American legal scholar, describes how racism structures a law exam. The exam required students to argue a case based upon a decontextualized version of Shakespeare's Othello, "in which Othello is described as a 'Black militaristic African leader' who marries the 'young white Desdemona' whom he then kills in a fit of sexual rage" (1991, p. 80). To answer the exam, students had to enter into the untenable terms of "the law," where the fact pattern offered dismisses the historical motivations of the play, contemporary history, and the interpretive capacities and different subject positions of the reader. Williams writes:

The problem presents a defendant who is black, militaristic, unsophisticated, insecure, jealous, and sexually enraged. It reduces the facts to the very same racist generalizations and stereotypes this nation has used to subjugate black people since the first slave was brought from Africa. Moreover, it places an enormous burden on black students in particular who must assume, for the sake of answering these questions, these things about themselves—that is the trauma of gratuitous generalization. The frame places blacks in the position of speaking against ourselves. It forces us to accept as "truth" constructions that go to the heart of who we are. (p. 82)

Williams goes on to document the structuring imperatives of racism, sexism, and heterosexism of law exams across the country and the particular construction of equality that veils the dismissal of history and social location. In this context, equity seems to mean making available to every student the dominant identity of white, male, heterosexual law professors. And yet, the assumption of such identities is not an equal opportunity. Upon analyzing these examples, Williams writes a detailed critique to her colleagues; their response "is not good" (1991, p. 91). Like the student who complained about the above "Othello" exam only to be labeled "an activist" by the examiner, Williams is labeled "didactic, condescending, too teacherly" (p. 91). Those she works with wonder why she cannot be "objective" and why she imposes her own "personal" agenda on something as "innocent" as an examination. Again, difference is viewed by her colleagues as something that disrupts their seamless narrative: equality signifies order while difference means social chaos.

Diana Fuss, a white lesbian feminist theorist, offers another version of how difficult it is to deconstruct the binary opposition between the struggle for equality and the struggle for difference. Fuss writes:

> Recently a student in a class on postcolonialism objected to another student's interest in the social and structural forms of non-Western homosexual relations; "what on earth does sexual preference have to do with imperialism?" the angry student charged. The class as a whole had no immediate response to the indictment and so we returned to the "real" issue at hand (race and ethnicity); the gay student was effectively silenced. (1989, p. 116)

Fuss addresses the underside of identity politics, where the demarcation of relevance often collides with a view of identities as hierarchical, relegating "otherness" to irrelevant spaces. The assumption is that there is an order to the chaos of imperialism; to focus on race and ethnicity means that the unruly questions of sexuality must be set outside. Fuss goes on to say, "What we see in this ordering of identities is none other than the paradoxical and questionable assumption that some essences are more *essential* than others" (1989, p. 116). In such a formulation, the binary opposition between equity and difference sets the criteria for who is bestowed with relevancy and redundancy.

As several poststructuralist theorists have already pointed out (e.g., Althusser, 1971; Gilroy, 1987; Larrain, 1982; Pecheux, 1982; Thompson, 1986), it is through systems of belief and representation—what Stuart Hall (1978) terms cultural maps—that people live in imaginary ways their real conditions of existence. The idea is that no one has unmediated and equal access to "the real." Likewise, "the real" does not telegraph pre-existent and unmediated meanings. However, the focus on systems of belief and representation—on the social imaginary—does not deny the real and the sufferings of people. Rather we want to underscore the fact that "the real" must be constructed continuously in order to be recognized as such. The student in Patton's class, for instance, believed she had described the "real Miami." The law examiner in Williams's narrative felt he was merely presenting an unmediated Othello. The student in Fuss's class dismissed homosexuals as not real to the issue at hand. Yet, as shown above, despite claims to be univocal and homogeneous—that everyone "gets" the same message from the same phenomena—these systems of representation are never monolithic. To a certain extent they cannot escape the contentious and dialogic character of the social clashes they are imagining to be otherwise:

> As you enter an ideological field and pick out any one nodal representation or idea, you immediately trigger off a whole chain of connotative associations. Ideological representations connote—summon—one another....Nor is the terrain of ideology constituted as a field of mutually exclusive and internally self-sustaining discursive chains. They contest one another, often drawing on a common, shared repertoire of concepts, rearticulating and disarticulating them within different systems of difference or equivalence. (Hall, 1985, pp. 104–105)

Given the ubiquity of these conditions of existence, no aspect of everyday life is left untouched. But the magnitude of an idea's materiality and the force of its capacity for convocation lie not only in the pervasiveness of "triggering whole chains of connotative associations." The power of ideas also derives from the fact that these ideological clusters are the very basis of all communities and group identities. The substance of the latter is the seemingly dispassionate—and, therefore, inherent and genuine—prerogative to command the loyalty of the community's members, while defining the boundaries of its membership and the otherness of nonmembers (Thompson, 1986). The delineation of membership depends upon, for example, notions of territoriality and geographic claims, ethnocentricities, gender centering, sexual identities, age-delineated subcultures, professional and class-specific forms of identification, and so on. Much of this delineation also depends upon the privileging of one social marker, such as race, at the cost of another, such as sex. While such categories are always social constructions, their persuasiveness derives from their seeming factuality and from the deep investments individuals and communities have in setting themselves off from the "others" that they must then simultaneously and imaginatively construct (Anderson, 1983).

Such a process marks the ever-functional appeal of the universal, of fashioning the world as the reign of universal categories ("all homosexuals are diseased," "a kinder and gentler nation," "the truly needy," ad infinitum) in order to imagine one's own community or group identity as the universal norm for the rest of the world (Ross et al., 1988). The problem is that these projects are materializing in an era in which all universals are crumbling even as they scramble to rearticulate themselves and partially gain new, though fractured, currency, under different forms. It is this contradictory process, of asserting old identities in the guise of the new, that we believe the teaching of multiculture must address.

Nightmare on Elm Street and Other Fictions of Community

We now shift our analysis to explore the tensions between the imagined and the real in the context of compulsory education. In the fall of 1989 one of the authors taught a student teaching graduate seminar.[1] A central assignment required student teachers to team teach a high school literature lesson. The lesson was videotaped and then presented to the seminar participants. Two young women, Erica, an African American, and Kathleen, an Anglo American, decided to teach a lesson in Kathleen's largely white English classroom. They both identify as feminists, are concerned with issues of social justice, and are articulate about the perplexing social relations that make up any classroom.

Erica entered graduate school with a focus on English education, determined to introduce African American literature to high school students. Her own school biography lacked not just African American literature, but any admission of the controversies of race, gender, sex, and class. In an early assignment that asked students to examine their "English education autobiography," Erica identified the painful representations that had been available to her and her peers. These representations were emblematic of the binary opposition between equity and difference.

> My English 10X class was full of rich kids, and I felt a bit out of place being the only Black person in the class....As a young teenager, I felt that I was not accepted as equally bright among white students, neither by my peers nor by my teachers. Yet, I was considered too smart to be "cool" by most of my Black peers, the majority of whom were non-Regents tracked due to behavior, not ability. (My theory)
>
> That year I...did a report on Gwendolyn Brooks. It had embarrassed me that of all her work, we only read, "We Real Cool," when I was the only Black person in the class. I had a very awkward feeling that all eyes were on me, that such a poem was supposed to reflect my experiences or one typical of my race (opposed to the human race).

Kathleen, who is bilingual in English and Spanish, entered teacher education with a background in community activism, political street theater, and work in the area of domestic violence. She hoped English education would provide a space to explore the relationship between the performing and expressive arts and social change and thus entered teacher education with an explicit commitment to the process of consciousness raising. At the same time Kathleen was concerned with what her students had to say about the world and wondered about the relationship between her own political commitments and the process of learning to teach. While these two commitments are not mutually exclusive, their enactment was far more contradictory than Kathleen had ever imagined.

During their planning session these student teachers decided to focus on how positions of power and desire are constructed in literature and in the student's world.

These themes, they believed, might move students onto the more contradictory terrain of how power and desire are lived as a relation of domination and subordination, beyond the easy dualism of equity and difference. They decided to work with the African American writer Ann Petry's story "Like a Winding Sheet." Erica had studied this story in an undergraduate course on black women's writing, and in that seminar the story had spurred lively debate. Both students were pleased to create a linguistic space for an African American woman writer and, through their focus on themes of power and desire, to implicate everyone in questions of race, gender, and, to some extent, sexuality. Their two-day plan focused on discussing Petry's story and then having the students rethink the story as a group by "writing a different ending." They hoped to signal, through the selection of the story, the methodology enacted, and their own commitments to anti-racist and feminist practices, that this would not be an ordinary lesson; students would have to deal with concepts not usually addressed in the classroom and do so in a way that hopefully would transform their own views of social life.

Ann Petry's story "Like a Winding Sheet" complicates the unstable meanings of race, class, gender, heterosexuality, power, and desire. It magnifies one day in the life of a black working-class couple, and while the narration is omniscient, the story trails the point of view of the male character, Johnson. Johnson and his wife, Mae, worked the night shift in different factories. On the late afternoon of Friday the thirteenth, they reluctantly left for work. Johnson arrived late and his boss, a white woman, racialized the meaning of his lateness by calling him a "nigger." With clenched fists, Johnson told the boss: "You got the right to get mad...You got the right to cuss me four ways to Sunday but I ain't letting nobody call me a nigger." He realized how easy it would be to strike her, yet despite the "curious tingling in his fingers," which continued to haunt him throughout his shift, managed to suppress his physical anger. When his shift ended, Johnson walked to the subway and stopped at a diner for coffee. He waited in a long line but upon his turn to be served, the white waitress at the counter told him the coffee urn was empty. Again, Johnson felt the sensation of wanting to hit this white woman for refusing a black man a cup of coffee, but reasoned with himself and walked out, not seeing her make a new urn of coffee. He returned home exhausted, as did his wife, Mae. They began to argue about small things and Mae attempted to cajole him: "You're nothing but an old hungry nigger trying to act tough and...." Seized again by the tingling in his hands, Johnson "sent his fist shooting straight for her face." And while the idea of hitting his wife appalled him, he could not stop himself. "Like a Winding Sheet" ends with Johnson repeatedly hitting Mae.

A very short discussion initiated by Erica began with the question of "what was bugging Johnson." The only African American student in the class, a young man, said he thought racism hurt Johnson. A white female student adamantly disagreed; she maintained that the story was not about race. "What made you think it was a race issue?", Erica softly asked the young man. "She called him a nigger," he replied in a barely audible voice. Carefully, Erica responded, "Yes, so that's something that could point to race." Neither Erica or Kathleen questioned the white female who refused to view the racial terms of the story. However, both student teachers were puzzled by the meanings of such a denial. But partly due to the circumstances of time, and, perhaps in Erica's case, partly due to the painful experience of dealing with the denial of race, Erica asked another question, "What does it mean that all of Johnson's confrontations were with women?" That question was lost; students were restless and wanted more to listen to each other's endings than to discuss the story.

The narrative endings the students came up with in group sessions represent two rejoinders to both the Petry story and the student teachers' pedagogical efforts.

Narrative I

He overdosed on PCP that he had been taking all along (that he bought from Lester). Then he proceeded to the local pub and got rather drunk. He then returned home. Mae was rather perturbed because he was quite late. She started complaining. He yelled, "Shut up...." Then went crazy. He pulled out a butcher knife, stabbed her 69 times, raped her because she was still warm. Took her and threw her over a bridge. [He] then decided to jump to be with her because he really did love her, but before he did he savagely and brutally murdered 7 white nuns with a razorblade studded garden hose.

Narrative II

But he stopped, he realized he couldn't hit her. He told Mae everything that happened. Then he went crazy. He went around the house slamming down everything in his way. After a half hour, he stopped, dropped to the floor and Mae after standing by watching, letting him get his anger out, comforted her husband. The next day he quit his job. Within the week he found another job. One which he liked and from then on he and Mae lived in peace and happiness.

Both narratives unleashed "whole chains of connotative associations" for everyone involved, and as we will see, turned out to be different sides of the same coin. However, at the end of the performance, it was the first narrative that caused Erica to exclaim amid the uproar, "That's really sick." She later expressed her shock: "After hearing that story, I just didn't have any words." Both student teachers knew they could not end their lesson with these narratives and planned a final lesson that asked students to return to their narratives and describe the cultural codes that governed their respective endings. In this way, both Erica and Kathleen believed that while they could not control how students expressed meanings, they at least could ask them to articulate the rules that structured meaning.

BETTER TO HEAR IT?

Compulsory education often leads to the assigning of blame to teachers for their failures to create tidy and efficient moments of learning. According to this enlightenment logic, learning is an orderly progression from ignorance to knowledge; ignorance is thus understood as an originary state, not as an effect of the knowledge one holds, and so typically, making space for ignorance is not an educational priority. However, Stuart Hall underscores the imperative of structuring classroom discourse and practice in ways that make room for the chaotic, for ignorance, and for the unleashing of "the unpopular."

> What I am talking about here are the problems of handling the racist time-bomb and doing so adequately so that we can connect with our students' experience and can therefore be sure of defusing it. That experience has to surface in the classroom even if it's pretty horrendous to hear: better to hear it than not because what you don't hear you can't argue with. (1981, pp. 58–59)

Whatever Erica and Kathleen felt lacked in their lessons—the ever-looming "what ifs...?"—it must be understood that theirs was an act of heroism. What was particularly true for Erica, whose biography made this experience all too familiar, was also working through the tensions raised by Patton, Williams, and Fuss. Given the myth pervasive to classroom learning that rationality leads to sensitivity, these educators understand its failure. Rationality, or the seeming neutrality of knowledge, can assault people's sensitivities, especially of those educators who are in different ways marginalized. What becomes suspect, along with their teaching authority, is their very identity. And in compulsory-education settings, when a teacher's authority becomes suspect student resistance is often virulent. For instance, it may well be that had Fuss been in a high school classroom the complaining student not only would have consigned the question of homosexuality to the realm of the irrelevant but more than likely would have called the other student a "faggot."

The commitment to rationality—and to rational persuasion—is antithetical to teaching multiculture. It actively erases the complex, contested, and emotionally charged investments students and teachers confront when their subject positions are called into question. It does this by positioning all participants as equal, as if one could choose to be unencumbered by larger dynamics of domination and subordination. Both narratives called into question the identities of these student teachers in very particular ways. At the same time, the narratives exposed the limitations and ignorance of these high school students, in a way that no rational discussion of race or gender ever could.

The first narrative invokes a pastiche of racist and sexist stereotypes that criminalizes the black male, brutalizes the black female, and renders white females as virgins and victims. Such positionings, dependent as they are on the process whereby identities become essential explanations for social failure, are very much an effect of these students' academic socialization: lacking sustained opportunities to see themselves as sexed, classed, raced, and gendered and thus unable to consider the contradictory relations of these markers, in whatever form, in terms of their social effects. Consequently they cannot make sense of the identities of others except through the matrix of intelligibility offered by virulent and readily available racist and sexist fantasies. And yet their "ignorance" of how identities work is, in actuality, an effect of the "knowledge" these students already hold, namely that race, class, gender, and sex are the explanations of "trouble" and "discomfort" and thus are best left alone. The trouble is challenging the immutability of these categories. Unlike Judith Butler, who considers categories of identity to be "stumbling blocks" precisely because they are constructed, these students perceive identity itself—and not how it is represented—as the source of trouble.

Both narratives are familiar. In the first narrative the student writer imagines that these identity markers, in and of themselves, lead to and explain social disorganization and individual failure; while in the second narrative safety and individual success can only occur when these markers of race, sex, and gender have been defused. Whereas the first narrative intrinsically victimizes "blacks" and ironically represents these white female students' fear of victimization, the second narrative represses the dynamics of any subordination by asserting the value of free markets and equal opportunity. Something else occurs in the first narrative and this is the conflative understanding of racist violence as tempted by heterosexual love. "Johnson" is a trope of the first narrative's contradictory fantasies. The second narrative offers a rejoinder: there, heterosexual love saves Johnson from systemic racism and ensures Mae's domestic bliss as predicated on Johnson's happiness.

If multicultural education is structured to engage and confront the unpopular in order to "defuse" the ideological violence lurking beneath the surface of sites of learning, it must also confront the ongoing tendencies of the subjects themselves to engage in another type of dispersal, namely avoidance. The second narrative, in effectively erasing discomforting identity markers, is these students' attempt to recast an explosive situation by rendering it familiar, safe, and oddly, an equal opportunity endeavor. To refer to Hall once more, the issue these narratives point to is how, in complex and precarious ways, unpopular moments in the classroom are everywhere in general but nowhere in particular.

RETHINKING "THE REAL" IN TEACHING MULTICULTURE

What regimes of truth structured the lesson and the students' narratives? By providing the students with the encouragement to move beyond merely harvesting meanings already planted in the text, the student teachers attempted to transform the literal reading strategies that structure talk in traditional literature classrooms. They mistakenly assumed that students would affectively cooperate with these new goals. At the same time, there is nothing literal about the Petry story; it is, we would argue, a particularly gritty and overdetermined story of representation, a critical fiction, so to speak. The difficulty, then, lay in the regime of truth these student teachers assumed, grounded in general on the persuasive capacities of reason and specifically anchored by the particular reason of feminist and anti-racist pedagogy. Supposedly this new rationality was to surface through the compelling presentation of factual data as each student worked at transforming the text. And yet where and how would such factuality emerge?

Enlightenment attempts of this sort tend to locate social prejudices within the realm of the illusory or the mistaken and as problems of individual attitudes. The view is that by presenting students with the effects of racism and sexism, via the Petry story, students would be capable of substituting the unsavory falsehoods that populate their own cultural maps (namely racism and sexism) with the healthy truth of an anti-sexist and anti-racist knowledge. Hopefully, this reasoning goes, to produce an appropriate ending to the story would permit the hardworking student to "experience" the substance of what it means to be "woman" and "black"—to step into the shoes of "the other," to be "the other of the day"—and in this way to access some inner truth already residing in this experience. In this manner each student would be able to work on, through, and with the stable, regulatory borders of race, gender, class, and sexuality that the Petry story was supposed to expedite. Such an enlightenment narrative assumes, on the one hand, that students will already want to recognize and transform oppressive relations and the bad old stereotypes that sustain them, and, on the other hand, that such knowledge—if indeed it can be made accessible—immediately leads to progress. Clearly, the students' narratives offered different cultural maps.

Despite the student teachers' desire to go beyond the naturalistic versions of social conflict in the Petry story, there were larger forces at work structuring the lesson's social effects. Their authority was partly suspect because of their "pseudo" status as teachers, and because they implicitly signaled to students social concerns that situated them in an unfamiliar political space. Like Patton, the two student teachers "did not bear the authority" of mainstream knowledge and experiences, and like Williams, they had a rationale for the lesson that was vulnerable to accusations of being inappropriate, political, and—oddly, in a literature class—too subjective. Erica and Kathleen wanted imaginary things such as racial freedom and gender justice; such desires evidently located them outside the teacher identities and the knowledge students were expecting. In other words, to the students in this class, these student teachers were not real. Like the question raised by the gay student in Fuss's class, their feminist and anti-racist concerns were not "the real issue at hand." The real issues, as the high school narratives offered and the above-mentioned classroom events demonstrated, were racial hierarchies, women's subordination, and compulsory heterosexuality. Each situation represented the refusal to complicate a tidy and familiar sense of the world.

Yet if the meanings, the identities, the experiences, and the knowledge being discussed had not been represented as being stable or as "real" by these student teachers—as opposed to being imagined and, therefore, constructed—then perhaps the students' normative responses could have been anticipated and addressed in more fruitful ways. That is, gesturing toward the constructed real—of the narratives, of the classroom dynamics, of the identities of every participant, and of the Petry story—may have allowed students to perceive experience otherwise, in more ambivalent and contested ways. They might have understood experience as made possible by the regimes of truth and the disciplinary technologies that fashion the ways in which "race," "gender," "sexuality," and "class" are uncomfortably lived and read through relations of domination and subordination (Foucault, 1985). This would have implied that identities such as "black woman," "black man," and "white woman," for instance, could not be adequately understood as essential explanations. It might require, in the case of the Petry story, the consideration of how these markers racialize and sexualize the knowledge and cultural maps of readers who are always already socially located. For this space to open, the problem would have to shift from one of rewriting the Petry story to reconstructing and renegotiating just what exactly students and teachers were responding to and what representations they had to borrow to do this work. In other words, the social effects of representation would have to become central.

MULTICULTURE AND THE TROUBLE WITH KNOWLEDGE

The teaching of multiculture must be coupled with the attempt to create or expand the space and time in the classroom to discuss race, class, gender, and sexuality with attention to what it is that structures these social markers as explanatory and with, as Wallace argues, a concern with the demystification of the old dualism of equity and difference. For instance, the new high school curricular reforms could argue for the need to address social differences as still being lived at present in socially conflictive and painful ways, despite the fact of civil rights legislation. This would mean *not* representing particular identities and cultures as evolving within a mellifluous present that has resulted from strife and discord that lie completely behind us. Much of the current reforms in multiculture continue to be "Disneyfied" by the normative imperatives of social and class harmony (McCarthy, 1990)—as if high school students of history, society, and culture could be whizzed through several centuries of U.S. and world experience, like visitors at the Epcot Center, smiling all the way (see, for example, Wilson, 1985).

From a different vantage point, many of the present reforms continue to be structured by the ever-present fear, as Michelle Fine (1991) has illustrated, that to mention things like racism, sexism, heterosexism, and class domination will either reproduce these narratives or somehow discourage students from the normative thought that they can succeed by their own individual efforts. To move beyond these kinds of normalizations, curricular efforts would have to address, as Samuel Delany suggests, that "the real is not a pregiven state that reproduces itself by means of the political but rather is political production itself" (1991, p. 56). This formulation, so necessary to the teaching of multiculture, couples knowledge and power.

Perhaps, then, the more pertinent issue—relevant to each classroom event previously discussed—is the conceptual gymnastics the students had to perform to shut out difference. This is reminiscent of Toni Morrison's question about the Western canon: "What intellectual feats had to be performed by the author of his critic to erase me from a society seething with my presence...? What are the strategies of escape from knowledge?" (1989, p. 12). These necessary questions suppose that knowledge and ignorance are imbricated with relations of power and thus disrupt any pretense of textual innocence. From a similar vantage point, those who practice multiculture should consider Eve Kosofsky Sedgwick's argument that "ignorance" is an effect of knowledge:

> Insofar as ignorance is ignorance of a knowledge—a knowledge that may itself...be seen as either true or false under some other regime of truth—these ignorances, far from being pieces of the originary dark, are produced by and correspond to particular knowledges and circulate as part of particular regimes of truth. (1990, p. 8)

These critical orientations suggest there are no innocent or unmediated readings and that the representations drawn upon to maintain a narrative as fact, or as fiction—as the real or the imaginary—are a function of the approximative power of any knowledge. From this anti-essentialist perspective all categories are unstable, all experiences are constructed, all reality is imagined, all identities are produced, and all knowledge is approximative. So only the social effects of such conditions and contexts could be determined and never with any certainty; that is, never without any argument. These troublesome fictions must become central to our practices, if multiculture is to make a difference in how the binary split between equity and difference is lived and if multiculture is to move beyond the normative impulse to maintain the social markers of identity as explanatory phenomena.

As these lessons illustrate, when the silences of race, gender, sexuality, and so on "speak verbosely of [their] own silences [and] take great pains to relate in detail the things they do not say" (Foucault, 1980, p. 8), the narratives of social life that are unleashed can hardly be expected to take on the imperatives of civility, compassion, or social justice. Any attempt to deconstruct any kind of repressive ideology of the real always holds the potential not only to colonize social imagination—that is, to bring many back to the place of departure—but also to disorganize the efforts of those who intervene. It behooves us to prepare for both possibilities, given that meanings cannot deliver the stabilities we hope and given that identities suggest more about social effects of political production than they do about essential selves. We need to consider how power circulates as knowledge in any representation and within this context ask: How might pedagogy address the messy process of producing knowledge and offer strategies for the critique of the representations that can and cannot be produced? In other words, once unpopular things have the floor, what might it take to make sense of their contradictory beckonings in ways that refuse the seductions of essentialism?

NOTES

1 For a different version of the classroom incident discussed in this chapter, see Britzman, et al., 1991 and Britzman, 1992.

REFERENCES

Althusser, L. (1971). *Lenin and Philosophy and Other Essays.* London: New Left.

Anderson, B. (1983). *Imagined Communities: Reflections on the origin and spread of nationalism.* New York: Verso.

Britzman, D. P. (1992). Decentering discourses in teacher education, or, the unleashing of unpopular things. *Journal of Education,* 173 (3), 60–80.

Britzman, D. P., Santiago-Valles, K., Jimenez-Munoz, G., & Lamash, L. (1991). Dusting off the erasures: Race, gender and pedagogy. *Education and Society,* 9 (2), 88–99.

Butler, J. (1991). Imitation and gender insubordination. In Fuss, (pp. 13–31).

Delany, S. (1991). Twilight in the Rue Morgue. *Transition,* 54, 36–56.

Dyer, R. (1988). White. *Screen,* 29 (4), 44–64.

Cohen, P. (1988). Tarzan and the jungle bunnies: Class, race, and sex in popular culture. *New Formations,* 170 (3), 25–30.

Ellsworth, E. (1989). Why doesn't this feel empowering? Working through the repressive myths of critical pedagogy. *Harvard Educational Review,* 59 (3), 297–324.

Fine, M. (1991). *Framing Dropouts: Notes on the politics of an urban public high school.* Albany: State U of New York P.

Foucault, M. (1979). *Discipline and Punish: The birth of the prison.* New York: Vintage.

_____. (1980). *The History of Sexuality: Volume I.* New York: Vintage.

_____. (1985). *The Use of Pleasure: Volume II.* New York: Pantheon.

Fuss, D. (1989). *Essentially Speaking: Feminism, nature, and difference.* New York: Routledge.

_____. (ed). (1991). *Inside/Out: Lesbian theories, gay theories.* New York: Routledge.

Gilman, S. (1991). *The Jew's Body.* New York: Routledge.

Gilroy, P. (1987). *"There Ain't No Black in the Union Jack": The cultural politics of race and nation.* London: Hutchinson.

Hall, S. (1981). Teaching about race. In A. James & R. Jeffcoate (eds.), *The School in the Multicultural Society* (pp. 58–69). London: Harper.

_____. (1985). Signification, representation, ideology: Althusser and the post-structuralist debates. *Critical Studies in Mass Communication,* 2 (2), 91–114.

_____. (1988). New ethnicities. In *ICA Documents 7: Black Film and British Cinema.* London: Institute of Contemporary Art.

Hall, S., et al. (1978). *Policing the Crisis: Mugging, the state, and law and order.* London: MacMillian.

Larrain, J. (1982). On the character of ideology: Marx and the present debate in Britain. *Theory, Culture, and Society,* 1 (1), 5–22.

Mariani, P. (ed.). (1991). *Critical Fictions: The politics of imaginative writing.* Seattle: Bay.

Marks, E. (1984). Feminism's wake. *Boundary 2,* 12 (2), 99–110.

McCarthy, C. (1990). *Race and Curriculum: Social inequality and the theories and politics of difference in contemporary research on schooling.* Philadelphia: Falmer.

Mercer, K. (1991). Skin head sex thing: Racial difference and the homoerotic imaginary. In Bad Object Choices (eds.), *How Do I Look: Queer film and video* (pp. 169–210). Seattle: Bay.

Morrison, T. (1989). Unspeakable things unspoken: The Afro-American presence in American literature. *Michigan Quarterly Review,* 28 (1), 1–34.

Patton, C. (1990). *Inventing AIDS.* New York: Routledge.

Pecheux, M. (1982). *Language, Semantics, and Ideology: Stating the obvious.* London: Macmillan.

Ross, A. (ed.). (1988). *Universal abandon? The Politics of Postmodernism.* Minneapolis: U of Minnesota P.

Sedgwick, E. K. (1990). *Epistemology of the Closet.* Berkeley: U of California P.

Simon, R. (1990). Jewish applause for a Yiddish shylock: Beyond the racist text. *Journal of Urban and Cultural Studies,* 1 (1), 69–86.

Spivak, G. C. (1988). Can the subaltern speak? In C. Nelson & L. Grossberg (eds.), *Marxism and the Interpretation of Culture* (pp. 271–313). Urbana: U of Illinois P.

Thompson, K. (1986). *Beliefs and Ideologies.* London: Tavistock.

Trinh, T. M. (1989). *Women, Native, Other: Writing postcoloniality and feminism.* Bloomington: Indiana UP.

Wallace, M. (1991). Caliban speaks to Prospero: Cultural identity and the crisis of representation. In Mariani, pp. 66–71.

Wicomb, Z. (1991). An author's agenda. In Mariani, pp. 13–16.

Williams, P. (1991). *The Alchemy of Race and Rights.* Cambridge, MA: Harvard UP.

Wilson, A. (1985). The betrayal of the future: Walt Disney's EPCOT Center. *Socialist Review,* 84, 41–54.

15 I Pledge Allegiance: The Politics of Reading and Using Educational Films

Elizabeth Ellsworth

EACH DAY THOUSANDS of teachers and students view educational films and videos on subjects from AIDS to teenage pregnancy to the NASA space program. Yet questions about how knowledge is constructed and represented in educational films are seldom raised by educational researchers who study curriculum materials and classroom practice. Innovative programs in critical media studies do exist in schools and teacher education programs in Great Britain and Australia. But these programs and authors in the field of media education focus on popular and news media, rather than educational film or television, and they seek to define strategies for teaching critical viewing skills rather than to intervene in curriculum theory and development (Masterman, 1985; Lusted and Drummond, 1985). In the United States critical media studies and scholarship on the ideology of representation are virtually nonexistent. Film scholars also perpetuate this critical and theoretical blind spot. Operating in much of their work is the long-standing assumption that educational films subordinate aesthetic expression and formal innovation to such an extent that these films are insignificant.

When educators do discuss educational films and videos, they usually focus on accuracy of content, measurable effects on learning, and meeting of educational objectives (Kemp, 1985; Salomon, 1981). Such an approach gives film the status of a transparent, neutral carrier or stimulus of educational content. Yet for more than twenty years, film scholars have rejected this view because it could not address how form and viewing experience actively shape meaning (Cook, 1985). Researchers in both curriculum studies and cinema studies have failed to come to terms with the cultural and educational importance of a film practice that pervades one of the most contested institutions of socialization in American culture, the school.[1]

This essay reports on part of a larger study of how visual representation and language in educational films organize knowledge through discourses of truth, desire, and control and inflect that knowledge with meanings that support particular gender, race, and class interests. I want to address the contradictions within educational films and particularly how the ideological positions they offer to teachers and students both support and resist unequal power relations within schools and society.

Educational documentaries offer the kinds of social positionings I want to trace here.[2] To a much greater degree than educational dramatizations or classroom lesson films, educational documentaries invite students to see themselves in *relation* to the "outside" world—that is, the social world outside of the classroom. They do this by using argumentative evidence. In contrast, educational dramatizations use narrative conventions that emphasize individual lives, emotions, and interpersonal relations; and classroom lesson films borrow forms and presentation styles from other instructional practices. (Only rarely do lesson films offer even cursory references to the social consequences of the ways in which the curriculum appropriates its objects of study.) Unlike educational dramatizations or lesson films, educational documentaries make it clear that students exist within a social context and that knowledge about that context carries specific implications for their future behavior as social actors.

In this essay I want to show that classical educational documentaries assume a particular politics of their own reading and use. That is, in order to "make sense" of and use an educational documentary *on its own terms*, the viewer must at least temporarily and imaginatively align her/himself with the specific set of power relations that underpin the logic of the film's forms and styles. It is important to emphasize that I am talking about the film's implied audience, and not the specific experience of actual individual viewers. My goal here is to understand the process and terms by which these films "attempt to make sense of us, by offering us positions from which we are invited to see experience in particular ways" (Masterman, 1985, p. 228). As I have argued elsewhere (Ellsworth, 1987, p. 36), educational films do not themselves cause students to make interpretations and invest emotions in ways intended by the filmmakers. Recent audience studies have produced ample evidence that "audiences work upon texts in complex and different ways, just as much as texts work upon audiences. Neither audiences nor texts pre-exist…their interactions with one another" (Masterman, 1985, p. 227). As many film theorists have argued, oppositional "readings" are always possible, and it is unlikely that any individual student (or teacher) will actually experience a particular film the way the filmmaker seems to intend (pp. 217–229). But it is still important for educators to understand how the production and use of educational films support the emergence and acceptance of particular educational ideologies and practices. And it remains important to investigate how media texts mobilize representations and meanings circulating within the culture and how filmmakers attempt to encourage students and teachers to invest recognition, allegiance, and assent in some knowledges rather than others. As Len Masterman argues, media education must center on explicating the techniques producers employ when they attempt to "win assent to and complicity with their ways of seeing." What remains open "is the audience's and the students' interpretations and acceptance of this text" (p. 219).

Here I am interested in how mainstream educational documentaries encourage the viewer's allegiance to the film's authority/voice, and by implication to the larger social formation. Using textual analysis and drawing evidence from the forms, styles, and use of language in a sample of films, I argue that educational documentaries offer students a viewing experience that attempts to make pleasurable a particular social position: that of subject-of-paternalism. They do this by orchestrating aesthetics and rhetorics of protection, progress, certainty, and goodness, and then link these to racist, sexist, monoculturalist, authoritarian, and other dominant interests in ways that make such interests appear to be natural and for the common good.[3] This kind of analysis can be used to draw conclusions about how educational films confirm, extend, and sometimes contradict prevailing assumptions and logics about the proper role of schools in society.

The analysis that follows is based on a study of thirty classical educational documentaries drawn from a three-year investigation of 150 educational films produced for classroom use between 1930 and 1965. These are part of the collection of the American Archives of the Factual Film at Iowa State University, Ames, IA. They represent the efforts of major educational film producers during the time when the dominant style of educational films became fully established, and before significant changes in curriculum practices and educational film norms began to take place. Preliminary analyses of contemporary educational films suggest that after 1965 conventions of form and style changed significantly in response to influences from cinema verité, television, and the cultural and curricular upheavals brought on by the civil rights, antiwar, countercultural, and feminist movements. Yet, as I discuss later, despite changes in conventions of form and style, contemporary educational films continue to be organized in ways that imply viewing experiences and a politics of reading similar to those of the "classical" educational films studied (Ellsworth, 1987, pp. 43–45).

Within cinema studies, analyses of non-educational documentaries have generated widely accepted definitions of the formal, stylistic, and ideological norms of documentary films (Kuhn, 1978; Nichols, 1976–77). For this study I asked how educational documentaries depend upon and depart from the norms of documentaries not intended for use in schools, that is, documentaries produced for theatrical and independent distribution to general and special interest audiences. Because of their formal and stylistic similarity to educational documentaries, I compare educational documentaries to social issue documentaries that used voice-over narration and were produced between 1930 and 1965. Through this comparison I want to find both similarities and differences between educational and non-educational documentaries in the ways they use language, form, and style to limit what can be said and delimit new statements about social issues and events. At various points in the films I studied, their language, film form, and style function both to join together and to separate two social practices: "education" and "documentary." These rhetorical and representational moments indicate points at which the ideological goals of the schools and educational film industries coincide with and diverge from those of individuals and institutions that produce non-educational documentaries. By locating points of divergence and analyzing the terms of their difference, I hope to begin to define the ideological project of educational documentaries and to discover how it is given representational form.

THE POLITICS OF READING SOCIAL ISSUE DOCUMENTARIES AND PROPAGANDA FILMS

The notion of a "politics of reading" has emerged in the wake of feminist critiques of science[4] and poststructuralist rejections of Truth as an absolute, transcendental, ahistorical given that is immanent within and immediately recognizable from texts, and indeed the world (Aronowitz, 1987–88; Henriques, Holloway, Urwin, Venn, and Walkerdine, 1984; Lather, 1987; Weedon, 1987). Both the feminist and poststructuralist critiques emphasize the multiple and contradictory social positions that people inhabit and from which they "read" or make sense of their worlds. As John Hartley argues from within a poststructuralist perspective, a truth "is not produced by the mere act of utterance, by whatever authority, in whatever medium. A truth is produced in the act of reading" (1987, p. 45). "Truth" is therefore a product of a particular kind of relationship between reader (social actor) and text (interpretations of the world)—namely, one that is characterized by recognition, allegiance, and assent between the addressor and the addressee (p. 46). It is the "end product (hopefully) of a mixture of fact, fiction, fabrication and faking whose chief characteristic is that the audience—with much encouragement—continues to believe in it despite the odds" (p. 41).

As technologies, both educational and non-educational documentaries are amenable to this kind of interpretation because both use representation and rhetoric to encourage a relationship of allegiance between addressor and addressee. However, the aims of the documentary tradition (Jacobs, 1971) and of educational institutions differ significantly. The "mixtures of fact, fiction, fabrication and faking" they use vary because they are designed to produce different terms of allegiance. Furthermore, mixtures of forms, styles, and images used by educational documentaries are not arbitrary or random combinations, but rather appropriate some of the aesthetic sensibilities and conventions of representation and "evidence" circulating within the culture at any given historical moment. While such conventions enjoy varying degrees of power and legitimacy, the specific appropriations of any given educational documentary are calculated to encourage the kind of allegiance—therefore "Truth"—that best serves the particular educational project in question.

Classical educational documentaries, like other educational films, were initially produced as part of a film culture dominated by Hollywood features and the British-American documentary tradition. In the 1940s a researcher of educational film effectiveness argued that if producers wanted students who typically attended feature films at their neighborhood theaters at least once a week to consider educational films watchable and believable, they would have to imitate Hollywood's dramatic structures and high production values (Hoban, 1982). Then, as today, educational dramatizations incorporated Hollywood techniques of characterization, plot structure, camera work, lighting, and editing. They used conventions associated with feature films to encourage students to identify with characters in emotionally charged situations and thereby relate the new knowledge presented in the film to their own lives. The characters then modeled the "proper use" of new knowledge relevant to the personal and interpersonal issues raised by the films, and happy endings sought to motivate students to do the same.

U.S. and British documentaries provided the educational film industry with widely recognized and accepted models and standards for making films about social issues or problems. The documentary method enjoyed popularity and credibility, status as a serious and responsible use of the film medium, and financial support from state institutions, including agencies of the United States and British governments, the U.S. Office of War Information, and the United Nations (Barsam, 1973; Lovell and Hillier, 1972; Nichols, 1981). Stuart Hall, as quoted by Annette Kuhn (p. 53), characterized the "representational machinery" of British documentary in the 1940s as "cutting across journalism, photojournalism, cinema, and social commentary, informed by a 'structure of feeling' constituted by social democracy and populism" (quoted in Kuhn, 1981, p. 53). For our purposes here, Hall's description can be applied to social issue documentaries produced in the United States as well, including *Power and the Land* (1940), *The Land* (1942), *The City* (1939), *People of the Cumberland* (1938), *Valley Town* (1940), *On the Bowery* (1956), the *"See It Now"* series on CBS television in the early 1950s, and *Harvest of Shame* (1960) (Barnouw, 1974; Barsam, 1973).

Social issue documentaries orchestrated a wide range of seemingly heterogeneous material. These can include actuality footage, reenactments, maps and charts, music, documents, and interviews. Such materials are organized "around conceptual patterns or social processes, bringing together images from diverse places and times with the final guarantee of unity located in a disembodied voice-over, a voice-over of knowledge, the documentary Voice-of-God" (Wolfe, 1984, p. 13). As defined by filmmakers and scholars of the documentary tradition, the purpose of social issue documentaries has never been to simply "report" or provide "factual data." It has always been to solicit allegiance from the viewer in support of an interpretation about the social significance of an event, issue, or situation existing in the world outside of the film itself (Grierson, 1966; Jacobs, 1971). The primary goal has been to persuade the viewer that the film's interpretation is true, i.e., worthy of allegiance, by incorporating into it language and representational styles that connote "observational neutrality," "neutral academic discourse," "dramatic realism,"[5] fixed signifiers of common sense meanings ("the human condition," "virtue," "heroism"), and/or "nonpartisan" discourses of democracy and populism (Colls and Dodd, 1985).

While the exact political agendas that social issue documentaries attempted to follow varied according to historical moment and particular filmmaker or production institution, they all attempted to produce allegiance of a particular type. Language, form, and style write the viewer into the film's discourse as a member of a collectivity or community designated as "we." Viewers are assigned membership in this "we" explicitly with the use of the first-person plural in the voice-over narration, or implicitly through camera work and voice-over that places them physically and ideologically "on the side" of the narrator (Ellsworth, 1987). Depending on the film and the historical moment, definitions of "we" may shift from "humanity" to "the free world" to "the nation" to "the common citizen." But in the populist tradition of social issue documentaries, "we" is always some form of "we the people,"[6] united by a social conscience that informs citizenship dedicated to the good of *all* people.

In the U.S. and Great Britain the conscience of the documentary tradition entailed advocacy for a unity that extended "the good" to all men and women in the face of intractable divisions across race, class, and gender. The target audiences of most classical social issue documentaries were those groups already unified into "we the people"— those who have access and resources to participate in and influence that unity, namely white, middle-class audiences and government officials. The strategy is to use documentary's representational machinery to take this audience into a world unknown to and often unseen by them—the world of victims of social problems such as poverty, ignorance, natural disaster, discrimination, or poor working conditions (Colls and Dodd, 1985). The goal is to use the representational machinery of documentary to promote populist feeling in order to encourage middle-class audiences to recognize and agree that the problems of these victims were social, not personal, but that they nonetheless affected the physical prosperity and moral integrity of the larger community. The documentary films I studied thus imply that extending membership in "we the people" to all citizens was in the best interests of the white, middle-class citizens/viewers who made up the target audiences, especially when membership is portrayed as a matter of giving those who were currently excluded the opportunity to adopt white, middle-class, patriarchal values and attitudes and to be assimilated into the unity as already defined by dominant discourses (Hill, 1985).

It is important to distinguish here between the documentary tradition and the superficially similar practices of the propaganda film. Propaganda films strive to produce in audiences types of allegiance and encouragement that are different from those of social issue documentaries. These differences raise significant implications for understanding educational documentaries. Propaganda films mobilize the same machineries of representation used by documentaries—actuality footage, reenactments, maps, voice-over narration, and so on—but into discursive configurations that project a different politics of reading. Documentaries give the viewer the "benefit of the doubt" and assume he/she has actively taken up membership on the side of the populist-defined "we the people." The viewer's ignorance of the causes and effects of the social problems depicted is assumed to be innocent (albeit at times the result of a lapse in the exercise of responsible citizenship). Ignorance, not malice, is the problem. If only the viewer understood the threat that social problems posed to "we the people," he/she would act to remedy the situation.

Propaganda, however, is produced within contexts of historically specific struggles against an "outside" enemy and assumes the viewer's prior knowledge and experience of that context. Because of this ongoing context of struggle, viewers are addressed by filmmakers as already passively or actively supporting one side over the other. They are not innocent. The purpose of propaganda is to demarcate battle lines between "us" and an "intolerable other" that must be destroyed (Neale, 1977, p. 33). Thus, in contrast to documentary, propaganda not only assumes a viewer's preexisting position in relation to a particular struggle but specifies what action viewers must take to destroy the enemy. A film may call for literal destruction, as in war propaganda, or symbolic destruction, as when the viewer is encouraged to identify with the film's commentary as Truth and to reject the perspective of the "intolerable other" as falsehood.

Like documentary, propaganda constitutes viewers as a collectivity, a "we." But this "we" is not defined as documentary's populist conscience, supposedly shared among white, middle-class men in positions of civic responsibility. Rather, propaganda's "we" is formed by collective opposition to an outside enemy, an opposition that of necessity must be shared by all people regardless of race, class, gender, education, or other differences. As a result, in propaganda the terms in which the intended audience must be addressed require appeals to a much broader range of social positions and competencies than in the documentary. Simple declarative sentences without analysis, coupled with appeals to emotions through popular-cultural images, predominate in propaganda. This "technology" of representation serves the situation's demands for clear-cut demarcation of good/bad, friend/enemy. And it also serves the pedagogical stance of the propagandist vis-à-vis an audience of people presumed to be "less educated" than the assumed middle-class, urban norm.

In contrast, social issue documentary constitutes viewers as a collectivity threatened from *within* by a failure to extend membership in the community of "we the people" to everyone by assimilation into the dominant culture. Given a positive view of democracy and its institutions, social problems are constituted not as the "intolerable other" demanding action for the sake of either the viewers' or victims' survival. (After all, how could a democratic system—even if flawed—produce abominations?) Rather, social problems are portrayed as unfortunate but temporary and surmountable stumbling blocks on the way to the democratic ideal. Seldom portrayed as a matter of life or death, social problems in documentaries are interpreted as matters of higher or lower standards of living. Therefore, if viewers are to be motivated to act to rectify the problem, it is their populist conscience (a common sense notion of a commitment to democratic ideals), not their instincts for survival, to which the film must appeal. Documentaries address white, middle-class audiences as if they already have that conscience—the problem is not them, their ideals, or their "democracy" but rather ignorance or misinformation. They therefore do not propose "the transformation of a social structure whose constitutive principle is that of inequality" but instead offer solutions that take the form of "tinkering" with living standards, political agendas, social policies, or institutional practices (Hill, 1985, p. 35).

Documentary constitutes its viewers as members of a democracy who have the right and responsibility to deliberate and define action. Unlike propaganda then, documentary forfeits the option to specify what action must be taken to solve the problems it identifies. Its role in social reform is limited to touching the conscience already in place with film images of a world otherwise hidden from the view of government officials, the middle class, and the privileged. The goal is to stimulate the democratic process that is likewise already adequate and in place, to provoke discussion and decision making within channels already constituted and adequate. It is therefore unnecessary for the documentarist to describe the direction that must be taken, because any outcome of the democratic process undertaken with a populist conscience can only enhance the common good. In fact, unlike the makers of propaganda, it is preferable to the ideological project of social issue documentaries that the documentarist falter at the point of prescribing a solution and course of action: "the author-as-documentarian establishes his credentials, earns our trust, by declaring himself inadequate to the task at hand. To perceive gaps and contradictions in his commentary is to confirm his honesty, a success that could be won no other way" (Wolfe, 1987, p. 67). The documentarian is inadequate to the task at hand because his/her perspective is limited and potentially partisan as a result of his/her particularity. In contrast, "we the people," once we are made aware of the existence of a problem, are adequate to the task because of our collectivity, our common ideals, and our established democratic process of decision making.

THE POLITICS OF READING EDUCATIONAL DOCUMENTARIES

Like social issue documentaries, educational documentaries unify diverse materials, including actuality footage, animated charts and graphics, and docudrama, through an everpresent voice-over narrator. In contrast to social issue documentaries, in which the narration, form, and style organize subject matter and aesthetic appeals through the logic of the social problem (temporary, surmountable disparities among living standards), and unlike propaganda's organization through the logic of the "intolerable other" (enemy outside, threatening to annihilate "we the people"), educational documentaries are organized through the logic of "positive" social consequences of new knowledge. While the subject matters of the educational documentaries studied ranged from industrialization of the Mohawk Valley to racial prejudice, those subjects are always interpreted and dramatized in terms of what has changed, must change, or will change for the betterment of particular social groups or the people as a whole as a result of new knowledge. For example, in *Water Power* (1933) and *Mohawk Valley* (1927), new technologies and agricultural and industrial development improve efficiency and production, and therefore the standard of living. In *What Color Are You?* (1967), a genetic explanation of difference in skin color is offered as the "answer" to unstated but implied questions that have their roots in racism, and the new biological knowledge is presented in a way that implies that prejudice is now obsolete. In *Rural Women* (1951), the new practices of female agricultural extension agents bring meaning, independence, and political power to the lives of rural women that have otherwise been characterized by isolation and unnecessary drudgery.

Educational documentaries do not designate enemies within or without. As in social issue documentaries, if the film refers to problems or threats to the people as a whole or to particular social groups, it does so without imputing blame. Problems such as unemployment (*Wastage of Human Resources*, 1947), "underdevelopment" (*Pueblo Dwellers*, 1931), and classism (*Social Class in America*, 1957) are the products of innocent ignorance—a "natural" and temporary, if unfortunate, step along "man's" path of scientific progress and mastery of nature. *Wastage of Human Resources*, for example, documents a litany of social problems that deplete human resources in the U.S.: infant mortality, accidents, public health problems, poverty, child neglect, rural underdevelopment, delinquency, job safety hazards, alcoholism. Yet there is no attempt to account for these conditions.

Rather, the project of the educational documentary is to announce the good news that a problem has already been solved by the discovery and use of new knowledge. Debate about the problem's nature and origin are thus irrelevant. *What Color Are You?* is typical of this. The film explains the genetic basis of differences in skin color through a docudrama depicting the already achieved and flourishing friendship between Anglo

American, African American, and Asian American boys. The narrator explains that genetically all human beings share the same ancestor, and racial differences are "only skin deep." The docudrama implies that the boys' friendships have been made possible and racism has been eradicated by behavior based on this new understanding of the biological reasons for racial difference: the boys treat each other as equals, and their tri-racial friendship draws no stares or comments as they visit their local zoo together. Because the problem is "solved" through a scientific explanation of racial difference, there is no need or room for consideration of social, ideological, historical, and economic "causes," which would require social changes that go beyond simply educating people out of their misunderstandings or ignorance of the genetics of skin color.

The predominant use of the past tense to structure educational documentaries is significant. Most educational documentaries take on a problem-solution structure. Knowledge *has been* discovered, applied, and shown to alleviate a social problem that resulted from innocent, disinterested misunderstanding or ignorance. In *Social Class in America,* Ted's "problem" of experiencing class inequality is portrayed as "solved" when he is able to achieve upper-class status by acting on what he learns from the narrator, who addresses Ted directly at one point in the film. Specifically, he learns that vertical mobility is possible if only he develop his talent, character, and abilities and be willing to move to another geographical location.

This way of presenting problems and their solutions has important implications for the implied role of the film's viewers. The new knowledge represented in educational documentaries has been produced and applied successfully elsewhere—prior to the film's viewing and without need for the audience's participation. This is in contrast to social issue documentaries, which refer to futures when the democratized audience enters the public sphere and contributes, in ways left unnamed by the film, to the democratic process of solving social problems. Educational documentaries therefore place no responsibility on the student for participating in social action outside the school. She or he is not asked to join in a struggle for survival or to enter the "public" sphere outside the classroom to engage in the democratic process of debating possible courses of action or applications of new knowledge. According to the terms set by the film, there is nothing left for the student to do but to consume the new knowledge, that is, to "know" it and use it.

The student's responsibility to consume and use new knowledge might appear similar to the propaganda viewer's responsibility to follow the exhortation of a leader and destroy the enemy. However, the kinds of allegiance entailed by propaganda and educational documentaries differ significantly. In place of propaganda films' emphasis on the leader as the source of the new knowledge, educational documentaries offer the Academic Expert. The Voice of the Academic Expert combines the address of the social issue documentary (Voice of the People) with that of propaganda (Voice of the Leader), and this combination can produce internal contradictions in the logic of the film. The significance of these contradictions will be explored later. Here, it is important to note that unlike the Voice of the Leader, the Voice of the Expert is constructed in a way that attempts to make the student's consumption and application of knowledge fit within democratic principles and alleviate the propagandistic tendencies of such an address.

The propagandistic tendencies of educational documentaries are tied to the fact that the Expert has already determined, without the participation of students, the truth of a situation and the consequences it raises for social groups. Further, the films make it clear that the Expert's understanding carries with it implications for action that may require changes in the student's future behavior. In *What Color Are You?*, for example, the genetic basis for differences in skin color is explained by a white male voice-over while we watch three boys from three different racial groups enjoying a day together at the zoo.

The film's narration states that differences in skin color are "only skin deep" and "we" all have the same ancestry, and the docudrama offers "evidence" that the boys are indeed the same—they enjoy the same things, play well together, and care for each other. These boys are acting according to the knowledge offered by the film and we see that it works: they are happy and free of prejudice. The narrator's direct address to the audience ("Imagine a world where everything is the same color...rather dull, isn't it?") and the film's happy ending make it clear that students should imitate the behavior of the film's characters.

Educational documentaries "prescribe" action by modeling "knowledgeable" or "informed" behavior. But unlike propaganda films, the prescribed action is not justified through a logic in which the extratextual context of threat to survival is so immediate that there is no time to use the democratic process to define the nature of the situation and deliberate appropriate action. Rather, the context of educational documentary production legitimizes the authority of the Expert by giving his already achieved knowledge and prescribed action status as both the *culmination* and *guarantee* of the democratic process itself. The films draw on the larger culture's ideas about the scientific method and of public policy formation, which already define experts as those who are objective, rational, and fully informed. In addition, traditional (or mainstream/ conventional/dominant) educational discourses define the Academic Expert as unbiased by allegiance to one or another faction of the People, presenting him as one who has taken into account all evidence, all voices. This association is reinforced by the participation of universities and research centers as consultants in the production and review of educational films. These institutions position themselves as democratic institutions composed of unbiased academic experts who sift and winnow the multiple and contesting voices in order to find those that best serve the common good as demonstrated by social scientific research. The opening credits of many educational documentaries refer explicitly to the authority of this extratextual context and borrow its legitimacy by naming the scientific and academic credentials of experts consulted in the film's production. Because educational institutions present the truth that results from a search based on the assumptions and methods of an "unbiased" scientific rationalism, they also are able to claim that such truth can only serve the common good. Yet new knowledge and prescriptions for change remain potentially threatening—they raise serious questions. Given the new knowledge, are we all right, or must we change the way we are doing things? What does this new knowledge mean for how we understand ourselves? What is our relation to it? What are the consequences of implementing this new knowledge in our individual and collective identities and daily lives?

Educational institutions in the U.S. claim as their imperative the production of citizens capable of making educated choices through democratic deliberation. Educational documentaries must encourage students to consume and use knowledge without being seen as manipulative or propagandistic, or they will not be adopted for use in schools. The Academic Expert's use of the scientific method aids in this because the scientific method is associated with democratic practice. They share the assumptions that "truth" or "right" will inevitably triumph in a free marketplace of ideas. Thus the result of the Expert's efforts will only make us more democratic.

The message of educational documentaries is always that the prescribed actions are not really changes at all, only improvements on what we already are—a better way to do what we are already doing, a better way to be who we already are. As in social issue documentaries, "who we are" becomes the assumed mythical norm into which "others" are to be assimilated. While social issue documentaries attempt to motivate viewers to work democratically for conditions in which all citizens can be assimilated into a white, middle-class, gender-specific standard of living and values, educational documentaries encourage students to accept particular ways of making sense of the world that also support and legitimize that mythical norm. (In fact, it is a mythical norm, since no individual person will "fit in" perfectly or unproblematically, and few will actually embody all of the traits associated with it.) The power of this norm as the vision shaping the future is so great that without exception, even in the occasional films about subjects traditionally identified with white, middle-class girls and women, the narrator of educational documentaries speaks from the position and knowledge of a man who is white, middle-class, able-bodied, heterosexual, Christian, and a scientist. Educational documentaries thus encourage students to understand the world and determine how to act in it by taking up allegiance to an academic science that serves the interests of that position. And that allegiance is privileged even when its expression undermines the film's apparent message.

Sometimes this undermining is caused by a conflict between the narrator's words and the film conventions used to illustrate them. For example, while the new knowledge offered in *What Color Are You?* is that "we are all the same, despite skin color," its language, visual representations, and narrative structure organize and represent that new knowledge from the position of the mythical norm. As the apparently white male narrator enumerates the "three main colors" of skin, we see three images to illustrate his point: a high-angle shot of an African American family buying balloons from a vender at the zoo, followed by an extreme low-angle shot of an Anglo American man selling the balloons, followed by a slight low-angle shot of an Asian American buying balloons. Conventionally, high-angle shots connote some sort of subjugation of the person represented vis-à-vis the viewer/narrator, as the camera offers the viewer a physical position that is above that of the subject. Likewise, an extreme low-angle shot connotes the dignity, nobility, or authority of the subject. In this film, then, the Anglo-American man selling the balloons to the African American and Asian American buyers is put in a position of representational superiority. Furthermore, when the narrator traces skin colors to their "origins" in particular parts of the world, his description is accompanied by drawings of the three "racial groups" in their "native" environments. The drawing of Africans depicts a woman wearing beads and standing, unoccupied, in the foreground. She is surrounded by children in a village setting. African men recede into the background, holding spears. The "world's first" light-skinned man is drawn as a powerful figure standing upright, gazing upward, filling the foreground, as other white men go about fishing in the background. Asians are drawn as though on display for the viewer's gaze, as they are unoccupied, positioned frontally, and staring wide-eyed and expressionless at the viewer. The "light-skinned man" then, is the only figure depicted as an active, effective subject rather than the object of our gaze—as a dynamic individual with lofty goals, as represented by his upward gaze. Similarly, in the docudrama of the boys' visit to the zoo, shots of their activities are consistently composed in a way that places the Anglo-American boy at the focal point (top, center) of the image, while the other boys bracket him or enter and leave the frame. The positioning of the Anglo-American boy at the "center" of our attention is just one representational strategy that supports an interpretation of his color as the norm from which others are defined in the film as deviations.

Early Settlers of New England (Salem 1626–1629) (1940) suggests how a film's narrative can support the perspective of the group defined as the norm. In this film the narrator offers a history of the settlement that is intelligible only from the position of and for the purpose of perpetuating the mythical norm, as when he describes the success of the "settlers'" harvest as "thanks partly to the Indians who abandoned land even before settlers came."

Educational documentaries encourage students to give allegiance to this particular way of making sense of the world by showing them the positive results of acting in accordance with new knowledge constructed from the position of the mythical norm. At some point in a typical educational documentary, a docudrama in which hypothetical scenarios are presented as if they were documents of actual events will depict people putting their new knowledge into action and enjoying unqualified success in solving some problem or improving their lives. While their lives are often improved dramatically, these changes are portrayed as technical, leaving unchanged the fundamental values and political arrangements that support the mythical norm and those whom it privileges.

In *Rural Women*, for example, although the agricultural agent has successfully transformed farm women's lives from ones of isolation, drudgery, and subordination to men, the narrator reassures us that their journey from "their kitchens to the world" has not upset the social/patriarchal contract between farm men and women. Ann, one of the women depicted, has started to give home demonstrations of food preservation and other domestic skills, she now speaks up at town meetings and votes according to her own judgment rather than her husband's, and she meets with other farm women to discuss world affairs. Yet this should be no surprise, for as the narrator states, "the farm women have always known that the family must come first. Now they know how the family could reach out to include the world." The narrator assures the viewer that Ann's husband is proud of her, and now Ann and her husband "share something besides social gossip." The changes are presented as only newer expressions of values that were always there—expressions that cement existing relationships—rather than as disruptive innovations.

Thus rather than showing "us" a "them" who is either an intolerable other or a social group that has been inadequately incorporated into "we the people," educational documentaries show us ourselves after we begin acting on our new knowledge. The threat of new knowledge is managed through dramatic representations of a future whose happiness is ensured by action based on that knowledge. The films thus provide paternalistic reassurances that its consequences are knowable and known and have proven to be benevolent—and that the "changes" are not really changes at all.

The goal of democratic education is the achievement of the common good through "improvement" and "progress," not social transformation. That good will be served only if students put the film's new knowledge—democratically arrived at and proven to work—into use without negotiation or revision. At this point in their logic, educational documentaries reveal a fundamental contradiction in their attempts to articulate educational practice with documentary practice: they must prescribe action for needed social and political change from within educational institutions that must be made to appear apolitical and noncoercive.

Because educational documentaries are aimed at students, their producers must deal with problems of audience that the makers of propaganda films or social issue documentaries do not confront. The democratic process requires fully informed citizens able to suspend self-interest in the name of the common good. Yet educational institutions cannot realistically position presumably immature and inadequately informed elementary and secondary students as members of "we the people," capable of or responsible for participating in democratic deliberation over choices and interpretations. (If nothing else, the continuation of students' schooling rests on the assumption that they are not yet fully ready for their roles as citizens.) Furthermore, because the schools are conventionally defined as apolitical institutions isolated from the political arena, the makers of educational documentaries cannot link students directly to the "public sphere" of political controversy and debate. They therefore face difficulties in approaching topics that do, in the world beyond the classroom, have implicit or explicit political significance.

The most common way for educational documentaries to negotiate this terrain is to make references to the world "outside" of the school only in the most noncontroversial, decontextualized terms. For example, in *Social Revolution* (1952), the role of the U.S. in industrializing the "underdeveloped" world is addressed by a docudrama in which an engineer who is an American originally from Europe explains to his wife why he must go abroad for several months to help build dams in "Asia." Although in reality the notion of a "social revolution" is a highly contested one and the engineering project described in the film is fundamentally political, the film's discussion never raises these issues. Instead, the project is described largely through the structure of the romance narrative and the individual engineer's dilemma about leaving his wife. This effectively removes the issues from the public sphere and places them within the logic of heterosexual romance and individualism. The engineer states that the new tools for peaceful social revolution are "a little education, reason, compromise, and understanding among men." "We have to show all people of the world initiative and freedom—this country can set the example." These abstractions are asserted without debate and bear little resemblance to the actual stakes and interests surrounding policies of "development."

While educational documentaries cannot refer to their extratextual contexts of negotiation, interpretation, and contestation, neither can educational discourses purporting to be democratic tolerate the propaganda film's positioning of students as choiceless followers of actions prescribed for them by the leader's voice. Positioned as the consumer of knowledge already achieved in her/his name through a democratic process, the student is addressed neither as a citizen who must actively participate in negotiating power relations within a specific social formation nor as a passive follower who must obey a leader. Although the People and the Leader represent contradictory forms of authority, the voice of the Academic Expert in educational documentaries allows the partial and imperfect interconnection of the two. This uneasy alliance is accomplished through the Expert's paternalistic address, which positions the student to receive "protection" in exchange for allegiance to the Expert's point of view. The Academic Expert seeks new knowledge on behalf of those as yet unable to do so for themselves (children, the uneducated) and offers it for the purpose of improving and protecting their lives. In return, the student is expected to consume the new knowledge offered by the Academic Expert. While the student is sometimes encouraged to think "critically" about the Expert's knowledge, s/he is seldom given permission or tools to challenge the authority of scientific rationalism, the basis of the Expert's expertise. In oblique recognition of the fact that educational institutions and documentaries are regulated by and act upon the world "outside" of the classroom, the paternalistic address of educational documentaries and of schools in general holds the private and the public in uneasy, yet effective tension. The Academic Expert is both white, middle-class father (private) and white, middle-class patriarch (public).

Sometimes, however, the contradictions inherent in the film's address break through. In *Pueblo Dwellers*, for example, silent footage of the everyday life of Pueblo Indians in a village is intercut with titles describing and interpreting their activities ("The home of the Pueblo Indian is his castle," "Making tamales"). In the final six shots, the film abruptly changes location and we see young Pueblo Indians in militarylike uniforms, standing in straight rows and marching outside of a building. The final intertitle states: "Indians in government schools advance rapidly." Here the inability of the white, middle-class Academic Expert's paternalistic address to contain its own contradictions and political project results in a film text whose logic is ruptured beyond repair. In the village the Indians demonstrate traditional activities of brick building, food preparation, basket weaving, harvest dancing, hair dressing. The images are composed using conventions that connote "documentation," "description," and "neutral observation," such as positioning the camera at a distance from the action, with the belief that this has a less intrusive effect on the action. The camera is also held motionless so as not to "interpret" the action by calling attention to the cameraperson's reactions to it. The narration uses language that encourages students to interpret the culture of the Pueblo Indians "positively" ("The hot oven bakes quickly," "Only settled peoples make pottery," "Special dances mark each season"). Neither the images nor the narration indicates any need—in health, "standard of living," or elsewhere—for "advancement" through new knowledge acquired in militaristic boarding schools. Yet images of the "positive" culture of Pueblo Indians are juxtaposed with images that imply its complete erasure: the marching students in uniform bear no resemblance to the Pueblo Indians of the rest of the film. This erasure is inexplicably represented as "advancement." Or rather, it is inexplicable until we consider the role of educational documentaries in helping to establish the authority and legitimacy of paternalistic educational institutions.

For social issue documentaries what is at stake in the attempt to win allegiance to "we the people" is the survival of the democratic process. That process is seen to break down at the point where the film is unable to motivate those with a populist conscience to enter the public sphere and participate in the democratic process. For propaganda what is at stake is the outcome of a struggle for survival. The struggle is lost if the film fails to motivate viewers to define themselves as part of the group threatened from the outside and to join the fight for survival.

Because they are produced to be used within the context of educational institutions, something else is at stake in educational documentaries like *Pueblo Dwellers*. The power and legitimacy of educational institutions themselves to act as guarantor of democracy and progress toward ending human suffering ride on the film's attempts to win allegiance from viewers to the knowledge of the Academic Expert. Progress and democracy are interrupted if students do not consume and use the new knowledge. But the paternalistic address of the Academic Expert embodies contradictorily the outcome of the democratic process worked on behalf of students. Therefore, what is at stake is a vision of the present and future in which paternalistic education is the central actor that guarantees the common good, the democratic process, and progress. This is actually stated outright in *The Negro American* (1966): "The most powerful tool in gaining freedom for the Negro was knowledge. Through education and only through education could the American Negro advance himself, and this meant education of the white man too. Many of the injustices were due to ignorance of white men. Superstition and ignorance can be wiped out only by education of all Americans, Negro and white."

Educational documentaries mobilize powerful and legitimated aesthetic and rhetorical appeals such as romantic narrative, problems solved, docudramas offering characters with whom students can easily identify, happy endings, paternalistic guarantees of protection and unqualified success, and progress through democratically applied scientific rationalism. The films use these appeals to encourage allegiance to scientific rationalism and the mythical norm of social identity. Unlike the allegiances demanded by social issue documentaries or propaganda, the terms of the allegiance sought by educational documentaries are consumption and use, without negotiation, of knowledge arrived at elsewhere, democratically, for the good of those unable—because of youth and inexperience—to participate in that process themselves. Educational documentaries attempt to offer a viewing experience that makes being a subject of paternalism pleasurable (or at least comfortable): someone has your safety, success, and happiness in mind. An expert has solved problems for the student viewer, who is therefore no longer threatened by the consequences of ignorance or misunderstanding about this particular issue. Positive outcomes are certain, progress is ensured, nothing can stop us from becoming safer, happier, or richer. The power that the father/patriarch/ teacher/mythical norm has over the viewer is only benevolent.

THE POLITICS OF USING EDUCATIONAL DOCUMENTARIES

At this point in an ideological analysis of educational documentaries, critical educators (Masterman, 1980, 1985) often prescribe a set of "critical viewing" strategies. Media educators offer such strategies to ensure "active" negotiation of the films' texts rather than the "uncritical" consumption assumed of uneducated viewers (Masterman, 1980, 1985). Like sociologists of education (Apple, 1979), they would suggest that educators and students ask "whose knowledge" is selected for inclusion in curriculum materials and textbooks, "for whose benefit," as a way to expose and ultimately reject the hidden curriculum that perpetuates the dominance of particular groups within a culture. For researchers in educational media, such questions would be framed by an investigation of how media messages are constructed, thereby enabling students and teachers to understand how mechanisms of form, style, address, and rhetoric are used by media producers in attempts to authorize particular readings by the student (Masterman, 1980, 1985).

These approaches are valuable for demonstrating the ideological nature and processes of educational media. But while educational researchers are well on the way to understanding how discourses of knowledge and power operate in textbooks and other curriculum materials, the existence and significance of discourses of pleasure and desire in educational materials remain virtually untheorized (Henriques, et al., 1984). Although these are important questions for film theorists, the literature on educational media has so far failed to address how the aesthetic nature of the educational film viewing experience mobilizes discourses of pleasure, desire, and fantasy circulating within its historical context and links them to discourses of knowledge and power. The need for such an analysis becomes acute in the case of educational film and video, because students' experiences of other noneducational media guarantee that school material is always viewed and interpreted in relation to popular film and television culture. The combination of student expectations and film- or videomakers' intentional use of conventions drawn from popular culture results in classroom viewing experiences that always include elements of entertainment, fantasy, and escape.[7]

The economic success of popular media is predicated on their ability to identify socially produced and historically varying structures of hope, anxiety, and desire, and then provide appropriate and compelling resources (images, narratives, music, etc.) for audiences to consume and use to produce meanings and pleasures that they find salient to their lives (Fiske, 1988). Educational documentaries likewise appeal to structures of feeling and offer similar "encouragements" to students to regard the resources the film offers for producing meanings as credible and salient. As in popular media, these encouragements draw their power from historically specific pleasures, desires, hopes, and fears: fear of American Indians as the other in *Pueblo Dwellers*, hope for success and upward mobility in *Social Class in America*, heterosexual desire in *Social Revolution*, pleasure in identifying with happy characters whose problems are solved in *What Color Are You?* And in addition, as described above, educational documentaries encourage students to produce meanings that confirm their allegiance to academic scientific rationalism as a way of making sense of the world and acting in it, and to the paternalism of educational institutions as a way of being incorporated (as children or as the "uneducated") into the body politic.

The above analysis of the politics of reading educational documentaries implies a classroom practice that would use and interpret those films in ways that refuse to enter into the paternalistic relation between the student and the Academic Expert who serves to perpetuate the mythical norm. The terms of such a refusal would depend only in part on an ideological analysis of whose knowledge is legitimated for whose interests. It would also need to problematize the experiences of pleasure, desire, and fantasy that these films encourage when they mobilize aesthetic conventions available from popular (film) culture. Such a refusal would focus on how an educational documentary uses aesthetic conventions to make pleasurable and desirable a relationship of dependency and protection in exchange for allegiance to the way a scientist who is white, middle class, male, and in other ways a member of the dominant culture knows the world.

As I have discussed elsewhere (Ellsworth, 1987), since 1960, some conventions of narration in educational films have changed. Influences from cinema verité and television styles, along with cultural upheavals brought on by the civil rights, antiwar, environmental, and feminist movements, have rejected the position of white male scientists as privileged sources and enunciators of knowledge. A detailed analysis of how contemporary educational films have modified aesthetic appeals to encourage particular types of allegiances is beyond the scope of my present study. Yet preliminary comparisons of educational documentaries currently in use with classical educational documentaries suggest that such films continue to employ aesthetic appeals designed to offer a viewing experience that makes pleasurable the position of subject-of-paternalism.

As an example, let us look briefly at *Too Young Too Far: The Facts about Teenage Sex and Pregnancy* (1987), produced by Northeastern Wisconsin In-School Telecommunications and funded in part by public agencies such as the Wisconsin Department of Health and Human Services. This educational documentary enjoys wide distribution and exhibition in Wisconsin public schools. *Too Young* uses a combination of docudrama, interviews, role playing, and footage of public speeches by experts in an attempt to, as the teacher's guide puts it, "trigger forethought, or at least some recall that will cause teens to alter their behavior" when they consider being sexually active. It is easy to identify the behavior sought by the film: for students to "control their own sexuality and prevent unwanted pregnancies." This documentary is especially interesting for the degree to which it constructs an aesthetic of fear and desire in its effort to motivate teenagers to interpret the film's discourse as "truth" and to act to prevent pregnancy.

The film opens with an extreme close-up of an African American teenage boy. A subtitle superimposed on his image reads "Myth." He looks directly into the camera and says: "You can't get pregnant the first time you have sex." Immediately, special effects graphics in the form of jagged teeth enter the image from each side and meet in the center of the screen. A jarring sound effect suggests the echo shock of prison doors slamming shut. The teethlike graphic wipe replaces the close up of the boy's face with a medium shot of the same boy standing, looking stunned, holding a baby in his arms. The next six shots repeat this pattern using different "myths" spoken by different teenagers— each ending up standing silently, holding a baby. The documentary then incorporates a docudrama depicting the lives of two white teenage parents, Kim and Rob. They act out scenes of everyday life (work, childcare, interpersonal disagreements) that portray loneliness, deprivation, entrapment, despair, isolation, interpersonal conflict. These portrayals are reinforced by the lifeless and somber manner in which the teenagers deliver their voice-over commentaries and by shot compositions that place the characters in claustrophobic tight frames or frames within frames.

Fear of isolation, loneliness, deprivation, and the "prison" of unwanted parenthood is constructed in *Too Young* and then appealed to in order to "encourage" students to accept as credible and salient the "facts" about teenage sex and pregnancy offered by adults who appear in the documentary. Although their historical and cultural referents are not mentioned, these encouragements refer to historically and culturally specific pleasures and hopes associated with adolescence: new independence from parental authority, economic power, romance and intimacy, freedom to define one's own identity. Each of these is portrayed as threatened or lost—Rob and Kim must buy diapers instead of albums, the stress of parenthood robs their relationship of romance and intimacy, they are trapped in a daily grind of low-paid physical labor and unpaid childcare. The pleasures and desires of adolescence are portrayed as threatened because of Rob's and Kim's ignorance of the scientific facts about the relation between sexual activity and pregnancy and/or their failure to think rationally about the social and economic consequences of teenage pregnancy. They have also been threatened by the students' "disobedience" to the father/patriarch/teacher as represented by the adult authorities who deliver the "facts" in the film; by their failure, as those authorities put it, to "act responsibly," to "control their sexuality," to possess "motivation, assertiveness, and conviction." In other words, they have failed to act as the adults/parents who address them from the documentary presumably do. Obviously the on-screen narrator has acted responsibly, and she enjoys economic security, respect, and personal and cultural power. She is Diann Burns, an African American woman who, in real life, works as a news broadcaster for ABC News in Chicago. While she does not embody the voice of the white, male, middle-class, scientist narrator of classical educational documentaries, she speaks from that position. In her final address to the audience, she exhorts students to set the same goal she set for herself, at the urging of her parents: namely, to "make life better for the next generation of your family." And she reassures them that this is an "easy goal," if only students become "sexually responsible." As a final warning, she reminds students that living according to the facts and logics offered by the tape will protect their lives in this age of AIDS.

Too Young constructs an aesthetic calculated to evoke fear about loss of individual happiness and freedom. This is a rendering, in film form and style, of the dominant ideological project underlying contemporary sex education in the schools. As Bonnie Trudell demonstrates, in current sex education curriculums the "problem" of teenage pregnancy has been defined as one of individuals. This problem arises when individuals act against what are taken to be prevailing social mores and produce what are assumed to be unwanted personal outcomes for all parties concerned (Trudell, 1985).

> Once the "problem" has been defined individually, the "solution" becomes changing certain characteristics of individuals via education, rather than changing larger social or economic factors that might be involved. For example, focusing on the percentage of out-of-wedlock births to black teens, 55% in 1979, compared to 9.3% for white teens..., obscures the role of cultural differences in the meaning of this event to a black teenager as well as economic inequities such as higher unemployment and lower average wages for blacks. We might well ask whether it is these systematic patterns of economic discrimination or instead teenage pregnancy that represents the larger problem for the black community. (p. 13)

Speaking to sex educators, Trudell writes: "Like our early counterparts, we perpetuate via the classroom the erroneous notion that our views represent public consensus on what constitutes 'responsible' sexuality when no such consensus actually exists" (1985, p. 13).

Thus, as with the classical documentaries, *Too Young* portrays the knowledge of the patriarch/father/teacher as true and safe, as capable of delivering more pleasure and profit than that of the students themselves and others in their subculture. This "good" knowledge is a result of scientific rationalism and a definition of responsibility that hinges on individuals who control their bodies and are motivated to achieve middle-class social and economic status.

Part of the goal of this study has been to demonstrate the need for research that would examine how educational documentaries, both classical and contemporary, orchestrate an ideology of protection, progress, certainty, and goodness, and then link that ideology to racist, sexist, monoculturalist, authoritarian, and other dominant interests. Such an understanding would necessarily require educators who are willing and able to confront their own implications in the paternalistic project of education. While the specifics of classroom practices tied to such a confrontation would change from context to context, they would have to share the ability to address the ways fear and desire are used in classrooms and curriculum materials in order to encourage childlike allegiances to curriculum projects.

NOTES

1 For what appears to be the first volume that seeks to question the uses and ideological work of representation in media intended for classroom use, see Ellsworth and Whatley, eds., 1990.

2 For discussions of educational dramatizations, see Ellsworth, 1987, 1988. For an analysis of "trigger films," see Orner, 1988. For analyses of classroom lesson films, see Kennard, 1988, and Erdman, 1988.

3 For a discussion of how media texts naturalize dominant interests, see White, 1987.

4 As Sandra Harding and others have argued, Western definitions of "science" as the unbiased search for truth have long disguised the fact that the scientific method actually promotes a particular set of dominant interests (Harding, 1987).

5 For analyses of the representational and filmic conventions associated with documentary and connotating observational neutrality (such as location shooting in natural light, following the spontaneous movements of subjects in the film, filming relatively unobtrusively with a two- or one-person crew, recording unscripted sounds and speech, and direct address to the audience), see Kuhn, 1978, and Nichols, 1976-77.

6 In her analysis of *Desert Victory* (1943), Annette Kuhn argues that the populism informing classical documentaries constitutes spectators as a collectivity, specifically as "the people," "a group politically united by ties of nationhood, undivided by class—or for that matter gender or race" (1981, p. 58).

7 A number of film and television theorists working from feminist and other perspectives concerned with the place of media in social change have focused on how viewing pleasure relates to social relations of power. For examples of this work, see Doane, 1987; de Lauretis, 1987; Fiske, 1988; Kaplan, 1987; Hebdige, 1988.

FILMOGRAPHY

Each of the films included in this study, with the exception of *Too Young, Too Far,* is part of the collection of the American Archives of the Factual Film, Iowa State University, Ames, IA. *Too Young, Too Far* is available through Northeastern Wisconsin In-School Telecommunications (NEWIST/CESA #7), University of Wisconsin-Green Bay.

The Negro American. (1966). Baily Films Inc.
Early Settlers of New England. (Salem 1626–1629) (1940). Encyclopedia Britannica Films.
Mohawk Valley. (1927). Encyclopedia Britannica Films.
Pueblo Dwellers. (1931). Encyclopedia Britannica Films.
Rural Women. (1951). United States Information Service.
Social Class in America. (1957). McGraw-Hill Book Co.

Social Revolution. (1952). Encyclopedia Britannica Films.
Too Young, Too Far. (1985). NEWIST.
Wastage of Human Resources. (1947). Encyclopedia Britannica Films.
Water Power. (1933). Encyclopedia Britannica Films.
What Color Are You? (1967). Encyclopedia Britannica Films.

REFERENCES

Apple, M. W. (1979). *Ideology and Curriculum.* London: Routledge.
Aronowitz, S. (1987–88). Postmodernism and politics. *Social Text,* 18, 99–113.
Barnouw, E. (1974). *Documentary: A history of the non-fiction film.* New York: Oxford UP.
Barsam, R. M. (1973). *Non-Fiction Film: A critical history.* New York: Dutton.
Colls, R. & Dodd, P. (1985). Representing the nation: British documentary film, 1930–45. *Screen,* 26 (1), 21–33.
Cook, P. (ed.). (1985). *The Cinema Book.* (1st U.S. ed.). New York: Pantheon.
de Lauretis, T. (1987). *Technologies of Gender: Essays on theory, film and fiction.* Bloomington: Indiana UP.
Doane, M. A. (1987). *The Desire to Desire: The woman's film of the 1940s.* Bloomington: Indiana UP.
Ellsworth, E., & Whatley, M. W. (eds.), (1990). *The Ideology of Images in Educational Media: Hidden curriculums in the classroom.* New York: Teachers College.
Ellsworth, E. (1987). Educational films against critical pedagogy. *Journal of Education,* 169 (3), 32–47.
_____. (1988). Educational media, ideology, and the presentation of knowledge through popular cultural forms. *Curriculum and Teaching,* 3 (1 & 2), 19–31.
Erdman, B. (1988, April). Curricular form and the classroom teaching film, 1930–1960. Paper presented at the annual meeting of the American Educational Research Association, New Orleans.
Fiske, J. (1988). *Television Culture.* London: Routledge.
Grierson, J. (1966). *Grierson on Documentary.* (Forsyth Hardy, ed.). London: Faber.
Harding, S. (ed.). (1987). *Feminism and Methodology: Social science issues.* Bloomington: Indiana UP.
Hartley, J. (1987). Regimes of truth and the politics of reading: A *Blivit. Cultural Studies,* 1 (1), 39–58.
Hebdige, D. (1988). *Hiding in the Light: On images and things.* London: Comedia.
Henriques, J., Hollway, W., Urwin, C., Venn, C., & Walkerdine, V. (1984). *Changing the Subject: Psychology, social regulation, and subjectivity.* New York: Methuen.
Hill, J. (1985). The British "social problem" film: "Violent Playground" and "Sapphire." *Screen,* 26 (1), 34–48.
Hoban, C. F. (1982). *Focus on Learning: Motion pictures in the schools.* Washington, DC: American Council on Education.
Jacobs, L. (ed.). (1971). *The Documentary Tradition: From "Nanook" to "Woodstock."* New York: Hopkinson.
Kaplan, E. A. (1987). *Rocking around the Clock: Music television, postmodernism, and consumer culture.* London: Routledge.
Kemp, J. E. (1985). *Planning and Producing Audio Visual Materials.* New York: Harper.
Kennard, M. (1988, April). Producing a sponsored film on menstruation: The struggle over meaning. Paper presented at the annual meeting of the American Educational Research Association, New Orleans.
Kuhn, A. (1978). The camera "I": Observations on Documentary. *Screen,* 19 (2), 71–84.
_____. (1981). *Desert Victory* and the people's war. *Screen,* 22 (2), 45–68.
Lather, P. (1987, Oct.). Educational research and practice in a postmodern era. Paper presented at the Ninth Conference on Curriculum Theory and Classroom Practice, Dayton.
Lovell, A. & Hillier, J. (1972). *Studies in Documentary.* London: Secker.
Lusted, D. & Drummond, P. (eds.). (1985). *TV and Schooling.* London: British Film Institute.
Masterman, L. (1980). *Teaching about Television.* London: MacMillan.

_____. (1985). *Teaching the Media*. London: Comedia.

Neale, S. (1977) Propaganda. *Screen*, 18 (3), 9–40.

Nichols, B. (1976–77). Documentary theory and practice. *Screen*, 7 (4), 34–48.

_____. (1981). *Ideology and the Image: Social representation in the cinema*. Bloomington: Indiana UP.

Orner, M. (1988, April). Trigger films and the construction of knowledge. Paper presented at the annual meeting of the American Educational Research Association, New Orleans.

Salomon, G. (1981). *Interaction of Media, Cognition, and Learning: An exploration of how symbolic forms cultivate mental skills and affect knowledge acquisition*. San Francisco: Jossey Bass.

Trudell, B. (1985, Spring-Summer). The first organized campaign for school sex education: A source of critical questions about current efforts. *Journal of Sex Education and Therapy*, 10–15.

Weedon, C. (1987). *Feminist Practice and Poststructuralist Theory*. Oxford: Blackwell.

White, M. (1987). Ideological analysis and television. In R.C. Allen (ed.), *Channels of Discourse: Television and contemporary criticism*. Chapel Hill: U of North Carolina P.

Wolfe, C. (1984). Modes of discourse in thirties social documentary: The shifting "I" of *Native Land. Journal of Film and Video*, 36, 13–18.

_____. (1987). Direct address and the social documentary photograph: "Anne Mae Gudger" as negative subject. *Wide Angle*, 9 (1), 59–70.

Zelnik, M. & Kanter, J. (1980). Sexual activity, contraceptive use and pregnancy among metropolitan area teenagers: 1971–1979. *Family Planning Perspectives*, 21 (5), 230–237.

16 Toni Morrison Teaching the Interminable

Susan Huddleston Edgerton

Toni Morrison's *Beloved*—a novel painfully working with a vast archetypal tradition showing step-parents and parents knowingly or innocently destroying their own children—evokes multiple discourses as Morrison's characters shriek and speak with one another, and with the listening reader. Morrison too speaks, of course, to the reader, and the attentive reader is finally forced to listen to her/himself, in a collusion of tongues recalling a contemporary Pentecost. Embedded in *the novel* is a pedagogical imperative that functions through these multiple discourses or layers of (knowledge) production. The teaching proceeds through a listening, a non-telling, a non-*mastery*, in each layer.

In Shoshana Felman's essay "Psychoanalysis and Education: Teaching the Terminable and Interminable," she articulates Lacan's "discipleship" to Freud's "discovery" not of the application of psychoanalysis to pedagogy, but of the "*implication* of psychoanalysis in pedagogy and of pedagogy in psychoanalysis." Morrison's *Beloved* demonstrates the problematics of such an implication through the particular forms that learning/teaching take between and within the above-mentioned pedagogical layers. Through a continuous excavation and unfolding of a past simultaneously repressed by social and individual forces, the characters of the novel inhabit and exchange roles with one another as teacher and student, thereby creating a dynamic "new condition of knowledge" for all involved.

It is this "new condition of knowledge" that I wish to explore in terms of its possibilities for teacher education classrooms. Morrison's novel gestures toward "teaching as a literary genre," or teaching as an interpretive act in which knowing is viewed as dynamic and always predicated on unique situations of listening—a listening that I have risked coupling with the loaded idea of "love." Such awareness for the conditions of a "knowledge that is not in mastery of itself," or knowledge in which the knower is aware of her own implication in that knowledge arises, Felman suggests, only through a kind of preliminary self-investigation. In my own pre-service teacher education classes my students and I have attempted such self-investigation through literary readings and autobiographical writings that follow social theoretical readings about schooling in the United States. I propose to combine my readings of Morrison's *Beloved* and Felman's article with a brief discussion of this classroom experience.

FICTION AND IDENTITY

Recently I moved to Chicago from Baton Rouge. On the way to Chicago my driving partner and I tuned in to a number of country music radio stations. Our first stop was to be his new home, a small town in Missouri. Since I knew nothing about the place and was apprehensive, a song expressing bitterness about life in a small town caught my ear: "In this town we believe the world is flat, 'cause when people leave here they don't ever come back." I grew up in a small northern Louisiana town, and this made some sense to me.

Later a student of mine in Chicago introduced himself to the class explaining that he had just returned from a small town in Arizona where he had worked as a journalist. I commented, "a small town in Arizona can be very small." "Indeed," he replied. "On what did you report?" I asked. "That was just the problem," he said. "I've tried to leave Chicago several times and I always come back. I guess the world *is* round." I was curious. "Round?" I asked. "What about the small town in Arizona? What do they think of the earth?" He had a ready answer. "There, it is flat."

Cognitive theorists want answers to the question "How do we arrive at our conclusions about reality?" In Chicago we know that the earth is round: in parts of Arizona, Missouri, and Louisiana we don't. Some (cognitive theorists and others) may ask, "How is it that some of us know and some of us don't?" But a question less often considered is, "How is it that some things come to be sources of knowledge and some things do not?" I prefer, in this paper, to look at those *unauthorized* sources of knowing and/or knowledge and at how they come to be considered nonauthorities at the same time that they profoundly influence those who encounter them. My student did not really say exactly what I related above; I invented part of it to make my point. Perhaps it is important that I tell you that. I suspect that it is not. My story is a "practical fiction." Besides popular music and other popular cultural forms, one of those nonauthoritative sources of knowing and/or knowledge (about pedagogy, culture, "social science") is popular literature. Another is autobiography, or, if you will, autobiographical fiction, or, in the words of Jo Anne Pagano, "practical fiction" (1990). The politics of identity is reflected in and produced by, in significant part, just such nonauthoritative sources.

Peter Taubman writes of three registers of identity formation (forthcoming). In the first register identity emerges as a construct of language and, thus, as a kind of fiction that can alienate one from the complex interplay of differences within oneself and between oneself and others. It can be viewed from a psychoanalytic perspective as a product of the Lacanian "mirror stage." In isolation this fictional register functions through a self-essentializing movement in which boundaries between self and not-self, margin and center, are rigidly drawn and assumed stable, while at the same time, contradictorily, a kind of fusion is sought (i.e., the other is the *same* as me). In this register the site of resistance to knowledge can be found in the boundaries between a dominant and an unauthorized discourse.

The second register, which Taubman calls the "communal as an identity-in-motion" involves group membership and all that it implies for identity as it emerges in the relations among and between individual, group, and society. The term "identity-in-motion" derives from Henry Louis Gates Jr.'s explanation of the "mask-in-motion," exemplified by the Yoruba mask, which only produces meaning when worn in front of an audience of initiates. This production of meaning evokes a sense of interior cohesion for the group involved in the process. Taubman explains,

> Within the communal register identity is made the ground for action. The identity is not taken as a formation of language but as an identity-in-motion....In such a world only those who are members can explore the meaning of the identity. (forthcoming)

The socially marginalized stand to benefit from the solidarity that such identity formation generates. It is through this register that multicultural education is approached as, for example, an Afrocentric curriculum. However, this register also risks essentializing identity, freezing it into mere group membership, if its relationship to other registers is lost.

The third register Taubman describes is the autobiographical. To explicate the subtle difference he intends between this register and the others requires that I quote him at length.

> Within the autobiographical register, unlike the fictional register, the narrative which the subject constructs does not create the real experience of living but rather posits the possibility of external validation. One's recounted autobiography therefore does not create one's experience but captures it. Thus autobiography as a means to self-knowledge is possible since a dialectic exists between narrative and actual experience. This autobiography is both the ground for action and what is to be transformed. (forthcoming)[1]

The ways in which groups, individuals, and ideas come to be marginalized in a given culture, society, and/or place has much to do with what is considered to be knowledge and who is considered to possess it, who is perceived as knower and who as known. Clearly education is deeply implicated in these processes, which are themselves deeply implicated in the formation of identities or subject positions. Too often approaches to multicultural education have systematically neglected the notion of identity formation across multiple registers. As Taubman observes,

> Not only have they failed to address how identity is formed, what it might mean and how it functions, but they have also left unexplored the way the approaches themselves consciously or unconsciously are used to create identities. (forthcoming)

Much of the most intricate and sophisticated theorizing I have read that has been produced around multicultural education in recent times has favored the second register of identity formation, the communal, to the virtual exclusion of the other two. At the same time such theorizing has not explicitly or sufficiently acknowledged the significance of something called "identity" to its own project. We hear about identity much more frequently in other discourses on education: feminist, phenomenological, psychoanalytic, and reflective or autobiographical studies, to name a few. I choose to devote the first and largest part of this essay primarily to the fictional register, specifically within the context of notions of multiculturalism in their relationships to race, identity, and representation. However, it will become evident that to isolate the fictional register from the others is not possible in any complete sense. I do this work through intertextual readings primarily of Toni Morrison's *Beloved* (1987) and Shoshana Felman's essay "Psychoanalysis and Education: Teaching Terminable and Interminable" (1987). The communal register comes into play through a demonstration of the ways in which literature, in this case Morrison's *Beloved*, is in dialogue with various traditions at the same time it works to "translate tradition" (Nadel, 1988). I will also mention briefly some student autobiographical work but, due to space limitations, will not point toward this register, or more fully develop this theme, as I have elsewhere (1992).

PEDAGOGY, LOVE, AND RESISTANCE TO KNOWING

In the realm of pedagogy, Felman articulates Lacan's "discipleship" to Freud not in terms of the application of psychoanalysis to pedagogy but in terms of the *"implication* of psychoanalysis in pedagogy and of pedagogy in psychoanalysis" (1987, p. 75; original emphasis). More precisely,

> what is unique about Freud's position as a student is that he learns from, or puts in the position of his teacher, the least authoritative sources of information that can be imagined: he knows how to derive a teaching, or a lesson, from the very unreliability— the very *nonauthority*—of literature, of dreams, or patients. (p. 92; original emphasis)

It is this lesson, according to Felman, that Lacan learns from Freud. The nonauthority of the study of teaching can be read in such a way as well, like (and through) a literary text. Like the psychoanalytic discipline, the study of teaching produces "a knowledge that does not know what it knows and is thus not in possession of itself" (p. 92; original emphasis). Such a knowledge holds certain advantages. It puts us in better stead for exploring the problems of hierarchy, of transference or love, and of translation across difference, what I call (from the example of philosopher John Rajchman [1991]) "translation without a master."

The pedagogical and psychoanalytic *risk* of love, transference love, is the displacement or deconstruction of hierarchized love (as in, for example, agape vs. eros, or love of others vs. love of self) and is a prerequisite for translation without a master. The implications that psychoanalysis holds for pedagogy are suggested by the significance of love to both. Henceforth in this writing love functions as an analogy for teaching/ learning at the same time that it is often, as in psychoanalysis, more than an analogy; it is a very real and necessary condition for the pedagogical situation. This (transference) love "occupies the middle spot between knowledge and ignorance" (Serres, 1982, p. 246).

Love (in the sense of "in love") effects a stifling of imagination (as in "love is blind") at the same time that it totally disrupts. It is a dangerous moment at the same time that it renews. "One speaks [of love (one learns; imagination returns)] only after the fact" (Kristeva, 1987, p. 3). It subverts and problematizes language, providing an opening for translation across differences. It makes one unique and special (particular) at the same time that it blurs boundaries between self and other. Fear shares its symptoms. Indeed, love is "fear of crossing and desire to cross the boundaries [margins] of the self" (p. 6). And, like learning, it is schizophrenic.

> In love "I" has been an *other*. That phrase, which leads us to poetry or raving hallucination, suggests a state of instability in which the individual is no longer indivisible and allows himself to become lost in the other, for the other. Within love, a risk that might otherwise be tragic is accepted, normalized, made fully reassuring. The pain that nevertheless remains bears witness to this experience, which is indeed miraculous—the experience of having been able to exist for, through, with another in mind. (Kristeva, p. 4)

Like learning/teaching, these are dangerous territories, disruptive, unsettling, risking blowing apart all that is official or certain. Love and learning are marginal passages. Love (learning) calls into question the very notion of identity. Julia Kristeva suggests that love dissolves "the limits of one's own identity." At the same time it tests the "referential and communicative power" of language to reach across this uncertain border (p. 2). These are two quite different points—love both joins us (limits vanish) and separates us (language stops working). What do we mean by "love"? Searching the question reveals a "linguistic profundity": love, which is "solitary because incommunicable," is nonetheless translatable. Versions of love (languages of love) "commune [only] through a third party: ideal, god, hallowed group" (p. 3). Can a classroom be one such third party, political problematics and all? Kristeva writes:

> Love probably always includes a love for power. Transference love is for that very reason the royal road to the state of love; no matter what it is, love brushes us up against sovereignty. (p. 9)

Transference takes place through a granting of authority by the analysand (student? teacher?). We ask our students to "suspend disbelief" in our competence. We ask them to grant us authority. It is we, the teachers, who are "presumed to know." And "as soon as there is somewhere a subject presumed to know, there is transference" (Lacan cited in Felman, 1987, p. 85).

But it is *they* who are to listen as we tell our stories. Here lies the "swerve" in this analogy. The swerve is the surplus, the place of nonsense, the uncultivated (Serres, 1989). The swerve gives us time, "breathing space" (p. 11) from which to complicate the psychoanalytic analogy. This particular swerve means *sovereignty is not complete.* If it is *they,* our students, who listen, are they not the analysts and we the analysands in this analogy?

Yet such complications are true to the Lacanian psychoanalytic paradigm. Psychoanalysis proceeds, as does teaching, through a kind of "mutual apprenticeship" (Felman, 1987, p. 83). The analyst "attempts to learn from the students his own knowledge" (p. 83). Love, then, is two-way. Lacan insists:

> I deemed it necessary to support the idea of transference, as indistinguishable from love, with the formula of the subject presumed to know.

and

> The question of love is thus linked to the question of knowledge.

and

> Transference *is* love…I insist: it is love directed toward, addressed to, knowledge. (All three citations in Felman, 1987, p. 86)

Or, one could say, listening is love; love pays attention. Thus it occurs only in an open system—that is, an interactive, intertextual system. Kristeva writes, "As implied in modern logical and biological theories dealing with so-called 'open systems,' *transference* is the Freudian self-organization" (1987, p. 14). With this, as Felman reminds us,

> the position of the teacher is itself the position of the one who *learns,* of the one who teaches nothing other than *the way he learns.* The subject of teaching is interminably—a student; the subject of teaching is interminably—a learning. (1987, p. 88, emphasis in original)

The articulation of learning/love is also indefinitely deferred. A coincidence between findings of psychoanalysis and of modern physics (Heisenberg's uncertainty principle) led Lacan to the following pedagogical principle:

> Until further notice, we can say that *the elements do not answer in the place where they are interrogated.* Or more exactly, as soon as they are interrogated somewhere, it is impossible to grasp them in their totality. (cited in Felman, 1987, p. 78; emphasis in original)

This principle is concretely evidenced, for example, by those students who return later to marvel at what they learned in a class and how little they realized it at the time: it is always after the fact, always deferred.

What does it mean to defer love, to defer learning? "Under its sway, one does not speak *of*" (Kristeva, 1987, p. 3). The rapture of love or learning, as it happens, is unspeakable. Yet as it happens "one simply has the impression of speaking at last, for the first time, for real" (p. 3). Instances and consequences of deferral are vividly addressed in Toni Morrison's novel *Beloved.* Such deferral takes different forms and different *distances* (in time/space) from that which "is" or becomes manifest or palpable or articulable. When that distance becomes too great, as Morrison's characters seem to testify, little good and much harm can come of it. Still, the "right distance" (Taubman, 1990) is not clear, nor does Morrison's writing presume to discover that distance as a general principle.

What her novel does, as does good pedagogy generally, is to call into question knowledge that claims to be its own authority. As Lacan has suggested, the only true teaching is that which provokes the desire to know in its listeners—a desire that can only emerge when they have apprehended "the measure of ignorance as such—or ignorance...in the one who teaches....What I teach you does nothing other than express the conditions which make it possible to learn" (cited in Felman, 1987, p. 81). Or, as Taubman puts it, "the teacher/analyst who engages in midspeak [positions her/himself at the right distance to/from the student] teaches the subject to recognize his own *méconnaissance*. His art 'must be to suspend the subject's certainties until their last mirages have been consumed' so that the subject/student gains true speech" (1990, p. 128).[2]

LOVE AND "REMEMORY" IN MORRISON'S *BELOVED*

Here is Morrison in *Beloved*:

> She shook her head from side to side, resigned to her rebellious brain. Why was there nothing it refused? No misery, no regret, no hateful picture too rotten to accept? Like a greedy child it snatched up everything. Just once, could it say, No thank you? I just ate and can't hold another bite? I am full God damn it of two boys with mossy teeth, one sucking on my breast the other holding me down, their book-reading teacher watching and writing it up. Add my husband to it, watching above me in the loft—hiding close by—the one place he thought no one would look for him, looking down on what I couldn't look at at all. And not stopping them—looking and letting it happen. But my greedy brain says, Oh thanks, I'd love more—so I add more....I don't want to know or have to remember that. I have other things to do: worry, for example, about tomorrow, about Denver, about Beloved, about age and sickness not to speak of love....Loaded with the past and hungry for more, [her brain] left her no room to imagine, let alone plan for, the next day....Working dough. Working, working dough. Nothing better than that to start the day's serious work of beating back the past. (1987, pp. 70, 73)

This passage from *Beloved* refers to an incident at a slave-holding antebellum plantation in Kentucky, "Sweet Home," where the "good-hearted" master has died and been replaced by a man who is a former teacher with an interest in science and a propensity for sadism—Schoolteacher, he is called. Schoolteacher is performing one of his experiments; it is unclear to what end. Sethe, the victim and narrator here who is recalling the incident, leaves soon after. She escapes to Ohio, pregnant, close to delivering, and injured by the beating she received just prior to leaving. Her other three children have been sent ahead of her to her freed mother-in-law, Baby Suggs. Sethe's husband, who may have left before her, is never heard from. Sethe delivers her fourth child en route with the help of a runaway poor white girl, Amy Denver. Sethe makes it to Suggs's house with her new baby girl, Denver.

After some time, Schoolteacher shows up (there was no legal protection for escaped slaves in Ohio) with the intent to take Sethe and her children back to Kentucky. Seeing him, Sethe commits an incredible act. She begins systematically murdering her children. She succeeds with the older girl-child but is stopped before she can kill her two boys and her new baby girl. She explains, "I took and put my babies where they'd be safe" (Morrison, 1987, p. 164). The white slave master is stunned into retreat. Sethe spends some time in a local jail and later returns to Baby Suggs and Denver and her sons. The ghost of the dead child, Beloved, is everpresent in the house. The two sons, who are old enough to know why the ghost is there and who are, as a consequence of that knowledge, scared of Sethe, run away never to be heard from. One day another former slave from "Sweet Home," Paul D, shows up at Sethe's doorstep. He and Sethe begin an attempt at love together—an attempt that is interrupted by the fleshly appearance of the ghost Beloved. Paul D, Sethe, and Denver, Sethe's only remaining child, must deal with the ghost before their relationship can become something for them all to count on. Dealing with Beloved means unearthing a repressed past for all three of them.

Sethe's brain refuses nothing, Morrison writes, but in articulating that (non)refusal she discovers the site of her resistance. And in learning, with the help of her teachers Beloved, Denver, Paul D, and Baby Suggs, to situate and articulate her own resistance, she comes to recognize, and to forgive in a sense, that of her husband, of her lover, and of her daughter, and finally to forgive, but not to forget, her own action. It is, for Sethe, a new way of reading the world. It offers the "permission to desire," to go beyond merely "loving small" (as it had been too dangerous to love larger).

Beloved is the ghostly embodiment of both the analyst and the situation of analysis for Sethe, Paul D, and Denver. She teaches Paul D to open his "red tin" (his heart) and Sethe how to be "her own best thing"; Denver, who has been trapped "inside," in introspection and fantasy, learns her "outside" from Beloved—all through love. In what follows I describe Sethe's cycle of countertransference with Beloved and how this cycle has to be broken by those others who have learned from Beloved and who loved Sethe and, finally, with help from the community that formerly scorned and ostracized Sethe.

LOVE AND ANALYSIS

Paul D is suspicious and frightened of loving too big or too much. Sethe's love often seems all-consuming and without boundaries. Paul D first becomes aware of and is alarmed by Sethe's seemingly boundless mother-love when she attempts to apologize for Denver's rudeness to him, and then to forbid him to confront Denver directly about it. He feels that it is "very risky...for a used-to-be-slave woman to love anything that much" given the fate of so many relationships under slavery. One must "love...everything, just a little bit [so that] maybe you'd have a little love left over for the next one" (p. 45). Later, upon discovering that Sethe murdered her baby girl, Paul D is horrified and cannot comprehend the source, meaning, and implications of such love. Here is Paul D:

> This here Sethe talked about love like any other woman,...but what she meant could cleave the bone. This here Sethe talked about safety with a handsaw. This here new Sethe didn't know where the world stopped and she began....More important than what Sethe had done was what she claimed. It scared him.
>
> "Your love is too thick"...
>
> "You got two feet, Sethe, not four," he said, and right then a forest sprang up between them; trackless and quiet. (pp. 164–165).

The murderous spectacle put on for the white inquisitors was indeed sufficient to save Sethe and her other children from returning to slavery. (Spectacular expressions, such as a woman's response to her first bidder at the slave auction by chopping off her own hand with a hatchet, were not so uncommon to slave women [Fox-Genovese, 1988, p. 329].) Finally she is heard. But the incident is permanently inscribed in the memory of herself, her sons, and the community as a horrifying reminder of the tenuousness of their integrity as a community, as loving individuals, as families. She buries the memory with the child, purchasing a headstone with yet another indignity—selling her body to another white exploiter.

With the unexpected arrival of Paul D the task becomes for Sethe, Paul D, and Denver that of dealing somehow with this repressed past that interferes with their abilities to feel for themselves and one another. Paul D always "dealt" with his own past by moving around, effectively denying it. But now he wants to stop and settle with the person who had known him longer than anyone else.

The (non-embodied) ghost of Beloved, who was earlier psychically maintaining Sethe and Denver without serious challenges, has now been run off by Paul D. Sethe, Denver, or both have to bring her back in a form that Paul D cannot deny. Beloved's (re)appearance at a crucial point in the development of the love relationship between Sethe and Paul D has the effect of deferring the painful process of love/analysis. Paul D and Sethe have been serving as one another's analysts, but a new analyst has to enter the picture for the "cure" to be effected.

The analysis proceeds "pathologically." Paul D participates in exhuming this past by impregnating the ghost, the analyst, Sethe's past. This act of his can be seen as a response to *fear of love*—fear, indeed, of the object of Sethe's love, knowing what her love can lead to. On the other hand, he provides her past, her ghost, with possibilities (pregnant with possibilities), but in doing so this ghost, Beloved, almost consumes Sethe. With Beloved as analyst, Sethe's transference love quickly escalates out of control. As this love of Sethe's further diminishes the boundaries between herself and the one she loves obsessively, Beloved, her "self" declines mentally and physically to a dangerously marginal place. Boundaries dissolve to the point that Sethe's love must be a kind of self-love, neurotic narcissism.

But what is Denver's stake in all this? She is *fascinated* with the ghost (Sethe made?). Why? Sethe, the one Denver loves, is afraid of her own love, understandably, and that fear/love takes the form of the ghost. Denver is fascinated with the "abject"—the object of her mother's fear and love. Kristeva writes that the abject is at the margins of life/death, "the edge of non-existence," and is signified by waste, corpses (ghosts?) (Kristeva, 1982, pp. 1–11).

The novel's climactic moment comes when an older white male acquaintance shows up at the gate. Beloved has practically consumed Sethe, growing larger and larger as Sethe physically shrinks. All Sethe can see in the man at the gate is Schoolteacher. Yet this time, instead of attacking Beloved, she moves toward the white man in a murderous rage. She is stopped by the appearance of members of the community who have given up spite for Sethe and have come to rescue her from Beloved, whom one community member calls "a grown-up evil...with a grudge" (Morrison, 1987, p. 257). The sight of a daughter (Denver), a lover, and a community who have all grown, learned, and are there in support of her stops Sethe cold. Beloved disappears—grown-up evil with a grudge, Sethe's past—now "re-repressed," but also re-read.

IGNORANCE, REPRESENTATION, AND THE PEDAGOGICAL IMPERATIVE

Education is always repressing something(s), someone(s). In "the serious work of beating back the past" (Morrison, 1987, p. 73), past repressions effect present ones for the sake of survival. Survival is difficult for a brain that "refuses nothing" (p. 70). Examining the desire itself—the desire to repress memory—Sethe, Paul D, and Denver discover a new way of reading the world, themselves, and one another. "Not to need permission for desire" (p. 162) is the prerequisite for being able to love at all. It is the prerequisite, therefore, for being able to learn, to teach, to give and take. (How often do we force our students [and ourselves] to protect themselves and to "love small"?)

The plantation master from whom Sethe and Paul D ran away is called "Schoolteacher" in the book. Schoolteacher fancies himself a scientist doing experiments on slaves, likening slaves in his written observations, his diagrams, and his practices to barnyard animals. We may know more and talk more than we once did about the fallacies of applying "technical" or "scientific rationality" to life, to the study of education and school practices, but not unlike Schoolteacher we still try to define and overdefine (for tenure dossiers, promotion, a "voice" in the "debate") our "methodology," "coherent programs," and "line of research," closing the gates against thinking. And if we are victimized by this, then what must our students feel from us as we "go about the serious work of beating back the past" to come up with a cool approach (scientific, even) that is no longer in need of the past—of interpretation, that is.

On the other hand, what is education, Freud reminds us, if not repression? Is the alternative to "method" only to release children, students, ourselves from the bonds of systems, trusting our fates to something larger? To who knows what? To ourselves in whom sleeps, presumably, a previously untapped in-born goodness? To the anti-structure? Collapsing all, as Taubman writes (1990), into the Imaginary? Do we have a choice?

Felman writes: "The Freudian pedagogical imperative [is] the imperative to learn from and through the insight which does not know its own meaning, from and through the knowledge which is not entirely in mastery—in possession—of itself" (1987, p. 96). Yet somewhere in this there is method. There *is* system. To the extent that I understand the term *listen,* to be acquainted enough with the writing produced about the psychology, history, philosophy, and social and cultural contexts of learning, to know that people do not like to be "told what to do" at the same time that they crave a kind of *telling*—but a telling that is not in mastery of itself, a sort of bold humbleness; this is the extent, ideally, to which I teach through a system and with a method. And that does not come simply with something glibly referred to as "life experience." It comes from practiced reading of literature, social science, philosophy, psychology, natural science, history, and so on, and from thinking, and from conversation, and from acting out or working "against the grain."

Like the poet who writes beyond herself, beyond what she "knows," the poetic pedagogy lives through language (saying and listening and reading) and interpretation and reinterpretation (resaying, relistening, rereading) interminably. It is only through this notion of the interminability of the impossible task of teaching that our choices come to some meaning. What does this mean for me in the "real" world of teaching? It means I go to my classes often having "overprepared" for the day's work, and that we almost always talk, in part or wholly, about something else. The preparation, however, is absolutely essential. For me. For my students. Preparation is interminable.

Nor does the critique ever stop. Sometimes we and our students seem to wish that it would. Cameron McCarthy, for example, related to me a story about a seminar on multicultural education that he conducted recently (personal communication, July 1991). He offered his students a critique of, among other things, the film *Dances With Wolves* (1991), in which he suggested that the story being told was still a representation of the marginalized produced and displayed from the perspective of a white male, albeit a guilty one. Students, dismayed, responded in what I imagine were hurt tones that the Lakota themselves had expressed approval in their evaluation of *Dances with Wolves* as the best film treatment yet. It was as if the students felt that the movie represented, finally, atonement or correct representation—"doing the right thing." It felt good. The critique could end here. But students also tend to confuse critique with polemic—with destruction. Of course, this is a long-observed and overly noted point. What is not so overly noted is our own implication as their teachers in this mistake. Not that we do not notice this mistake in our students and try to point it out to them; it is more that we are guilty ourselves of the mistake. The requirements of critique render it hard work. We may think that once we have mastered a particular critical language we are expert at it, no longer surprised by anything. But it is this very lack of surprise that signals the danger, that gets us into trouble, that incites others to charge us with being, for example, "politically correct dogmatists" (cheap phrase though that is).

Just as Freud recommended that the analyst return to analysis periodically in order to best understand and deal appropriately with her own countertransference, teachers do everyone a favor by returning, interminably, to examine their own theoretical and linguistic fixity. To examine their own *desire,* to reread and reinterpret on the basis of that examination, and to examine on the basis of that rereading and reinterpretation. Lacan writes:

> If it is true that our knowledge comes to the rescue of the patient's ignorance, it is not less true that, for our part, we, too, are plunged in ignorance. (Lacan, cited in Felman, 1987, p. 82)

I am suggesting that the very *nonauthority* of literature (as a resource for "social science" research, as a source for reading the self) can call our language use and emotional and cognitive stasis into question.

INTERTEXTUALITY AND TRANSLATION

Rereading ourselves is of a similar order of thinking as rereading the canon. We might reread Morrison, for example, by reading her rereading of the canon (e.g., 1989). This moves the notion of tradition, that which some scholars want to defend against "multiculturalism," into what Alan Nadel calls "translating tradition" (1988). Such a movement is analogous to moving from the fictional to the communal register of identity formation, and recalls Taubman's use of the Yoruba mask as symbol for the communal. This mask-in-motion only exhibits its effects in the ritual, the dance, the movement of challenging tradition at the same time it embodies it. It is humor, love. Such movement calls into question a canon or tradition that is in mastery of itself—an authoritative source and body of knowledge.

One such canonical work is Mark Twain's *The Adventures of Huckleberry Finn.* Just as Sethe learns to reread, Morrison is rereading Twain (among others). Love and the pedagogical imperative that live in this novel are not confined to expressions among characters within the text. That is, Sethe "speaks" beyond the pages of *Beloved*; she speaks to Twain and his readers. Readings of such conversations by myself and another (Moreland, 1991) follow.

SOUTHERN GHOSTS

It has been said of the American South that we are obsessed with the past, but that it is a romanticized mythical past that we remember and that as such is ahistorical. Still, our history presents itself in daily life in hidden ways. It surfaces in the form of a violence and guilt that some theorists say is peculiar to the South. We seem torn between what W. J. Cash called a "frontier" mentality of radical individualism and what are sometimes suffocating community ties ([1941]1969). If this is so, and we suffer as a society from a repression of collective memory, perhaps the South needs a kind of social psychoanalysis, as William Pinar has suggested (1991). Perhaps novelists, as I've taken some effort so far to suggest, are capable of being an important part of that analysis.

Twain seems to be addressing the well-worn conflict between radical individualism and community responsibility that takes a particular form in the South. He does this, according to Richard Gray, by "dissecting the Southern myths and exposing their faults and weaknesses" (1986, p. 115). However, Jim's story is not told and, at the end of *Huck Finn*, Gray suggests that Twain seems even to give up on his hero. As Gray states, "Huck is pushed to one side of the action, Tom Sawyer is permitted to play his familiar games, and the issue of Jim's slavery is reduced to the level of farce. For all Huck's occasional protests at Tom's behavior, or his famous final cry of defiance, the comedy loses its edge, the moral problems are minimised" (p. 115). Here is where, perhaps, Morrison picks up the story one hundred years after Twain.

Just as Sethe, Paul D, and Denver begin to trust in the possibility of a new life together, the past comes back inexorably to haunt them. The novel *Beloved* itself is a kind of ghost signifying upon generations of blocked readings of *Huck Finn*. An "innocent" (prior to *Beloved*) reading of *Huck Finn* and perhaps other Southern literature might lull us into complacency before we can fully confront our repressed past(s). Morrison teaches us that past suffering is most scarring in the present only so long as it is repressed. Confronted, that repressed past can become a source of wisdom—an opening for a "line of flight" (Deleuze and Guattari, 1983).

Huck's painful childhood experiences take him on a line of flight (of sorts) of often solitary excitement and adventure. But, one might ask, where is Jim's line of flight? Huck is able to do this because he has discovered his "invisibility" at a social and historical moment when a young white boy on a raft is not particularly noticeable. This assurance affords him a freedom of movement not available to a black runaway slave. Ralph Ellison's *Invisible Man* (1952) is able to discover the benefits of such invisibility only because he lives in mid-twentieth-century inner-city New York. But, as Nadel explains, "Ellison's imagery highlights the dilemma of which both he and Twain were well aware—that there was no place for Jim to go" (1988, p. 132). As Morrison's story reveals, the most marginalized are able to attain a line of flight of sorts only through a sort of internal search coupled with the assistance and cooperation of a community. Invisibility of the sort that Huck (and later, Invisible Man) is able to utilize is unavailable to Jim or Sethe or Paul D. On the other hand, Huck seems less able to look "inward" (or "outward") than are, ultimately, Morrison's characters.

Still, this inner search in which a repressed past is exhumed is not without danger. The past can take over the present, as it did for a time in the novel when Denver had to shift her protective efforts from Beloved to Sethe (as did the rest of the community). Southern ahistorical (hysterical?) obsession with the past must be confronted with history. That history lives in the present, in part, *through* that obsessiveness. When love (such as Sethe's love for Beloved) and historical consciousness become overwhelmed by (obsessive) guilt, growth is no longer possible. In order to be a mobilizing force the past must be exorcised from its dwelling "under the skin," so to speak, but not from "conscious" memory. The ambiguously positive ending of Beloved seems to hold the possibility of that promise both for the novel's characters and for the reader.

SETHE'S (JIM'S?) STORY

In *Beloved*, Sethe, a pregnant woman who had just suffered a severe beating by her master, runs away from slavery by crossing the Ohio River from Kentucky into Ohio. But before she makes it across, exhausted, hungry and about to deliver, she collapses, where she might die except that a young, poor, white runaway girl, Amy Denver, happens upon her, takes care of her, and helps to deliver the child. As Richard Moreland notes (1991), there are parallels between Sethe and Amy's relationship and between Huck and Jim's, a difference being that it is the journey of Sethe (Jim's counterpart), not Amy (Huck's counterpart), that is of primary concern. Furthermore, Sethe and others find a voice in Morrison's story. Neither Huck nor Jim is ever able fully to articulate his position in Twain's story.

Moreland reads Morrison's "put[ting] his [Twain's] story next to hers" (1991, p. 2). The beginning of this process is marked by "a-signifying ruptures," which Moreland sees as represented by the frustration repeatedly provoked in generations of *Huck Finn* readers—frustrations born of the persistent resistance of Twain's novel to providing satisfactory resolutions. Language and style that were needed to express such resolutions were not available to *Huck Finn* until Morrison's text entered it.

> This work in progress, drawing out the frustrated duet in Huck's (and the canon's?) monologue, involves not only exploring more of the runaway slave's own parallel, separate consciousness…but also tracing Denver's task for herself and her communicating her mother's story for herself and her community (and for us?) in a different form with different, more bearable, more liveable consequences. (1991, p. 25)

Knowledge then emerges through dialogue. Morrison is in dialogue: with her characters, with the reader, and with other literary works. In my readings of her she seeks to situate the will to ignore (the will to ignorance) and the resistances to knowledge and memory within all those conversations. Her conversation with and translation of Mark Twain (and with Ralph Ellison, at the same time Ellison and Twain converse—but those are other stories) reveal to us other ways of reading Morrison, and Twain, and Ellison. These other ways illustrate the pedagogical imperative in Morrison's work as well as the possibility for such an imperative in literary works more generally.

Indeed, Morrison rewards such readings of her novels by explicitly addressing, outside her fictional writing, her project of translating whiteness in white American literature (with blackness as the unsayable common ground) into its heretofore implicit "American Africanism." She demonstrates for us the ways in which the novel as pedagogue is both revealer and perpetrator of particular historical consciousnesses. Of Jim's role she writes:

> If Jim had been a white ex-convict befriended by Huck, the ending could not have been imagined or written: because it would not have been possible for two children to play so painfully with the life of a white man (regardless of his class, education, or fugitiveness) once he had been revealed to us as a moral adult. Jim's slave status makes play and deferment possible—but it also dramatizes, in style and mode of narration, the connection between slavery and the achievement (in actual and imaginary terms) of freedom. Jim seems unassertive, loving, irrational, passionate, dependent, inarticulate (except for the "talks" he and Huck have, long sweet talks we are not privy to—but what did you talk about, Huck?). It is not what Jim seems that warrants inquiry, but what Mark Twain, Huck, and especially Tom need from him that should solicit our attention. In that sense the book may indeed be "great" because in its structure, in the hell it puts its readers through at the end, the frontal debate it forces, it simulates and describes the parasitical nature of white freedom. (1992, p. 57)

Again, the role of the novel as "revealer" is elevated only through such reexamination, reinterpretation, dialogue, and translation.

To Teach/Learn Through the Literary: A Style

The novel teaches us through the pedagogical situation that is set up for its characters. We are enabled as readers to discover our own resistance to memory, to knowing, to difference, to the play of *differance*, as the characters struggle to discover their resistances. In reading students' autobiographical writings in the context of the "new condition for knowledge" offered by Morrison and Felman, we have together attempted to locate resistances to knowing and the "nonauthoritative" texts that have helped to produce that.

Through her reading of the first volume of African American author Maya Angelou's autobiography, *I Know Why the Caged Bird Sings* (1969), my student Donna arrives at a moral judgment for herself, against her intolerance, her lack of empathy. At the end of the semester Donna writes:

> I've tried and tried to title this writing, but I just can't find one that is suitable. So, I'll just jump straight into what I want to say. This is a combination of me, Donna, trying to explain both to myself, and to you, my teacher, what this class has taught me about "otherness," and how it has changed my vision of myself as a teacher.
>
> I have always been a very prejudiced person, although that is something I never would have admitted, perhaps even to myself, before this course. My prejudices, although they include racial ones, are certainly not exclusive to them. I have grown up with the belief that I was better than "others." "Others," in my life, were people who looked different, acted different, wore the wrong kind of clothes, drove the wrong car, held the wrong job, had a poor ACT score, a bad perm, a strange accent. The list is almost endless. I would certainly never have voiced my opinion; that would be tacky, cruel. No one that knows me would ever accuse me of being unkind, stuck-up, or even prejudiced. But in my mind, these feelings lived.
>
> When I made the decision to teach, I began to see the potential conflict between my desire to be a good teacher, and the intolerance I felt....How could I be a good teacher, change students' lives, be someone they respected and hold on to these beliefs. I couldn't....
>
> Maya Angelou's *I Know Why the Caged Bird Sings* spoke...directly to my heart. This was a wonderful, brilliant child....I read Maya Angelou's book twice; I couldn't get enough of it the first time. I began to look at the people around me differently. Why did I have so little patience with others? Wasn't that why I wanted to teach, to bring something to someone who did not have it before?...
>
> I also have had to face up to why this class was so difficult for me to engage in throughout the semester. This was trying ground for me to cover, new ground.

Trish discovers her own complicity in patriarchy after reading Annie Dillard's *An American Childhood* (1987) and exploring her own propensity for falling in love with her male mentors. The passage from Dillard that she explicitly cites is "They [boys] had been learning self-control. We [girls] had failed to develop any selves worth controlling" (p. 91). Trish writes:

> What a scary, scary passage. Does it really start that young? How many things must be *undone* to expose this conditioning that is begun so early? Is it possible? I know that this feeling exists in me and I reject it to the point of meanness. This is not a good solution! So what can be done about something that is so prevalent in our society?

We discovered together through private conversations that Trish's "meanness" consists in the idea that her female teachers must work much harder than her male ones to win her respect. Female teachers that she had liked as an elementary and high school student had been likable because they were "sweet," but all too often this sweetness was manifested in low expectations for students, particularly girl students. Trish, it seems, resented this as she grew older and discovered her own mind. That resentment resulted in a pre-judgement of female teachers and a kind of subconscious requirement that they work harder now, for atonement. Through further writing and in personal conversation I read Trish as deeply disturbed at her own complicity in patriarchy implicit in this attitude.

Beverly writes of her startling discovery of the consequences of difference. She describes how two girl children with whom she attended grade school were constantly abused by other students, and sometimes even faculty. One had a severe harelip and cerebral palsy, and the other had Down's Syndrome. The guilt she had felt for running with the abusive (popular) crowd and for not defending these children was brought dramatically home to her as an adult when she gave birth to a child who suffered from *all* of the physical problems that those two children had. Her initial wish that her child would die compounded her guilt. (Like Sethe, to "save" the child?) The profound learning that took place through her subsequent love of that child was echoed for her in her literary readings through difference as a general idea.

One might argue that, in the context of multicultural education, this practice of identifying resistances to learning is nothing other than the "human relations approach" (Sleeter and Grant, 1987) that sought to generate harmony across difference without ever interrogating the historical and cultural sources of genuine conflict or without altering policy—an approach that has been soundly and justly criticized. Ultimately, we *are* talking about human relations, but not the sort of human relations that will us to ignore larger contexts of the social, the cultural, the historical, and the political. Indeed, most of what we do and learn involves "human relations," insofar as economic, social, and cultural patterns and structures are human and relational. My students, in these examples, I believe, are discovering the ways in which culture is "made" as well as the problematics of the very meaning of culture and its relationship to the self. They discover the fallacy of viewing tradition as a monocultural commodity to be consumed rather than a dynamic transformation produced by encounters between and among cultures as well as individual readers. We are produced not only by what we "do to" others but also by their responses to that and vice versa. To read "tradition" as simply "common culture" (Hirsch, 1987) becomes absurd from this perspective. When tradition is understood as dynamic and as a result of multiple and ongoing cultural encounters and transformations, the gates are pried open a bit between "bounded" groups, offering spaces for coalition building among teachers and students both within and outside schools.

I do not pretend that my students and I are practicing psychoanalysis on ourselves or on one another, nor that we *should* be. I do suggest, as does Felman, that we can learn from the insights of the psychoanalytic process and its implications for and in pedagogy, and that we might do this through reflective readings of literature, both marginalized and canonical. Neither do I suggest that taking literature seriously as a source of knowledge means taking it literally. That is, I would not celebrate the "discovery" that the earth is flat or that ghosts return to us in the flesh, or even that historical fiction tells absolute historical truth. More interesting is the exploration of the ways and places in which we resist knowing and effectively will our own ignorance, and the ways in which this ignorance shapes what is considered "worth knowing" and how we represent ourselves and others to ourselves and others. More interesting are the ways in which teachers and students are mutually implicated in resistances to "knowing."

NOTES

1 I have argued elsewhere (Edgerton, 1992), differing from Taubman, that rather than operating in *dialectical* tension with one another, while these registers cannot be thought separately, neither is dialectical "synthesis" appropriate or possible. A *deconstruction* is called for in writing these registers. I am referring to deconstruction in the sense that I read it from Derrida in his *Of Grammatology* (1976), and *The Ear of the Other: Otobiography, Transference, Translation* (1985). At the certain risk of gross oversimplification of both dialectical and deconstructive approaches I provide my rationale for distinguishing them below.

A dialectical approach assumes that the processes by which events take place are knowable and, somehow, sensible. Thus, it must assume a certain transparency of language (through to reality). Analysis or investigation that proceeds through dialectical thinking is indeed complex and dynamic. In that sense it is not mired in chains of certainty or predetermined outcomes. However, in a total sense, such analysis can proceed only through a kind of faith in the knowable—an epistemological faith. Dialectical thinking as it is often characterized in contemporary theory is dependent on a notion of structure that presupposes a center of meaning of some sort (even those structuralist theories that regard social formations as a "decentered" structure). "This center governs the structure but is itself not subject to structural analysis (to find the structure of the center would be to find another center)" (Selden, 1989, p. 87). A dialectical approach depends on conceptualization as direct connection to the real—thus giving rise to the possibility for synthesis or incorporation. It is a movement between concepts in search of the knowable. The concepts with which it deals are necessarily assumed to be opposites, at least in key aspects. This would imply that to some extent the concepts (in this case the three registers) can be thought outside one another. (Derrida's notion of the supplement in deconstructive thinking denies this possibility.)

Deconstruction is based in rereadings—the refusal of final meaning (or synthesis), even momentarily. It proceeds in search of a space between concepts—a marking of the unknowable. Realist representation that can emerge from dialectical thinking and synthesis is viewed as an illusion of presence. Not unlike notions of power for Foucault, for deconstruction meaning is not inherently a problem until it becomes (viewed as) static, and asymmetric in its stasis. As such, a deconstructive approach may sometimes be inappropriate to particular problems of an immediate, daily, or local nature (problems that Jacques Daignault refers to as difficulties [personal communication]) because of its infinite deferral and lack of closure. That is, to think of it as a "method" that is applied to difficulties whereby "solutions" are perpetually deferred can result in a nihilism and passivity.

Deconstruction also acknowledges the extent to which Taubman's registers cannot even be thought outside or apart from one another, at the same time they are not collapsed onto one another. For a dialectical approach, a kind of sublation among registers is the goal. Such an approach is unable to take into account breaks and discontinuities in meaning. A deconstructive approach to the three registers would seek spaces between, by virtue of these breaks and discontinuities in meaning, that defy categorization (knowledge), but that nonetheless mark a persistence that is unsayable. Its expression in words (or otherwise) is not possible by any direct approach. Such expression is found in literary works, for example, where direct and positive categorization of "messages" or "morals" cannot be drawn, but where, perhaps, a sensibility remains—where a good reading leaves in its wake the trace of cross-cultural experience, a partial translation that is never final but always open to rereading, reinterpretation, retranslation. It is not an attempt to subsume through synthesis, incorporating differences and discovering oneself in every other.

2 In order not to go too far afield of my project in this writing I must end here my characterization of Taubman's argument. But I do so with the knowledge that by stopping where I do I implicitly oversimplify that argument in that, for example, Taubman argues with Lacan and Felman at points, and does not end with a definition of "true speech." I defend my choice to stop here by expressing my intent, or at least my hope, to convey the spirit of his argument in my reading of Morrison.

REFERENCES

Angelou, M. (1969). *I Know Why the Caged Bird Sings*. New York: Random.

Cash, W. J. ([1941]1969). *The Mind of the South*. New York: Vintage.

Deleuze, G. & Guattari, F. (1983). *Anti-Oedipus: Capitalism and schizophrenia* (R. Hurley, M. Seem, & H. R. Lane, Trans.). Minneapolis: U of Minnesota P.

Derrida, J. (1976). *Of Grammatology* (G. C. Spivak, Trans.). Baltimore: Johns Hopkins UP.

_____. (1985). *The Ear of the Other: Otobiography, transference, translation* (P. Kamuf, Trans.); and *Otobiographies: The teachings of Nietzsche and the politics of the proper name* (A. Ronell, Trans., C. V. McDonald, Ed.). New York: Schocken.

Dillard, A. (1987). *An American Childhood*. New York: Harper.

Edgerton, Susan H. (1992). *Cultural Studies and the Multi-Cultural Curriculum*. Louisiana State University. Unpublished dissertation.

Ellison, R. W. (1952). *Invisible Man*. New York: Vintage.

Felman, S. (1987). Psychoanalysis and education: Teaching terminable and interminable. In *Jacques Lacan, the Adventure of Insight: Psychoanalysis and contemporary culture* (pp. 69–97). Cambridge, MA: Harvard UP.

Fox-Genovese, E. (1988). *Within the Plantation Household: Black and white women of the old South.* Chapel Hill, NC: U of North Carolina P.

Gray, R. (1986). *Writing the South: Ideas of an American region.* New York: Cambridge UP.

Hirsch, E. D. (1987). *Cultural Literacy: What every American needs to know.* Boston: Houghton.

Kristeva, J. (1982). *Powers of Horror: An essay on abjection* (L. S. Roudiez, Trans.). New York: Columbia UP.

Kristeva, J. (1987). *Tales of Love.* New York: Columbia UP.

Moreland, R. (1991). "He wants to put his story next to hers": Twain's *Huckleberry Finn* and Morrison's *Beloved.* Unpublished manuscript. Louisiana State University, Baton Rouge, LA.

Morrison, T. (1987). *Beloved.* New York: Knopf.

_____. (1989). Unspeakable things unspoken: The Afro-American presence in American literature. *Michigan Quarterly Review,* Winter, 1–34.

_____. (1992). *Playing in the Dark: Whiteness and the literary imagination.* Cambridge: Harvard.

Nadel, A. (1988). *Ralph Ellison and the American Canon: Invisible criticism.* Iowa City: U of Iowa P.

Pagano, J. (1990). *Exiles and Communities: Teaching in the patriarchal wilderness.* New York: SUNY.

Pinar, W. F. (1991). Curriculum as social psychoanalysis: On the significance of place. In J. Kincheloe & W. F. Pinar (eds.), *Curriculum as Social Psychoanalysis: The significance of place* (pp. 165–186). New York: State U of New York P.

Rajchman, J. (1991). *Philosophical Events: Essays of the 80's.* New York: Columbia.

Selden, R. (1989). *A Reader's Guide to Contemporary Literary Theory.* Lexington, KY: UP of Kentucky.

Serres, M. (1982). *The Parasite* (L. R. Schehr, Trans.) Baltimore: Johns Hopkins UP.

_____. (1989). *Detachment* (G. James & R. Federman, Trans.). Minneapolis: Minnesota UP.

Sleeter, C., & Grant, C. (1987). An analysis of multicultural education in the United States. *Harvard Educational Review,* 57, 421–444.

Taubman, P. (1990). Achieving the right distance. *Educational Theory,* 1, (1), 121–133.

Taubman, P. (forthcoming). Separate identities, separate lives: Diversity in the curriculum. In W. Pinar & L. Castenell (eds.), *Understanding Curriculum as a Racial Text.* New York: State U of New York P.

Twain, M. ([1884]1985). *Adventures of Huckleberry Finn.* Berkeley: U of California P.

17 Encoding White Resentment: Grand Canyon— A Narrative for Our Times

Hazel Carby

This is an age of the world when nations are trembling and convulsed. A mighty influence is abroad, surging and heaving the world, as with an earthquake. And is America safe? Every nation that carries in its bosom great and unredressed injustice has in it the elements of this last convulsion....Not by combining together, to protect injustice and cruelty, and making a common capital of sin, is this Union to be saved, but by repentance, justice and mercy; for, not surer is the eternal law by which the millstone sinks in the ocean, than that stronger law, by which injustice and cruelty shall bring on nations the wrath of Almighty God!
Harriet Beecher Stowe, *Uncle Tom's Cabin or, Life Among the Lowly*

We live in chaos....Everyone is trying to control their fear.
"Davis" in Lawrence Kasdan's film *Grand Canyon*

The destruction of the racist complex presupposes not only the result of its victims, but the transformation of the racists themselves, and consequently, *the internal decomposition of the community created by racism.*
Etienne Balibar (with Immanuel Wallerstein), *Race, Nation, Class: Ambiguous Identities*

FOR A HUNDRED AND THIRTY YEARS, Harriet Beecher Stowe's novel *Uncle Tom's Cabin* has been closely associated in the North American cultural and political imagination with the Civil War that followed on the heels of the book's publication in 1852. Indeed the association is now so close that Stowe's words appear prophetic of the bloody conflagration that was to come. In the same way, Lawrence Kasdan's film *Grand Canyon* (1991) has become haunted by the specter of the rebellion in the streets of Los Angeles that began on the night of April 29, 1992.

The general concern of this essay is with the various ways in which narrative is essential for the production of what Etienne Balibar (1991) has called "genealogies" of race and nation, what Toni Morrison (1992) has referred to as the inscription of national issues of black bodies, and what Michael Rogin (1992) has described as "the surplus symbolic value of blacks, the power to make African Americans stand for something beside themselves." These narrative genealogies, in their production of this symbolic power, have significant political resonance when they are produced in response to a perceived crisis in the formation of a society. The process of inscribing national issues on black bodies accomplishes the ideological work that is necessary for the everyday maintenance of systems of racial injustice and inequality.

However, I am particularly interested in popular narratives that work as pedagogic texts exhibiting an explicit and self-conscious didacticism in their production, reproduction, or reconstruction of the meanings of race in order to create new genealogies, new surplus symbolic value, and new inscriptions of national concerns specific to a particular historical moment. The main focus of my attention is Kasdan's *Grand Canyon*, which I regard as one such contemporary narrative. Like Stowe's *Uncle Tom's Cabin*, *Grand Canyon* is a text that is not only self-conscious of addressing the historical moment of its production but also explicitly pedagogic in intent and didactic in tone. However, these genealogies are each specific to their time: Stowe invents her genealogy of race and nation within a crisis of modernity, while Kasdan is re-imagining relations between race and nation in ways that are symptomatic of a crisis in what is now frequently referred to as our postmodern moment.

A basic assumption of *Grand Canyon* is that we are living through a national crisis, a moment in history when the nation, as Stowe described it in 1852, "is trembling and convulsed," with its people on the brink of civil war. Indeed, the possibility of an imminent descent into chaos is a consistent visual and verbal motif of the film. Juxtaposing Stowe's description of the national tensions of the 1850s to Kasdan's filmic response to the social and political conditions of the 1990s is not a superficial gesture; the relation between these two cultural producers, even though they are separated by history and by ideological belief, is deeper than their shared premonitions of national disaster. Both *Grand Canyon* and *Uncle Tom's Cabin* are cultural texts that fear for the continued secure existence of the white and middle-class America to which they and their authors belong. Kasdan and Stowe each construct a racially defined and class-specific worldview, a worldview that is also, and not incidentally, the same class-specific and racially specific context that enables and secures the cultural production of their text; both are motivated by a desire to expose injustice and inequality; and each actively tries to construct a radical, political, and interventionist narrative of protest.

Grand Canyon and *Uncle Tom's Cabin* are texts that display a Dickensian urge to transform the existing social order through moral and ethical exhortation. Both appeal to the hearts and minds of the privileged to intervene in the lives of those less fortunate than themselves. However, what appear to be appeals to undertake acts of *selfish* charity need also to be identified as selfish acts motivated by a desire to preserve both individual and group privilege. While stark inequalities of wealth, power, and privilege are identified in each text as being a threat to the continued existence of the social fabric, neither Stowe nor Kasdan calls for a dramatic change in the social organization of power and powerlessness, nor do they argue for a redistribution of wealth to end economic injustice. Rather, both texts seeks to preserve the powers and privileges of the white middle class by attempting to demonstrate why it is the self-interest of that class to become the patrons of the underprivileged. Acts of patronage are appealing, I would argue, because the power of the patron is secured at the same moment that those subjected to patronage are confirmed in their powerlessness. Further, Stowe and Kasdan each construct the terms and conditions of a national crisis in their texts so that the representation of the acts of white individuals, acts that are enacted upon black bodies, not only serve the self-interest of the white middle class but are simultaneously interpreted as acts that serve the national interest. In the face of imminent chaos, Stowe and Kasdan construct genealogies that attempt to secure and confirm racialized national identities and, in doing so, to bring narrative coherence and cohesion to the incoherence and fragmentation of their own historical time.

First I want to briefly discuss what I mean by the creation of a narrative genealogy, an inscription of national concerns onto black bodies, in relation to Stowe's *Uncle Tom's Cabin*. Planter paternalism was founded through the doctrines and practices of Anglicanism in the British mainland colonies and, by the antebellum period, was the dominant ideology that both justified and resolved the social contradictions that arose from the enslavement of African peoples in North America. Stowe directly confronted and, indeed, utilized the glaring contradictions that arose from a doctrinal emphasis on sentiment, charity, and love within the Christian ethical system but seemed blind to the everyday acts of violence that were perpetrated upon black bodies.[1]

Stowe became an Anglican as an adult. In 1851, she wrote, while she was taking communion she had a vision of "a saintly black man being mercilessly flogged and praying for his torturers as he died" ([1852] 1981, p. 8). This vision and the novel that subsequently grew from it speak to the heart of one of the major contradictions in the ideology of planter paternalism. Stowe mobilized sentiment, charity, and love explicitly against two forms of social violence: against the violence of the slave system and against the potential violence of concerted acts of African rebellion. To enable her fictional act of dissent from the discourse of the dominant ideology of planter paternalism, Stowe actually had to reinscribe major portions of it. Paternalism is not so much undermined as revised and reinforced. The creation of the character of Uncle Tom, the figure who can pray for his torturers while they torture him, is crucial to this process of revision.

Tom is consciously constructed as a de-Africanized figure; he is an embodiment of the African spiritual holocaust accomplished through Christianization. The process of Christianization attempted to inscribe an alternative ethnicity upon the de-Africanized African, and Stowe reproduced this fictive ethnicity for her protagonist. The surplus symbolic value of the future of Uncle Tom consists of a fictive ethnicity that has the power to dislodge blackness from its association with perpetual disobedience and rebelliousness. At the same time, Tom's restraint, his refusal to take revenge on those who abuse him, epitomizes absolute obedience to the Christian ethic and subordination to the will of his persecutors. In other words, the figure of Tom is granted moral authority and occupies the ground of moral superiority only because he complies with the central doctrine of absolute obedience. The mechanism of his submission is Christianity, which, while it separates Tom from those despised traits of African degeneracy, confirms the existence of degeneracy in the un-Christianized. In this genealogy of race and nation Tom has an ideal existence in the category of humanity. The resolution of Stowe's grand narrative asserts simultaneously the necessity for the Christianization of Africans and the necessity to exclude them from the national entity that reinforces the insurmountable racial difference of their social existence. At the end of the novel George, his family, and Topsy are re-Africanized outside of the boundaries of America and returned to Africa as Christian zealots and African patriots—a fictive ethnicity that denies the possibility that they could be imagined as American patriots.[2]

In the face of the institutional crisis and antagonistic social relations of the antebellum period, Stowe's narrative accomplishes the ideological work necessary for a realignment of the national hegemonic structures of her time.[3] *Uncle Tom's Cabin* reconstructs a past, an alternative narrative of the meaning of slavery, in order to imagine an alternative national future: a future in which a paternalistic racial formation can be maintained under the hegemonic control of the white, Northern middle class. This re-imagining of the past, this new genealogy, is produced in conjunction with the production of fear: a fear of supernatural retribution and a fear of the chaos that would inevitably result from the dissolution of the social order. It is this fear of what will happen in the present as a consequence of the slavery of the past that provides the motivation for action. Fear is Stowe's tool of persuasion: it inspired the white middle class to act in the interest of their own class security, and for Stowe these class interests are synonymous with the national interest.

•

A blank screen is all we can see. Within the darkness the audience can gradually hear the unmistakable pulsating sound of chopper blades. My mind, like so many others of my generation, is conditioned to make an immediate connection between this sound and a particular social and geographic space. For more than twenty years, the noise made by a low-flying helicopter was used by film and television studios to signify the presence of Americans in the war zones of Southeast Asia; but I am unable to remember when, in the last few years, I stopped associating the rhythmic sweep of these blades with Vietnam or Korea and started instead to link the sound to Los Angeles.[4] Thus, although I knew nothing about the subject of the film *Grand Canyon*, when I started to watch it I knew, because of this sound, that the blank screen would be replaced by the symbolic landscape of a black urban neighborhood.

For Hollywood filmmakers the black neighborhoods of Los Angeles are important sites not just for the representation of death and destruction but for the enactment of social and political confrontations that constitute a threat to national stability. These neighborhoods are as fascinating in their exoticism, potential danger, and commerical marketability as Vietnam. In the United States, until quite recently, Southeast Asia has been culturally produced as the primary site of a national nightmare: a landscape through which North Americans moved under constant surveillance by a subhuman population of menacing "gooks." The "enemy" masqueraded as ordinary men, women, and children, but, within the heart of the nightmare, these people were never ordinary and never innocent. This haunting vision has been supplanted in the popular cultural and political imagination by images of black inner-city neighborhoods—neighborhoods that are spaces in which to enact the current national nightmares of the white suburban middle class, nightmares that are inscribed on the bodies of, and patrolled by, the Bloods and the Cripps.

Lawrence Kasdan's film *Grand Canyon* exemplifies the fascination of Hollywood with the black inner city as the symbolic space of suburban anxiety. The film conceals its role in the actual production of white fear of black aggression under the guise of merely confirming the already existing material reality of the threat that underlies the nation's anxieties. As Fox Video's promotional material describes this process, "*Grand Canyon* is director Lawrence Kasdan's powerful and uplifting film about real life and real miracles...and about how, after the millions of choices we make in life, one chance encounter can change it all."

The source of *Grand Canyon* is *Sullivan's Travels*, written and directed by Preston Sturges in 1941, in which a wealthy and very successful Hollywood director, John L. Sullivan, disguised as a tramp, sets off on a journey to discover what it is like to live like a poor and homeless person during the Depression. Sullivan's intention is to educate himself so that he can translate experience into art by making realistic films about despair and deprivation. What he learns while serving a six-year sentence to hard labor for assault is that the poor and oppressed do not want films of despair but on the contrary need to laugh. Upon his return to Hollywood Sullivan commit himself to make comedies for the masses. However, it is not only *what* Sullivan learns that is of significance to Kasdan and to the making of *Grand Canyon*; what is also important is *where*, when, and in what form Sullivan learns his lesson. The moment of Sullivan's greatest despair is when he is confined to a sweat box as punishment for reading a newspaper, the headlines of which announce his own death. Although his "death" is in one sense untrue, in another sense it dramatically marks the demise of the convictions of the former John L. Sullivan and allows for a process of his rebirth. Sullivan experiences his revelation in the cradle, as it were, of a black community.

What begins for Sullivan as a largely existential journey culminates in the torture of his body and mind. The moment of his greatest distress is followed by one of the most surprising and powerful climaxes in any movie of its time. The plot of the film, up until this moment, has not been concerned at all with issues of race in relation to either its visual or vocal exploration of the sufferings of the poor. Only one black character, a cook, has previously appeared, and his entire performance was confined to a slapstick comedy routine. Nothing that has already occurred in the movie, then, has prepared the audience for the racially encoded site of an epiphany. Chained to each other, the convicts are taken to a local black church to see a picture show. Before they arrive the preacher exhorts his congregation to show every courtesy to the people who are about to come among them:

> We're going to share our pleasure with neighbors less fortunate than ourselves....I'm going ask you once more neither by word, nor by action, nor by look to make our guests feel unwelcome. Nor draw away from them, nor act high-toned, for we is all equal in the sight of God.

Sturges incorporates a visually powerful and emotionally moving rendition of "Let My People Go" into this scene to emphasize and secure the common ground of oppression, understanding, and, in the preacher's terms, a bond of brotherhood between the convicts and the black community that has already been established through the words of exhortation to his congregation. The church doors swing open, and the convicts shuffle into the body of the church in tempo with the singing of the black community. Sullivan's personal revelation occurs as he watches a Mickey Mouse cartoon that produces laughter in every member of the audience. The screen is filled with the smiling faces of the respectable black poor and the convicts forming, in cinematic terms, a visual embodiment of a democratic political and spiritual community.

Kasdan pays homage to *Sullivan's Travels* in a number of ways. In the opening scene of *Grand Canyon*, Davis, a film producer, lectures his best friend Mack,[5] an immigration lawyer, that life is chaos and that confronted by this chaos all anyone can do is try to control their fear. By the end of the film Davis is standing in the middle of a Hollywood movie lot berating his friend because he hasn't seen *Sullivan's Travels*:

> That's your problem, you haven't seen enough movies....All of life's riddles are answered in the movies. It [*Sullivan's Travels*] is about a man who loses his way, he's a filmmaker like me and he forgets for a moment just what he was set on earth to do. Fortunately, he finds his way back. That can happen Mack, check it out.

Kasdan is clearly concerned with the tensions and conflicts that arise between an urge to dissect and analyze the various components of human activity that shape material conditions, what I will call representing the real, and a desire to recreate a sense of human awe, wonder, and predestination in the face of the supernatural, what is continually referred to in the film as the miraculous and what I will call representing the religious.[6]

Mack, played by Kevin Kline, is the protagonist of *Grand Canyon* who, like John L. Sullivan, undertakes a transformative existential and physical journey. It is the existential journey that constitutes the main plot of the film, but it is initiated by an identification of and confrontation with the enemy.

At the beginning of the film Mack searches for a way of avoiding the heavy traffic leaving the Forum after a Lakers game. He strays into an area that is so alien to him that he will later categorically assure his family, "You have never been where I broke down." What happens to Mack is evocative of a journey into the "heart of darkness," a journey originally conceived in the context of European imperialism in Joseph Conrad's novel of that name and recreated by Hollywood in Francis Ford Coppola's *Apocalypse Now*. As Mack peers anxiously through his windscreen at the unfamiliar and to him menacing aspect of a black residential neighborhood, Warren Zevon's music plays in his car.

Music is very significant for Kasdan, as it was for Sturges. The Zevon song on the soundtrack, "Lawyers, Guns, and Money," for example, is significant in two ways. First, the plea to "send lawyers, guns, and money" signifies the danger facing Mack, but the song also acts to situate Mack in history. Zevon's music is a product of '70s, white, yuppie, southern California culture. Mack's familiarity with the words and apparent nostalgia for the song locate him within this culture and provide him with a history of who he is and where he comes from, a history that has so far been absent from the film.[7] Unlike Sturges who, in 1941, was using music to establish a vision of political and social unity, Kasdan, in the '90s, uses music to signal the fragmentation of social and political positionality. In Kasdan's hands music becomes not only a register of cultural conflict but the very ground of social and political contestation.

The words of "Lawyers, Guns, and Money" evoke with a wry liberal irony memories of the Cold War, of danger to Americans trespassing in exotic locales, and of covert U.S. intervention in other countries. Presumably, the intentions behind the careful selection of this song are the establishment of the liberal credentials of the protagonist, the creation of a mood of empathy for the way in which he has accidentally strayed into alien territory, and an understanding of the gravity of the situation in which he finds himself. As Mack's anxiety increases, so do the strategies for creating tension in the minds of the audience, who watch with an increasing sense of helplessness and panic if they identify with his plight. Mack switches off Zevon in order to concentrate more effectively on finding his way home, and like a mouse in a laboratory maze, he turns his car around in a futile effort to escape. As Mack drives ever deeper toward the "horror" that awaits, he begins to sing the words of the song himself as if by doing so he could summon help. As Mack mutters to himself, "send lawyers, guns, and money," his words are overwhelmed by the taunting voice of Ice Cube, "Ruthless, plenty of that and much more," emanating from what looks like a white BMW that slows down and drives beside him for a while. Music here is the prime vehicle for a cultural war that has encoded within it the political potential of a larger civil war. NWA is polarized against Warren Zevon, in a symbolic confrontation central to the narrative genealogy of race and nation that is about to be inscribed on the bodies of young black urban males. The musical battle produces and carries the wider class and racialized meanings of the scene and in the process confirms the dominant ideologies of our time about what is wrong with the inner city and what is wrong with America.

However, the process of representing this war is structurally as well as ideologically unjust, and this is clear if we analyze the unequal representation of the musical battle. In contract to the fragments of NWA's "Quiet on the Set," we have a much more complete sense of the Zevon narrative. The audience is not exposed to significant sections of a verse or even complete sentences of the NWA lyrics, and thus we are denied access to a narrative that is significantly different from Kasdan's scenario. Ice Cube's voice faces in and out in the cat-and-mouse game being played out on the screen, but what can be clearly distinguished, "ruthless, plenty of that and much more," is intended to confirm the menacing intentions of the occupants of the second car: five young black males who take careful note of the existence of an interloper. Mack responds to his surveillance by singing:

> I'm an innocent bystander...
> Send lawyers, guns and money
> The shit has hit the fan.

Mack's car coughs, splutters, stalls, and finally breaks down, and he becomes a man under siege. Mack uses his car phone in an attempt to get help, but on being asked for his location he hesitates: "I dunno...let's say...Inglewood," he decides, without much conviction, as the car phone also crackles and then dies. Having run to a convenience store to find a public telephone, Mack continues to find it difficult, if not impossible, to describe exactly where he is, or to continue the military analogy, to give his coordinates: "Buckingham, yes...but remember it's about half a mile west, I guess, of there." Mack is not only lost, he is in enemy territory; his very survival is at stake. On being told by roadside assistance that it will take a while to get to him, Mack responds that he understands but that "if it takes that long I might be like, ah, dead." Mack remains under surveillance and the NWA soundtrack changes to include fragments of "F*** tha Police," signifying presumably the imminence of the moment of confrontation. Mack returns to his car to wait for help, and the BMW pulls up behind him. What follows is a filmic moment in which the entire gamut of language, sound, and image that have been used up until this point to symbolize danger and to produce fear in the audience coalesce into an intense evocation of an American soldier coming down in enemy territory: "Mayday, Mayday. We're coming down." Mack vocalizes his own personal distress while he simultaneously gives voice to the anxieties of a wider constituency: a constituency of the white suburban middle class whose greatest fear is being stranded in a black urban neighborhood at night.

There is a great irony in what Kasdan excludes from his audience in this scene that only those who know the lyrics of "Quiet on the Set" and "F*** tha Police" would perceive. In fact, I would argue that Kasdan depends upon the ignorance of his target audience for this film. Those who know the album *Straight Outta Compton* would be aware that "Quiet on the Set" is actually about the power of performance and, specifically, about the potential power that a successful rap artist can gain over an audience. Power is, quite explicitly, the power of words over the body. For example, "ruthless, plenty of that and much more" is about controlling the movements of people on a dance floor and about the power to create "a look that keeps you staring and wondering why I'm invincible." But the invincibility is entirely the result of being able to persuade with words: "when you hear my rhyme it's convincible." Kasdan, however, disrupts NWA's intended narrative structure, and lines like "I'm a walking threat," and "I wanna earn respect" are transformed into a filmic representation of the contemporary figure of the disobedient and dangerous black male who believes that respect is only gained through the possession of a gun. Perhaps the greatest irony of all is that the NWA song, in fact, predicts the misuse of their words. Near the end of the rap an interesting dialogue occurs between Ice Cube and an unidentified voice that mimics the supposedly dispassionate, analytic tone of the sociologist or ethnographer. Ice Cube asserts that he can create "lyrics to make everybody say," and the voice responds: "They can be cold and ruthless, there's no doubt about that, but, sometimes, it's more complicated." And Ice Cube concludes: "You think I'm committing a crime, instead of making a rhyme."

A tow truck driver, Simon, played by Danny Glover, comes to Mack's rescue at the height of his confrontation with the "gang." Mack has just been forced out of the safety of his car when the blaze of oncoming headlights announces his imminent rescue. However, the camera tantalizes the audience as it hesitates to reveal the identity of the man who climbs out of the truck. The camera swings from the truck to Mack flanked by the young men and then back again to the tow truck driver's boots and then slowly pans upward. What Kasdan does here is to reproduce the low-angle shot that he used moments before to stress the menacing nature of the black male faces that lean toward Mack in his car. The rescuer is revealed to be black and armed with an enormous steel crowbar, the size of which is emphasized by the camera angle. Before we can completely see his face, he bends into the cab to reach for a cap: this second of uncertainty about his identity is a cinematically produced hesitancy about the possible allegiance of the tow truck driver. But the hesitation is only momentary. Once the face is revealed to be that of Glover, his filmic persona as LAPD's heroic cop Sergeant Murtaugh, from *Lethal Weapon I, II,* and *III,* so well established in our popular-cultural imagination, assures the audience that he is Mack's savior.

The ideology that Kasdan reproduces in his genealogy of race and nation works in a structurally similar way to the ideology that was reasserted by Stowe in which the imaging of the good black is dependent upon a rejection of an alien black presence. Though Africa no longer functions, as it did for Stowe, as a possible metaphoric and material place for disposing of the alien element that threatens to disrupt the formation of national unity, I would argue that prisons function in our political imaginations as an equivalent site. Kasdan produces a visual narrative of what happens when disobedient, disaffected, and aggressive black males are pitted against a lone, liberal, and well-meaning white male who made an innocent, if foolish, mistake.

Glover's character, Simon, will become the means for solving the dilemma at the center of this racial national narrative: How exactly does the white middle class distinguish between the good and the bad black male? Indeed, Kasdan grants Simon the moral authority to exclude the five young men from all acceptable definitions of what it means to be human. This moral authority is acquired gradually and in a number of ways. First, Simon manages to extract Mack and himself from the clutches of the young men without resorting to violence. He establishes who made the call and then continues to talk to Mack about the problem with the car as if the others aren't there. This behavior is quickly identified by the young men as a sign of disrespect. Next, Simon tried to persuade them that he is just doing his job. As the young men are unresponsive to the terms of the work ethic, Simon tries another tactic: he identifies the young man he supposes is the leader and takes him aside. He explains that he is responsible for the truck, Mack's car, and Mack himself and asks a favor, to be allowed to go on his way. This exchange is a very important moment because it establishes the ground upon which Simon's role as a mouthpiece for the philosophy of the film will be built. The young man asks: "Are you askin' me a favor as a sign of respect, or are you askin' me a favor 'cos I got the gun?" Simon pauses and then replies:

> Man, the world ain't supposed to work like this, maybe you don't know that but this ain't the way it's supposed to be. I'm supposed to be able to do my job without asking you if I can. That dude is supposed to be able to wait with his car without you ripping him off. Everything is supposed to be different than what it is.

The young man is clearly puzzled by this response and says, "So, what's your answer?" To which Simon states, "You don't have the gun, we ain't having this conversation," which gets the response, "That's what I thought, no gun, no respect, that's why I always carry the gun."

Having confirmed that Simon can vocalize the moral codes and ethics of the middle class and can, simultaneously, be streetwise, the film also uses Simon to dehumanize the young men. In a conversation with Mack that takes place back at the service station while waiting for the car to be fixed, Simon adopts a folksy persona reminiscent of Zora Neale Hurston, a persona that many Americans find so comforting, and compares the young men to predatory sharks. Simon explains to Mack that what happened to him was a matter of chance, that "one day, just one particular day you bump into the big shark."

> Now the big shark don't hate you, he has no feelings for you at all, you look like food to him....Those boys back there, they got nothing to lose. If you just happen to be swimming along and bump into them, well...It might not be worth worrying about. It's like being in a plane crash.

Having been dismissed from the realm of humanity, these boys can be conveniently forgotten. They do not appear again in the film, and presumably they can disappear into jail, say, or be absorbed into statistical evidence of urban homicides, for do we really care or even think about what happens to sharks as long as they are contained and prevented from preying upon us?

What is to be feared has been identified and given a body, but no name. Now that the young black men presented as a "gang" have served their purpose, the conversation of Mack and Simon can shift to a more general level and establish the wider concerns of the film. For the confrontation of Mack and the five young black men are a coda, a means to address what ails this nation. As Mack says, "There just seems to be so many ways to buy it, particularly in this city. I'm amazed at the end of this day that anybody's alive. And on other days I think that maybe people aren't so fragile."

These musings about the strengths and vulnerabilities of humanity, or, I should say, about those people privileged enough to be allowed to remain in the category of humanity, developed into one of the two major themes of the film, and are a prelude to the other major concern of Kasdan—the miraculous. Again, it is Simon who is the vehicle for articulating a folk philosophy and for exposing the existential meaning behind the title *Grand Canyon* for the film:

> The thing that got me was sitting on the edge of that big old thing [the Grand Canyon]. Those rocks, those cliffs and rocks are so old, it took so long for that thing to look like that. It ain't done either, it happens right while you're sitting there watching it. It's happening right now while we're sitting here in this ugly town.

> When you sit on the edge of that thing you just realize what a joke we people are, and what big heads we've got thinking that what we do is going to matter all that much, thinking that our time means diddley to those rocks. Just a split second we've been here…just a piece of time too small to give a name.

> Those rocks were laughing at me. I could tell, me and my worries. It's real humorous to that Grand Canyon. Hey you know what I felt like? I felt like a gnat that lands on the arse of a cow that's chewing its cud next to a road that you drive by at seventy miles an hour.

The analogy with the gnat is not meant to indicate the helplessness of people. Rather, the gnat signifies the importance for human beings of being able to recognize when they are in the presence of a miracle. It is this recognition that can change the course of their lives. Mack's rescue is the first of many miraculous incidents that include the finding of a baby under a bush and that grows in spiritual significance as the film progress. Mack recognizes his rescue by Simon as a miracle that has to be played out in terms of developing a long-term friendship with him. But what constitutes this friendship is that Simon becomes the means for Mack himself to attempt to change the lives of others. When he hears that Simon's sister and her son and daughter live near where he broke down, he arranges for them to move to another part of town. He also successfully arranges for a new sexual partner for Simon.

To fully understand what black bodies mean in this film, it is necessary to return to a discussion of the opening credits. When the noise of the helicopter fades, a basketball net appears, surrounded by black hands reaching upward. In a black-and-white opening sequence on an urban basketball court, the camera strays over sections of the bodies of the black players, torsos, legs, hands, and feet. There is a clear visual analogy with the second half of the credit sequence that takes place in the Forum and is filmed in color. However, the force of the analogy is not established in the black-and-white communality of the basketball court, a site that is reserved for the safe portrayal of intimacy between men. Rather, the analogy works through the similarities between the straying gaze of the camera over black male bodies in the first sequence and the sexually desiring gaze of Mack cross the court at the women who walk by. In this part of the credit sequence again the camera lingers over sections of bodies, particularly the torsos and breasts of the walking women.

Certainly the blatantly sexual and somewhat predatory stare of Mack at these passing female bodies is intended to lock him into heterosexuality and to act as an early closure of the possibility of interpreting his later desire for Simon as homosexual. But these opening sequences and the scenes of black-white urban confrontation that follow do establish the cultural spaces designated by the film as safe. Safe spaces are sites in which whites can be in close proximity to, perhaps be intimate with, and gaze at black bodies. Both opening sequences prefigure the establishment of a close relationship between Simon and Mack; a friendship that comes to a cinematic climax when they play basketball with each other in Mack's driveway.

But as *Grand Canyon* constantly juxtaposes safe and dangerous spaces, it also treads in some dangerous spaces. The genealogy of race and nation cannot entirely explain the contradictions of the urban existence it portrays. The problem with using the Grand Canyon as a place to find salvation is that it also occupies a very contradictory space in the movie as a symbol of the distance between rich and poor. As Davis argues in justification for why he should continue to make films that contain graphic scenes of violence:

> There is a gulf in this country, an ever-widening abyss between the people who have stuff and the people who don't have shit. It's like this big hole has opened up in the ground, as big as the fucking Grand Canyon and what's come pouring out...what's come out of this big hole is an eruption of rage, and rage creates violence, and the violence is real, Mack, and nothing is going to make it go away, until someone changes something, which is not going to happen. And you may not like it, even I may not like it, but I can't pretend it isn't there because that is a lie, and when art lies it becomes worthless. So, I've got to keep telling the truth even if it scares the shit out of me, like it scares the shit out of you....I tell you this though, there's so much rage going around we're damn lucky to have the movies to help us vent a little of it....There's always been violence, they'll always be violence, violence and evil and men with big guns. My movies reflect what's going on, they don't make what's going on. And if I happen to make them better than anyone then I have a bigger responsibility than anyone to serve it up.

The final scene of *Grand Canyon* attempts to resolve the social and political contradictions that exist in the narrative, but, I would argue, this resolution points to both a crisis in and the limitations of the liberal middle-class political imagination embodied in its genealogy.

The end of the film turns away from the wider social and political implications of Davis's statement, a statement that however briefly directs our attention to economic injustice, about which he says nothing can be done. Instead, our attention is directed to the role of film in representing the real. The resolution we are offered uses black bodies as a means to white salvation.

Stowe made the black male body of Tom safe in two important ways. Stowe feminized him—Tom embodies all of the virtues of "true womanhood"—and she de-Africanized him through his Christianization. In *Grand Canyon* Kasdan situates black bodies in both safe and very dangerous spaces—they are both that which is most desired, as long as this desire is desexualized, and that which is most feared. For Kasdan, as a representative of the white liberal intelligentsia, the surplus symbolic value of black bodies is that they can be made to embody the anxieties of the white middle class. In his film these black bodies have to be acted upon, manipulated, and made malleable in order for the Macks of this world to be renewed, to be reborn, and to define and reinforce their identity. But for this to be accomplished, these black bodies have to remain on the surface, to be represented in superficial terms, to be in wait on the margins ready and willing to be acted upon for the salvation of the white soul. Indeed, it is in the process of becoming patrons to these safe black bodies that the reasons to retreat from the edge of the abyss, from chaos, will be given meaning.

NOTES

1 In a historical account of the process of the "Christianizing of the American people," Jon Butler(1990) dramatically describes how, in the eighteenth century, Christianity directly shaped the system of slaveholding and led to what he calls an African spiritual holocaust in North America: "a spiritual holocaust that effectively destroyed traditional African religious *systems*, [if] not all particular or religious practices." An "emerging Anglican understanding of slavery," Butler argues, "fitted with uncanny precision the degraded condition of captive Africans after 1680....The law that guaranteed liberty to English men and women became the seal of slavery for Africans." It was Anglican concepts of authority that "shaped a paternalistic ethic among planters," an ethic

> that not only coalesced with the doctrine of absolute obedience but made it all the more palatable and attractive....[Anglican] clergymen helped planters explain slave "misbehavior" in ways that solidified the masters' prejudices about slave degradation...[and] transformed planter views about laziness, lust, and lying among slaves into powerfully detailed pictures of African depravity.

This paternalistic ethic, continues Butler, rooted as it was in the doctrine of absolute obedience, "reinforced the growing violence of eighteenth-century slaveholding."

> It encouraged owners to excuse nearly all discrete instances of violence towards slaves. Ironically, paternalism loaded owners with obligations that were difficult to fulfill in a competitive, erratic economy where there were few effective restraints on the owners' treatment of their labor. Even "ethical" owners mistreated slaves. Worse, both "ethical" and unethical owners could readily agree that slaves disobeyed. A rigid doctrine fostered rigid responses. The stress on absolute obedience turned minor infractions of planter authority into major confrontations, and the result brought forth the first fixing of an indelible image in American race relations—the perpetually disobedient black....The meanings of blackness and disobedience had already begun to converge....

> The emergence of absolutist, paternalistic, and violent slavery gave Christianity as thoroughly a different cast as Christianity had given to slaveholding. Christianity's interpretation of social behavior and religious ethics produced a distended emphasis on sentiment, charity, and love utterly uncharacteristic of the society in which it was propounded. (pp. 153, 144, 146, 147)

2 The concepts of "fictive ethnicity" and genealogies of race and nation are drawn from Balibar and Wallerstein, 1991.

3 See Wallerstein, "Construction of Peoplehood: Racism, Nationalism, Ethnicity": "Pastness is a mode by which persons are persuaded to act in the present in ways they might not otherwise act. Pastness is a tool persons use against each other" (1991, p. 78).

4 It is clear that this association between the war zones of Southeast Asia and Los Angeles has been progressively established. Of particular importance to this process are the three *Lethal Weapon* films that, like *Grand Canyon,* starred Danny Glover. *Lethal Weapon III* is a culmination of the themes of the previous two: policing is indistinguishable from military intervention, and the burning of a housing complex is visually evocative of the burning of villages in Vietnam. Our reading of this scene of fire is, of course, directly influenced by *Apocalypse Now,* which reinforces my sense that Hollywood did and continues to mediate and inform this process of transition in the political imagination of the culture industry.

5 In the film none of the characters are given surnames. I would argue that this very deliberate omission is not just a "folksy" feature, but is an attempt to create a space for increased identification of the audience with the response of the characters to the series of incidents that happen to them. The lack of a "complete" identity enables the process of identity formation on the screen to include this generic component.

6 I am following Jon Butler's definition of religion outlined in his introduction to *Awash in a Sea of Faith*. He states that throughout his book:

> Religion is taken to mean belief in and resort to superhuman powers, sometimes beings, that determine the course of natural and human events. This is what philosophers of religion call a "substantive" rather than "functional" conceptualization. It describes what religion is rather than what religion does....Religion here is associated with supernaturalism, with supernatural beliefs, and with the conviction that supernatural beings and powers can and do affect life as humans know it. (1990, p. 3)

The religious is represented in a variety of ways throughout *Grand Canyon*. When Claire, who is married to Mack, finds a baby under a bush when she is out running, it becomes one of a number of incidents that are interpreted as a miracle. Mack feels that he is twice snatched from the jaws of death by strangers, and when Simon becomes the second of these saviors Mack concludes that this intervention has a supernatural aspect to it that cannot be ignored. The development of a friendship with Simon is seen by Mack as a necessary response to the presence of supernatural powers that are shaping his life. In addition, dream-life is very important, including a scene in which Mack flies over Los Angeles and in which his forbidden desires for Simon and Melissa are expressed. It is significant that Claire's dreams take place on the ground and are entirely confined to the enactment of desires and fears that constitute her identity as mother.

7 This superficial way of locating Mack is of course a postmodern substitute for history. See Jameson, 1991, pp. 6, 67–68.

REFERENCES

Balibar, E. & Wallerstein, I. (1991). *Race, Nation, Class: Ambiguous identities*. London: Verso.

Butler, J. (1990). *Awash in a Sea of Faith: Christianizing the American people*. Cambridge, MA: Harvard.

Jameson, F. (1991). *Postmodernism, or the Cultural Logic of Late Capitalism*. Durham: Duke UP.

Morrison, T. (1992). *Race-ing Justice, Engendering Power: Essays on Anita Hill, Clarence Thomas and the construction of social reality*. New York: Pantheon.

Rogin, M. (1992) Blackface, White Noise: The Jewish jazz singer finds his voice. *Critical Inquiry*,18 (3), 417–44.

Stowe, H. B. ([1852]1981). *Uncle Tom's Cabin Or, Life Among The Lowly*. New York: Penguin.

CULTURAL INTER-VENTIONS IN RACE RELATIONS IN SCHOOL AND SOCIETY

18

Multiculturalism and Oppositionality

MICHELE WALLACE

MANY INDIVIDUAL EVENTS on the current cultural landscape conspire to make me obsessed with contemporary debates over "multiculturalism" in both the art world and the culture at large. My concern is grounded first and foremost, however, in my observation of the impact of present material conditions on an increasing sector of the population. These material conditions, which include widespread homelessness, joblessness, illiteracy, crime, disease (including AIDS), hunger, poverty, drug addiction, alcoholism, the various habits of ill-health, and the destruction of the environment are (let's face it) the myriad social effects of late multinational capitalism.

In New York City, where I live, the population most affected by these conditions consists largely of people of African, Latino, or Asian descent, some of whom are gay: blacks either from, or one or two generations removed from, the South, the Caribbean, or Africa, or Latinos of mixed race from the Caribbean or Central or South America, or Asians from Korea, the Philippines, or China. In other parts of the country, the ethnic composition of the population that is most economically and politically disenfranchised may vary to include more poor whites, women and children of all races and ethnicities, gays, Native Americans, and Chicanos. In New York City this population, which accounts for more than half the population of the city, is menaced in very specific ways by inadequate and formidably expensive housing and medical care, by extremely shoddy and bureaucracy-ridden systems of social services and public education, by an inefficient, militaristic police force, and by increasing street violence and crime promoted by drug trafficking and high rates of drug addiction.

One of the immediate consequences of this system is that except for those people who are rich, white, and male (and therefore virtually never leave the Upper East Side), people live in fear in New York City. And contrary to the impression that one might get based on the overreporting of those incidents that involve black-on-white crime, it is women, children, old people, and especially young men of color who live under the greatest and most constant threat. In the spring and summer of 1991, even as multiculturalism was being debated in the cultural pages of the Sunday New York Times and celebrated by a variety of cultural events in the art world, New York City's non-white community was doubly menaced by a series of events. Their symbolic and/or political weight tended to endow these events with a certain quality of hyperreality, however fleeting.

These events were 1) the black boycott of the Korean fruit market in Flatbush, held in response to high prices and the alleged ill-treatment of a Haitian woman; 2) the trials of the murderers of Yusef Hawkins; 3) the trials of the Central Park rapists; and 4) the story of producer Cameron MacKintosh's resistance to the Actors Equity Association's decision that the white, British actor Jonathan Pryce should be replaced by an Asian as the lead in the Broadway version of the musical *Miss Saigon*. Perhaps the media representation of each of these events deserves its own analysis at some point, although I am not sure that any one of them significantly departs from well-established media patterns in racializing various kinds of "news" stories, especially those stories that include underlying gender issues.[1] Rather in this instance I wish to invoke them, and their extraordinary coverage in the mainstream media, as a background to the present discussion of "multiculturalism."

The character of the response—in the media and in the streets—to the trials of the Central Park rapists and the murder of Yusef Hawkins, the *Miss Saigon* debate and the Korean store boycott begins to give us some idea of the complex and contradictory attitudes in the dominant culture toward events that take place at the interstices of racial and social difference. The Central Park rape incident was first portrayed as "wilding" by New York City newspapers—a term apparently relevant only to the gang violence of black male youths, for it was not used to describe the attack by white male youths on Hawkins in Bensonhurst.

As for the black boycott of the Korean store in Flatbush and MacKintosh's refusal to bring *Miss Saigon* to Broadway, given the insistence on the part of Actors Equity that Pryce be replaced by an Asian, New York City press handled the former event as though it were a transparent case of black-on-Asian racism, whereas the latter event was reported as a blow for "artistic freedom," "freedom of expression," and even "multiculturalism." In the process a mockery was made of the history of Asians in the American theater: Yul Brynner in "The King and I," as well as the white actor who played Charlie Chan, were paraded as positive examples of "nontraditional casting."

While it is not surprising to encounter these contradictory attitudes in the mainstream, it is interesting to note how related ideological conflicts are played out in the programming and attitudes of the art world and the cultural left. Thus far this particular arena of multicultural discourse has centered around attempts by writers, artists, and others to establish relationships or kinships between issues of gender, sexuality, and ethnicity. In the past the problem for cultural activists has been how to theorize links between and establish commonalities among diverse constituencies. The current cultural-left and art-world versions of multiculturalism respond to this problem by circumventing theoretical discourse altogether in favor of a virtually unrestricted inclusiveness. I suspect that the link multiculturalism is trying to establish between discourses on feminism, sexual preference, and ethnicity could be more usefully viewed as a pragmatic political coalition: the cultural left version of Jesse Jackson's Rainbow Coalition against the rising tide of the conservative right.

While multiculturalism's inclination toward unrestricted inclusiveness as opposed to hierarchical exclusiveness doesn't automatically lead to significant structural changes in existing aesthetic and critical priorities and institutional discourses of power, it could offer and thus far has offered more opportunities for critical discussion outside the dominant discourse, and dissent and debate within, than its present aesthetic and critical alternatives. These alternatives I see as 1) a "color-blind" cultural homogeneity that originates in liberal humanist ideology; 2) separatist aesthetics and politics such as "Afrocentrism"; and 3) racist/sexist aesthetics, which range from the cultural fascism of a Hilton Kramer in *The New Criterion* to the social fascism of such right-wing vigilantes as the Ku Klux Klan and the youth gangs that attacked Hawkins in Bensonhurst and the female jogger in Central Park. Thus, despite my reservations about multiculturalism, I have become a reluctant supporter of it. At the same time it is crucial to its usefulness that we view multiculturalism not as an obdurate and unchanging ideological position but as an opportunity for ongoing critical debate.[2]

In an essay on "Endangered: Art and Performance by Men of Color" (a series of performances and exhibitions at Intermedia Arts Minnesota in 1990 that included work by Marlon Riggs and Essex Hemphill, Sansei Japanese American cultural critic and poet David Mura (1990) juxtaposes the exemplary multiculturalism of this series with *New York Times* critic Richard Bernstein's remarks on the threat of multiculturalism in an article entitled "The Arts Catch Up With A Society in Disarray" (1990). Reading Mura's essay, I am reminded that my remarks about multiculturalism are designed to invert Bernstein's. Mura summarizes Bernstein, who characterizes multiculturalism as "the new tribalism," in this way:

> Bernstein quotes Arthur Schlesinger's remark that the melting pot has yielded to the "Tower of Babel." In a seeming effort to complicate Schlesinger's observation, Bernstein admits there is a necessary connection between "artistic matters and the harsh world of the streets, where things seem to be getting conspicuously worse." What follows is a litany of the recent racial cases which have rocked New York—the rape and assault of the Central Park Jogger, the incident in Bensonhurst, Tawana Brawley, the picketing of Korean grocers, Washington, D.C. Mayor Barry's drug trial. Through such a listing, Bernstein creates an unspoken association in the reader's mind: Minority artists find their sources in the violence of the streets; this is the main difference between minority artists and mainstream tradition. A further implication: minority arts represent the anger and violence of the barbarians at the gate, figures of chaos and dissolution. (1990)

While Mura goes on to talk about other issues surrounding multiculturalism, I would like to reclaim here Bernstein's image of social chaos as the basis for any successful multiculturalism. The politicization of art against which he rails is precisely what is absolutely necessary. As for a society in disarray: when has American society ever been in order for people of color and people of sensitivity, for those who are visibly and invisibly other? For the poor, the gay, the women, the children, the disabled, the elderly, the not-white? "Society" is now in disarray for Bernstein only because he, and those of his cast of mind, have been forced to recognize that they are not the only ones on this planet, that they are, in fact, a distinct although not yet endangered "minority."

In the following remarks I want to analyze three contemporary instances of multicultural programming and artwork: the panel and film series "Sexism, Colonialism, Misrepresentation: A Corrective Film Series" (1988) held at the Dia Art Foundation and the Collective for Living Cinema in New York City and organized by feminist film critic Bérénice Reynaud and filmmaker Yvonne Rainer; "The Decade Show" (1990), a joint exhibition of the New Museum of Contemporary Art and the Museum of Contemporary Hispanic Art, that were at the time across the street from each other in Soho, and the Studio Museum in Harlem; and Rainer's film *Privilege* (1990). These events exemplify an interrelated set of issues relevant to current multicultural practice in the art world: the problematic elision of race within dominant psychoanalytic models of criticism, the accompanying lack of work by people of color that theorizes the relation of race to issues of class and gender, and finally, the tendency in multicultural programming to rely on artists and writers of color as the "subject matter" whose experience is then reconstituted through the theoretical elaboration of white intellectuals.

I want to begin by considering the controversy surrounding the coverage of "Sexism, Colonialism, Misrepresentation" by the Cuban American critic and curator Coco Fusco in the pages of *Afterimage* and *Screen* (1988; the same articles also reviewed the 1988 "Celebration of Black Cinema" conference in Boston). The event consisted of a series of three panels and the screening of forty films from Africa, Australia, the Middle and Far East, Latin America, and Europe. These films included, in addition to many films by people of color, films by white feminists and even one film by a white male on the French left. Instead of addressing the films—a possibly endless discussion given the range of aesthetic and critical issues arising from any series of independent films—or even all three of the panels, I would like to focus on Fusco's criticism of one of the panels, "The Visual Construction of Sexual Difference," and on the defense of the series by Rainer and Reynaud.

Before going any further, I should say that not only was I involved in the "Sexism, Colonialism, Misrepresentation" conference, but I am acquainted and friendly with Reynaud and Rainer and a close friend of Fusco. As such, it would be both impossible and ill-advised for me to attempt to engage in a thorough critique of their works or their intentions, especially since I am wholly sympathetic to their various endeavors. It is my assumption that Coco, Bérénice, Yvonne, and I are on the same side in matters having to do with gender, culture, and the mythologies and realities of "race."

Fusco begins her discussion by reminding us that "the blossoming of multicultural media events" is a response to the "perceived need to redress the effective ethnic segregation of the art world" (1988, p. 6). The particular division of labor that she describes is one in which white, "avant-garde" intellectuals "theorize about racism while ethnic film and video producers supply 'experiential' materials in the form of testimony and documentation, or in which the white intelligentsia solicits token third world intellectuals to theorize about the question—that is, the problem of the Other—for the white intelligentsia" (p. 7).

Much more insidious to me than the problem of white intellectuals theorizing nativist "data" is the problem of "whiteness" itself as an unmarked term in such conferences and discussions. This was particularly noticeable in the discussions that followed the panel on "The Visual Construction of Sexual Difference." A large portion of time was given over to arguing about what could be expected of psychoanalysis in terms of cultural resistance, whether or not psychoanalysis could be historicized, and whether it could be made to do political readings of cultural production. For the most part the participants seemed thoroughly convinced that such a combination would be unthinkable.

What Fusco says about the problem of this panel is that, first, "to ignore white ethnicity is to redouble its hegemony by naturalizing it. Without specifically addressing white ethnicity there can be no critical evaluation of the construction of the other" (1988, p. 9). Second, she says, "it did not officially include any interrogation of the Eurocentric prioritization of sexual difference" (p. 9). Of the conference overall, she further says, "there operated a Eurocentric presumption that sexual difference could be separated from other forms of difference and that the theoretical models that privilege gender-based sexual difference could be used to understand other difference" (p. 9).

My view, however, is that the challenge of multicultural criticism cannot be met simply by prioritizing other kinds of difference to the exclusion of gender but rather by theorizing sexuality, the body, and gender from other cultural perspectives. The solution is not to reject Freudian, Lacanian, and Foucauldian discourses about sexual difference out-of-hand in order to return to the pragmatics of race and class, for then we confront the old problem of a reductive "social realism" hamstringing critical analysis. Moreover, we don't want to neglect the contribution that feminist thought on the left (in both cultural studies and psychoanalytic film criticism) has made to thinking about cultural responsibility—specifically the idea that gender and sexuality are socially and culturally constructed, yet individual desire is never fully described or subsumed or determined by such constructions.

It is true that the left feminist avant-garde has had a rocky and uneven history (which needs to be recorded) in dealing with its own tendencies toward racism, elitism, and cultural apartheid. But it is also true that this sector, unlike any other, has been instrumental in foregrounding a political discourse on art and culture, thus fostering a climate in which it becomes at least hypothetically possible publicly to review and interrogate that very history of exclusion and racism.

The problem remains, however, that within the various progressive political and cultural positions there is an almost total lack of theoretical discourse that relates "race" to gender and sexuality. It is not often recognized that bodies and psyches of color have trajectories in excess of their socially and/or culturally constructed identities. What is needed to achieve effective social change is some intervention in the present deployment of these bodies and psyches, an intervention that demands a sophisticated level of theorization of racial and social identity. This is where the extraordinary, thus far almost insuperable difficulty arises in effecting concrete social transformation through discussions of cultural interpretation. In the rush to analyze, many of us not only reinscribe Eurocentric dominance and hegemony but also stifle the possibility of more pragmatic interpretations based on the belief that psychoanalytic and other forms of theory simply can't deal with racial differences.

For me the most interesting thing said in the panel was Joan Copjec's commentary, drawing from the work of African psychoanalyst Frantz Fanon, *Black Skins, White Masks* (1967). "The most insidious effect of the colonizing enterprise is that it constructs the *very desires* of the colonizing subject. The danger lies in the implied assumption that the content of desire is defined by the apparatuses of domination," Copjec argued, paraphrasing Fanon. "Psychoanalysis has never claimed that the subject is totally mastered by the social order. Psychoanalysis is the discourse which obliges us to think the *subversion of mastery*—not only of the subject by itself, but also the subject by the social" (in Benamou, Copjec, Gever, hooks, and Koch, 1990, p. 46).

Such ideas seem crucial to reconceptualizing the black female subject, black feminist cultural resistance, and a multicultural consciousness. And yet the discussion that followed Copjec's remarks seemed extremely uneasy about the relevance of such a discourse to other than middle-class, white, feminist women, as though a culturally relativist perspective would preclude any attempt at psychoanalytic interpretations of subjectivity.

The problem arises in conversations such as this from a basic misunderstanding. Despite the general critique of essentialism in many feminist discussions, when Reynaud asked the panelists and the audience, "So which father are we talking about? Are we talking about the heterosexual repressive father, about the white father, about the master of language, about the colonialist father, the capitalist father? We are constructing these fathers, and we are constructed by them. When we talk about patriarchy, what are we talking about? Who is the enemy?" (Benamou, Copjec, Gever, hooks, and Koch, 1990, p. 42), she implicitly identified herself and other white feminists on the left with the "colonized." Yet neither bell hooks nor Isaac Julien nor Kobena Mercer, in their subsequent comments, felt as though they could afford to confuse the position of white women in discourse with the position of the racially and ethnically colonized. "How does the canon of psychoanalytic discourse deal with the absence of black women in these new forms [TV, film] of representation?" Julien asked. "I think the Law of the Father is different from the Law of the Land," Julien further proposed, "and this is an inseparable identity for black subjectivity" (p. 45).

In such exchanges everyone is far too polite to come out and say the thing that needs to be said first—women are not to be trusted just because they're women, any more than blacks are to be trusted because they're black, or gays because they're gay, and so on. Unfortunately, what proves this position, besides the glaring examples of women, blacks, or gays who are profoundly reactionary, is precisely such superficially progressive discourses as feminist psychoanalytic film criticism, which one can read for days on end without coming across any lucid reference to, or critique of, "race."

How am I to understand this discourse as oppositional if it seems to do even less than the classic film tradition it reflects upon to challenge or interrogate racial/cultural apartheid? If racism (racial stereotyping and/or the confinement of black characters to the margins of the plot) is one of the most fundamental features of the Hollywood classic film tradition, and moreover, if the way in which such racism was imposed upon black female characters is eminently describable, how are we to regard the exclusion of such material altogether from what purports to be an ideological critique?

When Constance Penley suggests in a discussion that "we have to accept psychoanalysis in terms of its quite modest claim. It is a theory of sexual difference. It may not be easily articulable to the other kinds of differences discussed today" (Benamou, Copjec, Gever, hooks, and Koch, 1990, p. 43), I can only respond that I am unwilling to cede sexual difference to white women. Sexual difference is something that women of color, poor women, and gay women share with white, middle-class, heterosexual women. How am I supposed to regard a theory of sexual difference that doesn't apply to women of color? To my mind such theoretical discourses, in which "race" is marginalized, trivialized, and excluded, provide the component parts for the structure of racism in the dominant discourse. This has meant and continues to mean that as you turn to the cultural left you are greeted by the emphatic symbolic representation of your own invisibility. At least "race" is real to the reactionary right.

I'd like to suggest that there may be opportunities for control and theorizing that are not being adequately seized by people of color. People of color need to be engaged in critical and/or theorizing practices around multiculturalism as it is currently being developed in cultural institutions, in universities, and in public schools. Where I see the most intensive theorizing going on among African American critics, for example, is in academia and in response to texts, particularly historical literary texts. Although such activity is important and necessary, I also think that given the political/economic context in which we're living we have a responsibility to reach a broader audience by making connections between the interpretation of canonical texts, tradition building, and what has been happening in the Supreme Court and the Middle East in recent years.

Rainer's film *Privilege* (1990) is a laudable effort on the part of a white, feminist avant-garde filmmaker to integrate issues of race and ethnicity into her work. Yet however intriguing the result is, the film is still depressing for its inability to take seriously the subjectivities of women of color. Again, I want to emphasize that what is at issue here is not whether or not bodies of color are included on the set or in the film (or on the panel). In this case the shortcoming of multiculturalism is a structural dilemma. In order to believe that the subjectivities of women of color have been taken seriously, I have to see a structural change in the ways in which their voices are incorporated into the cultural discourse.

I am also disturbed by the feeling that I need to do this kind of postmortem on a work of art, because right or wrong, I still believe that artists are special and that the cult status of the work of art is not all bullshit. And I definitely don't believe in censorship. To the contrary, I wish more white feminist cultural producers and artists would foreground "race" in their work. On the other hand, if I haven't the right as a black feminist to critique what they've done, then the positive effects of the effort are canceled.

Although *Privilege* is in an entirely different league from such mainstream filmic attempts to deal with race as *The Long Walk Home* (1990), *Cry Freedom* (1987), *Betrayed* (1988), *Mississippi Burning* (1988), *Round Midnight* (1986), or *Bird* (1988) in that Rainer allows women of color to speak from a variety of positions, the filmmaker still shows no concrete interest in having the women of color themselves theorize race, or class, or gender. The positions from which women of color speak in the film are qualitatively different from, and inferior to, the positions from which white women, white men, and men of color speak.

The ideological positions from which white men speak in the film are the least complex and interesting. Although the lawyer who works in the district attorney's office is portrayed as a humane character, he's still a racist and a sexist. The "white male" medical authorities (some of whom are women) that pervade the film's documentary sections are almost comic in their inflexible pathologizing and palpable ignorance of female sexuality. Nevertheless and needless to say, white men come across with as much authority as ever.

The white women—from the character Jenny whose storytelling structures the film's plot to the former anarchists who are interviewed about their experience of menopause—are repeatedly humanized through close-ups, point-of-view shots, and dialogue. As viewers we are encouraged to identify with Jenny's anxiety about aging, her fantasies about men, her guilty admission that she lied under oath in order to get the Latino Carlos convicted of rape. The interviews with the former anarchists, in which they weave aspects of their political lives into their reflections on menopause, are equally fascinating. The women emerge completely triumphant over the symptoms the white male doctors describe.

The men of color, much like the white men, are highly inflexible and one-dimensional. Almost everything they say is quoted from a text by a male author of color—Piri Thomas, Eldridge Cleaver, Fanon, etc.—selected precisely for their authors' inability to conceptualize black female subjectivity. Moreover, the film dwells on the issue of whether black men or Latino men want to rape white women, a question that I find both irritating and uninteresting. Rainer's film attempts to deal with issues of race and gender but ignores the historical rape of the black woman—which literally founded the African American race and the African diaspora. What interests me is the larger issue of how dominant ideologies and discourses of power continue to structure desire. This is particularly true for men, black, white, and brown, but it is also true for women.

Which brings us to the women of color in the film. The film begins with a documentary-style interview with a nameless black woman, a "native," about menopause. That woman is my mother, Faith Ringgold. Ringgold is an important African American artist and one of the key early black feminist voices in antiwar, anti-racist, and feminist art-world activism. Yet she isn't asked to talk about the impact of race on menopause, or race in the art world or the film world, or anything that might identify her as who and what she is—a highly opinionated and influential black female subject. Three other interviews with black women, at least two of whom were recommended by Ringgold, are interspersed within the main narrative. Ringgold's statement that "Getting older is a bitch" opens the film because it foreshadows the main character Jenny's perspective on aging, not because it problematizes racial privileges. Rainer admits in a recent interview to having "missed an opportunity to ask the women of color in the film how they felt race impinged on their aging and on their treatment by the medical establishment" (quoted in Easterwood, Fairfax, and Poitras, 1990, p. 9).

Novella Nelson plays the black character Yvonne Washington, whom we are supposed to conceive of as a kind of alter ego of the white Yvonne Rainer. The black Yvonne, we are told, is the "author" of the documentary on menopause for which Ringgold and other black women are interviewed but not asked about race. But despite the apparent promotion of a fully developed alternative subjectivity, or alternative position in discourse, Yvonne serves largely as a foil or straight man for Jenny's narcissistic reveries. In interviews Rainer has credited Nelson with having influenced the final form of the film by improvising lines, which she chose to leave in. Nelson's desire to intervene in the script doesn't surprise me at all, given the film's equation, at one point, of racial and gender difference with feces and blood, as an explanation for why white men find "blacks and women" equally contemptible. As far as I'm concerned, this theory of racism, which Rainer borrows from Joel Kovel (1970), is thoroughly inadequate because it discounts the historical accomplishments of African American culture and other cultures of the African diaspora. For the most part, the alternative subjectivities of women of color are a product of precisely such cultures.

Finally, the representation of Digna (Gabriella Farrar), the Latina who is beaten up by Carlos and subsequently incarcerated in Bellevue mental hospital, is perhaps the most deeply problematic. The antithesis of madness to "voice" is not sufficiently interrogated. Digna "speaks" from Bellevue in a straitjacket about how Latinas are more likely than white women to be diagnosed as schizophrenic. But not only is the viewer never told where this information comes from; also there is no suggestion that this woman might be able to resist or subvert such a deadly cultural hegemony. More to the point: women of color don't generally speak from madhouses. Is the voice and visualization of Digna, a Latina, so deeply problematic for Rainer that she can only be figured "speaking" under the profound erasure of a straitjacket and incarceration in a mental hospital?

Does this mean that Digna is the most oppressed? Is she meant to represent a kind of extreme antithesis to "privilege": the subject who is completely without privilege? Rainer establishes a hierarchical continuum along which the individual's potential capacity for racial and gendered privilege and victimization is carefully calibrated. According to this view, white men can't be victims any more than a Latina can have privilege. In summation, my point is that while women of color were ostensibly allowed to "speak in their own voices" in *Privilege,* they were not empowered to structure the discourse of the film. Nor will women viewers of color be empowered to imagine themselves as structuring subjects of the film discourse. Or if they are (and this would be the best scenario) it will be to rebel against Rainer's invisible but nevertheless real authority as a preeminent feminist filmmaker, as well as that of other well-meaning artists, theorists, and academic intellectuals.

If we move from Ranier's film to the exhibition "The Decade Show: Frameworks of Identity in the 1980s," we encounter an instance of "multicultural" programming that seems intensely engaged by issues of authority, authenticity, who speaks for whom, and how discourses that flatten and trivialize difference are constructed. But there is a level of failure in this exhibition that, again, demonstrates the failure of the present potential for multicultural discourses as processed by white feminists.

"The Decade Show" is an example of programming and theorizing by white feminists. When I speak of white feminists I mean Marcia Tucker, the director of the New Museum, whose background in the art-world left goes back to the 1960s, and Laura Trippi and Gary Sangster, who were the New Museum's curators for this exhibition. Although curators and personnel were involved at the other two institutions, in their catalogue statements they made clear that what they hoped to achieve is distinctly pragmatic (Herzberg, 1990; Patton, 1990). In contrast, the New Museum's conception of the show is self-consciously theoretical. Sharon F. Patton, the Studio Museum's curator for "The Decade Show," begins by writing:

> For the Studio Museum in Harlem, The Decade Show is a curatorial endeavor to
> insert artists of color, especially African American artists, into the history of
> contemporary art in the United States. The institutional agendas were clear: first, to

present in a national arena African American artists; and second, to affirm cultural pluralism within the theater of the art world. The exhibition is a response, albeit not unique nor the first, to the exclusion of many African American artists from the critical art literature, art history, and exhibitions on American art. Many of the represented artists have been denied, or have had limited access to "mainstream" modernist and postmodernist documentation in terms of professional recognition (other than peers) and legitimization. (1990, p. 77)

In the context of "socially conscious art," which Patton says is the "agenda of the eighties" (1990, p. 77), she is talking about African American artists getting their piece of the economic pie, sharing in the enormous wealth of the art world. Except with regard to her critique of racial exclusion, Patton is not advocating any profound alteration in the structure of the mainstream.

The same is true of the essay by the curator from the Museum of Contemporary Hispanic Art. While Julia P. Herzberg invokes the necessity for "meaningful cross-cultural dialogue" and "comprehensive inclusion" (1990, p. 37), her essay, even more than Patton's, provides an inventory of artists of the minority group in question that focuses intensively on the value and originality of their art, in other words, on their ability to produce the transcendent art object upon which the cult value and the market value of art are based.

It is Trippi and Sangster, curators at The New Museum, who take on the task of providing the theoretical overview, the context for interpreting the conjunction of cultural practices, cultural production, and economic, political, and social realities.

> A cornerstone of modern Western aesthetics—with its impressionisms and expressionisms, on the one hand, and its ideal of disinterested, universal judgement on the other—the idea of the autonomous self helped provide a base for the larger edifice of modernity, an edifice built for the benefit of a largely white, largely male few, at the expense of the many. The application of dialogic models to considerations of identity suggested that the self be understood not as an entity but as a provisional construction, a weave of differing dialogic, or discursive, threads. (1990, pp. 64–65)

This exhibition, Trippi and Sangster argue, whether the artist is gay, or feminist, or a person of color, or some combination, is not really about "identity" as a unified, monological field but about "identities." They quote from and heavily rely upon Stuart Hall for this observation. As Hall wrote in *ICA Documents 6* in an essay called "Minimal Selves,"

> It may be true that the self is always, in a sense, a fiction, just as the kinds of "closures" which are required to create communities of identification—nation, ethnic group, families, sexualities, etc.—are arbitrary closures; and the forms of political action, whether movement, parties, or classes, those too, are temporary, partial, arbitrary. It is an immensely important gain when one recognizes that all identity is constructed across difference. (1987, p. 45; quoted in Trippi and Sangster, 1990, p. 65)

The extraordinary and ironic thing about the authority of Hall's remarks in this context is that although the ideas come from poststructuralist thought, they are filtered through the imagination of a very committed political activist who happens also to be black and originally from the Caribbean. Needless to say, he is not identified as such by Trippi and Sangster's essay. So Hall speaks here not only about ideas but also about material realities. In a very concrete and specific sense, the so-called "identity" of the diasporic subject is constructed from a plurality of "wheres" and "whats," as well as where and what one is not. As Hall, Gayatri Spivak, Cornel West, Hortense Spillers, bell hooks, Trinh T. Minh-ha, and so many other people of color who are interested in what is vaguely called "theory" might remind us, the nature of the "overview" changes depending upon "the politics of location" of the "author." For instance, in Trippi and Sangster's essay the reality of the art world in the 1980s is described in terms of the metaphor of a board game called Trivial Pursuit, and the art of making a deal is discussed in the sense that Donald Trump might use the word "deal." How real is this picture for artists of color or for critics or museum administrators of color? Where is the overview of artists and cultural critics of color on the left emanating from marginal theories and practices themselves? Don't we need one? Who will write it?

Published with the permission of the author. This essay first appeared in *Afterimage,* 19 (3) (October 1991), 6–9.

NOTES

1 In each case gender provides an underlying impetus for an explicitly racial story: in the Korean fruit market boycott a black woman was allegedly struck by an Asian male; in the Central Park rape a white woman was raped by black and Puerto Rican boys and men; in the Yusef Hawkins murder, we were told the initial provocation had to do with the suspicion that a white Bensonhurst girl was dating a black boy. In the case of the Cameron MacKintosh/*Miss Saigon* debacle, the part that Jonathan Pryce played was a pimp who sells sex with Vietnamese women to mostly white American GIs. See Joan Didion's interesting article in the *New York Review of Books* (1991) on why the rape or murder victim in nationally reported crime cases is always a "young, white attractive female" (p. 45).

2 As the 1990 debates on culture in the mainstream press tended to center on censorship, the following year's round of debates centered on the notion of "political correctness." Interestingly enough, if one sees the censorship debate and the political correctness debate as stages in a larger, ongoing multiculturalism debate, then one will also see that the continuous underlying motivation of the dominant discourse is to delay and/or forego the validation of alternative subjectivities and discourses as long as possible in favor of reconsolidating the center as one in which all debates are between "the left" and "the right," both of which are viewed as white (they have no ethnicity or "race"). Of course, racial issues are continually subsumed by the so-called larger debates of censorship or political correctness, and in the process, blacks are neatly objectified (from the naked, black male bodies in Robert Mapplethorpe's photographs to Jules Feiffer's cartoon about political correctness in which a black female college student gloats over having been able to function as a racist for a semester).

REFERENCES

Benamou, C., Copjec, J., Gever, M., hooks, b., & Koch, G. (1990). The visual construction of sexual difference. *Motion Picture,* 3 (3–4) [special issue documenting the proceedings of the conference "Sexism, Colonialism, Misrepresentation"], pp. 34-48.

Bernstein, R. (1990, Sept. 2). The Arts catch up with a society in disarray. *The New York Times,* Sec. 2, pp. 1, 12-13.

Didion, J. (1991, Jan. 17). New York: Sentimental journeys. *New York Review of Books,* pp. 45-51.

Easterwood, K., Fairfax, S., & Poitras, L. (1990). *Interview with Yvonne Rainer.* In *Yvonne Rainer: Declaring stakes.* San Francisco: San Francisco Cinematheque.

Fanon, F. (1967). *Black Skin, White Masks.* New York: Grove.

Fusco, C. (1988). Fantasies of oppositionality. *Afterimage,* 16 (5), 6–9; *Screen,* 29 (4).

Hall, S. (1987). Minimal selves. In L. Appignanesi (ed.), *ICA Documents* 6 (pp. 44–46). London: Institute of Contemporary Art.

Herzberg, J. P. (1990). Re-membering identity: Visions of connections. In Museum of Contemporary Hispanic Art et al.

Kovel, J. (1970). *White Racism: A psychohistory.* New York: Pantheon.

Mura, D. (1990, Nov.). The minority artist and the nature of difference: or, Caliban speaks. *Public Art Review.*

Museum of Contemporary Hispanic Art, New Museum of Contemporary Art, Studio Museum in Harlem. (1990). *The Decade Show: Frameworks of identity in the 1980s.* New York: Authors.

Patton, S. F. (1990). The agenda in the eighties: Socially conscious art. In Museum of Contemporary Art et al.

Trippi, L. & Sangster, G. (1990). From trivial pursuit to the art of the deal: Art making in the eighties. In Museum of Contemporary Hispanic Art et al.

19 Black Studies, Cultural Studies, Performative Acts

Manthia Diawara

One of the most important, and appealing, aspects of cultural studies is its critical, or even polemical, attitude toward every form of theoretical orthodoxy. The term *elabore*, used by Antonio Gramsci to stretch and test the limits of Marxism, captures the sense of critical attitude I have in mind here. Elaboration has become, within cultural studies, a means to make use of some of the approaches and methodologies of poststructuralism while being critical of it as an institutionalized discipline.

Cultural studies often delineates ways of life by elaborating them quite literally, embarrassing and baffling previous theoretical understanding of those forms of life. This ethnographic approach has helped cultural studies ground some of its key concepts in material conditions—for example, uneven development, cultural articulation, positionality, and specificity. Through the "literal reading of event," cultural studies explicates the material bases and implications of worldviews we assume and analyzes identity politics as moments of difference and rupture in the hegemonic status quo described by the discourses of Marxism or psychoanalysis.

I want to follow the evolution of the practice of elaboration from its development by early practitioners at the Centre for Contemporary Cultural Studies, University of Birmingham, through its use by London-based black artists and writers, to its deployment in the United States, particularly in departments of black studies and in feminist studies. I would like to distinguish what I call the London-based black British cultural studies from the tradition derived from work at Birmingham Centre. In the 1960s and 1970s researchers at the Birmingham Centre were mainly interested in the British working class and in an attempt to constitute an unique and alternative British Marxist theory around that subject. They were concerned to generate a British Marxism that would challenge the theoretical work of Louis Althusser, Claude Lévi-Strauss, and the Frankfurt School. In contrast, in the 1980s black filmmakers, artists, photographers, and writers were decomposing and restructuring the terms of Britishness, using race as the modality through which to read class. Black British cultural studies took as its main subject the elaboration of black Britishness over and against ethnic absolutism in Britain, the construction of a hegemonic blackness by black Americans, and other manifestations of diasporan aesthetics.

London-based black cultural workers found the language specific to their condition of black Britishness by submitting to a critical reading not only the texts of the white left, which often ignored facts, but also texts from the black diaspora. Some of the most fascinating moments in Paul Gilroy's *There Ain't No Black in the Union Jack* (1987) involve a critique of the work of George Orwell and Raymond Williams for their black ethnocentrism. In order to carve out a space for blackness in Britain, Gilroy had to denounce Williams and Orwell in a way similar to how he denounced British right-wingers such as Enoch Powell for their nostalgic celebration of a mythic, homogeneous way of life of the English working class. Isaac Julien similarly developed his film language through a critical reading of white avant-garde cinema. Julien states:

> On the left of avant-gardism is pleasure, which the avant-garde itself denies, clinging to the purism of its constructed ethics, measuring itself against a refusal to indulge in narrative or emotions and indeed, in some cases, refusing representation itself, because all these systems of signs are fixed, entrenched in the "sin or evil" of representation. The high moral tone of this discourse is based on a kind of masochistic self-censorship that relies on the indulgence of a colonial history and a post-colonial history of cinema or white representations based on our black absence. The problematic that surfaces when black filmmakers experiment with the idea of black film text and the subjective camera, is that subjectivity implies contradiction. But this is not, in itself, fixed. (1988, p. 36)

Black British cultural workers also engage with the black American culture of the 1960s and 1970s and elaborate it into something energetic and specifically British. Some of the most significant diasporic influences on black British cultural studies have been the works of black Americans such as June Jordan, whose *Civil Wars* (1981) helped young black British thinkers to theorize "policing" in their own context, Manning Marable, Cedric Robinson, James Baldwin, Toni Cade Bambara, Ntozake Shange, and Toni Morrison. Caribbean influences included C. L. R. James, George Lamming, Wilson Harris, Frantz Fanon, Aimé Césaire, Edward Braithwaite, and Derek Walcott, and African influences included Ngũgĩ wa Thiong'o and Ousmane Sembène. But these diasporic texts were articulated with black Britishness to create new approaches that were attentive to the fluidity of identities, class, and sexual politics in the British context.

While the distinction between the "Birmingham school"—an economic or class-based cultural studies—and a "black British school"—a race or ethnic identity-based cultural studies—may be difficult to maintain in light of the fact that figures such as Stuart Hall, Gilroy, and Dick Hebdige played and continue to play key roles in our understanding of both these strands of thought, it is a useful distinction to consider if we want to understand why in the U.S. academic context there appear to be two different kinds of "cultural studies" even though both are said to be derived from "British cultural studies."

One prevalent strain of cultural studies in the U.S. posits race at its center and uses metaphors of racial construction to bring to light the ways of life of oppressed groups. It is concerned with issues such as black appropriation of the discourse of modernism, the performative character of the construction of identity, crossover texts, cultural ambivalence, and sexism and homophobia in black communities. Thus it combines elements of what we might call "oppression studies"—historical and sociological work that has concerned itself with uncovering the various modes of oppression of black men and women, the black family, etc.—with descriptive and semiotic studies of the ways of life and artifacts of black individuals and communities. Writers such as bell hooks, Michele Wallace, Marlon Riggs, Wahneema Lubiano, Tommy Lott, Henry Louis Gates Jr., Houston Baker Jr., Cornel West, Jane Gaines, Cora Caplan, Hazel Carby, and Herman Gray, to name a few, have entered into dialogue with the strand of black British cultural studies that focuses on issues of hybridity, essentialism, etc.—for example, with the work of Gilroy, Kobena Mercer, Sonia Boyce, David Balley, Sankofa, and the Black Audio Film Collective. The December 1991 conference "Black Popular Culture," organized by the Dia Center for the Arts in New York City, brought together many of these critics and reasserted the centrality of the discourse of blackness to cultural studies. The proceedings have been edited into a book of the same title by Gina Dent.

The other cultural studies in the U.S. explicitly links itself to the Birmingham Centre for Contemporary Cultural Studies. Taking as one of its primary projects the description of people's ways of life, it focuses on cultural practices and texts such as rock music, Hollywood and independent films, and so-called new ethnicities. Practitioners of this form of cultural studies also describe the impact on culture of, for example, the medical profession, leisure industries, and corporate control of electronic media. While these theorists maintain a strong anti-essentialist perspective, their abstract discourse belies the fact that they have been more influenced by certain strains of poststructuralism than by recent developments in the black strand of cultural studies. The conference "Cultural Studies Now and in the Future," held at the University of Illinois at Urbana-Champaign, April 4-9, 1990, represented not only the best and highest levels of abstraction in the discourse of this brand of cultural studies but also its tendency to evacuate race and gender as primary issues.

This genealogy of cultural studies obviously oversimplifies the field: for example, the forms I have described are not simply in opposition; many cultural workers cross the boundaries of many of these approaches. The purpose of constructing a typology is that comparing and analyzing the foci of each form facilitates exposing its advantages as well as its limitations. For example, British cultural studies theorists have criticized some black cultural workers for essentializing blackness by reifying black ways of life even as they debunk the ethnic absolutism they associate with Englishness and black nationalism. This anti-essentialist critique of black cultural work suggests how an emphasis on identity politics can encourage people to forego the project of coalition building and actually fragment revolutionary struggle.

Similarly, contradictions within U.S. cultural studies underline the fact that the importation of the theoretical traditions of the Birmingham Centre to the U.S. must include an engagement with the material conditions of culture in the U.S. Unfortunately, a good deal of U.S. cultural studies that invokes the Birmingham tradition disengages theory from its spaces of application. The perspectives of the Birmingham school cannot simply be lifted and applied to the U.S.—where traditions of family, nation, and spectatorship, for example, are quite different—without a negotiation and reapplication of the tools of ethnography and analysis in the context of U.S. social and material conditions. In their attempt to replace deconstruction with cultural studies as a new academic discipline, its practitioners have made anti-essentialism their strongest critical tool and turned their backs on the theoretical and methodological contributions of Marxism, feminism, and black studies. The anti-essentialism of this cultural studies has become an essentialism of its own kind: the reification of discourse.

At the same time, practitioners of the Birmingham school tradition in Britain and of black British cultural studies have much to learn from black studies and feminist studies as they have been developed in the U.S. Black British writers studying, for example, the implications of postmodern films or theories of global systems might do well to look at work that has been done in such areas as African studies, Asian studies, and Latin American studies before declaring that we are beyond history, development, and recovery. The perspective of British cultural studies researchers on such issues as essentialism and binarism would also be complicated by examination of case studies produced by U. S. feminists and African American scholars on racism, oppression, and exclusion.

The challenge for black Americans is now to engage British cultural studies and to develop cultural work that addresses issues such as the plight of inner-city youth, as well as what Cornel West calls the "institutions of caring" in the black community. (1991, p. 223). To effectively analyze the specificity of the black public sphere in the U.S., black studies must engage both the ethnographic approach of the Birmingham school and the race-centered approach of the black British school. We must ground our cultural studies in material conditions. We cannot wait for Hall or Gilroy or Boyce or Julien to tell us how to do this. On the contrary, we have to elaborate the U.S. context in light of the work of Hall and other British scholars, not find replications of their ethnographies or abstractions. We must read their work in such a way that they do not recognize themselves. Cultural studies in our hands should give new meaning to terms such as hybridity, essentialism, ambivalence, identity politics, and the black community.

BLACK STUDIES IN THE U.S.

If the Dia "Black Popular Culture" conference is any indication, the careful integration of elements from both strands of British cultural studies promises to enable black studies in the U.S. to expand in purview as well as depth, shifting its emphasis from "oppression studies" to what I call "performance studies."

"Oppression studies" has historically done much to uncover and decipher the exclusion of blacks from the inventions, discourse, and emancipatory effects of modernity, and much still needs to be said about this. A great deal of contemporary work seeks to continue this line of study, and it is furthermore concerned to respond to the critiques of poststructuralism and cultural studies. In an effort to break down the so-called "black community," these theorists focus analysis on subgroups delineated through such categories as class, sexuality, gender, etc. The importance of specificity in narratives about discrimination and oppression is undeniable. However, the identification of study subjects as "the black woman," "the young endangered black male," "the black gay or lesbian," "the middle-class black," within the larger political context has posed a danger to black studies. The fragmented perspective of such narratives can exacerbate political divisions in responses to events such as the Mike Tyson trial or the Clarence Thomas/Anita Hill hearings that may call for unity across lines of class, gender, and sexual orientation.

Furthermore, "oppression studies" need not overshadow the actions of black people that helped to refine the tools of modernity and advance its democratic ideals. Black "performance studies" would mean study of the ways in which black people, through communicative action, created and continue to create themselves within the American experience. Such an approach would contain several interrelated notions, among them that "performance" involves an individual or group of people interpreting an existing tradition—reinventing themselves—in front of an audience, or public; and that black agency in the U.S. involves the redefinition of the tools of Americanness. Thus, the notion of "study" expands not only to include an appreciation of the importance of performative action historically but to include a performative aspect itself, a reenaction of a text or a style or a culturally specific response in a different medium. At the "Black Popular Culture" conference, for example, Greg Tate explored a new realism of black urban life by adding his knowledge of jazz, funk, and science fiction to his familiarity with the dramatic, audience-involving traditions of preaching and music within black communities. Such a "performance" is both political and theoretical: it refers to and draws on existing traditions; represents the actor as occupying a different position in society; and interpellates the audience's response to emerging images of black people.

In the U.S. today young writers, artists, and performers like Trish Rose, Lisa Kennedy, Jacqui Jones, and Tate are interested less in what legal scholar Regina Austin has called crossover dreams and the narrative of the "dream deferred" as in the notion of a black public sphere. These cultural workers are heirs of the civil rights movement and the black nationalist movements of the '60s, but they differ significantly in focus and perspective from both. They are different from civil rights intellectuals and activists in that they are not as concerned with forwarding integration and the development of "oppression studies" that dominated black studies, women's studies, and Chicano studies in the '70s. Their ideology is also significantly different from the black nationalism of the '60s, which in the context of white supremacism developed strong strains of sexism, racism, and homophobia.

These thinkers are motivated by the social and economic changes among black communities occasioned by the combination of post-World War II patterns of migration and urbanization and the civil rights movements. This period saw the growth of an unprecedented mass literacy among blacks, who earlier depended on the church and popular music as their primary arena for cultural and political debate. This broad cultural shift to a new black public sphere set the stage for an environment in which books, films, the visual arts, and music no longer principally exhibit an interest in the project of integration or in belonging to the society of the "good life," which is increasingly recognized as being white. Instead, seeing one's life reflected at the center of books, film, visual arts, and music takes precedence.

Indeed, the shift to the new black public sphere has been accompanied by the evolution of a new version of black nationalism. The traditional exclusionary themes of black nationalism are transformed in the works of writers such as Terry McMillan and filmmakers as diverse as Reginald Hudlin, Spike Lee, Julie Dash, and Charles Burnett into the themes of a black "good life"; elements of black nationalism are reinscribed in contemporary material and cultural conditions to construct a different black version of the American dream. Today black artists, from rap musicians to filmmakers and writers, are deriving fame and success from exploiting the themes of a black public sphere, or as Public Enemy puts it, a "black planet." The consumers of art about the black "good-life" society not only are both black and white but exist internationally. This "good life" has become the object of interest, and even envy, of Americans of different origins and races.

Civil rights activists feared that black nationalism would enhance ghettoization. But white youth and an international audience have become increasingly fascinated by cultural production that calls itself authentically black. Reasons for this attraction range from the pull of the exotic to the incorporation of liberatory themes into resistance to parent ethnic cultures that position themselves as universal. Rap, for example, has moved from the underground toward the center, making it the subject of incorporation by white pop musicians as well as the object of parody by "Deadheads" and country musicians.

As the work of younger scholars has already shown, cultural studies of the black British variety can make an important intervention in the analysis of the new arts produced about the black good-life society. Emphasis on hybridity, crossover, and the critique of homophobia yields some tools with which to check the regressive consequences of any nationalism. Black British cultural workers have a love and hate relationship with black American culture; this both enables the British to use American culture as raw material for its own critical and artistic endeavors and prompts the British to criticize American culture for being obsessed with the discourse of race and slavery, for being nationalistic in the worst sense, and for not being reflexive or self-critical. Black British viewers do not identify with the notion of a black good-life society, let alone with the consumers of a Spike Lee film.

I submit that a measure of identification with the U.S. black public sphere, its cultural consumers and reproducers, is necessary for the production of engaging texts on the black good-life society and its arts. In addition, it is not sufficient to analyze only the art of the black good-life society and the consumers of that product. One must understand the forms of life of blacks and whites in the U.S. in order to appreciate the techniques that black artists engage in transforming well-established white meanings.

Conditions of black life in the U.S. have resulted in a black American response to modernity that is both innovative and antimodern. Blacks have constantly redefined the meanings imposed on the tools and products of modernization by a linear and often destructive Eurocentrism. For example, the acts of black leaders such as Ida B. Wells, Frederick Douglass, and Martin Luther King, Jr., served as the background to the rewriting of laws that were written to protect the rights of whites only. At the same time, by being situated at the margins, black people observed the advancement of the most efficient modernity in the world upside down. As a result, black people have provided—and continue to provide—some of the most important critiques of modernity through what might be called techniques of reversibility. Take, for example, black people's iconoclastic redirection of instruments used in classical music and army bands, which violated many levels of order to create jazz, the music of modernity.

I suggested earlier that the civil rights movement contributed to mass literacy among black people, but the failure of civil rights politics of integration has left this mass starved for black-centered books, films, painting, music, etc. At the same time, black nationalism's legacy of emphasis on identity, political struggle, and self-determination cannot be placed in the shadows, for it survives in the structures of the new black public sphere. In fact, many black thinkers have a suspicious attitude toward poststructuralism and postmodernism in part because they interpret the emphasis that these theoretical projects put on decentering the subject politically as a means once again to undermine the black subject. The historical and ideological discontinuities between those giving voice to the black good-life society and their predecessors in the civil rights and black nationalist movements urgently need to be addressed in order for the black public sphere to continue to develop its black-centered perspectives and techniques.

To reproduce itself, the new black public sphere needs both an economic base that provides jobs for young people and definitions and discussions of the culture it is producing daily. U.S. black studies can develop performance studies as a mode of interpellating people in the black cultural sphere, positioning the people of the black good-life society as its "ideal readers." Such a method of elaboration promises a way to narrate the break with the tenets of the civil rights movement and black nationalism and move on to higher levels of abstraction along the lines of sexual politics, class, and labor relations.

This essay first appeared in *Afterimage,* 20 (3) (October, 1992), 6–9.
Published with the permission of the author.

References

Dent, G. (ed.). (1990). *Black Popular Culture.* Seattle: Bay.

Julien, I. (1988). In M. Attille et al., Aesthetics and politics: Working on two fronts? *Undercut,* p. 36.

West, C. (1991, Spring). Nihilism in black America. *Dissent,* pp. 221–227.

20 Opposition and the Education of Chicana/os

LAURA ELISA PÉREZ

CAUTION: The following essay models itself upon the rather *rasquache* image of a bunch of cans tied to the back fender of a veteran vehicle that's got a lot of gas in the tank. A ride through the neighborhood never promises to be smooth or straightforward; on the contrary, its purpose is to check out the many goings-on of the friends, family, and strangers that inhabit its *recorrido*. It needn't be dangerous to your health.

ONE OF THE LAST HOOPS that I was to jump through as an undergraduate at a well-known private university in Chicago, in order to be admitted into a BA/MA joint degree program, was to interview with the department's chairman. The memory of that emblematic encounter remains with me in ways that perhaps would not altogether surprise that old professor. I sat before him in his cramped office, on the other side of his desk, as he looked from file to me and back again to file, occasionally emitting small sounds that finally resolved themselves into what seemed to be the heart of that particular live reading: "I'm going to admit you," he began hesitantly in his Eastern European-inflected English, "but you must promise that you aren't going to get mixed up in all that Chicano stuff." With an interrogating expression, he surveyed me over his reading glasses as he continued to elaborate his concern. Completely taken aback, I realized that he was not joking as he scrutinized me for some bodily sign of the truthfulness of the "No, of course not," that my survival instincts had somehow automatically produced. It was not merely to literary studies that the chairman was referring. We were both perfectly aware that the Department of Romance Languages and Literatures only taught Spanish and Latin American literatures, that Chicano literature was clearly not an option and therefore not the issue. Across our *desencuentro* (dis-encounter) in that purported academic interview, it became evident that something other than the file before him attesting to my academic abilities and "good character" held the concerned attention of this professor whose final say determined whether or not I would be admitted into the predoctoral program to which I sought access. It would seem that the more demanding and prestigious academic route I was attempting to pursue required another sort of credential in my particular case: an approved politics that, specifically, included none of that "Chicano stuff." I believe I correctly understood this university "official" to be subtly intimating to me—precisely because I was "understood" to be a special case, a Chicana—that there was a correct "minority" politics involved in securing access to and success in our society's higher institutions of education. Now assuaged and showing signs of affability, the chairman concluded the interview, transforming the earlier admonition into friendly, paternal advice: "Remember, none of that Chicano stuff, eh?"

If I have dwelled on this anecdote it is because it enacts the contradictory character of power relations in the educational system. For ironically, power produces not only oppression but its opposition—and opposition, in turn, avails itself of power's blind spots and loopholes. The educational system's greater or lesser discriminatory and dehumanizing constructions of the "third world"-origin minority "identity" elicit the minority subject's destabilization of dominant ideology's logic, while oppression and discrimination in turn create the oppressed's desire for empowerment, equality, and justice. Within present structures of power relations in the U.S. educational system, the minority, as a member of a socially, economically, politically, and culturally oppressed *group*,[1] does not at present have the power socially to transcend dominant ideology's discourse of differential identity. S/he does, however have varying degrees of tactical ability to subvert, to attempt to bring to crisis the dominant other's constructions of (both minority and dominant) self through expressions of self that are dissonant with and destabilizing of this discourse. Think, for example, of the Chicana student, teacher, or administrator who identifies unapologetically as such, and expresses aspects of, let's say, working-class Mexican and Mexican American forms of speech, dress, and socializing that enable others to rethink these customs' construction in the dominant culture as essentially vulgar, tacky, or unsophisticated. On the level of curricula this approach has been used to appraise minority scholarship and aesthetics from within their own concerns and specific circumstances, rather than judge them by neocolonizing standards of European and Euroamerican values and interests.[2] Within the educational system, depending of course on the type of institution and our position within it, there are specific social and class privileges available to minorities that can be exploited. We have, for example, the power to pacify and undermine "authorities" representing dominant ideologies, in order to gain and secure the power necessary to undermine the logic that constructs us as "minority" to begin with. Put another way, proceeding as we do from communities that historically have been and continue to be multiply oppressed and disempowered, minorities cannot transcend or effectively ignore the dominant discourse of identity; nonetheless, we can practice an oppositional, tactical politics of identity aimed at eventually constructing a new discourse of multiple, mobile, and unhierarchized identities.[3]

In what follows I consider some of the specific ways in which minority identity is currently constructed through dominant social, educational, and academic practices. I then examine the claim—interestingly, made by conservatives and leftists alike—that minority identity politics are ultimately counterproductive or even obsolete. It is because of ongoing oppressive beliefs and practices within U.S. society, its educational system, and its intellectual culture that I critique both the rejection of identity politics altogether and the refurbishing of a nationalistic minority politics. I argue instead for a partial, tactical identity politics, for practices that attempt to rearticulate oppressed cultural and social differences in oppositional ways, as specific acts that resist and transform dominant paradigms of minority identity. The claim that identity politics are today counter-productive presupposes both that we can produce a paradigmatic shift in material practices outside of dominant culture politics and, further, despite the vastly different and complex social positioning of minorities and "whites," that minorities can transcend the dominant identity politics that on a daily and inescapable basis operate upon them. With respect to the educational system and intellectual culture, a transformative and not merely reactionary opposition by U.S. minorities continues to be necessary at the very sites of power's ideological and material production of us as culturally inferior and socially disempowered subjects. To this end I examine the statistics and demographics of social and educational conditions specific to the vast majority of Chicana/os. I conclude by turning to recent formulations of identity and politics by Chicana/o intellectuals and teachers Chela Sandoval (1991) and Tomás Ybarra-Frausto (1991) on, respectively, "oppositional consciousness" and the politics of the *rasquache* aesthetic.

MODERNIZING THE PRODUCTION OF MINORITY IDENTITIES

Precisely because the minority subject cannot fully transcend the exploitive construction of her/his being as such in dominant U.S. culture, one effective tactic continues to be the defense and affirmation of cultural difference, but in ways that construct that difference as neither essentializing nor totalizing nor intrinsically inferior or superior. By choosing to identify—among other identifications—with the Chicana/o, for example, one does not necessarily promote a dualistic nationalism that would invert power relations or promote ethnic separatisms—i.e., that reproduce the current logic of hierarchy. What is sought and produced is the empowerment of those communities that across their heterogeneity still share conditions of oppression signified by such words as "Chicana/o," "African American," "Native American," or "Asian American." Nor is inclusion for one's self or one's community based on cultural "difference" that is implicitly understood to be unequal difference—a "mixed but unequal" version of earlier claims to "separate but equal." Today defense of the cultural difference of the oppressed is not necessarily nationalistic, nor does it necessarily function to reproduce myths of unified national identity or Manichaean logics. However, affirmation of the cultural differences of oppressed minorities *continues* to destabilize *ongoing*, fundamentally racist and dehumanizing mythologies of identity and nationality that the dominant culture produces to ensure hierarchical power relations and its hegemony within them.

I agree with the department chair at the university in Chicago that there was good reason to worry about the interference of politics in my education on the basis of my "minority identity." Our constructions of my identity as minority were not only different but heavily invested in a *difference of interests*. In that encounter I realized that success in the higher echelons of the educational institution was not blind to my social status as minority, that it in fact depended on approval of "me" as a Chicana, and that this in turn depended on our mutual erasure of my own active and self-affirming constructions of self in a discourse of constant assurance to the authorities that in fact I would be a good and grateful *chicanita,* amiably jumping through all the hoops necessary to the racist, dominant culture's approval.

It is ironic that the hierarchically differentiated process of my education "politicized" me. I was made aware that, regardless of my field of study or academic accomplishments, a racist, generic "minority identity" already existed for me in the university, as it did in society, a social and political identity through which I was perceived. This identity was not of my own making. Historically crafted, this identity was continually redrafted, modernized in subtle forms, invoked for and by me on the basis of my physical appearance and "Mexican" ethnicity.[4] Dominant ideological practices within the educational system function to construct the minority as such and thus to (re)produce our cultural differences as unequal within the vaster social and economic structure of dominant culture's exploitive power relations. It is within these conditions that a minority politics affirming minority cultural differences that are effaced and dehumanized in the dominant culture *is* oppositional.

Within the logic of the educational system's dominant ideological practices, Chicana/o honor students at the primary and secondary school levels, like students and faculty in higher education, are viewed and taught to view themselves as intellectually exceptional to the Chicana/o community, though rarely with respect to nonminority peers. However, the ideological education of Chicana/os is of course complex, and differs vastly in ways that depend, for example, upon the wealth and degree of public autonomy of institutions, the percentage of minorities they have enrolled historically, the presence and history of minorities in the school's community or regional location, the presence of institutions of empowerment for Chicana/os like Chicano studies programs, departments, or courses, and of course, even more specific variables like the liberal or conservative cast of a given educational administration and influential individuals within an institution. From another point of view, dominant-culture stereotypes and discriminatory practices will rarely be as disempoweringly blunt at the college or university levels as they can be with respect to children and adolescents in the educational system, or with respect to the working and lower classes, to which the vast majority of Chicana/os continue to belong.

The growing recognition in the university system at large of the importance of Chicana/o studies departments, programs, and courses and the equally growing visibility of Chicana/o intellectuals in current theoretical debates, as well as of writers in the mainstream culture, speak to a shift in the nature of discriminatory and oppressive practices on the one hand, and Chicana/o opposition on the other. The shift—effected precisely during the Reagan and Bush administrations—toward the visible inclusion of selected Chicana/os in mainstream culture, the educational system, and the government functions on one level to create the illusion of equal access and proportionate representation of minorities throughout the society at large. On another level, crucially, the shift operates to neutralize minority identity politics, that is, politics that are shaped by the social significance of existing as a "minority" in the U.S., as practiced since the civil rights era. The struggle over minority representation is being waged from both oppressive and oppositional "interests." The dominant ideology's defense of the conservative minorities it constructs through the media as minority "spokespeople," like Clarence Thomas or Linda Chavez,[5] who support or promote anti-affirmative-action politics, rests on the claim that minority watchdog organizations and oppositional minority politics *no longer* represent the majority of their communities. What is of course implied is that these more media-visible, privileged, middle- and upper-middle-class conservatives are somehow in fact really more representative of the interests of minorities. What is obscured here is that minority status and the communality of minority experiences are produced as much through ongoing social marginalization and exacerbated economic exploitation as by common cultural or ethnic traditions. Contrary to Richard Rodriguez's assimilationist arguments in his influential *Hunger of Memory* (1982), social status for the U.S. minority does not merely depend upon class and cultural affiliations that might distance him or her from the majority of the minority community of his or her origin. The claim by minority conservative "spokespeople" that the solution to discrimination and oppression lies in removing ourselves from our communities through assimilationist politics is yet another strategy for reproducing the dominant racist logic, but among minorities, as it cynically encourages us to shift the burden of social responsibility away from the state onto our people. These minority conservatives have also been instrumental to the currently ruling Republican Party's attempt to dismantle affirmative action legislation and programs and to discredit community watchdog organizations such as the NAACP, by being made to illustrate the success of the up-by-your-bootstraps national mythology—while glossing over the fact that the road to the present successes of the Thomases and Chavezes of this country was paved by affirmative action policies, and almost unthinkable before them.

The claim that identity politics has failed wholesale is currently circulating throughout the university as well. That gains continue to be made for a miniscule percentage of certain kinds of Chicana/os in higher social, cultural, and educational spheres is undeniable. But not all Chicana/os mistake these gains as representative of gains for the still predominantly working- and lower-middle-class communities from which we come. The Chicana/o community as a whole continues to live subtle and blunt forms of discrimination and exploitation based on the dominant culture's racist identity politics. Chicana/os, like other oppressed minority groups and women as a whole in this country, are still fighting for our civil rights. Given the prevalence of unchallenged racist assumptions behind many educational and social practices, it is vital that we continue to practice oppositional and multiple-identity politics—that is, a politics shaped by the understanding that social and personal identity is created by a multiplicity of interests, positions, and desires that are, in varying degrees, subject to change. It is also crucial that we reformulate our tactics to address and undermine the renewed strategies of dominant ideologies that continue to discriminate and oppress even as they represent themselves to be anti-racist, multicultural, and "equal opportunity." Neither society nor its educational system is blind to difference; it is we as a whole who are perhaps less able to detect the modernization of its strategies or discern the ideological interests behind the dominant culture's representations of an egalitarian, democratic society in which we may all supposedly choose to participate whenever we come of cultural age.

At subtler levels, how much *has* changed since the civil rights movement with respect to the presence and education of Chicana/os in the country's educational system? Along with the more visible important gains, there has been a widespread anti-affirmative action backlash, some of whose scenarios are all too common in the day-to-day practices of higher education institutions. In my recent experiences, for example, it has become more common to hear or be told by leftist and liberal students and faculty of their resentment of colleagues supported by affirmative action funding and hiring policies; of their doubts concerning their minority peers' academic merit and credentials; or of their suspicion of the importance of their intellectual work, minority focused or otherwise. Within this climate all minority students and professors identified as such are felt to be *and* feel suspect in ways that others are not, and in ways that are disempowering: Do they really deserve to be here, or are they here as mere tokens? Is their work really important? Is it intellectually and/or theoretically sophisticated enough? Minority intellectuals in the university are themselves defensively drawn into an implicit game of legitimation, given that affirmative action is used in the university's construction of our identities as minorities. Educational affirmative action policies have been made to function as double-edged swords, a door to opportunity and empowerment that is nonetheless stigmatized. But further, all minorities are suspected of unfairly benefiting from affirmative action policies, and thus, through the circular logic of racism, we are tainted yet again, precisely because we have been socially constructed as minorities. Academic minority scholarships or fellowships are not taken as serious indicators of intellectual talent but dissolved into an indistinguishable pool of financial aid. In the minority experience at the university, it becomes a commonplace that one is guilty of some kind of intellectual inadequacy or incompetence until one proves otherwise, or until one successfully deploys a politics of assuagement; that is, until one's politics—conservative or progressive—are approved.

Many other intellectual and ideological forms of resistance important to minority empowerment and self-representation have emerged. Note, for example, the well-known "Western culture" or "great books" debates in which the claim is made that an impoverished and politically "illiberal education" is emerging from "the politics of race and sex on campus," to quote from Dinesh D'Souza's (1991) book title. Or the "political correctness" ("PC") debate, in which conservatives have attempted to construct ethnic and women's studies and the critique of traditional patriarchal and Eurocentric educational canons and epistemologies as the dictates of fringe, radical leftists. Perhaps less clearly understood than these more visible strategies to destabilize the empowerment of minority groups and women has been a general anti-intellectual backlash. Male and female critics, minorities and "whites," have in varying degrees contributed to a wholesale discrediting of "theory," whether it be poststructuralist, postcolonial, postmodernist, feminist, or some combination thereof—a debilitating reaction at best, given that these theories and academic practices have decisively contributed to challenging patriarchal, Eurocentric, imperialist, and hierarchically differential philosophical constructions of knowledge, power, identity, and society. To further complicate the academic state of affairs, some, as I have mentioned earlier, who support theoretical propositions for politics of difference have recently "moved beyond" identity politics, regardless of the different social and local loci that minorities and nonminorities occupy. It is especially counterproductive to attempt to settle these debates through an appeal to greater theoretical "authority" about "key" texts. Knowledge and modes of knowing produced within specific historical conditions and discursive locations by subjects who do not, for example, speak for or to conditions or productions of U.S. minorities can of course be extremely useful in Chicana/o and other minority formulations, but it should not be difficult to see that this is not necessarily so. There is no logical reason for anyone to expect that precisely the differences of minority experiences, productions, and practices should be addressed with the same concerns, methodologies, or politics as are the European or Euroamerican. Working with, for example, literary or other cultural productions of individuals or collectives from oppressed minorities involves many methodologies from which a fuller and basic uncovering of texts can emerge and be understood on their own terms and theorized within their own specificities, as the work of Gates (1988) and Ybarra-Frausto (1991) shows. An oppositional minority politics—shaped by the difference of minority interests—cannot delimit the understanding of difference to the tokenized presence of the physical bodies of minorities. It must, more profoundly, be mindful and supportive of the differences manifested in the intellectual, pedagogical, and political practices of minorities *as such*. Ready-made "correct" minority identities and approved politics are produced by both progressive and conservative "authorities" who attempt to speak both for and about us—but above our own perceptions and constructions. Again, it is not clear to me than any of us must or can practice an all-or-nothing, static identity politics that is necessarily dualistic and essential.

The representation of "tokenization" itself needs to be challenged as well, as Spivak (1990, p. 61) suggests. There is, for example, no reason to assume that Chicana/os should only teach in the field of Chicana/o studies (despite a more than reasonable fear that if we do not no one else will). Nor is there any reason to assume that those who do not are necessarily assimilationist "coconuts." It seems to me that the position Chicana/o intellectuals, like Chicana/o studies, occupy in academia remains a precarious one. Neither the field nor we who practice in it are fully legitimized yet. I have seen traditional departments reject job candidates, deny promotion or tenure, and stymie the institutionalization of courses and programs using the claim that the work and field are overly specialized or insufficiently significant contributions of new knowledge. I fail to see how yet another article or book on canonized authors, periods, or phenomena could a priori be deemed more significant than the production of knowledge on altogether new types and fields of inquiry that are, furthermore, vital in their social, political, and epistemological relevance.

While I have seen Chicana/os and progressive allies struggle around hirings, tenure, and the institutionalization of courses and programs, I think we must also address the on-the-surface "kinder and gentler" discriminatory logic, practices, and institutional structures that define our identity as minority within the educational system and delimit the standards of quality and relevance around our work. How and where we research, when we publish, and what institutions we graduate from or currently work in are traditionally received criteria that must also be rethought if we are to increase the presence of Chicana/os in postsecondary institutions as both teachers and students. The vastly unequal privileged educations of wealthier individuals or affirmative action-funded minorities in elite institutions does not in itself produce intellectually acute people. It does, however, construct their possibilities for success in the status quo. Challenging elitist assumptions about the quality of one's education and scholarship is fundamental to the security and support of Chicana/o intellectuals and studies, as well as to the dismantling of patriarchal, Eurocentric, and imperialist structures of thought and practice. It is through both the erasures and the dehumanizing inscriptions in educational institutions and its bodies of information that the ongoing repression and oppression of minority intellectuals and communities are produced.

The new or updated strategies and rhetoric that have emerged in the educational system, which I have only briefly and partially addressed here, have functioned, as in society at large, to put a "kinder, gentler" mask on the production of modernized discourses of racism—and their internalization by minorities as well as "whites." However, old strategies of racist, classist, and gendered discrimination continue to bar minorities such as Chicana/os from access to equal and quality education at every level. Despite a seemingly proportionate representation of minorities in postsecondary education, since 1978, for example, Chicana/os have actually lost ground or made no significant gains in enrollment, retention, and graduation from high school through doctoral programs. While the presence of highly educated and professionally successful individuals like myself would seem to suggest otherwise, the conditions of the general Chicana/o community are vastly different.

THE EDUCATIONAL PRODUCTION OF CHICANA/OS AS MINORITIES

I would now like to look more closely at some of the historical circumstances and current demographics of Chicana/o presence in the United States that are vital to understanding current conditions for Chicana/os in the educational system. The history of education of Chicana/os in this country dates to early discriminating and colonizing practices toward Mexicans following Texas's declaration of independence from Mexico in 1836 and the U.S.–Mexico War of 1846-48. Kenneth J. Meier and Joseph Stewart Jr. (1991) open the brief but well-documented historical section of *The Politics of Hispanic Education: Un paso pa'lante y dos pa'tras* with the following observations, which, despite regional and historical differences, hold in Texas, New Mexico, Arizona, and California:

> Given the Anglo efforts to dominate Mexican Americans politically and economically..., we should not be surprised that education was used for similar purposes. Economic and political domination is enhanced when the educational system reproduces and reinforces the inequities in society. Policies of denying equal access of Mexican Americans to educational opportunities, therefore, were consistent with the overall relationship between Mexican Americans and Anglos in the United States. Mexican Americans, while not subject to "separate, but equal" laws in quite the same form that blacks were, were routinely denied access to education or were provided with only inferior segregated education. (p. 60)

The denial of access to equal education continues to this day through various exclusionary practices—disproportionate tracking into lower-level and lower-quality programs of study; disproportionate exclusion from honors and higher-level programs; and disproportionate suspensions and expulsions—that fundamentally contribute to the conditions summarized in the concluding remarks of the National Council of La Raza's (NCLR) *Hispanic Education, A Statistical Portrait 1990*:

> *Hispanic undereducation has reached crisis proportions.* By any standard, Hispanics are the least educated major population in the United States; Hispanic students are more likely to be enrolled below grade level, more likely to drop out, less likely to be enrolled in college, and less likely to receive a college degree than any other major group. (1990, p. 95; original emphasis)

"Of all Hispanic subgroups," the report specifies, "Mexican Americans have the lowest levels of educational attainment, and Cubans the highest."[6] Despite the fact that the Hispanic population is growing five times as fast as the non-Hispanic population, the report states, the educational gap between these groups continues to widen (pp. 1–2). "At ages 18–19 almost one-third of Hispanics (31.3%) are [high school] dropouts, compared to about one in six Blacks (17.9%) and one in seven Whites (14.3%)" (p. 36). At the college level, in 1986, only four percent of Latina/os were enrolled in four-year PhD-granting institutions, and fifteen percent at "less-than two-year institutions" (p. 77). In 1988 Latina/os aged eighteen to nineteen years old made up only 6.7 percent of total college enrollment, compared to 9.2 percent for blacks and 86.6 percent for whites, with enrollments highly concentrated in Florida and the Southwest (p. 78). With respect to postsecondary degrees awarded to Hispanics at large, the NCLR reported the following:

> In 1987 only 2.7% of all Bachelor's degrees were earned by Hispanics, who comprised 5.3% of the undergraduate population in 1986, compared to 2.3% in 1981. Hispanic students comprised about 3.2% of graduate school enrollment in 1986, yet they earned only 2.4% of all Master's and only 1.9% of Doctoral degrees awarded in 1987....Between 1976 and 1987, the percent of Hispanic-earned Bachelor's degrees did not change significantly. (p. 83)

Chicana/os are by far the largest of the diverse Latina/o subgroups that together were estimated at 20.1 million, that is, 8.2 percent of the total "legal" U.S. mainland population, according to 1989 Census Bureau figures. Documented, that is "legal" Mexican Americans comprise 12.6 million (62.6 percent) of all Latina/os in the U.S., yet the income, employment status, and educational attainment levels for the majority of Chicana/os, together with those of mainland Puerto Ricans, are among the lowest in the Latina/o community, and in the U.S. at large. To cite a few examples: the per capita income of Chicana/o families is $7,956 compared to $13,896 for "whites"; one-quarter (24.9 percent) of the Chicana/o population lives below poverty level; 37.8 percent of Chicana/o children live in poverty; and of the 19 percent of Chicano families that are headed by women, over half of these, 52 percent, live below poverty level (NCLR, 1990, pp. 5–15). Meier and Stewart (1991) confirm that Chicana/o primary and secondary students are in significant disproportion held back grades and tracked into programs for slow learners or the mentally retarded or "special" inferior academic or vocational tracks. In this same fashion they are excluded from gifted and college preparatory programs. Meier and Stewart term these and other disciplinary and unequal segregatory practices "second-generation educational discrimination" in their study of the educational crisis for Hispanic students.[7]

It is from the perspective gleaned from statistics like these that the current dominant rhetoric of equal educational conditions and access to meaningful, enabling education must be unmasked as cynically inaccurate. It seems to me crucial to the continuing reproduction of the demographics I have just cited that Mexican Americans like Rodriguez, Chavez, and other relatively "privileged" individuals buy the up-by-your-own-bootstraps, anti-affirmative-action narratives, given that opportunities and services are manifestly unequal for us *as a whole*. It also seems to me crucial that we not simply dismiss them, that we attempt to understand and demystify the types of rewards with which assimilationist minority politics are compensated. *Hunger of Memory: The Education of Richard Rodriguez* (1982), to which I referred earlier, can be read not only as a memoir testifying on behalf of assimilationist, antibilingual education; it is also a testament to the dehumanizing and painful education of minorities in order fundamentally to maintain us as such. For the Chicana/o, "Americanization" does not mean equal status. Regardless of educational, social, and economic attainments, the Chicana/o is never fully "excepted" from her/his dehumanized, "sub-European" community of origin, nor fully accepted within the dominant culture that constructs minorities as essentially and socially unequal while promising full, melting-pot inclusion. Under current conditions, politics of assimilation are a painful politics of self-annihilation and loathing; this Rodriguez's memoir makes quite clear. It is, in his case, more likely to be the politics of the Chicana/o acting in good faith, buying the myths of equal opportunity and the "equality of all *men*," that has led to a guilt-laden identification with a Eurocentric, middle-class culture that alienates him from Mexican and Mexican-American cultures and, more specifically, from his family. Rodriguez's book is a fascinating attempt to rationalize that alienation within the very logic that underwrites it. One of the racist, dominant culture's most effective ideological strategies has been to educate us *all*—minorities and non-minorities—to the national myths of equality, democracy, and freedom for all. We are taught that these principles are attainable realities in the U.S., and furthermore, as minorities we wish that this were true. We wish somehow, at some point, to be able to avoid the discrimination and oppression rationalized on the basis of our cultural and supposed "racial" differences. It is within our power as students, educators, and administrators to educate minorities and nonminorities alike to question the construction of national mythologies and predefined stereotypes or "identities" that underlie *our* "national romance" (to use Doris Sommer's [1991] phrase with respect to nineteenth-century Latin American literary and national fictions).

OPPOSITIONAL IDENTITY, AESTHETICS, AND EDUCATION

In response to the exclusionary practices of the Euroamerican feminist movement, Chela Sandoval (1991) has recently theorized a "differential mode of oppositional consciousness" in U.S. third world feminist politics. Her formulations are useful in suggesting a politics that can be similarly conceived with respect to the education of Chicana/os and others. In particular, her notion of a mobile, "tactical subjectivity," variably allied with or opposed to hegemony, helps us to develop other Chicana/o oppositional practices. For Sandoval,

> U.S. third world feminism represents a central locus of possibility, an insurgent movement which shatters the construction of any one of the collective ideologies as the single most correct site where truth can be represented. (p. 14)

Conceiving both politics *and* identity as mobile and tactical can be liberating and empowering, as well as a defense, for the minority within the educational system. A Chicana/o politics, for example, might only be partially and momentarily "nationalist." Much more to the point here is the recognition that Chicana/o cultural and political differential practices are in themselves models of a mobile, irreverent politics with respect to dominant culture ideology and practices. This kind of politics depends precisely on the exploitation of loopholes and blind spots within the structures and practices of institutions, and the broad building of alliances based on intersections of interests rather than on orthodox allegiances that cannot respond to the difference and array of Chicana/o interests. Just as crucially, more transformative tactical politics can be deployed *within* the Chicana/o community itself so that it is understood as a plurality of interests and conditions that can include—at certain moments, around specific issues—the concerns of middle-class, heterosexual, male liberals together with those of leftist, feminist, working-class women of different sexual orientations.

The "hierarchization" of cultural and individual differences is socially and historically constructed, as are the oppositional responses of those oppressed through its practices. Thus minority identities and political practices themselves are contingent, first, upon the existence of oppression and exploitation, and second, upon our ability to recognize and oppose the ways in which we are socially produced as such. Ybarra-Frausto's essay "*Rasquachismo*: A Chicano Sensibility" (1991) suggests ways of working toward emancipatory, quotidian practices brought to bear within the educational system. Addressing himself to the make-do-with-what's-at-hand politics of Chicana/o popular aesthetics that are deemed "tacky" and "vulgar" on both sides of the border, Ybarra-Frausto observes:

> Very generally, *rasquachismo* is an underdog perspective—a view from *los de abajo*, an attitude rooted in resourcefulness and adaptability, yet mindful of stance and style....
>
> To be *rasquache* is to be down, but not out (*fregado pero no jodido*). Responding to a direct relationship with the material level of existence or subsistence is what engenders a *rasquache* attitude of survival and inventiveness. (p. 156)

The *rasquache* is perceived as such by others because of hierarchical class and cultural differences or alliances, and it therefore can be oppositional in vitally embodying what dominant culture(s) would wish to erase or predefine as unacceptable. To meet the censorious glare of dominant cultural tastes and norms irreverently outfitted in a *rasquache* aesthetics/politics is clearly to disable its power over us and over curious bystanders; to be Chicana/o on one's own terms within the educational system is to be *rasquache* with respect to it. We should enlist everything that can be used productively for the purposes of securing equal access to quality education for Chicana/os and other U.S. minorities. We should devise creative tactics for beating the odds against the admission, retention, and quality education of minority students, and the hiring, promotion, and protection of minority teachers and administrators. And with the image in our hearts of an inner-tube flower pot on a cluttered front yard somewhere in Aztlán or its "diaspora," we must creatively continue to exploit unexpected sources in the construction of identities and politics that challenge the norms of thinking and practices within the educational system.[88]

NOTES

1 "Membership" in a "minority" group may reflect choice, as in the decision to identify as Chicana rather than Mexican American; however, minority identity is always imposed within the dominant culture on the individual perceived to be of "third world" origin. Thus conservatives or liberals who would argue an assimilationist politics of ethnicity are, ironically, themselves qualified in the dominant culture as "conservative minorities," "conservative blacks," "conservative Hispanics," and the like. My usage throughout this essay of the term "minority" refers to its function in the dominant culture; it refers not merely to individuals who belong to ethnic population groups that are numerically in the minority in the U.S., such as Lithuanian Americans, but rather

exclusively to those whose ethnic origins lie in "third world" countries. It is precisely the neocolonizing, racist logic of designating "third world" origin, i.e., non-"white," peoples as "minority," but not those of "first world" origin, to which I am interested in calling attention.

2 With respect to African American vernacular traditions and literature, see, for example, Henry Louis Gates, Jr. (1988); with respect to a general working-class-origin Chicana/o aesthetic, see Tomás Ybarra-Frausto (1991).

3 Referring to Marx, Robert Meister (1991) observes: "He identified himself as a socialist among others, but, unlike the others, he knew that a politics is not merely a set of transcendent ideals or goals. Having a politics also means articulating the relationship between one's views about the world and one's position within it. Marx's approach to political analysis committed him to the view that one's politics is a matter of identity that is not merely given, and not wholly chosen" (p. 24).

4 In Chicago during the 1970s and 1980s, the "-American" part of social identity was completely dispensed with. The thorough, timeless otherness of how we were perceived was marked by labels of supposed national identity like "Mexican," "Puerto Rican," "Pole," and "Italian," which of course helped to reinforce our otherness by splitting our allegiances between U.S. and "homeland." I remember going to Mexico and realizing quite clearly that I was not in fact a "Mexican" like those Mexicans. In many ways I had more in common with Latina/os of other national origins and even with the Polish Americans in my neighborhood, whose working-class parents spoke little English like my own.

5 The Mexican-American Republican Linda Chavez (1991), former president of the "English Only" antibilingual, proassimilationist movement during the 1980s, recently published *Out of the Barrio: Toward a New Politics of Hispanic Assimilation* (1991), which Lourdes Torres (1992) reviewed in *The Women's Review of Books*. "In Chavez' conspiracy theory," writes Torres, "the 'power brokers,' as she calls the Latino leaders, are to blame. Cynically she claims that these unscrupulous leaders are more interested in expanding their power base than helping the Latino people succeed. If it were not for them, the bad statistics and the continuing influx of Latin Americans, everyone would see that Latinos are progressing just like all immigrant groups before them" (p. 10).

6 "As of 1989, only 49.8% of the young adult Mexican American population (25 to 34) have completed four or more years of high school, compared to 70.2% of Central and South Americans, 75.9% of Puerto Ricans, 83.8% of Cubans, and 77.0% of Other Hispanics. About 38.0% of all Mexican Americans 35 and over have completed four or more years of high school, compared to 41.6% of Puerto Ricans, 57.9% of Cubans, 62.7% of Central and South Americans, and 56.2% of Other Hispanics. College completion rates for Mexican Americans are extremely low. Only 6.2% of young adult Mexican Americans—and the same percentage of adults 35 and older—have completed four or more years of college. A substantially higher proportion of the young adult Central and South American population (22.2%)—and nearly 14% of those 35 and over—have completed four or more years of college" (NCLR, 1990, p. 89).

7 Meier and Stuart's (1991) findings and proposals are summarized on pp. 201–222.

8 Versions of this paper were presented at the Colloquia on Critical Theory at the University of Michigan, Ann Arbor, March 18, 1992, and the Twentieth Annual Conference of the National Association of Chicano Scholars, March 27, 1992. I would like to express my thanks to Ali Behdad, Ross Chambers, and Elie D. Hernández for many stimulating exchanges around topics raised in this essay. My thanks also to Cameron McCarthy for many useful editorial suggestions.

REFERENCES

Chavez, L. (1991). *Out of the Barrio: Toward a new politics of Hispanic assimilation.* New York: Basic.
D'Souza, D. (1991). *Illiberal Education: The politics of race and sex on campus.* New York: Free Press.
Gates, H. L., Jr. (1988). *The Signifying Monkey: A theory of African American literary criticism.* New York: Oxford UP.
National Council of La Raza (1990). *Hispanic Education: A statistical portrait 1990.* [Prepared by Denise de la Rosa and Carlyle E. Maw.] Washington, DC: Author.

Meier, K. J. & Stewart, J., Jr. (1991). *The Politics of Hispanic Education: Un paso pa'lante y dos pa'tras*. New York: State U of New York P.

Meister, R. (1991). *Political Identity: Thinking through Marx*. Cambridge, MA: Blackwell.

Rodriguez, R. (1982). *Hunger of Memory: The education of Richard Rodriguez: An autobiography*. Boston: Godine.

Sandoval, C. (1991). U.S. third world feminism: The theory and method of oppositional consciousness in the postmodern world. *Genders*, 10, 1–24.

Sommers, D. (1991). *Foundational Fictions: The national romances of Latin America*. Berkeley: U of California P.

Spivak, G. C. (1990). *The Post-Colonial Critic: Interviews, strategies, dialogues* (S. Harasym, ed.). New York: Routledge.

Torres, L. (1992). The price of assimilation. *The Women's Review of Books*, 9 (5), 9–10.

Ybarra-Frausto, T. (1991). *Rasquachismo:* A Chicano sensibility. In R. G. del Castillo, T. McKenna, & Y. Yarbro-Bejarano (eds.), *Chicano Art: Resistance and affirmation, 1965–1985* (pp. 155–162). Los Angeles: Wright Gallery, U. of California, Los Angeles.

21 Decolonization and the Curriculum of English

Patrick McGee

IN RECENT YEARS curriculum reform has become an issue in English departments throughout the United States, and my department is no exception. In our case, "reform" was apparently felt by some faculty members to be too strong a word, so a committee was constituted with the mission of *revising* the curriculum. The statement of goals that first emerged from this committee says that *revision* means "*to see again*—to look at what we are doing now, to see it again in the light of the changes in the discipline—and to build a curriculum for the future based on that new vision" (Committee, 1990, p. 1). These words sound promising; but if one reads the document they introduce, one may have the sense that "revision" essentially means making minor adjustments to an already established and fundamentally unquestioned program. The logic appears to be that "if it isn't broken, why fix it?" In a vote the faculty of my department expressed its approval of this statement.

I will paraphrase the goals for the undergraduate English major in the document to which I refer:

> 1) English majors should be proficient writers able to write, revise, edit, employ rhetoric, distinguish among styles, and do research.

> 2) They should be skilled readers, able to paraphrase and read closely, grasp patterns, structures and themes, identify conventions, summon historical and other outside contexts, and relate these to the interpretation of an entire work.

> 3) They should be able to produce critical analysis that connects and differentiates texts, styles, genres, authors, and periods of literary history and culture—that recognizes how text and context interact, how values are determined, how canons are produced, and the range of critical approaches to interpretation.

> 4) Most important, English majors should be knowledgeable readers, having read "works in the traditional canon of British and American literature, and works offering perspectives not always included in the traditional canon—such as works by women, African Americans, other ethnic and racial minorities, and Anglophone authors beyond Great Britain and the United States." (Committee, 1990, p. 5)

The document concludes with this sentence: "Through their writing, reading, and thinking about these processes, English majors should come to see themselves as shaping and sustaining the literary culture they study" (p. 5).

My colleagues wrote this document in good faith, and I believe that it reflects the assumptions behind the curriculum in many English departments today. I will try to state them briefly. If we teach our students how to write, how to read, and how to classify what they write and read—if we familiarize them with a tradition and, since we are fair-minded, with those works that for suspect or clearly invalid historical reasons were excluded from the tradition (the only response to exclusion being an inclusion that reauthorizes the tradition itself)—if we enable them to choose from the whole range of critical approaches, then we will have shaped and sustained a literary culture by inducting them into the same process of shaping and sustaining. Our job, it seems, is to reproduce that literary culture but not in a form that is self-identical. Each generation makes a difference. So, for example, today it is no longer possible to keep politics out of the English department since the final justification for programs like women's studies, African American literature, cultural studies, and so forth, is necessarily political. Yet curiously, inclusion becomes a form of exclusion and has the effect of depoliticizing the organization of English studies itself. Every time a threatening political formation rears its head, a new field is created and the problem is contained. As Gerald Graff writes, "The field-coverage principle made the modern educational machine friction free, for by making individuals functionally independent in the carrying out of their tasks it prevented conflicts from erupting which would otherwise have had to be confronted, debated, and worked through" (1987, p. 7).

These problems may be debated at conferences on cultural studies, which are becoming more frequent, and in a few unusually democratic English departments, but a casual glance at the catalogues would indicate that not much of this "talk" gets translated into practice. Curricula are revised but rarely transformed from the inside out. For the most part students hear only rumors about institutional conflicts and are encouraged not to concern themselves with the uncertainties underlying the program of studies they have undertaken. As Graff stresses, "The tacit assumption has been that students should be exposed only to the *results* of professional controversies, not to the controversies themselves, which would presumably confuse or demoralize them" (1987, p. 8). In other words, though most academics admit that English studies today is an arena of conflict and radical disagreement, they insist, usually in the name of pluralism, that the members of the profession must agree to disagree because they share the common goal of shaping and sustaining a literary culture that somehow transcends political differences, if only to become the ground where such differences can be asserted without destroying one another. The present organization of English studies assumes that, despite our conflicts, we share a common culture as the basis of a common world.

But there are, we sometimes hear, other worlds. For example, in 1968 Ngũgĩ wa Thiong'o and some of his colleagues at the University of Nairobi called for and actually brought about the abolition of the English department. No one is surprised to hear that Africans object to the primacy of English literature and culture in a curriculum designed for the education of Africans. The argument was that "education is a means of knowledge about ourselves." Politically, such knowledge works to reverse colonialism's impact on the social construction of African reality: "With Africa at the centre of things, not existing as an appendix or a satellite of other countries and literatures, things must be seen from the African perspective" (Ngũgĩ, 1972, p. 150). This politically motivated curriculum reform, coming only a few years after Kenyan independence, still operates within the first of what Edward Said identifies as "two distinct political moments during the nationalist revival" of a formerly colonized territory. These are the moment of "nationalist anti-imperialism" and, what surely follows, the moment of "liberationist anti-imperialist resistance" (1990, p. 76). Obviously, in a postcolonial nation, these two moments can coexist in a relation of nonsynchrony between subjects of different class positions and political formations. Ngũgĩ's own history illustrates the relation between these two moments rather well.

By abolishing the English department, Ngũgĩ and his colleagues simply brought to its logical conclusion a process of decolonization that required, according to Said, "a theoretical assertion of the end of Europe's cultural claim to guide and/or instruct the non-European or non-mainland individual" (1990, p. 76). However, nationalism historically turns out to be the symptom of a deeper longing for human liberation that may find itself frustrated after independence by the domination of a national bourgeoisie that simply reproduces "old colonial structures...in new national terms" (p. 74). As Said insists, following Frantz Fanon, liberation eventually requires "a transformation of social consciousness beyond national consciousness" (p. 83). In the case of Ngũgĩ, by 1976 he was writing that education cannot limit itself to reproducing and preserving a national literature. It is necessary to choose between two opposing aesthetics: "the aesthetic of oppression and exploitation and of acquiescence with imperialism; and that of human struggle for total liberation" (Ngũgĩ, 1981, p. 38). Eventually the struggle for liberation required that Ngũgĩ step outside the university and carry literary production and education into the community. He began to write in the language of the community—in this case, the Gĩkũyũ language—so that he could speak not *for* but *with* the people. This community activism led finally to his imprisonment and exile by the Kenyan government. In his second Gĩkũyũ novel *Matigari* (1987), most of which was written in England, Ngũgĩ says to the reader/listener: "May the story take place in the country of your choice!" (p. ix).

The spectacle of this Gĩkũyũ novel written in England, published in Kenya, and then suppressed and confiscated by the Kenyan government dramatically illustrates the political nature of literature in the postcolonial context. Is there any way to apply this lesson to our own situation in U.S. or other Western universities? Several recent studies suggest an affirmative answer to this question. In *Resistance Literature* (1987), Barbara Harlow uses Ngũgĩ's distinction between an aesthetic of oppression and an aesthetic of liberation as the basis of a critique of literary criticism and pedagogy in the West. She argues that such a distinction "contests the ascendancy of sets of analytic categories and formal conventions," including categories of genre, nationality, and historical period, or even the general categories determined by elementary distinctions between fiction and nonfiction, literature and nonliterature (p. 9). To a large extent these categories characterize the goals of my own and most other English departments. This formal or analytic structure of curriculum creates the illusion of an autonomous cultural process that can include the political but is never governed by it. By contrast, a Kenyan writer and educator like Ngũgĩ "proposes...a different organization of literary categories, one which is 'participatory' in the historical processes of hegemony and resistance to domination" (p. 9). Harlow's point, I think, is not to abolish analytical categories but to resituate them in the historical context so that they become the instruments and not the objects of literary study. As a result, the literary text is not reduced to a decontextualized set of formal properties without a social purpose or aim but rather is read as a dimension of that intertext of historical-cultural relations from which it emerged in the first place.

From a different perspective, Gauri Viswanathan's *Masks of Conquest* (1989), argues that the academic study of English literature did not arise as a logical category in the inevitable reproduction of a national culture. In fact, English studies did not begin in England or North America but in British India. As Viswanathan stresses, the history of this discipline "shows that certain humanistic functions traditionally associated with literature—for example, the shaping of character or the development of the aesthetic sense or the disciplines of ethical thinking—were considered essential to the processes of sociopolitical control" (p. 3). Viswanathan is not claiming that the historical origins of English studies as an instrument of colonial domination vilify its present organization through some simple and reductive logic of contamination or causality. The historical rise of Eurocentric literary curriculum in colonial contexts, she insists, is not some naive expression of Western superiority but "a vital, active instrument of Western hegemony in concert with commercial expansionism and military action" (pp. 166–67). This leads her to the following conclusion that bears on our curricular debates today:

> Until curriculum is studied less as a receptacle of texts than as activity, that is to say, as a vehicle of acquiring and exercising power, descriptions of curricular content in terms of their expression of universal values on the one hand or pluralistic, secular identities on the other are insufficient signifiers of their historical realities. (p. 167)

Again, Viswanathan's point is not some simple negation of English studies as a project but rather a call to grasp English studies through its historical formation as an institution with a political purpose, even if that purpose is only the reproduction of cultural norms.

These historical lessons point to the need for more than a revision of the curriculum of English studies. Although we must continue to fight for expansions of the curriculum to include more literature by women, African Americans, and postcolonial writers, we should use these curricular gains to ground a critique of the discipline as an instrument of hegemonic processes. We have not challenged the fundamental organization of English studies along the lines of canonicity and tradition simply by introducing new programs with new canons. For example, the statement of the goals for the English major I summarized earlier suggests several areas where more critical investigations should be undertaken.

First, this statement takes for granted that the subject of literary education is an autonomous individual who can be inserted in the process of shaping and sustaining literary culture without any direct interference in his or her own political formation. A student can be made into a proficient writer and a skilled critical reader without taking into account his or her formation along lines of class, race, and gender and the relation to culture determined by that formation. Minority students, it is argued, should be exposed to "their" traditions, but only on the condition that these be integrated with a more "universal" tradition that it is the business of the university to preserve and inculcate. The subjective autonomy presupposed by these "canonical" views completely disregards the actual social trajectories of many students and the dynamics of class in the classroom. Students in this context are not unitary points of identity that either accept or reject the information presented to them; rather, the differential play of multiple ideological tendencies enters into their makeup. The social drama that emerges in the classroom suggests that, as Cameron McCarthy points out, "schooling…constitutes a site for the production of the politics of difference" (1988, p. 275). McCarthy describes this politics with the term *nonsynchrony*. The feminist theoretician Emily Hicks (1981), to whom McCarthy refers, elaborates on this concept derived from the theoretical work of Ernst Bloch: "By nonsynchrony I mean the concept that individuals (or groups), in their relation to their economic and political system, do not share similar consciousness of that system or similar needs within it at the same point of time" (p. 221). The relations of race, class, and gender intersect within the individual or group through a complex pattern or knot and "have contradictory effects even in similar institutional settings" (McCarthy, 1988, p. 275).

From this perspective the value of multiculturalism in the classroom may have to do less with giving so-called "minorities" a voice than with grasping and responding to the "contradictory effects" of cultural norms. The commonplace assumption is that students are either prepared or not prepared, have either a proper or an improper cultural background, to learn what they need to learn in the school or university. There is little effort made to understand how students actually relate to institutionalized culture and how their social trajectories determine this mode of relating. Students are never without a background, and no background is purely negative. The classroom is always a scene of class struggle, though it is essential that we not oversimplify the nature of this conflict. From a theoretical perspective, for example, the traditional Marxist principle of a synchronous contradiction between the productive forces of human labor and capitalist property relations has to be qualified by those nonsynchronous contradictions that characterize the postmodern and postcolonial conditions: the complicated interrelations between race, class, and gender across the international division of labor. Bloch (1977), still in a mainstream Marxist tradition, argued that the "proletarian voice of synchronous dialectics remains decidedly the leading one; but both above and below this *cantus firmus* (fixed hymn) run disorderly emissions which can only be related to the *cantus firmus...*by its relating itself to them—in a critical and non-contemplative totality" (p. 38). It seems to me that such "polyphonous dialectics" (p. 38) have been overtaken today by the dialectic of nonsynchrony itself. The world cannot be reduced to a single narrative or even a polyphonic text, in Bloch's metaphor; it must be understood as the differential play of nonsynchronous social texts without a center. Or at most the center would be the international division of labor, which should be thought of not as a unitary structure or contradiction but as a disruptive and shifting social process revealing a historical tendency like what Fredric Jameson (1981) names the political unconscious. However, such a cultural unconscious is not really a single collective narrative, as Jameson suggests, but the differential play of narratives constructing subjects as a set of mobile positions in the world historical process.

No teacher who has faced a contemporary American classroom with its complicated configurations of sexual, racial, and class differences can be blind to the effects of nonsynchrony on his or her students. It is easy to point out the gaps in their knowledge of history but much more difficult to discover their lived relation to the historical process as it is mediated by their personal narratives. I am not suggesting that teachers investigate the private lives of their students, but they should be sensitive to the personal fictions that emerge in the classroom and the narrative resistances to which they point. When students say they cannot do something, they are doing something—living out the fictions on which their lives are based. When institutional pedagogies center on canonical norms to which students must conform through either their mastery of the norm or their failure to master the norm, these pedagogies necessarily reinforce hegemonized subjectivities and the exclusion of those forms of subjectivity that resist the so-called dominant culture. Of course, students from marginalized social backgrounds should not be deprived of exposure to the "dominant" culture; but this exposure should be critical and not naive as it frequently is in curricula that take for granted the self-evident nature of tradition.

This points toward a second area in need of critical investigation: the concept of tradition itself. In my opinion, such an investigation will first require that this concept be distinguished from that of history, though history in its textbook form is often nothing more than a representation of tradition. Tradition, as Raymond Williams has stressed, is always *selected* and thus presents us with a system of values disguised as a natural and transcendent process of cultural development (1977, p. 115). History, on the other hand, exists in what Walter Benjamin called the "time of the now" (1969, p. 263) and articulates the past through the mediation of a critical relation to the present that ruptures tradition. By basing curriculum on the concept of tradition and canon, even if minority works are included as candidates for canonization, English studies mediates the process of cultural hegemony without consciously and critically participating in it.

What do I mean by "participation" in the context of the Western university? I certainly do not mean that teachers must become the doctrinaire agents of a narrowly conceived "political correctness." This term has been used by culturally conservative academics, journalists, and politicians to label the pedagogical goals of so-called liberal and radical professors in U.S. universities. The academics of the right would claim that Western culture itself is under attack by the forces of multiculturalism, although they totally ignore the fact that the different cultures identified by multicultural concepts of curriculum are, for the most part, either subcultures within Western culture (such as African American, Latino, Native American, and so forth) or historically produced hybrids (such as postcolonial literatures in English, French, Spanish, and Portuguese). Obviously, American culture is a dynamic process undergoing constant change, and it is virtually impossible to conceive of it without taking into account the influence of African, Asian, Native American, and marginalized European cultures. The pace and significance of cross-cultural exchanges in the postmodern/postcolonial world of the last thirty years has forced the university to transform itself in response to the needs and values of a culturally diverse student body in an increasingly complicated and diverse Western culture. By identifying the study of English in the university as a hegemonic process, therefore, I am not suggesting that the function of this study is simply to reproduce a narrow and narrowly defined set of cultural values. The university is simultaneously the site of social reproduction, social change, and counter-hegemonic social resistance. Bringing the hegemonic process into the consciousness of institutional education simply means that the institution, and those of us who are institutional agents, must begin to take responsibility for the social effects of our pedagogical and curricular decisions. In order to assume this responsibility in a world that is now undergoing the long-term process of decolonization, it is necessary to recognize what Susan Miller has powerfully demonstrated in a recent study of the politics of composition-instruction in the American university: "Colonizations begin, and remain, at home" (1991, p. 26).

In other words, a pedagogy that would critically "participate" in the hegemonic cultural process would be one that is not focused primarily on maintaining a selected tradition against all those forces that would seem to challenge it in the modern university. Rather it would center the curriculum of English on the historical formation of literature as an institution and on those other writing practices that to some degree challenge the naturalness or inevitability of that formation. I have no objection to courses on English Renaissance poetry, Shakespeare's tragedies, Romantic poetry, or Pound's *Cantos;* but the teachers of such courses should take on the responsibility of situating these works not only in the immediate historical context of the author but also in the context of the history of the author's canonization or of the author-function itself. For example, if I am teaching Conrad's *Heart of Darkness,* I must take responsibility for the institutional functions of this text both as a brilliant example of the modernist will-to-style and as an ambivalent critique of European imperialism. This novella, because it is frequently reprinted in the introductory anthologies that are used in basic courses, has a specific history as an exemplary work for teaching literary form and value. Yet Chinua Achebe has called it a racist text and insisted that the universal teaching of it in the West has had a pernicious effect on the image of Africa and Africans (1988, p. 8). It is not necessary that one agree with Achebe, but such criticism of *Heart of Darkness* should not be buried in the teaching of it. It should be confronted and analyzed and not in the privacy of the study but in the open space of the classroom. Students should be made aware of the fact that literary texts do not transcend historical contexts (both the contexts in which they are written and the contexts in which they are read) but are the grounds of contention and debate and the sites of historical contradictions.

At the same time the study of literature as an institution should be situated in the study of noncanonical and popular forms of cultural expression, including the study of nonliterary writing in general. Progress has been made lately in the study of popular or mass culture, but it remains extremely difficult to break down the wall between the study of literature and the study of institutionally unvalued writing confined to the problematic area of composition. In *Textual Carnivals*, Miller reveals the extent to which the formation of literary studies within the university was dependent on the codification of composition as the institutional site of the "low": "Composition and 'literature'…were joined [in English departments] to provide a necessary distinguishing boundary, a way to stratify diverse participants in one of America's dominant functional interests, writing" (1991, p. 54). As U.S. universities became more democratic, they also took over the function of distinguishing the "high" students from the "low" in order to reproduce the order of a class society. Literature, as Matthew Arnold had foreseen, took the place of religion as the repository of universal values that could provide a ground for the moral authority of the bourgeois subject:

> To colonize and save the isolated souls of its passively constituted individual and "expressive"…human subjects, literary study logically must be dissociated from textual production. The history of "literature" must by definition be told as a history of *authorship* and of the authorized voice, whose origins, successes, and privileges are not bound to the material circumstances of either readers or writers. (Miller, 1991, p. 27)

The result is that students—and especially students from the least privileged cultural backgrounds—are institutionally identified as lacking authority, as lacking a legitimate voice and style. In casting the net of words around the African other, Marlow, in Conrad's *Heart of Darkness*, announces that "mine is the speech that cannot be silenced" ([1899]1988, p. 38). Perhaps in saying so, he also speaks for the authority of Conrad's literary style—an authority that can be documented by the history of English studies. But the domination of literary value in the field of English also leads to the institution of composition as, in Miller's phrase, "a national course in silence" (1991, p. 55).

As the debate over the curriculum continues in my department, I have repeatedly heard professors claim that they only want what is best for the students. Invariably what is best for the students is that they be required to take traditional and canonical courses in English literature. Those who make these claims are frequently the ones who teach the courses they believe should be required. Yet they claim for themselves a "disinterested" view of what the curriculum ought to be. Every teacher, of course, has an ethical obligation to engage in pedagogical practices and make decisions about curriculum that he or she believes are in the best interests of the students. But those who teach in the field of English must come to terms with the fact that there is no longer any fixed consensus about what those "best" interests are. My response to this situation has been to design and teach courses that require students to articulate their own cultural values in a critical context. I do not hide my politics or critical methodologies from students, but I work at constructing for them a space in which they can challenge my position as teacher as well as their own values. In practice, I try to share my pedagogical authority with students by having them actually participate in the process of teaching the class. I also try to teach myself how to listen to them from the viewpoint of a learner—something I have to work at. However problematic it may be at times, this reversal of classroom authority is crucial.

For by privileging "correct" student writing and the authority of the teacher, teachers fail to recognize the validity of student viewpoints and their way of relating to literature and language. They refuse to have a dialogue with their students and to engage in the process of communicative exchange. Ironically, as a result they teach them that cultural knowledge is a matter of institutional authority and not a process of negotiation, exchange, compromise, and like it or not, struggle. Since English teachers do not deal in objective facts but culturally and historically determined values, they mislead their students in presenting themselves as the archons of good taste and the patriarchs of universal traditions. It may be true, as some argue, that teachers have an obligation to teach their students how to write standard English or how to appreciate the values of the dominant culture. Nevertheless, if students have to write standard English or play the language games of the "dominant" culture, they should be given the opportunity to learn these practices in a critical and historical context.

A multicultural curriculum should not be a carnival of minority discourses but a rigorous program built on the theory of knowledge as a social and historical process. Cultural difference is not a phenomenon that the liberal academy should encourage us to tolerate but one of the fundamental grounds of significant human knowledge. From culturally conservative academics one hears the call these days for a "knowledge-based" curriculum. What they mean, however, is a curriculum based on the unquestioned belief in the authority of *selected tradition*. Such a curriculum, whatever its good intentions, is neither knowledge based nor historical in the critical sense. English studies should no longer be the domain of a monological voice but the field of open debate and dialogue between different voices, backgrounds, and subjectivities. Teachers from both the left and the right must learn how to challenge their assumption that knowledge is a one-way street. Radical or oppositional teachers, in particular, must learn that transforming the hegemony also means deploying it. Through counter-hegemonic intervention from within, the hegemony itself becomes the medium of articulation for those who have never had a political voice.

Only by centering the curriculum on a historical relation to literary production and reception can we actively participate in the hegemonic process and direct it toward a future that promises the possibility of human liberation and global decolonization. Such a political aesthetic is consistent with a *radical* pluralism such as that argued for by Ernesto Laclau and Chantal Mouffe. Whereas liberal humanist pluralism takes for granted the authority of tradition and the metaphysical stability of the so-called "free" subject, radical pluralism suggests that no subject is free until it has come to terms with its own political formation in a historical process. In the words of Laclau and Mouffe,

> Pluralism is *radical* only to the extent that each term of this plurality of identities finds within itself the principle of its own validity, without this having to be sought in a transcendent or underlying ground for the hierarchy of meaning of them all and the source and guarantee of their legitimacy. (1985, p. 167)

A curriculum with radical pluralism as its goal would have to surrender the "natural" authority of literary periods and traditional aesthetic categories to the radical questioning of a "new" historical consciousness. It would have to emphasize critical debate over field coverage, cultural critique over tradition, politics over "pure" aesthetics.

REFERENCES

Achebe, C. (1988). *Hopes and Impediments: Selected essays, 1965–1987*. London: Heinemann.

Benjamin, W. (1969). Theses on the philosophy of history. In H. Arendt (ed.), *Illuminations* (pp. 253-264). (Harry Zohn, Trans.) New York: Schocken.

Bloch, E. (1977). Nonsynchronism and the obligation to its dialectics. *New German Critique*, 11, 22–38.

Committee for the Revision of the Undergraduate Curriculum. (1990). *Goals and Objectives for the English Curriculum*. Department of English, Louisiana State U.

Conrad, J. ([1899]1988). *Heart of Darkness*. (Robert Kimbrough, ed.). 3rd ed. New York: Norton.

Graff, G. (1987). *Professing Literature: An institutional history*. Chicago: U of Chicago P.

Harlow, B. (1987). *Resistance Literature*. New York: Methuen.

Hicks, E. (1981). Cultural marxism: Non-synchrony and feminist practice. In L. Sargent (ed.), *Women and Revolution: A discussion of the unhappy marriage of Marxism and feminism* (pp. 219–238). Boston: South End.

Jameson, F. (1981). *The Political Unconscious: Narrative as a socially symbolic act.* Ithaca: Cornell UP.

Laclau, E., & Mouffe, C. (1985). *Hegemony and Socialist Strategy: Toward a radical democratic politics.* (W. Moore and P. Cammack, Trans.). London: Verso.

McCarthy, C. (1988). Rethinking liberal and radical perspectives on racial inequality in schooling: Making the case for nonsynchrony. *Harvard Educational Review,* 58 (3), 265–279.

Miller, S. (1991). *Textual Carnivals: The politics of composition.* Carbondale: Southern Illinois UP.

Ngũgĩ wa Thiong'o. (1972). *Homecoming: Essays on African and Caribbean literature, culture and politics.* London: Heinemann.

_____. (1981). *Writers in Politics: Essays.* London: Heinemann.

_____. (1987). *Matigari.* (Wangũi wa Goro, Trans.). Oxford: Heinemann.

Said, E. (1990). Yeats and decolonization. In T. Eagleton, F. Jameson, & E. Said, *Nationalism, Colonialism, and Literature* (pp. 69–95). Minneapolis: U of Minnesota P.

Viswanathan, G. (1989). *Masks of Conquest: Literary study and British rule in India.* New York: Columbia UP.

Williams, R. (1977). *Marxism and Literature.* Oxford: Oxford UP.

22

After the Canon
Knowledge and Ideological Representation in the Multicultural Discourse on Curriculum Reform

CAMERON MCCARTHY

Instead of a transformative nation with an identity all its own, America in this new light is seen as preservative of diverse alien identities. Instead of a nation composed of individuals making their own unhampered choices, America increasingly sees itself as composed of groups more or less ineradicable in their ethnic character. The multiethnic dogma abandons historic purposes, replacing assimilation by fragmentation, integration by separatism. It belittles *unum* and glorifies *pluribus*.
Arthur M. Schlesinger, Jr., *The Disuniting of America*

It is in...ideology that we live, move, and have our being....It is indeed a peculiarity of ideology that it imposes (without appearing to do so) obviousnesses as obviousnesses which we cannot fail to recognize and before which we have the inevitable and natural reaction of crying out (aloud or in the "still small voice of conscience"): "That's obvious! That's right! That's true!"
Louis Althusser, "Ideology and Ideological State Apparatuses"

If one reverses...the binary opposition of [East and West], our turn towards the West—the so-called non-West's turn towards the West is a *command*.
Gayatri C. Spivak, *The Post-Colonial Critic*

SPURRED FORWARD by pressure from African Americans, Native Americans, Latinos, Asian Americans and other marginalized groups for fundamental reforms in race relations in education and society, and by the efforts of mainstream educators to provide practical solutions to the problem of racial inequality in the United States, multicultural education emerged in the late 1960s as a powerful challenge to the Eurocentric foundations of the American school curriculum (McCarthy, 1988, 1990, 1991; McCarthy and Apple, 1988). Multiculturalism is therefore a product of a particular historical conjuncture of relations among the state, contending racial minority and majority groups, educators, and policy intellectuals in the United States when the discourse over schools became increasingly racialized.

For a brief period (early 1960s to early 1970s) in the United States' educational history, subaltern racial groups fought a limitedly successful but very intensive "war of position" (Gramsci, 1971) within the institutions of education themselves. It is this period that Sylvia Winter (1992) calls the "glorious decade of Black Studies." Of particular significance was the connection that subaltern school critics made between knowledge and power. These critics pointed specifically to the deep imbrication of traditional, canonical school knowledge in the legitimation of authority and inequality in society. In this sense canonical knowledge was official knowledge, which undergirded official stories about social stratification and minority educational marginalization. In contrast to the dominant preoccupations of traditional educators, African Americans and other minority groups emphasized a variety of transformative themes, insisting that curriculum and educational policy address the vital questions of community control, the distribution of power and representation in schools, and the status of minority cultural identities in curriculum organization and arrangements. Of course, minority cultural identities are not fixed or monolithic but multivocal, and even contradictory. These identities are indeed "fluid" and are theorized here as the effects and consequences of the historically grounded experiences and practices of oppressed minority groups, as well as the processes by which these practices and experiences come to be represented, reconstructed, and reinvented—in daily life, in the school, in the workplace, in the symbolic media, in textbooks, and in the school curriculum. Minority identities are therefore defined in the context of inter- and intragroup conflicts, encounters, and struggles between minorities and dominant white groups on the ideological terrain of education and in the production and circulation of common sense meanings in establishment and popular culture.

Within the last two decades these transformative themes in the multicultural movement have been steadily "sucked back into the system" (Swartz, 1990). Appropriated by dominant humanism, multicultural education is now entrenched in highly selective debates over content, texts, and attitudes and values. As Warren Crichlow argues, "this ideological encirclement currently serves to mute more fundamental challenges to the symbolic mechanisms and scholarly operations by which dominant knowledge is historically legitimated and subordinated traditions are repressed" (1991, p. 1). As departments of education, textbook publishers, and intellectual entrepreneurs push more normative themes of cultural understanding and sensitivity training, the actual implementation of a critical emancipatory multiculturalism in the school curriculum and in pedagogical and teacher-education practices in the university has been effectively deferred. (Critical multiculturalism is defined here as the radical redefinition of school knowledge from the heterogeneous perspectives and identities of racially disadvantaged groups—a process that goes beyond the language of "inclusivity" and emphasizes relationality and multivocality as the central intellectual forces in the production of knowledge.)

Conservative educators and commentators have responded vigorously to the multicultural challenge, and within the past few years there has been a virulent reaffirmation of Eurocentrism and Western culture in debates over the school curriculum and educational reform (Bloom, 1987; D'Souza, 1991; Ravitch, 1990; Schlesinger, 1992). As we shall see, proponents of multicultural education also "claw back" (Fiske and Hartley, 1978) from the radical themes associated with subaltern challenges to the white-dominated school curriculum and school system, emphasizing instead a normative rhetoric that accepts the broad structural and cultural parameters and values of American society and the American way. By "clawing back," I refer to the way in which some multicultural educators tend to graft the theme of diversity onto the negotiated central concerns and values of this society—the values of possessive individualism, occupational mobility, and status attainment—leaving completely untouched the very structural organization of capitalism in the United States. (This criticism can also be made of the more emergent discourse of Afrocentrism in that proponents such as Molefi Asante [1987] fail to offer any serious class analysis of American capitalism.) Within this framework the emancipation of the minority individual is fulfilled when he or she becomes a good capitalist. It is the nonthreatening social centrality of the "good bourgeois life" for the minority poor that the multiculturalist ultimately seeks to promote.

In what follows I offer a critique of current multicultural approaches to education in order to discover and extend the best intuition of their adherents: namely, that any discussion of curriculum reform must address issues of representation as well as issues of unequal distribution of material resources and power outside the school door. I will conclude by outlining an alternative approach to multicultural education that draws directly on some of the more critical insights in the curriculum and cultural studies literatures (Giroux, 1985, 1992; Hall, 1988, 1992; JanMohamed and Lloyd, 1987; Said, 1992). Let me say from the outset that there are subtle and important variations within the field of multiculturalism with respect to general perspectives, core ideological assumptions, and desired outcomes advanced by its proponents. Multiculturalists do vary in the ways they mobilize the themes of race, diversity, and culture. It is therefore possible to identify three different types of multicultural discourses on racial inequality as embodied in various school curriculum and preservice teacher-education programs guides, as well as in the articulated theories of some multicultural advocates.

First, there are those proponents who articulate discourses of *cultural under-standing*. Discourses of cultural understanding are inscribed in various university-supported human relations programs that place a premium on "improving communications" among different ethnic groups. The fundamental stance of this approach to ethnic differences is that of cultural relativism. Within this framework, all social groups are presumed to have a formal parity with each other. The matter of ethnic identity is understood in terms of individual choice and preference—the language of the shopping mall (Olneck, 1989).

This stance of cultural relativism is translated in curriculum guides for ethnic studies in terms of a discourse of reciprocity and consensus: *We are different but we are all the same.* The idea that racial differences are only "human" and "natural" is, for example, promoted in the teaching kit *The Wonderful World of Difference: A Human Relations Program for Grades K–8* in which the authors "explore the diversity and richness of the human family" (Anti-Defamation League of B'nai B'rith, 1986, p. iv). In a similar manner, Iris Tiedt and Pamela Tiedt, in their *Multicultural Teaching: A Handbook of Activities, Information, and Resources* (1986) require students to make up a list of cultural traits that would be characteristic of Sue Wong. Students are then told to complete the sentence "Sue Wong is…" (p. 144). This tendency to focus on the acceptance and recognition of cultural differences has led in recent years to a movement for the recognition of the cultural uniqueness of white ethnic groups, Poles, Swedes, Norwegians, and so forth, in order to counterbalance demands for the study of African American, Latino, and Native American cultures (Banks, 1988; Gibson, 1984; Sleeter and Grant, 1988).

A second emphasis in the multicultural field is that of *cultural competence*. Underpinning this approach to education is a fundamental assumption that values of cultural pluralism should have a central place in the school curriculum. This concept of social institutions as sites for the confluence of a plurality of ethnic interests was formulated in the 1960s by liberal social scientists such as Nathan Glazer and Daniel Patrick Moynihan (1975). Some educators, such as James Banks (1988), contend that there is a general lack of cross-cultural competencies, especially in the area of language, among minority and majority groups in the American populace. The American Association of Colleges of Teacher Education (AACTE), in their often-cited "No One American Model," makes a particularly strong case for cultural pluralism in education. AACTE maintains that

> Multicultural education is education which values cultural pluralism. Multicultural education rejects the view that schools should merely tolerate cultural pluralism. Instead, multicultural education affirms that schools should be oriented toward the cultural enrichment of all children and youth through programs rooted to the

preservation and extension of cultural alternatives. Multicultural education recognizes cultural diversity as a fact of life in American society, and it affirms that this cultural diversity is a valuable resource that should be preserved and extended. (1973, p. 264)

Educators who promote the idea of a cultural competence approach to curriculum reform argue for various forms of bilingual and ethnic studies programs based on pluralist values that would help to "build bridges" between America's different ethnic groups (Sleeter and Grant, 1988). These programs aim at preserving cultural diversity in the United States, particularly the language and identity of minority groups such as Native Americans and Hispanics. It is expected that white students will also acquire knowledge and familiarity with the languages and cultures of minority groups. It is felt that such cross-cultural interaction will contribute to reduced racial antagonism between majority and minority students.

Third, models of *cultural emancipation* go somewhat further than the previous two approaches in suggesting that a reformist multicultural curriculum can boost the school success and economic futures of minority youth. Theorists such as James Rushton (1981) and Jim Cummins (1986) argue that a reform-oriented curriculum that includes knowledge about minority history and cultural achievements would reduce the dissonance and alienation from academic success that centrally characterize minority experiences in schooling ("Considerable research data suggest that, for dominated minorities, the extent to which students' language and culture are incorporated into the school program constitutes a significant predictor of academic success" [Cummins, 1986, p. 24]). Such a reformed school curriculum is expected to enhance minority opportunities for academic success and better futures in the labor market. This thesis of a "tightening bond" between multicultural education and the economy is summarized in the following claim by Rushton:

> The curriculum in the multicultural school should encourage each pupil to succeed wherever he or she can and strive for competence in what he or she tries. Cultural taboos should be lessened by mutual experience and understandings. The curriculum in the multicultural school should allow these things to happen. If it does, it need have no fear about the future career of its pupils. (1981, p. 169)

Multicultural educators who promote the idea of cultural emancipation therefore hold a great deal of faith in the redemptive qualities of the educational system and its capacities to influence positive changes in the job market and in the society.

TOWARD A CRITICAL EMANCIPATORY MULTICULTURALISM

Though these three types of multicultural discourse significantly differ in emphasis, it is generally the case that their proponents attach an enormous significance to the role of attitudes in the reproduction and transformation of racism. Human relations and ethnic studies programs based on these approaches pursue what Banks (1988) calls the "prejudiceless goal." The strong version of these multicultural paradigms directly targets white students and teachers as the flawed protagonists in their racial relations with minorities. It is expected that negative white attitudes toward minorities will change if these prejudiced individuals are exposed to sensitivity training in human relations and ethnic studies programs.

In my view the three multicultural paradigms identified here do not provide adequate theories of or solutions to the problem of racial inequality in schooling. Within these frameworks school reform and reform in race relations depend almost exclusively on the reversal of values, attitudes, and the human nature of social actors understood as "individuals." Schools, for example, are not conceptualized as sites of power or contestation in which differential resources and capacities determine the maneuverability of competing racial groups and the possibility and pace of change. In significant ways, too, the proponents of multiculturalism fail to take into account the differential structure of opportunities that helps to define race relations in the United States. A case in point is the tendency of proponents to lean toward an unwarranted optimism about the potential impact of the multicultural curriculum on the social and economic futures of minority students. Indeed, the linear connection between academic credentials and the job market asserted by some multicultural theorists is problematic. The assumption that higher educational attainment and achievement via a more sensitive curriculum would lead to a necessary conversion into jobs for black and other minority youth is frustrated by existing racial practices in the job market itself. Barry Troyna (1984), in an incisive analysis of the British job market, challenges the myth that there is a necessary "tightening bond" between education and the economy. In his investigation of the fortunes of educated black and white youth in the British job market, Troyna concludes that racial and social connections, rather than educational qualifications per se, "determined" the phenomenon of better job chances for white youth even when black youth had higher qualifications than their white counterparts. The tendency of employers to rely on informal channels or word-of-mouth networks, and the greater likelihood that white youth would be in a position to exploit such networks, constitute one of the principal ways in which the potential for success of qualified black youth in the labor market is systematically undermined. Stokely Carmichael and Charles Hamilton (1967) and Manning Marable (1983) have made similar arguments about the racial disqualification of black youth in the job market in the United States. In a more recent ethnographic study of youth crime and work in the inner city, Mercer Sullivan (1990) documents the frustrations of black "Projectville" and Puerto Rican "La Barriada" youth in the job market. He maintains that there is a racialized job ceiling that limits the working futures of these racial minority youth. Further, Sullivan's study corroborates the claims that Carmichael and Hamilton made three decades ago with respect to the unfair advantages that help to boost job opportunities for white youth in the labor market. In sharp contrast to their minority counterparts, white working-class kids from "Hamilton Park" were able to secure early "off-the-books" jobs in their neighborhood and high-wage union-protected jobs later. DiLeonardo (1990) points to a further significance of Sullivan's work:

> Sullivan offers...well-documented surprises. White, Puerto Rican and black kids had similar education levels, even though the white neighborhood had family incomes roughly twice as high as those in Projectville and La Barriada. Blacks valued education most highly, and returned most often to work on G.E.D.s and gain college credits. (p. 672)

Sullivan's findings introduce a necessary caution with respect to the multicultural optimism about the responsiveness of the job market to curriculum change in the multicultural area.

Another issue for examination is the status of the multicultural text itself and what Stuart Hall (1984) calls the "semiosis of encoding and decoding." Various studies have shown that the drive toward the elimination of prejudice through exposing white teachers and students to sensitivity training has not produced the intended result of the prejudiceless goal. Indeed, as studies of student responses to a University of Wisconsin human relations program (Fish, 1981) and the British educational television series "The Whites of their Eyes" have demonstrated, white students often make "aberrant decodings" of multicultural texts (Buckingham, 1984). Indeed, Joel Fish's study of the Wisconsin human relations program showed that prejudice against blacks had *increased* by the end of the field-experience component of the semester-long human relations program administered at that university in 1981. (For a more recent account of the unintended effects of sensitivity programs see Christine E. Sleeter's essay in this volume.)

Besides these concerns, it must be noted that multicultural proponents do not systematically pursue the very premise that set the multicultural project in education in motion in the first place: the interrogation of the discourse of the Eurocentric basis of the American school curriculum that links the U.S. to Europe and to "Western civilization." Indeed, within the past few years contemporary conservative educators such Allan Bloom (1987), Dinesh D'Souza (1991), E.D. Hirsch, Jr. (1987), and Dianne Ravitch (1990) have sought to gain the upper hand in the debate over curriculum reform by reinvigorating the myth of Westernness and the role of Europe in the elaboration of American institutions and culture. No one puts this more directly than George Will:

> Our country is a branch of European civilization...."Eurocentricity" is right, in American curricula and consciousness, because it accords with the facts of our history, and we—and Europe—are fortunate for that. The political and moral legacy of Europe has made the most happy and admirable of nations. Saying that may be indelicate, but it has the merit of being true and the truth should be the core of the curriculum. (1989, p. 3)

In response to these frontal attacks on multicultural education, proponents have tended to propose models that emphasize the addition of "new" content about minority history to the school curriculum. The multiculturalist strategy of adding diversity to the dominant school curriculum serves, paradoxically, to legitimate the dominance of Western culture in educational arrangements in the United States. Multiculturalists have simply failed to provide a systematic critique of the ideology of "Westernness" that is ascendant in curriculum and pedagogical practices in education. Instead, proponents articulate a language of inclusion.

Rethinking Multiculturalism

Where does this multicultural strategy of inclusion leave us with respect to the question of race and the curriculum? How should we begin to rethink current approaches to the issue of race and curriculum organization? What are the elements of a new critical approach to multicultural education? Because of limitations of space, I will only be able to draw the outlines of a critical approach to multiculturalism.

First, such a new approach must begin with a more systematic critique of the construction of school knowledge and the privileging of Eurocentrism and Westernness in the American school curriculum. The rather philistine assertion of Eurocentrism and Westernness on the part of conservative educators is itself a wish to run away from the labor of coming to terms with the fundamental historical currents that have shaped the U.S.—a wish to run away from the fundamentally "plural," immigrant, and Afro-New World character that defines historical and current relations among minority and majority groups in the United States (Jordan, 1985, 1988). To claim a pristine, unambiguous Westernness as the basis of curriculum organization, as Bloom, Hirsch, Ravitch, and others suggest, is to repress to the dimmest parts of the unconscious a fundamental anxiety concerning the question of African American and minority identities and "cultural presence" in what is distinctive about American life. The point I want to make here is similar to one that John Berger makes in *Ways of Seeing* (1972) and Toni Morrison develops and extends in her book *Playing in the Dark* (1992): There is nothing intrinsically superior or even desirable about the list of cultural items and cultural figures celebrated by traditionalists like Hirsch and Bloom. It is to be remembered that at the end of the last century the English cultural critic Matthew Arnold did not find it fit to include in the "the best that has been thought and said" (Arnold, 1888, 1971; Czitrom, 1983) any existing American writer. This powerfully reminds us that what is "Western" is not synonymous with what is "American," no matter how hard some people may try. It also reminds us that the notion of Westernness is a powerful ideological construct—one thoroughly infused with ongoing struggle over meaning and values (Bernal, 1987). What is Western is therefore highly problematic, as June Jordan (1985) has argued. How is it that African Americans who have been in the Americas for at least as long as whites—how is it that the history, and writings, and culture of African Americans are non-Western? Who is demarcating the West? Do we, for instance, want to say that Ernest Hemingway is in and Alice Walker is out? Where is the line of the Western to be drawn within the school curriculum? Where does Westernness end and where does Americanness begin? Multiculturalists have tended to counter the Western civilization movement by insisting on "diversity" and cultural pluralism. But this approach leaves untouched the very premise of the interchangeability of the culture of the U.S. and Europe and the notion that there is an easy fit between white America, the West, and Europe. It is this easy fit that needs to be questioned.

This brings me to my second departure from the multicultural models discussed earlier. A critical approach to multiculturalism must insist not only on the cultural diversity of school knowledge but on its inherent relationality. School knowledge is socially produced, deeply imbued with human interests, and deeply implicated in the unequal social relations outside the school door. A critical multiculturalism should therefore be more reflexive with respect to the relationship between different social groups in the United States and the relationship of developments in the United States to the rest of the world. This would mean, for instance, that we begin to see the issue of racial inequality in global and relational terms—in the context of what Immanuel Wallerstein (1990) calls "world systems theory." The links between America's development and the underdevelopment of the third world and the links that African Americans have had in terms of their intellectual and political engagement with the peoples of the Caribbean, Africa, and Asia must be emphasized. For example, the civil rights movement in the United States has had profound multiplier effects on the expansion of democratic practices to excluded groups in Australia, the Caribbean, Africa, and England, as well as in the United States itself. In a related sense too, a world systems approach would call attention to the fact that the development of "Western" industrialized countries is deeply bound up in the underdevelopment and the exploitation of the third world. C.L.R. James (1963), for example, points out that in the 1770s, at the time when the French government was helping to bankroll the American Revolution, its West Indian colony in Haiti was generating two-thirds of France's overseas trade.

By emphasizing the relationality of school knowledge, one also raises the question of the ideological representation of dominant and subordinate groups in education and in the popular culture. By representation I refer not only to mimesis or the presence or absence of images of minorities and third world people in textbooks. By representation I refer to the question of power that resides in the specific arrangement and deployment of subjectivity in the artifacts of the formal and informal culture. This is what Louis Althusser (1971) calls the "mise-en-scène of interpellation"—the way in which the orchestration of cultural form in textbooks and in the popular culture generates the capacity to speak for whole groups, to arraign these groups, as it were, before a deeply invested court of appeal, draining social life of its history and naturalizing dominant/subordinate relations in the process. This is, by and large, what textbooks do as a matter of course. For example, as Edward Said (1978) has pointed out in his brilliant book

Orientalism, contemporary Western scholars arbitrarily draw a line of demarcation between "East" and "West," "West" and "non-West," the "North" and the "South," the "first world" and the "third world." This arbitrary line of demarcation is stabilized by the constant production and reproduction of attributions, differences, desires, and capacities that separate the West from the non-West. The West is rational. The third world is not. The West is democratic. The third world is not. The West is virtuous, moral, and on the side of good and right. The third world is vicious, immoral, and on the side of evil. Indeed, the electronic media images generated on the recent Persian Gulf conflict exploited many of these dichotomies in order to help the American viewer separate the cause of the allies of the West from that of the bad guys of the East—Saddam and the Iraqis (Schechter, 1992). This was a case of the Crusades all over again.

It is therefore possible to find in textbooks used in the U.S. schools very negative social constructions of the third world. The production and arrangement of images in textbooks draw intertextually on a media language that saturates the popular culture outside and inside the school. More significant than simple stereotyping, then, is the characterization of the relationship of developed countries like the U.S. to third world countries such as Panama and Guatemala in Central America. As *Interracial Books for Children Bulletin* notes about textbooks currently in use in schools across the U.S.:

> Textbooks distort the role of the U.S. in Central America, portraying it only as the perennial "helper." The U.S. has repeatedly intervened in the internal affairs of Central American nations. Rarely are these interventions mentioned. The 34 U.S. military interventions in the area from 1898-1932—and the numerous interventions [once every year and half since WWII], overt and covert, since then—are ignored. ("Central America," 1982, p. 5)

A striking example of this kind of vigorous fast-and-loose historical accounting of the United States' relationship to Latin America is illustrated in the misleading treatment many textbooks give to the topic of the overthrow of Jacobo Arbenz's government in Guatemala in 1954. The following passage taken from Thomas Flickema and Paul Kane's *Insights: Latin America* is typical:

> Jacobo Arbenz was the president of Guatemala from 1950 to 1954. While he may not have been a Marxist, he was in favor of them [sic]. Arbenz was defeated, though, before he had a chance to make long-lasting changes in Guatemala. (1980, pp. 106–107).

Brief accounts such as this misrepresent history. Arbenz was elected in 1950 by sixty-three percent of the Guatemalan electorate. As Stephen Kinzer wrote in his essay "Isthmus of Violence" in the *Boston Globe Magazine*:

> [In 1954] Jacobo Arbenz won congressional approval for an agrarian program aimed at giving poor Guatemalan peasants access to land for the first time. Soon after the law was passed, Guatemala's National Agrarian Department began to expropriate the vast unused properties [some 400,000 acres] owned by United Fruit Company. This was too great an outrage for the then Secretary of State John Frances Dulles to accept. Instinctively hostile to Arbenz anyway because of Guatemala's leftist drift, Dulles agreed that the regime would have to be overthrown. Dulles' brother Allen, director of the Central Intelligence Agency, had successfully deposed the government of Iran just a year earlier. He was called upon to duplicate the feat in Guatemala, and he went about the job with gusto. Agents established clandestine radio stations to spread misinformation in Guatemala, American pilots flew unmarked planes that bombed military and civilian targets, and the CIA put together a motley "Liberation Army" of exiles and mercenaries under the control of a disgruntled Guatemalan colonel. President Arbenz, already unpopular in many quarters [because of his progressive policies], was no match for the CIA juggernaut. On June 27, 1954, he resigned. (1981, p. 4)

In contradistinction to this historical account, social studies textbooks present the role of the U.S. almost always as benign, encouraging students to be "shocked" if they hear about anti-American sentiment ("Central America," 1982, p. 6).

It is very interesting how these textbook representations of the third world corroborate and reinforce images in the popular culture, particularly in the area of film. Though the treatment of Central America and the third world in social studies textbooks leaves much to be desired, starker examples of the marginalization and the manipulation of difference are reproduced in the popular film culture in the United States. In adventure films such as *Rocky, Red Dawn,* and *Rambo First, Second,* and *Third Blood* and in space operas such as *Aliens,* thousands of alien people die in seconds on the screen and whole cultures are wiped out. One cannot but note the way in which these films anticipate the kind of high-tech war that the United States and the armies of the major Western countries waged upon Iraq in the Persian Gulf.

Within the past few years, we have seen the re-emergence of what I wish to call the nostalgia film. Examples of this film genre are *Dances with Wolves* (1990), *Bonfire of the Vanities* (1990), and *White Palace* (1990). Each of these films specializes in the rewriting and recoding of American history and contemporary reality in ways that allow a new-age yuppie male to assume the mantle of "victim." Set in the 1860s, Kevin Costner's *Dances with Wolves* features the spiritual, even cosmic, conversion of a union soldier, Lieutenant John J. Dunbar, from the world of a war-mongering crusader on the western frontier to the idyllic life of a naturalized citizen of Sioux Country. Dunbar does this without missing a beat. One day, while holding down an outpost on the edge of Sioux country, he runs into a group of Indians, and the rest is history. He takes on their cause, their history, and their culture, almost with more dignity and panache than they do. Fleeing white civilization, which will eventually claim all in its path, including the Native Americans, he discovers a transcendent, idyllic, and romantic life with a white woman who was captured and raised by the Sioux (matchmaking in this film is racially unbesmirched). White meets white against the backdrop of Indian culture, somewhat reminiscent of Robert Redford meeting Meryl Streep in *Out Of Africa* (1985). Like Dunbar, she takes on an inimitable Indian name, "Stands with a Fist." She too takes on the mantle of displaced Indian victim—as noble as the Sioux. *Dances with Wolves* glibly reworks the history of the Sioux and the struggle against imperialism and domination on the plains. The story, like that of *Mississippi Burning* (1988), becomes one of the triumph, the conversion, the moral resources and individuality of the white man. The Sioux merely provide the punctuation marks, the cut-and-paste cardboard types that help to accent the story of a reflexive, new-age John Wayne, always on the side of the good against the evil. One could go on to discuss films like *Bonfire of the Vanities,* in which the principal character, Sherman McCoy, a Wall Street stockbroker, takes a wrong turn in the South Bronx and his plush, middle-class life goes down the tubes. He too becomes a victim, this time of black underclass harassment and deception.

All of these are examples of a larger system of representation and production of images in the media and popular culture and school texts that position minorities, women, and third world people in relation to dominant whites. In many cases our students depend on the media, more so than on textbooks or the classroom, for their understanding of existing relations of dominance and subordination in the world. We must therefore find some way dynamically to interrogate the current production of images in the popular culture; we must find some way critically to examine film, TV, the newspaper, and popular music in classroom.

A third point of consideration is the status of the conceptualization of the race category within the multicultural paradigm. Current multicultural formulations tend to define racial identities in very static or essentialist terms. By this I mean that proponents tend to treat racial identities as a settled matter of physical, cultural, and linguistic traits. Minority groups are therefore defined as homogeneous entities. For example, as we discussed earlier, Tiedt and Tiedt's (1986) fictional character, "Sue Wong," is presented in their handbook for preservice teachers as a generic Chinese American. She is defined by the presumed invariant characteristics of the group. A critical approach to multicultural education requires a far more nuanced discussion of the racial identities of minority and majority groups than currently exists in the multicultural literature. This critical approach would call attention to the contradictory interests that inform minority social and political behavior and that define minority encounters with majority whites in educational settings and in society. These discontinuities in the needs and interests of minority and majority groups are expressed, for example, in the long history of tension and hostility that has existed between the black and white working class in this country. Also of crucial importance within this framework are the issues of the "contradictory location" (Wright, 1978) of the "new" black middle class within the racial problematic and the role of neoconservative black and white intellectuals in redefining the terrain of contemporary discourse on racial inequality toward the ideal of a "color blind" society (McCarthy, 1990). Just as important for a nonessentialist approach to race and curriculum is the fact that, because of the issue of gender, minority women and girls have radically different experiences of racial inequality from those of their male counterparts. A non-essentialist approach to the discussion of racial identities allows for a more complex understanding of the educational and political behavior of minority groups.

In South Africa, as Michael Burawoy (1981) and Mokubong Nkomo (1984) make clear, the economic divide between the black underclass from the Bantustan and their more middle-class counterparts working for the South African state (police officers, nurses, etc.) often serves to undermine black unity in the struggle against apartheid. Similar examples exist in the United States, where some middle-class minority intellectuals have spoken out against affirmative action and minority scholarship programs in higher education, suggesting that such ameliorative policies discriminate against white males. A case in point is the 1990 ruling by the U.S. Department of Education's former Assistant Secretary for Civil Rights, Michael Williams, that maintained that it was illegal for a college or university to offer a scholarship only to minority students (Jaschik, 1990). The irony of this situation is underlined by the fact that the former Assistant Secretary for Civil Rights is a black man. Tragically, without these scholarships a number of very indigent minorities would not be able to pursue higher education. Here again, the "point man" on a policy that effectively undermines the material interests of African Americans and other minority groups is a neoconservative member of the emergent minority middle class. The point that I want to make here is that you cannot read off the political behavior of minority groups from assumptions about race pure and simple. Different class interests within minority groups often cut at right angles to racial politics. In a related sense, to predicate multicultural education on the basis of static definitions of what white people are like and what minorities are like can lead to costly miscalculations that can undermine the goal of race relations reform in education itself.

DEMOCRATIC INITIATIVES

A new approach to multicultural education must go much further than a critique of current definitions of racial identity. A critical approach to the fostering of multi-culturalism must also seek to promote democratic initiatives in curriculum and pedagogical practices and social relations in schools. In this matter, certain facts have become painfully clear. There is now considerable documentation in both the mainstream and radical literature indicating stagnation and, in some cases, reversals in the educational fortunes of black, Hispanic, and Native American youth in the emerging decade of the 1990s (Gamoran and Berends, 1986; Grant, 1984, 1985; Hacker, 1992; Sudarkasa, 1988). These studies also draw attention to some of the most pernicious ways in which current curriculum and pedagogical practices—not simply content—militate against minority success and alienate minority students from an academic core curriculum. For instance, studies show the following: that minority girls and boys are more likely than their white peers to be placed in low or non-academic tracks (Fordham, 1988; Grant, 1984); that teachers' encouragement and expectations of academic performance are considerably lower for black and Latino students than for white students (Ogbu and Matute-Bianchi, 1986); that black students have access to fewer instructional opportunities than white students (Gamoran and Berends, 1986); and that ultimately black, Latino, and Native American youth are more likely to drop out of school than white youth (Here they come, 1986). These racial factors are complicated by dynamics of gender (black girls fare better academically than black boys but are more likely to be denied the academic and social status accorded to white girls and white boys in desegregated classrooms [Grant, 1984, 1985; Ogbu, 1978]) and dynamics of class (increasingly, black youth from professional middle-class backgrounds are abandoning predominantly black institutions and opting for white-dominated state colleges and Ivy League universities, thereby imperiling the autonomy and the survival of black institutions and raising disturbing questions about cultural identity [Marable, 1985]).

As we have seen, multicultural proponents have stressed attitudinal models of reform. In this manner these proponents have tended to paste over the central contradictions associated with race and the curriculum, promoting instead a professional discourse of content addition. These approaches to curriculum and educational reform have consequently had the effect of stabilizing rather than challenging the modus operandi of schooling and curriculum practices such as ability grouping and tracking— the principal mechanisms through which minorities are culturally excluded from an academic core curriculum and "prepared" for the secondary labor market. These practices of curriculum differentiation—the teaching of different types of curricula to different groups of students—also constitute the core processes of racial marginalization and subordination of minority students in the institutional culture of the school. Fundamentally, then, mainstream educators and policy makers have failed to engage teachers and students in a sustained examination of the sociological and racial dimensions of current curriculum and pedagogical practices of tracking and ability grouping (Bastian, Fruchter, Gittell, Greer, and Haskins, 1986). All students should have access to an academic curriculum. The fact that disproportionate numbers of America's African American, Latino, and Native American youth are now alienated from such a curriculum in the public schools is both intolerable and indefensible.

The idea of a general academic curriculum also poses direct political questions about the selective tradition in curriculum organization. As school populations become more ethnically diverse, and as minorities become the majorities in many school districts across the country, the moral and practical support for the hegemony of Eurocentrism in the curriculum has been imperiled (Schmidt, 1989). The hegemonic truce that has existed over the years between school authorities and the rapidly diversifying constituencies they serve has become frayed. Minority youth and women have begun to offer a more systematic challenge to the structure of existing school knowledge and the assumptions and practices that undergird the curricula of colleges and universities in the

U.S. Questions are being raised about "traditional dichotomies such as the division between the hard 'masculine' subjects like mathematics and the sciences, and the soft 'feminine' arts subjects" (Sarup, 1986, p. 17). Minority students are once again mounting "new" demands for democratization and diversity in the curriculum and course offerings of dominant educational institutions across the country. It is at this point of rupture within the dominant curriculum paradigm that more radical demands for critical anti-racist and anti-sexist curriculum materials and pedagogical practices can be introduced. As school critics such as Bob Connell (1987) and Madan Sarup (1986) have argued, the school curriculum for minority and majority youth should have an organic link to other experiences and struggles within the society, with respect to such issues as the loss of infrastructural supports and jobs in minority communities in the inner cities. Such a new critical approach to the multicultural curriculum would also "celebrate the contributions of working people, women, and minorities to our general cultural pool" and would be the point of departure "for providing students with their own cultural capital" (Wood, 1985, p. 107). By insisting that radically diverse cultural knowledge(s) rooted in the social bases and experiences of oppressed groups be introduced into the school curriculum, we can move beyond the "benign" pluralism and cultural relativism that is now embodied in certain innocuous forms of multicultural education. For as Abdul JanMohamed and David Lloyd (1987) argue, "Such pluralism tolerates the existence of salsa, it even enjoys Mexican restaurants, but it bans Spanish as a medium of instruction in American schools" (p. 10).

But merely moving beyond simplistic models of cultural relativism is not enough to "invert the hegemony" (Connell, 1987, p. 15) of Eurocentrism in the curriculum. We must go further than the compensatory strategy of simply adding diverse cultural knowledges to the dominant curriculum. A critical approach to the transformation of school knowledge requires a second strategy, one aimed at promoting difference and heterogeneity as what Bob Connell (1987) calls a program of "common learnings." Such a strategy aims at reconstructing the dominant curriculum—which we now know legitimates the experiences and practices of the white middle class—by bringing the uninstitutionalized experiences of marginalized minorities and working-class women and men to the "center" of the organization and arrangement of the school curriculum. The ultimate objective of a "common learnings" educational strategy is to seek the generalized diffusion throughout the whole system of schooling of counter-hegemonic knowledge based on the experiences and perspectives of the disadvantaged. Connell argues for such a proactive and generative approach to "universalizing" the hetero-geneous experiences of oppressed groups in the curriculum. His arguments rest on two important principles. First, he suggests that a political and ethical principle of positive social justice should inform the selection of knowledge in the school curriculum. In practice this implies that a "new" critical curriculum should privilege the human interests of the least advantaged. Second, he maintains that the racial transformation of the school curriculum should be based on epistemological principles that affirm the validity of the points of view of marginalized minorities and working-class men and women. It is useful to quote him in some detail here:

> In principle there are many possible common learnings programs, though in a particular historical setting only a few are likely to be of great practical importance. A minimal criterion for choice among them, and a minimal defence of the strategy of inverting hegemony, is the criterion of social justice. We can accept with Rawls that social justice means taking the standpoint of the least advantaged, though we can do without his fantasy that this might occur in ignorance of one's social position....But this is only a minimal defense. There are stronger reasons for seeking an educational

program constructed in this way. Different standpoints yield different views of the world and some are more comprehensive and powerful than others....If you wish to teach about ethnicity and race relations, for instance, a more comprehensive and deeper understanding is possible if you construct your curriculum from the point of view of the subordinated ethnic groups than if you work from the point of view of the dominant one. "Racism" is a qualitatively better organizing concept than "natural inferiority," though each has its roots in a particular experience and embodies a social interest. [Another] case is provided by the growth of knowledge about gender. There has long been a body of information and discourse about the family, women's employment, children's social development, masculinity and femininity, which remained for decades a backwater in social sciences hegemonised by the interests of men. The standpoint of the least advantaged in gender relations, articulated in feminism, has transformed that. Modern feminism has produced a qualitatively better analysis of a large domain of social life through a range of new concepts (sexual politics, patriarchy, the sexual division of labor, etc.) and new research informed by them. The implications of this conceptual revolution are still to be felt across much of the curriculum. (pp. 16–18)

Connell's arguments for reconstructing the curriculum from the standpoint of those "carrying the burdens of social inequality" (Connell, 1987, p. 17) are well founded. A critical multicultural curriculum, which emphasizes anti-racist and anti-sexist change and social reorganization and utilizes the points of view and experiences of oppressed minorities and working-class women and men as the primary bases for a core curriculum, would constitute a fundamental step in the direction of preparing students for democratic participation in a complex and differential world.

Of course, we must be ever mindful of the dangers that Paulo Freire (1970) pointed us to in his volume, *Pedagogy of the Oppressed*—that is, that the oppressed "are at one and the same time themselves and the oppressor whose consciousness they have internalized" (p. 32). There are no simple guarantees in political or educational life, and critical multicultural educators must avoid the tendency to reify the oppressed through an activism shrouded in "monologues, slogans and communiques" (p. 52). In this sense Connell's common learnings approach still reflects significant limitations. For the production of knowledge and cultural forms among the oppressed does embody an encounter and a double reading of dominant knowledge. It is this process that Paul Gilroy (1988-89) calls "popular modernism"—the process by which the oppressed decode and deconstruct the meaning of style of the oppressor and respond with their own counter-hegemonic forms. A very good example of this is Derek Walcott's recently completed epic poem, *Omeros* (1990), in which he reworks the inherited tradition of colonial literature prosecuted in the Caribbean school system. In this extraordinary work, Homer's *Odyssey* becomes the vehicle for the literary exploration of the middle passage of the peoples of the African diaspora. This, however, is a middle passage in reverse, in which the Caribbean peoples reclaim their history and their landscape and, most importantly, the tools of language. In a similar manner, Zora Neale Hurston, in *Their Eyes Were Watching God* (1978), discovers in the everyday speech of her black characters Janie and T-Cake, and others, the liberating power of a dialect that reorders the world in the language of the people in the margins of the South. It would be interesting to have a ninth-grade literature class compare and contrast Mark Twain's use of dialect in *Huckleberry Finn* with Hurston's use of dialect in *Their Eyes Were Watching God*. I say all that to say this: Multicultural changes in the curriculum to address the present and the future of race relations in the United States must be founded in the recognition that knowledge is socially produced and is systematically relational and heterogeneous—the product of human beings in what the Marxist novelist George Lamming (1960) calls "their rendezvous with history." Efforts to redefine the curriculum in the name of multiculturalism must get beyond the narrow prescription of content addition and replacement. A critical approach to curriculum reform must make salient the connections between knowledge and power and must build on the deconstructive and relational analysis already on the way in third world and indigenous scholarship and cultural production. Such an approach would bring the entire range of traditional and contemporary material and symbolic arrangements in the school curriculum into focus for examination with a view toward transformation.

REFERENCES

Althusser, L. (1971). Ideology and ideological state apparatuses. In *Lenin and Philosophy and Other Essays* (pp. 127–186). London: Monthly Review.

American Association of Colleges for Teacher Education. (1973). No one American model. *Journal of Teacher Education*, 24, 264–265.

Anti-Defamation League of B'nai B'rith. (1986). *The Wonderful World of Difference: A human relations program for grades K-8*. New York: Author.

Arnold, M. (1888). *Civilization in the United States: First and last impressions of America*. Boston: Cupples.

_____. (1971). *Culture and Anarchy: An essay in political and social criticism* (ed. I. Gregor). Indianapolis: Bobbs-Merrill.

Asante, M. K. (1987). *The Afrocentric Idea*. Philadelphia: Temple UP.

Banks, J. (1988). *Multiethnic Education: Theory and practice*. Boston: Allyn.

Bastian, A., Fruchter, N., Gittell, M. Greer, C., & Haskins, K. (1986). *Choosing Equality*. Philadelphia: Temple UP.

Berger, J. (1972). *Ways of Seeing*. London: Penguin.

Bernal, M. (1987). *Black Athena: The Afroasiatic roots of classical civilization* (vol. 1). London: Free Association Books.

Bloom, A. (1987). *The Closing of the American Mind*. New York: Simon.

Buckingham, D. (1984). The whites of their eyes: A case study of responses to educational television. In M. Straker-Welds (ed.), *Education for a Multicultural Society* (pp. 137–143). London: Bell.

Burawoy, M. (1981). The capitalist state in South Africa: Marxist and sociological perspectives on race and class. In *Political Power and Social Theory*, (vol. 2) (pp. 279–335). Greenwich, CT: JAI.

Carmichael, S. & Hamilton, C. (1967). *Black Power*. New York: Vintage.

Central America: What U.S. educators need to know [special double issue]. (1982). *Interracial Books for Children Bulletin*, 13 (2 & 3), 1–32.

Connell, R. W. (1987). *Curriculum, Politics, Hegemony, and Strategies of Change*. Unpublished manuscript, Macquarie University, Department of Sociology, New South Wales.

Crichlow, W. (1991). *Theories of Representation: Implications for understanding race in the multicultural curriculum*. Unpublished manuscript. University of Rochester, School of Education.

Cummins, J. (1986). Empowering minority students: A framework for intervention. *Harvard Educational Review*, 56 (1) 18–36.

Czitrom, D. J. (1983). *Media and the American Mind: From Morse to McLuhan*. Chapel Hill: U of North Carolina P.

diLeonardo, M. (1990, May 14). Who's really getting paid? *The Nation*, 672–676.

D'Souza, D. (1991). *Illiberal Education: The politics of race and sex on campus*. New York: Free Press.

Ellsworth, E. (1989). Why doesn't this feel empowering? Working through the repressive myths of critical theory. *Harvard Educational Review*, 59 (3), 297–324.

Fish, J. (1981). The psychological impact of field work experiences and cognitive dissonance upon attitude change in a human relations program. (Doctoral dissertation, University of Wisconsin-Madison, 1981). *Dissertation Abstracts International*, 42/08B3494.

Fiske, J. & Hartley, J. (1978). *Reading Television*. London: Methuen.

Flickema, T. & Kane, P. (1980). *Insights: Latin America*. Columbus: Merrill.

Fordham, S. (1988). Racelessness as a factor in black students' school success: Pragmatic strategy or pyrrhic victory? *Harvard Educational Review*, 58(4), 4–84.

Freire, P. (1970). *Pedagogy of the Oppressed* (M. B. Ramos, Trans.). New York: Seabury.

Gamoran, A. & Berends, M. (1986). *The Effects of Stratification in Secondary Schools: Synthesis of survey and ethnographic research*. Madison: National Center on Effective Secondary, University of Wisconsin–Madison.

Gibson, M. (1984). Approaches to multicultural education in the United States: Some concepts and assumptions. *Anthropology and Education Quarterly*, 15, 94–119.

Gilroy, P. (1988-89 Winter). Cruciality and the frog's perspective. *Third Text*, 5, 33–44.

Giroux, H. (1985). Introduction. In P. Freire, *The Politics of Education: Culture, power, and liberation*. South Hadley, MA: Bergin.

_____. (1992). Resisting difference: Cultural studies and the discourse of critical pedagogy. In Grossberg, Nelson, & Treichler (pp. 199–212).

Glazer, N. & Moynihan, D. P. (eds.). (1975). *Ethnicity: Theory and experience*. Cambridge: Harvard.

Gramsci, A. (1971). *Selections from the Prison Notebooks* (ed. Q. Hoare & G. Nowell-Smith). London: Lawrence.

Grant, L. (1984). Black females' "place" in desegregated classrooms. *Sociology of Education*, 57, 98–111.

_____. (1985).*Uneasy Alliances: Black males, teachers, and peers in desegregated classrooms:* Unpublished manuscript, Southern Illinois University, Department of Sociology, Carbondale.

Grossberg, L, Nelson, C., & Treichler, P. (eds.). (1992) *Cultural Studies*. New York: Routledge.

Hacker, A. (1992). *Two Nations: Black and white, separate, hostile, and unequal*. New York: Scribner's.

Hall, S. (1984). Encoding/decoding. In S. Hall, D. Hobson, A. Lowe & P. Willis (eds.), *Culture, Media, Language: Working papers in cultural studies, 1972–79* (pp. 128–138). London: Hutchinson.

_____. (1988). New ethnicities. In *ICA Documents 7: Black film and British cinema* (pp. 27–30). London: Institute of Contemporary Arts.

_____. (1992). Cultural studies and its theoretical legacies. In Grossberg, Nelson, & Treichler (pp. 277–294).

Here they come ready or not: An *Education Week* special report on the ways in which America's population in motion is changing the outlook for schools and society. (1986, May 14). *Education Week*, pp. 14–28.

Hirsch, E. D. (1987). *Cultural Literacy: What every American needs to know*. Boston: Houghton Mifflin.

Hurston, Z. N. (1978). *Their Eyes Were Watching God*. Chicago: U of Illinois P.

James, C. L. R. (1963). *The Black Jacobins: Toussaint L'Ouverture and the San Domingo revolution*. New York: Vintage.

JanMohamed, A. & Lloyd, D. (1987). Introduction: Minority discourse—What is to be done? *Cultural Critique*, 6, 5–17.

Jaschik, S. (1990). Scholarships set up for minority students are called illegal. *The Chronicle of Higher Education*, 37(15), A 1.

Jordan, J. (1985). *On Call: Political essays*. Boston: South End.

_____. (1988). Nobody mean more to me than you and the future life of Willie Jordan. *Harvard Educational Review*, 58(2), 363–374.

Kinzer, S. (1981, August 18). Isthmus of violence. *Boston Globe Magazine*, p. 4.

Lamming, G. (1960). *The Pleasures of Exile*. London: Joseph.

McCarthy, C. (1988). Reconsidering liberal and radical perspectives on racial inequality in schooling: Making the case for nonsynchrony. *Harvard Educational Review*, 58(2), 265–279.

_____. (1990). *Race and curriculum*. London: Falmer.

_____. (1991). Multicultural approaches to racial inequality in the United States. *Oxford Review of Education*, 17(3), 301–316.

McCarthy, C. & Apple, M. (1988). Race, class and gender in American educational research: Toward a non-synchronous parallelist position. In L. Weis (ed.), *Class, Race, and Gender in American Education* (pp. 9–39). Albany: State U of New York P.

Marable, M. (1983). *How Capitalism Underdeveloped Black America: Problems in race, political economy, and society.* Boston: South End.

_____. (1985). *Black American Politics.* London: Verso.

Morrison, T. (1992). *Playing in the Dark: Whiteness and the literary imagination.* Cambridge, MA: Harvard UP.

Nkomo, M. (1984). *Student Culture and Activism in Black South African Universities: The roots of the resistance.* Westport, CT: Greenwood.

Ogbu, J. U. (1978). *Minority Education and Caste: The American system in cross-cultural perspective.* New York: Academic.

Ogbu, J. U. & Matute-Bianchi, M. (1986). Understanding sociocultural factors in education: Knowledge, identity, and school adjustment. In California State Department of Education (ed.), *Beyond Language: Social and cultural factors in schooling language minority students.* (pp. 73–142). Los Angeles: Evaluation, Dissemination and Assessment Center, California State University.

Olneck, M. (1989, March). *The Recurring Dream: Symbolism and ideology in intercultural and multicultural education.* Paper presented at the annual meeting of the American Educational Research Association, San Francisco.

Ravitch, D. (1990). Diversity and democracy: Multicultural education in America. *American Educator,* 14(1), 16–48.

Rushton, J. (1981). Careers and the multicultural curriculum. In J. Lynch (ed.), *Teaching in the multicultural school* (pp. 163–170). London: Ward Lock.

Said, E. (1978). *Orientalism.* New York: Vintage.

_____. (1992). Identity, authority, and freedom: The potentate and the traveller. *Transition,* 54, 4–18.

Sarup, M. (1986). *The Politics of Multiracial Education.* London: Routledge.

Schechter, D. (1992, Jan./Feb.). The gulf war and the death of T.V. news. *The Independent,* pp. 28–31.

Schlesinger, A. M., Jr. (1992). *The Disuniting of America.* New York: Norton.

Schmidt, P. (1989, Oct. 18). Educators foresee "renaissance" in African studies. *Education Week,* p. 8.

Sleeter, C. E. & Grant, C. A. (1988). *Making Choices for Multicultural Education: Five approaches to race, class and gender.* Columbus: Merrill.

Spivak, G. C. (1990). *The Post-Colonial critic: Interviews, Strategies, Dialogues.* (S. Harasym, ed.). New York: Routledge.

Sudarkasa, N. (1988). Black enrollment in higher education: The unfulfilled promise of equality. In National Urban League (eds.), *The State of Black America 1988.* New York: National Urban League.

Sullivan, M. (1990). *Getting Paid: Youth crime and work in the inner city.* Ithaca: Cornell UP.

Swartz, E. (1988). *Multicultural Curriculum Development.* Rochester, NY: Rochester City School District.

_____. (1990, April). Cultural Diversity and the School Curriculum: Context and practice. Paper presented at the annual meeting of the American Educational Research Association, Boston.

Tiedt, I., & Tiedt, P. (1986). *Multicultural Teaching: A handbook of activities, information, and resources.* Boston: Allyn.

Troyna, B. (1984). Multicultural education: Emancipation or containment? In L. Barton & S. Walker (eds.), *Social Crisis and Educational Research* (pp. 75–97). London: Croom.

Walcott, D. (1990). *Omeros.* New York: Farrar.

Wallerstein, I. (1990). Culture as the ideological battleground of the modern world system. In M. Featherstone (ed.), *Global Culture: Nationalism, globalization and modernity* (pp. 31–56). Beverley Hills: Sage.

Will, G. (1989, Dec. 18). Eurocentricity and the school curriculum. *Morning Advocate* (Baton Rouge), p. 3.

Williams, M. (1982). Multicultural/pluralistic education: Public education in America "The way it's 'spoze to be," *Clearing House*, 3, 131–135.

Winter, S. (1992, April). The Challenge to our Episteme: The case of the California textbook controversy. Paper presented at the annual meeting of the American Educational Research Association, San Francisco.

Wood, G. (1985). Schooling in a democracy: Transformation or reproduction. In F. Rizvi (ed.), *Multiculturalism as an Educational Policy*. Geelong, Victoria: Deakin UP.

Wright, E. O. (1978). *Class Crisis and the State*. London: New Left.

23 The Politics of Knowledge

EDWARD SAID

LAST FALL I was invited to participate in a seminar at a historical studies center of a historically renowned American university. The subject of the seminar for this and the next academic year is imperialism, and the seminar discussions are chaired by the center's director. Outside participants are asked to send a paper before their arrival; it is then distributed to the members of the seminar, who are graduate students, fellows, and faculty. They will have read the paper in advance, precluding any reading of a lecture to them by the visitor, who is instead asked to summarize its main points for about ten minutes. Then for an hour and a half, there is an open discussion of the paper—a fairly rigorous but stimulating exercise. Since I have been working for some years on a sequel to *Orientalism* (Said, 1978)—it will be a long book that deals with the relationship between modern culture and imperialism—I sent a substantial extract from the introduction, in which I lay out the main lines of the book's argument. I there begin to describe the emergence of a global consciousness in Western knowledge at the end of the nineteenth century, particularly in such apparently unrelated fields as geography and comparative literature. I then go on to argue that the appearance of such cultural disciplines coincides with a fully global imperial perspective, although such a coincidence can only be made to seem significant from the point of view of later history, when nearly everywhere in the colonized world there emerged resistance to certain oppressive aspects of imperial rule like theories of subject races and peripheral regions and the notions of backward, primitive, or undeveloped cultures. *Because* of that native resistance—for instance, the appearance of many nationalist and independence movements in India, the Caribbean, Africa, the Middle East—it is now evident that culture and imperialism in the West could be understood as offering support each to the other. Here I referred to the extraordinary work of a whole range of non-Western writers and activists, including Tagore, Fanon, C.L.R. James, Yeats, and many others, figures who have given integrity to anti-imperialist cultural resistance.

The first question after my brief resumé was from a professor of history, a black woman of some eminence who had recently come to the university but whose work was unfamiliar to me. She announced in advance that her question was to be hostile, "a very hostile one in fact." She then said something like the following: For the first thirteen pages of your paper you talked only about white European males. Thereafter, on page fourteen, you mention some names of non-Europeans. "How could you do such a thing?", she asked. I remonstrated somewhat and tried to explain my argument in greater detail—after all, I said, I was discussing European imperialism, which would not have been likely to include in its discourse the work of African American women. I pointed out that in the book I say quite a bit about the response to imperialism all over the world; that point was a place in my argument where it would be pertinent to focus on the work of such writers as—and here I again mentioned the name of a great Caribbean writer and

306

intellectual whose work has a special importance for my own—C.L.R. James. To this my critic replied with a stupefying confidence that my answer was not satisfactory since C.L.R. James was dead! I must admit that I was nonplussed by the severity of this pronouncement. James indeed *was* dead, a fact that needn't, to a historian, have made further discussion impossible. I waited for her to resume, hoping that she might expatiate on what she meant by having suggested that even in discussions of what dead white European males said on a given topic it was inappropriate to confine oneself to what they said while leaving out the work of living African American, Arab, and Indian writers.

But she did not proceed, and I was left to suppose that she considered her point sufficiently and conclusively made: I was guilty of not mentioning living non-European nonmales, even when it was not obvious to me or, I later gathered, to many members of the seminar, what their pertinence might have been. I noted to myself that my antagonist did not think it necessary to enumerate what specifically in the work of living non-Europeans I should have used, or which books and ideas by them she found important and relevant. All I had been given to work with was the asserted necessity to mention some approved names—which names did not really matter—as if the very act of uttering them were enough. I was also left unmistakably with the impression that as a non-white—a category, incidentally, to which as an Arab I myself belong—she was saying that to affirm the existence of non-European "others" took the place of evidence, argument, discussion.

It would be pointless to deny that the exchange was unsettling. Among other things I was chagrined at the distortions of my position and for having responded to the distortions so clumsily. It did not seem to matter that a great deal of my own work has concerned itself with just the kind of omission with which I was being charged. What apparently mattered now was that having contributed to an early trend, in which Western and European intellectuals were arraigned for having their work constructed out of the suffering and deprivations of so many people of color, I was now allegedly doing what such complicit intellectuals had always done. For if in one place you criticize the exclusion of Orientals, as I did in *Orientalism*, the exclusion of "others" from your work in another place becomes, on one level, difficult to justify or explain. I was disheartened not because I was being attacked, but because the general validity of the point made in *Orientalism* still obtained and yet was now being directed at me. It was *still* true that various Others—the word has acquired a sheen of modishness that has become extremely objectionable—were being represented unfairly, their reality distorted, their truth either denied or twisted with malice. Yet instead of joining on their behalf, I felt I was being asked to get involved in an inconsequential academic contest. I had wanted to say, but didn't, "Is all that matters about the issue of exclusion and misrepresentation the fact that *names* were left out? Why are you detaining us with such trivialities?"

To make matters worse, a few minutes later in the discussion I was attacked by a retired professor of Middle Eastern studies, himself an Orientalist. Like me, he was an Arab, but he had consistently identified himself with intellectual tendencies of which I had always been critical. He now intervened to defend imperialism, saying in tones of almost comic reverence that it had accomplished things that natives couldn't have done for themselves. It had taught them, among other things, he said, how to appreciate the cuneiform and hieroglyphics of their own traditions. As he droned on about the imperial schools, railroads, hospitals, and telegraphs in the third world that stood for examples of British and French largesse, the irony of the whole thing seemed overpowering. It appeared to me that there had to be something to say that surrendered neither to the caricatural reductiveness of the two positions by then arrayed against me, and against each other, nor to that verbal quality in each that was determined to remain ideologically correct and little else.

I was being reminded, by such negative, flat-minded examples of thinking, that the one thing that intellectuals *cannot* do without is the full intellectual process itself. Into it goes historically informed research as well as the presentation of a coherent and carefully argued line that has taken account of alternatives. In addition there must be, it seems to me, a theoretical presumption that in matters having to do with human history and society any rigid theoretical ideal, any simple additive or mechanical notion of what is or is not factual, must yield to the central factor of human work, the actual participation of peoples in the making of human life. If that is so then it must also be true that, given the very nature of human work in the construction of human society and history, it is impossible to say of it that its products are so rarefied, so limited, so beyond comprehension as to exclude most other people, experiences, and histories. I mean further that this kind of human work, which is intellectual work, is worldly; that it is situated in the world and about that world. It is not about things that are so rigidly constricted and so forbiddingly arcane as to exclude all but an audience of like-minded, already convinced persons. While it would be stupid to deny the importance of constituencies and audiences in the construction of an intellectual argument, I think it has to be supposed that many arguments can be made to more than one audience and in different situations. Otherwise we would be dealing not with intellectual argument but either with dogma or with a technological jargon designed specifically to repel all but a small coterie or handful of initiates.

Lest I fall into the danger myself of being too theoretical and specialized, I shall be more specific now and return to the episode I was discussing just a moment ago. At the heart of the imperial cultural enterprise I analyzed in *Orientalism*, and also in my new book, was a politics of identity. That politics needed to assume, indeed needed firmly to believe, that what was true about Orientals or Africans was *not*, however, true about or for Europeans. When a French or German scholar tried to identify the main characteristics of, for instance, the Chinese mind, the work was only partly intended to do that; it was also intended to show how different the Chinese mind was from the Western mind.

Such constructed things—they have only an elusive reality—as the Chinese mind or the Greek spirit have always been with us; they are at the source of a great deal that goes into the making of individual cultures, nations, traditions, and peoples. But in the modern world considerably greater attention has generally been given to such identities than was ever given in earlier historical periods, when the world was larger, more amorphous, less globalized. Today a fantastic emphasis is placed upon a politics of national identity, and to a very great degree this emphasis is the result of imperialistic experience. For when the great modern Western imperial expansion took place all across the world, beginning in the late eighteenth century, it accentuated the interaction between the identity of the French or the English and that of the colonized native peoples. And this mostly antagonistic interaction gave rise to a separation between people, as members of homogenous races and exclusive nations, that was and still is one of the characteristics of what can be called the epistemology of imperialism. At its core is the supremely stubborn thesis that everyone is principally and irreducibly a member of some race or category and that that race or category cannot ever be assimilated to or accepted by others—except as itself. Thus came into being such invented essences as the Oriental or Englishness, as Frenchness, Africanness, or American exceptionalism, as if each of those had a Platonic idea behind it that guaranteed it as pure and unchanging from the beginning to the end of time.

One product of this doctrine is nationalism, a subject so immense that I can treat it only very partially here. What interests me in the politics of identity that informed imperialism in its global phase is that just as natives were considered to belong to a different category—racial or geographical—from that of the Western white man, it also became true that in the great anti-imperialist revolt represented by decolonization this same category was mobilized around, and formed the resisting identity of, the revolutionaries. This was the case everywhere in the third world. Its most celebrated instance is the concept of *négritude,* as developed intellectually and poetically by Aimé Césaire, Léopold Senghor, and, in English, W.E.B. DuBois. If blacks had once been stigmatized and given inferior status to whites, then it has since become necessary not to deny blackness, and not to aspire to whiteness, but to accept and celebrate blackness, to give it the dignity of poetic as well as metaphysical status. Thus *négritude* acquired positive Being where before it had been a mark of degradation and inferiority. Much the same revaluation of the native particularity occurred in India, many parts of the Islamic world, China, Japan, Indonesia, and the Philippines, where the denied or repressed native essence emerged as the focus of, and even the basis for, nationalist recovery.

It is important to note that much of the early cultural resistance to imperialism on which nationalism and independence movements were built was salutary and necessary. I see it essentially as an attempt on the part of oppressed people, who had suffered the bondage of slavery, colonialism, and—most important—spiritual dispossession, to reclaim their identity. When that finally occurred in places such as Algeria, the grander nationalist efforts amounted to little short of a reconstructed communal political and cultural program of independence. Where the white man had once only seen lazy natives and exotic customs, the insurrection against imperialism produced (as in Ireland for example) a national revolt, along with political parties dedicated to independence, which (like the Congress party in India) were headed by nationalist figures, poets, and military heroes. There were remarkably impressive results from this vast effort at cultural reclamation, most of which are well known and celebrated.

But while the whole movement toward autonomy and independence produced in effect newly independent and separate states constituting the majority of new nations in the postcolonial world today, the nationalist politics of identity has nonetheless quickly proved itself to be insufficient for the ensuing period.

Inattentive or careless readers of Frantz Fanon, generally considered one of the two or three most eloquent apostles of anti-imperialist resistance, tend to forget his marked suspicions of unchecked nationalism. So while it is appropriate to draw attention to the early chapters on violence in *The Wretched of the Earth* (Fanon, 1963), it should be noticed that in subsequent chapters he is sharply critical of what he called the pitfalls of national consciousness. He clearly meant this to be a paradox: for the reason that while nationalism is a necessary spur to revolt against the colonizer, national consciousness must be immediately transformed into what he calls "social consciousness," just as soon as the withdrawal of the colonizer has been accomplished.

Fanon is scathing on the abuses of the postindependence nationalist party: on, for instance, the cult of the Grand Panjandrum (or maximum leader), or the centralization of the capital city, which Fanon said flatly needed to be deconsecrated, or most importantly, the hijacking of common sense and popular participation by bureaucrats, technical experts, and jargon-wielding obfuscators. Well before V.S. Naipaul, Fanon was arguing against the politics of mimicry and separatism that produced the Mobutus, Idi Amins, and Saddams, as well as the grotesqueries and pathologies of power that gave rise to tyrannical states and praetorian guards while obstructing democratic freedoms in so many countries of the third world. Fanon also prophesied the continuing dependency of numerous postcolonial governments and philosophies, all of which preached the sovereignty of the newly independent people of one or another new third world state and, having failed to make the transition from nationalism to true liberation, were in fact condemned to practice the politics, and the economics, of a new oppression as pernicious as the old one.

At bottom, what Fanon offers most compellingly is a critique of the separatism and mock autonomy achieved by a pure politics of identity that has lasted too long and been made to serve in situations where it has become simply inadequate. What invariably happens at the level of knowledge is that signs and symbols of freedom and status are taken for the reality: You want to be named and considered for the sake of being named and considered. In effect this really means that just to be an independent postcolonial Arab, or black, or Indonesian is not a program, nor a process, nor a vision. It is no more than a convenient starting point from which the real work, the hard work, might begin.

As for that work, it is nothing less than the reintegration of all those people and cultures, once confined and reduced to peripheral status, with the rest of the human race. After working through *négritude* in the early sections of *Cahier d'un retour* ([1947]1969), Césaire states this vision of integration in his poem's climactic moment: "no race possesses the monopoly of beauty, of intelligence, of force, and there is a place for all at the rendez-vous of victory."

Without this concept of "place for all at the rendez-vous of victory," one is condemned to an impoverishing politics of knowledge based only upon the assertion and reassertion of identity, an ultimately uninteresting alternation of presence and absence. If you are weak, your affirmation of identity for its own sake amounts to little more than saying that you want a kind of attention easily and superficially granted, like the attention given an individual in a crowded room at a roll call. Once receiving such recognition, the subject has only to sit there silently as the proceedings unfold as if in his or her absence. And, on the other hand, though the powerful get acknowledged by the sheer force of presence, this commits them to a logic of displacement, as soon as someone else emerges who is as, or more, powerful.

This has proved a disastrous process, whether for postcolonials, forced to exist in a marginal and dependent place totally outside the circuits of world power, or for powerful societies, whose triumphalism and imperious willfulness have done so much to devastate and destabilize the world. What has been at issue between Iraq and the United States is precisely such a logic of exterminism and displacement, as unedifying as it is unproductive. It is risky, I know, to move from the realm of interpretation to the realm of world politics, but it seems to me true that the relationship between them is a real one, and the light that one realm can shed on the other is quite illuminating. In any case the politics of knowledge that is based principally on the affirmation of identity is very similar, is indeed directly related to, the unreconstructed nationalism that has guided so many postcolonial states today. It asserts a sort of separatism that wishes only to draw attention to itself; consequently it neglects the integration of that earned and achieved consciousness of self within "the rendez-vous of victory." On the national and intellectual level the problems are very similar.

Let me return therefore to one of the intellectual debates that has been central to the humanities in the past decade, and that underlies the episode with which I began. The ferment in minority, subaltern, feminist, and postcolonial consciousness has resulted in so many salutary achievements in the curricular and theoretical approach to the study of the humanities as quite literally to have produced a Copernican revolution in all traditional fields of inquiry. Eurocentrism has been challenged definitively; most scholars and students in the contemporary American academy are now aware, as they were never aware before, that society and culture have been the heterogeneous product of heterogeneous people in an enormous variety of cultures, traditions, and situations. No longer does T.S. Eliot's idea of the great Western masterpieces enduring together in a constantly redefining pattern of monuments have its old authority; nor do the sorts of patterns elucidated with such memorable brilliance in formative works like *Mimesis* (Auerbach, 1953) or *The Anatomy of Criticism* (Frye, 1957) have the same cogency for today's student or theorist as they did even quite recently.

And yet the great contest about the canon continues. The success of Allan Bloom's *The Closing of the American Mind* (1987), the subsequent publication of such works as Alvin Kernan's *The Death of Literature* (1990) and Roger Kimball's *Tenured Radicals* (1990), as well as the rather posthumous energies displayed in journals like *The American Scholar* (now a neoconservative magazine), *The New Criterion*, and *Commentary*—all this suggests that the work done by those of us who have tried to widen the area of awareness in the study of culture is scarcely finished or secure. But our point, in my opinion, cannot be simply and obdurately to reaffirm the paramount importance of formerly suppressed or silenced forms of knowledge and leave it at that, nor can it be to surround ourselves with the sanctimonious piety of historical or cultural victimhood as a way of making our intellectual presence felt. Such strategies are woefully insufficient. The whole effort to deconsecrate Eurocentrism cannot be interpreted, least of all by those who participate in the enterprise, as an effort to supplant Eurocentrism with, for instance, Afrocentric or Islamocentric approaches. On its own, ethnic particularity does not provide for intellectual process—quite the contrary. At first, you will recall, it was a question, for some, of adding Jane Austen to the canon of male Western writers in humanities courses; then it became a matter of displacing the entire canon of American writers like Hawthorne and Emerson with best-selling writers of the same period like Harriet Beecher Stowe and Susan Warner. But after that the logic of displacement became even more attenuated, and the mere names of politically validated living writers became more important than anything about them or their works.

I submit that these clamorous dismissals and swooping assertions are in fact caricatural reductions of what the great revisionary gestures of feminism, subaltern or black studies, and anti-imperialist resistance originally intended. For such gestures it was never a matter of replacing one set of authorities with another, nor of substituting one center for another. It was always a matter of opening and participating in a central strand of intellectual and cultural effort and of showing what had always been, though indiscernibly, a part of it, like the work of women, or of blacks and servants—but which had been either denied or derogated. The power and interest of—to give two examples particularly dear to me—Tayib Salih's *Season of Migration to the North* ([1969]1980) is not only how it memorably describes the quandary of a gifted young Sudanese who has lived in London but then returns home to his ancestral village alongside the Nile; the novel is also a rewriting of Conrad's *Heart of Darkness* ([1899]1967), seen now as the tale of someone who voyages into the heart of light, which is modern Europe, and discovers there what had been hidden deep within him. To read the Sudanese writer is of course to interpret an Arabic novel written during the late '60s at a time of nationalism and a rejection of the West. The novel is therefore affiliated with other Arabic novels of the postwar period including the works of Naguib Mahfouz and Yusuf Idris; but given the historical and political meaning of a narrative that quite deliberately recalls and reverses Conrad—something impossible for a black man at the time *Heart of Darkness* was written—Salih's masterpiece is necessarily to be viewed as, along with other African, Indian, and Caribbean works, enlarging, widening, refining the scope of a narrative form at the center of which had heretofore always been an exclusively European observer or center of consciousness.

There is an equally complex resonance to Ghassan Kanafani's *Men in the Sun* ([1956]1978), a compelling novella about the travails of three Palestinian refugees who are trying to get from Basra in Iraq to Kuwait. Their past in Palestine is evoked in order to contrast it with the poverty and dispossession of which they are victims immediately after 1948. When they find a man in Basra whose occupation is in part to smuggle refugees across the border in the belly of his empty watertruck, they strike a deal with him, and he takes them as far as the border post, where he is detained in conversation in the hot sun. They die of asphyxiation, unheard and forgotten. Kanafani's novella belongs to the genre of immigrant literature contributed to by an estimable number of postwar writers— Rushdie, Naipaul, Berger, Kundera, and others. But it is also a poignant meditation on the Palestinian fate, and of course eerily prescient about Palestinians in the current Gulf crisis. And yet it would do the subject of the work and its literary merit an extraordinary disservice were we to confine it to the category of national allegory, to see in it only a mirroring of the actual plight of Palestinians in exile. Kanafani's work is literature connected both to its specific historical and cultural situations and to a whole world of other literatures and formal articulations, which the attentive reader summons to mind as the interpretation proceeds.

The point I am trying to make can be summed up in the useful notion of worldliness. By linking works to each other we bring them out of the neglect and secondariness to which for all kinds of political and ideological reasons they had been previously condemned. What I am talking about therefore is the opposite of separatism, and also the reverse of exclusivism. It is only through the scrutiny of these works *as* literature, as style, as pleasure and illumination, that they can be brought in, so to speak, and kept in. Otherwise they will be regarded only as informative ethnographic specimens, suitable for the limited attention of experts and area specialists. *Worldliness* is therefore the restoration to such works and interpretations of their place in the global setting, a restoration that can only be accomplished by an appreciation not of some tiny, defensively constituted corner of the world but of the large, many-windowed house of human culture as a whole.

It seems to me absolutely essential that we engage with cultural works in this unprovincial, interested manner while maintaining a strong sense of the contest for forms and values that any decent cultural work embodies, realizes, and contains. A great deal of recent theoretical speculation has proposed that works of literature are completely determined as such by their situation, and that readers themselves are totally determined in their responses by their respective cultural situations, to a point where no value, no reading, no interpretation can be anything other than the merest reflection of some immediate interest. All readings and all writing are reduced to an assumed historical emanation. Here the indeterminacy of deconstructive reading, the airy insouciance of postaxiological criticism, the casual reductiveness of some (but by no means all) ideological schools are principally at fault. While it is true to say that because a text is the product of an unrecapturable past contemporary criticism can to some extent afford a neutral disengagement or opposed perspective impossible for the text in its own time, there is no reason to take the further step and exempt the interpreter from any moral, political, cultural, or psychological commitments. All of these remain at play. The attempt to read a text in its fullest and most integrative context commits the reader to positions that are educative, humane, and engaged, positions that depend on training and taste and not simply on a technologized professionalism, or on the tiresome playfulness of "postmodern" criticism, with its repeated disclaimers of anything but local games and pastiches. Despite Lyotard and his acolytes, we are still in the era of large narratives, of horrendous cultural clashes, and of appallingly destructive war—as witness the recent conflagration in the Gulf—and to say that we are against theory, or beyond literature, is to be blind and trivial.

I am not arguing that every interpretive act is equivalent to a gesture either for or against life. How could anyone defend or attack so crudely general a position? I am saying that once we grant intellectual work the right to exist in a relatively disengaged atmosphere and allow it a status that isn't disqualified by partisanship, we ought then to reconsider the ties between the text and the world in a serious and uncoercive way. Far from repudiating the great advances made when Eurocentrism and patriarchy began to be demystified, we should consolidate these advances, using them so as to reach a better understanding of the degree to which literature and artistic genius belong to and are some part of the world where all of us also do other kinds of work.

This wider application of the ideas I've been discussing cannot even be attempted if we simply repeat a few names or refer to a handful of approved texts ritualistically or sanctimoniously. Victimhood, alas, does not guarantee or necessarily enable an enhanced sense of humanity. To testify to a history of oppression is necessary, but it is not sufficient unless that history is redirected into intellectual process and universalized to include all sufferers. Yet too often testimony to oppression becomes only a justification for further cruelty and inhumanity, or for high-sounding cant and merely "correct" attitudes. I have in mind, for instance, not only the antagonists mentioned at the beginning of this essay, but also the extraordinary behavior of an Elie Wiesel who has refused to translate the lessons of his own past into consistent criticisms of Israel for doing what it has done and is doing right now to Palestinians.

So while it is not necessary to regard every reading or interpretation of a text as the moral equivalent of a war or a political crisis, it does seem to me to be important to underline the fact that whatever else they are, works of literature are not merely texts. They are in fact differently constituted and have different values, they aim to do different things, exist in different genres, and so on. One of the great pleasures for those who read and study literature is the discovery of longstanding norms in which all cultures known to me concur: such things as style and performance, the existence of good as well as lesser writers, and the exercise of preference. What has been most unacceptable during the many harangues on both sides of the so-called Western canon debate is that so many of the combatants have ears of tin and are unable to distinguish between good writing and politically correct attitudes, as if a fifth-rate pamphlet and a great novel have more or less the same significance. Who benefits from leveling attacks on the canon? Certainly not the disadvantaged person or class whose history, if you bother to read it at all, is full of evidence that popular resistance to injustice has always derived immense benefits from invidious distinctions made between ruling-class and subservient cultures. After all, the crucial lesson of C.L.R. James's *Black Jacobins* (1963) or of E.P. Thompson's *Making of the English Working Class* (1966; with its reminder of how important Shakespeare was to nineteenth-century radical culture) is that great antiauthoritarian uprisings made their greatest advances not by denying the humanitarian and universalist claims of the general dominant culture but by attacking the adherents of that culture for failing to uphold their own declared standards, for failing to extend them to all, as opposed to a small fraction, of humanity. Toussaint L'Ouverture is the perfect example of a downtrodden slave whose struggle to free himself and his people was informed by the ideas of Rousseau and Mirabeau.

Although I risk oversimplification, it is probably correct to say that it does not finally matter *who* wrote what, but rather *how* a work is written and *how* it is read. The idea that because Plato and Aristotle are male and products of a slave society they should be disqualified from receiving contemporary attention is as limited an idea as suggesting that *only* their work, because it was addressed to and about elites, should be read today. Marginality and homelessness are not, in my opinion, to be gloried in; they are to be brought to an end, so that more, and not fewer, people can enjoy the benefits of what has for centuries been denied the victims of race, class, or gender.

Published with the permission of the author. This essay first appeared in *Raritan*, 11 (1) (Summer 1991), pp. 17-31.

REFERENCES

Auerbach, E. (1953). *Mimesis: The representation of reality in Western literature*. (W. R. Trask, Trans.). Princeton: Princeton UP.

Bloom, A. (1987). *The Closing of the American Mind*. New York: Simon.

Césaire, A. ([1947]1969). *Cahier d'un retour au pays natal*. [Return to my native land]. (A. Berger & J. Bostock, Trans.). Baltimore: Penguin.

Conrad, J. *Heart of Darkness*. ([1899]1967). In *Great short works of Joseph Conrad* (pp. 211–292). New York: Harper.

Fanon, F. (1963). *The Wretched of the Earth*. (H. Kirkpatrick, Trans.) New York: Grove.

Frye, N. (1957). *Anatomy of Criticism: Four essays*. Princeton: Princeton UP.

James, C. L. R. (1963). *The Black Jacobins: Toussaint l'Ouverture and the San Domingo revolution* New York: Vintage.

Kanafani, G. ([1956]1978). *Men in the Sun*. Washington, DC: Three Continents.

Kernan, A. B. (1990). *The Death of Literature*. New Haven: Yale UP.

Kimball, R. (1990). *Tenured Radicals: How politics has corrupted our higher education*. New York: Harper.

Said, E. (1978). *Orientalism*. New York: Pantheon.

Salih, T. ([1969]1980). *Season of Migration to the North*. Washington, DC: Three Continents.

Thompson, E. P. (1966). *The Making of the English Working Class*. New York: Vintage.

Index

315

NOTES ON CONTRIBUTORS

Michael W. Apple is John Bascom Professor of Curriculum and Instruction and Educational Policy Studies at the University of Wisconsin, Madison. A former president of a teacher's union, he has worked with dissident groups, unions, and governments to democratize educational research, policy, and practice. Among his many books are *Ideology and Curriculum* (1979; second edition 1990), *Education and Power* (1985), *Teachers and Texts* (1988), and *The Politics of the Textbook* (1991). He is the editor of the Critical Social Thought series published by Routledge.

Ali Behdad teaches cultural studies at the University of Rochester. He has published several articles on colonial discourses of the nineteenth century and is currently completing a book on the micropractices of Orientalism.

Deborah P. Britzman, Associate Professor of Education, teaches English Education and Multicultural Education in the School of Education and Human Development, State University of New York at Binghamton. She is the author of *Practice Makes Practice: A Critical Study of Learning to Teach* (State University Press of New York, 1991) and has published in the *Journal of Curriculum Theorizing*, the *Harvard Educational Review*, and the *Journal of Education*.

Hazel Carby is Professor of English and Afro-American Studies at Yale University. She is the author of *Reconstructing Womanhood: The Emergence of the Afro-American Woman Novelist*, published by Oxford University Press.

Warren Crichlow is Assistant Professor of Teaching and Curriculum in the Graduate School of Education and Human Development at the University of Rochester. His major areas of interest are social studies education, social and cultural theory of urban education and educational reform, and the study of urban neighborhoods, families, and adolescent development. He has published articles and book reviews in the *Boston Journal of Education*, *The Journal of Negro Education*, and *Afterimage*. He currently serves as editorial adviser for *Urban Education*.

Manthia Diawara is Professor of Comparative Literature and Film and is the Director of Africana Studies at New York University.

Susan Edgerton is Assistant Professor of Education in the Department of Curriculum, Instruction, and Evaluation at the University of Illinois at Chicago. Her theoretical interests are currently around poststructuralist studies, cultural studies, and feminist studies of pedagogy. She teaches courses in curriculum, multicultural education, and the politics of identity.

Elizabeth Ellsworth is Associate Professor of Curriculum and Instruction at the University of Wisconsin-Madison. She teaches courses in cultural studies, media studies, and education. She is currently co-authoring a book with Mimi Orner on media, classroom practices, identity, and difference.

Lawrence Grossberg is a professor at the University of Illinois at Urbana-Champaign in the Department of Speech Communication, the Institute of Communications Research, and the Unit for Criticism and Interpretive Theory. His most recent book is *We Gotta Get Out of This Place: Popular Conservatism and Postmodern Culture* (Routledge, 1992). He has also recently co-edited *Cultural Studies, Sound and Vision: The Music Video Reader* and *Rock and Popular Music: Politics, Policies and Institutions.* He is the international coeditor of the journal *Cultural Studies.*

Richard Hatcher is Senior Lecturer in Education Studies at the University of Central England in Birmingham, England. He is currently researching the implications of market reforms in English education for issues of social class and (with Barry Troyna) racial equality.

Glenn M. Hudak is Assistant Professor of Education at the State University of New York at Albany. His areas of research are curriculum theory and social education. His article "On the Limits of Visual Communication" is published in *Paradigms Regained* (1991), D. Hlynka and J. Belland (Eds.). He is also a senior associate and a project director at The National Center for Teaching and Learning of Literature, SUNY Albany. His project is titled "Popular Media in the Literary Experience of High School Students."

Laura M. Lamash teaches in elementary education with the Binghamton Public School District. She has taught for six years and is an active community organizer. Her interests include the uses of autobiography in education, critical pedagogy, and the development of children's gendered identities. She has published in *Education and Society.*

Patrick McGee is Associate Professor at Louisiana State University. He has published two books: *Paperspace: Style as Ideology in Joyce's "Ulysses"* and *Telling the Other: The Question of Value in Modern and Postcolonial Writing.*

Cameron McCarthy teaches curriculum theory and media studies at Colgate University in Hamilton, New York. He has published widely on the topics of cultural politics and problems with neo-Marxist and poststructural theories on race in journals such as *Harvard Educational Review, Oxford Review of Education, Education and Society, Contemporary Sociology, Interchange,* and the *European Journal of Intercultural Studies.* McCarthy is the author of *Race and Curriculum* (1990) published by Falmer Press. With Chris Richards of the Institute of Education at the University of London and Glenn M. Hudak of SUNY Albany, he is currently working on a book on popular music and adolescent identities, entitled *Sound Identities,* to be published by Routledge next year.

Gladys Jiménez-Múñoz is Assistant Professor of Women's Studies at the State University of New York at Oneonta. She was a school teacher in Puerto Rico. Her articles include "The Crossroads of Gender and History," in *Integrating Latin America and Caribbean Women into the Curriculum and Research* (1990), and the "Work of Juan Sánchez: Dismantling the U.S. Cracker Jack" exhibition catalogue, University Art Museum, SUNY Binghamton. Her dissertation analyzes the textual practices in the debate on women's suffrage in Puerto Rico during the 1920s.

Roxana Ng immigrated to Canada in 1970 and obtained her B.A. (Hon.) and M.A. from the University of British Columbia. After working as a community worker in Vancouver, where she began to develop her work on immigrant women, she returned to graduate studies and obtained her Ph.D. in 1984. She has been active in immigrant women's organizing since the mid-1970s, and continues to refine her conceptualization of race, gender, and class relations based on her organizing experiences. She now teaches sociology at the Ontario Institute for Studies in Education.

Michael Omi is a sociologist who teaches Asian American Studies and Ethnic Studies at the University of California, Berkeley. He is the coauthor, with Howard Winant, of *Racial Formation in the United States.*

William F. Pinar teaches curriculum theory at Louisiana State University. With William M. Reynolds, he is editor of *Understanding Curriculum as Phenomenological and Deconstructed Text* (Teachers College Press, 1992).

Laura Elisa Pérez is an Assistant Professor in the Department of Romance Languages and Literatures and a Faculty Associate of the Program of American Cultures at the University of Michigan, Ann Arbor. She is currently a postdoctoral fellow at the Susan B. Anthony Center for Women's Studies at the University of Rochester.

Catherine Raissiguier is currently a visiting assistant professor of Women's Studies at the University of Oregon. She has taught Women's Studies and Sociology of Education at University of Michigan, SUNY Buffalo, and Middlebury College. She is currently working on a book entitled *Becoming Women/Becoming Workers: Identity Formation in a French Vocational School.*

Fazal Rizvi is Associate Professor of Education at the University of Queensland, Australia. Before joining the University of Queensland in 1991, he was working in Victoria at Deakin University. He obtained his Ph.D. in Philosophy of Education from Kings College, University of London, and over the past eight years has utilized this background to explore a range of cultural and political issues in education. He has written extensively on ethics and educational administration, problems of democratic reforms in education and racism, and the politics of multicultural education.

Leslie Roman is Assistant Professor in the Department of Social and Educational Studies at the University of British Columbia in Vancouver. She is the author of numerous essays on the construction of feminine sexuality in popular culture, particularly in youth subcultures and feminist materialist ethnography. She coedited with Linda Christian-Smith and Elizabeth Ellsworth *Becoming Feminine: The Politics of Popular Culture* (Sussex: Falmer, 1988). She is also coeditor with Dennis Dworkin of an international anthology, *Views Beyond the Border Country: Raymond Williams and Cultural Politics* (Routledge, 1992), which critiques the work of Williams in light of feminist and postcolonial interventions into cultural studies. Her ethnography, *A Tenuous Sisterhood: Women in an American Punk Subculture*, is also forthcoming with Routledge.

Edward Said is Parr Professor of English and Comparative Literature at Columbia University. His books include *Orientalism, The Question of Palestine*, and *The World, The Text, and the Critic.*

Kelvin Santiago-Válles is Assistant Professor of Sociology and of Latin American and Caribbean Area Studies at the State University of New York at Binghamton. His research and teaching address race, class, gender, sexuality, nationality from sociohistorical and postcolonial perspectives. He is the author of the forthcoming *"Subject People"* and *Colonial Discourse: Economic Transformation and Social Disorder in Puerto Rico, 1898–1947* (Albany: State University New York Press, forthcoming) and has published in *Historia y Sociedad* (Mexico), *Proceso* (San Juan), and *Centro* (Hunter College-CUNY).

Christine E. Sleeter is Associate Professor of Teacher Education at the University of Wisconsin-Parkside. She was formerly a teacher in Seattle Public Schools, and received her Ph.D. at the University of Wisconsin-Madison. She has published extensively on issues related to multicultural education. Her articles appear in journals such as *Harvard Educational Review, Journal of Education, Teachers College Record*, and *Educational Researcher*. Her books include *Keepers of the American Dream, Empowerment through Multicultural Education* (with Carl Grant), and *After the School Bell Rings* (with Carl Grant).

Barry Troyna is Senior Lecturer in Education at the University of Warwick in England. Among the latest of his publications on anti-racist education is *Racism and Education: Research Perspectives* (Open University Press, 1993). With Richard Hatcher he is currently researching the impact of the 1988 Education Reform Act on racial equality issues in England.

Michele Wallace is Associate Professor at the City College of New York. She teaches courses in Afro-American literature and literary criticism and black feminist theory. She is the author of *Black Macho and the Myth of the Super Woman* and *Invisibility Blues: From Pop to Theory*.

Cornel West is Professor of Religion and Director of Afro-American Studies at Princeton University. His most recent books are *The American Evasion of Philosophy* and *Breakin' Bread: Insurgent Black Intellectual Life* (with bell hooks). *The Ethical Dimensions of Marxist Thought, Prophetic Criticism* is forthcoming.

Howard Winant is Associate Professor of Sociology at Temple University, Philadelphia, Pennsylvania. He is the coauthor, with Michael Omi, of *Racial Formation in the United States*.